Deuteronomy

Reformed Expository Commentary

A Series

Series Editors

Richard D. Phillips
Philip Graham Ryken

Testament Editors

Iain M. Duguid, Old Testament
Daniel M. Doriani, New Testament

Deuteronomy

Trent Casto

P.O. BOX 817 • PHILLIPSBURG • NEW JERSEY 08865-0817

Printed in the United States of America

Library of Congress Cataloging-in-Publication Data

Names: Casto, Trent author
Title: Deuteronomy / Trent Casto.
Description: Phillipsburg, New Jersey : P&R Publishing Company, [2025] | Series: Reformed expository commentaries | Includes bibliographical references and index. | Summary: "Christians need to understand Old Testament theology to fully appreciate the New-and Deuteronomy, the Old Testament's central theological text, is the best place to start"-- Provided by publisher.
Identifiers: LCCN 2025015963 | ISBN 9781629959726 hardcover | ISBN 9781629959733 epub
Subjects: LCSH: Bible. Deuteronomy--Commentaries
Classification: LCC BS1275.53 .C37 2025 | DDC 222/.1507--dc23/eng/20250610
LC record available at https://lccn.loc.gov/2025015963

In loving memory of Rev. M. Jack Bohman
(May 11, 1944–January 23, 2022),
evangelist, church planter, preacher, and—above all—pastor.

To Hudson, Anna Kate, William, and the children
of Covenant Church of Naples,
with prayers that you will pass these things on to your children also.

And to Emily,
whose love reflects the covenantal faithfulness at the heart of this book.

Contents

Series Introduction

In every generation there is a fresh need for the faithful exposition of God's Word in the church. At the same time, the church must constantly do the work of theology: reflecting on the teaching of Scripture, confessing its doctrines of the Christian faith, and applying them to contemporary culture. We believe that these two tasks—the expositional and the theological—are interdependent. Our doctrine must derive from the biblical text, and our understanding of any particular passage of Scripture must arise from the doctrine taught in Scripture as a whole.

We further believe that these interdependent tasks of biblical exposition and theological reflection are best undertaken in the church, and most specifically in the pulpits of the church. This is all the more true since the study of Scripture properly results in doxology and praxis—that is, in praise to God and practical application in the lives of believers. In pursuit of these ends, we are pleased to present the Reformed Expository Commentary as a fresh exposition of Scripture for our generation in the church. We hope and pray that pastors, teachers, Bible study leaders, and many others will find this series to be a faithful, inspiring, and useful resource for the study of God's infallible, inerrant Word.

The Reformed Expository Commentary has four fundamental commitments. First, these commentaries aim to be *biblical*, presenting a comprehensive exposition characterized by careful attention to the details of the text. They are not exegetical commentaries—commenting word by word or even verse by verse—but integrated expositions of whole passages of Scripture. Each commentary will thus present a sequential, systematic treatment of an entire book of the Bible, passage by passage. Second, these commentaries are unashamedly *doctrinal*. We are committed to the Westminster Confession of Faith and Catechisms as containing the system of doctrine taught in the Scriptures of the Old and New Testaments. Each volume will teach, promote, and defend the doctrines of the Reformed faith as they are found in the Bible. Third, these commentaries are *redemptive-historical* in their orientation. We believe in the unity of the Bible and its central message of salvation in Christ. We are thus committed to a Christ-centered view of the Old Testament, in which its characters, events, regulations, and institutions are properly understood as pointing us to Christ and his gospel, as well as giving us examples to follow in living by faith. Fourth, these commentaries are *practical*, applying the text of Scripture to contemporary challenges of life—both public and private—with appropriate illustrations.

The contributors to the Reformed Expository Commentary are all pastor-scholars. As pastor, each author will first present his expositions in the pulpit ministry of his church. This means that these commentaries are rooted in the teaching of Scripture to real people in the church. While aiming to be scholarly, these expositions are not academic. Our intent is to be faithful, clear, and helpful to Christians who possess various levels of biblical and theological training—as should be true in any effective pulpit ministry. Inevitably this means that some issues of academic interest will not be covered. Nevertheless, we aim to achieve a responsible level of scholarship, seeking to promote and model this for pastors and other teachers in the church. Significant exegetical and theological difficulties, along with such historical and cultural background as is relevant to the text, will be treated with care.

We strive for a high standard of enduring excellence. This begins with the selection of the authors, all of whom have proved to be outstanding communicators of God's Word. But this pursuit of excellence is also reflected in a disciplined editorial process. Each volume is edited by both a series editor and a testament editor. The testament editors, Iain Duguid for the Old Testament and Daniel Doriani for the New Testament, are accomplished pastors and respected scholars who have taught at the seminary level. Their job is to ensure that each volume is sufficiently conversant with up-to-date scholarship and is faithful and accurate in its exposition of the text. As series editors, we oversee each volume to ensure its overall quality—including excellence of writing, soundness of teaching, and usefulness in application. Working together as an editorial team, along with the publisher, we are devoted to ensuring that these are the best commentaries that our gifted authors can provide, so that the church will be served with trustworthy and exemplary expositions of God's Word.

It is our goal and prayer that the Reformed Expository Commentary will serve the church by renewing confidence in the clarity and power of Scripture and by upholding the great doctrinal heritage of the Reformed faith. We hope that pastors who read these commentaries will be encouraged in their own expository preaching ministry, which we believe to be the best and most biblical pattern for teaching God's Word in the church. We hope that lay teachers will find these commentaries among the most useful resources they rely on for understanding and presenting the text of the Bible. And we hope that the devotional quality of these studies of Scripture will instruct and inspire each Christian who reads them in joyful, obedient discipleship to Jesus Christ.

May the Lord bless all who read the Reformed Expository Commentary. We commit these volumes to the Lord Jesus Christ, praying that the Holy Spirit will use them for the instruction and edification of the church, with thanksgiving to God the Father for his unceasing faithfulness in building his church through the ministry of his Word.

Richard D. Phillips
Philip Graham Ryken
Series Editors

Preface

Ignorance of the Old Testament constricts our Christian faith. To understand what Isaiah, Jeremiah, Jesus, Paul, or James said, we need to be thoroughly grounded in the same texts as they were. If we desire to understand the theology of the Old Testament to live more faithfully as Christians in the present day, there is no better text to study than Deuteronomy. Deuteronomy is the central theological text of the Old Testament. Thus, I intend to show in this commentary how the theology and themes of love and loyalty developed in Deuteronomy are expressed throughout the rest of the Bible.

The book of Deuteronomy presents itself to us as the words of Moses. This commentary will approach it as such, while recognizing that someone else must have put the book into its final form, as evidenced by occasional references to Moses in the third person[1] and an account of his death in chapter 34. But the words of the book are the words of Moses. At its most basic structural level, Deuteronomy is a series of three messages that Moses preached to the people of Israel on the plains of Moab at the end of their wilderness wanderings. More helpfully, the book follows the general pattern of Hittite suzerain-vassal treaties from the second millennium B.C., and its similarities to those treaties helps us date the book to the time of Moses or shortly thereafter. It therefore functions as a renewal of the covenant made at Sinai to prepare the people of God for life in the land after Moses.

Following that treaty framework, Deuteronomy 1:1–5 is the preamble that introduces Moses as the one who speaks on behalf of God as the mediator of this covenant. Deuteronomy 1:6–4:40 forms the historical prologue, reminding the people of Israel what God had done for them in the past, and

1. Deut. 1:1, 3, 5; 4:41, 44–46; 5:1; 27:1, 9, 11; 29:1–2; 31:1, 7, 9–10, 14, 16, 22, 24–25, 30; 32:44–45, 48; 33:1, 4; 34:1, 5, 7–10, 12.

what he would continue to do in the future. The stipulations of the covenant are found in the large middle section of Deuteronomy 5:1–26:19. These are the laws that God expects his people to abide by as a show of their loyalty to him and their recognition of his ownership of them, the land, and everything in it. I will interpret and apply the law by making use of the moral, civil, and ceremonial law categories as described in the Westminster Confession of Faith, while also recognizing the limitations of that framework. We are no longer under the terms of the covenant that God made with his people at Sinai, but the law of God continues to be of tremendous use to us as those under the terms of the new covenant, and his moral law forever binds all people. Following the Hittite treaty pattern, the blessings for obedience and curses for disobedience are laid out next in chapters 27–28. Witnesses are called in chapter 30, and in chapter 31 the people are commanded to assemble occasionally to be reminded of what is in this document. Finally, chapters 32–34 close with the transition of leadership from Moses to Joshua.

The basis of this commentary was a series of sermons I preached to the people of Covenant Church of Naples. I felt a burden to preach through this book long before I had the courage to finally do it. For those pastors and Bible teachers who are considering doing so, I pray that this book will be an encouragement for you to go forward. It never ceased to amaze me or the people of our church how much God had to say to us through this profound book. At its core, the book of Deuteronomy is about what it means to live as the covenant people of God. Here Moses recounts God's love for his people expressed in their rescue from Egypt, preservation in the wilderness, and instruction in the law. All the while, Deuteronomy calls forth a loving response from God's people: to remember what he has done in the past, to trust him in the present, and to obey him going forward into the future. My prayer for you is that this commentary, alongside your study of Deuteronomy, will likewise lead you to remember, trust, and obey.

Trent Casto
Naples, Florida

Acknowledgments

Preaching through Deuteronomy requires tremendous patience and effort for any pastor. But it may require even more from his congregation! I want to acknowledge the people of Covenant Church of Naples for their patience with me as I attempted to preach my way through this tremendous book of Moses. Your insatiable hunger for God's Word gave me the confidence to launch into a deep exposition of this book. Thank you for the inspiration and your encouragement along the way. All proceeds from this book return to Covenant Church for the advancement of the gospel from Naples to the ends of the earth.

Writing a book on Deuteronomy required the help of many people, only some of whom I can mention here. I first want to acknowledge my wife, Emily, and our children, who have continually supported me in my writing, even though it means that I'm in my study or away from home more often than I would be otherwise. Without the stability and love that you each contribute to our home, a project such as this would not be possible. Thank you for your part in holding me up and helping this book come to life. I love you and our life together.

Additionally, without the ministry provided by our elders, our deacons, and the tremendously gifted people I serve with on staff at Covenant Church, I could not have attempted a work such as this. My fellow pastors were a constant source of encouragement and helpful feedback in improving the original content undergirding the book. I especially want to thank Sarah Adams for her daily commitment to supporting me in this ministry, for ensuring that I have everything I need when I need it, and for laboring as long as I have over edits to this manuscript. Thank you to James, Harriette, Peggy, and Alisha, who graciously read chapters and identified remaining errors.Also, Jennifer Denard has been a faithful friend and editor for years and made countless improvements to this book before it ever reached our formal editors. Thank you, all.

When our editors did finally get their chance to work on this manuscript, they did their work thoroughly, for which I am deeply grateful. Iain Duguid and Rick Phillips offered excellent feedback, corrections, and suggestions, and Karen Magnuson and John Hughes continue to amaze me by their ability to take an already finely edited book and make it even better. Thank you.

I also want to acknowledge my parents, Jerry and Vickey Casto, who did their best to embody Deuteronomy 6:6–7 in our home and who continue to live sacrificially in obedience to the Great Commission. Finally, I want to thank God for Pastor Jack Bohman, who faithfully shepherded my family for many years. Long after I left my childhood home, Pastor would continue to call on occasion to check in on me. In our last conversation, I was able to share with him the vision for this book and hear some of his thoughts. Though he's no longer here on earth to see the book in print, it wouldn't exist except for his long and faithful ministry at the Buckhannon Alliance Church. May the gospel seed he sowed continue to bear fruit for generations to come.

Abbreviations

ApOTC — Apollos Old Testament Commentary

BDB — Francis Brown, S. R. Driver, and Charles A. Briggs, *The New Brown-Driver-Briggs Hebrew and English Lexicon* (Hendrickson, 2005)

CBQ — *Catholic Biblical Quarterly*

CSB — Christian Standard Bible

EDEJ — *Eerdmans Dictionary of Early Judaism*, ed. John J. Collins and Daniel C. Harlow (Eerdmans, 2010)

EPSC — Evangelical Press Study Commentary

ESV — English Standard Version

IC — Interpretation Commentary

ISBE — *International Standard Bible Encyclopedia*, ed. Geoffrey W. Bromiley, 4 vols. (Zondervan, 1979–88)

JETS — *Journal of the Evangelical Theological Society*

JPSTC — Jewish Publication Society Torah Commentary

JSOT — *Journal for the Study of the Old Testament*

KJV — King James Version

NAC — New American Commentary

NASB — New American Standard Bible

NBD — *New Bible Dictionary*, ed. I. Howard Marshall, A. R. Millard, J. I. Packer, and Donald J. Wiseman, 3rd ed. (InterVarsity Press, 1996)

NDBT	*New Dictionary of Biblical Theology*, ed. T. Desmond Alexander, Brian S. Rosner, D. A. Carson, and Graeme Goldsworthy (InterVarsity Press, 2000)
NIBC	New International Biblical Commentary
NICOT	New International Commentary on the Old Testament
NIDOTTE	*New International Dictionary of Old Testament Theology and Exegesis*, ed. Willem A. VanGemeren, 5 vols. (Zondervan, 1997)
NIV	New International Version
NIVAC	NIV Application Commentary
NSBT	New Studies in Biblical Theology
s.v.	*sub verbo, sub voce* ("under the word")
TOTC	Tyndale Old Testament Commentaries
WCF	Westminster Confession of Faith
WLC	Westminster Larger Catechism
WSC	Westminster Shorter Catechism

Deuteronomy

Remember, Trust, and Obey: Living as God's Covenant People

1

God's Covenant People

Deuteronomy 1:1–5

Beyond the Jordan, in the land of Moab, Moses undertook to explain this law. (Deut. 1:5)

The world as we're experiencing it right now is not the way it's supposed to be: the scenes of devastation caused by a seemingly endless series of natural disasters, the sad stories of violence and repressive regimes always on the move, and the constant reports of the latest flu or other virus threatening the population. It wasn't supposed to be like this. It won't always be like this. But right now, the world is enslaved in the clutches of sin and death (1 John 5:19). Our estate of misery is a consequence of our rebellion against the one true God. Yet despite our rebellion, God loves his creation, and he has a plan to redeem his covenant people, to bring us into a place of rest, and to bless us with his presence forever.

In the book of Genesis, after humanity rebelled against him, God made a promise to the serpent who had lured Eve into rebellion against God: "I will put enmity between you and the woman, and between your offspring and her offspring; he shall bruise your head, and you shall bruise his heel" (Gen. 3:15). The story of history is going to be a story of conflict between the offspring of the serpent and the offspring of the woman. The serpent and his offspring represent evil and everything that has gone wrong with God's good creation. The woman and her offspring represent God's covenant people, and one offspring in particular who will bruise the serpent's head. The serpent will be defeated. But how is this going to take place? The rest of the Bible tells the story.

A Promise of Land, People, and Blessing

In Genesis 12, God called a man named Abram who was worshiping idols in the city of Ur, and God made this promise to him:

> Go from your country and your kindred and your father's house to the land that I will show you. And I will make of you a great nation, and I will bless you and make your name great, so that you will be a blessing. I will bless those who bless you, and him who dishonors you I will curse, and in you all the families of the earth shall be blessed. (Gen. 12:1–3)

God promised Abram a land, a people, and a blessing so that he would be a blessing. God chose one man to begin his project of redemption, but with the intention to bless all the families of the earth in him.

In Genesis 15, God made a covenant with Abram. At this point in the story, Abram was not a great nation. In fact, he did not even have a single child or one parcel of land. So God brought him outside and reaffirmed the promise of offspring: "Look toward heaven, and number the stars, if you are able to number them. . . . So shall your offspring be" (Gen. 15:5). Then God reaffirmed the promise of land: "I am the Lord who brought you out from Ur of the Chaldeans to give you this land to possess" (v. 7). Abram believed God, but also asked God how he could know for sure that he would have this land. So God instructed Abram to cut some animals in half, leaving a little path for walking between them. Then as the sun was going down, Abram fell asleep and God spoke:

> "Know for certain that your offspring will be sojourners in a land that is not theirs and will be servants there, and they will be afflicted for four hundred years. But I will bring judgment on the nation that they serve, and afterward they shall come out with great possessions. As for you, you shall go to your

> fathers in peace; you shall be buried in a good old age. And they shall come back here in the fourth generation, for the iniquity of the Amorites is not yet complete."
>
> When the sun had gone down and it was dark, behold, a smoking fire pot and a flaming torch passed between these pieces. On that day the LORD made a covenant with Abram, saying, "To your offspring I give this land, from the river of Egypt to the great river, the river Euphrates, the land of the Kenites, the Kenizzites, the Kadmonites, the Hittites, the Perizzites, the Rephaim, the Amorites, the Canaanites, the Girgashites and the Jebusites." (Gen. 15:13–21)

God told Abram in advance how his descendants were going to go into a land of affliction without mentioning Egypt specifically. But God also promised to bring them out and then bring them into the land currently occupied by the various nations listed. Then, just a couple of chapters later, God reaffirmed the covenant with Abram again, changing his name to Abraham and giving him the covenant sign of circumcision. God promised:

> And I will establish my covenant between me and you and your offspring after you throughout their generations for an everlasting covenant, to be God to you and to your offspring after you. And I will give to you and to your offspring after you the land of your sojournings, all the land of Canaan, for an everlasting possession, and I will be their God. (Gen. 17:7–8)

As a sign of these covenant promises to make Abraham a great nation, to give him a land, and to be the God of his descendants, every male in Israel was to be circumcised.

As we fast-forward through the rest of Genesis, we see God give Abraham a son, Isaac, who would be the inheritor of these great promises. Isaac fathered Jacob, and Jacob fathered many sons, who would become a great people in the land of Egypt where they went to escape famine. The family of Abraham was afflicted for four hundred years in the land of Egypt, exactly as God had said it would happen in Genesis 15:13. But God did not forget his promise. Exodus tells the story of how God raised up a redeemer to set his people free from their slavery in Egypt. Through Moses, God poured out ten different plagues on the most powerful nation on the earth, humiliating their so-called gods. Just as God promised, they did come out of slavery with great possessions.

But what next? If we suppose that these newly liberated slaves were just going to go and start a new nation from scratch, we underestimate the impact of four hundred years of slavery. The Israelites knew nothing about war or governance or nation building. Sandra Richter helps us appreciate just how improbable it would be for Israel to succeed:

> In addition to their theological confusion, the people of Israel had been shaped by generations of slavery. Pause to consider the long-term effects of such conditions. Stripped of the opportunity to organize their own lives and society, illiterate, abused and dominated, how would this mob become a nation? By what laws would they rule themselves, structure their religion, organize their calendar? How would they be shaped into a fighting force that had any chance of conquering Canaan?[1]

They had a number of high hurdles to overcome if they were going to be a light to the nations as God intended. So what did God do? He brought them out of Egypt, and he led them to a desert place in the Sinai Peninsula called Horeb. (Outside Deuteronomy, it is normally referred to as Mount Sinai.) There at Horeb, Yahweh, the God of Israel, defined the relationship for his people. At Horeb, God established the descendants of Abraham as a new nation by making a covenant with them. The events are recorded beginning in Exodus 19.

The Establishment of God's Covenant People

To understand God's covenant relationship with his people in the book of Deuteronomy, we need to understand the suzerain-vassal treaty. When Deuteronomy was written, sometime around 1400–1200 B.C. (depending on when the exodus is dated), there was a common kind of covenant relationship called a suzerain/vassal treaty. In this arrangement, the suzerain was the greater military power and the vassal was the lesser. The suzerain would take authority over the vassal kingdom, demanding its submission. The suzerain had authority over the people and the land of the vassal nation and ultimately

1. Sandra L. Richter, *The Epic of Eden: A Christian Entry into the Old Testament* (IVP Academic, 2008), 83.

owned everything they produced. Some portion of that produce was required as tribute from the vassal nation. The suzerain ruler then bound himself to protect his vassal and to fight for it if an enemy arose. If the vassal called for help and salvation from an enemy, the suzerain was expected to come. In return, the vassal was to remain loyal to the suzerain and not make any other alliances. This kind of loyalty had a name in Hebrew: *ḥesed*. We typically translate it as "steadfast love," but at its heart the word refers to "covenant faithfulness."[2] If the vassal did not remain loyal, the suzerain would turn his power against the vassal, and likely take away the land grant and send the people into exile.[3] Typically in this kind of covenant arrangement, the suzerain-vassal would be referred to as father/son or lord/servant. To keep the covenant was "to love" one's suzerain, and to break the covenant was "to hate" him.[4] Does any of this sound familiar?

This background is so important because in the 1950s, biblical scholars studying these Hittite suzerain-vassal treaties made the compelling case that God's covenant with his people follows the same pattern, and it can be seen in the structure of the book of Deuteronomy.[5] These treaties were common and had a standard form, much like a marriage license or a bill of sale today. Here are the standard components of a second-millennium B.C. Hittite suzerain-vassal treaty: (1) *Preamble*: In the preamble, the suzerain identified himself, frequently using language such as this: "These are the words of . . ." (2) *Historical prologue*: In the historical prologue, the suzerain reminded his vassal of the basis of his obligation to the suzerain. Usually, it was a reminder of how the suzerain had saved, protected, or provided for the vassal. (3) *Stipulations*: These were the detailed expectations required of the vassal in terms of economics, warfare, and so on, as well as the expectations of loyalty to the suzerain. (4) *Blessings and curses*: Blessings were promised if the vassal remained faithful and loyal to the suzerain, and curses promised if not. (5) *Witnesses*: Typically, deities were called on to witness the covenant that was made to ensure the loyalty of all the parties involved. After oaths

2. Richter, 75.

3. Richter, 74.

4. Richter, 79.

5. J. A. Thompson, *Deuteronomy: An Introduction and Commentary*, TOTC (InterVarsity Press, 1974), 17. The pattern can also be seen in Exodus 19:1–23:19, an event being recounted here in Deuteronomy.

were made and sacrifices offered to seal the covenant, each partner was to go home with a copy of the covenant and instructions to read it periodically so that everyone would remember the deal.[6]

Deuteronomy as a Covenant Treaty

When we look at the big picture of Deuteronomy, we see that it is laid out very much like a Hittite suzerain-vassal treaty. In other words, the idea of a suzerain's forming a covenant with his vassal people was not something that God created to advance redemptive history. But by God's providence, the covenant concept was already prevalent in the ancient world when God entered into a covenant with Israel in Exodus. God co-opted the concept of covenant to communicate his plan of redemption to his people.[7] He is the suzerain, and his people are the vassals.

In Deuteronomy 1:1–5, the preamble introduces Moses, who speaks on behalf of God as the mediator of this covenant. Deuteronomy 1:6–4:40 forms the historical prologue. It reminds the people of Israel what God has done for them in the past, and what he will continue to do in the future. The question raised in this section is not whether God will be faithful to keep his promises, but whether his people will be faithful to their God. Success in taking the land is going to depend on their relationship to their suzerain more than on their military might.[8] The stipulations of the covenant are found in the large middle section of Deuteronomy 5:1–26:19. These are all the laws that God expects his people to abide by as a show of their loyalty to him and their recognition of his ownership of them, the land, and everything in it. The sheer breadth and diversity of laws illustrate that no area of life is unimportant in this covenant community.[9] The people that the Lord rescued from Egypt are not just any people; they are his people, and they are to learn to live as his people in every area of life. The blessings

6. Peter Craigie rightly understands the covenant structure of Deuteronomy to be the key to interpreting its theological significance. For a helpful overview of some of the key theological themes following the basic breakdown of the covenant form, see Peter C. Craigie, *The Book of Deuteronomy*, NICOT (Eerdmans, 1976), 36–45.

7. Richter, *Epic of Eden*, 82.

8. Craigie, *Deuteronomy*, 92.

9. Craigie, 43.

for obedience and curses for disobedience are laid out in chapters 27–28, and then in chapter 30 witnesses are called:

> I call heaven and earth to witness against you today, that I have set before you life and death, blessing and curse. Therefore choose life, that you and your offspring may live, loving the LORD your God, obeying his voice and holding fast to him, for he is your life and length of days, that you may dwell in the land that the LORD swore to your fathers, to Abraham, to Isaac, and to Jacob, to give them. (Deut. 30:19–20)

These are the words of a suzerain to his vassal, the words of God to his people. If they reject this covenant, they are choosing death, and neither they nor their children will remain in the land. Finally, in chapter 31 there is a command to assemble the people periodically to reread the words of this covenant and remember them.

Why are we considering this information so closely? Because Deuteronomy presents God to us as a suzerain king fulfilling his promises to his vassal people, and posing the question whether his people are going to be faithful to him and experience life or reject his ways and end in death. These questions still confront every reader of Deuteronomy today because God still demands of us the same love and loyalty as he did of the people of Israel: will we remember what he has done, trust him to be faithful to his promises, and obey his commands?

The Long Way of Disobedience

That background information brings us to the opening words of Deuteronomy 1:1, "These are the words that Moses spoke to all Israel beyond the Jordan in the wilderness, in the Arabah opposite Suph, between Paran and Tophel, Laban, Hazeroth, and Dizahab." Deuteronomy's opening words serve as the title of the book in Hebrew: "These are the words." Deuteronomy consists of the words that Moses spoke to the people of Israel before they began their conquest of the promised land under Joshua. In fact, it is basically three speeches that can be delineated by key words of introduction: 1:1–4:43; 4:44–28:68; 29:1–30:20. Where does Moses deliver these speeches? Deuteronomy 1:1 says, "These are the words that Moses spoke to all Israel beyond the Jordan in the wilderness, in the Arabah opposite Suph, between Paran and Tophel, Laban, Hazeroth, and Dizahab." But verse 5 states, "Beyond the Jordan, in the land of Moab, Moses undertook to explain this law." So which is it? It is probably best not to see this as an either/or situation. The place names mentioned in verse 1 are difficult to identify, although most likely they refer to various places in the Sinai Peninsula or perhaps the Arabah south of the Dead Sea.[10] It is possible that Moses originally delivered some of the content of Deuteronomy at these places along the way over the course of the Israelites' forty years of wandering.[11] But now here on the plains of Moab (1:5), he is summing it all up and preaching to them these messages in preparation for their entry into the land as God's covenant people. In other words, the content of Deuteronomy is not necessarily new to the Israelites when Moses delivers it here on the plains of Moab. Rather, Deuteronomy is a renewal of the covenant that God made with his people at Sinai nearly forty years earlier.[12] In fact, our English word "Deuteronomy" comes from a word in the Greek translation of Deuteronomy 17:18, *deuteronomion*, which means "second law." Deuteronomy is not a second law, but an exposition of the law that God gave at Sinai forty years earlier. As we read Deuteronomy, we recognize that it is Moses' exposition of the law to God's people. Why is it necessary for Moses to preach this law to them and remind them of this covenant?

The answer is cleverly crafted in Deuteronomy 1:2 and easy to miss if we are not paying attention: "It is eleven days' journey from Horeb by the way of Mount Seir to Kadesh-barnea." "Horeb" is Deuteronomy's preferred name for Mount Sinai.[13] Moses says that it is an eleven-day journey from Horeb to Kadesh-barnea by the way of Mount Seir.[14] Since we do not know exactly

10. See Jeffrey H. Tigay, *Deuteronomy*, JPSTC (Jewish Publication Society, 1996), xlv, for possibilities. Craigie, *Deuteronomy*, 90, locates these places in the general region of the Transjordan.

11. Tigay, *Deuteronomy*, 3.

12. Christopher Wright, *Deuteronomy*, NIBC: Old Testament 4 (Hendrickson, 2007), 1.

13. The only place in Deuteronomy where "Sinai" is used is in Deuteronomy 33:2. Everywhere else, it is referred to as Horeb. Outside Deuteronomy, "Horeb" is used only a handful of times.

14. If Mount Seir is located southeast of the Dead Sea at Jebel Esh-Shera as some believe, it is not clear why the Israelites would have gone there before going to Kadesh-barnea. Yet the Hebrew word for "mount" frequently refers not to a particular mountain, but to a highlands or hill country region (such as the familiar "hill country of Ephraim" used throughout the Old Testament). Additionally, route names in the Bible are usually designated by their terminating points. Much as a subway line in the city is identified by its terminating point, so "the way of Mount Seir" was likely a road that ran through Kadesh-barnea and ended at Mount Seir or in the Seir Highlands. For more, see Tigay, *Deuteronomy*, 4.

where Horeb was located, it is impossible for us to identify this road. But we know that it is supposed to be only an eleven-day journey from Horeb, where Israel received the law, to Kadesh-barnea, which is on the southern border of the promised land. But verse 3 tells us that Moses is speaking in the "fortieth year." Why does Moses mention this little detail, juxtaposing the eleven days' journey with its being the fortieth year since the exodus? He does so to serve as a reminder to Israel and to us that the people's last thirty-eight years of wandering in the wilderness were completely unnecessary. The death of that whole generation was completely unnecessary. If the people of God had only remembered that God delivered them from the mighty power of Egypt, if they had only trusted in God to fight for them as their suzerain, if they had only obeyed his command to go up and take the land, they could have avoided the suffering of the last thirty-eight years. It needed to be only an eleven-day trip!

It is like a family road trip in south Florida from Naples to Miami. One day a family sets out from Naples, and thirty-eight years later they arrive in Miami. An observer notes, "It's only a two-hour drive to Miami from Naples." But the observer does not say it to the parents who started out on the journey, because they died in the Everglades along the way! Instead, their children are wondering, "How did a two-hour trip turn into thirty-eight years?" And the answer is this: by not following directions. Or to put it more biblically: disobedience resulting from a failure to trust resulting from a failure to remember. If we were one of the people in this new generation poised to enter the promised land now, we would not want to repeat the same mistake as the last generation. But of course, this remains to be seen.

Deuteronomy 1:3–5 sets the scene for the rest of the book:

> In the fortieth year, on the first day of the eleventh month, Moses spoke to the people of Israel according to all that the LORD had given him in commandment to them, after he had defeated Sihon the king of the Amorites, who lived in Heshbon, and Og the king of Bashan, who lived in Ashtaroth and in Edrei. Beyond the Jordan, in the land of Moab, Moses undertook to explain this law.

It has now been forty years since God freed the Israelites from slavery in Egypt and established his covenant with them. Rather than going in immediately and taking the land as God's vassal nation, they did not remember, they did not trust, and they did not obey, as we will see in coming chapters. They have spent thirty-eight years wandering in the wilderness, and now they are about to get a second chance at taking the land that God promised them. On the eastern border of the promised land, they have just defeated two kings, Sihon and Og. It is a good sign that their suzerain, God, is fighting for them and will give them more victories going forward. But before they go in, Moses reminds them of this covenant that God made with them to be his people when he brought them out of Egypt. Over the course of our study of this book, we are going to learn in detail what God has promised to do for his people as their suzerain, and what it means to remember, trust, and obey as his covenant people. But right at the outset, we are reminded of the consequences of not remembering, not trusting, and not obeying.

Living as God's Covenant People Today

We are no longer under the terms of the covenant that God made with his people at Sinai, but we *are* under the terms of the new covenant, a covenant that is far greater than the covenant God made at Sinai. Despite Moses' best intentions for the people of Israel, he knew that they were not going to live up to the terms of this covenant. They were going to seek out other suzerains and ultimately bring the curses of the covenant upon themselves and be exiled from the land that God had given them. But God was not yet done with his covenant people.

After repeated generations of his people failed to keep his covenant, God initiated the new covenant. Knowing that all his people were so corrupted by sin that none of us could be faithful, God himself stepped out of heaven and into human flesh in the person of Jesus Christ, and in our place, Christ fulfilled the requirements of the covenant for us. Then he took the curses that a covenant-breaker deserves upon himself. The effect is that for those who trust in Jesus, there remains only covenant blessing, which Christ deserved and earned for us.

Now we are in Jesus Christ and he is the Mediator of God's new covenant, and those who trust in Christ as their Lord and Savior are God's covenant people. Under the old covenant, God rescued his people from slavery in Egypt and, with the blood of sacrificial animals, sealed his promise to be their God and to have Israel as his people. Under the terms of the new covenant,

God has rescued us from our greater slavery to sin and the fear of death and has sealed that covenant with his own sacrificial blood. He is our suzerain Lord, and we are his vassal people. He is the Mighty One who fights for us, and we are his treasured possession, and no one can snatch us out of his hands. Though we falter and fail, he will never send us into exile, for Jesus has already taken the whole curse for us. We are safe and secure in him.

In grateful response to his entering into covenant with us, like Israel, we are now called to live as his covenant people. Every single part of our lives is to be brought into alignment with God's good purposes for us and his creation. Though we no longer live under the terms of the covenant made in Deuteronomy, our study of this book will help us learn more deeply what it means to remember, trust, and obey and live as God's covenant people.

2

The Gifts of God for the People of God

Deuteronomy 1:5–18

See, I have set the land before you. Go in and take possession of the land that the Lord *swore to your fathers, to Abraham, to Isaac, and to Jacob, to give to them and to their offspring after them.* (Deut. 1:8)

I can still vividly remember that morning. It was my birthday, and I wanted only one thing—the one thing that I was pretty sure I would never get. A horse. For about two years, it was all I thought about. I remember watching Westerns on TV, not because I was interested in the storylines, but just because I wanted to see the horses. I dreamed about horses, I daydreamed about horses, and I asked my parents for a horse nonstop. On one beautiful August morning, they called me to come outside, where I got the gift of a lifetime: my own horse. I loved that horse—for a while.

I loved to ride him, brush him, and feed him. Sometimes I would just go out and lie on him as he wandered around, eating grass. But he was not a perfectly trained horse. He did not trot when he was supposed to, he frequently tried to buck me off, and he had a knack for stepping on my feet. His favorite trick, though, was to puff out his stomach while I was saddling him up. When we would set out on a ride and he was no longer pushing his stomach out, the saddle would loosen. Typically, when we started to gallop, both saddle and rider would slide right off the horse onto the ground. This did not put us on good terms. The less time and effort I put into him, the worse he got and the less I enjoyed him. Eventually, the gift stopped feeling so much like a gift and started feeling more like a burden. It was not long before the horse found a new home at a farm down the road.

Some gifts are like that. They are good gifts, but to enjoy them requires effort. If I had invested a little more time and effort into that horse, I would have enjoyed the gift a whole lot more. Sometimes God's gifts are that way. Contrary to what we might think, possessing God's good gifts does not free us *from* effort, but calls us *to* effort to truly enjoy them. In this passage, Moses is recounting when God told the people of Israel that they had been at Horeb long enough. It was time for them to move forward into the good future that he had prepared for them. He had good gifts that he was eager to give them, namely a great land, a great people, and a great law. But right from the beginning, we can see that these good gifts are going to require effort if they are to be enjoyed. The same is true for God's gifts to us today. In this chapter, we will consider those gifts and what they mean for us.

The Gift of a Great Land

Deuteronomy 1:5 helpfully locates the setting of this book with these words: "Beyond the Jordan, in the land of Moab, Moses undertook to explain this law." The people are currently on the east side of the Jordan River, just north of the Dead Sea on the plains of Moab. Before they go in and take the land that God promised to them, Moses sets about renewing the covenant that God made with them at Horeb when he brought them out of Egypt nearly forty years before. The book of Deuteronomy is framed as a suzerain-vassal treaty, and here Moses begins to remind the people of their history with God as their suzerain. Throughout the course of his series of sermons, he will remind them not only of what God has done for them, but also of what God requires of them as his people, as well as the specific blessings and curses that await them, depending on their willingness to abide by God's covenant terms. As Alec Motyer writes:

> The theological truth here is that those who have been redeemed by the blood of the lamb must come to the place where they hear the law of the Lord: his law is not a system of merit whereby people, by good works, seek divine favour; but a divinely revealed way of life whereby those who have already been brought into his favour by redemption can live according to his will: it is a lifestyle of responsive obedience for the redeemed.[1]

So now Moses takes them back nearly forty years. After rescuing his people from their slavery in Egypt, God led them down the Sinai Peninsula to Horeb, where he entered into a covenant with them and gave them his law. After they spent a year there, God said that it was time to move on. We read in Deuteronomy 1:6, "The LORD our God said to us in Horeb, 'You have stayed long enough at this mountain.'" God's words to the people at Horeb suggest that he was eager for the Israelites to enter the land. The fact that it took forty years is portrayed here not as God's intention, but rather as the result of Israel's failure to trust and obey him.[2] Horeb was an incredible place. God met with his people there in astounding ways, and through Moses, he gave them his law. But as amazing as Horeb was, it was not God's final destination for his people—just an essential stop along the way. If they had settled there, they could not have received all that God had promised them. To be fully blessed so that they could become a blessing, they needed to move on.

This is instructive for us as Christians too. There are times in our Christian lives when God says, "You've been here long enough." We get comfortable where we are, but God has more to give us, and we cannot receive it without leaving what we know and going forward. Sometimes that means a call to a new and unfamiliar vocation or ministry. It may mean a change of location. Or it could be a move from singleness to marriage or from marriage to widowhood. But in each case, what he intends to give us is not for ourselves

1. Alec Motyer, *Roots: Let the Old Testament Speak*, ed. John Stott (Christian Focus, 2009), 62.
2. Jeffrey H. Tigay, *Deuteronomy*, JPSTC (Jewish Publication Society, 1996), 8.

only, but so that we might be a blessing to others. So he calls the Israelites to go forward and take hold of what he has promised them: namely, a land. We read in Deuteronomy 1:7–8:

> Turn and take your journey, and go to the hill country of the Amorites and to all their neighbors in the Arabah, in the hill country and in the lowland and in the Negeb and by the seacoast, the land of the Canaanites, and Lebanon, as far as the great river, the river Euphrates. See, I have set the land before you. Go in and take possession of the land that the LORD swore to your fathers, to Abraham, to Isaac, and to Jacob, to give to them and to their offspring after them.

As we saw in the previous chapter, God had promised Abraham that he would give him the land of Canaan for a dwelling place, and the same promise was given to his children.[3] Here in Deuteronomy 1, they are on the verge of taking hold of that promise.

Notice that the land is being given to God's people in fulfillment of the promise. It is a gift—yet Israel still must go in and take it. God asserts: "See, I have set the land before you. Go in and take possession of the land" (Deut. 1:8). Just because God gives us something as a gift does not mean that there is no effort involved in enjoying that gift. Here is a principle of the Christian life: God's promises do not preclude human effort but rather establish and motivate it. God's promise of the land to Israel was to motivate the people to go in and take it, knowing that it had been given. The fact that God had sworn it to them should have given them all the confidence and assurance they needed. But they still had to go up and fight and take it. Christopher Wright reminds us that "God's gift of grace needed to be appropriated by faith, obedience, and action. Centuries later, prophets would threaten that the gift could be lost again through unbelief, disobedience, and complacency."[4]

Likewise, God has given incredible gifts to us Christians, who are his covenant people. But it does not mean that no effort is required to enjoy them. This is not to say that we can earn God's gifts; we most certainly cannot. But enjoying them requires effort. Dallas Willard famously wrote: "The path of spiritual growth in the riches of Christ is not a passive one. Grace

3. Genesis 12:1; 15:7, 18–21; 17:8.

4. Christopher Wright, *Deuteronomy*, NIBC: Old Testament 4 (Hendrickson, 2007), 25.

is not opposed to effort. It is opposed to earning. Effort is action. Earning is attitude. You have never seen people more active than those who have been set on fire by the grace of God."[5] One of God's good gifts of grace to us is our sanctification, the progressive process by which we become increasingly like Christ. This is a gift. At the same time, we have an active role to play in putting off the things in us that do not accord with Christlikeness and putting on those things that are Christlike (see, e.g., Col. 3:1–17). In a similar way, eternal life is a gift given to those who trust in Christ. Yet this gift is not something that we simply passively acknowledge, but one that we are to actively take hold of. That is precisely what Paul commands in 1 Timothy 6:12: "Take hold of the eternal life to which you were called." We are called to eternal life, but we must also take hold of it even as the Israelites needed to take hold of the land that was promised to them. As we will see, the Israelites fail to do that on their first attempt. God has given them a gift, but the people are not ready to take hold of it.

Is God holding out to us any gifts today that we are not yet willing to take hold of because it requires effort? Or has God made promises, but we are content to settle for less? If we were to chart out the boundaries of the land mentioned here, it is an area far larger than anything that Israel ever laid claim to in its history. Even when the people went in and took the land, they never grasped all that God had for them. So too in our Christian lives, how often do we live with less than what God has promised to us simply because receiving the promise requires effort? Let us not leave anything of what God has promised to us sitting on the table unclaimed. Instead, may we take hold of all of it, not only for our own sake, but for the sake of our missionary purpose, so that through us his blessings would flow to the nations.[6]

The Gift of a Great People

God was keeping his promise to give Abraham a land and to make him a nation. Now at Horeb, God told Moses that it was time for Israel to go and take the land. But before the people could leave Horeb, Moses needed some leadership help. God had so abundantly kept his promise to Abraham

5. Dallas Willard, "Live Life to the Full," *Christian Herald* (UK), April 14, 2001, https://dwillard.org/articles/live-life-to-the-full, accessed September 2, 2021.

6. Wright, *Deuteronomy*, 25–26.

that the people were more than Moses could handle on his own. The gift of more people required the effort of raising up leaders. Moses highlights the problem in Deuteronomy 1:9–12: "At that time I said to you, 'I am not able to bear you by myself. The LORD your God has multiplied you, and behold, you are today as numerous as the stars of heaven. May the LORD, the God of your fathers, make you a thousand times as many as you are and bless you, as he has promised you! How can I bear by myself the weight and burden of you and your strife?'" The growth of God's people was a good thing. In fact, Moses recounts here the promise of God to Abraham in Genesis 15:5: "Look toward heaven, and number the stars, if you are able to number them. . . . So shall your offspring be." God was fulfilling his promise and giving them the gift of being a great people. But that gift meant work!

Moses prayed that God would bless the Israelites even more in this way, but they were already beyond his ability to manage on his own. Leaders needed to be raised up. We read in Deuteronomy 1:13–15:

> "Choose for your tribes wise, understanding, and experienced men, and I will appoint them as your heads." And you answered me, "The thing that you have spoken is good for us to do." So I took the heads of your tribes, wise and experienced men, and set them as heads over you, commanders of thousands, commanders of hundreds, commanders of fifties, commanders of tens, and officers, throughout your tribes.

The leaders who were to be chosen by the people needed to possess both ability and standing in the community. The sense of the Hebrew word translated "experienced" is that they are well known, and therefore seen as trustworthy.[7] These men needed to have a reputation in the community. Notice that it is the communities that choose their leaders; Moses does not impose leaders on them. After the communities chose them, Moses divided them up in such a way as to help spread out the load of the leadership of the people.

As we continue to read through our Bibles, we see something similar play out in the New Testament. When the early church was born in the book of Acts, God's promises resulted in the extraordinary growth of the church. After Peter's sermon on the day of Pentecost and the church's remarkable

7. BDB, s.v. "יָדַע," 394.

display of sacrificial love for one another, new believers were being added to their number every day. It was not long before the growth of the church resulted in some disputes and organizational challenges that were more than the apostles could handle on their own. So they followed the pattern set down here by Moses. We read in Acts 6:2–3: "And the twelve summoned the full number of the disciples and said, 'It is not right that we should give up preaching the word of God to serve tables. Therefore, brothers, pick out from among you seven men of good repute, full of the Spirit and of wisdom, whom we will appoint to this duty.'" The characteristics that they were looking for in the leaders were similar: men of good reputation who were known for their wisdom. As in the selection of those who came alongside Moses, the wise selection of elders and deacons enables our churches to grow without overtaxing any one person or leader. Now, as then, the choosing of these people is the responsibility of the people. Growth is a gift that calls for effort.

In an interview with *The Christian Century*, the late pastor Eugene Peterson lamented the sorry state of churches in the early 2000s. In his view, part of the issue was that churches had money and people, but they were not being properly pastored. He felt that a church really ought not to be more than five hundred people.[8] The challenge of shepherding and leading a large church is real, and a case could certainly be made for Peterson's suggestion. But rather than capping the size of the growth of the people of God in any particular church, the biblical witness across both the Old and New Testaments is that we ought to be raising up more leaders to help carry the pastoral load. Growth is a blessing, but it comes with challenges. Our privilege is to identify leaders among us who meet the qualifications laid out in Scripture, and to equip them to help shepherd the flock.[9] Likewise, men ought to be doing everything in their power to become the kind of wise, godly, seasoned men of reputation who can help to shepherd the flock.

The Gift of a Great Law

God kept his promises to give Abraham a land and to make him a nation. Then at Horeb, after giving his law, God told Moses that it was time for Israel

8. David J. Wood, "The Best Life: Eugene Peterson on Pastoral Ministry," *Christian Century*, March 13, 2002, https://www.christiancentury.org/article/2002-03/best-life, accessed September 2, 2021.

9. See 1 Timothy 3 and Titus 1 for the specific qualifications for an elder or deacon in the church.

to go and take the land. But before God's people left Horeb, Moses gave special instructions to the judges. God himself is the Judge who rules with righteousness and justice, and therefore he makes it clear that his people are to be known by these qualities as well:

> And I charged your judges at that time, "Hear the cases between your brothers, and judge righteously between a man and his brother or the alien who is with him. You shall not be partial in judgment. You shall hear the small and the great alike. You shall not be intimidated by anyone, for the judgment is God's. And the case that is too hard for you, you shall bring to me, and I will hear it." (Deut. 1:16–17)

The appointment of these judges was to help with the administration of justice among the people of God. God gives his people the gift of his law to show his wisdom and goodness to the nations as embodied in this distinct people. But a law in a land is ultimately only as good as those who administer it. Therefore, those who judge in Israel need to do so in accordance with God's character.

It is easy for us to take these characteristics of judges for granted because we live in a culture grounded on these very principles, but we should not take these qualities for granted. We can gather the following principles from these verses:

1. *Judges must judge righteously.* They must rule based on what the law says is right, not based on who the parties of the case are. Judges of God's people should be so shaped by God's Word that they will have wisdom to know what is right in any given situation.

2. *Judges must not show partiality.* It does not matter if the case is between two Israelites, or between an Israelite and a foreigner among them. What is right is right, and a person's ethnicity does not factor into the judgment. Judges are not to show partiality in what cases they are willing to hear, nor in how they decide those cases. God shows no partiality, and if his judges do, they are misrepresenting him.

3. *Judges must not be intimidated.* In other words, some people will try to manipulate these judges through their wealth, strength, position, or influence. But among God's people, judges are to fear God more than men so that nothing will keep them from doing what is right. As Patrick Miller

writes, "fearfulness leading to partiality places the judge before a greater threat than the powerful defendant or plaintiff."[10] God does not take the perversion of justice lightly.[11]

We see right here at the beginning of Deuteronomy that how the law is administered is as important as the content of the law itself. It does little good to have a great law if that law is administered unrighteously. Old Testament scholar ChristopherWright observes:

> This corresponds well with a growing awareness in our own day that people, especially the powerless, the poor, the illiterate, the immigrant, the asylum seeker[,] are as often hurt by the cumbersome and complicated *process* of the law, even good law, as they are victims of bad law or deliberate injustice. Legal processes that are delayed, demeaning and discriminatory, or simply unaffordable by the poor, are as bad as active injustice and oppression.[12]

In other words, by biblical standards of justice, our own (American) legal system falls short. We are likely better off than most other nations, and yet built into our system is a bias against those who are poor and vulnerable. The practical implication of this deficiency is that even when our laws themselves are just, we may have injustice because of faulty administration of those laws. In an article for the American Bar Association, Liane Jackson writes:

> At criminal courts across the country, poor defendants can't afford competent counsel; many succumb to unfavorable plea deals for financial reasons; and public defenders are underresourced and overworked. There is a de facto dual justice system in the United States—one for the well-off and one for the poor—and it undermines our commitment to the rule of law.[13]

Thankfully, the Sixth Amendment of the United States Constitution guarantees Americans legal representation, even if we cannot afford it. But

10. Patrick D. Miller, *Deuteronomy*, IC (John Knox Press, 1990), 30.

11. Job himself apparently functioned as a righteous judge among his people in earlier days (Job 29:7–17).

12. Christopher J. H. Wright, *Old Testament Ethics for the People of God* (InterVarsity Press, 2004), 304.

13. Liane Jackson, "Balance of Power: Money and Inequity in the Judicial System," *ABA Journal*, September 1, 2019, https://www.abajournal.com/magazine/article/balance-of-power, accessed September 2, 2021.

the odds of a good outcome are far better if we can afford our own legal counsel. I can remember a few years ago when a well-known celebrity was arrested for driving under the influence and getting into an accident. As soon as I read about it, I said, "There is no way he ends up with a DUI." Within a few short months, the celebrity had a lesser charge because our legal process helps those who can afford it the most. To be clear, the poor are far better off in the United States legal system than in nearly any other nation, but biblically speaking, our legal system is fraught with injustice. Christians should care about this kind of thing.

Several years ago, a regular attender of our church was pulled over for having a brake light out. He lacked proper documentation and was taken to a detention center in Miami. After spending months locked away in limbo, his oldest son had to drop out of school to take over the business and support the family. The son brought this to our attention, and we prayerfully considered the matter as elders. Our elders wanted to help and offered to pay for the family's legal representation out of their own pockets. It was not a statement that the man was innocent, but rather a recognition that without money for legal aid, this family did not have a chance. So at their own expense, our elders hired competent legal counsel for this family. By God's grace (and the best justice that money can buy), this man was released and is now a legal member of our community, and his family is thriving. But without the intervention of our elders, it is almost certain that the man would have been deported, leaving his family alone in the United States to plunge into abject poverty. Money makes a difference in our legal system, and that is a problem in the biblical concept of justice. The same is true in many other nations of the world today. Israel was not to be that way, and neither should our system—and to the degree that we can help, it is our Christian calling to do so. God has given us his standard of justice, but this gift calls for effort from his people. Because God is just and loves justice, his people must pursue justice.

In the church, elders are tasked with the charge of deciding cases among God's people. In fact, as much as possible, believers should settle their disputes within the church and not take cases to the government legal system. The apostle Paul admonishes in 1 Corinthians 6:1–7:

> When one of you has a grievance against another, does he dare go to law before the unrighteous instead of the saints? Or do you not know that the saints will

> judge the world? And if the world is to be judged by you, are you incompetent to try trivial cases? Do you not know that we are to judge angels? How much more, then, matters pertaining to this life! So if you have such cases, why do you lay them before those who have no standing in the church? I say this to your shame. Can it be that there is no one among you wise enough to settle a dispute between the brothers, but brother goes to law against brother, and that before unbelievers? To have lawsuits at all with one another is already a defeat for you. Why not rather suffer wrong? Why not rather be defrauded?

God has given us his Word, and he has given us elders who can decide cases among his people. But before it escalates that far, Paul stresses, as believers we should prefer to be defrauded rather than to take a case to a court outside the church. (We're talking about civil cases here. Criminal cases need to be handled by the court system because the church does not have authority to act in that sphere.) But here is how the gospel transforms even this: rather than insist on our rights, the gospel sets us free to suffer wrong without retaliation. We have a right to seek for wrongs to be made right in the context of our churches, and we have a responsibility to point out to a brother or sister when that person has sinned against us (Matt. 18:15–17). But we are not to utilize a secular court to get our way. Why not? Because the cross assures us that ultimate justice is coming. Christ died on the cross to satisfy the demands of justice. Every sin of ours was laid on Christ, and he bore the justice we deserved, so that we who trust in Christ might receive forgiveness and grace. We know that if God's commitment to justice was so great that he would send his Son to face what our sins deserved, nothing in this universe will ultimately escape his justice. We will seek justice for others and demand it in our society because it reflects the character of our God. But for ourselves in the church, we would rather be defrauded, entrusting our souls to our faithful Creator, who sees all and will make all things right in the end.

God has gifted his people in extraordinary ways, as Deuteronomy 1 reminds us, but those gifts do not release us from working hard. Rather, God's gifts call us to make every effort to take hold of them, knowing that the one who promised them is faithful and will do what he has said. Jesus is the perfect example of being motivated by God's promise to possess the promise. As the writer of Hebrews proclaims, "For the joy that was set before him [Jesus] endured the cross" (Heb. 12:2). He knew the promise of the redemption of his people; he would have his bride for himself. But he did not simply sit back and receive the promise. He was moved to action—moved to endure the cross in order to possess the promise—in order to possess us. He showed us what it looks like to trust the Father and to obey his commandments, even to the point of death on a cross. Because he did not shrink back from obedience, he will not lose one of his own. Jesus left no blessings on the table unclaimed, no promises unpossessed, and no promised land unoccupied. He will have all the new creation, filled with people from every tongue, tribe, and nation. He will possess every inch of creation for himself, and he will possess us as well.[14]

In light of this, let us take hold of the promises offered to us in the gospel. As he blesses us with the gift of growth in our churches, let us faithfully raise up more leaders. As we grow in our knowledge of his Word, let us faithfully pursue its vision of justice until the day he returns to establish perfect liberty and justice for all.

14. I am indebted to Covenant Church of Naples member Rachel Dube for sharing her reflections with me of how Jesus models the faithful response to God's promises.

3

The Problems or the Promises?

Deuteronomy 1:19—33

Yet you would not go up, but rebelled against the command of the Lord your God. And you murmured in your tents and said, "Because the Lord hated us he has brought us out of the land of Egypt, to give us into the hand of the Amorites, to destroy us." (Deut. 1:26–27)

Success does not come without challenges. No one plants a church, builds a booming business, starts a school, or breaks a world record without overcoming a mountain of obstacles and problems along the way. Successful people are not people who never face problems, but they see their problems differently. One of the keys to their success is that they view the opportunity in front of them as bigger than the obstacle. Another key is that they do not face all their obstacles at once but take them one at a time. Consider, for example, the tennis star Novak Djokovic. When he came on to the world tennis stage, Roger Federer and Rafael Nadal were already well established as the kings of tennis, setting records that seemed impossible to break. But tournament after tournament, year after year, Djokovic kept showing up and, as of the time of this writing, has surpassed Federer and Nadal with twenty-four Grand Slam titles. To win that many titles is to climb an enormous mountain with countless obstacles that would discourage even the most promising players. So what do successful people have to do? They take one obstacle at a time, and they keep their focus on the opportunities before them.

In this passage, Moses recounts how God had set an incredible promise in front of his people: the promise of a great land of their own that was exceptionally productive. He told them to go in and take it and assured them of success. But of course, this did not mean that there would not be challenges. It simply meant that they would overcome those challenges and obtain the promise if they would remember, trust, and obey. Of course, such things are easier said than done. We are all inclined to focus on the problems before us rather than the promises of God. We all struggle with the temptation to let the obstacles before us loom larger than the opportunities. But if we do not check this tendency, we will never take possession of all that God intends for us to possess. This not only means that we are missing out on the blessing that God intends for us personally, but also means that we are not extending the blessing of God to others. God has set before us some incredible promises and likewise calls us to attempt great things in this world for his glory and the good of others. But if we are focused on the problems and obstacles rather than the promises of God, we will likely never attempt any of them. This passage teaches us to fix our eyes on the promises, not on the problems.

The Promises

Remember, at this point in Deuteronomy, Moses is reminding the Israelites of their history with God. After he rescued them from Egypt, he led them to Horeb, where he gave them his law. Then Moses appointed various leaders and judges to help manage the astounding growth that God had given the people in fulfillment of his promise to Abraham. Now God is ready for them to go up and take the land he had promised them. We read in Deuteronomy 1:19: "Then we set out from Horeb and went through all that great and terrifying wilderness that you saw, on the way to the hill country of the Amorites, as the Lord our God commanded us. And we came to Kadesh-barnea." As we saw earlier (Deut. 1:2), it is an eleven-day journey from Horeb to Kadesh-barnea. Kadesh-barnea, on the southern border of the promised land, was going to be the Israelites' point of entry. The word "Amorites" sometimes refers to one of the people groups living in Canaan, and sometimes it stands for all the inhabitants of Canaan that God intended to judge through Israel's conquest. God described them specifically in Genesis 15:16 as those whose sins were not quite enough in the days of Abraham to justify the destruction that Israel was later to bring to them. But now that time has come.

We continue in Deuteronomy 1:20–21: "And I said to you, 'You have come to the hill country of the Amorites, which the Lord our God is giving us. See, the Lord your God has set the land before you. Go up, take possession, as the Lord, the God of your fathers, has told you. Do not fear or be dismayed.'" God is giving them this land in fulfillment of the promises he made to Abraham, Isaac, and Jacob hundreds of years beforehand (Gen. 15:18–21), but they must still go up and take it. God's promises do not preclude our action but establish and motivate it. The Israelites are explicitly commanded by Moses, "Do not fear or be dismayed" (Deut. 1:21). Of course, this command tells us that there is going to be something scary or discouraging up ahead, but they are not to let it shatter them. They are not to let it keep them from doing what is right. Implied in this command is that although they will meet frightening and challenging problems, God is with them.[1]

Before they go up and take the promised land, the people want to scout out the best way to go up. We read in Deuteronomy 1:22–23: "Then all of you came near me and said, 'Let us send men before us, that they may explore the land for us and bring us word again of the way by which we must go up and the cities into which we shall come.' The thing seemed good to me, and I took twelve men from you, one man from each tribe." We can agree with Moses that this seems harmless. But the account of this story as we read it here differs from how it is told in Numbers 13. Because of this difference, some critical scholars see a contradiction. According to Numbers 13:1–2, "The Lord spoke to Moses, saying, 'Send men to spy out the land of Canaan.'" Yet in Deuteronomy, it was the men of Israel who came to Moses, asking to send spies into the land. So is it a contradiction? It certainly does not

1. In other similar passages where Israel is commanded, "Do not fear or be dismayed," God's presence is explicitly cited as the reason for their confidence: Deut. 31:8; Josh. 1:9; 1 Chron. 28:20.

have to be. It is entirely possible that what Moses records as a word from God in Numbers came to him not by direct revelation, but rather through a suggestion of the people.[2] It is also possible that the people suggested the plan and it was then approved and ordered by the Lord.[3]

John Calvin understands the event as God's condescending to the weakness and fear of his people. Because God saw that the people were hesitating and not inclined to go up and take the land, he allowed them to send in the spies to see how great the land was to provide a stimulus for them to go up and take it.[4] We read in Deuteronomy 1:24–25: "And they turned and went up into the hill country, and came to the Valley of Eshcol and spied it out. And they took in their hands some of the fruit of the land and brought it down to us, and brought us word again and said, 'It is a good land that the Lord our God is giving us.'" Based on the report of the spies, the land was everything that God had told them it would be. It was from this valley that the Israelites took a cluster of grapes so large that it had to be carried on a pole held between two men (Num. 13:23). Clearly, God was giving them the land. Clearly, the land was good. Clearly, they had nothing to be afraid of as they went in to take the land because God was going to be with them. Clear promises such as these should have filled their vision and motivated their faithful obedience to God's commands. But that is not exactly what happened. Looming larger in their minds than the promises were the problems.

The Problems

Even though the land was good, and despite God's promise to be with the people, we read in Deuteronomy 1:26, "Yet you would not go up, but rebelled against the command of the Lord your God." The intent of this verse is to astound the present generation of Israelites hearing Moses' words. Remember, the events that he is describing here happened thirty-eight years earlier. All the adults who would not go up were now dead. But Moses is addressing the people of this generation as if they were the ones who

2. Christopher Wright, *Deuteronomy*, NIBC: Old Testament 4 (Hendrickson, 2007), 29.

3. John D. Currid, *Deuteronomy*, EPSC (EP Books, 2006), 41.

4. John Calvin, *Commentaries on the Four Last Books of Moses Arranged in the Form of a Harmony*, trans. Charles William Bingham, Calvin's Commentaries (Baker, 2005), 4:54.

would not go up. There is a solidarity among the generations, and the same tendencies and temptations that plagued the former generation will plague this generation if these issues are not overcome. The same is true for us. God makes astonishing promises, yet somehow, we still rebel and disobey. Psalm 106:24 captures the heart of the issue: "Then they despised the pleasant land, having no faith in his promise." In the face of the problems, they did not remember God's faithfulness, they did not trust his promise, and they did not obey his command.

But that is not all. We read in Deuteronomy 1:27–28: "And you murmured in your tents and said, 'Because the LORD hated us he has brought us out of the land of Egypt, to give us into the hand of the Amorites, to destroy us. Where are we going up? Our brothers have made our hearts melt, saying, "The people are greater and taller than we. The cities are great and fortified up to heaven. And besides, we have seen the sons of the Anakim there."'" We did not hear this in the report given in verse 25. But clearly, the spies had more to say in their report than simply that the land was good.[5] Two primary problems stood between Israel and the possession of God's promised land: the giant people and their fortified cities. Moses uses similar language to describe the problems later in 9:1–2 that the nations are greater than Israel, the people are bigger, and the cities are heavily fortified. The issue is not that the report about the problems is untrue; the issue is that they believed this report to be decisive. The spies were not wrong to define the problem, but they were wrong to allow the problem to define the situation.

Calvin writes that "we should in all points have our mouths shut when God speaks, and our ears open to receive whatsoever he says to us."[6] Once God has spoken, we ought to shut our mouths unless it is to say "Amen" and "thank you." How often do we read God's promises in the Scripture and rather than saying "amen, thank you," we say, "But what about . . . ?" God declares in his Word: "Therefore, if anyone is in Christ, he is a new creation. The old has passed away; behold, the new has come" (2 Cor. 5:17). Yet we say, "But I don't feel like a new creation." God's Word directs: "Do not be anxious about your life. . . . But seek first the kingdom of God and

5. The fuller report can be found in Numbers 13:27–33.

6. John Calvin, "The Sixth Sermon upon the First Chapter on Saturday the 15th of April 1555," in *Sermons on Deuteronomy*, https://www.monergism.com/sermons-deuteronomy-ebook, 83.

his righteousness, and all these things will be added to you" (Matt. 6:25, 33). Yet we say, "But I don't know how God is going to provide." The Lord Jesus declares in his Word: "I am the way, and the truth, and the life. No one comes to the Father except through me" (John 14:6). Yet we say, "Surely there must be another way for some people." But where God has spoken, we must shut our mouths. As soon as we begin to doubt the sure words of God, we also quickly begin to doubt his goodness and love.

The account in Numbers reveals that ten of the twelve spies who were supposed to engender confidence in the beauty of God's promise instead magnified the size of the problem and inspired terror in the hearts of the people. No matter how clear the promise from God, unbelieving people will attempt to overshadow the promises of God with the size of the problems before us. Those people might be the voices living inside our own heads. We ought, therefore, to surround ourselves with people who will remind us of the goodness and grandness of the promises so that we can keep the size of the problems we face in their proper perspective. This is one of the functions of being involved in a church community. Here, more than anywhere else, we want to be surrounded by people who have their eyes fixed on the promises and power of God, not on the size of the problems. We are not to be ignorant of the opposition or the challenges that lie before us, but if we are not careful, we can quickly grow the problems and shrink the promises. That is exactly what Israel did here. The people grew the problems, shrank the promises, and acted in fear rather than faith.

They asked, "Where are we going up?" (Deut. 1:28). The sense of this phrase is "what kind of place are we going to?"[7] The suggestion is that something is wrong with the land; it is one that devours its inhabitants (Num. 13:32). The very statement demonstrates how perverse their thinking had become, since any objective survey of the land revealed it to be wonderful, "flow[ing] with milk and honey" (v. 27). Their focus on the problems warped their view of the promises rather than allowing the promises to shape their view of the problems. But this is not the only place where their vision got skewed.

We read in Deuteronomy 1:27, "And you murmured in your tents and said, 'Because the LORD hated us he has brought us out of the land of Egypt, to

7. Jeffrey H. Tigay, *Deuteronomy*, JPSTC (Jewish Publication Society, 1996), 16.

give us into the hand of the Amorites, to destroy us." This is one of the most exceptionally ridiculous statements recorded in all the Bible. Christopher Wright comments:

> The very events that had been the greatest proof of God's love for them and of God's faithfulness to the promise to their ancestors are inverted into proof of God's malevolence. . . . It is sadly typical that even the people of God turn on God in accusation and blame when things go wrong, when obstacles seem insuperable, or when prolonged frustration leads to exhaustion.[8]

The spies reported that the land that God was giving them was amazing. God had told them to go up and take it. Yet the people's response was: "It's because he hates us. He brought us out of our four hundred years of slavery in Egypt so that he could lead us to the land he promised and kill us by the hand of the Amorites." If they had paused just one second to listen to themselves, they might have heard the absurdity of their grumbling. Does it make any sense that God would go through the trouble of bringing them out of Egypt just to kill them in the promised land? Why not just kill them by the hands of the Egyptians? Why did he bring them to Horeb and give them his law to govern their life in the land if his intention was to kill them before bringing them in? It makes no sense whatsoever—and neither does our own grumbling against the Lord. Rather, the grumbling reveals the heart of their issue and ours.

Underneath their failure to go up and possess the land was a lurking fear. Yes, there was fear of the big people and the fortified cities. But a deeper fear was revealed in this murmuring: "God doesn't really love us. It's all a sham. God actually hates us and wants to ruin us." Let us consider that underneath our failure to trust and obey God's commands lurks the same fear that the Israelites had. We think it could not be possible that God would actually love us and desire our good. We are too bad and too broken, and there are too many failures in our past to be truly loved by him. We suspect that he is just putting up a front because he is supposed to be loving, but that we really cannot trust him.

Our fundamental problem is that we know that we are sinners and do

8. Wright, *Deuteronomy*, 30.

not deserve God's loving care, protection, and provision. We have known it since the days that Adam and Eve hid themselves among the trees in the garden. Our guilt is blocking our view of the promise so much that we cannot bring ourselves to believe that "whoever comes to me I will never cast out" (John 6:37). "That may be true for some people," we think, "but not for me." As a result, our greatest struggle in life is simply to believe the plain truth that God loves us. If we could just get that fundamental lesson planted deep in the core of our being, it would change everything. We do not have much trouble believing that God loves us when life is good, but when we are faced with problems, challenges, and struggles, we fall back on our deeper underlying conviction: "It is because God does not love me. Why are my kids going astray? Why am I struggling with this sin? Why am I sick? Why do I not have meaningful employment? Why is my marriage hard? It is because God does not love me, or perhaps because I do not deserve God's love." We may not say those words, but the ideas lie beneath the surface of our grumbling, murmuring, and discontent.

What more could God have done to show the Israelites his love? He had rescued them from being slaves. He had judged their enemies. He had given them his law. He had promised to give them a land. Yet still they thought he hated them! How deep is that brokenness? Then consider this: God has demonstrated his love for us even more clearly than he did for them: "But God shows his love for us in that while we were still sinners, Christ died for us" (Rom. 5:8). There is no surer way that God could show his love for us than that while we were sinners, he gave his beloved Son to die on the cross in our place. If he gave Jesus to die when we were good, we might think that when we were not good, God would change his mind about us. But he did not give his Son to us when we were good. He gave him for us at our worst. He loved us at the bottom of the barrel. Dare we doubt his love now that we have been reconciled through the work of Christ?

We should all settle this question once and for all: does God truly love me? We really should know. If he does not love us, it is better to find out now and live our lives in light of that fact. If he does not love us, it means that we are on our own. But if he does love us, then we need to quit the crazy ups and downs of "he loves me, he loves me not" that characterize so much of our Christian lives and disobedience. If we fix our eyes on the problems we face, it will skew our view of God's promises and even of his love. But if we fix our eyes on the promises, especially his promises of love, it will helpfully shape how we view our problems.

The Plea

Moses hears the craziness coming out of the people's mouths, and he pleads with them in Deuteronomy 1:29, "Then I said to you, 'Do not be in dread or afraid of them.'" The command is plain enough: do not be in dread or afraid of the inhabitants of the land, including the sons of the Anakim. It is one thing to tell people not to be afraid. It is another thing to give them legitimate reasons not to be afraid. I can appreciate the challenge of facing the sons of the Anakim. I am pretty sure that I once sat next to a descendant of the Anakim on a flight from Boston to Atlanta. The New England Patriots football team had recruited him to play defensive end for them, and somehow he ended up in the middle seat of a commercial flight. If God called me to take on a city filled with people like him, I would probably hesitate. It would not be enough to tell me not to worry about him. I would need reasons. Here Moses gives the people three legitimate reasons not to be afraid of these the sons of the Anakim—these same three reasons remain true to this day because the Lord has not changed.

First, the Israelites should not be in dread or fearful of the problems before them because the Lord is a fighter. Deuteronomy 1:30 says, "The Lord your God who goes before you will himself fight for you, just as he did for you in Egypt before your eyes." The same God who demonstrated his fighting power against the Egyptians, who were far more powerful than any of the peoples in the promised land, is going to fight for them against these enemies. He did those amazingly mighty wonders in front of their eyes. They saw the boils, the gnats, the frogs, the hail, and the death of all the firstborn in Egypt (Ex. 7–12). They saw the waves come crashing down on the Egyptian army when they tried to pursue Israel across the Red Sea (14:26–29). The Lord is a Warrior, and he is going to go with them; therefore, they do not need to be afraid.

Second, the Israelites should not be fearful of the problems before them because the Lord is a father. Deuteronomy 1:31 goes on: "and in the wilderness, where you have seen how the Lord your God carried you, as a man carries his son, all the way that you went until you came to this place." God had miraculously provided for his people during their time in the wilderness, supplying food and water in a place where neither was normal. God had carried them. What Father would carry his son through the desert just to give him up to his enemies to destroy him? It makes no sense. So they have every reason to trust in the mightiness of God and to trust in the goodness of God as they step forward in faith to possess the land he promised them. But they do not.

Third, the Lord is also a forerunner. We read in Deuteronomy 1:32–33, "Yet in spite of this word you did not believe the LORD your God, who went before you in the way to seek you out a place to pitch your tents, in fire by night and in the cloud by day, to show you by what way you should go." The very same God who miraculously led them out of Egypt, and guided them through the wilderness with a cloud by day and fire by night, they refused to believe. The very cloud and fire that have guided them thus far are still right there, visible to their own eyes, tangible signs of God's presence with them. Yet they still ignore the evidence of God's care and guidance—because their eyes are fixed on the problems and not on the promises.[9] If we fix our eyes on the problems before us, the obstacles, and all the reasons why we cannot do what God is calling us to do, we will act out in disobedience, just like Israel. But if we remember the promises of God, if we remember his love, if we remember that he is a fighter and a Father and a forerunner that we can trust, then we will go up in obedience and possess all that he intends for us, so that we might be a blessing to the nations.

The example of Jesus himself is instructive here. Hebrews 12:2 calls us to look to Jesus, "the founder and perfecter of our faith, who for the joy that was set before him endured the cross, despising the shame, and is seated at the right hand of the throne of God." Jesus did not set his eyes on the problem of the cross or its shame, though he was certainly conscious of both. Instead, he fixed his eyes on the joy set before him, which enabled him to endure the cross and its shame and secure all the promises of God for us. Likewise, Peter instructs Christians in 1 Peter 1:13, "Therefore, preparing your minds for action, and being sober-minded, set your hope fully on the grace that will be brought to you at the revelation of Jesus Christ." He was talking to people who were encountering persecution, and the encouragement he gave

9. Tigay, *Deuteronomy*, 18.

them was to look forward to what they could see not with their physical eyes but only with the eyes of faith. That is where they were to set their hope. Nowhere in the Bible are we commanded to fix our eyes on the size of the problems or the size of the challenges before us. Rather, we are called to walk by faith and not by sight.

I was overwhelmed by launching out into a sermon series on the book of Deuteronomy because all I saw was the sheer size of it, the work it would require, the challenges I would encounter, and the real pain involved in giving birth to all these messages. Focusing on the problems crushed my joy and my resolve to do the work. I had to set my eyes on what I could not see: the innumerable blessings that God pours out on his people each week when his Word is opened up Sunday after Sunday. I needed to remember all the ways in which he has faithfully provided in the past, trust that he would continue to supply in the future and walk in obedience to this call to preach the Word. When I set my hope on what he can do, my joy in the work increases, and so does my strength for the work.

Where is our focus on the problems robbing us of the joy of the promises? Where is our focus on the challenges skewing our confidence in the Father's love? Let us fix our eyes on Jesus, who is God's "yes" to every promise he has made, and with joy, let us go up and possess all the good that God has prepared for us.

4

The Consequences of Unbelieving Rebellion

Deuteronomy 1:34–46

Not one of these men of this evil generation shall see the good land that I swore to give to your fathers, except Caleb the son of Jephunneh. He shall see it, and to him and to his children I will give the land on which he has trodden, because he has wholly followed the Lord! (Deut. 1:35–36)

Sometimes seeing isn't believing. Several years ago, David Rakoff was featured on an episode of National Public Radio's *This American Life.*[1] One of his first jobs out of college was working for an advertising agency in Japan. It was 1986. The agency was working on a computer network that would allow expatriates living in Tokyo to be able to talk to one another over computers. David remembers thinking, "What kind of loser would log onto a computer to talk to someone?" In what he describes as the only moment of decisiveness in his entire life, he walked in

1. The following is all taken from the transcript of *This American Life*, "472: Our Friend David," aired August 17, 2012, https://www.thisamericanlife.org/472/transcript, accessed September 16, 2021.

to work the next day and quit his job. He went on to say: "All I could think was like, sayonara, suckers! You know, good luck with your network. And we know exactly what the network was. It was the internet." But that's not the only thing that David saw and didn't believe. He goes on to tell the story of seeing a young lady in concert in Michigan in the early 1980s. He came away, saying, "Boy, is she lousy!" That young woman was Madonna, who went on to become an international icon. Later, when he was working as an editorial assistant for a publishing company, David was given a manuscript to read. He read it and then wrote on it, "Subliterate, borderline misogyny, an easy pass." Someone else in the company decided to give it a read as well. It turns out that the book was *Men Are from Mars, Women Are from Venus*, a runaway *New York Times* bestseller.

It is hard to believe that one man could have seen such things and come away in each case not believing. Who knows how his life might have been different if he had believed what he saw? But what about us? Have we not all had opportunities in which we saw something, did not believe that it would be successful, and then missed the opportunity? How many people would like to go back and be early investors in that little store that started in Bentonville, Arkansas (Walmart), or to have put some early money into that fruit company making computers and phones (Apple)? Of course, in those cases our failure to believe had only financial consequences. But when it comes to our relationship with God, unbelief carries the direst consequences both in this life and for eternity.

In this passage of Deuteronomy, we begin to see the consequences of Israel's unbelieving rebellion. Because the people were so focused on the problems of entering the land, they failed to believe the promises of God and rebelled against his commands. Now Moses is reminding the next generation of Israelites of the failure of their parents so that they, and we, learn that unbelieving rebellion has consequences. Therefore, in contrast, we must faithfully follow the Lord.

Unbelieving Rebellion Rouses the Judgment of God

When the Israelites fail to believe the promises and murmur against the Lord, it is not a harmless little trifle. It is a full-on rebellion against their suzerain Lord, the King of kings. So we read in Deuteronomy 1:34–35,

"And the LORD heard your words and was angered, and he swore, 'Not one of these men of this evil generation shall see the good land that I swore to give to your fathers.'"

Do you realize that God gets angry? It is possible for us to err in so many ways when we think about God. On the one hand, some people's impression of God is that he is angry all the time and just yearning for people to mess up so that he can smite them. Alternatively, some people's view of God is that he is such a nice guy that we cannot imagine his ever getting mad.[2] The truth is that God does get angry, but not as we do. J. I. Packer writes: "God's wrath in the Bible is never the capricious, self-indulgent, irritable, morally ignoble thing that human anger so often is. It is, instead, a right and necessary reaction to objective moral evil. God is only angry where anger is called for."[3] From this passage we see that when God heard Israel's unbelieving murmuring, he got angry. To disbelieve God's Word of truth *is* objective moral evil. So God swore an oath: just as he had sworn that his people would possess the land, now he is swearing that this generation will not even see it. God's decree of judgment matches the people's offense: if they do not *want* to go into the land, they *will not* go into the land.[4] It may sound like an overreaction, but in fact God is just giving them what they asked for. In Numbers 14:2, the people lamented, "Would that we had died in this wilderness!" And in Numbers 14:28–29, God declared, "What you have said in my hearing I will do to you: your dead bodies shall fall in this wilderness." Sometimes God's judgment is to give us exactly what we want.[5]

Occasionally people caricature Reformed theology by saying that we believe that God drags people "kicking and screaming" into heaven. Or, conversely, that God sends people kicking and screaming to hell, which is their way of saying that since God is sovereign, people have no choice. But neither of those pictures is an accurate description of people's entering

2. Martin Luther writes: "We must know how to teach God's Word aright, discerningly, for there are divers sorts of hearers; some are struck with fear in the conscience, are perplexed, and awed by their sins, and, in apprehension of God's anger, are penitent; these must be comforted with the consolations of the gospel. Others are hardened, obstinate, stiff-necked, rebel-hearted; these must be affrighted by the law, by examples of God's wrath: as the fires of Elijah, the deluge, the destruction of Sodom and Gomorrah, the downfall of Jerusalem. These hard heads need sound knocks." *Table Talk of Martin Luther*, trans. William Hazlitt (Lutheran Publication Society, n.d.).

3. J. I. Packer, *Knowing God* (InterVarsity Press, 1973), 136.

4. Jeffrey H. Tigay, *Deuteronomy*, JPSTC (Jewish Publication Society, 1996), 18.

5. Packer, *Knowing God*, 139.

into their eternal reward or judgment. To be sure, God does send people to hell as surely as he sent the Israelites back into the wilderness. But it is also true that God gives people what they want. C. S. Lewis wrote in *The Great Divorce*, "There are only two kinds of people in the end: those who say to God, 'Thy will be done,' and those to whom God says, in the end, '*Thy* will be done.'"[6] God gives us what we want. Unbelieving rebels want their sin. They want to hang on to their unbelief, their self-pity, their sinful lusts and desires, and what they get is the judgment of hell as surely as the Israelites got the wilderness. It is not just the unbelieving Israelites who experience the judgment of God and are not allowed into the promised land.

We read in Deuteronomy 1:37, "Even with me the LORD was angry on your account and said, 'You also shall not go in there.'" Moses himself would not enter the land on account of the unbelieving rebellion of the people. This verse has been a source of consternation for students of the Bible. We know from Numbers 20:10–13 that Moses would not enter the land that God had promised, but it does not directly have to do with this incident at Kadesh-barnea. In the Numbers account, Moses is not permitted to enter the land because he struck the rock when he was commanded by God to speak to the rock. But here in Deuteronomy, he says that it is on account of the people of Israel that God was angry with him.[7] So which is it?

We should probably avoid seeing the two viewpoints as mutually exclusive, unlike critical theory, which sees Numbers 20 and Deuteronomy as representing two independent traditions explaining why Moses does not get to enter the land.[8] First, the event in Numbers when Moses struck the rock would have never even happened if it were not for this event of rebellion in Deuteronomy.[9] So the Israelites were partly responsible for Moses' later failure. But something bigger is being shown here. Moses is being implicated in the sinful rebellion of the people of Israel. Even though he did not personally rebel against God's command, he was the mediator of this

6. C. S. Lewis, *The Great Divorce* (Macmillan, 1946), 72.

7. Moses makes this point again in Deuteronomy 3:26 and 4:21. Deuteronomy 32:51 highlights the event described in Numbers 20:10–13.

8. Tigay, *Deuteronomy*, 425.

9. Raymond Brown, *The Message of Deuteronomy: Not by Bread Alone*, The Bible Speaks Today (InterVarsity Press, 1993), 43.

covenant. His identification with the people of Israel as their leader meant that he would also share in the result of their failure.[10] Moses is describing his own suffering as a result of Israel's sin. As Christopher Wright puts it, "He entered into the suffering of his people and of the God of his people in a way that, like so much else in his life, foreshadowed that future servant of Yahweh who would indeed offer a blameless life for the sins of us all."[11]

Truly there was another Servant of the Lord coming who would be the Mediator of a new covenant. Under the old covenant, the sinful failure of the people was enough to bring the judgment of God on Moses, the mediator of that covenant. But under the new covenant, the faithful obedience of our covenant Mediator, Jesus, is sufficient to overcome all our sinful failures! While Israel's failure kept Moses out, Jesus' success brings us in.

So because of the unbelieving rebellion of the people, that whole generation of Israelites and even Moses himself—experiences the judgment of God. None of them are getting in. But there is an exception: "Caleb the son of Jephunneh. He shall see it, and to him and to his children I will give the land on which he has trodden, because he has wholly followed the LORD!'" (Deut. 1:36). Caleb is the exception (and also Joshua, as we will see in Deuteronomy 1:38). All the rest of the spies who went up into the land saw the land and its astounding fruitfulness. They saw the cities, and they saw the giant people living in the land and ultimately determined that God could not deliver on his promise. Caleb, however, stood out because he had his eyes fixed on the promises of God. He knew that God could not lie and that if God told them that they would have this land, then it did not matter how big the giants or how fortified the cities; they were going to have it! Caleb took God at his word.

We need Calebs in our midst—people who, when all we see are the problems, remember the promises. Moreover, when we have Calebs in our midst who remind us faithfully of the promises of God, we need to have the humility to listen to them. Look carefully at what this text tells us about Caleb: he "wholly followed the LORD" (Deut. 1:36). Most translators believe that Caleb's name is a form of *kelev*, "dog," and could be short for "dog of God."[12] To call someone a "dog" in Jewish culture was typically a harsh

10. Peter C. Craigie, *The Book of Deuteronomy*, NICOT (Eerdmans, 1976), 105.
11. Christopher Wright, *Deuteronomy*, NIBC: Old Testament 4 (Hendrickson, 2007), 42.
12. Tigay, *Deuteronomy*, 347n110.

insult and often directed toward Gentiles.[13] And interestingly, Caleb does seem to have had Gentile origins. He is presented in Numbers 32:12 as "Caleb the son of Jephunneh the Kenizzite" and as a descendant of Kenaz, who was a grandson of Esau.[14] (Remember that God's promise to Abraham was coming not through Esau but through his brother, Jacob.) But Caleb was so thoroughly integrated into the life and faith of God's people that he is the chosen representative of Judah and is one of only two of the twelve spies who was faithful to the Lord. He was more Israelite than the Israelites. Herein we see the meaning of Caleb's name turned upside down. If a dog has one particular virtue, it is this: it follows its master. As Charles Spurgeon remarked about Caleb, "Never has a dog so followed his master as Caleb followed his God."[15] May we all aspire to the kind of loyalty that this dog showed to his Master. He wholly followed the Lord.

Some of us are unhappy because we are not wholly following the Lord. We are partially following the Lord and partially doing our own thing. In short, we are divided. In his book *Christian Perfection*, François Fénelon speaks of this condition. While we reject Fénelon's Christian perfectionism, his insights in the following quotes help us see that the more fully we give ourselves to following the Lord, the deeper our joy in him will be: "Those who are God's are always glad, when they are not divided, because they only want what God wants and want to do for him all that he wishes. They divest themselves of everything, and in this divesting find a hundredfold return."[16] In other words, only when we are fully devoted to God's cause can we experience true joy in the Christian life. Contrary to the view of Christian perfectionists, we should understand that in this life, our devotion to God will remain alloyed with self-interest. But many of us are afraid to begin denying our own will in this world to devote ourselves fully to God's. Fénelon rightly says that this is irrational: "What folly to fear to be too entirely God's! It is to fear to be too happy. It is to fear to have too much courage in the crosses which are inevitable, too much comfort

13. See, e.g., Deut. 23:18; 2 Sam. 16:9; Phil. 3:2; Rev. 22:15.

14. Daniel I. Block, *Deuteronomy*, NIVAC (Zondervan, 2012), 73n8.

15. Charles H. Spurgeon, "Caleb—The Man for the Times," no. 538, preached November 1, 1863, Spurgeon Sermon Collection, Accordance electronic ed. (OakTree Software, 2012).

16. Quoted in Richard J. Foster and James Bryan Smith, eds., *Devotional Classics: Selected Readings for Individuals and Groups*, rev. ed. (Zondervan, 2005), 48.

in God's love, and too much detachment from the passions which make us miserable."[17] To fear to give ourselves wholly to God's cause makes no sense because we are leaving ourselves attached to the very things that actually rob us of our joy! Finally, Fénelon warns those who want to live for themselves and for God:

> Woe unto those weak and timid souls who are divided between God and their world! They want and they do not want. They are torn by passion and remorse at the same time. They fear the judgments of God and those of others. They have a horror of evil and a shame of good. They have the pains of virtue without tasting its sweet consolations. O, how wretched they are![18]

Here is a perfect description of those ten faithless spies. They were miserable because they were divided. On the other hand, Caleb was happy and ultimately satisfied because he wholly followed the Lord. In addition to Caleb, one more person will enter the land. We read in Deuteronomy 1:38: "Joshua the son of Nun, who stands before you, he shall enter. Encourage him, for he shall cause Israel to inherit it." Moses will not enter the land, but God is raising up another who will lead his people into all that he has promised. His name is Joshua. Many readers will know that the Hebrew name "Joshua" when translated into the Greek language of the New Testament is "Jesus." While Joshua will lead the people into the land, it would take another "Joshua" to lead God's people into the ultimate rest that God intended for us—not rest from our physical enemies but ultimate rest from our spiritual enemies in the new heavens and earth. Unbelieving rebellion rouses the judgment of God, but those who faithfully follow the Lord can fully expect to enjoy all that God has promised.

Unbelieving Rebellion Forfeits the Promises of God

That is exactly what the older generation of Israelites did: they forfeited their share in the promises of God. God declares in Deuteronomy 1:39: "And as for your little ones, who you said would become a prey, and your children,

17. Quoted in Foster and Smith, 50.
18. Quoted in Foster and Smith, 51.

who today have no knowledge of good or evil, they shall go in there. And to them I will give it, and they shall possess it." The people of Israel had attributed their refusal to go up and take the land that God promised to them to the premise that it would be bad for the children. They justified their disobedience to God by saying that it was in the best interests of the kids.

Does this still happen? Do parents still disobey commands from God and then justify it by saying, "We're doing it for the kids"? Perhaps we justify our lack of generosity by saying that it is so that we can afford things for our children. This is not to say that we should not buy nice things, or have nice experiences, or even leave a nice inheritance for our kids. But we should be careful about using our kids as an excuse for disobeying God. Or how about regularly neglecting the gathered worship of God's people on Sundays because we have various other extracurricular activities to attend to? It is for the kids, right? Or maybe we have felt the clear call of God to serve him in a difficult place or under difficult circumstances and we have balked because we "have to look out for the kids." If the Lord is calling us to do something, we cannot let fear for how it might hurt our children keep us away. The safest place for our children is in a home with parents who wholly follow the Lord. Let us learn from this text to never disobey God under the pretext of looking out for the best interests of our children.

As we see here, it is the offspring of the exodus generation who will go in and possess the land, not the parents. We read in Deuteronomy 1:40, "But as for you, turn, and journey into the wilderness in the direction of the Red Sea." Those whom God had brought out of Egypt were now rejected as heirs of the promise to their fathers.[19] God had not forgotten his promise, but this generation's people had forfeited their share of it. What is clear through both the Old and New Testaments is that no one will inherit God's promises apart from faith. Faithless people will not share in the blessings promised to Abraham because it is by faith that we become the children of Abraham. As Paul writes in Galatians 3:7, "Know then that it is those of faith who are the sons of Abraham." Similarly in Galatians 3:14, Paul writes that "in Christ Jesus the blessing of Abraham might come to the Gentiles, so that we might receive the promised Spirit through faith." What stands between us and the reception of all of God's promises is our unbelief. The

19. Block, *Deuteronomy*, 74.

writer to the Hebrews picks up on this theme and these very events in Israel's history. He writes in Hebrews 3:7–19:

> Therefore, as the Holy Spirit says,
>
> "Today, if you hear his voice,
> do not harden your hearts as in the rebellion,
>   on the day of testing in the wilderness,
> where your fathers put me to the test
>   and saw my works for forty years.
> Therefore I was provoked with that generation,
> and said, 'They always go astray in their heart;
>   they have not known my ways.'
> As I swore in my wrath,
>   'They shall not enter my rest.'"
>
> Take care, brothers, lest there be in any of you an evil, unbelieving heart, leading you to fall away from the living God. But exhort one another every day, as long as it is called "today," that none of you may be hardened by the deceitfulness of sin. For we have come to share in Christ, if indeed we hold our original confidence firm to the end. As it is said,
>
> "Today, if you hear his voice,
> do not harden your hearts as in the rebellion."
>
> For who were those who heard and yet rebelled? Was it not all those who left Egypt led by Moses? And with whom was he provoked for forty years? Was it not with those who sinned, whose bodies fell in the wilderness? And to whom did he swear that they would not enter his rest, but to those who were disobedient? So we see that they were unable to enter because of unbelief.

Here we see that the reason that they could not enter into the promises of God was their unbelief. The same remains true today. The one thing that stands between us and all that God has promised to us in his Word is our unbelief. Consider how significant this sin of unbelief truly is. Matthew Henry writes, "It was not the breach of any of the commands of the law that shut them out of Canaan, no, not the golden calf, but their disbelief of that promise which was typical of gospel grace, to signify that no sin will ruin us but unbelief, which is a sin against the remedy."[20] God's remedy for our sin is the life, death, and resurrection of his Son, Jesus Christ, in our place on the cross. Jesus comes to every one of us today and presents himself to us as the Lamb of God who takes away the sins of the world, the one all-sufficient sacrifice that could pay the debt for our sin. How will we respond to him? John writes: "[Jesus] was in the world, and the world was made through him, yet the world did not know him. He came to his own, and his own people did not receive him. But to all who did receive him, who believed in his name, he gave the right to become children of God" (John 1:10–12). Only those who believe in his name are given the right to become children of God. We must believe in the name of Jesus! To believe in the name of Jesus makes us partakers of all the blessings and promises of God, and it is the only way to be a partaker of all the promises of God. Not to believe in Jesus, however, is to forfeit the promises, including the promise of eternal life.

Unbelieving Rebellion Presumes on the Grace of God

After the people heard God's word of judgment on their unbelieving rebellion, they feigned some kind of repentance. We read in Deuteronomy 1:41: "Then you answered me, 'We have sinned against the Lord. We ourselves will go up and fight, just as the Lord our God commanded us.' And every one of you fastened on his weapons of war and thought it easy to go up into the hill country." The emphasis in the Hebrew is on the phrase "we ourselves." In other words, it is we who will go up and take the land, not the next generation.[21] Now that God had forbidden them from entering the land, they determined that they were going to go forward. This is just another manifestation of unbelieving rebellion. God had told them to enter the land, and they wanted to go back to Egypt. Now God told them to go back toward Egypt, and they determined that they wanted to go into the land. You can see why Moses was losing his mind with these people! But God

20. Matthew Henry, "Complete Commentary on Deuteronomy 1," in *Henry's Complete Commentary on the Bible*, https://www.studylight.org/commentaries/eng/mhm/deuteronomy-1.html.

21. Tigay, *Deuteronomy*, 21.

graciously warned them about their foolish plan in verses 42–43: "And the LORD said to me, 'Say to them, Do not go up or fight, for I am not in your midst, lest you be defeated before your enemies.' So I spoke to you, and you would not listen; but you rebelled against the command of the LORD and presumptuously went up into the hill country." The people of Israel failed to appreciate that God was no longer in their midst. God had withdrawn his presence from them and was not going to go up and fight for them. But in their unbelieving rebellion, they now thought it would be easy to go up and take the land on their own. This is the sin of presumption. They presumed on the grace of God. Yes, they had sinned, but now that they said they were sorry, surely God would fight for them. But they found out the hard way what happens when we presume on God's grace in verses 44–46: "Then the Amorites who lived in that hill country came out against you and chased you as bees do and beat you down in Seir as far as Hormah. And you returned and wept before the LORD, but the LORD did not listen to your voice or give ear to you. So you remained at Kadesh many days, the days that you remained there."

It is easy to imagine what this defeat looked like if we have ever seen someone being chased by a hive of bees. Apart from the Lord's presence, the people of Israel didn't have a chance! God desires a people like Caleb who wholly follow after him. These people were not that. As a result of their unbelieving rebellion, they ended up wandering around in the desert for about thirty-eight years. They were essentially a death camp in which the chief sound they heard every day was that of wailing and mourning for the dead.[22] That is the price of unbelieving rebellion: ultimately death. Unbelieving rebellion rouses the judgment of God, forfeits the promises of God, and presumes on the grace of God, leading to death and separation from the presence of God. But it does not have to be that way. Israel did not have to go out like that, and Moses is reminding the people of that truth so that the next generation does not make the same mistakes.

What is the antidote to unbelieving rebellion? It is to remember, trust, and obey. Our share in the promises of God is dependent not on our own faithfulness, but rather on our faith in the faithfulness of Jesus. In Christ, we obtain our inheritance of all that God has promised. That inheritance is

22. Block, *Deuteronomy*, 75.

available to all of us today, to all those who will believe the good news. God does not call us to earn anything. He rather calls us to believe that Christ has done all for us. Do not rebel against God's love; do not refuse to receive the gift. Rather, open the empty hands of faith, trust in the finished work of Christ, and give yourself wholly to following the Lord.

5

The Lord Provides for You

Deuteronomy 2:1–23

For the Lord your God has blessed you in all the work of your hands. He knows your going through this great wilderness. These forty years the Lord your God has been with you. You have lacked nothing. (Deut. 2:7)

Legend has it that following the end of World War II, the Allied soldiers collected large numbers of hungry and homeless children and put them into camps. The soldiers provided abundantly for the children, and they were well fed. But at night, the children did not sleep well. They were fearful and restless. A psychologist sized up the situation and came up with a solution. He suggested that after the children were fed and put into bed, each child should be given a slice of bread. The children could have more food if they needed it, but this particular slice of bread was not to be eaten; they were simply to hold it while they slept. The bread had excellent results. As the children lay in bed, holding their piece of bread, they had the confidence that there would be something to eat tomorrow. This confidence allowed the children to sleep in peace.[1]

While it may be an apocryphal story, we are not so different from those kids. We too struggle with doubts from time to time about whether there will be enough of what we need tomorrow. Each year, the American Psychological Association conducts a survey to determine the primary sources of stress in the lives of Americans. Each year, money is first or second on the list.[2] It is well known that one of the chief causes of breakdown in marriage has to do with disagreements about money. One of the chief causes of stress in churches is money. The same is true of corporations, schools, and nations. Money represents provision, security, and a future. The lack of money represents the opposite. What money represents for us, land represented for the people of Israel.

In Deuteronomy 2, Moses is continuing his address to the people of Israel on the plains of Moab as they prepare to cross the Jordan. Provision will be among their chief concerns. Will God supply their needs and give them the land that their enemies currently possess? In this passage, Moses recounts for them how God provided for them everything they needed in the wilderness to encourage them to remember, trust, and obey. Now the question is: Will the Israelites trust God to provide all that he has promised to his people? And will we?

In terms of the structure of this passage, the thirty-eight years that Israel spent in the wilderness is going to be passed over in just one verse (Deut. 2:1). Then God will direct the people to go up the eastern side of the Dead Sea because their conquest of Canaan would happen from the east rather than from the south as originally planned (Kadesh-barnea). But passing alongside the eastern side of the Dead Sea meant that they would pass through the territory of multiple nations, namely, Edom/Seir, Moab, and Ammon. So God will specifically instruct the Israelites that they are not to attack any of these nations, for reasons that we will see. The fundamental reason that

1. Charles L. Allen, *God's Psychiatry* (Revell, 1988), n.p., taken from Craig Brian Larson and Phyllis Ten Elshof, eds., *1001 Illustrations That Connect: Compelling Stories, Stats, and News Items for Preaching, Teaching, and Writing* (Christianity Today International, 2008), 463.

2. See, e.g., American Psychological Association, *Stress in America 2019* (November 2019), https://www.apa.org/news/press/releases/stress/2019/stress-america-2019.pdf, accessed July 15, 2023.

they are not to attack them—and the primary lesson of this passage—is that God's covenant people can trust him to provide what he has promised.

WHAT IF WE DO NOT TRUST GOD TO PROVIDE?

We know from what we have already seen that God cares deeply about his people's trusting him. In fact, we have seen the great truth from Hebrews 11 illustrated in living color in Deuteronomy: "without faith it is impossible to please him" (Heb. 11:6). But specifically in this passage, we see three negative results of not trusting God to provide.

First, if we do not trust God to provide, we will not possess what he has promised. This truth is illustrated by the faithless generation of Israelites who refused to go up and take the promised land at Kadesh-barnea, as described in Deuteronomy 1. We pick up with the results of their unbelieving rebellion in verse 1: "Then we turned and journeyed into the wilderness in the direction of the Red Sea, as the LORD told me. And for many days we traveled around Mount Seir." In just a few words, Moses passes over the thirty-eight years of wilderness wanderings that the people of Israel suffered on account of their refusal to trust in God's provision of the land for them. That faithless generation was told that its people would not possess the land because of their unbelief, and so God made all the people wander around in the wilderness until every last one of that generation dropped dead (except for Caleb and Joshua). We are given more detail on this situation down in verses 14–15: "And the time from our leaving Kadesh-barnea until we crossed the brook Zered was thirty-eight years, until the entire generation, that is, the men of war, had perished from the camp, as the LORD had sworn to them. For indeed the hand of the LORD was against them, to destroy them from the camp, until they had perished." Not only did their unbelief mean that they forfeited their share in God's promises, but because of their unbelief the Lord's hand was against them.

Second, if we do not trust God to provide, we will be tempted to grumble. Our text does not refer to Israel's grumbling, but the concept is there between the lines. The text is silent on it because Israel's grumbling is not the focus of what Moses is trying to communicate. When we read the fuller account of this period in Israel's history, however, we discover that it was the people's failure to trust in God's provision that tempted them to grumble, which ultimately resulted in severe discipline coming from the Lord. We read in verses 4–6 of Deuteronomy 2:

> You are about to pass through the territory of your brothers, the people of Esau, who live in Seir; and they will be afraid of you. So be very careful. Do not contend with them, for I will not give you any of their land, no, not so much as for the sole of the foot to tread on, because I have given Mount Seir to Esau as a possession. You shall purchase food from them with money, that you may eat, and you shall also buy water from them with money, that you may drink.

God was sending the people of Israel through the land of Edom, but the Edomites did not want them to pass through. So rather than going through Edom, the Israelites "went on, away from our brothers" (Deut. 2:8), and skirted the edge of Edom, as we read in Numbers 21:4. But skirting the edge of Edom meant that there was no food or water to buy. Thus we read in Numbers 21:4–5: "And the people became impatient on the way. And the people spoke against God and against Moses, 'Why have you brought us up out of Egypt to die in the wilderness? For there is no food and no water, and we loathe this worthless food.'" This sounds remarkably similar to what the people said in Kadesh-barnea and betrays the same underlying fear in their heart: God does not really love us. This murmuring and grumbling about the Lord's lack of care at Kadesh-barnea caused them to spend the next thirty-eight years in the wilderness. They still did not learn the lesson, however, so here the Lord sends another form of discipline to teach them about the consequences of their lack of trust in his loving care:

> Then the Lord sent fiery serpents among the people, and they bit the people, so that many people of Israel died. And the people came to Moses and said, "We have sinned, for we have spoken against the Lord and against you. Pray to the Lord, that he take away the serpents from us." So Moses prayed for the people. (Num. 21:6–7)

Despite their sin, however, God made a provision for his people to be saved from the consequences of their disobedience. Moses was to make a bronze serpent and put it on a pole. When anyone was bitten by one of the fiery serpents, if he would look at the bronze serpent, he would live. This bronze serpent can be seen by Christians as a type of Christ. Though we have been bitten by the serpent, sin, those who look to Christ, who has been lifted up on the cross on our behalf, will be saved. But there is more that we are to learn from the example of the Israelites. The apostle Paul picks up this theme in 1 Corinthians 10:6, 9–11:

> Now these things took place as examples for us, that we might not desire evil as they did. . . . We must not put Christ to the test, as some of them did and were destroyed by serpents, nor grumble, as some of them did and were destroyed by the Destroyer. Now these things happened to them as an example, but they were written down for our instruction, on whom the end of the ages has come.

We are meant to learn from the bad example of the people of Israel neither to be grumblers nor to put God to the test. When are we tempted to grumble? When we are not trusting God to provide. If we think about our own lives for a moment, reflecting on when we are prone to grumble and complain, we may find that it is when we are not trusting in God's provision. Are we putting Christ to the test, suggesting that he will not provide for us what we need? Consider how seriously this sin is taken in this Old Testament example written for our instruction. Discontent reveals a lack of trust in God and invites God's discipline. We must root out all grumbling from our lives as we settle firmly into the confidence that God loves us and will provide for us whatever we need for life and godliness (2 Peter 1:3).

Third, if we do not trust God to provide, we will be tempted to take what God has not given. In other words, if we do not think that God is going to give us what we need, then we will be tempted to take for ourselves what we want. For example, suppose that a man is facing financial hardships at home. He has prayed and yet still does not have what he needs. He feels that God has not provided. So he decides to take what God has not given, either through old-fashioned stealing or a more sophisticated approach. Or perhaps a woman is married but experiencing no satisfaction in her marriage. She feels that God is letting her down and not providing what she needs. She decides to take for herself through adultery what she thinks God is not giving her in her marriage. Or perhaps someone is single and desiring to be married. Maybe this person has been praying for God to provide for years, and yet no one seems to be qualified. If this person is not believing that God will provide a Christian spouse, he or she may be tempted to settle for a nice woman or man who is not a Christian. Tired of waiting, this person may just take for himself or herself what God has not provided.

Rather than doing any of these things, we need to continue to entrust ourselves to God and do what is good. We need to trust that he will provide what we need, and if he has not provided it yet, then we must trust that we do not need it yet. But we certainly cannot act contrary to his Word and provide for ourselves what he has not yet seen fit to give us.

God specifically warns Israel against taking what he has not given in terms of the land. He has promised to give the Israelites the land of Canaan; therefore, they are not to take the land that belongs to the Edomites, the Moabites, or the Ammonites:

> You are about to pass through the territory of your brothers, the people of Esau, who live in Seir; and they will be afraid of you. So be very careful. Do not contend with them, for I will not give you any of their land, no, not so much as for the sole of the foot to tread on, because I have given Mount Seir to Esau as a possession. (Deut. 2:4–5)

The first country that Israel is going to pass through is that of the people of Esau, the Edomites (sometimes called Seir or Edom). God wants the Israelites to remember that the Edomites are their "brothers." Recall that Abraham had Isaac and Isaac had two sons: Jacob and Esau. The Israelites are descended from Jacob and the Edomites from Esau. Even though they are not part of God's covenant people, God still gave the Edomites a land—and Israel was not to take it from them.

God gave Esau's descendants land just as he did Jacob's. The same is true for Moab and Ammon. God continues to be involved in the history of every nation on earth.[3] We can go further and say that every nation that exists has ultimately received its land under the sovereign providence of God. This does not mean that every nation has its land lawfully. Fair questions can be

3. Jeffrey H. Tigay, *Deuteronomy*, JPSTC (Jewish Publication Society, 1996), 24.

raised about the legality or morality of the methods used by early Americans in taking possession of Native American lands, for example. But there is nothing that happens in the affairs of men that God is not sovereign over. One implication of this passage is that because God has given each nation its land, one nation should not seek to displace another nation and take its land. To do so will ultimately invite the Lord's judgment.[4]

This raises questions for Israel's possessing of the promised land that will be considered in the next chapter. For now, God is still sovereignly working out his plans in the affairs of nations. The focus of the church in every age and nation should not be to encourage military conquest, but should be love of neighbor, inside and outside the nation's borders. This passage reminds us that nations and lands come and go. As the people of God, we are to seek the welfare of the nations in which we live, but we must not fix our eyes on earthly kingdoms and lands. Instead, we must set our hopes on the coming kingdom that will never be shaken (Heb. 12:27–28). We must live for that one, and not these.

After passing through Edom, Israel is going to come to another land. We read in Deuteronomy 2:8–9: "And we turned and went in the direction of the wilderness of Moab. And the LORD said to me, 'Do not harass Moab or contend with them in battle, for I will not give you any of their land for a possession, because I have given Ar to the people of Lot for a possession.'" The Israelites are not to take the land of Moab either. The Moabites are distant relatives of Israel. Abraham had a nephew named Lot. Through an incestuous encounter with his daughters, Lot fathered two sons (Gen. 19:30–38). One of them was the father of the Moabites, and the other was the father of the Ammonites. God gave these people their land as surely as he is giving the Israelites theirs.

After passing through Moab, Israel will come to the land of Lot's other son, Ammon. But before the people go into the Ammonite land, one other thing had to happen:

> So as soon as all the men of war had perished and were dead from among the people, the LORD said to me, "Today you are to cross the border of Moab at

4. John Calvin makes the same point in "The Twelfth Sermon Which Is the Second upon the Second Chapter on Friday the 25th of April 1555," in *Sermons on Deuteronomy*, https://www.monergism.com/sermons-deuteronomy-ebook.

> Ar. And when you approach the territory of the people of Ammon, do not harass them or contend with them, for I will not give you any of the land of the people of Ammon as a possession, because I have given it to the sons of Lot for a possession." (Deut. 2:16–19)

Only after the last of the unbelieving generation was dead could the people cross into the land of the Ammonites. But the people of Israel are not to take the land of the Ammonites because God had given that land to them. In each case—Edom, Moab, and Ammon—Israel demonstrates confidence in God's ability to provide by not taking the land of these other nations.[5] This is what trusting him to be our Provider means. We remember who he is, we trust his character, and we obey his commands.

Why Should We Trust God to Provide?

Moses gives the people of Israel multiple reasons in this passage to trust God's provision of land and everything else they need, reasons that continue to be relevant to us today. First, we should trust God to provide because he is sovereign. Remember, Moses is trying to convince the Israelites that they can trust God to provide land for them. He points out God's power to do that in an understated way. In most Bibles, Deuteronomy 2:10–12 is in parentheses, indicating that the verses are giving some background information. The Lord is describing how he gave the land of Ar to Moab in verses 10–12:

5. This seemingly insignificant passage takes on great importance in another seemingly insignificant passage in Judges 11:4–28. Some three hundred years after the events described in this Deuteronomy passage, the Ammonites made war on the Israelites living in Gilead. The elders of Gilead called on Jephthah to come and defend them. So Jephthah sent messengers to the Ammonites, asking them why they were attacking his people. The Ammonites justified their attack by saying that when Israel came out of Egypt in the exodus, they took land that belonged to the Ammonites. But Jephthah knew his Deuteronomic history. He proceeded to explain to the Ammonites that the people of Israel most certainly had not taken Ammonite land. Nor had they taken Edomite or Moabite land. They had taken only Amorite land, and that was only after the Amorite kings attacked them first. Furthermore, Jephthah wants to know why they waited three hundred years to raise their concern. Ultimately, Jephthah concluded his great speech by saying that the Ammonites had no right to try to take the land from Israel. Of course, despite Jephthah's having the facts, the Ammonites were not satisfied and ended up getting defeated by the people of Israel in battle. This passage in Judges, along with Deuteronomy 2, raises some fascinating questions about God's sovereignty over the affairs of nations and the distribution of lands. Additionally, in 2 Chronicles 20:10–11, Jehoshaphat prays and reminds God of these events as he asks for divine aid in repelling the coordinated attack of Ammon, Moab, and Mount Seir.

> (The Emim formerly lived there, a people great and many, and tall as the Anakim. Like the Anakim they are also counted as Rephaim, but the Moabites call them Emim. The Horites also lived in Seir formerly, but the people of Esau dispossessed them and destroyed them from before them and settled in their place, as Israel did[6] to the land of their possession, which the LORD gave to them.)

God gave Ar to Moab, but when he did so, people called the Emim[7] were already living there. These people were as tall as the Anakim, the very people that the Israelites were so afraid of that they disobeyed and refused to go into the land. Yet Moab was able to overcome them because God had given them the land. Not only that, but there were also people who lived in Seir before the people of Esau went in. But God had given the people of Esau the land, and they were able to take it. If God was willing and able to give land that was inhabited by fearsome enemies to the people of Esau, Moab, and Ammon, then how much more can his covenant people trust him to deliver what he has promised to them?

Now, as if this were not enough, God emphasizes the same point again after talking about the land he gave to the Ammonites:

> (It is also counted as a land of Rephaim. Rephaim formerly lived there—but the Ammonites call them Zamzummim—a people great and many, and tall as the Anakim; but the LORD destroyed them before the Ammonites, and they dispossessed them and settled in their place, as he did for the people

6. "As Israel did" is written as though Israel had already taken possession of the land. Moses did not cross over the Jordan, so if this account was not written until after the conquest, Moses did not write it. Was this written after Israel took possession of the land, therefore requiring a late post-Mosaic final composition of Deuteronomy? Peter Craigie argues that verses 10–12 of Deuteronomy 2 were added to the text sometime later in Israel's history, though exactly who wrote it and when are uncertain. Peter C. Craigie, *The Book of Deuteronomy*, NICOT (Eerdmans, 1976), 110–11. If that is the case, then the purpose of the insertion is either to explain how God worked out his will for his people through history or to give the people of Israel fresh courage for whatever trial they may have been facing at the time. Tigay, *Deuteronomy*, 26. Eugene Merrill summarizes two other possibilities: (1) This could be a "perfective of confidence" that speaks of a future event as being as good as completed; or (2) Moses may have written this in reference to the possession of the lands of Sihon and Og that they had already taken possession of. Eugene H. Merrill, *Deuteronomy*, NAC 4 (Broadman & Holman, 1994), 94. Each of the views has issues, but what is clear is that the presence of this verse does not require a late final composition of Deuteronomy.

7. The word "Emim" means something like "fearsome ones." Tigay, *Deuteronomy*, 27.

> of Esau, who live in Seir, when he destroyed the Horites before them and they dispossessed them and settled in their place even to this day. As for the Avvim, who lived in villages as far as Gaza, the Caphtorim, who came from Caphtor, destroyed them and settled in their place.) (Deut. 2:20–23)

The Zamzummim[8] were also tall like the Anakim, and the Lord destroyed them before the Ammonites, who took their land. Then, seemingly out of nowhere, he mentions the Avvim, who were living over on the Mediterranean Sea. Moses points out that the Caphtorim destroyed them and took their place. He does so to show us that God is sovereign and can be trusted to give his people what he has promised, and that nothing can stand in his way.

Second, we should trust God to provide because he is gracious. Going back to Deuteronomy 2:7, after God has told the people that they are going to need to buy food and water as they pass through Edom, he reminds them, "For the LORD your God has blessed you in all the work of your hands." The meaning of this blessing is that God has made them prosperous; they have what they need. They are prosperous not because they are deserving, but because God is gracious. As surely as the Lord graciously provided for his people's needs in the wilderness, he is graciously willing to supply our needs. With our basic needs met, we are—or ought to be—content. The apostle Paul models that humble posture of contentment for the Christian when he writes in 1 Timothy 6:8, "But if we have food and clothing, with these we will be content." God is sovereign and he is gracious; if all we have is food and clothing, it is not because he cannot give us more or because he is stingy. It is because he loves us. Out of his grace he will provide for our needs.

Third, we can trust God to provide for us because he is all-knowing. Moses assures the people, "He knows your going through this great wilderness" (Deut. 2:7). God was not unprepared for the Israelites to go through the wilderness where there would not be provision for them. Nor is he unprepared for our wilderness. He knows exactly what we need and when we need it. We can trust him to supply what we need when we need it.

Fourth, we can trust God to provide because he is faithful. Moses reminds the people of Israel in Deuteronomy 2:7: "These forty years the LORD your

8. The word "Zamzummim" means "confusing/threatening sound." Daniel I. Block, *Deuteronomy*, NIVAC (Zondervan, 2012), 84.

God has been with you. You have lacked nothing." He calls them to remember how God has faithfully provided for them. Likewise, he also calls us to remember how he has been with us all these years. God carried his people through forty years of wilderness wanderings, and they lacked nothing. This does not mean that they had everything they wanted, but they had everything they needed. So too we can count on God to be the same today as he was yesterday and will be forever. He intends for us to learn from the Israelites' experience that as surely as they could trust him to be faithful to provide, so also can we.

I do not know what you are lacking or where you are feeling that the Lord is not providing. But remember the story of those children in the camp after World War II. They went to bed at night and held on to those pieces of bread, and just clutching the bread gave them assurance that they would have what they needed tomorrow. We do not always have bread to hold, but we have something far better. We have the promises and character of God. When we lay our heads down on our pillows and we are feeling restless, discontent, or fearful, let us take hold of the Bread of God's Word. Let us take hold of these promises and remind ourselves of these four truths about God's character that were true for Israel and are true for us today. We can trust God in this wilderness because he is sovereign, he is gracious, he is all-knowing, and he is faithful. The cross reminds us that he loves us. If we do not yet have what we think we need, it is because we do not need it yet. The Lord will provide. Meanwhile, we will remember who he is, we will trust his love and character, and we will obey his gracious commands.

6

The Lord Fights for You

Deuteronomy 2:24—3:29

You shall not fear them, for it is the Lord *your God who fights for you.* (Deut. 3:22)

The practice of psychological operations in warfare is not a new one. From ancient times, nations have sought to "psych out" their enemies through various strategies of intimidation. In his book *Head Game*, author Tim Downs describes a tactic that Alexander the Great used. On one occasion, Alexander and his army were in retreat from a larger army. As they were running, Alexander ordered his armorers to make oversized breastplates and helmets that would fit men who were seven or eight feet tall. Then, as his army was on the run, he would leave behind these gigantic pieces of armor for the enemy to discover. When items that were far larger than any normal-sized man would wear were discovered, the pursuing army would become demoralized and give up their pursuit, not wanting to tangle with such giant foes.[1]

Psychological operations are not new, and they are not limited to human warfare. Our enemy Satan also likes to conduct psyops against us, and too

1. Tim Downs, *Head Game* (Thomas Nelson, 2007), 309.

frequently we are susceptible to the fear and doubt that he seeks to create in us. He overwhelms us with the reminder of the power of remaining sin in our lives. He magnifies the size of the problems before us, whether relational, financial, or spiritual, in hopes of demoralizing or discouraging us.

In this passage, Israel is commanded to go up and fight two different kings. The kings are not Edomite, Moabite, or Ammonite. They are Amorite, the very people that God has said he is going to use Israel to judge (Gen. 15:16). Now, these people are no pushovers and, in some cases, reflect relation to the kind of giant people that Israel has been afraid of. In fact, Moses points out in Deuteronomy 3:11 that Og the king of Bashan is descended from the Rephaim and that his bed of iron was nine cubits in length and four cubits wide (approximately thirteen and a half feet long by six feet wide).[2] Perhaps the bed was overkill, but Moses mentions it to give some indication of Og's size. In purely human terms, the Israelites were not wrong to think themselves outmatched by Sihon, Og, or any of the peoples living in the promised land. Like Israel, we often face foes too great for us. Who are we to stand up to, let alone to overcome, the world that stands opposed to God, the power of indwelling sin that remains in us, the power of death under which we will all one day fall, and the power of the devil himself? But in Deuteronomy 3:22, God gives his covenant people our marching orders: "You shall not fear them, for it is the LORD your God who fights for you." Therefore, we must not be intimidated by Satan's psyops campaigns against us—not because of anything that is true about us, but because of what is true about the Lord who fights for us. Yes, our enemies are big, but the Lord fights for his people, and he is fighting for us today. Do not fear, but remember, trust, and obey.

THE CALL TO WAR

Now the Israelites are to cross the Arnon. To the north and west lies territory belonging to Sihon the Amorite, and to the north and east is territory belonging to the Ammonites. Remember that they were not to

2. Some scholars believe that this may be a reference not to his bed but to his sarcophagus. Peter C. Craigie, *The Book of Deuteronomy*, NICOT (Eerdmans, 1976), 120. In either case, it indicates an abnormally large and terrifying human whose bed or sarcophagus is now on display because God gave him into the hand of Israel (Deut. 3:2).

attack the Ammonites because of their relation and also because God had given them those particular lands to inhabit. But when it comes to Sihon and the Amorites, it is a different story. The Lord urges in Deuteronomy 2:24–25:

> Rise up, set out on your journey and go over the Valley of the Arnon. Behold, I have given into your hand Sihon the Amorite, king of Heshbon, and his land. Begin to take possession, and contend with him in battle. This day I will begin to put the dread and fear of you on the peoples who are under the whole heaven, who shall hear the report of you and shall tremble and be in anguish because of you.

God is going to use the people of Israel to bring his judgment on the Amorites (Gen. 15:16). His instruction here (which began in Deuteronomy 2:17) is that Israel is to take possession of the land of Sihon and contend with him. As a result, the Israelites are assured that God has given him and his land into their hand. Furthermore, God has put fear into the hearts of all the peoples who will hear the report of the Israelites and tremble.[3] God has his own psyops campaign against his enemies. Just as the Israelites returned to obedience in 2:1, so now God is returning to the fulfillment of his promise to fight for them in 2:25.[4] We read in verses 26–27, "So I sent messengers from the wilderness of Kedemoth to Sihon the king of Heshbon, with words of peace, saying, 'Let me pass through your land. I will go only by the road; I will turn aside neither to the right nor to the left.'" Based on what God instructed in verses 24–25, we do not expect Moses to send messengers to Sihon with "words of peace." The message he sends to Sihon in verses 28–29 is the same one he sent to the people of Esau, which God had commanded him to do (Deut. 2:6). But with Sihon they were to contend. So were Moses and the people being disobedient by offering terms of peace? Deuteronomy does not present it that way. Rather, it is presented as a demonstration. Israel is not attacking Sihon unprovoked. Israel is being reasonable, and Sihon is presented as getting what he deserves.[5]

3. The evidence of this is found in Rahab's words in Joshua 2:9–11.

4. Christopher Wright, *Deuteronomy*, NIBC: Old Testament 4 (Hendrickson, 2007), 38.

5. As to the bigger question whether this land east of the Jordan was considered part of the promised land, it is difficult to speak with certainty. On the one hand, God clearly gave this land to Israel under Moses' leadership, and they were Amorite peoples who were defeated, as God promised Abraham

We read of Sihon's resistance in Deuteronomy 2:30–31: "But Sihon the king of Heshbon would not let us pass by him, for the LORD your God hardened his spirit and made his heart obstinate, that he might give him into your hand, as he is this day. And the LORD said to me, 'Behold, I have begun to give Sihon and his land over to you. Begin to take possession, that you may occupy his land.'" Sihon will not let Israel pass, and the specific reason given is that "the LORD your God hardened his spirit and made his heart obstinate" (Deut. 2:30). God is actively involved in this situation, hardening Sihon's heart. Seen from one angle, God is going to judge Sihon for not allowing Israel to pass, but it was God himself who hardened Sihon's heart so that he would not let Israel pass. That may seem unfair to us, but this is not the first time we see such a thing described in the Bible. In fact, this passage is explicitly linked to the story of the exodus in order to show that this event is the continuation of God's redemptive plan for his people.[6] Earlier, in the book of Exodus before Israel is rescued from Egypt, Pharaoh's heart is described multiple times as being "hardened."[7] Sometimes it is said that Pharaoh hardened his heart, and sometimes it is said that God hardened Pharaoh's heart. We are not explicitly told that Sihon hardened his heart, but the connection with the story of Pharaoh suggests that it is the case.

In short, Sihon and Pharaoh were both responsible for hardening their hearts, even though they did so in accordance with God's sovereign decree. Modern readers tend to think either that God is sovereign or that people are responsible for the decisions they make. But the Bible never poses these two things as exclusive of each other. The Bible teaches throughout the Old and New Testaments that God is sovereign over all the affairs of men, and it also teaches that humans are completely responsible for the choices that we

---

in Genesis 15:16–19. On the other hand, if we follow the course of these lands through the rest of Israelite history, we see that numerous problems arise between the tribes separated by the Jordan River. Additionally, Ezekiel's later vision of the people of Israel restored to the promised land leaves out the Transjordanian region (Ezek. 47:15–20). For more on the case against this region's being considered part of the promised land, see Daniel I. Block, *Deuteronomy*, NIVAC (Zondervan, 2012), 108.

6. John D. Currid, *Deuteronomy*, EPSC (EP Books, 2006), 66.

7. The term "hardened" or "harden" occurs thirty-seven times in the ESV across the Old and New Testament. It is worth taking some time to look up each of these passages and see how this idea of heart hardening is used throughout the Bible. The passages listed first in Exodus are the ones referring to Pharaoh's heart. See Ex. 4:21; 7:3, 13–14, 22; 8:15, 19, 32; 9:7, 12; 9:34–10:1; 10:20, 27; 11:10; 14:4, 8, 17; Deut. 2:30; 15:7; Josh. 11:20; 1 Sam. 6:6; 2 Chron. 36:13; Job 9:4; Ps. 95:8; Isa. 63:17; Dan. 5:20; Mark 6:52; 8:17; John 12:40; Rom. 11:7; 2 Cor. 3:14; Heb. 3:8, 13, 15; 4:7.

freely make. The Westminster Confession of Faith attempts to capture both aspects of this truth: "God, from all eternity, did, by the most wise and holy counsel of his own will, freely, and unchangeably ordain whatsoever comes to pass: yet so, as thereby neither is God the author of sin, nor is violence offered to the will of the creatures" (WCF 3.1). In other words, nothing happens except what God has decreed, including the free choices of people. At the same time, God does not violate the wills of people to make free choices. Rather, the free choices of people ultimately serve to accomplish the sovereignly decreed will of God. As a result, people will be held responsible for the free choices they have made, including hardening their hearts against God.

A clear example of this truth is in Luke 22:22, where Jesus declares, "For the Son of Man goes as it has been determined, but woe to that man by whom he is betrayed!" In other words, God determined that Jesus would be handed over and crucified for the salvation of his people—God is sovereign. But this does not absolve Judas of betraying him—man is responsible for his choices. So also here in the case of Sihon and Og. Yes, God had foreordained that they would harden their hearts so that Israel would bring God's judgment on them and take their land. But Sihon and Og are completely responsible for hardening their hearts against God and his people—and so are we. While it may be tempting to continue wrestling with this interesting theological question, it will be more profitable to heed the warning given to Israel and later to readers of the New Testament: "Today, if you hear his voice, do not harden your hearts" (Heb. 4:7). As surely as Sihon suffered for hardening his heart against God and his covenant people, so also will we if we do the same.

The Battle Belongs to the Lord

God's intention is to give Sihon and his land into Israel's hand, and that is exactly what he does after Sihon comes out to attack Israel. We read in Deuteronomy 2:32–36:

> Then Sihon came out against us, he and all his people, to battle at Jahaz. And the Lord our God gave him over to us, and we defeated him and his sons and all his people. And we captured all his cities at that time and devoted to destruction every city, men, women, and children. We left no survivors. Only

> the livestock we took as spoil for ourselves, with the plunder of the cities that we captured. From Aroer, which is on the edge of the Valley of the Arnon, and from the city that is in the valley, as far as Gilead, there was not a city too high for us. The LORD our God gave all into our hands.

Clearly, Deuteronomy 2:33 ascribes this victory to the Lord's fighting for the people of Israel and giving Sihon over to them. But this raises another difficult question for us. Israel defeats Sihon but does not defeat just the men of war. The Israelites take all the cities of Sihon and devote "to destruction every city, men, women, and children" (Deut. 2:34). They leave no survivors. This is not the only time the people of Israel do this. After defeating Sihon, they do exactly the same thing to Og the king of Bashan, as described in 3:1–7. Again, every man, woman, and child of Og's people is "devoted . . . to destruction."[8] But the livestock and other spoils of the cities the people of Israel kept for themselves. To be clear, God commanded Israel to do this explicitly. We read his instructions to Israel about what to do to Og in 3:2: "But the LORD said to me, 'Do not fear him, for I have given him and all his people and his land into your hand. And you shall do to him as you did to Sihon the king of the Amorites, who lived at Heshbon.'"

The destruction of these people and the later destruction of the peoples of Canaan described in the book of Joshua are commonly raised as reasons why the God of the Bible is not worthy of worship. Is God evil for commanding the destruction of women and children? How does this correlate with the biblical teaching to "love your neighbor" (e.g., Rom. 13:9)? Is there any defense of what we read in these passages?

First, we should appreciate the fact that these texts are included in the Bible without apology. The same Bible that teaches love for neighbor, and even our enemies, includes these passages as well without a sense of contradiction. In other words, we in the twenty-first century may be somewhat embarrassed by these texts, but Moses was not, the New Testament writers were not, and God is not. We should not be either. We also should not overlook the fact that the man who leads the conquest of Canaan and the destruction of the Canaanites is named Joshua; this is the Hebrew form of the name that God

8. The Hebrew root is *ḥāram*. "It involves consecration of something or someone as a permanent and definitive offering for the sanctuary; or in war, the consecration of a city and its inhabitants to destruction and the carrying out of this destruction." Jackie A. Naudé, *NIDOTTE*, s.v. "חָרַם," 2:269.

commanded Mary and Joseph to name their son. Joshua was heralded as a savior, not a monster, and that is why Jesus receives that name (Matt. 1:21).

Second, we must recognize that the biblical concept of love of neighbor does not mean simply being "nice" to all people in all situations. At the familial level, love of neighbor sometimes involved discipline, such as a parent's disciplining a child. It was loving not only for the child, but for all the future people that the well-disciplined child would one day encounter. At the community level, sometimes love of neighbor meant exposing the idolatry or apostasy in a neighbor, and in other cases loving one's neighbors involved the sanctioned execution of the most heinous offenders.[9] A repeated phrase in Deuteronomy that is also picked up by the apostle Paul in the New Testament is "Purge the evil from among you."[10] That command is not incompatible with love of neighbor but is rather a specific application of the command to love your neighbor. Under the terms of God's covenant with the people of Israel, purging evil from among them meant executing idolaters and other sinners who sought to lead God's people astray.

The apostle Paul, in 1 Corinthians 5:13, still embraces the principal idea here, but rather than executing people, the church is to excommunicate them. To fail to do so in a local church is a failure to love our neighbors. In the broader context of God's intention to bless all the nations through Israel, we can see that God's justice executed on the Canaanites is not incompatible with the command to love.[11] Rather, love of neighbor required the utter destruction of the Canaanites.[12] This was an act of God's judgment to advance his redemptive plan of love for all the nations. This was not to be a judgment that Israel made for itself, but was to be one that God determined and commanded. It was not Israel's normal practice in other wars, and even in the conquest there were exceptions to total destruction, such as Rahab (Josh. 6:17). This passage is most certainly not a justification for later crusades that the church initiated in the Middle Ages, or even for the

9. Wright, *Deuteronomy*, 227.

10. See, e.g., Deut. 13:5; 17:7, 12; 19:19; 21:21; 22:21–22, 24; 24:7; 1 Cor. 5:13.

11. Wright, *Deuteronomy*, 227.

12. Christopher J. H. Wright, *Old Testament Ethics for the People of God* (InterVarsity Press, 2004), 473–74.

European conquest of the Americas and destruction of its native peoples under the banner of "manifest destiny."[13]

Third, we need to understand this whole concept within the suzerain-vassal framework of Deuteronomy. Israel is God's vassal people, and he is the suzerain Lord. The vassal pledges loyalty to the suzerain, and the suzerain promises protection for his loyal subjects. A suzerain in the ancient Near East would primarily go to war for two purposes: (1) to protect or rescue his vassals from their enemies and (2) to do battle against those resisting his sovereignty, whether they were erring vassals or just plain enemies.[14] The first case is what happened in the exodus when God waged war on Egypt to rescue his people from slavery. The second case is what he is doing here in the conquest of the promised land. He is bringing his promised judgment on the wicked nations that are resisting his will, and he is going to take their land and give it to his faithful subjects, as he promised Abraham.[15] Those vassals are bound by covenant to join in the fight with their suzerain Lord. (Later in Israel's history when God's vassal people go astray and worship idols, he will use Babylon and Assyria to bring judgment on his own people and give their land to others.)

The primary takeaway from this passage is that God is the sovereign power in this universe, and is dead set against the forces of evil. He has waged war on evil, and he will not be defeated. He has also made it clear that in the end, there will be a final judgment on all wickedness and evil and that there will be a final rescue for all those who are loyal to him and bow the knee in submission to this sovereign suzerain.[16] We read in 2 Thessalonians 1:7–9 of that day "when the Lord Jesus is revealed from heaven with his mighty angels in flaming fire, inflicting vengeance on those who do not know God and on those who do not obey the gospel of our Lord Jesus. They will suffer the punishment of eternal destruction, away from the presence of the Lord and from the glory of his might." In other words, God is going to judge and remove from his land all the wicked and give it to his people. He will execute

13. Block, *Deuteronomy*, 98.

14. J. A. Thompson, *Deuteronomy: An Introduction and Commentary*, TOTC (InterVarsity Press, 1974), 72.

15. Deuteronomy 9:4–5 makes explicit this twofold purpose of (1) judgment and (2) deliverance on his promises to Israel.

16. Thompson, *Deuteronomy*, 73.

perfect justice, and every knee will bow before him (Phil. 2:9–10). But his gracious invitation to all peoples today is to acknowledge his lordship as the rightful King of the universe. We are called to confess that we have been rebels against his will and to turn from our rebellion and devote ourselves to him and his ways. He has made peace with his enemies through the blood of Jesus Christ, his Son, and all people everywhere are called to trust him and obey him. Those who do will experience God's perfect mercy and pardon. Those who do not will ultimately face God's perfect justice.

One for All and All for One

The phrase "one for all and all for one" was made famous by *The Three Musketeers*, but Israel was practicing the concept long before. Now that the land is taken, it is to be divided. We read in Deuteronomy 3:12–13 that the land is given to the tribe of Reuben, the tribe of Gad, and the half-tribe of Manasseh. This would be their inheritance of the promised land. But they are not just to settle into it and leave their brothers to go and fight on their own. They are to join in the fight, as we read in verses 18–20:

> And I commanded you at that time, saying, "The Lord your God has given you this land to possess. All your men of valor shall cross over armed before your brothers, the people of Israel. Only your wives, your little ones, and your livestock (I know that you have much livestock) shall remain in the cities that I have given you, until the Lord gives rest to your brothers, as to you, and they also occupy the land that the Lord your God gives them beyond the Jordan. Then each of you may return to his possession which I have given you."

The wives, children, and livestock of Israel can settle into the cities that they have just taken from Sihon and Og, but the warriors need to join the campaign to take all the rest of the land that God is giving them on the western side of the Jordan. Only after every tribe has received its allotment could any tribe settle into its rest. This mutual obligation to one another remained an ideal for the people of Israel, and also carried on into the time of the early church. In fact, in the service of communion, one of the things that we remember is that because we all share in Christ, we all have mutual obligations to one another (1 Cor. 12:12–26). If one of us is in need, we all feel the need. If one of us is grieved, we all share the grief. If one of us rejoices, we all share in the rejoicing. In the early church, when there were needs among the people of God, some went so far as to sell property belonging to them to be able to give and make their fellow brothers and sisters whole (Acts 4:34–35). We continue to uphold this ideal first presented in the Old Testament and confirmed in the New Testament, that we belong to the Lord first, and therefore we also belong to one another, which carries the responsibility to care for one another. For the people of God, the battles we fight in this world are one for all and all for one.

Moses gives Joshua and the people some final words of courage:

> And I commanded Joshua at that time, "Your eyes have seen all that the LORD your God has done to these two kings. So will the LORD do to all the kingdoms into which you are crossing. You shall not fear them, for it is the LORD your God who fights for you." (Deut. 3:21–22)

Here is the fundamental point that the people of Israel need to grasp: it is the Lord your God who fights for you. He has given this new generation a fresh illustration of the strength of the Lord as a Warrior. Sihon and Og were no slouches; remember Og's bed! But God is no slouch either, and he has given both these kings into the hand of the Israelites! They are explicitly told to remember this reality as they head across the Jordan so that they will trust the Lord as they go forward into battle and obey all his commands.

A Final Request

There is one final piece of unresolved business. Moses has seen the victories that God gave his people over Sihon and Og, and he wants to be a part of helping take the rest of the land. He recalls how he pleaded with God: "And I pleaded with the LORD at that time, saying, 'O Lord GOD, you have only begun to show your servant your greatness and your mighty hand. For what god is there in heaven or on earth who can do such works and mighty acts as yours? Please let me go over and see the good land beyond the Jordan, that good hill country and Lebanon'" (Deut. 3:23–25). We sympathize with Moses. He has led these people for nearly forty years in the wilderness. He has put up with so much foolishness and sinfulness. He has interceded with God on behalf of the people numerous times and is even referred to as the meekest man on the earth (Num. 12:3). He knows that God is only getting started in showing his great power to his people, and he wants to see more of that as well as the good land that God is giving. But God has already made his decision on the matter, and we read in Deuteronomy 3:26–27: "But the Lord was angry with me because of you and would not listen to me. And the Lord said to me, 'Enough from you; do not speak to me of this matter again. Go up to the top of Pisgah and lift up your eyes westward and northward and southward and eastward, and look at it with your eyes, for you shall not go over this Jordan.'" Again, Moses points out that it is on account of his identification with the people of Israel that the Lord is not listening to his plea. Not only that, but God tells Moses that he does not want to hear about it anymore. It feels a little bit like a parent in the grocery store with a little child. The child sees the candy on the shelf once they walk into the store, and the child is asking over and over, "Can I get some candy?" The parent has already told the child "no" before they even entered the store. Eventually, the parent says, "I'm not changing my mind; do not ask me about this again." This is what God has done with Moses here. He is not changing his mind.

How do we compare this response with Jesus' teaching on prayer and the importance of being persistent in our prayers to God?[17] In short, both are true. So long as we are not asking for what we know is contrary to his will, we should bring our requests to God. As far as we know, we should bring our requests to God repeatedly. But there may come a point when we become aware that we are no longer to continue praying the same way. (How we know that God is communicating to us this way is a matter of discernment. But we can rest assured that the Lord knows how to speak in such a way that we will hear him.) If he does say to us what he said to Moses, then we ought to stop praying in the same way.

The apostle Paul had a similar experience in 2 Corinthians 12. Paul had a thorn in his flesh that caused him great suffering. He responded as he should have, by bringing it to God in prayer. We read of his experience in 2 Corinthians 12:8–9: "Three times I pleaded with the Lord about this, that it should leave me. But he said to me, 'My grace is sufficient for you,

17. As taught, for instance, in Luke 11:1–13 and 18:1–8.

for my power is made perfect in weakness.'" In other words, Jesus told him to stop asking for the removal of the thorn and to begin trusting in the sufficiency of his grace to enable him to endure the suffering. Commenting on Moses' prayer, Daniel Block writes, "The measure of faith is not necessarily established by what we can get God to do for us; sometimes strong faith means simply casting ourselves into his loving and gracious arms, trusting him to be with us even in grief."[18] Instead of leading the people into the promised land himself, Moses is to charge, encourage, and strengthen Joshua to lead the people into all that God has promised. That is what he does in Deuteronomy 3:28–29, and unlike the rest of the generation that died in the wilderness, God shows Moses the grace of allowing him to go up to the top of the mountain, where he got a great view of the land of promise. Not only that, but later in the New Testament we read that he was granted the privilege of being with Jesus and Elijah on the Mount of Transfiguration in the promised land (Mark 9:2–8).

In the New Testament conception, God still fights for his people. But one of the things that is progressively revealed is that our battle is not against flesh and blood. Paul writes in Ephesians 6:12, "For we do not wrestle against flesh and blood, but against the rulers, against the authorities, against the cosmic powers over this present darkness, against the spiritual forces of evil in the heavenly places." God has waged war on our spiritual enemies, even the ones residing inside our own flesh. The question is, how can God destroy the evil residing in us without destroying us? The way that he ultimately accomplishes this victory is through the cross of Christ. We read in Colossians 2:13–15:

> And you, who were dead in your trespasses and the uncircumcision of your flesh, God made alive together with him, having forgiven us all our trespasses, by canceling the record of debt that stood against us with its legal demands. This he set aside, nailing it to the cross. He disarmed the rulers and authorities and put them to open shame, by triumphing over them in him.

The principal weapon that our enemy wielded against us was our record of debt: the endless list of ways in which we have resisted and rebelled against God, the sovereign Ruler. Justice demanded that we pay the debt we owed

18. Block, *Deuteronomy*, 111.

to him, and Satan the accuser would point to that list, demanding our utter destruction to satisfy justice. The great mystery that neither Satan nor any of his minions saw coming was that God would cancel that debt. How? He ripped it out of Satan's hands and nailed it to the cross. Jesus took the record of debt upon himself and paid it through his death. Now Satan has no more weapon to wield against us. Our sins are forgiven, and we are no longer condemned. Christ fought for us the ultimate battle by dying on the cross and then rising again in victory on the third day. Now he proclaims peace and pardon to all who will come to him in faith. No matter how long our list of debts, Jesus has paid it all for all who will come.

With the close of these verses in Deuteronomy 3, we come to the end of the main section of the historical prologue. In this section, Moses has reminded the people of their history with God, of the loyalty that they owe him for his deliverance of them, and also of two great and fresh victories he gave them in overcoming Sihon and Og. In Deuteronomy 4, Moses will begin to transition from the historical prologue to exhort Israel to live in a particular kind of way as God's covenant people when they go in to take the land that he is giving them. They are not to be afraid, but instead to remember that it is the Lord who fights for them. Therefore, they can trust him and obey his commands as they go forward, and so can we. Paul asks rhetorically in Romans 8:31, "If God is for us, who can be against us?" The answer is "No one." God definitively declared that he is for us when he gave us his Son. No enemy can stand against us: not the devil, not our indwelling and remaining sin, not even death. But in Jesus Christ, the God who fights for us, we have ultimate victory over them all. So then let us remember these things, let us trust the God who fights for us, and let us walk in joyful obedience to all his commands.

7

The Gift of God's Word

Deuteronomy 4:1–8

Keep them and do them, for that will be your wisdom and your understanding in the sight of the peoples, who, when they hear all these statutes, will say, "Surely this great nation is a wise and understanding people." (Deut. 4:6)

A five-year-old girl was sent to her room for disobeying her mother. After a few minutes of "alone time," the mother went to talk with her about what she had done. The teary-eyed girl asked, "Why do we do wrong things, Mommy?" Her mother said: "Sometimes the devil tells us to do something wrong and we listen to him. We need to listen to God instead." The little girl sobbed, "But God doesn't talk loud enough!"[1]

Indeed, sometimes it feels that way. The compulsion to do what is wrong is strong, not only because of the influence of our adversary, but because of the corruption of sin that remains even in the hearts of those redeemed by

1. Craig Brian Larson and Phyllis Ten Elshof, eds., *1001 Illustrations That Connect: Compelling Stories, Stats, and News Items for Preaching, Teaching, and Writing* (Christianity Today International, 2008), 453.

Jesus Christ. Despite those realities, we cannot say that God has not spoken loudly enough. Among the greatest gifts that God has given to his people are the Old and New Testaments. According to the third question and answer of the Westminster Shorter Catechism: "What do the Scriptures principally teach? The Scriptures principally teach what man is to believe concerning God, and what duty God requires of man." God's Word reveals his perfect character as well as what he requires of us. We do not have to wonder who he is, what he is like, what he has done for us, or what he asks of us. This is an extraordinary gift! We can proclaim with the psalmist, "I rejoice at your word like one who finds great spoil" (Ps. 119:162). Scripture is an incredible treasure! That is what Moses claims in this passage: God's Word is a gift, and we must be diligent to obey it.

At the end of Deuteronomy 3, Moses recounted his request to go into the promised land and God's refusal based on the sins of Moses and the people. Now in chapter 4, he exhorts the people of Israel to follow the law that they are about to receive so that they can go into the land and take possession of it—a privilege that Moses and the previous generation will miss because of their unfaithfulness. This helps us understand why Moses is so adamant that they pay attention to put into practice what he teaches. Reflecting on the significance of this passage, Gary Millar writes, "Moab is the new Kadesh: Israel cannot afford to let it become the new Baal-Peor."[2] In this chapter, Moses is not going to tell us what the laws are; that will come later, starting in chapter 5 and running through chapter 26. But in this chapter, he emphasizes the importance of and the reasons for obeying. From this passage we glean two things that the people of God must remember about the gift of God's Word.

Remember the Priority of Obedience to God's Word

Moses says in Deuteronomy 4:1, "And now, O Israel, listen to the statutes and the rules that I am teaching you, and do them, that you may live, and go in and take possession of the land that the Lord, the God of your fathers, is giving you." The first words of this verse, "And now," refer us back to the main section of the historical prologue (Deut. 1:6–3:29) that recounted God's

2. J. Gary Millar, *Now Choose Life: Theology and Ethics in Deuteronomy*, NSBT 6 (Apollos, 1998), 76.

faithfulness to Israel.[3] His appeal to obey is predicated on Israel's history with God.[4] The stipulations that are to come in chapters 5–26 are for the life and protection of God's covenant people.

Israel is to listen and keep the statutes and rules that God is teaching the people. The words "the statutes and the rules" are synonyms referring to the whole of the law revealed in Deuteronomy 5–26.[5] This is a call not to blind obedience but to common sense.[6] As we follow the text, we see two reasons for obeying God's Word: (1) that you may live and (2) that you may go in and take possession of the land that the Lord is giving you.

The first reason given for obedience is so that God's people may live. This concept of obedience bringing life while disobedience brings death is a "Deuteronomic principle,"[7] and it is repeated in this book (e.g., Deut. 30:15–18), other books in the Old Testament (e.g., Ezek. 18:1–9), and the New Testament. In his conversation with the rich young ruler, Jesus affirms the Deuteronomic viewpoint: "And behold, a man came up to him, saying, 'Teacher, what good deed must I do to have eternal life?' And he said to him, 'Why do you ask me about what is good? There is only one who is good. If you would enter life, keep the commandments'" (Matt. 19:16–17). Jesus is affirming what Moses taught in Deuteronomy. He makes it clear in Matthew 19:18–21: "He said to him, 'Which ones?' And Jesus said, 'You shall not murder, You shall not commit adultery, You shall not steal, You shall not bear false witness, Honor your father and mother, and, You shall love your neighbor as yourself.' The young man said to him, 'All these I have kept. What do I still lack?' Jesus said to him, 'If you would be perfect, go, sell what you possess and give to the poor, and you will have treasure in heaven; and come, follow me.'" Jesus was not teaching that salvation can be earned by keeping the commandments, but was instead that obeying the commandments is an expression of trust as a proper response to God's gracious salvation, resulting in life-giving blessings. This is the same lesson found in Deuteronomy.

3. J. A. Thompson, *Deuteronomy: An Introduction and Commentary*, TOTC (InterVarsity Press, 1974), 102.

4. The place of 4:1–8 in the context of Deuteronomy as a whole signals the beginning of a transition between God's faithfulness to Israel in the past and the necessity of Israel's faithfulness to God if its people want to have a pleasant future in the land.

5. Peter C. Craigie, *The Book of Deuteronomy*, NICOT (Eerdmans, 1976), 129n2.

6. Patrick D. Miller, *Deuteronomy*, IC (John Knox Press, 1990), 54.

7. Thompson, *Deuteronomy*, 102.

The second reason given for why the Israelites should listen and obey God's Word is so that they may go in and take possession of the land. Israel's entrance into the land is not based on military strength or strategy, but it is connected to the people's commitment to God's Word. So too is their ongoing enjoyment of that land and the relationship it signifies. When we look carefully at these words, we see a tension here. On the one hand, there is the command to obey, and the possession of the land seems to be conditional on their obedience. On the other hand, the promise of the land is unconditional because God had promised it and is already in the process of giving it to Israel. How do we hold this tension together? It is probably best to understand the unconditionality and conditionality of these promises in the context of the father-son relationship that exists between God and his covenant people. Their sonship is unconditional, and they cannot earn it. But their sonship also calls them to particular obligations of obedience to God their Father.[8] As Christopher Wright puts it: "Behind everything stands the unconditioned grace and faithfulness of God to the divine promise. The land would be given. But secure possession of it, long life, and enjoyment of it were dependent in each generation on the people's response of committed loyalty and obedience."[9]

We are called to live as God's covenant people in obedience to his Word. Like Israel, we should remember that there are good reasons to do so. For one thing, it makes sense. For example, ignoring God's good commands regarding human sexuality is not only sinful, but also just not smart. The consequences of living without God's gracious guardrails for our sexual desires are evident to those who have disregarded them. Likewise, those who have been rescued from worshiping our cultural gods of money, power, and fame see the folly in such a way of life. This is true on an individual level and also a societal level. A community that disregards God's commands around honesty experiences the consequences when trust is eroded. A society that ignores God's commands regarding marriage and family will experience the disintegration of the family and the societal ills that result from broken homes. There are good practical reasons for obeying God's Word.

An essential component of obeying God's Word is to preserve it unaltered.

8. Christopher Wright, *Deuteronomy*, NIBC: Old Testament 4 (Hendrickson, 2007), 59.
9. Wright, 46.

Moses asserts in Deuteronomy 4:2, "You shall not add to the word that I command you, nor take from it, that you may keep the commandments of the LORD your God that I command you." It is common to apply this verse (as well as Revelation 22:18–19, which may derive from it) to all the Scripture of the Old and New Testaments. Nothing is to be added to it, nor is anything to be taken away from it. God's Word is not a buffet from which we can choose what we like and reject parts that we do not like. Nor can we add things that we think should be there. The "word that I command you" in this context is the law that Moses is about to give in Deuteronomy 5–26.[10] This prohibition against adding to the Word did not mean that there could be no further revelation after this point, and clearly, further revelation was given through the prophets, the apostles, and Jesus himself. Additionally, the reference to not adding to or taking away from the law had to do with the essence of the law as well as the letter of the law. If we compare the Ten Commandments in Exodus 20 and Deuteronomy 5, we will find some slight differences in wording, but the essence of the laws and their meaning are the same.[11] Furthermore, when Jesus begins to proclaim the gospel, he makes it clear that he is not offering something different from the law that God gave through Moses. He declares in Matthew 5:17–19:

> Do not think that I have come to abolish the Law or the Prophets; I have not come to abolish them but to fulfill them. For truly, I say to you, until heaven and earth pass away, not an iota, not a dot, will pass from the Law until all is accomplished. Therefore whoever relaxes one of the least of these commandments and teaches others to do the same will be called least in the kingdom of heaven, but whoever does them and teaches them will be called great in the kingdom of heaven.

The ministry of Jesus and the teaching of the New Testament are not additions to the law that God gave to Moses but rather the fulfillment of it.

Not only is the priority of obeying God's Word highlighted in the positive with regard to the promise of life and the possession of the land, but a negative example is also held up before the people in Deuteronomy 4:3:

10. Craigie, *Deuteronomy*, 130.
11. Craigie, 130n7.

"Your eyes have seen what the LORD did at Baal-peor, for the LORD your God destroyed from among you all the men who followed the Baal of Peor." Baal-peor is mentioned as a warning and as an encouragement for the Israelites to keep God's law. The last verse of chapter 3 tells us that the people of Israel "remained in the valley opposite Beth-peor" (Deut. 3:29). They were just a short distance away in terms of location, and the events of Beth-peor (also called Baal-peor as in 4:3) had happened within weeks of the words that Moses is speaking. The story is recounted in Numbers 25. The short version is that the Israelites began to engage in sexual sin with the women of Moab, which also opened them up to worshiping the gods of Moab, namely, Baal and Asherah. In response, the Lord brought a plague until the participants in this idolatry were executed. Some twenty-four thousand people died. The story is a vivid illustration that "the wages of sin is death" (Rom. 6:23).

It is only by God's mercy that he does not destroy us all immediately when we rebel against him. His patience with our provocations is beyond fathoming. Moses recounts the events of Baal-peor to encourage the people to cleave to the Lord. Moses reminds them of this event to warn them what happens if they disregard the gift of God's Word: it leads to death. Maybe not today, because God is patient in wanting all to reach repentance (2 Peter 3:9). But ultimately, death is the end of disobedience. Then Moses contrasts that example of the disobedient dying with Deuteronomy 4:4, "But you who held fast to the LORD your God are all alive today." Follow after false gods and you will perish. Hold fast to the true God and you will live. That is the message of Deuteronomy.[12]

The eighteenth-century Scottish pastor Ralph Erskine put it this way: "When you see a dog following two men, . . . you know not to which of them he belongs while they walk together; but let them come to a parting road, and one go one way, and the other another way, then you will know which is the dog's master."[13] Circumstances will arise, as they did for Israel at Baal-peor, that require us to choose: follow the Lord and hold fast to

12. This whole chapter is considered the theological heart of Deuteronomy, giving us a concise summary of the importance of worshiping God only and avoiding idolatry. Jeffrey H. Tigay, *Deuteronomy*, JPSTC (Jewish Publication Society, 1996), 41.

13. Quoted in "Impossible to Serve God and Mammon," Bible Hub, https://biblehub.com/sermons/pub/impossible_to_serve_god_and_mammon.htm, accessed January 13, 2025.

him as Master, or follow the world. Verse 5 of Deuteronomy 4 continues to emphasize the same point as verse 1.

How can we know whether we are holding fast to our God? He has given us one very clear test. In John 14:21, Jesus notes, "Whoever has my commandments and keeps them, he it is who loves me." The test of our love and commitment to God is not our studying of his Word, as important as that is. The test of our love of and commitment to God is not our intellectual assent to his Word, as important as that is. The test of our love of and commitment to God is not our verbal praising of his Word, as much as it is worthy. The test of our love of and commitment to God is whether we actually obey his commands. We need to be honest with ourselves, starting with those of us who teach. It is easy to tell others week after week what God requires of us. It is easy to spend hours reflecting on the implications of God's Word for our lives today, and then not spend thirty seconds being ruthlessly honest in our own assessment of doing God's Word. The people of God who followed the Baal of Peor knew what God required; what separated them from the rest of Israel was that though they knew God's command, they did not obey it. Remember the priority of obedience to God's Word!

Remember the Missional Purpose of God's Word

Turning from the personal and communal reasons why the people of God need to hear and obey God's Word, Moses now addresses God's missional purpose in giving his Word to his people. Moses writes in Deuteronomy 4:6, "Keep them and do them, for that will be your wisdom and your understanding in the sight of the peoples, who, when they hear all these statutes, will say, 'Surely this great nation is a wise and understanding people.'" As God's people faithfully live by God's Word, others take notice, and that is God's intention. Remember, God chose Abraham and his descendants so that they would become a blessing to the nations. As they lived according to God's Word, the nations would ask questions. But only as his people reflected the ethical qualities laid out in God's Word would the nations be interested in Israel's God.[14] So it is also today. Jesus told his followers in Matthew 5:13–16:

14. Wright, *Deuteronomy*, 49.

> You are the salt of the earth, but if salt has lost its taste, how shall its saltiness be restored? It is no longer good for anything except to be thrown out and trampled under people's feet.
>
> You are the light of the world. A city set on a hill cannot be hidden. Nor do people light a lamp and put it under a basket, but on a stand, and it gives light to all in the house. In the same way, let your light shine before others, so that they may see your good works and give glory to your Father who is in heaven.

If our lives as God's people are not different from the world around us, then there is no reason for the world to seek what we have. The church is to be a picture of humanity as God intended it to be—not perfectly so, but distinctively so. "The missional goal of God's people is not fulfilled with precise theological formulas, but through the life-giving and transforming power of the divine Word."[15] In other words, it is not our theological statements that primarily impact the world, but our communal embodiment of the theological truths that we claim to believe. Do we model concern for the vulnerable populations among us, as God's Word instructs? Do we model love for one another and even for our enemies in the culture around us? Are we a people primarily defined by our anger and the things we are against, or are we zealously pursuing and rejoicing in what is good? Do we reflect the anxieties of the world around us and the mob mentality so prevalent, or are we a people marked by peace and civility in our private and public discourse? Are we a graceless people who reject all those who are different from us, or do we hold tightly to our theological convictions while extending a warm welcome to all those who are not yet fully devoted followers of Jesus Christ?

Moses continues to describe how the gift of God's Word embodied in God's people causes them to stand out from the rest of the peoples in Deuteronomy 4:7: "For what great nation is there that has a god so near to it as the Lord our God is to us, whenever we call upon him?" The distinctiveness of God's people would be seen in the intimacy that they shared with him. Other great nations of the earth did not have a god so near as Israel's God. When Israel called on him, God answered. He still answers today!

God's people would also stand out among the nations because of the quality of God's Word, as we read in Deuteronomy 4:8: "And what great

15. Daniel I. Block, *Deuteronomy*, NIVAC (Zondervan, 2012), 123.

nation is there, that has statutes and rules so righteous as all this law that I set before you today?" The commands and statutes that God has given reflect his righteous character. The invitation here is for all the peoples to hold Israel's law up against anyone else's law in the world and to compare them. As for righteousness, there is no competition. When we move through chapters 5–26, we will see the wisdom and the righteousness of God on display in his statutes and rules.

King David writes in Psalm 19:7–11:

> The law of the LORD is perfect,
> reviving the soul;
> the testimony of the LORD is sure,
> making wise the simple;
> the precepts of the LORD are right,
> rejoicing the heart;
> the commandment of the LORD is pure,
> enlightening the eyes;
> the fear of the LORD is clean,
> enduring forever;
> the rules of the LORD are true,
> and righteous altogether.
> More to be desired are they than gold,
> even much fine gold;
> sweeter also than honey
> and drippings of the honeycomb.
> Moreover, by them is your servant warned;
> in keeping them there is great reward.

Like David, we should see the wisdom and righteousness of God's law. His Word should be more desirable than money to us. Only those for whom the Word is their delight will live in obedience to it. We must receive God's Word as the faithful ones in Israel received God's Word: with joy. Commenting on a common misperception that Christians have of God's law, Wright notes:

> The least one can say about people who express such enthusiastic sentiments for the law is that they were not grovelling along under a heavy burden of

> legalism. They were not anxiously striving to earn their way into salvation and a relationship with God through punctilious law-keeping. They were not puffed up with the claims of self-righteousness or exhausted with the efforts of works-righteousness. They did not, in short, fit into any of the caricatures that have been inflicted upon the Old Testament law by those who, misunderstanding Paul's arguments with those who had *distorted* the law, attribute to the law itself the very distortions from which Paul was seeking to exonerate it.[16]

While the law called people to obedience and warned about the consequences of disobedience, God's Word was not the basis of their acceptance or rejection by God. They were already in a relationship with God by virtue of his saving of them in Egypt while they were slaves. They were not to try to keep God's commands in order to be saved, but were to obey God because he had saved them. It was a response of love and gratitude.

It is the same for us as the people of God under the terms of the new covenant. We are called to walk in obedience to God's Word, namely, the two Great Commandments to love God and to love people. If we think our relationship with God is dependent on how well we do those two things, we will not love God or people well. Either we will reject God and his commands altogether when we realize that we cannot live up to them or, like the Pharisees in the New Testament, we will focus intently on outward conformity to God's laws and the things that are easily measurable while our hearts are dead to God and to people. But when we understand that our relationship with God is wholly dependent on our faith in Jesus Christ and what he accomplished for us at the cross, we are free to love God and people from the heart—not to get something, but because of the extraordinary gift that we have already been given. Then obeying God is not a chore, but is our delight. As we live in obedience to his Word, his missional purpose for us to be a light to the nations will come to fruition as we share Jesus with others.

God's Word is an incredible gift. In light of what he has done for us, let's prioritize obedience to it and fulfill our missional calling to show the world the greatness and righteousness of our God.

16. Christopher J. H. Wright, *Old Testament Ethics for the People of God* (InterVarsity Press, 2004), 282.

8

Cheating on a Jealous God

Deuteronomy 4:9–31

Take care, lest you forget the covenant of the Lord your God, which he made with you, and make a carved image, the form of anything that the Lord your God has forbidden you. For the Lord your God is a consuming fire, a jealous God. (Deut. 4:23–24)

Some things should never be done. You don't spit into the wind. You don't test an electrical outlet with a butter knife. And you most certainly don't get between a mama bear and her cub. Along those same lines, we might add this: you don't cheat on a jealous God. It is strange to think about cheating on God. But in fact, the Bible describes this as happening in many places. Much of the book of Hosea is devoted to this theme, and large parts of Ezekiel and Jeremiah. The people of God are described not only as his servants, his children, and his treasured possession, but also as his bride. As his people, we owe him our exclusive love, loyalty, and devotion. Biblically speaking, the primary way by which we cheat on God is through idolatry. Idolatry is putting something ahead of God in our life, or worshiping something in place of God. It was a major problem in the Old Testament, and it remains a continual temptation today.

In this passage, Moses is still setting us up for the giving of the law that will formally begin in Deuteronomy 5. In the previous chapter, we saw that as God's people live faithfully by God's law, they will function as a light to the nations. The primary threat to Israel's witness to the nations—and the people's relationship with God—is idolatry. In these verses, Moses provides strong words about idolatry and commands God's people in multiple ways to "take care" not to engage in it.

This passage reveals that we are not naturally alert to the spiritual dangers of idolatry, and so we are repeatedly warned: "Watch yourselves very carefully" (Deut. 4:15); "beware lest you act corruptly by making a carved image for yourselves" (v. 16); "beware lest you raise your eyes to heaven, and . . . be drawn away" (v. 19); "Take care, lest you forget the covenant of the Lord your God, . . . and make a carved image" (v. 23). We can run headlong into this sin, but we can also get subtly drawn into it without realizing it. In the same way that an adulterous affair typically develops little by little, so also we tend to slide into idolatry imperceptibly. Moses commands God's covenant people to take care not to forget God's covenant, lest we find ourselves cheating on a jealous God.

Take Care Not to Forget: Our God Is a Speaking God

The first warning comes in Deuteronomy 4:9: "Only take care, and keep your soul diligently, lest you forget the things that your eyes have seen, and lest they depart from your heart all the days of your life. Make them known to your children and your children's children." Moses warns the people not to forget what their eyes have seen, lest the memories depart from their hearts. The faith of God's people in the Old Testament is not based on speculative thoughts about what God might be like, but it is based on their lived experience of God.[1] They are to recount to themselves and to their children the works that their eyes have seen God do so that the significance of those works does not depart from their hearts.

1. Jeffrey H. Tigay, *Deuteronomy*, JPSTC (Jewish Publication Society, 1996), 46. Tigay goes on to quote Abraham Joshua Heschel, *God in Search of Man: A Philosophy of Judaism* (Jewish Publication Society, 1959), 140: "The essence of Jewish religious thinking does not lie in entertaining a concept of God but in the ability to articulate a memory of moments of illumination by His presence. Israel is not a people of definers but a people of witnesses."

People from the United States take care not to forget some things. For example, we are careful to remember our veterans each year on Veterans Day and those who gave their lives in battle on Memorial Day. We have set those days apart so that we do not forget. Likewise, in the church, we set apart Sundays to remember who God is and what he has done. Most Christians also observe Christmas and Easter for the same reasons. God wants his people to remember. For the Israelites, remembering includes God's mighty rescue of them in the exodus and the miracles associated with that event, along with his acts of judgment on Egypt. Moses recalls in Deuteronomy 4:10–11

> how on the day that you stood before the LORD your God at Horeb, the LORD said to me, "Gather the people to me, that I may let them hear my words, so that they may learn to fear me all the days that they live on the earth, and that they may teach their children so." And you came near and stood at the foot of the mountain, while the mountain burned with fire to the heart of heaven, wrapped in darkness, cloud, and gloom.

Moses is specifically reminding the Israelites not to forget what they experienced at Horeb after God rescued them from Egypt. It was there that God descended on the mountain in fire and the mountain smoked like a kiln (Ex. 20:18). The imagery of fire suggests God's holiness and the illumination he brings, and yet that fire is wrapped in darkness, cloud, and gloom, suggesting his transcendence and mystery.

From that place of fire in darkness and gloom we read in Deuteronomy 4:12: "Then the LORD spoke to you out of the midst of the fire. You heard the sound of words, but saw no form; there was only a voice." God spoke out of the fire, and what was most significant about it is that the people saw no form. They only heard a voice. God reveals himself to his people by his voice. God speaks—and verse 13 tells us what he said that day: "And he declared to you his covenant, which he commanded you to perform, that is, the Ten Commandments, and he wrote them on two tablets of stone."[2]

2. Many people typically think of the two tablets of stone as being necessary to contain all the Ten Commandments. But it is more likely that this reflects the ancient Near Eastern practice of producing two covenant treaty documents: one for the suzerain and one for the vassal. According to the second-millennium B.C. Hittite documents, the vassal's copy was to be placed in the temple of the vassal's

God spoke to his people from the fire that day because he desired for them to listen and obey. Not only that, but he wanted to instill in them a sense of reverence and holy fear so that they would not sin. In Exodus 20:20, "Moses said to the people, 'Do not fear, for God has come to test you, that the fear of him may be before you, that you may not sin.'" The first phrase says, "Do not fear." But immediately Moses points out that the reason for God's coming to them at Horeb was so that the fear of him would be before them. In other words, they were not to be terrified of God, but they were to revere him. Jeffrey Tigay writes: "Reverence is man's response to God's power. It consists of both respect and awe at His grandeur and dread of His power, which serves as a deterrent to disobeying Him. It is one of Moses' main aims in Deuteronomy to instill reverence for God as a guiding principle in the people's lives."[3]

God is no less holy today than he was in the days of Moses, and he is no less worthy of reverence. Some people think of reverence as being reflected in the clothing we wear, the music we sing, or the expression on our faces. Those things may express reverence, but not necessarily. The best way to reverence God is by listening to his Word and obeying it. God has not only spoken by Moses, but also spoken through the prophets and the apostles. Even more so, the writer of Hebrews tells us that in these last days, he has spoken to us by his Son (Heb. 1:2). God reveals himself through his Word. Jesus is God's Word to us not to fear, but also to stand in awe and reverence of our God. Like the Israelites, our greatest battle is not going to be with the Canaanites or the culture out there in the world. Our greatest battle will be fighting our proclivity to forget who God is and what he has done.[4] That is why this call to take care and watch ourselves is so important. It tells us that remembering that we have a God who speaks, and also remembering to obey what he says, will not be easy. We must be diligent to remember the significance of what God has accomplished for us in salvation history.[5]

---

chief god. But for the people of Israel, since their suzerain was their God, both copies of the covenant were kept in the ark of the covenant, which would ultimately be placed in the Holy of Holies of the temple. See Daniel I. Block, *Deuteronomy*, NIVAC (Zondervan, 2012), 128–29.

3. Tigay, *Deuteronomy*, 46–47.

4. Block, *Deuteronomy*, 126.

5. J. Gary Millar, *Now Choose Life: Theology and Ethics in Deuteronomy*, NSBT 6 (Apollos, 1998), 163.

TAKE CARE NOT TO FORGET: OUR GOD IS A JEALOUS GOD

In verses 15–29 of Deuteronomy 4, Moses focuses on the second commandment of the Decalogue and warns us of the temptation, the foolishness, and the consequences of idolatry.

The Temptation to Idolatry

Moses writes of the temptation to idolatry in Deuteronomy 4:15–16: "Therefore watch yourselves very carefully. Since you saw no form on the day that the LORD spoke to you at Horeb out of the midst of the fire, beware lest you act corruptly by making a carved image for yourselves." Moses warns that God's people need to keep a close watch on themselves because they are going to be tempted to this sin. The specific warning here is against making a carved image to worship. The reason given is that God's people did not see any form of God at Horeb and therefore should not try to make an image of him. Instead of making something visual, they should worship the one who revealed himself through his Word by obeying. It was this conviction that led sixteenth-century Reformers such as John Calvin to simplify worship spaces, removing colorful vestments, stained-glass windows, icons, and statues, while placing the pulpit in the middle of the congregation. In this way, "the Word of God and the message of salvation in Jesus Christ might sound forth in all its clarity and beauty. This was an aesthetic discerned by the sense of hearing rather than of sight."[6] Faith comes by hearing, not by the viewing of images.

The rest of Deuteronomy 4:16–18 describes the kinds of things that Israel might be tempted to make images of for the purpose of worship, while verse 19 warns against assigning divinity to created things, such as the sun.[7] The end of verse 19 is sometimes seen as one of the most difficult phrases in the book. After mentioning the sun, moon, and stars, the text reads "things that the LORD your God has allotted to all the peoples under the

6. Scott M. Manetsch, *Calvin's Company of Pastors: Pastoral Care and the Emerging Reformed Church, 1536–1609*, Oxford Studies in Historical Theology (Oxford University Press, 2013), 37.

7. Peter C. Craigie, *The Book of Deuteronomy*, NICOT (Eerdmans, 1976), 137. The righteous Job recognizes the wickedness of being drawn away to worship aspects of creation rather than the Creator in Job 31:24–28.

whole heaven" (Deut. 4:19). Some take this verse to mean that God assigned the rest of the nations to worship created objects such as the sun and moon while keeping Israel for himself. Such a view runs counter to the grain of the rest of the Old Testament as well as the New Testament. It makes more sense to understand Moses as saying here that sun, moon, and stars were given to all the nations to bless them by giving light, heat, and order to the universe while proclaiming the glory of God.[8]

Notice also that the order of the possible forms that idols might take in Deuteronomy 4:16–19 is given in exactly the opposite order that these objects are introduced in the creation story of Genesis 1:14–26: humans, animals, birds, creeping things, fish, and the heavenly bodies. It hardly seems likely that this reversal is coincidental. Instead, what Moses is pointing out through this literary feature is the way in which idolatry ultimately turns the created order upside down.[9] In giving in to the temptation to idolatry, the people of Israel submit themselves as vassals to the very objects of creation that they were called to rule over as God's viceregents.[10] The five connected verbs in Deuteronomy 4:19 show the regression of idolatry: "raise your eyes," "see," "be drawn away," "bow down," and "serve."[11] Idolatry makes us worshipers of creation rather than rulers of creation.

The Foolishness of Idolatry

After warning the people to watch out for their tendency to make idols and visible forms to worship, Moses shows why idolatry is so foolish in Deuteronomy 4:20: "But the Lord has taken you and brought you out of the iron furnace, out of Egypt, to be a people of his own inheritance, as you are this day." God gave all the nations the benefits of the heavenly bodies, but he rescued Israel alone out of Egypt to be his special possession.[12] It is utterly foolish for Israel to join in the futility of worshiping the idols that the rest of the nations venerate, whether carved images or representations

8. See John D. Currid, *Deuteronomy*, EPSC (EP Books, 2006), 94.

9. Christopher Wright, *Deuteronomy*, NIBC: Old Testament 4 (Hendrickson, 2007), 51.

10. Block, *Deuteronomy*, 129.

11. Currid, *Deuteronomy*, 93.

12. The order of the words in Hebrew emphasizes the contrast from Deuteronomy 4:19: "But you all the Lord took and brought out you all" (my translation).

of gods or by assigning divinity to the objects of creation, when its people have been rescued by the true God. Exchanging the God who has rescued them to worship things that God's hands have made is foolish enough. Worse yet is to worship the work of their own hands.[13] But the full scope of the folly of disregarding God is seen when Moses relates in verses 21–23 that he is not going to be entering the promised land on account of God's anger. He does not want the people to miss out on the promised blessings by forgetting the covenant and being disobedient as those of the previous generation were. So he commands them again in verse 23, "Take care, lest you forget the covenant of the LORD your God, which he made with you, and make a carved image, the form of anything that the LORD your God has forbidden you." To make an image for the purposes of worship in any form is ultimately to forget the covenant that God has made with his people.[14] This is at the heart of cheating on a jealous God, and it is incredibly foolish.

As Moses warns in Deuteronomy 4:24, "For the LORD your God is a consuming fire, a jealous God." We tend to think of jealousy as a bad thing, and it certainly can be. But in the Old Testament, this word usually refers to the legitimate passion that arises when a third party threatens a proper relationship. It is a husband or wife's proper reaction to the intrusion of a lover into the relationship. God treasures his people and is radically committed to our good and his glory. Our highest good is God himself. When something threatens that relationship and we begin to go after other lovers in the form of idols, God's passion for our well-being is going to be seen.[15] The same God who rescued his people out of the iron furnace in Egypt can also be a consuming fire toward his own if they break his covenant.[16] Nor has God changed. The writer of Hebrews urges, "Let us offer to God acceptable worship, with reverence and awe, for our God is a consuming fire" (Heb. 12:28–29). Not only must we not go astray after idols, but we must worship God with appropriate reverence and awe. We must not take him lightly. As we come into worship, we ought to prepare our hearts and minds, remembering

13. See, e.g., Isa. 40:18–31; Jer. 10.
14. Craigie, *Deuteronomy*, 138.
15. Block, *Deuteronomy*, 132.
16. Eugene H. Merrill, *Deuteronomy*, NAC 4 (Broadman & Holman, 1994), 125n176.

who it is that we serve. If we do give in to the temptation to idolatry, we should expect to reap the consequences.

The Consequences of Idolatry

God lays out the consequences of idolatry in Deuteronomy 4:25–28. He warns in verse 26 that the people of Israel will perish from the land rather than live in it. In verse 27, he says that he will scatter them among the peoples in exile. Then we read in verse 28, "And there you will serve gods of wood and stone, the work of human hands, that neither see, nor hear, nor eat, nor smell." If the people of Israel want to serve gods that humans have made, then that is exactly what they will do. If we want to worship idols and cheat on a jealous God, God will give us what we want. The more we debase ourselves in the worship of idols, however, the more debased we will become.

The apostle Paul also explains that if we insist on worshiping idols, God will let us reap the consequences:

> Claiming to be wise, they became fools, and exchanged the glory of the immortal God for images resembling mortal man and birds and animals and creeping things. Therefore God gave them up in the lusts of their hearts to impurity, to the dishonoring of their bodies among themselves, because they exchanged the truth about God for a lie and worshiped and served the creature rather than the Creator, who is blessed forever! Amen. (Rom. 1:22–25)

When we refuse to honor God, taking him lightly, when we fail to give him thanks and worship him as he deserves, we will become fools. When we begin to think that our own ideas make more sense than what the Scripture says, we will think we are wise even as we become more foolish. God may give us over to such foolishness. According to Romans 1, a people that refuses to worship God will not only be marked by unnatural attractions (Rom. 1:26–27), but also "filled with all manner of unrighteousness, evil, covetousness, malice. They are full of envy, murder, strife, deceit, maliciousness. They are gossips, slanderers, haters of God, insolent, haughty, boastful, inventors of evil, disobedient to parents, foolish, faithless, heartless, ruthless. Though they know God's righteous decree that those who practice such things deserve to die, they not only do them but give approval to those who practice them" (vv. 29–32).

These are the consequences of idolatry. Nearly all the sins listed here are sins not only against God, but also against people. That is not surprising. When we exchange the true worship of God for worship of false images of God, we debase ourselves and one another.

In the creation story, we discover that there is only one permissible image of God: people. People were made to represent what God is like in the world, and our original mandate was to rule the world as God's representatives. Wood and stone cannot image the living God; only people can. As Patrick Miller writes, "If we would look for something that in some way 'images' God in a way accessible to our experience, we will have to deal with one another."[17] We were created to mirror God's likeness and image into the world. Of course, on account of sin, we are all broken mirrors. It is because we are made in God's image that even in the worst people, if we look carefully enough, we can discover traces of God's design and glory. But because of sin, even the best people are still cracked, and if we look carefully enough, we will see how they provide a distorted reflection of what God is really like. Since humans are the image of God, we cannot say that we love God, whom we cannot see, while we hate our brother, whom we can see (1 John 4:20). When we love God rightly, we will also love one another, even if we are cracked distortions of who we were made to be.

Ignoring the words of a speaking God and cheating on a jealous God have serious consequences. But even amid the consequences of disobedience, there is hope. When we are dwelling in the miserable consequences of sin, we must not forget God's mercy.

Take Care Not to Forget: Our God Is a Merciful God

Moses has lived with these people for forty years. Despite all his pleading with the people, he knows that they are going to fall short, go astray, and be scattered among the nations. But he holds out this hope in Deuteronomy 4:29–30: "But from there you will seek the LORD your God and you will find him, if you search after him with all your heart and with all your soul. When you are in tribulation, and all these things come upon you in the latter days, you will return to the LORD your God and obey his voice." Listen to what

17. Patrick D. Miller, *Deuteronomy*, IC (John Knox Press, 1990), 61.

he is saying to Israel in effect: "Even when you fail, God can still be found by you if you seek him with all your heart. Even amid trial and trouble on account of your rebellion, it is not too late to remember, trust, and obey."

I knew a man, a follower of Jesus, who got caught up in idolatry. In his case, a woman who was not his wife became more precious to him than his God. He not only engaged in an affair with this other woman but told his wife and children that he was leaving them for her. He knew that he was throwing away so much, but this woman had become more important to him than anything else. That is what happens in idolatry: we become willing to suffer the loss of everything but our idol. Biblically, the only thing in the universe worthy of that level of devotion from us is God himself. He is the only thing or person that we should be unwilling to lose, no matter what it costs. This man made a shipwreck of his life, ignoring the pleas of those who love him. I sent him a message reminding him of what he seemed to have forgotten: "You have made a colossal mess here, but you don't have to go on making the mess worse. This failure does not have to be final. You can turn around. Don't keep going forward with this. I don't know if your marriage can be saved at this point, but one thing I know: you will never be better off going deeper into sin. . . . What I'm saying, brother, is that there's a way forward with Jesus. There's forgiveness with Jesus. There's redemption and the making of things new with Jesus." How could I give such encouragement to a man who had so flagrantly shaken his fist in God's face? Because Deuteronomy 4:31 is still true: "For the LORD your God is a merciful God. He will not leave you or destroy you or forget the covenant with your fathers that he swore to them."[18] Our God is a merciful God! He has not changed.

How do we understand God's mercy and jealousy together? Christopher Wright explains it this way:

> The apparent contradiction between verse 24 and verse 31 is in reality a vital consistency. For mercy functions precisely in the context of judgment. It was the fire of God's jealousy that protected the strength of God's mercy and covenant faithfulness to this people. In rebellion and idolatry they would

18. Which covenant is being referred to here? Daniel Block rightly identifies it: "The covenant he remembers is the one made with Abraham, extended to his descendants at Horeb, and about to be confirmed with this generation on the Plains of Moab." Block, *Deuteronomy*, 136.

> find the God of verse 24. In return and obedience they would find the God of verse 31. This is the same unchanged God, responding to a tragically changeable people.[19]

To be sure, he is a jealous God, a consuming fire, and those who cheat on him will experience him as such. But even the worst offenders who repent will discover that our God is full of mercy toward sinners.

My wayward brother in Christ eventually concluded that he might have lost his family, his reputation, and everything else that was dear, but that the one thing he could not live without was God himself. He left his idol, he returned to the Lord, and that family is working to rebuild on the mercy of God what idolatry nearly destroyed.

The people of Israel learned very early in their history that their survival could not depend on their ability to keep God's covenant, but depended on God's mercy and his commitment to keep his promises. Their hope and future were grounded not in their character but in God's.[20] So is ours. We will fail, we will go astray, we will fall short, and we will experience the consequences of cheating on a jealous God. But we do not have to stay there. We must take care not to forget that we serve a merciful God. No matter where we are, the path back to him is wholehearted repentance. God is a consuming fire to rebels, but he is rich in mercy toward the repentant.[21]

What does it mean that God is rich in mercy toward repentant sinners? In his book *Gentle and Lowly*, Dane Ortlund writes:

> That God is rich in mercy means that your regions of deepest shame and regret are not hotels through which divine mercy passes but homes in which divine mercy abides. It means the things about you that make you cringe most, make him hug hardest. It means his mercy is not calculating and cautious, like ours. It is unrestrained, flood-like, sweeping, magnanimous. . . . It means our sins do not cause his love to take a hit. Our sins cause his love to surge

19. Wright, *Deuteronomy*, 53. In the same place, he writes: "The fire of Yahweh as a jealous God is the fire of an exclusive commitment to this people that demands an exclusive commitment in return. It is, in short, the fire of redeeming love that had brought them out of the fires of bondage . . . and would therefore tolerate no rival."

20. Wright, *Deuteronomy*, 54.

21. J. A. Thompson, *Deuteronomy: An Introduction and Commentary*, TOTC (InterVarsity Press, 1974), 108.

> forward all the more. It means on that day when we stand before him, quietly, unhurriedly, we will weep with relief, shocked at how impoverished a view of his mercy-rich heart we had.[22]

Some might still be struggling with the idea of thinking of God as merciful. Perhaps we have been suffering a long time. Perhaps we have a seemingly endless stream of relational pain. Perhaps our life feels like a series of disappointments, heartaches, or betrayals. We may be looking around at our life and saying, "If this is what mercy looks like, God can keep it." But as Ortlund has written, "the evidence of Christ's mercy toward you is not your life. The evidence of his mercy toward you is his—mistreated, misunderstood, betrayed, abandoned. Eternally. In your place. If God sent his own Son to walk through the valley of condemnation, rejection, and hell, you can trust him as you walk through your own valleys on your way to heaven."[23]

As God's covenant people, believers must take care not to forget that we serve a God who speaks and who has called us to obedience in his Word. We must take care not to forget that we serve a jealous God who will tolerate no rivals to our love for him. When our corrupted hearts lead us astray in pursuit of idols and we experience the miserable consequences of idolatry, no matter how far we have gone away, we must not forget that we serve a merciful God who stands ready to receive us and shower his mercy on us in his Son.

22. Dane Ortlund, *Gentle and Lowly: The Heart of Christ for Sinners and Sufferers* (Crossway, 2020), 179–80.

23. Ortlund, 179.

9

No Other God

Deuteronomy 4:32–43

To you it was shown, that you might know that the Lord *is God; there is no other besides him.* (Deut. 4:35)

You may have seen the movie *Talladega Nights: The Ballad of Ricky Bobby.* If you have not seen it (and I do not recommend it), Ricky Bobby is a professional race car driver whose car crashes during a race. Ricky thinks he is on fire, and he begins to run around the track, crying out: "Help me, Jesus! Help me, Jewish God! Help me, Allah! Help me, Tom Cruise! . . . Help me, Oprah Winfrey!" It is intended to be a ridiculous scene, and it is. But in its own ridiculous way, the scene captures a common approach to religion in the ancient world and even today. In short, the idea is that when it comes to needing help from a god, you should not rely on just one.

In his book *The Problem of God*, Mark Clark describes this approach: "One god doesn't necessarily exclude the other gods, so don't limit yourself to just one when you can believe in all of them at once! This concept has its roots in Hindu and Eastern philosophy, and has largely been adopted in Western culture."[1] He then goes on to describe how this approach is reflected in contemporary society by quoting several people:

1. Mark Clark, *The Problem of God: Answering a Skeptic's Challenges to Christianity* (Zondervan, 2017), 205.

> "I am absolutely against any religion that says one faith is Superior to another. I don't see how that is anything different than spiritual racism." (Rabbi Shmuley Boteach) "My position is that all great religions are fundamentally equal." (Mahatma Gandhi) "One of the biggest mistakes humans make is to believe there's only one way. Actually, there are many diverse paths leading to God." (Oprah Winfrey)[2]

Most of the people that Moses was speaking to, and most of us reading today, are not likely to embrace syncretism as a biblical approach to a relationship with God. But as we saw in the previous chapter, idolatry is frequently subtle, the kind of thing that we slip into little by little more often than we intentionally choose it. For example, we pray to God and seek his guidance, but we might take a look at the horoscope just to see whether we can find some more immediate answers there. Or we ask God for healing, but we ask our Hindu friend whether he will pray to his gods for us too. We know that God alone can satisfy, but we also look to our earning potential, a significant other, or a social media–worthy life to fill the void in our hearts. When we fail to remember what God has done for us, or when we underestimate the unique and incomparable things he has done in salvation history for his people, we will be more inclined to turn to other gods—not necessarily in place of God, but in addition to God. That is a road that leads to death, however, not to life. So in this passage Moses reminds Israel and us that there is no other god than God and that because of this we must walk in his ways and keep his commandments. Moses invites the people to examine the historical facts about their relationship with God, to contemplate the theological conclusions of those facts, and to embrace the ethical implications of those conclusions.

Examine the Historical Facts

The Hebrew particle *ki* ("For") beginning in verse 32 of Deuteronomy 4 serves to connect it with the preceding passage. There Moses assured the Israelites that even when they fall or run into idolatry and they are exiled (Deut. 4:27), they will find the Lord when they seek him with all their hearts

2. Quoted in Clark, 205.

(v. 29). The reason for this assurance is God's mercy and his commitment not to forget the covenant that he made with their fathers (v. 31). In verse 32, Moses gives further assurance of the mercy that God will show them, and it is grounded in their unique experience of God's revelation and salvation (vv. 32–34). He writes in verse 32, "For ask now of the days that are past, which were before you, since the day that God created man on the earth, and ask from one end of heaven to the other, whether such a great thing as this has ever happened or was ever heard of." Moses invites the people to look as far back in history as the beginning of the world, and then to look as far around the world as they are able and see whether anything as great as what God has done for them has ever been done. Clearly, the expected answer is "no." The whole act of God in history for his people, including their rescue from Egypt, the establishment of the covenant with them at Horeb, and their beginning to take possession of the land through the defeat of Sihon and Og, was unique and unprecedented.[3] Two things are certain, to which Moses points the people back for examination.

First, God's revelation to Israel was unique: "Did any people ever hear the voice of a god speaking out of the midst of the fire, as you have heard, and still live?" (Deut. 4:33). Further evidence of their uniqueness was in the fact that they had heard God's voice speaking to them out of the fire at Horeb and lived. To have heard God's voice as Israel did would ordinarily have led to death. (We will learn more about this when we get to Deuteronomy 5.) But God, in his mercy, spared Israel from being consumed by the holiness of his revelation of himself.

Deuteronomy 4:36 adds color to God's revelation: "Out of heaven he let you hear his voice, that he might discipline you. And on earth he let you see his great fire, and you heard his words out of the midst of the fire." God let the people hear his voice and see his great fire, "that he might discipline" them? That phrase sounds like a bad thing to most of us. But while the Hebrew conception of discipline included correction and punishment, it also spoke of instruction in the context of relationship. The same verb is used later in Deuteronomy when Moses says, "Know then in your heart that, as a man disciplines his son, the LORD your God disciplines you" (Deut. 8:5). Once again, in Psalm 94:12, "Blessed is the man whom you discipline,

3. Peter C. Craigie, *The Book of Deuteronomy*, NICOT (Eerdmans, 1976), 142n1.

O LORD, and whom you teach out of your law." Both verses suggest that the discipline in view here is not of a punitive nature, but is the kind of training and instruction that exists in a healthy relationship between a father and a son. God speaks to Israel as his son, making the people aware of the nature of their relationship and what he requires of them. Did he reveal himself this way to any other people? No, he did not.

Second, God's salvation of Israel was unique. Moses asks a second rhetorical question in Deuteronomy 4:34: "Or has any god ever attempted to go and take a nation for himself from the midst of another nation, by trials, by signs, by wonders, and by war, by a mighty hand and an outstretched arm, and by great deeds of terror, all of which the LORD your God did for you in Egypt before your eyes?" Israel had a unique experience of God's salvation. No other nation had ever experienced the kind of deliverance from another nation that Israel did through the miraculous working of God by way of trials, signs, wonders, and everything else he did. Here we see not only the uniqueness of Israel in experiencing God's saving acts, but also the uniqueness of God in doing these saving acts. Not only had no god ever demonstrated the kinds of miraculous, saving works that the Lord did for Israel, but no god had even *attempted* such a thing. It raises the question why the people would go after other gods.

God did these works uniquely for the people of Israel, and he had a purpose in doing so, as we will see. But for now, consider the basic facts once more. Why can the people be confident that even when they are in exile on account of their idolatry, God will be merciful to them if they return wholeheartedly? Because they are precious to God, as seen by the fact that he revealed himself to them in a way that he had not to any other people on earth. That they were precious to God is seen in how he rescued them from a nation in a way that had never been done or even attempted. Moses explains this in Deuteronomy 4:37–38: "because he loved your fathers and chose their offspring after them and brought you out of Egypt with his own presence, by his great power, driving out before you nations greater and mightier than you, to bring you in, to give you their land for an inheritance, as it is this day." God loved the fathers of Israel. That includes Abraham, who handed over his wife to two different men to save his own skin. That includes Isaac, who did the same thing to his own wife. That includes Jacob, who was a conniver and swindler. Broken and messed up as they were, God loved those people. He can love us too. If we ask the question, "Why did God love these people?," we have no answer. *That* God loved them is evident as the motivating influence of his salvation, but *why* God loved them is not revealed. God simply chose to love them.[4]

One implication of this recounting is that God's people are not to be proud, arrogant, or haughty. That remains true to this day for those of us who are God's covenant people. We may be tempted to become self-righteous because of what we know as compared to "those people out there" who do not know. But as surely as Israel did not deserve God's love, neither do we. As surely as Israel did not deserve his revelation of himself, neither do we. As surely as Israel did not deserve his saving acts, neither do we. In fact, God seems to go out of his way to tell the Israelites that they were the least likely candidates for God's electing love.[5] Paul does the same thing in 1 Corinthians 1:26–31. Therefore, we should be humble when engaging with others who do not believe as we do. If we love God, it is because he first loved us.

So these are the historical facts. God revealed himself to the people of Israel at Horeb in a way that he did not do with any other people, treating them like a son. God also saved his people in a way that no other god even attempted, and he did so because of his love for their fathers and his choosing of this people. God's acting on their behalf in history was intended to lead Israel and ultimately all the nations to some theological conclusions.

Contemplate the Theological Conclusions

God was treating Israel as a son, and God was acting out of his love for Israel's fathers in saving the people. Moses wanted them to make two theological conclusions as a result of the exodus and Horeb. He says in Deuteronomy 4:35, "To you it was shown, that you might know that the LORD is God; there is no other besides him." What was shown here is God's self-revelation and saving power. After going over those two things again in verses 36–38, he brings them to the same conclusion with more flourish in verse 39: "know therefore today, and lay it to your heart, that the LORD is God in heaven above and on the earth beneath; there is no other." The

4. Christopher Wright, *Deuteronomy*, NIBC: Old Testament 4 (Hendrickson, 2007), 56.
5. See, e.g., Deut. 7:6–8; 9:4–29.

truths that we are about to see are not simply to be known intellectually, but Moses says to "lay it to your heart." These are truths worth contemplating and meditating on.

The first theological conclusion from these events is that the Lord is God. "Lord" (rendered with a capital and small capitals) is used in our English Bibles to note the Hebrew letters YHWH. This is the name that used to be transliterated *Jehovah*, but is more accurately transliterated now as *Yahweh*. In Exodus 3:15, God told Moses to tell the people of Israel to call him by this name. The events of the exodus and Horeb reveal that Yahweh is not just a powerful force in the universe. He is God. What is God? WSC 4 answers, "God is a Spirit, infinite, eternal, and unchangeable, in his being, wisdom, power, holiness, justice, goodness, and truth." That is a great answer and one worthy of laying to our hearts in contemplation.

Consider the fact that God is immutable. He does not change. Everyone and everything else in all creation changes. We have changed since the beginning of this chapter. But guess who has not changed since the beginning of this chapter and has never changed since before time began—the Lord. Every change for us makes us either somehow better or worse, but not so for God. He is perfect in all his attributes, and therefore it is impossible for him to change. He does not change. He is God.

God is also infinite. He has no boundaries and no limitations. There is no beginning to his life, and there is no end to his life. The same can be said of all his other attributes. There is no limit to his being, his knowledge, his wisdom, or his power. He is infinite in his holiness, infinite in his love, infinite in his justice, infinite in his mercy, and more. When we speak about God's eternity, we can do so with this definition from theologian Louis Berkhof: "His eternity may be defined as that perfection of God whereby He is elevated above all temporal limits and all succession of moments, and possesses the whole of His existence in one indivisible present."[6] While our lives are divided into past, present, and future, God's is not. He possesses the whole of his existence in one indivisible present. His covenant name, Yahweh, means literally "I am." The Lord is God.

6. Louis Berkhof, *Systematic Theology* (Banner of Truth, 1958), 60.

God self-exists.[7] Everything in creation derives its life or existence from something else. Everything in this universe had a beginning at some point. We each had a beginning; there was a time when we were not. Our nation had a beginning; there was a time when it did not exist. The Bible had a beginning; there was a time before it was written. The universe had a beginning. What was here before that? Was it nothing? It could not have been nothing! One thing that we can plainly observe is that *something* does not come from *nothing*, but that something comes from something. If there was truly nothing, then there would still be nothing. What was here before there was something, before there was a beginning, was God. He has always been and he will always be, and one day all creation will worship him and him alone. The events of the exodus and Horeb lead to the theological conclusion that the Lord is God.

The second theological conclusion we come to in Deuteronomy 4:35 and 39 is that there is no other god. God showed these mighty works to the people of Israel in order that they would know that the Lord is God. Not only that, but there is no other God.[8] If the Lord is God, then we should worship him. If there is no other god, then we should not worship any other gods. It is quite simple! God has no rivals, and he has no equals. No one else is worthy of our worship or our deepest love and devotion. The Lord is unique in all the universe. There is nothing and no one like him. There may be many so-called gods, and there may be many objects of worship, but there is no other god besides him.

God's intention was that these truths would be made evident, not only to Israel, but through Israel to all the nations. Many years later, the prophet Isaiah spoke on behalf of God to the Persian king Cyrus:

> I am the LORD, and there is no other,
> besides me there is no God;
> I equip you, though you do not know me,
> that people may know, from the rising of the sun
> and from the west, that there is none besides me;

7. In systematic theology, this attribute is referred to as God's *aseity*.

8. This theme is frequently repeated in the Old Testament. See, e.g., Ex. 8:10; 9:14; Deut. 33:26; 1 Kings 8:60; Isa. 45:5–6, 14, 18, 21–22; 46:9; Joel 2:27.

> I am the LORD, and there is no other.
> I form light and create darkness;
> I make well-being and create calamity;
> I am the LORD, who does all these things. (Isa. 45:5–7)

The Lord alone is God, and he desires not only his own people to know it, but all peoples to know it. How does he make these two realities known?

For the Israelites, the two primary sources of their knowledge of God were Horeb and the exodus.[9] In the exodus, God revealed his mighty power at work for their salvation, and at Horeb he spoke and revealed to his people who he is and what he required of them. As his covenant people walked in his ways, God was to be made known through them to the nations. Now these two events and the response he required of his people ultimately become paradigmatic for God's covenant people today.

In the New Testament, God has revealed himself more fully than he did in the Old Testament. In the Old Testament, God spoke to his people from the fire on the mountain, but in the New Testament, God has spoken to us through the incarnation of his Son. Jesus is the Word of God made flesh who came and dwelt among us (John 1:14). While the exodus demonstrated God's saving power from Egypt, the finished work on the cross demonstrated God's power to save his people even from sin and death. What the Lord began for Israel in the exodus, he brought to completion for the whole world through the cross of Jesus![10] Now all of us can be recipients of God's saving power by putting our trust in Jesus Christ. In the words of Peter Craigie, "while the Exodus and Sinai remain important, it is of the death and resurrection that it can be said, in the words of Moses' address: *you were shown this in order to know that the Lord, he is God. There is none other apart from him*."[11] Through the incarnation and the finished work of Christ, we know that the Lord is God and that there is no other. If we have seen God revealed to us through Jesus Christ of Nazareth as recounted in the Scriptures, and if we have experienced his saving power through faith in his finished work on the cross, why would we look to any other gods? For those of us who are Christians, why do we trust in anything or anyone

9. Craigie, *Deuteronomy*, 143.
10. Wright, *Deuteronomy*, 57.
11. Craigie, *Deuteronomy*, 143 (emphasis in original).

more than we trust in the God who has saved us? Why would we not be careful to heed every word that proceeds out of his mouth for our good? If the facts recounted in Israel's story are true, then we must contemplate the theological conclusions that we have come to. If our theological conclusions are true that the Lord is God and that he alone is God, then we must embrace the ethical implications.

Embrace the Ethical Implications

Verse 40 of Deuteronomy 4 brings this section to a head with the ethical response required of God's covenant people: "Therefore you shall keep his statutes and his commandments, which I command you today, that it may go well with you and with your children after you, and that you may prolong your days in the land that the Lord your God is giving you for all time." If the Lord is God, if there is no other God, if he has revealed himself to us and demonstrated his love for us in saving us, then we need to obey him. Moses has not even given the commands yet, but he is setting us up for them by laying the foundation of God's grace. God's grace is the foundation of our obedience to God's commands, not the goal of our obedience. As Herman Bavinck notes, "God gives Himself to His people in order that His people should give themselves to Him."[12]

As the people of God living under the terms of the new covenant, we frequently think of the commands of the law given under the Mosaic covenant as being harsh, burdensome, and joy-killing. Not only is that not how the people of God understood it under the Mosaic covenant, but it is also not how God intended it. As we see in this passage, God's intention in giving his people his law was so that life would go well with them and their children and so that they might prolong their days in the land. God's law was a blessing to his people, and we should still see it as such. Even if some things in his law are difficult for us, where else can we go? He alone has the words of eternal life (John 6:68). The good life for Israel, and for us, is still found in obedience to God's commands.[13] His aim in teaching the law to the people was not simply so that they would believe, but so that they would

12. Herman Bavinck, *Our Reasonable Faith*, trans. Henry Zylstra (Eerdmans, 1956), 24.
13. Craigie, *Deuteronomy*, 144.

believe and live out the ethical implications of that belief.[14] As they lived out the ethical implications of God's revelation and salvation, the nations would be blessed by their wise and godly ways.

The one who will not live by God's commands does not actually know God, regardless of what he might think. Jeremiah picks up on this connection between knowing God and demonstrating the same ethical commitments: "but let him who boasts boast in this, that he understands and knows me, that I am the Lord who practices steadfast love, justice, and righteousness in the earth. For in these things I delight, declares the Lord" (Jer. 9:24). To know God means to know the practice of steadfast love, justice, and righteousness. The promise of the new covenant would be that all of God's people would truly know him (31:34), which must mean something more than a type of spiritual or mystical knowledge. It means that we actually practice the things that reflect our true knowing of him.[15]

This brings us to the three cities of refuge that are mentioned in Deuteronomy 4:41–43. We are going to take up the significance of cities of refuge in more detail in Deuteronomy 19, but why do verses 41–43 appear right here in chapter 4? I propose that Moses is modeling what it looks like to obey God's commands. In Numbers 35:9–34, God told Moses that Israel would need to set apart three cities of refuge on each side of the Jordan, and here in this passage that is exactly what Moses does. He is living out the very thing that he is calling all Israel to do.[16] It is a great example to all of us who lead and who teach in the church or in the home, that we must lead in obedience primarily through our example. So let us go back to the historical facts of our salvation and consider again what God has done for us. Let us allow those facts to lead us to the theological conclusion that the God who saved us is the only God and therefore the only one worthy of our worship, trust, and devotion. Then let us live out the ethical implications of our confession, not only by worshiping the Lord our God, but by obeying his commands.

This is still the call of God's covenant people today, only now we have an even more amazing revelation of God and an even greater experience of

14. Jeffrey H. Tigay, *Deuteronomy*, JPSTC (Jewish Publication Society, 1996), 57.
15. For more, see Wright, *Deuteronomy*, 56.
16. John D. Currid, *Deuteronomy*, EPSC (EP Books, 2006), 108.

his salvation. Paul prayed for the church in Colossae, setting an example for our prayers, that we would

> be filled with the knowledge of his will in all spiritual wisdom and understanding, so as to walk in a manner worthy of the Lord, fully pleasing to him: bearing fruit in every good work and increasing in the knowledge of God; being strengthened with all power, according to his glorious might, for all endurance and patience with joy; giving thanks to the Father, who has qualified you to share in the inheritance of the saints in light. He has delivered us from the domain of darkness and transferred us to the kingdom of his beloved Son, in whom we have redemption, the forgiveness of sins. (Col. 1:9–14)

This spiritual fulfillment is what we have experienced from the Lord, so let us walk worthy of him, for he is God and there is no other.

10

How to Respond to God's Grace: Love God

Deuteronomy 4:44—5:15

I am the Lord your God, who brought you out of the land of Egypt, out of the house of slavery. You shall have no other gods before me. (Deut. 5:6–7)

Years ago, a series of studies set out to find out how a fence and a boundary affected the behavior of children playing on a playground. First, the researchers built a playground that had no fences. When they put the children on the playground to play, those kids stayed very near the center of the playground and never went beyond the playground structure itself. They seemed to be fearful of venturing out. The next thing the researchers did was to put up a fence around the playground. As soon as the fence was up, the children's behavior changed. Instead of fearfully staying in the center of the playground, they began to wander around, freely exploring the entire space within the fence. The researchers wrote: "The overwhelming conclusion was that with a given limitation, children felt safer to explore a playground. . . . With a boundary, in this case the fence, the children felt at ease to explore the space." As the writer relating this story concluded, "fences brought freedom. It was the absence of fences that created fear and apprehension."[1]

We tend to think of rules or commandments as being restrictive fences that narrow our enjoyment of life in this world. But every good parent knows that rules are key to a healthy and happy childhood and foundational to a satisfying life. In a loving family, parents give rules to their children not to make them miserable, but to protect them from danger and ruin. Ultimately, this is how the Ten Commandments function in the life of God's covenant people. We refer to them as the Ten Commandments, but that is not a totally accurate translation. In Hebrew, they are called the "Ten Words," sometimes translated into English as the "Decalogue." They were not given to be an arbitrary list of rules to restrict the freedom of God's people, but rather were given as protective boundary markers so that a people who had been set free from slavery and bondage could continue to live as free.

Historically, this is how the church has understood the Ten Commandments. They function as a summary of God's moral law, a short description of what God requires of all people in all times and places. When Jesus wants to give the rich young ruler a summary of God's commandments, he quotes from the Ten Commandments (Mark 10:19). The apostle Paul does something similar when he sums up what it looks like to live as a Christian (Rom. 13:8–9). Question 41 of the WSC asks, "Where is the moral law summarily comprehended?" The answer? "The moral law is summarily comprehended in the Ten Commandments." And not only the Westminster Standards, but also many other creeds, confessions, and catechisms have used the Ten Commandments as the primary tool for teaching children and new believers how to live as faithful followers of Christ. Pastor Kevin DeYoung writes:

> For centuries, catechetical instruction was based on three things: the Apostles' Creed, the Lord's Prayer, and the Ten Commandments. In other words, for virtually all of church history, when people asked, "How do we do discipleship?

1. Adapted from A. J. Swoboda, *Subversive Sabbath* (Brazos Press, 2018), 76. A summary of the research can be accessed here: https://www.asla.org/awards/2006/studentawards/282.html.

> How do we teach our kids about the Bible? What do new Christians need to know about Christianity?" their answers *always* included an emphasis on the Ten Commandments.[2]

The effect of this training throughout the world where Judaism or Christianity has been widely practiced for centuries is that the Ten Commandments have largely formed the moral consciousness of every Western nation, fostering prosperity and peace.

In recent years, however, this emphasis has been lost, and it has been lost to our detriment. One of the effects of this loss in the context of the church has been that our love for God has largely become a sentimental thing based primarily in the realm of our feelings. We think that the primary way by which we show love for God is by how we feel about him, by whether we experience something emotional when we come to corporate worship or engage in our quiet times of personal Bible reading or prayer. While having our affections stirred with love for God is an important part of the Christian experience, we should not lose sight of the fact that our affections for God are intended to lead us in a particular direction: namely, in the direction of obedience to his commands.

In the early 1990s, Gary Chapman published a very important and popular book called *The Five Love Languages*.[3] The basic point of the book is that not all of us experience love the same way. We all have our own love languages by which we hear or experience love from our mates, including acts of service, gift-giving, physical touch, quality time, and words of affirmation. As we seek to show love to the people we love, we should be intentional to communicate love to them such that they actually feel loved. So if quality time together is the primary way in which a wife experiences love from her husband, her husband should not insist that she feel loved because he keeps giving her gifts.

We can apply this concept to our relationship with God. What is God's love language? Obedience! We may insist that we love God by talking positively about him or to him or by bringing him gifts and offerings, but these are

2. Kevin DeYoung, "Do the Ten Commandments Have Authority over New Testament Christians?," The Gospel Coalition, October 23, 2018, https://www.thegospelcoalition.org/blogs/kevin-deyoung/ten-commandments-authority-new-testament-christians/, accessed November 4, 2021.

3. Gary Chapman, *The Five Love Languages: How to Express Heartfelt Commitment to Your Mate* (Northfield, 1992).

not the primary ways that God experiences love from his people. If we want to express our love to God, the most important way we can do so is by doing what he commands. Jesus said, "If you love me, you will keep my commandments" (John 14:15).

Moses continues to make the transition from reminding the people what God has done for them to laying out the stipulations of God's covenant with them. Because of God's grace, they are God's covenant people, and he is showing them how to live as such. Our proper response to God's grace as his covenant people is to love God by obeying his commands. We need to remember God's grace, and we need to respond to God's grace.

Remember God's Grace

In Deuteronomy 4:44–49, we are given some editorial comments that place the giving of these commandments in historical context. According to verses 45–46:

> These are the testimonies, the statutes, and the rules, which Moses spoke to the people of Israel when they came out of Egypt, beyond the Jordan in the valley opposite Beth-peor, in the land of Sihon the king of the Amorites, who lived at Heshbon, whom Moses and the people of Israel defeated when they came out of Egypt.

So that is where the Israelites are now as Moses begins to deliver the law to them a second time. They have been delivered from Egypt, and God has led them safely through the wilderness over the course of nearly forty years. He has given them the land of Og and Sihon, and he has promised to give them the rest of the land on the other side of the Jordan. It is in this context of God's gracious actions on behalf of his people that this law comes to them.

Then we read in Deuteronomy 5:1, "And Moses summoned all Israel and said to them, 'Hear, O Israel, the statutes and the rules that I speak in your hearing today, and you shall learn them and be careful to do them.'" In Hebrew, Moses' words to them begin with the same *Shema* phrase that we will see in Deuteronomy 6:4. Because of what God has done for them and what he is still going to do for them, they need to heed three particular imperatives: hear the statutes and rules, learn them, and be careful to do them. God has not given us his Word so that we would simply have it. He gave it to us so that we would be diligent to live our lives in conformity to it.

Then Moses goes on to remind the people of what God did for them after he brought them out of Egypt in Deuteronomy 5:2–3: "The LORD our God made a covenant with us in Horeb. Not with our fathers did the LORD make this covenant, but with us, who are all of us here alive today." When God rescued his people from Egypt, he brought them to Horeb (Sinai) in Exodus 19. There he revealed himself to them on the fiery mountain in thick clouds and smoke, and he constituted them as his covenant people. He told them who he was, and he told them what he required of them as his people (Ex. 19–24). But as Moses recounts what God did in the past, he says, "Not with our fathers did the LORD make this covenant, but with us, who are all of us here alive today" (Deut. 5:3). What does he mean when he states that God did not make this covenant with their fathers but with them who were present right then and there? Christopher Wright suggests that it may be more of a "with us especially" as opposed to a "with us only" kind of idea.[4] Clearly, the covenant was made with Israel's fathers at Horeb, and any of the people hearing Moses' words now either would not have been born or would have been just kids at the time. Along this view, Moses' point is that the covenant was made with this generation of God's people as surely as it was with the last, and in the present moment what counts is not that God made it with their fathers, but that he made it with the ones who are living right now. While this is true, it is not the most natural reading of the text. Exodus 19–24 says that God did make the covenant with those of the previous generation, who would have literally been their fathers.

But when Deuteronomy refers to "our fathers" or "your fathers," it almost always means the patriarchs: Abraham, Isaac, and Jacob.[5] God did have a covenant relationship with Abraham, Isaac, and Jacob, yet the particular covenant that Moses is recounting here in Deuteronomy was made not with Abraham, Isaac, and Jacob, but with those who were listening that day.[6]

4. Christopher Wright, *Deuteronomy*, NIBC: Old Testament 4 (Hendrickson, 2007), 62.

5. Jeffrey H. Tigay, *Deuteronomy*, JPSTC (Jewish Publication Society, 1996), 61.

6. Daniel Block acknowledges this view but believes that it is most natural to treat "your fathers" as the exodus generation. It is hard for me to see how that reading is most natural, given that Exodus 19–24 makes it clear that God *did* make the covenant with their fathers, but nowhere is it said that this covenant is made with *the* fathers. The use of "our fathers" occurs five times in Deuteronomy, including this use, and in each case it is a clear reference to Abraham, Isaac, and Jacob (Deut. 5:3; 6:23; 26:3, 7,

As blessed as their fathers were, God has been even more gracious to the people listening, who were poised to cross the Jordan to take possession of God's land.

We read what happened next in Deuteronomy 5:4–5: "The LORD spoke with you face to face at the mountain, out of the midst of the fire, while I stood between the LORD and you at that time, to declare to you the word of the LORD. For you were afraid because of the fire, and you did not go up into the mountain." So did God speak to his people face-to-face or through Moses? The answer is yes! These Ten Commandments were spoken by the Lord directly to his people, which was a unique feature of Israel's law. Jeffrey Tigay explains the significance of this fact:

> The belief that God is the author of the laws is a distinctive feature of Israelite law. Elsewhere in the ancient Near East the laws of society were believed to be the product of human minds. The source of law in Mesopotamia was the king. He claimed to have learned the principles of truth and justice from the gods, but to have turned those principles into specific laws himself. In the Bible not only the principles behind the laws but the laws themselves were believed to have been authored by God and revealed to Israel through His spokesmen, the prophets. This belief reflects the conviction that God is Israel's king, hence its legislator.[7]

The phrase "face to face" suggests intimacy and also a dangerous situation, given that God is the other party.[8] The people were understandably afraid, but these were words that God wanted to speak directly to his people. The rest of the law given in Exodus 20–23 was given by God to Moses to give to the people, but these Ten Commandments were from God's mouth to their ears.

---

15). Three of the references are to the land promise given to Israel. When we consider Deuteronomy's use of "your fathers," which is far more extensive, it could also be argued that every reference is ultimately to Abraham, Isaac, and Jacob (1:8, 11, 21, 35; 4:1, 31, 37; 6:3, 10, 18; 7:8, 12–13; 8:1, 3, 16, 18; 9:5; 10:15, 22; 11:9, 21; 12:1; 13:6, 17; 19:8; 27:3; 28:11, 36, 64; 29:13; 30:5, 9, 20; 31:16; 32:17). Both the simplest reading of the text and the use of "our/your fathers" in Deuteronomy support the view that the law that Moses is about to give the Israelites reflects their privileged position, even over against Abraham, Isaac, and Jacob.

7. Tigay, *Deuteronomy*, 60.

8. Though the exact Hebrew phrase is not used in each of these passages, the same idea is being communicated in Gen. 32:30; Ex. 33:11; Num. 14:14; Deut. 5:4; 34:10; Judg. 6:22; Jer. 32:4; 34:3; Ezek. 20:35.

And what does he say first? "I am the LORD your God, who brought you out of the land of Egypt, out of the house of slavery" (Deut. 5:6). This verse is a preface to the entire Decalogue and to the first commandment especially. Because the Lord is God, and he is their God, and he delivered them out of their slavery in Egypt, the Israelites are to obey the commands that he is about to give them. These commandments are not given as the basis of God's relationship to his covenant people. His relationship with them is one based purely on the grace of election. He did not say, "Keep the commandments, and based on how well you do, I will decide whether or not to rescue you out of your slavery in Egypt." Instead, he came and delivered them and set them free. In the context of their newfound freedom, he gave them his law. The purpose of the law was not to bind or enslave them; its purpose was to help them continue to live freely. The grace of God precedes the law of God and is the only proper context in which to view the law of God. What is more, the law of God does not nullify God's grace. We do not have to keep God's law to receive God's grace. Rather, we come and receive his grace so that we might have power to keep his laws.

When we come to God's moral requirements for his people, the same pattern we have seen all along still stands: remember what God has done for you, trust him, and obey his commands—not to get something from him, but as a response to what he has already done for you. God graciously saved them from their slavery, he preserved them in the wilderness, he revealed himself to them, he entered into covenant with them personally, and now he is going to show them how to respond to his grace and live as his covenant people. As Christians, we have been grafted into Israel's story, and Israel's history becomes our history, Israel's fathers our fathers. Through the person and work of Jesus, we have experienced God's grace even more personally and powerfully in his revealing himself to us and saving us from the power of sin and death. We also need to remember the grace we have received so that we will properly respond to that grace and live as God's covenant people.

Respond to God's Grace

Most of the rest of Deuteronomy consists of instructions on how to live as God's covenant people, but here in these Ten Commandments, that whole law is summarized. The Ten Commandments are usually divided between the first four commandments, which focus on our duty toward God, and the second six commandments, which relate to our duty toward man.[9] In this chapter, we will consider the first four commandments, and in the next chapter the remaining six. We will consider these commandments broadly in these two chapters and then explore their depths as Moses expounds them through the rest of Deuteronomy 5–26. So how should we respond to God's gracious salvation?

Love God by Having No Other Gods

God gives the first commandment in Deuteronomy 5:7, "You[10] shall have no other gods before me." This commandment is the first because everything else hangs on it. The point is not simply that God needs to be the first God of many gods in his people's lives. The point is that there are to be no other gods in their lives because there are no other gods like Yahweh. He alone is God, he is their God, and they must not bring any rival gods into this relationship. Israel's primary temptation (as well as ours) was not so much to worship Yahweh *or* some other god, but to worship Yahweh *and* some other god. But God will tolerate no rivals, and neither should we.

Imagine a wife's returning home to her husband one day, and she says: "Hi, honey; I want you to meet my new man. Don't worry, I'm not done with you, but he's going to be living with us. I think he's wonderful, and I know you two will get along together fine. Some nights I'll be with you and some with him. The three of us are going to have a great life together." How should the husband respond in this situation? Is he being unreasonable to say: "No, that's not acceptable. It's either me or him. You choose, but it's not going to be both of us"?[11] God calls for and deserves all our love and devotion, and he will not tolerate rivals. If we have any rival gods in our lives, we need to put them away. As Elijah challenged the people of Israel: "How long will you go limping between two different opinions? If the LORD is God, follow him; but if Baal, then follow him" (1 Kings 18:21). Is there anything competing

9. See, e.g., WLC 98 and Heidelberg Catechism 93.

10. The commandments are addressed to the singular "you," emphasizing the individual responsibility that each one of God's people has to obey. At the same time, the commandments are given in a public assembly, emphasizing their corporate responsibility. See Tigay, *Deuteronomy*, 62.

11. I am indebted to Kevin DeYoung for inspiring this illustration in Kevin DeYoung, *The 10 Commandments: What They Mean, Why They Matter, and Why We Should Obey Them* (Crossway, 2018), 33.

for our deepest affections? Do the goals we have for our lives reflect our embrace of this commandment? What about our approach to relationships or our aspirations in the workplace? Jesus addressed a common idol in Matthew 6:24: "No one can serve two masters, for either he will hate the one and love the other, or he will be devoted to the one and despise the other. You cannot serve God and money." Loving God means that we do not try to serve two masters.

Love God by Not Making Images to Worship

The second commandment is in Deuteronomy 5:8–9: "You shall not make for yourself a carved image, or any likeness of anything that is in heaven above, or that is on the earth beneath, or that is in the water under the earth. You shall not bow down to them or serve them." This command was further explained in 4:15–19. In short, God did not reveal himself to Israel with any kind of likeness, but only by his Word. Therefore, we should not make representations of him. It is a common practice in some parts of the church to have images of God or Jesus in places of worship and for people to bow down before those images. This commandment forbids that practice and forms the basis for the regulative principle of worship. Deuteronomy 5:9–10 gives specific reasons for not utilizing images in worship: "for I the LORD your God am a jealous God, visiting the iniquity of the fathers on the children to the third and fourth generation of those who hate me, but showing steadfast love to thousands of those who love me and keep my commandments." Worshiping an image provokes God's jealousy because representations of God are not God.

What about this concept of cross-generational retribution for hating God? Are the children to the third and the fourth generations punished on account of their parents' sins? Later, in Deuteronomy 24:16, it is clear that judicial authorities are not to put parents to death for the actions of their children, nor are children to be put to death for the actions of their parents, yet clearly, people are often better off or worse off because of the actions of their ancestors. God includes children in the covenantal blessings and curses that flow from their parents' choices. Noah's family is saved on account of Noah's righteousness. Abraham's descendants are blessed and given the land on account of his faith. David's descendants receive the throne because of God's promise to him. Likewise, the entire households of Achan, Dathan, and Abiram are put to death along with them for their sins, while the punishments due to David, Jeroboam, and Ahab fall on their descendants.[12] Yet Ezekiel 18:1–20 emphasizes that God is rewarding or punishing people only for their own acts.

So what do we do with all this? It is important to notice the qualifying phrases in verses 9–10 of Deuteronomy 5, "third and fourth generation of those who hate me, but showing steadfast love to thousands of those who love me and keep my commandments." It is quite likely that those phrases refer to the descendants themselves, meaning that the cross-generational rewards or punishments apply only to descendants who do the same things that their ancestors did. In the words of Jeffrey Tigay, "God punishes or rewards descendants for ancestral sins and virtues *along with their own* if they—the descendants—'continue the deeds of their ancestors.'"[13]

Love God by Honoring His Name

The third commandment is in Deuteronomy 5:11, "You shall not take the name of the LORD your God in vain, for the LORD will not hold him guiltless who takes his name in vain." The word "vain" is sometimes translated as "emptiness" or "nothingness."[14] This commandment literally prohibits taking the Lord's name for an empty, meaningless thing. In the ancient world, it was common to swear oaths in court situations or private conversations to back up the veracity of what one was saying with God's name. A person would declare, "By the life of the LORD, I will" or "May the LORD do such and such to me if I did."[15] The person using God's name in the oath is calling down God's curse on himself if he's not telling the truth. When a person swears a false oath, he is showing contempt for God by implying that the person is not concerned about God's judgment.[16] To take his name in vain is to bring guilt and judgment upon ourselves. Of course, honoring God's name would also mean not using it as an expletive or in some flippant manner. The psalmist writes, "You have exalted above all things your name and your word" (Ps. 138:2). We would do well to do the same by living in a way that

12. Tigay, *Deuteronomy*, 436.
13. Tigay, 437.
14. BDB, s.v. "שָׁוְא," 996.
15. Tigay, *Deuteronomy*, 67.
16. Tigay, 67.

advances the repute of God's name—even as we pray in the first petition of the Lord's Prayer, "hallowed be your name."

Love God by Not Slavishly Working

The fourth commandment in Deuteronomy 5:12–15 is the longest and, historically, the most difficult for Christians to understand. Verse 12 states, "Observe the Sabbath day, to keep it holy, as the LORD your God commanded you." The fourth commandment requires the setting apart of the seventh day, the Sabbath, as a holy day.[17] After Jesus rose from the dead on Sunday, Christians began to worship on Sunday and called it the "Lord's Day." Some continued to keep the Sabbath and also worshiped on the Lord's Day. In the Presbyterian tradition, Sunday is the Christian Sabbath and should be strictly observed.[18] Outside Presbyterianism, many Christians think of the Sabbath or the Lord's Day principally as a day of worship. But when we revisit the fourth commandment, we observe that the emphasis of the day was on stopping one's ordinary labor and not becoming a slave to work again. Moses goes on in verses 13–15:

> Six days you shall labor and do all your work, but the seventh day is a Sabbath to the LORD your God. On it you shall not do any work, you or your son or your daughter or your male servant or your female servant, or your ox or your donkey or any of your livestock, or the sojourner who is within your gates, that your male servant and your female servant may rest as well as you. You shall remember that you were a slave in the land of Egypt, and the LORD your God brought you out from there with a mighty hand and an outstretched arm. Therefore the LORD your God commanded you to keep the Sabbath day.

17. The same language of sanctifying or consecrating something or someone is used of Aaron (Ex. 28:3; Lev. 8:12), of the altar (Ex. 29:36), of the Lord (Num. 20:12; 27:14), and of the most holy things (1 Chron. 23:13).

18. For an example of this approach, see WLC 116–21. Heidelberg Catechism 103 may better capture the spirit of the fourth commandment for Christians: "What does God require in the fourth Commandment? In the first place, God wills that the ministry of the Gospel and schools be maintained, and that I, especially on the day of rest, diligently attend church, to learn the Word of God, to use the Holy Sacraments, to call publicly upon the Lord, and to give Christian alms. In the second place, that all the days of my life I rest from my evil works, allow the Lord to work in me by His Spirit, and thus begin in this life the everlasting Sabbath."

The specific motive attached to keeping the Sabbath day is that the Israelites were slaves. Now they are no longer slaves, and they should demonstrate their freedom by not working all the time. Multiple times in Deuteronomy, the covenant people are exhorted to remember their slavery as an encouragement to obeying God's law. The law is not a new type of slavery; rather, the law is given to help God's people stay free. If the people of God were to begin worshiping idols, they would become slaves again to whatever or whomever they served, including work.

It is hard to imagine a more relevant command for many of us. God's people should never say: "I don't have time to read God's Word. I don't have time to attend public worship. I don't have time to rest." If we can never stop to take a day for rest and worship, we need to ask ourselves what God we are really serving, because the God of the Bible commands his people to stop and rest.

In an agrarian society, ceasing to labor one day in seven is a serious act of faith. Farmers would have to trust God to provide. Not only were they not to work, but God commanded the ceasing from work also for children as well as servants, animals, and even foreigners living among them. It is a radical idea that slaves and foreigners should also share in the benefit of one day a week to cease from labor and turn their thoughts to God in grateful worship and rest. The gift of rest is not one that God gave to his people alone, but he gave it to all people to enjoy. What is more, he commanded us to observe it for our good.

We can sum up the first four commandments in the same way that Jesus did: "You shall love the Lord your God with all your heart and with all your soul and with all your mind" (Matt. 22:37).[19] It seems simple enough, and it is, but we should not think that we have kept these commandments in a way that meets God's righteous requirements. John Calvin reminds us that we never render to God the love that we lawfully owe him. Paraphrasing Augustine, he writes: "Love so follows knowledge that no one can love God perfectly who does not first fully know his goodness. While we wander upon the earth, 'we see in a mirror dimly'. . . . Therefore, it follows that our love is imperfect."[20] Indeed, that is a description of the best possible scenario. Most

19. The WLC does the same thing in Q&A 102.

20. John Calvin, *Institutes of the Christian Religion*, ed. John T. McNeill, trans. Ford Lewis Battles, Library of Christian Classics 20 (Westminster John Knox Press, 1960), 2.7.5.

of us are aware of how far short we fall of God's righteous requirements in our thoughts, words, and deeds. In fact, the law helps us see how far short we fall of God's glory. If just one sin or failure to keep God's law deserves God's wrath and curse, imagine what our endless list of sins deserves. But God so loved the world that he made a way out for sinners like us. What does God require of us—those who have fallen short of loving him as he deserves to be loved?

First, God requires that we put our faith in the life and death of Jesus, who bore the wrath and curse of God in our place before rising again from the dead. Second, God requires that we repent of our sin and turn to him with a commitment to walk in his ways as a response to the grace he has shown us through Christ. We turn from our sins and commit to walk in his ways, not as a way of earning God's grace, but because he has already given it to us. Third, God requires us to make use of the outward and ordinary means through which Christ gives us the benefits of what he accomplished. Those outward and ordinary means are to sit under the ministry of God's Word, to submit ourselves to baptism, to participate in the Lord's Supper, and to pray. God works through each of these to draw us to Christ, to make us more like Christ, and to keep us free in him until our final redemption.

If you know that you are a lawbreaker today, do not rely on the law as the basis of your relationship with God. "All who rely on works of the law are under a curse" (Gal. 3:10). Instead, rely on Jesus. Go to Jesus today and find sufficient grace to pay for all your sins. Then respond to that grace by turning from your sins, loving God, and doing what he commands.

11

How to Respond to God's Grace: Love People

Deuteronomy 5:16–21

And you shall not covet your neighbor's wife. And you shall not desire your neighbor's house, his field, or his male servant, or his female servant, his ox, or his donkey, or anything that is your neighbor's. (Deut. 5:21)

He was young, smart, wealthy, well connected, and influential. We can assume that he was also good-looking. He was a good man by all accounts. But he himself was not so sure. Yes, he worshiped as he was supposed to, and he was not a blasphemer or an adulterer or a murderer. But he felt that something was still missing inside. So he asked Jesus, "What good deed must I do to have eternal life?" (Matt. 19:16). Jesus replied, "If you would enter life, keep the commandments" (v. 17). The young man asked, "Which ones?" (v. 18). We read in Matthew 19:18–21:

> And Jesus said, "You shall not murder, You shall not commit adultery, You shall not steal, You shall not bear false witness, Honor your father and mother,

> and, You shall love your neighbor as yourself." The young man said to him, "All these I have kept. What do I still lack?" Jesus said to him, "If you would be perfect, go, sell what you possess and give to the poor, and you will have treasure in heaven; and come, follow me."

Those who are familiar with the story know that the young man went away sorrowful because he could not part with his possessions. While he professed to be keeping all the commandments, it became clear that he was not even keeping the first one, to have no other gods.

But Jesus did not point that out, and he did not mention any of the first four commandments. Instead, he mentioned five out of the six commandments regarding relationships to other people, and instead of giving the command about coveting, he summed up the whole law regarding love of neighbor. Why? John Calvin argues that when it comes to the first four commandments, obedience is largely in the intention of the heart. We could fool people and even ourselves that we truly loved God with all our hearts. But the works of love toward neighbor as summed up in the second part of the Ten Commandments are such that through them, we can *see* whether there is real righteousness.[1]

Do we really love God? How can we tell? We saw in the previous chapter that we can tell that we love God by whether we keep his commandments. In this chapter, we will see that those commandments involve loving people. Not just our people, but all people. First John 4:20–21 puts it starkly: "If anyone says, 'I love God,' and hates his brother, he is a liar; for he who does not love his brother whom he has seen cannot love God whom he has not seen. And this commandment we have from him: whoever loves God must also love his brother." So what does loving people look like? The rest of the Ten Commandments show us the way.

We should note at the outset that laws in and of themselves point us toward how a people should live, but they do not necessarily define the ideal. Rather, the law defines the minimum required behavior for a person to avoid bringing consequences upon himself. For example, the seventh commandment forbids adultery. But that's a minimum. Just because we do

1. John Calvin, *Institutes of the Christian Religion*, ed. John T. McNeill, trans. Ford Lewis Battles, Library of Christian Classics 20 (Westminster John Knox Press, 1960), 2.8.52.

not commit adultery does not mean that we have fulfilled the biblical vision of what it means to be a good husband or wife. It just means that we have not dropped below the minimum behavior that would require us to face some kind of punishment. Gordon Wenham describes this as the "gap between law and ethics." The law provides the baseline, the minimum. But the law is pointing us toward a much higher ethical ideal.[2] Jesus summarizes that ideal when he defines the two greatest commandments as loving God and loving people (Matt. 22:36–40), an ideal that we must keep in mind as we work through these commandments.

When we come to commandments 5–10 and look at them as a whole, we see that our first responsibility to other people starts with honoring our parents, which is the human counterpart to the honor due to God. It serves as the bridge between the first four commandments and the last five. The sixth commandment forbids taking a man's life, the seventh forbids taking his wife, the eighth forbids taking his property, the ninth forbids taking from him through bearing false witness, and the tenth forbids even *desiring* to take what is his.[3] So with the final six commandments as our guide, we will see how loving people is the proper response to God's grace.

We Love People by Showing Honor

The fifth commandment is given in verse 16 of Deuteronomy 5: "Honor your father and your mother, as the Lord your God commanded you, that your days may be long, and that it may go well with you in the land that the Lord your God is giving you." This is the bridge between loving God and loving people: learning to honor our parents, who, in many ways, represent God to us. Notice that honoring our father and our mother is an active command. Most of the commands in the Decalogue are prohibitions, but this one is a call to do something in particular: namely, honor our parents. We should not simply be waiting for opportunities to honor our parents, but should be actively seeking ways to honor them. In pondering this command in the past, I have thought of it as a duty to obey my parents when they ask me to do something. As Paul directs in Ephesians 6:1, "Children, obey

2. Gordon J. Wenham, "The Gap Between Law and Ethics in the Bible," *Journal of Jewish Studies* 48, no. 1 (Spring 1997): 17–29.

3. Jeffrey H. Tigay, *Deuteronomy*, JPSTC (Jewish Publication Society, 1996), 62.

your parents in the Lord, for this is right." That is a proper application of the fifth commandment, as Paul goes on to show. But while obeying our parents is essential to honoring them, we should not reduce honoring our parents to simple obedience. Honoring our parents also includes reverence and gratitude.[4]

How we honor our parents will change as we age through life. When we are children, we honor our parents by obeying them with cheerful hearts the first time they ask us to do something. We can make them gifts or cards on birthdays or other special occasions. We can speak to them (and about them to our friends) in ways that indicate our respect of them. We can say "thank you," and that is not true just when we are kids. When we are in the phase of raising our own children, we can continue to honor our parents by helping them establish relationships with their grandchildren. We can make room for them to visit in our homes. We can make an effort to see them at least occasionally around holidays or other special occasions. As they continue to get older, we can make a place for them in our homes and care for them as they once did for us. Or if they need more specialized care, we can sacrifice to place them in a facility that will care well for them. We can visit them as they age and have fewer and fewer friends. When they pass away, we can organize memorial services to honor them and their contribution to our lives and our world, however great or small it may have been. Such a service does not have to be a huge affair, nor does it have to be expensive. As with so many of the gifts we give to our parents from early childhood on, it is the thought that counts far more than the cost.

Honoring our parents is the first step toward learning to honor all who are in authority. Christians have long understood this commandment in that way. For example, WLC 124 says, "By *father* and *mother*, in the fifth commandment, are meant, not only natural parents, but all superiors in age and gifts; and especially such as, by God's ordinance, are over us in place of authority, whether in family, church, or commonwealth." We should not expect our kids to honor us in the home while we mock or deride the authorities over us in the church or state. Some of the political flags and bumper stickers prominently displayed in the United States are despicable and should never be displayed by Christians, regardless of how much we

4. See Calvin, *Institutes*, 2.8.36.

disagree with the president's politics or how harmful his policies might be. Calvin writes, "It makes no difference whether our superiors are worthy or unworthy of this honor, for whatever they are they have attained their position through God's providence."[5]

What about the promise attached, that those who honor parents will live long in the land? One of my cousins was talking to her little boy and teaching him the Ten Commandments. When he heard this commandment and the promise of long life attached to it, he said about our grandmother, "Mamaw must have been a really good girl as old as she is!" Of course, honoring one's parents does not necessarily mean in every case that we are going to live to old age. Some who honored their parents well have not lived long, while others who did not honor their parents have lived long. But generally speaking, it does go well for people who honor their parents, and it does not go well for those who do not honor their parents. Let us love people well by showing honor where honor is due (Rom. 13:1–7; 1 Peter 2:17).

We Love People by Promoting Life

The sixth commandment is found in Deuteronomy 5:17, "You shall not murder."[6] This command includes not only premeditated or intentional murder, but also the unintentional taking of life that our legal system calls manslaughter. The biblical command stands out from Babylonian laws in that the sixth commandment does not value life based on status, race, or gender. The life of every human is sacred.[7]

We should not think that just because we have not murdered someone or accidentally killed someone, we have fully kept this command. As we

5. Calvin, 2.8.36.

6. The ESV translation "murder" is the correct translation of the Hebrew verb *rāsah* (רצח). Unfortunately, for generations the primary translation of this command was the version found in the King James Bible, which reads, "Thou shalt not kill" (Deut. 5:17 KJV). To kill is obviously a much broader concept than to murder. As a result of this, people have used this commandment as a support for pacifism or as a basis for opposing the death penalty. While Christians may have reasons for pacifism or for opposing the death penalty, the sixth commandment should not form part of that basis. The very same law that contains this command also commands the death penalty for numerous offenses, as well as commanding war in particular circumstances. So the word in this context refers to taking a life, whether intentionally or unintentionally, outside the parameters laid down by God, such as war or capital punishment. See W. R. Domeris, *NIDOTTE*, s.v. "רָצַח," 3:1186.

7. Daniel I. Block, *Deuteronomy*, NIVAC (Zondervan, 2012), 166.

will see later in Deuteronomy, to keep the sixth commandment means not only avoiding killing anyone, but also actively seeking to preserve and protect life. The WLC says that it includes "all careful studies, and lawful endeavors, to preserve the life of ourselves and others."[8] Abortion is a sensitive topic in our culture, and there are many complicated issues surrounding unplanned pregnancies. But the Christian church has always recognized that abortion is a violation of the sixth commandment, dating all the way back to the *Didache* in the first century.[9] The sixth commandment not only means that we should not practice abortion as Christians, but also means that we actively work to protect life. We do not want to reduce that work to simply being involved in political activism and legislation, but it does not exclude this either. Christians should also be actively involved in helping to provide support to men and women who are tempted to abort, which we do through local pregnancy resource centers, partnership with organizations ministering to the poor, and providing support to those seeking to adopt children.

While abortion is the leading cause of death that Christians can combat to help preserve life, we should not ignore other issues. Gun violence and every other sort of violence should be of concern to us. We should be concerned to preserve the lives of immigrants and refugees, whether they are documented or not. We should be concerned about the impact of environmental and climate changes (whether man-made or not), particularly on the lives of the poor. We should be concerned about injustice when it comes to the application of the death penalty. We should be concerned about the causes of

8. It is worth quoting the answer in its entirety: "The duties required in the sixth commandment are, all careful studies, and lawful endeavors, to preserve the life of ourselves and others by resisting all thoughts and purposes, subduing all passions, and avoiding all occasions, temptations, and practices, which tend to the unjust taking away the life of any; by just defense thereof against violence, patient bearing of the hand of God, quietness of mind, cheerfulness of spirit; a sober use of meat, drink, physic [medicine], sleep, labor, and recreations; by charitable thoughts, love, compassion, meekness, gentleness, kindness; peaceable, mild and courteous speeches and behavior; forbearance, readiness to be reconciled, patient bearing and forgiving of injuries, and requiting good for evil; comforting and succoring the distressed, and protecting and defending the innocent." WLC 135.

9. In the first three hundred years of the church, not one single source condones either abortion or infant exposure. For a short overview, see David W. T. Brattson, "Abortion and the Early Church," Christians for Social Action, January 10, 2017, https://christiansforsocialaction.org/resource/abortion-and-the-early-church/, accessed November 10, 2021.

suicide and how we can help address those causes. Driving carefully, firearm safety, and safe workplaces are all included in this commandment. I am not suggesting that there is only one Christian approach to resolving these issues. But I am saying that our commitment to the sixth commandment should shape how we think about these issues more than any other commitment we may have to politics or policies.

Of course, we also need to take account of what Jesus says about the sixth commandment to appreciate the full scope of what this command means. In the Sermon on the Mount, he explains: "You have heard that it was said to those of old, 'You shall not murder; and whoever murders will be liable to judgment.' But I say to you that everyone who is angry with his brother will be liable to judgment; whoever insults his brother will be liable to the council; and whoever says, 'You fool!' will be liable to the hell of fire" (Matt. 5:21–22). He then goes on to say that if we have a broken relationship, we need to actively pursue reconciliation. To be angry with someone, to insult someone, to remain unreconciled with someone is a violation of the sixth commandment not to murder. Reflecting on the sixth commandment, we should ask this question: how can I love people by protecting and promoting life?

We Love People by Practicing Sexual Integrity

The seventh commandment is in Deuteronomy 5:18, "And you shall not commit adultery." The prohibition against adultery speaks specifically to inappropriate sexual contact between a married person and anyone besides the person's spouse. Adultery was a very serious offense in ancient Israel that carried the death penalty for both the male and female involved (Deut. 22:22). While death is not the punishment in our society, adultery does frequently bring about the death of a marriage and a family. This commandment calls us to practice sexual integrity, meaning that we abstain from sexual activity in mind and body outside marriage to a person of the opposite sex. Any sexual activity outside that context is sin. Jesus declares in the Sermon on the Mount: "You have heard that it was said, 'You shall not commit adultery.' But I say to you that everyone who looks at a woman with lustful intent has already committed adultery with her in his heart" (Matt. 5:27–28). Let us ask ourselves whether we are loving people well by preserving our own sexual integrity as well as our neighbor's, in heart, speech, and behavior.[10]

We Love People by Respecting Property

The eighth commandment is found in Deuteronomy 5:19, "And you shall not steal." The Ten Commandments do not list specific penalties for breaking them, though we see those penalties described elsewhere in Deuteronomy. But one of the things that stands out about this commandment is that it does not carry the death penalty as a punishment. In Israel, only stealing another person to sell him into slavery was punishable by death (Deut. 24:7). While personal property is important, it is not more important than human life. This stands in contrast to other ancient Near Eastern law codes that may have threatened death or mutilation for certain kinds of theft.[11]

The Bible does take stealing very seriously. Calvin writes that there are multiple ways in which we can steal from others, including by force, by deceit, and by seemingly legal means.[12] The first of those two are straightforward.[13] The third is a little harder to recognize. The Bible is clear that taxes are legitimate, and that Christians are called to pay taxes (Matt. 22:21). But some policies that politicians propose and people support amount to little more than legal attempts to take one person's goods and give them to another fueled by covetousness. At the same time, other policies seem to enable business practices that effectively rob laborers of profits that they should be sharing in. As Christians, we should aim to help protect the property of people and do our part to see to it that no one is robbed of what is due to him or her through injustice.

But not taking what belongs to our neighbor is not the fulfillment of the law. What the spirit of the law is pointing toward is a generous heart. That generosity needs to extend not only to our neighbors, but also to the Lord. In fact, the prophet Malachi makes it clear that failing to give to the Lord

10. WSC 71.

11. Christopher Wright, *Deuteronomy*, NIBC: Old Testament 4 (Hendrickson, 2007), 82.

12. Calvin, *Institutes*, 2.8.45.

13. Not only is outright theft prohibited by this commandment, but Proverbs 29:24 condemns being party to a theft and not reporting it: "The partner of a thief hates his own life; he hears the curse, but discloses nothing."

is stealing: "Will man rob God? Yet you are robbing me. But you say, 'How have we robbed you?' In your tithes and contributions" (Mal. 3:8). Not giving faithfully of your possessions to the Lord is to rob *him* of his possessions. Calvin's summary is helpful:

> We will duly obey this commandment, then, if, content with our lot, we are zealous to make only honest and lawful gain; if we do not seek to become wealthy through injustice, nor attempt to deprive our neighbor of his goods to increase our own; if we do not strive to heap up riches cruelly wrung from the blood of others; if we do not madly scrape together from everywhere, by fair means or foul, whatever will feed our avarice or satisfy our prodigality . . . and let us share the necessity of those whom we see pressed by the difficulty of affairs, assisting them in their need with our abundance.[14]

Are we loving God and neighbor by respecting what properly belongs to them?

We Love People by Upholding Truth

The ninth commandment is in verse 20 of Deuteronomy 5: "And you shall not bear false witness against your neighbor." The specific prohibition here relates to false accusations or lying in the context of a court proceeding. In the ancient world, eyewitness testimony was the primary source of evidence of a crime. It is still important today, but we also have access to video records, DNA testing, and other means to prove guilt or maintain innocence. But at that time, eyewitness testimony was everything. Breaking this commandment also frequently involved breaking the third commandment prohibiting taking the Lord's name in vain.[15] But while lying in the context of legal proceedings is chiefly in view here, the commandment extends beyond that. The call is ultimately to speak truth about ourselves and others and to avoid doing harm with our words. This would preclude all manner of slander and gossip as violations of this commandment. Calvin writes that "if a good name is more precious than all riches . . . we harm a man more

14. Calvin, *Institutes*, 2.8.46.
15. Wright, *Deuteronomy*, 84.

by despoiling him of the integrity of his name than by taking away his possessions."[16] This commandment calls us to be careful not to harm our neighbor's name or character with our words. When we hear someone being defamed privately, we should be diligent to protect the person's name. Are we doing what we can to love our neighbor by promoting truth and protecting our neighbor's name?

We Love People by Desiring Their Good

The final commandment is in Deuteronomy 5:21: "And you shall not covet your neighbor's wife. And you shall not desire your neighbor's house, his field, or his male servant, or his female servant, his ox, or his donkey, or anything that is your neighbor's." The tenth commandment differs from the rest in that it does not prohibit a particular action as much as it prohibits a particular kind of desire: the desire to have what belongs to another person. On the flip side, WLC 147 helps us see what this law requires: "such a full contentment with our own condition, and such a charitable frame of the whole soul toward our neighbour, as that all our inward motions and affections touching him, tend unto, and further all that good which is his."

Including coveting among the Ten Commandments shows us that conformity to God's law and being faithful to his covenant goes far deeper than external conformity to behavioral markers.[17] It is a matter of the heart. Jesus fully endorses this view in the New Testament: "Take care, and be on your guard against all covetousness, for one's life does not consist in the abundance of his possessions" (Luke 12:15). He recognizes that finding one's value and significance in possessions leads to a covetous heart. In her book on the Ten Commandments, Jen Wilkin breaks coveting down into basically three categories: desiring another person's stuff, another person's relationships, and another person's circumstances.[18] Who has not wanted another person's car, home, phone, yard, shoes, hair, or tennis racquet stringing machine? (I may be alone on that last one.) Have you ever looked at another person's spouse and said, "If only my husband were

16. Calvin, *Institutes*, 2.8.47.

17. Wright, *Deuteronomy*, 85.

18. Jen Wilkin, *Ten Words to Live By: Delighting in and Doing What God Commands* (Crossway, 2021), 143.

as helpful, as sensitive, as decisive, as thoughtful, as spiritually mature, as adventurous as hers" or "If only my wife were as productive, content, attractive, supportive, responsive, or low maintenance as his"? Or perhaps we find ourselves wishing, "I want their career, their vacations, their lifestyle, or even their problems." The apostle Paul recognizes that coveting is not just a matter of being discontent with what we have. It is far more sinister. He exhorts in Colossians 3:5, "Put to death therefore what is earthly in you: sexual immorality, impurity, passion, evil desire, and covetousness, which is idolatry." Covetousness is idolatry. This means that the Ten Commandments come back around full circle. To break the tenth commandment forbidding coveting is to break the first commandment forbidding idolatry.[19]

A French proverb says, "What makes us discontented with our condition is the absurdly exaggerated idea we have of the happiness of others."[20] I believe that social media has greatly exacerbated our problem of discontentment. As someone has said, "comparison is the thief of joy."[21] Comparing is exactly what many people find themselves doing while browsing a Facebook or Instagram feed. Research has shown that people who take a break from social media experience significant jumps in life satisfaction and positive emotions.[22] I do not believe it is sin to be on social media, and I have various accounts myself. But we really ought to ask ourselves why we are on there. If we are unhappy, we should definitely ask ourselves what we are doing on there because it is likely a key contributor to our unhappiness.

This tenth commandment is an interesting one particularly because of how it focuses so much on the heart's condition and the realm of desire. At some level, we have much more control over not killing someone than we do over not wanting what someone else has. I believe this is why the apostle Paul singles out this command as being the one that convinced him more than any other of his sinful condition. Not only did it convince him of his sinful condition, it exacerbated his sinful condition.[23] Even if we think we

19. Wright, *Deuteronomy*, 86.

20. Wilkin, *Ten Words to Live By*, 143.

21. This quote has been attributed to Mark Twain, Theodore Roosevelt, C. S. Lewis, and others. In short, no one knows who said it first.

22. Markham Heid, "You Asked: Is Social Media Making Me Miserable?," *TIME*, August 2, 2017, https://time.com/4882372/social-media-facebook-instagram-unhappy/, accessed November 9, 2021.

23. Romans 7:7–25 is a profound reckoning with how our sin takes something good, such as the law, and uses it to bring about something sinful.

have kept the commandments up to this point, we must acknowledge that we have not always desired our neighbor's good, which is a failure to love our neighbor. A failure to love our neighbor is a failure to love God, which is a failure to respond properly to his grace. WSC 82 reminds us that none of us perfectly keep God's commands but "daily break them in thought, word, and deed." Consequently, we are all under God's wrath and curse. But God has not left us.

God calls every one of us who are under his wrath and curse to recognize our helpless condition and run to Jesus. Jesus is the Savior of sinners; he died on the cross, bearing the curse of all our sins. He alone has kept the command to love God and neighbor perfectly. When we put our trust in Jesus, our record of lawbreaking becomes his, and his record of lawkeeping becomes ours. This cannot be earned; it is given. Jesus Christ is God's grace to us. Through him, our sins are taken away and our relationship with God secured. Now we are free to embrace all that God's commands mean without fear of condemnation. We may walk in obedience to the law as a response to God's grace, not as a means to try to earn it. Having seen all our needs met through Christ, we need no longer focus on the pursuit of our own interests, but may gladly seek the good of our neighbor.

The rich young ruler did not love either God or neighbor properly, which can be done only as a response to God's grace. The young man was not yet captured by the grace and love of God for him that would have freed him to give away all he had. Zacchaeus, on the other hand, is a picture of what grace does to a person. Formerly, he took advantage of others through his position as a tax collector. But after encountering the grace of Jesus Christ, the tightfisted thief of a man opened his fists, repaid four times what he had stolen from others to make them whole, and did so with joy (Luke 19:1–10).

Apart from God's grace, all we want to know is the least we have to do. But by God's grace, we are overwhelmed with the knowledge of what he has done for us. A graceless heart wants to know the minimum requirements; a grace-full heart overflows with joyful obedience and generosity. If we are asking about the minimum we need to do to keep God's law, it may be that we are not Christians and have never experienced the grace of God. Or it may be that we are Christians, but have forgotten what God has done for us. Love for God and others is a response to grace. As Calvin puts it:

> Hence it is very clear that we keep the commandments not by loving ourselves but by loving God and neighbor; that he lives the best and holiest life who lives and strives for himself as little as he can, and that no one lives in a worse or more evil manner than he who lives and strives for himself alone, and thinks about and seeks only his own advantage.[24]

Have we experienced the grace of God? If not, then we must run to Jesus today and find grace greater than all our sins. If we have received grace, then let us respond to that grace by loving God and our neighbor through obedience to his commands.

24. Calvin, *Institutes*, 2.8.54.

12

The Importance of Godly Fear

Deuteronomy 5:22–33

And you said, "Behold, the Lord our God has shown us his glory and greatness, and we have heard his voice out of the midst of the fire. This day we have seen God speak with man, and man still live. Now therefore why should we die? For this great fire will consume us. If we hear the voice of the Lord our God any more, we shall die." (Deut. 5:24–25)

In his book *A World of Ideas*, Bill Moyers quotes an observer of the Apollo 17 launch in 1975. Here is how he describes the experience:

It was a night launch. There were hundreds of cynical reporters all over the town drinking beer, wisecracking, waiting for this thirty-five-story-high rocket. The countdown came and then the launch. The first thing you see is this extraordinary orange light, which is just at the limit of what you can bear to look at. Everything is illuminated with this light. Then comes this

> thing slowly rising up in total silence because it takes a few seconds for the sound to come across. You hear a "WHOOOOOSH HHHHMMMM!" It enters right into you. You can practically hear jaws dropping. The sense of wonder fills everyone in the whole place as this thing goes up and up. The first stage ignites this beautiful blue flame. It becomes like a star, but you realize there are humans in it. And then there's total silence. People just get up quietly, helping each other up. They're kind. They open doors. They look at one another, speaking quietly and interestedly. These were suddenly moral people because the sense of wonder, the experience of wonder, had made them moral.[1]

What he refers to here as a "sense of wonder" from seeing the shuttle launch is similar to the biblical concept of "the fear of the Lord" that results from an encounter with the living God. The effect that the shuttle launch had on observers is similar to what God's revelation of himself at Horeb had on his people.

Whenever God reveals himself to people in the Bible, the revelation produces a dramatic effect. Abraham fell on his face to listen to God speak (Gen. 17:3). When Moses heard God speak from the burning bush, he hid his face (Ex. 3:6). When Isaiah had a vision of God in the temple, he cried out that he was undone (Isa. 6:5). Something similar happened to the people of Israel when God spoke the Ten Commandments from Horeb. This was intentional, as Moses wrote about "how on the day that you stood before the LORD your God at Horeb, the LORD said to me, 'Gather the people to me, that I may let them hear my words, so that they may learn to fear me all the days that they live on the earth, and that they may teach their children so'" (Deut. 4:10). God spoke directly to them so that they would learn to fear God and teach their children to do the same. Moses explains why this was so important in Exodus 20:20: "Do not fear, for God has come to test you, that the fear of him may be before you, that you may not sin." God intended to put the fear of God (literally) into his people so that they would not sin against him. Godly fear is an effective deterrent to sin.

1. Quoted in Craig Brian Larson, *750 Engaging Illustrations for Preachers, Teachers, and Writers* (Baker, 2007), 613.

But for contemporary people, "the fear of the Lord" is a relic of a bygone age. Even back in 1961, A. W. Tozer wrote: "The self-assurance of modern Christians, the basic levity present in so many of our religious gatherings, the shocking disrespect shown for the Person of God, are evidence enough of deep blindness of heart. Many call themselves by the name of Christ, talk much about God, and pray to him sometimes, but evidently do not know who He is."[2] Yet it is not merely a modern problem. The same issue plagued the people of God in the days of Moses. So in this chapter, we will consider the importance of godly fear under three headings: the source, the wisdom, and the hope of godly fear.

The Source of Godly Fear

After God delivers the Ten Commandments, we read in Deuteronomy 5:22–24:

> These words the LORD spoke to all your assembly at the mountain out of the midst of the fire, the cloud, and the thick darkness, with a loud voice; and he added no more. And he wrote them on two tablets of stone and gave them to me. And as soon as you heard the voice out of the midst of the darkness, while the mountain was burning with fire, you came near to me, all the heads of your tribes, and your elders. And you said, "Behold, the LORD our God has shown us his glory and greatness, and we have heard his voice out of the midst of the fire. This day we have seen God speak with man, and man still live."

The giving of the law at Horeb was an intense visual and auditory experience. Try to imagine the scene. The people of Israel are in a vast desert wilderness filled with craggy rocks and difficult terrain. They were recently rescued from Egypt and brought to this mountain, led by a cloud during the day and a fire by night. Now they see the glory and greatness of God revealed to them while they hear his voice speak out of the fire. This is a theophany.

Theophany comprises the Greek word for "God" and the verb "to show." A theophany is a manifestation of God's presence. The Bible records multiple theophanies, and each of them shares nine elements in common. We are going

2. A. W. Tozer, *The Knowledge of the Holy* (Harper & Row, 1961), 78.

to look at six of those nine elements to help us understand this theophany as well as the others in the Bible.[3]

Divine Initiation

When God reveals himself in history, it is always at his own initiation. In other parts of the ancient Near East, it was believed that strenuous effort could sometimes provoke a god to reveal himself (e.g., 1 Kings 18:23–29), but not so with Israel's God. No one can cause God to reveal himself; he must choose to do so.

An Impartation of Holiness

We know that God is holy. But when God reveals himself in a theophany, he also sanctifies the place where he is revealed. That is why, when God appears to Moses in the burning bush, he tells Moses to take off his shoes because he is standing on holy ground (Ex. 3:5). Likewise, when God speaks to his people from Sinai in Exodus 19:11–12, they are warned not to come near the mountain upon penalty of death. Because the Lord is there, the mountain is holy. God's presence makes the place holy.[4]

Revelation and Concealment at the Same Time

Because God is perfectly holy and people are sinful, a full revelation of God to sinful people would destroy them. The people of Israel understand this well (Ex. 20:19; Deut. 5:25; 18:16). So God reveals himself in fire but

3. Throughout this section, I am relying heavily on the excellent work of Jeffrey J. Niehaus, *NIDOTTE*, s.v. "Theophany," 4:1244–46. I am also including here the remaining three elements mentioned in Niehaus's article that are typical of a theophany with my own brief description of each. (1) *Temporariness.* God is always revealing himself at some level through the general revelation of creation, as described in Psalm 19:1–6. But a theophany is a very specific revelation of God at a particular time for a particular purpose. Once he has accomplished that purpose, he disappears again. Theophanies are temporary revelations. (2) *A bringing of salvation and/or judgment.* God often reveals himself in order to bring salvation or judgment, and these two things are frequently happening at the same time. In Deuteronomy 4:33–35, God explains the purpose of his revealing himself to them in Egypt and at Horeb, bringing salvation for his people and judgment on Egypt, that they might know that Yahweh is God. In the same way, when Jesus reveals himself at the end of the age in his glory, it will mean salvation for his people and final judgment for his enemies (2 Thess. 1:9–10). (3) *A foreshadowing of the end.* God's revelations of himself foreshadow his return at the end of the age, when he will reveal himself in final judgment on his enemies and salvation for his people.

4. In light of this, consider the fact that God's Spirit, his presence, dwells within the believer. Every believer is holy because God dwells within and imparts his holiness to us. We truly are the temple of the Holy Spirit (1 Cor. 6:19).

also conceals himself in a cloud and darkness. Likewise, in Matthew 17:5 on the Mount of Transfiguration, God speaks (revelation) from out of a bright cloud (concealment). Even in the incarnation there is revelation and concealment, and occasionally what is concealed breaks through. When the soldiers come with Judas to arrest Jesus in the garden of Gethsemane, Jesus asks, "Whom do you seek?" They reply, "Jesus of Nazareth." And Jesus declares, "I am he" (John 18:4–5). John writes, "When Jesus said to them, 'I am he,' they drew back and fell to the ground" (v. 6). For just a moment, what had been concealed was revealed in greater measure.

An Evocation of Human Fear

The typical reaction to God's revelation of himself is to cover one's face or fall down in fear before him (Ex. 3:6; 1 Kings 19:13; Isa. 6:5; Ezek. 1:28; Acts 9:3–4). When Daniel had a theophanic experience, although he alone saw the vision, the others with him were deeply affected too: "And I, Daniel, alone saw the vision, for the men who were with me did not see the vision, but a great trembling fell upon them, and they fled to hide themselves" (Dan. 10:7). Something similar happened to the traveling companions of Saul of Tarsus when he saw the risen Christ on the road to Damascus in Acts 9:4–7. As Jeffrey Niehaus writes, "Humans can only respond in awe and fear, not because of their humanity but because of their fallen nature, even in the presence of the God who saves them."[5]

An Occasion of Natural Upheaval

When God reveals himself, it not only affects human beings, but also disturbs the natural order. At Sinai when God descended on the mountain, the whole mountain trembled (Ex. 19:18). In 1 Kings 19:9–13, God revealed himself to Elijah at Sinai, and the effect was a strong wind that tore the mountains and broke rocks, followed by an earthquake and a fire. With that in mind, consider the description of Pentecost in Acts 2:1–3: "When the day of Pentecost arrived, they were all together in one place. And suddenly there came from heaven a sound like a mighty rushing wind, and it filled the entire house where they were sitting. And divided tongues as of fire appeared to them and rested on each one of them." The natural upheaval

5. Niehaus, "Theophany," 4:1246.

marks God's revelation of himself to accomplish his purpose of bringing about the salvation of the nations.

A Verbal Revelation

The verbal revelation is the most important part of a theophany because without it, the visual aspects of the revelation would be unexplained. When God appeared to Moses in Exodus 3, he explained that he was going to use him to rescue his people from Egypt. When he appeared to Isaiah (Isa. 6) and Ezekiel (Ezek. 1), it was to ordain them as prophets and commission them to carry his Word to a rebellious people. When God revealed himself at Pentecost and people did not understand what was happening, he spoke through Peter to explain what it was all about. The visual component of these theophanies is important and serves to inspire fear, but the primary purpose of the fear is for the people to heed what the Lord has to say. The theophany at Sinai was so that they would fear God and listen to his commandments. Likewise, at the Mount of Transfiguration, the revelation of Jesus' glory was to communicate this message: "This is my beloved Son, with whom I am well pleased; listen to him" (Matt. 17:5). We even see a type of theophany at the crucifixion of Jesus, where the revelation of who he is creates natural upheaval and the ones who crucify him give the verbal revelation of the significance: "When the centurion and those who were with him, keeping watch over Jesus, saw the earthquake and what took place, they were filled with awe and said, 'Truly this was the Son of God!'" (27:54).

These are six of the elements that commonly accompany a theophany. God reveals himself to his people to inspire godly fear in them so that they would obey his voice.

This is fine for people who experience a theophany, but what about the rest of us? We have not heard God's voice speaking out of the fire and cloud. We have not felt the earthquake or the whirlwind accompanying his voice. We have not seen the transfiguration of Jesus or the resurrection of him in his glory. Can we have godly fear? Yes, of course we can. We can rely on the eyewitness testimony of those who experienced these things. The next generation of Israelites was not going to hear God's voice from Sinai, but the generation who did hear him was commanded to tell the next generation about it as well as its significance. We are the recipients of that tradition. We have been blessed to live in an age when the canon of Scripture is completed, and God has revealed to us in his Word his complete plan for our salvation. Nothing needs to be revealed that has not been revealed. We may think that if God spoke to us himself from a mountain, or if he sent an angel to speak to us, we would be more inclined to listen and believe. But this is not likely the case. Jesus tells the story of the rich man in Hades pleading with Abraham to send Lazarus to go and speak to the rich man's brothers. Abraham says that it's not necessary because the rich man's brothers have Moses and the Prophets. The rich man replies, "'No, father Abraham, but if someone goes to them from the dead, they will repent.' He said to him, 'If they do not hear Moses and the Prophets, neither will they be convinced if someone should rise from the dead'" (Luke 16:30–31). We underestimate the sinfulness of the human heart. The very same people who trembled to hear God's voice at the mountain did not take long to break his commandments again (see Ex. 32). The question is, will we heed God's Word and obey it? The source of godly fear is God himself; he puts the fear of himself in our hearts, and he does so primarily by his Holy Spirit working by his Word.

The Wisdom of Godly Fear

We see the wisdom of godly fear in Deuteronomy 5:25–26: "Now therefore why should we die? For this great fire will consume us. If we hear the voice of the Lord our God any more, we shall die. For who is there of all flesh, that has heard the voice of the living God speaking out of the midst of fire as we have, and has still lived?" The theophany has had its effect. The people are in great fear of the Lord and are in a position to be able to receive the words as the commandment of God. After hearing God's voice, they are amazed to still be alive. Can any of us imagine hearing something that left such an impression on us that we felt lucky to be alive? I cannot. But the Israelites are confident that if they hear God speak any more, they will die. Hearing God's voice has made them aware of their own sinfulness. To see or hear something of God is to see or hear something of his holiness, and exposure to his holiness exposes our sinfulness. It is like the glass doors that lead out to the lanai of our home. When it is dark outside, the glass doors look perfectly clean. But when the afternoon sun begins to shine through the glass on the doors, all the fingerprints suddenly become visible. The prints were there all along, but they were not seen until the light exposed them. Like the sun on the windows, God's holiness exposes our sinfulness.

In another theophany in Isaiah 6, the prophet Isaiah has a vision of the Lord seated on his throne. The angelic beings known as seraphim are singing, "Holy, holy, holy" (Isa. 6:3). And then we read: "And the foundations of the thresholds shook at the voice of him who called, and the house was filled with smoke. And I said: 'Woe is me! For I am lost; for I am a man of unclean lips, and I dwell in the midst of a people of unclean lips; for my eyes have seen the King, the LORD of hosts!'" (vv. 4–5). This vision of God in his holiness exposes Isaiah's sinfulness and his need of cleansing from his sin. The people of Israel here at Horeb do not express it as explicitly, but this is the concern of being in the presence of the holy God. So they ask Moses to be a mediator for them in Deuteronomy 5:27: "Go near and hear all that the LORD our God will say, and speak to us all that the LORD our God will speak to you, and we will hear and do it." They do not want to hear from God directly again, but rather through a mediator, namely, Moses.

How will God feel about this? Will he be upset with them for no longer wanting to hear from him directly? No, it is quite the opposite! We read in verses 28–29 of Deuteronomy 5:

> And the LORD heard your words, when you spoke to me. And the LORD said to me, "I have heard the words of this people, which they have spoken to you. They are right in all that they have spoken. Oh that they had such a heart as this always, to fear me and to keep all my commandments, that it might go well with them and with their descendants forever!"

The people are right! God longs for them to have this kind of reverential heart always before him not because he needs it, but because they need it. God longs for them to always fear him because he loves them. He wants them to keep his commandments because he wants it to go well with them and their descendants forever. God exclaims in verse 29, "Oh that they had such a heart as this always, to fear me and to keep all my commandments, that it might go well with them and with their descendants forever!" God longs for his people to fear him and keep his commandments because he loves us. To disregard him, and therefore to disregard his commandments, is to bring sin and misery on ourselves. God knows that this is in Israel's future. But here in this moment, the people get it right. "The fear of the LORD is the beginning of wisdom" (Prov. 9:10), and the Israelites are on the right track.

That they recognize the significant gap between them and God is a gift of God's grace. As John Newton wrote in "Amazing Grace," "'Twas grace that taught my heart to fear."[6] When we recognize the gap between us and God, there is room for the fear of the Lord to grow. That fear can grow in one of two ways. When we see only the gap between God's holiness and our sinfulness, our fear of God is a kind of terror that causes us to run from God and hide, as Adam and Eve did in the garden of Eden. In some cases, our awareness of this gap might even cause us to resent or hate God for his holiness. This is the situation that afflicted Martin Luther during his years as a monk. No matter how much good he did, no matter how righteous he tried to be, no matter how much he confessed his sin, he fell short of what God required. His awareness of God's righteousness made him miserable, and he later recognized that he did not love God at all. God's righteousness was a terror to him.

Maybe some of us feel that way. We know that God is righteous and his law is good, and we are doing everything we can to measure up, but we still do not have a sense of peace. Maybe we are beginning to resent God and we find his commands burdensome. How do we properly recognize the gap between God's holiness and our sinfulness without running from God or resenting him?

The Hope of Godly Fear

The fear of the Lord can terrorize us and cause us to run, but the fear of the Lord can also grow another way. Notice in our text what the people ask for: they want a mediator. They do not want less of God, but they do not want to deal with God directly on their own because he is holy and they are sinful. So they ask Moses to be the middleman. Under this arrangement, they no longer need to fear being consumed by God's holiness but can still be in relationship to him. In a similar way, we need a Mediator between us and God. The exposure of our sinfulness in the light of God's holiness

6. John Newton, "Amazing Grace!" (1779).

should drive us to seek one. The only Mediator between God and man is Christ Jesus (1 Tim. 2:5). How does this work, exactly?

At Horeb, the Lord warned Moses: "Go down, and come up bringing Aaron with you. But do not let the priests and the people break through to come up to the Lord, lest he break out against them" (Ex. 19:24). The sinful people could not approach the Lord. In Exodus 20:19, the people were afraid even to hear God's voice on account of their sinfulness. We are told in verse 21, "The people stood far off, while Moses drew near to the thick darkness where God was." There was thick darkness in the place where God was dwelling at Sinai. The people stood far off, leaving Moses to enter the thick darkness alone as their mediator. Moses was warned that if anyone were to approach the holy mountain as a sinner, the Lord would break out against that person.

In this light, consider the New Testament teaching. When Jesus went to the cross, he went there as the only Mediator between God and man. We are told in Matthew 27:45 that when Jesus was hanging on the cross, there was darkness over the land during the middle of the day. Likewise, the disciples fled, leaving Jesus to enter the thick darkness alone. Bearing all our sin, Jesus went up the holy mountain in the darkness and experienced the Lord's breaking out against him on account of our sin, which he was carrying. The holy God brought down the full curse of the law on him. If the sinful people of Israel could not bear even to hear God's voice, no wonder Jesus' sweat was like drops of blood as he anticipated going into the presence of God with our record of sin on him.

After he bore the judgment for our sins, the curtain in the temple that served to protect the people of God from the holiness of God was torn in two. Through the propitiating death of Jesus, a sinful people can directly enter into the presence of the holy God without terrifying fear. We can ascend the hill of the Lord and hear his voice with joy because Jesus ascended the hill of the Lord and bore the terrors of judgment in our place. Again, to quote "Amazing Grace," "'Twas grace that taught my heart to fear, and grace my fears relieved." It is by the grace of God given to us in Jesus that our terror in the face of God's holiness can be relieved. That grace fuels our grateful response of obedience to God's commands.

When we understand that Jesus has done everything to reconcile sinful people to God's holiness, we are able to experience the reverential fear of the Lord that draws us to him rather than repels us. Jonathan Edwards described the difference between these two kinds of fears when he wrote, "Herein is the difference between . . . the fear of a godly man, and the fear of a sinner: the one fears the effects of God's displeasure, the other fears his displeasure itself."[7] The one who has not been reconciled through the mediation of Jesus is concerned with judgment and punishment. But the one who truly reverences the Lord is no longer driven by fear of judgment, for he understands that Jesus has taken all the judgment and that there is no more condemnation. Instead, Christians fear displeasing God himself because we love him for all that he has done for us.

When we have this kind of love for God, we are ready to hear his commandments and walk in his ways—not because we have to, but because we want to. As Daniel Estes describes it: "The one who fears Yahweh admits that the Lord alone possesses total knowledge and control in the universe he has made. Rather than questioning or rejecting the dictates of Yahweh, the reverential worshipper adopts the position of the submissive servant before him."[8] To see the holiness of God and to feel our sinfulness, and then to see Christ as the one who reconciles us, binds our hearts to him in loving loyalty.

If we are enslaved by fear so that the awareness of God's holiness causes us to want to flee, let us flee toward Jesus, in whom God has provided a refuge for sinners. This is the message of Hebrews 12:18–24:

> For you have not come to what may be touched, a blazing fire and darkness and gloom and a tempest and the sound of a trumpet and a voice whose words made the hearers beg that no further messages be spoken to them. For they could not endure the order that was given, "If even a beast touches the mountain, it shall be stoned." Indeed, so terrifying was the sight that Moses said, "I tremble with fear." But you have come to Mount Zion and to the city of the living God, the heavenly Jerusalem, and to innumerable angels in festal gathering, and to the assembly of the firstborn who are enrolled in heaven, and to God, the judge of all, and to the spirits of the righteous made perfect, and to Jesus, the mediator of a new covenant, and to the sprinkled blood that speaks a better word than the blood of Abel.

7. Jonathan Edwards, *The "Miscellanies": Entry Nos. a–500*, vol. 13 of *The Works of Jonathan Edwards*, ed. Thomas A. Schafer (Yale University Press, 1994), 376.

8. Daniel J. Estes, *Hear, My Son: Teaching and Learning in Proverbs*, NSBT 4 (Apollos, 1997), 37.

After the people ask for a mediator, God tells Moses in Deuteronomy 5:30–33:

> "Go and say to them, 'Return to your tents.' But you, stand here by me, and I will tell you the whole commandment and the statutes and the rules that you shall teach them, that they may do them in the land that I am giving them to possess." You shall be careful therefore to do as the LORD your God has commanded you. You shall not turn aside to the right hand or to the left. You shall walk in all the way that the LORD your God has commanded you, that you may live, and that it may go well with you, and that you may live long in the land that you shall possess.

What does God desire from those who fear him? That we remember what he has done for us and that we be careful to walk in his ways. We are to remember, trust, and obey so that it may go well with us and with our children after us.

As we move through Deuteronomy and the rest of the Old Testament, it becomes clear that the people who fear God at Sinai quickly lose that fear. Their fear of him comes in fits and starts, and so does their obedience to his commands. Consequently, though he desires to bless his people, they are constantly under his curse. But a day is coming when God will put into the hearts of his people a fear that lasts, and along with it a blessing that will never be removed. God holds forth the promise to his rebellious people in Jeremiah 32:39–40:

> I will give them one heart and one way, that they may fear me forever, for their own good and the good of their children after them. I will make with them an everlasting covenant, that I will not turn away from doing good to them. And I will put the fear of me in their hearts, that they may not turn from me.

13

Don't Forget

Deuteronomy 6:1—15

Hear, O Israel: The Lord our God, the Lord is one. You shall love the Lord your God with all your heart and with all your soul and with all your might. (Deut. 6:4–5)

I can still hear the sound of my dad's voice: "Don't forget to put oil in the car." I hear it better now than I did then. I was still a college student and driving my first car: a 1986 Nissan Pulsar. It was essentially a go-cart, but it was good enough for me, and the price was right. The only issue with the vehicle was that it burned oil. It burned so much oil that I kept an extra case of it in the car. Every time I filled the car with gasoline, I also needed to add a quart of oil.

On a chilly April evening, I set out to make an eight-hour drive through the night. I was doing everything I could to stay awake, from drinking coffee, to blasting music, to putting my head out the window at eighty miles per hour. I managed to stay awake, but I forgot to keep feeding the car oil. Somewhere in Kentucky at about four in the morning, I heard a loud *bang!* under the hood, followed by a persistent knocking sound. The car refused to go any farther. As I sat there by the side of the road, watching the smoke rise like noxious incense, I heard my dad's voice: "Don't forget to put oil in the car." I had forgotten. It cost me dearly.

We are all prone to forget. We forget to water the plants. We forget why we walked into a room. We forget our keys or wallet or sunglasses. We forget anniversaries and birthdays. We get busy or distracted, and at least temporarily we forget what is important. This is also true in the spiritual realm. Amid the busyness and distractions of everyday life, we can forget the things that are most important. Remembering was a continual challenge for the people of God in Moses' day, and it remains a continual challenge for us. While it may be costly to forget a wallet or an anniversary, forgetting the truths of this passage would be infinitely worse.

DON'T FORGET: GOD'S COMMANDMENTS ARE FOR OUR GOOD

In Deuteronomy 5, Moses laid out the Ten Commandments. Much of the rest of Deuteronomy will spell out the meaning of those commandments. But here in Deuteronomy 6, Moses reminds the people of God that the commandments are for their good. He writes in verse 1, "Now this is the commandment—the statutes and the rules—that the LORD your God commanded me to teach you, that you may do them in the land to which you are going over, to possess it." God gave the commandments recorded in Deuteronomy specifically so that the people would do them when they entered the promised land. The commandments show them how to live as God's people in God's land. Though God's land is no longer understood to be a particular region along the Mediterranean Sea, his commandments still show us how to live as his people wherever we may be. In these first three verses, we can see two reasons why God gave the commandments and how they serve our good.

First, God gave the commandments to instill reverence: "that you may fear the LORD your God, you and your son and your son's son" (Deut. 6:2). God gave Moses the commandments to teach the people to fear the Lord. In a similar way that God's revelation of himself at Sinai served to instill reverence in the people, so also the meditation on God's law should deepen our awe of the Lord.[1] Perhaps we can appreciate this idea by comparing it

1. Jeffrey H. Tigay, *Deuteronomy*, JPSTC (Jewish Publication Society, 1996), 75.

to something else. Recently, I reread *The Brothers Karamazov* by Fyodor Dostoyevsky. Every time I revisit one of his works, I find myself coming away freshly amazed and awe-inspired at the incredible talent of this man. Or when I relisten to Handel's *Messiah*, I am struck again by the genius of the work. In an even more profound way, meditation on God's law should leave us with an ever-deepening sense of awe at the wisdom and holiness of God as it is expressed in the law. This sense of reverence is not to stop with us. Rather, we are to pass it along to our children and our grandchildren. I have tried to help my children be captured with awe at the beauty and grace of Roger Federer's tennis strokes. I am still amazed by him after all these years, and naturally I communicate that amazement to my children. We are to communicate the same sense of awe and reverence and delight in God as he is revealed in his Word to the next generations.

The rest of Deuteronomy 6:2 teaches us how that reverence for God is to be expressed: "by keeping all his statutes and his commandments, which I command you, all the days of your life." God does not want us simply to marvel at his Word, but desires us to express our fear of him by keeping *all* his statutes and commandments, *all* the days of our lives. As those who live under the terms of the new covenant, we are not under the law of the Mosaic covenant. Many of the laws described in the Old Testament have found their fulfillment in Christ. But the moral law of God, summed up in the Ten Commandments, continues to be binding on all people at all times.[2] We properly reverence God when we are diligent to walk in obedience to all his commands, properly understood in their redemptive-historical context. Notice that last phrase: "all the days of your life." Reverencing God by keeping his commands is not something that we do only when we are children, or when we are in church, or when we are not feeling rushed or busy. We honor God by keeping all his commands, all the days of our lives. To do so instills and expresses our reverence.

The second reason that God gave the commandments was to enrich life. God attaches multiple explanations to help us understand how keeping his commandments leads to a richer life: "that your days may be long" (Deut. 6:2). We saw this same promise in Deuteronomy 5:33. In Israel, this typically had a literal fulfillment. When the people walked in the ways of God's commands,

2. WCF 19.5.

they usually lived longer because they had victory over their enemies, the rains came down, and the fields produced. When they were unfaithful and disobedient, their collective lives were shorter. Verse 3 of chapter 6 continues with the promises of enrichment: "Hear therefore, O Israel, and be careful to do them, that it may go well with you, and that you may multiply greatly, as the LORD, the God of your fathers, has promised you, in a land flowing with milk and honey." Obey God's commandments, that it may go well with you and that you may multiply greatly. As Christians, we understand that obeying God does not necessarily mean that we will live long lives, or that we will have children, or that life will be easy. Even the Old Testament book of Job disabuses us of simplistically equating obedience with a life free from challenge or tragedy. Though trials may come even when we obey, we can be certain that the way of obedience will lead to a rich life. We can be certain that we are not going to be less enriched than the covenant people of God were under the terms of the Mosaic covenant now that Christ has come and poured out his Holy Spirit on the church. We cannot know for certain all the ways in which God will enrich our lives as we individually and corporately commit ourselves to walking in his ways, but we can be certain that he will do it. Whatever else he may do, he will certainly enrich our lives by conforming us to the image of Christ (Rom. 8:28–29).

Look at how many times in these verses God emphasizes the personal benefit to his people of walking in his ways. He gives us his commands not to ruin us or to make our lives miserable, but to instill reverence for him and to enrich us. We might think of it this way: a physician tells us to get out and exercise. In the heat of a tough workout, we might think the physician hates us. But the opposite is true. A physician who encourages healthy eating and exercise wants us to live a full, rich, and healthy life. God's commandments may sometimes be challenging, but they are meant for our good.

DON'T FORGET: GOD CALLS FOR TOTAL ALLEGIANCE

The next verses express the heart of Deuteronomy, and indeed the whole Bible: "Hear, O Israel: The LORD our God, the LORD is one.[3] You shall love

3. The Hebrew literally reads: "YHWH our God YHWH one." The ESV supplies the following three alternative translations: "The LORD our God is one LORD"; "The LORD is our God, the LORD is one"; "The LORD is our God, the LORD alone."

the LORD your God with all your heart and with all your soul and with all your might" (Deut. 6:4–5). These two verses make up the beginning of what is called the *Shema*,[4] named thus because of the first Hebrew word of Deuteronomy 6:4, which means "hear." These verses are so important in Judaism that devout Jews have been reciting them every morning and evening since at least the first century, and probably longer. But despite its familiarity and significance, there are some interpretive difficulties.

One of the difficulties relates to how to translate Deuteronomy 6:4. In Hebrew, it literally says, "YHWH our God YHWH one." The statement lacks verbs. There are two ways of translating this. The first way is to understand it as it is translated in the ESV, "The LORD our God, the LORD is one"[5]—as a statement about the nature of God himself. The idea here is that God is indivisible, unique, and incomparable. These things are true, of course, but one issue with this translation is that we do not really need the second reference to "the LORD." Moses could have simply written, "The LORD our God is one" if that is his point. But the first and second halves of this phrase are communicating particular things.

A preferable translation would be, "The LORD is our God, the LORD alone." The first half is communicating that Yahweh and no other is our God. The second half is communicating that Yahweh is God alone. There are some challenges with translating it this way, but none that are insurmountable. While the word *ʾeḥād* normally means "one," in multiple instances it means "alone," such as in Zechariah 14:9: "And the LORD will be king over all the earth. On that day the LORD will be one and his name one." According to this verse, one day what is currently true of Israel will be true of all the earth. Clearly, the Lord is already "one," and so is his name. He is not going to be more "one" on that day than he is today. Rather, the idea is the same one in the *Shema*, that on that day the Lord will be recognized as God alone and his name will be the one exclusively called on in prayer and worship.[6] As Daniel Block helpfully explains the concept:

> Within the immediate and the broader contexts the purpose of this statement is not to answer the question, "How many is God?" but "Who

4. The *Shema* includes Deuteronomy 6:4–9; 11:13–21; and Numbers 15:37–41.
5. See Tigay, *Deuteronomy*, 438–40, for a succinct discussion of the various options.
6. See also Tigay, 438–40.

> is the God of Israel?" To this question the Israelites were to respond in unison and without compromise or equivocation, "Our God is Yahweh, Yahweh alone!" This is not strictly a monotheistic confession . . . but a cry of allegiance.[7]

Understood in this way, we can see why faithful Jews would confess this truth morning and evening. To confess that they believe in monotheism is important, but it seems unnecessary as a twice-daily practice. Yet it makes total sense that they would remind themselves that Yahweh is their God and nobody else. What a beautiful practice that takes into account our own weakness and proclivity to forget. As we sing in the beloved hymn, "Prone to wander—Lord, I feel it—prone to leave the God I love."[8] To make the *Shema* our pledge each morning upon rising and each evening before bed is a practice of remembrance.

Of course, this interpretation does not exclude this verse's being a statement about God's uniqueness either. In fact, when Mark recounts the story of Jesus' explaining the greatest commandment, he seems to hold both meanings together. We read in Mark 12:28–32:

> And one of the scribes came up and heard them disputing with one another, and seeing that he answered them well, asked him, "Which commandment is the most important of all?" Jesus answered, "The most important is, 'Hear, O Israel: The Lord our God, the Lord is one. And you shall love the Lord your God with all your heart and with all your soul and with all your mind and with all your strength.' The second is this: 'You shall love your neighbor as yourself.' There is no other commandment greater than these." And the scribe said to him, "You are right, Teacher. You have truly said that he is one, and there is no other besides him."

The Lord is unique and undivided, and he is also God all by himself. To confess the *Shema* carries with it some definite implications. If Yahweh is our God, and he is the only God, then multiple ramifications are spelled out in the next verses.

7. Daniel I. Block, *Deuteronomy*, NIVAC (Zondervan, 2012), 182.
8. Robert Robinson, "Come, Thou Fount of Every Blessing" (1758).

First, we must love the Lord with all that we are and all that we have. This is the gist of Deuteronomy 6:5, the greatest commandment in the Bible: "You shall love the LORD your God with all your heart and with all your soul and with all your might." To love the Lord with all our heart includes the affections, but in Hebrew the "heart" also includes the will and the mind. The term for "soul" has a wide lexical range, but here it is a reference to the source of one's life or vitality.[9] To love with the heart and soul means being fully devoted to God with everything that one has. That particular combination of "heart and soul" occurs quite frequently in Deuteronomy.[10] But the addition of the last term "might" is unique in this book.[11] The word literally means "muchness."[12] What does it mean to love the Lord with all our "muchness"? Because the word can refer to property, some Jewish rabbis believed that this meant that we are to love the Lord with all our wealth or possessions.[13] That is true. But it goes beyond that as well to include using everything we have, including our talents, our experiences, our relationships, our intellects, and anything else, to love Yahweh. If Yahweh is our God and he is the only God, then we are to direct all that we are and all that we have toward loving him. As Patrick Miller writes, "The oneness of the Lord your God is matched by the oneness and totality of your devotion."[14] But what does it mean to "love God"?

Interestingly, Deuteronomy is the first book of the Bible to speak of loving God. Other passages speak about the importance of revering him, but Deuteronomy introduces the command to love. In the book's historical context, as a covenant treaty document between a suzerain and his vassal people, "love" is not simply a feeling. Rather, "love" refers to the actions of loyalty, devotion, and faithfulness to the king. To love God in this sense means not only keeping his commandments, but also not going after other suzerain lords. It is not mere obedience, but deeply affectionate loyalty, which is not less than obedience.[15] The central theme of Deuteronomy is

9. J. A. Thompson, *Deuteronomy: An Introduction and Commentary*, TOTC (InterVarsity Press, 1974), 122.

10. Deut. 4:29; 10:12; 11:13; 13:3; 26:16; 30:2, 6, 10.

11. In fact, the only other time that "heart," "soul," and "might" appear together in the Old Testament is 2 Kings 23:25 as a description of Josiah, who returned to God in a fully devoted way, unlike any other king.

12. BDB, s.v. "מאד," 547.

13. Tigay, *Deuteronomy*, 77.

14. Patrick D. Miller, *Deuteronomy*, IC (John Knox Press, 1990), 103.

15. Robin Wakely, *NIDOTTE*, s.v. "מְאֹד," 2:818.

the call to covenant faithfulness and loyalty to the suzerain with all that we have and all that we are.

The second implication of the *Shema* is that we should saturate our lives and families with God's words. If Yahweh is so important that everything about who we are and what we have is to be brought into the service of actively loving him, and loving him means nothing less than obeying his commands, then it follows that we would imbue our lives with his words. That is the essence of the teaching in Deuteronomy 6:6–9:

> And these words that I command you today shall be on your heart. You shall teach them diligently to your children, and shall talk of them when you sit in your house, and when you walk by the way, and when you lie down, and when you rise. You shall bind them as a sign on your hand, and they shall be as frontlets between your eyes. You shall write them on the doorposts of your house and on your gates.

We must make sure that the words are written not simply on tablets of stone, but on our very hearts. We should memorize these words, meditate on them, and eat up this book so that it becomes part of the very fabric of our being and colors the way we see, hear, and feel. We should aim to see the Word become flesh in our own lives. We must recognize that the world, the flesh, and the devil are conspiring to draw us away from our love for God and his words, that we will be prone to forget his words, and so we must organize our lives in such a way as to remember. The text speaks of binding the words on our hands and between our eyes. Still to this day, many Jews take this verse literally and strap portions of the Torah to their foreheads and arms (*tefillin*) when they go to pray. Likewise, on their doors they hang *mezuzahs*, which are little boxes that contain the *Shema*. It is unlikely that this is what the passage is driving at, but we would do well to learn from this intentional effort to put the commands into practice. Gary Millar writes: "God's people, then, must immerse themselves totally in the atmosphere of the divine word, because they need to counter their innate tendency to forget. All kinds of visual and memory aids are necessitated by their weakness."[16]

16. J. Gary Millar, *Now Choose Life: Theology and Ethics in Deuteronomy*, NSBT 6 (Apollos, 1998), 166–67.

The call for us is to let the words of our King be always on our hearts. The whole Psalter begins with a description of the man who is blessed: "his delight is in the law of the Lord, and on his law he meditates day and night" (Ps. 1:2). The apostle Paul seems to pick up on this Deuteronomic theme when he writes in Colossians 3:16, "Let the word of Christ dwell in you richly, teaching and admonishing one another in all wisdom, singing psalms and hymns and spiritual songs, with thankfulness in your hearts to God." Clearly, there is an intentionality here. The Word of Christ will not dwell in you richly if you are not dwelling richly in the Word of Christ.

How do we let God's Word dwell in us richly? One thing we can do is to start a Bible-reading plan. There are many good options to help us be in the Word every day. We could read through the Bible in one year, but we do not have to do that. We could just read and meditate on a smaller portion every day. The key is that we are constantly going back to the Word and being reminded of the truth. The people of God in the Old Testament dwelt on the words delivered here in Deuteronomy and elsewhere. We can and should dwell on those same passages, but we can also dwell on the whole New Testament. As these words dwell richly in us and on our hearts, we will be far more inclined to teach them to our children, which will be the focus of the next passage.

Don't Forget: Fruitfulness Frequently Leads to Forgetfulness

We are just going to touch on this theme now, because we will cover it in much more detail when we get to Deuteronomy 8. But the warning comes in verses 10–12 of Deuteronomy 6:

> And when the Lord your God brings you into the land that he swore to your fathers, to Abraham, to Isaac, and to Jacob, to give you—with great and good cities that you did not build, and houses full of all good things that you did not fill, and cisterns that you did not dig, and vineyards and olive trees that you did not plant—and when you eat and are full, then take care lest you forget the Lord, who brought you out of the land of Egypt, out of the house of slavery.

Moses is warning his people that when they settle into the land and are prosperous and no longer counting on God to supply their daily bread, they need to be very intentional not to forget him. What an interesting problem of the human heart! When our lives are hard, we seek him. When our lives are easy, we drift away and forget. In a similar way, when Israel gets into the promised land and prospers, the people are going to have a serious proclivity to forget who brought them there and what life was like in the wilderness. They might start to worship the gods of the land. In our case, we might be inclined to worship the gods of material wealth, success, beauty, influence, and so on. We forget that it is God who gives us every good and perfect gift. So God in his mercy sometimes brings us into difficulty to help us remember. We must not let our fruitfulness lead to forgetfulness.

Moses points us back in the right direction and gives a solemn warning in Deuteronomy 6:13–15: "It is the LORD your God you shall fear. Him you shall serve and by his name you shall swear. You shall not go after other gods, the gods of the peoples who are around you—for the LORD your God in your midst is a jealous God—lest the anger of the LORD your God be kindled against you, and he destroy you from off the face of the earth." Yahweh is the only God we should be serving, and a morning-and-evening reminder from the *Shema* can help to keep us from forgetting. If we are tempted to go after the gods of the land, we will provoke the jealous anger of the Lord. When the people of Israel and Judah continually did so, he eventually destroyed many of them and sent the rest into exile out of his land. God does not take kindly to cheating! The Lord is our God, the Lord alone. Don't forget.

One final thing. Some Jewish theologians have used the *Shema* as a case against our Trinitarian understanding of God. But the apostle Paul, a Jewish scholar of the highest order, trained at the feet of one of the most preeminent Jewish rabbis of the day, did not see worshiping Jesus as being inconsistent with monotheism. Many excellent New Testament scholars believe that Paul was referring to the *Shema* in 1 Corinthians 8:6: "Yet for us there is one God, the Father, from whom are all things and for whom we exist, and one Lord, Jesus Christ, through whom are all things and through whom we exist." Here Paul does something stunning. He bifurcates the passage so that "God" refers to the Father and "Lord" refers to Jesus. In so doing, he makes it clear that he is not rejecting Jewish monotheism, but he redefines it to include Jesus Christ.[17]

The one God that we confess in the *Shema* is known to us through Jesus Christ our Lord. To keep the *Shema*, we must love the Lord our God with all our heart, soul, and strength, which means nothing less than being fully devoted to Jesus Christ—the same Jesus Christ who expressed his full devotion to us in taking on flesh, taking on the form of a servant to come and serve his people by becoming the ransom payment to set us free from our slavery to sin. Because we have been set free by Jesus' death and resurrection, it is only right and appropriate that we now devote ourselves fully to him with all our affections, with all our will, with all our capacity.

Don't forget: God's commandments are for our good, our God calls for total allegiance, and our fruitfulness can lead to forgetfulness. As we come to the Word each day, and as we come to the Lord's Supper in our worship services, may they both serve to remind us of the God who loved us with full devotion all the way to the cross and beyond, that we may love him with all that we have and all that we are.

17. Kim Huat Tan, "The Shema and Early Christianity," *Tyndale Bulletin* 59, no. 2 (2008): 204.

14

Teach Your Children Well

Deuteronomy 6:16–25

When your son asks you in time to come, "What is the meaning of the testimonies and the statutes and the rules that the Lord *our God has commanded you?" then you shall say to your son, "We were Pharaoh's slaves in Egypt. And the* Lord *brought us out of Egypt with a mighty hand."* (Deut. 6:20–21)

"Teach Your Children" was written by Graham Nash and later released in 1970 by Crosby, Stills, Nash & Young. For over fifty years now, that song has been calling parents to be intentional to teach their children well. As parents, we cannot help but teach our children. The question is, are we teaching our children *well*?

Years ago, my wife and I drew up a strategic plan for our family. We started the plan by asking this question: "On our last day as a couple, what do we want?" We wrote several answers to that question. For starters, we want to end our life as a happily married couple. We want to have good relationships with our children and with any grandchildren we may have. We want to have been used to bring many people into God's kingdom. We want to have been financially responsible with enough to share until the end. We also want to have a bank of fun memories and adventures we have shared together. But each time we revisit the question of what we want on our last day as a couple, the same thing comes up first. On our last day, what we want above everything else is to know that our kids are walking with the Lord. We want to have lived in such a way that, even after we are gone, our children will know how to follow Jesus. If we do nothing else, if we have nothing else, if we accomplish nothing else in this life, this is the one thing we desperately desire. Some of those reading this who have young children feel that desire intensely as well. Others who are older parents or grandparents are experiencing the joy of that desire fulfilled, or the heartache of unfulfilled desire.

Statistically, heartache is what most of us with grown children or grandchildren are feeling. Lifeway Research conducted a poll among young adults from twenty-three to thirty who regularly attended a Protestant church in high school. In 2017, it was found that 66 percent of those young people stopped attending church regularly for at least a year between eighteen and twenty-two. That is two out of every three regularly attending high schoolers. Most concerning about the study is that 71 percent of those who left did not make an intentional decision to do so.[1] They just drifted away. The good news is that among those who do drop out, 31 percent of them return after marriage or children. The bad news is that 69 percent stay gone.

So what is the problem? We can assign some of the drift to the fact that part of growing up is distancing from one's parents and establishing one's own identity. At the same time, if we were to measure how many kids grow up being lifelong fans of their dad's favorite sports team, the departure numbers would probably be much smaller. How many of our children would resonate with this description of a dad's influence?

> Among the myriad traits I inherited from my father, the most significant is not my eyes or my hands but rather my steadfast (often gut-wrenching) devotion to the New York Mets. My love of the Mets was instilled by my father like religion. I don't remember becoming a fan; it is simply who we were. I do remember the moment at which I defended my fandom—getting into a physical fight with a Yankees fan, a boy twice my size, during the tense 2000

1. Aaron Earls, "Most Teenagers Drop Out of Church When They Become Young Adults," Lifeway Research, January 15, 2019, https://lifewayresearch.com/2019/01/15/most-teenagers-drop-out-of-church-as-young-adults/, accessed January 6, 2022.

> Subway Series. Since then, I've worn my orange and blue proudly. (In fact, I think one of my happiest moments was when I overheard my dad boast to a peer, "My daughter bleeds orange and blue!") For me, it is a true joy to carry this legacy, even with all the pain that comes along with it.[2]

Would our children say the same thing about the legacy of faith that we are passing on to them? If so many of us desire that our children would continue following the Lord after they leave home, why do so many of them walk away? Or, to flip the question around: How can we effectively pass on our faith to our children? This is the question that our text begins to answer in Deuteronomy 6. As the people of Israel prepare to go into the promised land, God is concerned not only for the present generation's faithfulness, but for the next generation's as well.

Moses' intention in this passage is not to condemn, but to instruct and encourage. We younger parents can be a judgmental lot, quick to point out how our parents failed and quick to suggest that if a person had "just done this" or "not done that," then that person's children would be walking with the Lord. But it is simply not true. All of us parents have fallen short of the glory of God. Additionally, some great parents have children who walk away, and some terrible parents have kids who love Jesus to the end. But we are going to listen to God's Word to determine how, with our remaining years and influence, we can do our part to see to it that our children and grandchildren are walking with the Lord, even long after we are gone. How can we effectively pass on our faith to our children? The answer to the question comes in two parts: first, we must cause the question, and then we must tell the story.

We Must Cause the Question

The whole premise of this passage and of parents' passing on the faith to their children is based on the children's asking their parents a question. Deuteronomy 6:20 begins, "When your son asks you in time to come." The best opportunity we have for passing on the faith is when our children are intrigued enough by our lives to ask us about it. What does it take for our

2. "How Sports Fans Choose Their Teams: Readers Share Their Stories," *New York Times Magazine*, July 5, 2017, https://www.nytimes.com/2017/07/05/magazine/how-sports-fans-choose-their-teams-readers-share-their-stories.html, accessed January 6, 2022.

son or daughter or grandson or granddaughter to ask us this question, or another one like it? It takes at least two things. First, the child must see us conspicuously living out our faith. Moses writes in verse 16, "You shall not put the LORD your God to the test, as you tested him at Massah." The story of Massah is told in Exodus 17. The people of God had no water in the wilderness, and they tested the Lord, which means that they sought to have God prove that he was really among them (Ex. 17:7). They lacked confidence in his ability to provide, despite the extraordinary miracles he had already worked for them. They were probably making their obedience to his commands conditional on his doing what they wanted.[3] Rather than doing that, Moses commands in Deuteronomy 6:17–19:

> You shall diligently keep the commandments of the LORD your God, and his testimonies and his statutes, which he has commanded you. And you shall do what is right and good in the sight of the LORD, that it may go well with you, and that you may go in and take possession of the good land that the LORD swore to give to your fathers by thrusting out all your enemies from before you, as the LORD has promised.

We have seen these commands in other places already. The call is to be living their lives in accordance with God's commandments, which are spelled out throughout Deuteronomy. It is when God's people live their lives in alignment with God's commands that the next generation begins to ask questions.

Listen to the question that the son asks in Deuteronomy 6:20: "What is the meaning of the testimonies and the statutes and the rules that the LORD our God has commanded you?" The Hebrew of this question literally says, "What are the testimonies and statutes . . . ?" Most scholars agree that the son is not asking about the content of the laws, since he would already know them through his family's teaching (Deut. 6:7) and observance of them. That is why almost every English translation says something like "What is the meaning of the testimonies?"

Teaching opportunities like this one arise only when parents are conspicuously living in obedience to God.[4] If there is no practice of the

3. J. A. Thompson, *Deuteronomy: An Introduction and Commentary*, TOTC (InterVarsity Press, 1974), 125.

4. Christopher Wright, *Deuteronomy*, NIBC: Old Testament 4 (Hendrickson, 2007), 103.

faith, there are no questions. Faith is better caught than taught. It is when our children see us living differently from the world they see at school, or on the television, or at their friends' homes that they ask us these kinds of questions. "Why do we go to church every week when friends regularly use that time for sports or to catch up on things around the house? Why do we always give money to the church? Why don't we watch this movie or that show? Why do we care about the immigrant, the addicted, and the broken instead of trying to run them out of town or out of the country? Why do we always give thanks?"

These are the kinds of questions that Christian parents want to hear their children asking. We want our lives to be so compellingly different from the world they experience on a day-to-day basis that it causes them to ask the question, "Why do we live like this?" Now, be forewarned: especially when our children are little, they will ask us questions about the life that we live; it just may not be the questions we want to hear. "Dad, why do you always have a drink when you get home?" "Mom, why don't you and Dad sleep in the same room?" "Why don't you read the Bible to me?" If they are not asking these questions out loud, they are thinking them. Our life will cause questions; the question is, "What kinds of questions is our life causing?" We cause the questions we want to hear when our kids see a difference in our lives as we conspicuously live out our faith.

But before they can see us conspicuously living out our faith, they have to *see* us. This is the second key to causing the question that we want to hear as parents. For many of us, this is a greater challenge than conspicuously living out our faith. But it is fundamental to passing on our faith. Earlier in this passage, Moses gave more detailed instructions on how we can verbally pass on the faith to our children: "And these words that I command you today shall be on your heart. You shall teach them diligently to your children, and shall talk of them when you sit in your house, and when you walk by the way, and when you lie down, and when you rise" (Deut. 6:6–7). What do these opportunities to pass on our faith to our kids and grandkids have in common? They happen when we are with them. They happen when they see us and we see them. In order for us to have these kinds of questions, two conditions need to be met.

First, we must be around. Quality time happens in the context of quantity time. Between the demands of work, hobbies, church activities, and whatever else we are engaged in, sometimes being around is the hardest thing of all for us to be. Yet it is fundamental. Unless we are around, our children will not see us. I wonder sometimes if we are not around more often because we have made the unconscious decision to sacrifice our children to pursue the idols of our culture. Psalm 106:34–38 reminds us that when the Israelites came into Canaan, they did not live according to God's commands. Instead, they became like the culture around them: "They did not destroy the peoples, as the Lord commanded them, but they mixed with the nations and learned to do as they did. They served their idols, which became a snare to them" (Ps. 106:34–36). Now, that is bad enough, but look at what serving the idols of the culture around them cost them: "They sacrificed their sons and their daughters to the demons; they poured out innocent blood, the blood of their sons and daughters, whom they sacrificed to the idols of Canaan" (vv. 37–38). We may not be literally throwing our children into a fire, but are we giving them up to pursue the idols of our culture? One of our culture's biggest idols is the twin idea that we need it all and can have it all. Do we? Can we? Having a strategic plan for your family can be a helpful safeguard. As leaders of our families, we can decide (on paper, at least) that we do not want it all. We want first and foremost to follow Jesus and on our last day to know that our kids are following Jesus. What do we *really* need in order for that to happen? Rather than sacrificing our children to pursue the idols of our culture, how can we live differently so as to cause the kinds of questions we want to hear: "Mom and Dad, why do we live like this when it seems like everyone else is doing that?"

Second, we must be available. We know that there is a difference between being around and being present. For some of us, our kids are more familiar with the backs of our phones than they are with our faces. Or it may be the TV or our laptop that keeps us from being available. The sad truth is that unless we are intentional, there are a million things for us to be more available to than our children. Multitasking has been scientifically proved to be an illusion.[5] We cannot be mentally absorbed in one thing and also available to our children. It does not mean that we should *only* be available to our children, but we must be intentionally available to them.

5. Paul Atchley, "You Can't Multitask, So Stop Trying," *Harvard Business Review*, December 21, 2010, https://hbr.org/2010/12/you-cant-multi-task-so-stop-tr, accessed January 6, 2022.

I sometimes think that if the scene in Deuteronomy 6 were to play out in our homes today, and our son asked us, "Why do we live like we do?," we would answer with the smartphone grunt. It sounds like this: "Huhm?"

Son: "Dad, why do we live like we do?"

Dad: "Huhm? Hold on a second; let me finish this."

Dad, two minutes later: "All right, buddy, what did you say? You don't remember?"

The opportunity has been lost. Being available to the next generation is a matter of the heart. But recognize that it may require a change in our lives. As our kids and grandkids see our lives, it is the difference in our lives that compels them to ask the question. If we are available to them to answer, then we have the opportunity to tell the story.

We Must Tell the Story

Consider again the question that the son asks in verse 20 of Deuteronomy 6: "What is the meaning of the testimonies and the statutes and the rules that the Lord our God has commanded you?" We might expect that the answer would come in the words of verse 24: "the Lord commanded us to do all these statutes." Or in other words, "we do these things because God said to." Of course, "Because God said to" is a pretty good last word in any argument or discussion. But that is not what the father is to say, at least not at first. Others would answer the question "why do we do these things?" with the words at the end of verse 24: we do these things so "that [God] might preserve us alive." Or to put it another way, "we do these things so that God will . . ." Many of us answer that way, and we clearly have a biblical basis for doing so. The trouble is that this is not what we are supposed to say either, at least not first. When our kids ask us this question, our first response is not to say "because God said to" and it is not to say "so that God will," but rather, our response is to tell them a story about *what God has done*. More specifically, it is to tell them *our* story of what God has done.

Listen to how the father is to respond. The son asks, "Why do we live this way?" and the father is to say: "We were Pharaoh's slaves in Egypt. And the Lord brought us out of Egypt with a mighty hand. And the Lord showed signs and wonders, great and grievous, against Egypt and against Pharaoh and all his household, before our eyes" (Deut. 6:21–22). The first thing we say when our children ask why we do these things is "because God rescued us!" The answer to the "why do we obey God" question is the gospel! Until Jesus came, this was the most up-to-date version of the gospel that existed. Now, if this was true for the Israelites, how much more so is it true for those of us who have experienced the rescue of Jesus Christ! We were not slaves in Egypt, but we were slaves to sin. We were slaves to fear, to pride, to lust, to anger, to despair, to our possessions, to food, to drink, and to everything else. But Jesus Christ came and broke the chains of our bondage! The Israelites were set free from Egypt when God poured out judgment on the firstborn son of every Egyptian, but we were set free from sin when God poured out judgment on *his own firstborn Son* on the cross. Look how he loves us, that he would set us free at so high a price!

Only after we have related what God did will we then come to the "because God said so" answer. But the order is nonreversible. In Deuteronomy 6:23–24, the father is to continue: "And he brought us out from there, that he might bring us in and give us the land that he swore to give to our fathers. And the LORD commanded us to do all these statutes, to fear the LORD our God, for our good always." "Why do Mommy and Daddy do what we do? Because God loved us so much that he set us free, and now we want to do everything we can to love him back. He told us that this is how we can show our love for him, by obeying all that he commands." It gets even better than this. His laws and rules and commands are not arbitrary. Notice what the father says in verse 24, that these things are "for our good always." Keeping God's commands and living in obedience to him is in our best interests. But unless we understand what God has already done for us, we likely will not believe that. Therefore, we must start our explanation with the loving relationship that God has established with us by grace. We can trust a God who loves us like this.

Then comes the third part of the answer, the "so that" answer. The father continues in Deuteronomy 6:24–25: "that he might preserve us alive, as we are this day. And it will be righteousness for us, if we are careful to do all this commandment before the LORD our God, as he has commanded us." Why do we live this way? Because God loved us enough to set us free, and he has given us these commandments to show us how life works best, and he has told us that when we live in obedience to him, our lives will be blessed. Specifically, the parent is to say that "it will be righteousness for us, if we are careful to do all this commandment." Is this righteousness the basis of our relationship with God? It cannot be. The point being made in the whole passage is that obeying God's law is a grateful response to the saving work of God, which was entirely by grace. Jonathan Edwards explains the phrase in this way:

> 'Tis not meant this shall be esteemed as the thing which properly merits or recommends to God's favor and a title to happiness, but that this God shall as it were remember and set before his eyes in his providence as an evidence of our being righteous, and his treating us accordingly as good men, God's friends.[6]

The meaning of "righteousness," then, carries more of the passive meaning here, as in "we shall . . . enjoy the blessing of, everything being right—in our family, in our society, and in our relationship with God."[7] Parents, grandparents, it is so important that we give a complete answer to the question and that we give it in the right order, beginning with God's love for us as seen most clearly in the gospel and ending with obedience as the proper response of gratitude. Here are two problems with other approaches.

First, the problem with giving only the "so that God will bless you" answer is that recognizing God's blessing requires that we recognize *him*. As Laura Story reminds us in her song "Blessings," sometimes God's blessings come to us in the form of raindrops. Sometimes it takes a thousand sleepless nights to convince us that God is near. Trials are God's mercies in disguise.[8] But if we do not know him, we are not likely to recognize his mercies and blessings. As soon as our children encounter difficulty in the world, they will become disillusioned. They will say: "I did all the right things, I tried my best to obey all his commands, and this is what I get? Cancer? A life of singleness? My parents' divorce?" Some of us are angry with God because we have been obeying primarily so that he will bless us, but he has not given us the blessing we wanted. Our first reason for obedience cannot be "so that God will" but must be "because God has." Otherwise, we will not trust him

6. Jonathan Edwards, *The Blank Bible*, vol. 24 of *The Works of Jonathan Edwards*, ed. Stephen J. Stein (Yale University Press, 2006), 289.

7. Wright, *Deuteronomy*, 106–7.

8. Laura Story, "Blessings," Capitol Christian Music Group, 2011.

or obey him when things begin to happen that we do not understand. But if we are always living in light of the story of what he has already done, then when things happen that we do not understand, we can know that whatever is happening now is not happening because he does not love us. It is not happening because he does not intend to bless us. We can trust him in what he is doing now because we know him and what he has already done. As we pass down our faith to our kids, we must answer the "why do we do this?" question with the "because this is what God has already done" response first.

Second, the problem with starting with the "because God said so" answer is that while it encourages obedience in the short term, it does not do so in the long term, for us or our kids. Indeed, not only does it not encourage obedience, but it often produces the opposite. I once heard Josh McDowell say that "rules without relationship lead to rebellion." This is the reality in some of our homes. We set rules for our children, but we lack the relational context for those rules, and our kids ultimately rebel against them. If we know only in our heads that Jesus died on a cross, but we do not know in our hearts that Jesus died for us, we will not walk in obedience to God's commands. Some of us cannot tell the story of how God in his love set us free because we have not been set free. The fact is that we will never pass on a faith to our children that we do not possess ourselves. At best, we will pass on our dead faith.

Some of us are rebelling today, and we are Christians. Psalm 106:7 tells us why we are rebelling: "Our fathers, when they were in Egypt, did not consider your wondrous works; they did not remember the abundance of your steadfast love, but rebelled by the sea." Why did they rebel? Because they did not remember God's great love. Why are we rebelling today? Because we have forgotten how much he loves us. We have forgotten the gospel. We see the rules and understand how we are supposed to live, but we do not trust him because we have forgotten that his love for us was so great that he gave up his Son for us.

Some of us know the will of God for us in a certain situation, but we are dragging our feet to obey. We know what we should have done a long time ago, but we have not because we are afraid. The reason we are afraid is that we have forgotten how much he loves us. John writes: "There is no fear in love, but perfect love casts out fear. For fear has to do with punishment, and whoever fears has not been perfected in love" (1 John 4:18). When we grasp in our hearts the indescribable love with which he has loved us, to that degree we will fearlessly run to obey his commands. When the all-powerful God loves us like this, do we really think we have anything to fear by obeying him?

When we remember and fully embrace God's love in Christ, when the only thing we will is his will, the Holy Spirit will come and fill up our life, and we will exclaim with the psalmist, "I delight to do your will, O my God; your law is within my heart" (Ps. 40:8). The Spirit of Christ within us will say, as Jesus did, "My food is to do the will of him who sent me" (John 4:34). "I don't care about eating, let alone anything else; the joy and sustenance of my life is to obey my Father because I love him so much!" That kind of faith is contagious; that is the kind of faith that our kids and grandkids will catch.

They will ask us, "Why do you rejoice always, why are you always praying, why do you give thanks in all circumstances, why do you love those who hate you, why do you give till it hurts, why do you ask my forgiveness when you sin?" In response, we will say: "Oh, child, it is because God loves us so! We were slaves to our sin, but God loved us so much that he set us free through the death and resurrection of his own Son, Jesus. Now it is our highest honor and deepest joy to live a life of full devotion to his commands. He has promised that when we do obey, it will be for our good, and that his blessing will fill our lives and home. But even if his blessing should come in the form of bankruptcy, illness, or death, we will trust him because no God who has shown this much love could ever do anything but good to us."

Do we desire to pass on our faith to our children and grandchildren? Do we long to teach them well? Then no matter how old they may be today, let us live so as to cause the question. When they ask, "Why do you live life as you do?," then tell them. Tell them the story—the old, old story, of Jesus and his love.[9] In the telling, we will point them to the gospel, and we ourselves will find fresh motivation as we remember, to trust and obey.

9. Wright, *Deuteronomy*, 104.

15

Passionately Pursuing Holiness

Deuteronomy 7:1–26

For you are a people holy to the Lord *your God. The* Lord *your God has chosen you to be a people for his treasured possession, out of all the peoples who are on the face of the earth.* (Deut. 7:6)

Elections have consequences. That phrase is frequently bandied about in the United States each time there is a change of power. When a political party out of power takes the reins again, many things change. New appointments are made, new agendas are set, new policies are enacted, and different values are embraced. Elections have consequences.

In Deuteronomy 7, we can see that divine election also has consequences. God chose the people of Israel to be his very own "treasured possession" out of everybody on the earth. That election had definite consequences for how they were to live. The chief consequence was that because God is holy, and because he set his people apart as holy, they were to live as a holy people in accordance with his commandments. Much of Deuteronomy and the rest of the Bible spell this out. In the New Testament also, God's intention in electing and saving his people is so that we would live holy and distinct lives from the world. Paul summarizes it well in Titus 2:11–14:

> For the grace of God has appeared, bringing salvation for all people, training us to renounce ungodliness and worldly passions, and to live self-controlled, upright, and godly lives in the present age, waiting for our blessed hope, the appearing of the glory of our great God and Savior Jesus Christ, who gave himself for us to redeem us from all lawlessness and to purify for himself a people for his own possession who are zealous for good works.

This is a great description of the project that God was doing in Deuteronomy, and what God still desires from his covenant people today.

But do those phrases describe us? Are we a people renouncing ungodliness and worldly passions in every part of our lives? Are we demonstrating self-control in our words, our habits, and our thoughts on account of God's grace? If someone spent the next week with us, would that person come away with the impression that we are zealous for good works? An honest assessment will reveal areas in our lives where we have fallen short. We can all give thanks that God's grace is not dependent on our success. Rather, his grace is given to us precisely because of our failures. Where sin abounds, grace abounds all the more! But this free and abounding grace is not given to us so that we would rest content with our sin. God gives us grace to ignite our hearts in the passionate pursuit of holiness. If this is not true of us, then we need to go back for more training in the grace of God. In this passage, Moses gives us at least three reasons why God's covenant people should be passionately pursuing holiness.

God's Covenant People Must Passionately Pursue Holiness Because of What Sin Does

In Deuteronomy 6, Moses was calling God's people to devote themselves to him and to teach their children to do the same because of what God had done for them. Deuteronomy 7 continues that theme by explaining how they are to live in the land. The first thing that they are to do when they enter the land is to kill everyone:

> When the LORD your God brings you into the land that you are entering to take possession of it, and clears away many nations before you, the Hittites, the Girgashites, the Amorites, the Canaanites, the Perizzites, the Hivites, and the Jebusites, seven nations more numerous and mightier than you, and when the LORD your God gives them over to you, and you defeat them, then you must devote them to complete destruction. You shall make no covenant with them and show no mercy to them. (Deut. 7:1–2)

We addressed the issue of destroying entire populations back in Deuteronomy 2 and 3. Recall that Israel is being used by God as an instrument of judgment upon these people, whose practices were exceptionally wicked. Israel is to destroy the people living in Canaan, not because of their ethnicity or even their religious beliefs, but because of their wickedness. Furthermore, Deuteronomy is clear that if the people of Israel go after other gods and practice the same kinds of wickedness that these nations were practicing, they too would be devoted to destruction and removed from the land (Deut. 13:12–16).

What does the command to "devote them to complete destruction" mean? Christopher Wright reasons that "it is an absolute and irrevocable *renouncing* of things or persons, a refusal to take any gain or profit from them."[1] Wright believes that Israel could keep this command without literally destroying every person. If that is true, then the command to avoid intermarriage makes more sense. If everyone in these cities were killed, the prohibition against marrying them would appear superfluous.

While Wright makes a valid point, it is difficult to escape the conclusion that God is calling for the literal destruction of the entire people.[2] Marriage is prohibited, lest the Israelites think they can marry ones they have spared from destruction, contrary to God's decree. The effect of such marriages between God's people and idol worshipers would be disastrous, as we read in Deuteronomy 7:3–4: "You shall not intermarry with them, giving your daughters to their sons or taking their daughters for your sons, for they would turn away your sons from following me, to serve other gods. Then the

1. Christopher Wright, *Deuteronomy*, NIBC: Old Testament 4 (Hendrickson, 2007), 109.

2. For a discussion of various views in traditional and modern critical Jewish exegesis, see Jeffrey H. Tigay, *Deuteronomy*, JPSTC (Jewish Publication Society, 1996), 470–72.

anger of the Lord would be kindled against you, and he would destroy you quickly." This is not a prohibition against marrying people because they are from a different culture or race. Despite what some have believed through the ages, the Bible does not prohibit cross-cultural or interracial marriage. What the Bible does explicitly forbid is cross-religious marriages for God's people. The warning is clear: marry idol worshipers, and more likely than not, we will become idol worshipers. Sin ensnares. God's people are to make no peace with sin, and they are to make no covenants with idolaters because otherwise, in all likelihood, they will be led astray. Israel's history proves it repeatedly, with King Solomon as a prime example. First Kings 11:1–4 tells us:

> Now King Solomon loved many foreign women, along with the daughter of Pharaoh: Moabite, Ammonite, Edomite, Sidonian, and Hittite women, from the nations concerning which the Lord had said to the people of Israel, "You shall not enter into marriage with them, neither shall they with you, for surely they will turn away your heart after their gods." Solomon clung to these in love. . . . And his wives turned away his heart. For when Solomon was old his wives turned away his heart after other gods, and his heart was not wholly true to the Lord his God, as was the heart of David his father.

Take heed: Solomon's heart turned away when he was old. The effect of being in close partnership with idolaters over time was that he too eventually went after idols. Solomon was wiser than any of us, and even so celebrated a believer could not keep his heart from becoming ensnared by his partnership with idolaters. Why do we think it would be different for us?

If we have been walking with Jesus for years, we have likely seen a Christian fall in love with and get married to a non-Christian. In some occasional situations, the Christian leads the non-Christian to faith in Jesus. But more frequently, the Christian abandons his or her first love. God graciously warns his people not to yoke ourselves so intimately with nonbelieving persons, lest we be led astray.

The people of Israel were not to marry idolaters. Instead, they were to destroy all the traces of idolatry left in the land: "But thus shall you deal with them: you shall break down their altars and dash in pieces their pillars and chop down their Asherim and burn their carved images with fire" (Deut.

7:5). When the Israelites entered the promised land, they were to destroy the idolaters, avoid making covenants with them, and destroy all the remnants of their idolatry, lest they be ensnared by their sin. What do such drastic and violent measures have to do with people like us today?

We know that sin, particularly idolatry, still ensnares today. Yet we are not called to execute judgment on idolaters, as the nation of Israel was at that time in redemptive history. Nor are we to go out and destroy the idols that others have made. Neither Jesus nor the apostles did this, though idolatry and abominable practices were rife in their day. Rather, we are called to proclaim the good news of forgiveness of the sin of idolatry (and every other sin) to all peoples. But simply because we are not called to execute idolaters or smash their idols does not mean that we should think of sin as any less ensnaring today than it was then. While we are not called to put people to death, we are called to put sin to death. Where we see sin in our own lives, we must make no peace with it and show it no mercy. The apostle Paul commands a particular kind of violence in Colossians 3:5–6: "Put to death therefore what is earthly in you: sexual immorality, impurity, passion, evil desire, and covetousness, which is idolatry. On account of these the wrath of God is coming." The Puritan John Owen famously wrote, "Be killing sin, or sin will be killing you."[3] If we do not continually put sin to death by the Spirit, sin will be killing us. Our hearts are like a giant farm filled with trees and brush. A farmer cannot grow crops amid trees and brush. These must be cleared. If the farmer does not continually clear them, the trees and brush will eventually take over again. So it is with sin in the heart of the Christian. We must continually be clearing the heart of sin by the power of the Spirit.

Additionally, we must beware of close partnerships with nonbelievers, lest we be led astray into idolatry. Paul writes in 2 Corinthians 6:14: "Do not be unequally yoked with unbelievers. For what partnership has righteousness with lawlessness? Or what fellowship has light with darkness?" We are God's people, and as such we are not to yoke ourselves in close partnership with those who do not serve him. This includes marriage, but it may also include business or legal partnerships and other kinds of long-term binding relationships. To ignore this command is to expose ourselves to the ensnaring power of idolatry. We must passionately pursue holiness because sin ensnares.

3. John Owen, *The Mortification of Sin in Believers* (Religious Tract Society, 1799), 9.

God's Covenant People Must Passionately Pursue Holiness Because of Who We Are

Moses' explanation for why the Israelites are not to engage in the idolatry of the peoples they are driving out is found starting in verse 6 of Deuteronomy 7. He will explain that God's people are a consecrated people, a chosen people, and a covenanted people. He writes in verse 6, "For you are a people holy to the Lord your God." The opening word "For" (*kî*) indicates that he is now giving the reason for the preceding commands. The first reason is that they are a consecrated, or holy, people.[4] The primary idea of holiness is separation and distinctness. In this context, "holy to the Lord" refers to the fact that they have been "set apart" for him. But to be "set apart" for him also entails an expectation to live distinctively as those set apart. Moses expands on this in Leviticus 20:26: "You shall be holy to me, for I the Lord am holy and have separated you from the peoples, that you should be mine." They were set apart, or made holy, when God rescued them from Egypt, and they are to continue to live distinctly from the world in accordance with all of God's commands.[5] Likewise, Christians are made holy and set apart through the rescue of Jesus Christ and are also called to live as holy. Peter writes, "As obedient children, do not be conformed to the passions of your former ignorance, but as he who called you is holy, you also be holy in all your conduct" (1 Peter 1:14–15). We must pursue holiness because we are holy.

Second, God's people are a chosen people. Moses continues in Deuteronomy 7:6, "The Lord your God has chosen you to be a people for his treasured possession, out of all the peoples who are on the face of the earth." The word to describe Israel as God's "treasured possession" is *sĕgūllâ*. The word describes the private treasure of a king who owned everything but valued this private treasure as his prized possession.[6] As a child, I collected baseball cards. I had over a thousand cards at one point, all of which meant something to me. But my favorite baseball player at the time played third base for the Cincinnati Reds. His name was Chris Sabo. He was a good player, to be sure, but it would be hard to make the case that he was the best player on that early-1990s Cincinnati Reds team. Nevertheless, he was my favorite. I

4. The particular Hebrew phrase (*'am qādôš*) recurs in Deuteronomy 7:6; 14:2, 21; 26:19; 28:9.

5. D. G. Peterson, *NDBT*, s.v. "Holiness," 546.

6. Wright, *Deuteronomy*, 111.

literally, and inexplicably, loved him. While I valued all the baseball cards stuffed in my bottom drawer, I had a little velvet case that contained my most treasured possession: my Chris Sabo cards. They held a value for me that the others did not. I would give up all my other cards for those cards.

At a deeper and more profound level, we see God's posture toward his people. He owns everything, but among all that he has, he has chosen his people to be his treasured possession. He would give up everything else for them, including his only Son. This is the doctrine of unconditional election. Out of all the peoples of the earth, God chose Israel to be his treasured possession, special among all other people groups. God did not choose Israel on the basis of any conditions. The reason why God chose Israel is made clear in Deuteronomy 7:7–8:

> It was not because you were more in number than any other people that the LORD set his love on you and chose you, for you were the fewest of all peoples, but it is because the LORD loves you and is keeping the oath that he swore to your fathers, that the LORD has brought you out with a mighty hand and redeemed you from the house of slavery, from the hand of Pharaoh king of Egypt.

In other words, the reason why God chose Israel is that he loved Israel. What is more, the reason why he loved them is that he loved them. It was not because they kept his law or did anything else to deserve his love.[7] He simply set his love on them. According to Herman Bavinck: "The covenant relation did not depend on the observance of that law as an antecedent condition; it was not a covenant of works, but rested solely in God's electing love. It must, however, receive its proof and seal in conduct according to the Lord's law."[8]

We too have been chosen by God, not because of anything we have done, but unconditionally. He loved us because he loved us. We can say with Paul in Ephesians 1:3–5: "Blessed be the God and Father of our Lord Jesus Christ, who has blessed us in Christ with every spiritual blessing in the heavenly places, even as he chose us in him before the foundation of the world, that we should be holy and blameless before him. In love he predestined us for

7. Christopher J. H. Wright, *Old Testament Ethics for the People of God* (InterVarsity Press, 2004), 329.

8. Herman Bavinck, *Reformed Dogmatics*, ed. John Bolt, trans. John Vriend, vol. 3, *Sin and Salvation in Christ* (Baker Academic, 2008), 494.

adoption to himself as sons through Jesus Christ, according to the purpose of his will." We were chosen and predestined in love to be a holy people. Likewise, the apostle Peter takes this language that Moses uses to describe Israel, and he broadens it to include the whole church of Jewish and Gentile believers. He writes to Gentiles in 1 Peter 2:9–10:

> But you are a chosen race, a royal priesthood, a holy nation, a people for his own possession, that you may proclaim the excellencies of him who called you out of darkness into his marvelous light. Once you were not a people, but now you are God's people; once you had not received mercy, but now you have received mercy.

We too are a chosen race, a royal priesthood, a holy nation, a people for God's own possession. Our election carries definite implications: we are his people, that we might proclaim the excellencies of him who called us out of darkness into his marvelous light. We must pursue holiness because we were chosen by God for this purpose.

Third, God's people are a covenanted people. God entered various covenants with Israel, and Deuteronomy is a reminder and renewal of one of those covenants. As he calls the Israelites to holiness, he reminds them again of this fact in Deuteronomy 7:9–11:

> Know therefore that the LORD your God is God, the faithful God who keeps covenant and steadfast love with those who love him and keep his commandments, to a thousand generations, and repays to their face those who hate him, by destroying them. He will not be slack with one who hates him. He will repay him to his face. You shall therefore be careful to do the commandment and the statutes and the rules that I command you today.

God reminds them as people in covenant with him that there is extraordinary blessing for those who are faithful to his covenant, and tremendous disaster for those who break it. The sign of that covenant was circumcision. Circumcision was a reminder to the adults of what God had done for them in making them holy, and a promise to the children that he would do the same for them. As Christians, we are no longer under the Mosaic covenant, and we do not practice circumcision as God's covenant sign. But we are a covenanted people under the terms of the new covenant, and the sign of this covenant is baptism. We apply this sign to believers as a picture of all that God has done for us by grace through faith, and it also serves as a reminder of the new life in which we are to walk. We apply the sign to our children (as Israel did) to hold out the promise to them and invite them to embrace their call to be God's covenant people through faith in Jesus. To embrace God's covenant through faith in Jesus leads to blessing beyond measure, but to reject his covenant promises is to embrace a curse that endures forever. We who have been baptized into God's covenant family must pursue holiness because we are a holy people, we are a chosen people, and we are a covenanted people.

God's Covenant People Must Passionately Pursue Holiness Because of Who God Is

We have already seen that God is holy and that therefore we too must be holy. As surely as we are a covenanted people, God is a covenant-keeping God. Observe the clear link between being careful to keep God's covenant and the extraordinary blessings that God will pour out on his people. Moses explains in Deuteronomy 7:12–13: "And because you listen to these rules and keep and do them, the Lord your God will keep with you the covenant and the steadfast love that he swore to your fathers. He will love you, bless you, and multiply you." As they keep God's covenant, God will keep his covenant promises to bless them.

The passage goes on to describe how God's love, blessing, and multiplication will manifest itself: health (Deut. 7:15), wealth (vv. 13–14), and victory (vv. 16, 20–24). We have an appropriate skepticism today when someone begins talking about God's will for our health, wealth, and prosperity. We refer to it as the *prosperity gospel.* The prosperity gospel is a false gospel. It claims that faith and a relationship with God are a means to earning wealth and prosperity. In the true gospel, God himself is the goal, and various forms of prosperity are sometimes a byproduct. Fundamentally, prosperity theology fails to explain why sometimes the righteous are barren (Luke 1:5–7), sometimes the faithful suffer sickness and calamity (Job 1–2), and sometimes the godliest are poor (Matt. 8:20; Acts 3:6; 2 Cor. 8:1–5). But in our zealous refutation of the prosperity gospel, we may sometimes diminish God's promises of blessing on his people. This passage is full of descriptions about the ways in which God will prosper his faithful people. Ordinarily, health and prosperity of various sorts do accompany holiness. We do not pursue holiness in order to receive these blessings, but we pursue holiness because of who we are and who God is. Then we trust God for his blessing without prescribing for him the shape that this blessing must take, trusting that our Father in heaven knows best what we need.

As the people of Israel go into the land and start going toe-to-toe with these various enemies, they may get scared, as we read in Deuteronomy 7:17: "If you say in your heart, 'These nations are greater than I. How can I dispossess them?'" There are giants living in the land after all! What are the people to do when they are fearful and lack confidence that they can win? They are not to be afraid, but they are to remember. Look at verses 18–21:

> You shall not be afraid of them but you shall remember what the LORD your God did to Pharaoh and to all Egypt, the great trials that your eyes saw, the signs, the wonders, the mighty hand, and the outstretched arm, by which the LORD your God brought you out. So will the LORD your God do to all the peoples of whom you are afraid. Moreover, the LORD your God will send hornets among them, until those who are left and hide themselves from you are destroyed. You shall not be in dread of them, for the LORD your God is in your midst, a great and awesome God.

When they are doubtful of their ability to overcome these enemies, they are to remember the extraordinary victory that God already gave them over the Egyptians. In addition, God promises to send hornets! The bottom line is that he is a great and awesome God who will be in their midst, and that is all they need to know.

In our own pursuit of holiness, we may find ourselves discouraged or overawed by the power or pervasiveness of the sin that remains in us. We may be tempted to make peace with certain sins or idols remaining in our lives for fear that we cannot put them to death. We may have made peace with some besetting sins long ago. But we cannot be at peace with sin in our lives, nor are we to be cowed by its seeming strength. Instead, like Israel, when we are timid or fearful, we must remember what God has done. The cure for timidity in the pursuit of holiness is to remember what God has done in Christ. As surely as God's defeat of the Egyptians could give the Israelites confidence that they could overcome any enemy with God in their midst, so also Christ's defeat of sin and death through his death and resurrection should give us confidence that we can put any remaining sin to death.

The God of the Bible is no mousy figure, passively hoping that things will turn out okay for his people as he watches with bated breath while history plays out. The God of the Bible is a Warrior, who goes to battle against the sin that easily ensnares us, against the false gods that quickly enthrall us, and he fights to set us free. That victory has already been accomplished at the cross for all who believe. We have been set free, as surely as Israel was. Now we must live as free. Those who have been set free by a holy God passionately pursue holiness because of what sin does, because of who we are, and because of who God is. If we are not passionately pursuing holiness today, one of two reasons is likely.

First, we may not have been set free. We may not have experienced the liberating power of Christ's salvation. We might protest that we are not enslaved to anything. But some people in Jesus' day said the same thing. We read in John 8:31–36:

> So Jesus said to the Jews who had believed him, "If you abide in my word, you are truly my disciples, and you will know the truth, and the truth will set you free." They answered him, "We are offspring of Abraham and have never been enslaved to anyone. How is it that you say, 'You will become free'?"
>
> Jesus answered them, "Truly, truly, I say to you, everyone who practices sin is a slave to sin. The slave does not remain in the house forever; the son remains forever. So if the Son sets you free, you will be free indeed."

Call upon Jesus and he will set you free, and you will be free. The fact is that none of God's people kept the terms of the covenant he made with Moses, and none deserved the blessings of that covenant. So God made a new covenant with Jesus. Jesus kept God's covenant perfectly. Now, through faith in him, we are joined to Jesus and share in all the blessings that God has promised. No blessing is denied to us in Christ.

The second reason that we may not be passionately pursuing holiness is that we have forgotten that we are free. John Murray writes: "To say to the slave who has not been emancipated, 'Do not behave as a slave' is to mock his enslavement. But to say the same to the slave who has been set free is the necessary appeal to put into effect the privileges and rights of his liberation."[9] So let me remind you of what the apostle Paul writes in Romans 6:1–12:

> Are we to continue in sin that grace may abound? By no means! How can we who died to sin still live in it? Do you not know that all of us who have been baptized into Christ Jesus were baptized into his death? We were buried therefore with him by baptism into death, in order that, just as Christ was raised from the dead by the glory of the Father, we too might walk in newness of life.
>
> For if we have been united with him in a death like his, we shall certainly be united with him in a resurrection like his. We know that our old self was crucified with him in order that the body of sin might be brought to nothing, so that we would no longer be enslaved to sin. For one who has died has been set free from sin. Now if we have died with Christ, we believe that we will also live with him. We know that Christ, being raised from the dead, will never die again; death no longer has dominion over him. For the death he died he died to sin, once for all, but the life he lives he lives to God. So you also must consider yourselves dead to sin and alive to God in Christ Jesus.
>
> Let not sin therefore reign in your mortal body, to make you obey its passions.

Brothers and sisters, we have been set free; therefore, let us passionately pursue holiness because of what sin does, because of who we are, and because of who God is.

9. Quoted in Jerry Bridges, *The Discipline of Grace: God's Role and Our Role in the Pursuit of Holiness* (NavPress, 1994), 74.

16

Remembering the Lessons of the Wilderness

Deuteronomy 8:1–20

And he humbled you and let you hunger and fed you with manna, which you did not know, nor did your fathers know, that he might make you know that man does not live by bread alone, but man lives by every word that comes from the mouth of the Lord. (Deut. 8:3)

In the classic Western *Shenandoah*, Jimmy Stewart stars as a Virginian farmer trying to keep his family out of the Civil War. In one famous scene, Jimmy's character has his children all gathered around him at the table. He indicates that they should all bow their heads, and then he prays: "Lord, we cleared this land, we plowed it, sowed it, and harvested it. We cooked the harvest. We wouldn't be here, we wouldn't be eatin', if we hadn't done it all ourselves. We worked dog-boned hard for every crumb and morsel, but we thank you just the same anyway, Lord, for the food we're about to eat. Amen." Clearly, the prayer was more to honor the wishes of his deceased wife than to honor the Lord.

As the movie progresses, a series of tragedies strike the family. One son is mistaken for a soldier and captured. Another son and his wife are murdered. A third son is shot. When the family is around the table again, there are four more empty seats when Stewart begins his ritual prayer. But this time as he prays it, his voice quivers and breaks when he gets to the line "if we hadn't done it all ourselves." It seems that the wilderness has brought him to the realization that he is not the master of his own destiny. He stops his prayer, gets up, and leaves, knowing that he needs to turn to the Lord. But he is not ready to do so.

Journeys in the wilderness have a way of exposing us and breaking down our pride and assertions of independence. It could be a health crisis that reveals to us that we are not as strong as we thought. It could be a child going astray that exposes our inability to control things. It could be a series of tragedies that leaves us gasping for breath. Yet as difficult as these experiences are, they tend to drive us to the Lord, and we discover that he is our Provider, our Protector, and our Sustainer. The wilderness either makes us or breaks us.[1] If it does not break us, it makes us stronger by bringing us to the end of ourselves, where we encounter God in a more profound way.

But this strengthening only serves to prepare us for the test that is even greater than the wilderness: the test of prosperity. The only place harder for God's people to flourish spiritually than the land of hardship is the land of plenty. Benjamin Franklin observed, "Success has ruined many a man." He is right. We have known people to go through extraordinary seasons of calamity, illness, or financial devastation, drawing nearer to the Lord, only to drift away when peace, health, or prosperity returned. It is one of the great challenges of our fallen condition: to continue to lean on the Lord when it is not apparent that we need him.

In Deuteronomy 8, Moses is preparing the people for that day when they will enter the promised land and have plenty of everything that they need. He tells them in this passage that the key to living faithfully in the land of plenty is to apply the lessons learned in the wilderness. The text appears to be designed with a chiastic structure. The effect of the chiasm is to highlight

1. Peter C. Craigie, *The Book of Deuteronomy*, NICOT (Eerdmans, 1976), 185.

the central message of the passage to give thanks to the Lord and not forget the lessons of the wilderness when they enter the promised land.[2]

Learn the Lessons of the Wilderness

Moses is warning the people about the danger of forgetting the Lord in the land of plenty. He writes in Deuteronomy 8:1, "The whole commandment that I command you today you shall be careful to do, that you may live and multiply, and go in and possess the land that the Lord swore to give to your fathers." It is fitting that he begins with a reminder to keep the commandments, which serve a twofold purpose in the life of God's people: "the commandments are the practical expression of awareness of God and serve to foster it."[3] Accompanying the command to keep the commandments is the promise of the people's flourishing and entering the promised land. But as they go in, Moses reminds them of some of the lessons of the wilderness that will be essential to remember if they are going to flourish in the future: God leads us in the wilderness to humble us, and God disciplines us there because he loves us.

First, God leads us in the wilderness to humble us. We read in Deuteronomy 8:2, "And you shall remember the whole way that the Lord your God has led you these forty years in the wilderness, that he might humble you, testing you to know what was in your heart, whether you would keep his commandments or not." The phrase "that he might humble you" conveys purpose and intention. The Israelites' wandering in the wilderness was not an accident. They were there because of their disobedience, but they were also there because God wanted to do something good in them. Namely, he wanted to humble them.[4] Not all our wilderness experiences are a consequence of our sin, but all our wilderness experiences are intended to humble us.

God humbles us in the wilderness by exposing our hearts. We saw in verse 2 reference to a test that God was carrying out on Israel in the wilderness. Why does God test people? One commentator writes, "Because humanity has free will, God does not know how people will act, and He therefore tests

2. See Christopher Wright, *Deuteronomy*, NIBC: Old Testament 4 (Hendrickson, 2007), 121.

3. Jeffrey H. Tigay, *Deuteronomy*, JPSTC (Jewish Publication Society, 1996), 92.

4. The same word translated "humble" is used three times in this chapter (Deut. 8:2, 3, 16), indicating that it is a significant theme.

them."[5] Yet God is omniscient, and he knows the end from the beginning. To say that God learns how people will act from a test is to deny his omniscience. But although God does not learn from the test, those who are being tested do. The people of Israel discover what is in their hearts, as do all of us who have come after them. The test brings to light what is hidden to all except God himself. What this test would reveal is whether they would keep God's commandments.

Naval officers sometimes refer to the "integrity of the hull." When a submarine comes out of dry dock, the first exercise is called a "sea trial," which takes the submarine to depth in the ocean to test the integrity of the hull. If it is compromised in any way, such as a poor weld, the stress from the increased pressure of deep water will inevitably expose that weakness.[6] Hard times function similarly to expose our weaknesses; if there is a crack, the wilderness will expose it. Israel's testing revealed many weaknesses. The people failed the test at Sinai when they made the golden calf (Ex. 32). They failed at Massah and Meribah when they grumbled and rebelled (17:7). They failed in the matter of Baal of Peor when they fell prey to seduction (Num. 25). The tests of the wilderness humbled the Israelites by exposing their fickle devotion and wandering hearts.

The Puritan Thomas Case writes of how God uses difficulties: "In affliction God reveals the unknown corruptions in the hearts of his people: what pride, impatience, unbelief, idolatry, distrust of God, murmuring, and unthankfulness. Sin lies very close and deep and is not easily discerned until the fire of affliction comes. The furnace discovers the dross."[7] Those who have prolonged illness or suffering know how that wilderness exposes hidden sin in their hearts. Even something so small as a traffic jam that makes us late can expose what is wrong with us. Such experiences show us that we are not in control, that we are limited, and, frequently, that we are not as mature as we thought we were.

God also humbles us in the wilderness by teaching us dependence. Moses explains in Deuteronomy 8:3: "And he humbled you and let you hunger and fed you with manna, which you did not know, nor did your fathers know,

5. Tigay, *Deuteronomy*, 92.

6. Tim Irwin, *Impact: Great Leadership Changes Everything* (BenBella Books, 2014), 79.

7. Thomas Case, "A Treatise of Afflictions," in *Select Works* (Soli Deo Gloria, 1993), 28–32, quoted in *Voices from the Past: Puritan Devotional Readings*, ed. Richard Rushing (Banner of Truth, 2009), 146.

that he might make you know that man does not live by bread alone, but man lives by every word that comes from the mouth of the Lord." *God* humbled the Israelites, and *God* let them hunger, and *God* fed them with manna. God was involved in each part of that lesson. What he intended (same intention word as in verse 2) to teach them was that "man does not live by bread alone." Israel's hunger in the wilderness was not an accident. It was part of God's intentional training, or discipline, of Israel as a people. What they were to learn from these forty years is that there are some things more important than food or material provision. As surely as they depended on God for the bread he provided in the wilderness, even more they depended on every word that God spoke.

Jesus quotes these words when Satan comes to test him during his forty days of fasting. Jesus' own experience in the wilderness is patterned after Israel's. Israel was God's son and spent forty years in the wilderness, while Jesus as God's Son spends forty days in the wilderness also being tested (Luke 4:1–2). Israel hungered and thirsted, and so does Jesus. Satan says to Jesus, "If you are the Son of God, command these stones to become loaves of bread" (Matt. 4:3). Satan is asking him in effect: "If you are God's Son, why should you be hungry? Why should you have any unmet needs?" This is at the heart of the Israelites' own temptation in the wilderness, wondering why they were hungry and thirsty and why they had left Egypt to begin with. We can be tempted to wonder the same thing: "If I am God's child, why do I not yet have my healing? Why is life so hard? Why do I have unmet needs?" The devil may tempt us to resent God, to live for our physical desires, or to seek to gratify them in some way contrary to his Word. But Jesus shows us a better way. Whereas the old Israel stumbles and fails the test, Christ, the new Israel, passes.[8]

Jesus shows us that obedience to God's commands is even more important than gratifying our own needs, even a need as essential as eating.[9] He declares in John 4:34, "My food is to do the will of him who sent me and to accomplish his work." Like Jesus, we must live our lives in dependence on God's Word. Bread, or the satisfaction of our physical or emotional needs, is not the chief thing we need for life. Rather, our chief priority is to do the Father's will. We

8. R. T. France, *The Gospel of Matthew*, New International Commentary on the New Testament (Eerdmans, 2007), 128.

9. France, 131.

depend on God for our food, but even more, we depend on him to show us the way to live. William Gurnall reminds us, "The Christian is bred by the Word, and he must be fed by it."[10] God is the one we depend on for our daily bread, both literally and spiritually. God leads us in the wilderness to humble us by exposing our hearts and teaching us our absolute dependence on him.

Second, God disciplines us in the wilderness because he loves us. We read of God's loving intention in discipline in Deuteronomy 8:5: "Know then in your heart that, as a man disciplines his son, the LORD your God disciplines you." The comparison is between how a man disciplines his son and how the Lord disciplines Israel. The word for "discipline" (*yāsar*) appears frequently throughout the Old Testament, and its Greek counterpart (*paideuō*) appears repeatedly in the New Testament. In some contexts, the word is used to describe instruction with regard to behavior (Isa. 28:26). Discipline goes beyond instruction, however, and also refers to warnings seeking to bring someone back when the person has gone astray from living faithfully to God's covenant (8:11). What is more, in some contexts, it refers to corrective discipline inflicted on someone who is not heeding those warnings (Ps. 39:11). Healthy discipline in the context of a parent-child relationship begins with instruction because it is necessary for children to know what is required of them. If a child is rebelling, or perhaps unknowingly going astray from instruction, then come warnings. If the child persists in going astray, then more corrective forms of discipline come that increase in severity until the child returns to the safe path. God says that this method is how he disciplines his people.

Parents discipline their children in order to protect them and to help them grow to maturity. They do that because they love their children. The ultimate motive of a parent's discipline of a child, and God's discipline of his children, is love. More light is given in Proverbs 3:11–12: "My son, do not despise the LORD's discipline or be weary of his reproof, for the LORD reproves him whom he loves, as a father the son in whom he delights." Sometimes the wilderness is imposed because we have gone astray and need correction as Israel did when the people refused to go up into the promised land at Kadesh-barnea. Sometimes the wilderness is simply a proving ground, as

10. Quoted in I. D. E. Thomas, comp., *The Golden Treasury of Puritan Quotations* (Banner of Truth, 1989), 32.

it was for Jesus as he was preparing to launch into his earthly ministry. But in any case, when we find ourselves in a wilderness experience, we should pause and intentionally remember that God has led us here to discipline us because he loves us.

Recently a friend of mine has been dealing with perpetual and inexplicable pain. For some time, she simply resisted it and tried to make the pain go away. Then someone else asked her, "Have you considered what God may be trying to teach you in this?" The pain is still real, but now her perspective on the wilderness experience has changed, and she is seeking God, not just healing. When we find ourselves in the wilderness, our first instinct is to get out as quickly as possible. Instead, we should humble ourselves before God by allowing him to expose our hearts and teach us dependence. Further, we can trust that this wilderness involves his loving discipline intended to either correct us or train us for what is to come. When the training is complete, we will be ready for the greater test, living in the land of plenty.

Apply the Lessons of the Wilderness in the Land of Plenty

God is bringing Israel out of the wilderness, where the pressure exposes the people's hearts and they are consciously dependent on God, into a land of plenty that seems to be the opposite. Listen to the description in verses 7–9 of Deuteronomy 8:

> For the Lord your God is bringing you into a good land, a land of brooks of water, of fountains and springs, flowing out in the valleys and hills, a land of wheat and barley, of vines and fig trees and pomegranates, a land of olive trees and honey, a land in which you will eat bread without scarcity, in which you will lack nothing, a land whose stones are iron, and out of whose hills you can dig copper.

They are coming into a kind of paradise where all their needs will be abundantly met. Notice that it is not a sin that they are prosperous. Nor is it a sin for us to be well-off. We do not have to feel any more guilty for prospering or for living in the land of plenty than Israel did. But we must be on guard. The temptations of the land of plenty are even more hazardous to our life with God than the wilderness.

Have we not seen this truth in our own lives? Can we not say with the psalmist, "Before I was afflicted I went astray, but now I keep your word" (Ps. 119:67)? How many of us turned to the Lord for the first time amid a wilderness of affliction, or turned back to him again in the wilderness? It may have been a job loss, a divorce, a defeat, an addiction that was untamable, a health crisis, or the loss of someone dear. There we discovered that what we most needed was not the satisfaction of our natural desires, but fellowship with the Lord, to hear his voice through his Word, and to walk in his ways. How often have we seen that when God brings us through that wilderness to a place of flourishing and abundance, we turn away from following him and go our own way? Likewise, we tend to think of criticism as being the hardest thing to handle in life or leadership. But criticism is not the true test. The true test is how we handle praise. The writer of Proverbs says, "The crucible is for silver, and the furnace is for gold, and a man is tested by his praise" (Prov. 27:21). Learning to handle criticism is a sort of wilderness that God uses to prepare us for the greater test of handling man's praise. The more successful we are, the wealthier we are, the more things are going our way, the stiffer our test and the more important it is for us to apply the lessons of the wilderness. How can we do that practically?

First, we apply the lessons of the wilderness by walking in obedience in the land of plenty. The discipline of the Lord in Deuteronomy 8:5 is directly linked to the call to obedience in verse 6: "So you shall keep the commandments of the LORD your God by walking in his ways and by fearing him." When we find ourselves in the land of plenty and we have what we need and life is going our way, then we need to be especially diligent to walk in God's ways and honor him. If we learn to keep God's commandments in the afflictions of the wilderness, we are far more likely to go on keeping his commandments in the land of plenty. If we are more preoccupied with our physical well-being than with obeying every word from the Lord, we too will perish.[11]

Second, we apply the lessons of the wilderness by practicing gratitude in the land of plenty. Moses describes what it will be like after God brings

11. Daniel I. Block, *Deuteronomy*, NIVAC (Zondervan, 2012), 237.

Israel into this amazing land in Deuteronomy 8:10: "And you shall eat and be full, and you shall bless the LORD your God for the good land he has given you." Grammatically, the phrase "you shall bless the LORD" can be a statement of what will be, or a commandment of what to do. The second interpretation (given in the ESV) is more likely correct. The call here is for Israel to explicitly bless the Lord (which in this case means to give thanks to him) to avoid falling into ingratitude and idolatry.[12] Giving thanks to God for the blessings we enjoy is one of the ways in which we keep his blessings from becoming our gods. It is also one of the primary ways that we keep from becoming prideful. We need to make gratitude a discipline because the more accustomed we are to enjoying the land of plenty, the more likely we are to take God's gifts for granted.

In the church I pastor, we have had many years of positive financial reports. Each time we gather as elders, we get an update. Each time, the news is good. We are in the land of plenty. When we get that kind of good news every month, it is easy for us to slip into thinking that things will always be like this or, even worse, that this is a result of our good leadership. So it has become our practice after every financial report to pause our meeting and intentionally thank God for his blessings. But we must discipline ourselves to do it. If our financial reports were showing that we do not have two nickels to rub together and may have to shut down, we would not have to be disciplined about seeking God. We would do that instinctively because we would have nowhere else to turn. The greater test is to seek God when all our needs are met. What is true for us as church leadership is true for all our churches and our families as well. Make it a discipline to practice gratitude and so avoid the pitfalls of an ungrateful heart in the land of plenty.

The third way that we apply the lessons of the wilderness in the land of plenty is by remembering the Lord. Moses warns in Deuteronomy 8:11, "Take care lest you forget the LORD your God." He is not talking about forgetting that God *exists* but is cautioning about forgetting that God *matters*. How can we know whether we have forgotten the Lord amid our prosperity? The passage shows us three clear signs that we have forgotten him.

The first sign of forgetting is disobedience. Deuteronomy 8:11 continues, "Take care lest you forget the LORD your God by not keeping his

12. Tigay, *Deuteronomy*, 94–95.

commandments and his rules and his statutes, which I command you today." The most obvious sign that we have forgotten the Lord is that we are living as though he were not there. The more we disregard his commandments, the more we forget him.

The second sign of forgetting is pride. Verses 12–14 of Deuteronomy 8 continue:

> lest, when you have eaten and are full and have built good houses and live in them, and when your herds and flocks multiply and your silver and gold is multiplied and all that you have is multiplied, then your heart be lifted up, and you forget the LORD your God, who brought you out of the land of Egypt, out of the house of slavery.

When we are full and wealthy and satisfied in the land of plenty, our hearts will be lifted up as we forget the Lord. In Deuteronomy 8:15–16, Moses reminds the people of all that God has done for them, from their rescue from slavery to giving them food and water in the wilderness. If they forget what God did for them, they will become prideful. This is what it sounds like: "My power and the might of my hand have gotten me this wealth" (Deut. 8:17). We may not say it out loud, but in our hearts we believe that the abundant and good life we enjoy is our own doing. If we find ourselves unwilling to share with others, it may be a sign that we believe that our own power and might have gotten us our wealth. If we are reluctant to give to God's people and God's mission, it is a likely sign that we believe that our own power and might have resulted in our wealth. If we look down on people who have not been as diligent and successful as we have, and we have no compassion for those who suffer poverty, we likely believe that we are primarily responsible for our blessings. To be sure, our hard work, good decision making, and wise investing have likely all made a difference. But remember verse 18: "You shall remember the LORD your God, for it is he who gives you power to get wealth, that he may confirm his covenant that he swore to your fathers, as it is this day." It was God who gave us our parents, put us in the places where we were born, and gave us our brains, our emotional intelligence, our ability to delay gratification, our network of friends, a favorable economy, and the breath we have required at each step along the way. These are just a few examples, but remembering these things helps save us from the pride that flourishes in the land of plenty and tends to wither in the wilderness.

The third sign of forgetting is idolatry. We read in Deuteronomy 8:19–20: "And if you forget the LORD your God and go after other gods and serve them and worship them, I solemnly warn you today that you shall surely perish. Like the nations that the LORD makes to perish before you, so shall you perish, because you would not obey the voice of the LORD your God." We can be sure that we have forgotten the Lord when we go after other gods, such as money, success, comfort, and security, or when we put concerns for our physical needs above our spiritual needs, or when we disregard God's commands because we want something else more than to obey him. This passage is a warning that if Israel or we pursue other gods, Israel or we will perish as surely as the Canaanites did.

If we are in the wilderness today, let us humble ourselves before God and learn what God is teaching us. We must not be afraid to have our sin exposed, but rather know that through faith in the blood of Christ, all our sins are taken away. We may confess them to God freely, and freely receive fresh grace for today. We also must not fear that we are in this wilderness because God hates us or wants to ruin us. We are his beloved children, and he is using this wilderness to train us for that which is still to come. Christ has gone into the ultimate wilderness for us on the cross, he has borne all the judgment that our sins deserve, and the blows we receive in this life can be nothing other than our Father's loving care. Even if our wilderness may last the rest of this earthly life, we know that a new creation is coming where the wilderness will be no more.

Finally, let us take heart in the words that Moses used to remind Israel. God brought his people through the wilderness, according to Deuteronomy 8:16, "that he might humble you and test you, to do you good in the end." God's intention in the humbling and testing is to do good to his people in the end. It may not feel like that in the middle of the wilderness, but it will be clear in the end.

For those of us who find ourselves in the land of plenty, let us be especially diligent to heed and obey all of God's good commands. Let us practice gratitude and make it a discipline so that pride can find no safe haven in our hearts. Let us remember the Lord, lest we be tempted to disobey, to become prideful, or to go after idols. Though God may have blessed us with many things, there is only one thing that we truly need: him. Jesus declared:

> "It was not Moses who gave you the bread from heaven, but my Father gives you the true bread from heaven. For the bread of God is he who comes down from heaven and gives life to the world." They said to him, "Sir, give us this bread always."
>
> Jesus said to them, "I am the bread of life; whoever comes to me shall not hunger, and whoever believes in me shall never thirst." (John 6:32–35)

In the wilderness, or in the land of plenty, may this be our prayer: give me Jesus.

17

Memory: The Pride-Crusher

Deuteronomy 9:1–24

Know, therefore, that the Lord *your God is not giving you this good land to possess because of your righteousness, for you are a stubborn people. Remember and do not forget how you provoked the* Lord *your God to wrath in the wilderness.* (Deut. 9:6–7)

Imagine that you never forgot anything. At first, it sounds great. We would never lose our keys or forget someone's name or what we were trying to say. But having a memory that never forgets anything could also have its challenges. We know this because around sixty people in the world have a condition referred to as *highly superior autobiographical memory* (HSAM) and they remember almost everything. Jill Price is one of those people. In her fifties at the time of this writing, Jill can recall in vivid detail every single day of her life since 1980. She remembers what day of the week it was, where she was, who she was with, and what she was doing. Ask her what she was doing on August 29, 1980, and she will tell you, "It was a Friday, I went to Palm Springs with my friends, twins, Nina and Michelle, and their family for Labour Day weekend." Ask her when she drove a car for the third time and she will say: "The third time I drove a car was January 10, 1981. Saturday. Teen Auto. That's where we used to get our driving lessons from." When did she first hear Rick Springfield sing "Jessie's Girl"? Answer: "March 7, 1981." She was driving in a car with her mother, who was yelling at her.[1]

Most people consider Jill's condition to be a great gift. She considers it a burden. Though she has an amazing ability to remember good times, she can also remember every insult, every bad decision, every humiliating thing that has ever happened to her. She sometimes feels paralyzed and assaulted by these memories.[2] I wonder whether she also feels humbled by them. Most of us carry around a favorable opinion of ourselves. Part of the reason is that we forget most of our past thoughts, desires, and actions. What would we think of ourselves if we could remember them all perfectly? It is likely that such a memory would crush our pride.

In Deuteronomy 9, Moses does not call the people of Israel to remember every sinful and rebellious thing they have ever been guilty of, but he does call them to remember some of the lowlights. He calls them to remember just enough of them to protect them from one of the deadliest perils for God's people: the peril of pride and self-righteousness. The inherent danger in being the chosen people of God is that we begin to believe that we are chosen because of something good in us. We may start to think that there is something inherently better in us than others, and that we were chosen by God for a reason found in us. This kind of pride and self-righteousness not only is offensive to God and others, but robs us of the joys of knowing God's love and grace. It is this attitude that we see so prevalently displayed in the Pharisees of Jesus' day. It is this attitude that we still see creeping up in ourselves when we spend more time judging others than judging ourselves; when we see the sins of others more easily than our own; when we are less forgiving of others than we are of ourselves. Moses calls the people to "know" (Deut. 9:6) that it is not because of them that they are God's people. He further calls them to "remember and do not forget" (v. 7) the ways in

1. Linda Rodriguez McRobbie, "Total Recall: The People Who Never Forget," *Guardian*, February 8, 2017, https://www.theguardian.com/science/2017/feb/08/total-recall-the-people-who-never-forget, accessed February 4, 2022.

2. Joshua Harris, *Dug Down Deep: Unearthing What I Believe and Why It Matters* (Multnomah, 2010), 101.

which they explicitly do not deserve their favored position. As he does so, he also gives us two things that we ought to remember that keep pride at bay so that our joy might be full.

God Blesses Us Not for Reasons Found in Us, but for Reasons Found in Him

The whole passage we are considering is predicated on the events described in Deuteronomy 9:1–3. We will not revisit those verses here because we have seen their content elsewhere, but they remind us that God is going to bring the people of Israel into the promised land. There they will face the giants, the sons of the Anakim, who live in fortified cities that the people of Israel fear. But verse 3 explains what they need to know: "Know therefore today that he who goes over before you as a consuming fire is the Lord your God. He will destroy them and subdue them before you. So you shall drive them out and make them perish quickly, as the Lord has promised you." God will bless them with the victory over their enemies, and even though they have not yet stepped foot into the land, the victory is as good as done.

But now Moses turns his attention to a problem that will be even more challenging for the people to overcome than the sons of the Anakim: the problem of pride and self-righteousness. They will be tempted to believe that the reason for their success is in them, on account of their own righteousness. So Moses cuts them off at the pass in Deuteronomy 9:4: "Do not say in your heart, after the Lord your God has thrust them out before you, 'It is because of my righteousness[3] that the Lord has brought me in to possess this land,' whereas it is because of the wickedness of these nations that the Lord is driving them out before you."[4] It would be a very dangerous miscalculation to think that because the Israelites were God's instrument of judgment on

3. The Hebrew word is typically translated "righteousness." In this instance, it may refer specifically to loyalty or devotion. This meaning is attested elsewhere and would also be suggested by the fact that the rest of the chapter demonstrates the ways that Israel has not been loyal. See Jeffrey H. Tigay, *Deuteronomy*, JPSTC (Jewish Publication Society, 1996), 97.

4. The Hebrew text of this verse is somewhat ambiguous, and it is difficult to determine the reasons given in the heart for why God is giving the Israelites the land. In our ESV text, the reason given is the Israelites' righteousness. But some scholars (e.g., Tigay and Wright) believe that all of Deuteronomy 9:4 should be included in what the people of Israel say in their hearts. In that case, it would read like this: "it is because of my righteousness and their wickedness that God is driving out the nations." Ultimately, the meaning is not significantly altered either way.

the people of Canaan, this meant that they themselves were righteous.[5] The reasons for Israel's coming victory over the Canaanites was not to be found in the people themselves, but in God: "Not because of your righteousness or the uprightness of your heart are you going in to possess their land, but because of the wickedness of these nations the LORD your God is driving them out from before you, and that he may confirm the word that the LORD swore to your fathers, to Abraham, to Isaac, and to Jacob" (Deut. 9:5).

Two reasons are given for Israel's upcoming victory: God's justice and God's faithfulness. God is going to execute his justice against the wicked people living in the land, but this does not mean that Israel is righteous. Later in Israel's history, the prophet Habakkuk is going to have a hard time with the reverse of this. God will raise up the Assyrians to come and judge Israel, and Habakkuk complains that the Assyrians are not righteous. God answers the complaint and tells him that he will then raise up Babylon to judge Assyria. God can use unjust and wicked people to execute perfect justice.

There is also an implicit warning in this passage against equating military superiority with moral superiority. As Americans, we have been historically inclined to believe that when we wage war on another nation, we do so because we are morally superior. Or we may be tempted to think that another nation is more deserving of judgment than we are. But this passage should give us pause before we make such evaluations. War is sometimes necessary, but our posture as Christians in a nation at war should be a very humble and circumspect one. God has little patience with moral grandstanding.[6]

The second reason found in God for why his people will have victory is found in his faithfulness. God promised the patriarchs that he would give them the land, which he will. This is not because they deserve it, but because he promised, and he is faithful to deliver on his promise. When we put God's justice and faithfulness together, we can observe that God is not giving the Israelites what they deserve when he gives them the land. The land is a gift of grace in fulfillment of a promise because of God's faithfulness. At the same time, the removal of the Canaanites from the land is a demonstration of God's justice in which he is giving those people precisely what they do

5. Christopher Wright, *Deuteronomy*, NIBC: Old Testament 4 (Hendrickson, 2007), 131.
6. See Wright, 134.

deserve. God's gifts to us are given not because we are good, but because he is good.

We may think that when we receive good things in this life, we are getting what we deserve, and that when we experience hard things, we are getting what we do not deserve. But in fact, the good things we enjoy are gifts of God's grace. That is why in our successes, we should not boast as though it is primarily because of us that we have succeeded. Meanwhile, the hard things that we suffer and experience, as hard as they may be, are far less than we deserve. If we believe what the Bible tells us about our fallen and rebellious condition by nature, and that the least sin and rebellion against God is deserving of eternal punishment in hell, then we should be very slow to complain against God for any hardships we do experience. As challenging or heartbreaking as they may be, they are far less than what we would be experiencing if God dealt with us on the basis of justice alone. How we respond to hardship and trial will reveal much to us about what we think we deserve from God. The same is true for how we respond to success.

All of this can be applied to our understanding of our own salvation. When God brings us into a relationship with Christ, our posture is not one of saying, "Of course he did," as though the reason for his grace were in us. Rather, it is one of saying, "Can you believe this!?" because we know that the reason must be in him. Some friends at my church once brought me as their guest to an event hosted by the Fellowship of Christian Athletes. I did not deserve to be at the head table, but I was there because my friends had given me a gift. Seated next to me at the head table was Heisman-winning quarterback Tim Tebow. I can assure you that I was not thinking, "Of course Tim Tebow is sitting beside me." I was thinking: "Holy cow! Tim Tebow is sitting beside *me*!" I did not deserve to be sitting at that table with Tim Tebow; it was a gift. So also, when we find ourselves at Christ's table, we should not say, "Of course I deserve to be here." Rather, we exclaim: "Can you believe this? What a gift!" As Charles Wesley put it so well centuries ago: "And can it be that I should gain an int'rest in the Savior's blood? Died he for me, who caused his pain? For me, who him to death pursued? Amazing love! How can it be that thou, my God, shouldst die for me?"[7]

7. Charles Wesley, "And Can It Be That I Should Gain" (1738).

GOD BLESSES US NOT BECAUSE OF OUR RIGHTEOUSNESS, BUT DESPITE OUR SIN

Moses has established that the reason for the people's success was to be found not in themselves but in God. Now he goes on to show that not only is their victory not a result of their righteousness, it is a gift given despite their sin. Moses states in Deuteronomy 9:6–7:

> Know, therefore, that the LORD your God is not giving you this good land to possess because of your righteousness, for you are a stubborn people. Remember and do not forget how you provoked the LORD your God to wrath in the wilderness. From the day you came out of the land of Egypt until you came to this place, you have been rebellious against the LORD.

Not only are they not getting the land because of their righteousness, they are getting it despite their sinfulness.

There is something else to notice in these verses. If God is driving out the Canaanites on account of their pagan wickedness, we might expect to get a catalogue of all of the Canaanites' sins. But the sins of the pagans are not what the people of God need to remember. Instead of getting a list of examples of the wickedness of the Canaanites, we get a catalogue of the sins of God's people. We are taught by this that we should be far more concerned with our own sins and failures than we are with those of the pagan world around us. When we focus on the sins of the world around us, we tend to get self-righteous and become very ineffective at reaching the world with the gospel, or even grasping the gospel ourselves. But when we keep our focus on the ways that we have been unfaithful, our posture toward the world is humble and winsome.

In Deuteronomy 9:7, Moses gives two commands: "Remember and do not forget," which are two ways of saying the same thing with emphasis. Why is it so important that the Israelites remember and do not forget how they repeatedly provoked the Lord to wrath? It seems a little morbid and unhealthy to us to reflect on our past failures. Indeed, it can be so. When we wallow in the guilt of sin that has already been forgiven, we rob ourselves of the joy of the gospel. I do not believe that Moses is calling them to wallow in the guilt of sins forgiven, but believe that he is calling them to remember sins committed, lest they think more highly of themselves than they ought when they experience success and possess the land. It is a call to remember not only what they are capable of, but what they have actually done. The memory of sins committed, the memory of rebellion, and the memory of our stubbornness should serve to crush our pride.

The people of Israel are told that they have been rebellious from the beginning, from the day they came out of Egypt. Moses mentions five instances of their sinfulness, though he spends the majority of the time on the first one. Let us consider these five instances and what they can show us about how God blesses his people, not because of our righteousness, but despite our sin.

First, there is Horeb.[8] After God brought the people out of slavery in Egypt, he brought them to Horeb, where he gave them his law, that they might learn to live as his holy people. Moses went up onto the mountain for forty days and nights to receive the law from God. While he was up there, God spoke to him. We read in Deuteronomy 9:12: "Then the LORD said to me, 'Arise, go down quickly from here, for your people whom you have brought from Egypt have acted corruptly. They have turned aside quickly out of the way that I commanded them; they have made themselves a metal image.'" The metal image was the golden calf. Right after God saved them, before the dust on the freshly carved tablets of the covenant had blown away, the people of Israel were already breaking God's commands and worshiping an idol. Moses recalls in verses 15–17:

> So I turned and came down from the mountain, and the mountain was burning with fire. And the two tablets of the covenant were in my two hands. And I looked, and behold, you had sinned against the LORD your God. You had made yourselves a golden calf. You had turned aside quickly from the way that the LORD had commanded you. So I took hold of the two tablets and threw them out of my two hands and broke them before your eyes.

The breaking of the tablets on which the Ten Commandments were written not only expressed Moses' anger at the Israelites' egregious sin, but also had

8. The whole incident can be found in Exodus 32–34. Small discrepancies between the Exodus account and what we see here in Deuteronomy are easily accounted for by considering that the account in Deuteronomy is an abbreviated sermonic retelling with a particular aim.

legal significance. In Mesopotamian law, the cancellation of a contract was signified by breaking the clay tablets that it was written on, much as we might tear up legal documents today. When Moses smashed the tablets, he was communicating that the covenant between the suzerain God and his vassal people was annulled; relations were severed.[9]

But God in his grace, and in response to the intercession of Moses, willingly entered into covenant with the people once again, as we will see in the next chapter. God constituted them as his people not because they were faithful, but despite their unfaithfulness. But what about us? Have we ever been guilty of idolatry? Timothy Keller helpfully defines *idolatry* as "anything more important to you than God, anything that absorbs your heart and imagination more than God, anything you seek to give you what only God can give."[10] This means that idols can be our family, a relationship, a hobby, money, or a career. Let us remember the things we have put before God, what we have valued more than we have valued him, and let the remembrance of such foolishness humble our proud hearts.

Next, there is Taberah. In Deuteronomy 9:22, Moses mentions several place names: "At Taberah also, and at Massah and at Kibroth-hattaavah you provoked the LORD to wrath." "Taberah" refers to the events described in Numbers 11:1: "And the people complained in the hearing of the LORD about their misfortunes, and when the LORD heard it, his anger was kindled, and the fire of the LORD burned among them." God has rescued them from slavery and blessed them with his presence, yet they are still complaining. This kind of discontent against the Lord is sin. We count it a small thing even today to grumble about our circumstances and misfortunes, but look how it provokes God's wrath! I am embarrassed to say it, but my nickname as a child was "Whine-O." Sadly, I have made only marginal progress since then. The blessings that we enjoy come to us not because we are good, but despite our rebellion.

Third, there is Massah. The events of Massah are described in Exodus 17. We read in verses 2–3 that "the people quarreled with Moses and said, 'Give us water to drink.' And Moses said to them, 'Why do you quarrel with me? Why do you test the LORD?' But the people thirsted there for water, and the

9. Tigay, *Deuteronomy*, 100.

10. Timothy Keller, *Counterfeit Gods: The Empty Promises of Money, Sex, and Power, and the Only Hope That Matters* (Dutton, 2009), xvii.

people grumbled against Moses and said, 'Why did you bring us up out of Egypt, to kill us and our children and our livestock with thirst?'" Their fear over their physical needs led them to grumble against their spiritual leader and accuse him of intending their harm. Additionally, despite God's faithfulness to provide for them, they questioned his ability and willingness to provide what they needed. Have we ever found ourselves testing the Lord this way? In tough times, have we questioned his ability to provide what we have needed? Have we ever allowed our fears to make us quarrelsome? Have we ever accused God of intending to do us harm? Massah reminds us that it is not because of our righteousness but despite our sins that we experience God's blessings.

Fourth is Kibroth-hattaavah. "Kibroth-hattaavah" literally means "graves of craving." In Numbers 11, we learn that it is called by this name because this is where the people who had the craving for meat were buried. We read in Numbers 11:4–6:

> Now the rabble that was among them had a strong craving. And the people of Israel also wept again and said, "Oh that we had meat to eat! We remember the fish we ate in Egypt that cost nothing, the cucumbers, the melons, the leeks, the onions, and the garlic. But now our strength is dried up, and there is nothing at all but this manna to look at."

Of course, having a craving for meat is not in itself a bad thing. On the surface it is simply a complaint about food, but underneath it is a rejection of God's plans and a yearning to go back to slavery in Egypt. Have we ever found ourselves complaining about God's intentions for us, saying in the words of singer Sara Groves, "I've been painting pictures of Egypt, leaving out what it lacks; the future feels so hard and I want to go back"?[11] Have we experienced a craving for the things we left behind when we began to follow Christ? I have. Those cravings remind me that the blessings I enjoy today have been given not because of anything good in me, but despite the wrong that remains in me.

Finally, there is Kadesh-barnea. We considered Kadesh-barnea earlier

11. Sara Groves, "Painting Pictures of Egypt," SaraGroves.com, https://www.saragroves.com/song-lyrics/painting-pictures-of-egypt, accessed February 4, 2022.

in Deuteronomy. Moses relates in Deuteronomy 9:23–24: "And when the LORD sent you from Kadesh-barnea, saying, 'Go up and take possession of the land that I have given you,' then you rebelled against the commandment of the LORD your God and did not believe him or obey his voice. You have been rebellious against the LORD from the day that I knew you." It was to be the launching-off point for the conquest of the promised land, but the people were filled with fear and did not believe that God could do what he had promised. So they refused to go up and fight to possess what God had promised to deliver. Have we ever been hesitant to trust God's promises and move forward in obedience to his clear commands? Have we ever allowed the giants and obstacles before us to loom larger in our vision than God himself and his promises? Have we rebelled against his clear purposes? Yes, we have.

Like Israel, the blessings we enjoy are ours not because of our righteousness, but despite our sinfulness. This is all to the praise of God's glorious grace! The Puritan Thomas Goodwin writes, "The freedom of grace, and so the excellency of it in that particular, is shewn in this, that there is not only no worthiness, but nothing but unworthiness."[12] Not only is there nothing worthy in us to deserve God's grace, but there are only reasons why we should not receive it! And yet what does grace say? Goodwin goes on: "Grace comes with a sovereignty, and saith, Though he be stiff-necked, though he be obstinate, yet . . . 'I have seen his ways, and I will heal him.' I see he will never be better, I must mend him myself. This is the language of grace."[13] God has done this for us in giving Christ Jesus as our Savior and Lord.

We need to remember this. We do not remember our sin to glamorize it, nor do we remember it to wallow in our misery, but we remember it to bring about an appropriate level of self-loathing.[14] As Ezekiel writes, "Then you will remember your evil ways, and your deeds that were not good, and you will loathe yourselves for your iniquities and your abominations" (Ezek. 36:31). Too often we water down our sins. We minimize them. We shift the blame to others for them. We compare them with other people's sins and decide

12. Thomas Goodwin, *The Works of Thomas Goodwin*, vol. 2 (Tanski, 1996), 290–91.

13. Goodwin, 2:290–91.

14. "When we remember sin to renew our love to it,—that is damnable; but when we remember it to loathe it, and to loathe ourselves for it,—that is saving." Richard Steele, "Sermon XIV: What Are the Hinderances and Helps to a Good Memory in Spiritual Things?," in *Puritan Sermons 1659–1689 in Six Volumes* (Richard Owen Roberts, 1981), 3:350.

that we are not so bad. When we do that, we water down our grief over them. We also water down the gospel and, in turn, our joy in God's love and our astonishment at what he has done for us. Jack Miller writes, "When you are shocked by your sins and shocked by God's love in Christ, then you will be full of joy—joy you will want to share with others."[15] We remember our sins not in order to feel guilty over them again, but to be freshly humbled by the grace of God given to us in Christ, which is an effective deterrent against the pride and self-righteousness that rob us of joy.

The Scottish pastor-theologian James Denney had framed in his church vestry these words: "No man can bear witness to Christ and to himself at the same time. No man can give the impression that he himself is clever and that Christ is mighty to save."[16] As it was with Israel, so it is with us. We must either bear witness to the sovereign grace of God in our salvation or bear witness to ourselves and our goodness, but we cannot do both. As one of the old Puritan prayers puts it, "The memory of my great sins, my many temptations, my falls, bring afresh into my mind the remembrance of thy great help, of thy support from heaven, of the great grace that saved such a wretch as I am."[17]

One of the results of the fact that we are all sinners is that we all are inclined to forget our sins and to remember our good, with the effect that we forget the gospel and become proud and self-righteous. These are two qualities that God detests in his people. At the same time, we have an amazing ability to remember other people's sins and to forget their good. This also makes us even more proud and self-righteous. One of the evidences that we are being transformed by the grace of God is that we become increasingly mindful of our own sins, while becoming more forgetful of the sins of others. As we are transformed, we become increasingly humble ourselves and gracious toward others, while pride and self-righteousness melt away in the light of the gospel, making way for joy to abound.

Moses makes it very clear: despite the Israelites' rebelliousness, God gave them victory. They were going to take the land because of God's promise

15. C. John Miller, *Saving Grace: Daily Devotions from Jack Miller* (New Growth Press, 2014), 152.

16. Ajith Fernando, *Deuteronomy: Loving Obedience to a Loving God*, Preaching the Word (Crossway, 2012), 309.

17. Arthur Bennet, *The Valley of Vision: A Collection of Puritan Prayers and Devotions* (Banner of Truth, 2002), 71.

and Moses' intercession on their behalf, as we will see in the next chapter. We ourselves are saved not because of our righteousness, but despite our sinfulness. Even as unworthy sinners, our place is secure in God's family through his grace and the intercession of an even greater Mediator than Moses. Let us together remember our sin, that we might be more deeply humbled—and let us remember our Savior, that we may forever rejoice.

18

The Ministry of Intercession

Deuteronomy 9:25—10:11

I myself stayed on the mountain, as at the first time, forty days and forty nights, and the Lord listened to me that time also. The Lord was unwilling to destroy you. (Deut. 10:10)

Legend has it that President Thomas Jefferson and a group of companions were traveling the country on horseback when they came to a flooded river. The riders would have to ford the river in the deadly current. Another traveler who was not a part of the group was watching them from a distance. After seeing several of the riders cross safely, he walked up to the president, tapped his boot, and said, "Can I have a ride across the river?" The president agreed, the man climbed up onto the back of the horse, and the two of them made it safely across the river.

As the stranger got off the horse, a man in the group looked at him incredulously and inquired: "What were you thinking, asking the president of the United States for a ride across the river? Why didn't you ask one of us?" The stranger was shocked and said: "I had no idea he was the president of the United States. The reason why I asked him was that on some of your faces was written the answer 'no,' and on his face was the answer 'yes.' He had a 'yes' face, so I knew he would take me across."[1]

How do we perceive God's face? Does he have a "yes" face or a "no" face? How we perceive God's face toward us will determine whether we seek him in prayer, for ourselves or for others. In the previous passage, we saw Moses repeatedly remind the people of God that they were entering the promised land not on account of their righteousness, but despite their sin. The chief example of their sin was the golden calf: because of their idolatry, God was prepared to destroy his people. But he did not destroy them, and this passage shows us why he did not: it was due to the intercession of Moses the mediator. To intercede is to plead on behalf of someone who is in trouble, and Israel was in as much trouble as a people could be. But Moses knew that though the people were sinful and deserved judgment, God had a "yes" face toward his people, and so Moses went to God and pleaded for mercy. God did not destroy the people but renewed his covenant with them and continued to bring them into the promised land.

Like the people of Israel, we also have our Horebs, Taberahs, Massahs, Kibroth-hattaavahs, and Kadesh-barneas—places where it is evident that we do not deserve a share in the good future that God is preparing for those who love him. Our sins have provoked the righteous wrath of God, and we are helpless to save ourselves from the destruction we deserve. Do we have an Intercessor who will stand in the gap between us and God as Moses did for Israel? Are we prepared to stand in the gap for others who are under God's wrath? The story illustrates the need for intercession, the practice of intercession, and the future of intercession.

The Need for Intercession

We passed over some of the interchange between God and Moses in the previous chapter, but now we are going to return to it. As a result of Israel's worship of the golden calf while Moses was receiving the law, the Lord said to Moses: "I have seen this people, and behold, it is a stubborn people. Let me alone, that I may destroy them and blot out their name from under

1. Lightly adapted from Joseph O. Gouin, "God Always Has a 'Yes' Face," *Iron Mountain Daily News*, October 22, 2018, https://www.ironmountaindailynews.com/lifestyles/life/2018/10/god-always-has-a-yes-face/, accessed February 10, 2022.

heaven. And I will make of you a nation mightier and greater than they"[2] (Deut. 9:13–14). We might underestimate two things in the passage. The first is that God is genuinely prepared to destroy Israel and give Moses the opportunity to be the father of a nation greater and mightier. Moses could be the new Abraham. Moses knows how rebellious these people are; the prospect of starting over with new people is probably tempting. Yet Moses declines God's offer. He is committed not just to being a shepherd, but to being a shepherd of these people particularly. For those of us who serve as shepherds of God's flock, we should remember the example of Moses. God sometimes calls shepherds to new assignments, but we should be careful to discern that it is God leading us to change, and not simply a desire to start over with different people. After all, what the different people and the current people share in common is that they are people. This means that the different people have problems too. God's people may be stubborn and rebellious, but they are still God's people. Moses models the shepherd's heart toward them as their intercessor.

The second thing that we might underestimate in this passage is that God is so angry with Israel's stubborn rebellion that he is prepared to destroy the nation completely. We think God could never do such a thing, but Moses believed that God would do exactly as he had said. This was not an empty threat, and Moses knew it. That is why we read how Moses responds in Deuteronomy 9:25, "So I lay prostrate before the LORD for these forty days and forty nights, because the LORD had said he would destroy you." The people were under God's wrath and needed an intercessor. Sin and the wrath it provokes in the Lord are real, and so is the judgment that he is bringing because of it.

Likewise, Jesus declares, "Whoever believes in the Son has eternal life; whoever does not obey the Son shall not see life, but the wrath of God remains on him" (John 3:36). Jesus does not say that the wrath of God *will* come upon him, but says that the wrath of God *remains* on him. This is the condition of every human from birth; the apostle Paul tells us that we "were by nature children of wrath, like the rest of mankind" (Eph. 2:3). We were born under God's wrath on account of the original sin that we inherited as

2. The Lord's language is even stronger in Exodus 32:9–10: "And the LORD said to Moses, 'I have seen this people, and behold, it is a stiff-necked people. Now therefore let me alone, that my wrath may burn hot against them and I may consume them, in order that I may make a great nation of you.'"

the descendants of Adam and Eve. It is enough that our sin nature provokes God's wrath, but we further provoke him by engaging in the same kinds of sin as Israel did. We have loved other things more than we have loved God. We have not loved our neighbors as ourselves. We have deceived, coveted, lusted, and burned with resentment. As in Israel's situation, God's judgment is coming because of our sin. As surely as Israel needed intercession, so also do all people under God's wrath.

The Practice of Intercession

Moses becomes the intercessor for God's people, seeking for them what they cannot, or will not, seek for themselves. Moses models for us what faithful intercession looks like and sets the example for all of us who are called to intercede with God on behalf of others.

First, the intercessor humbles himself. Moses says in Deuteronomy 9:18, "Then I lay prostrate before the Lord as before, forty days and forty nights." Moses is so aware of the holiness of God and his burning wrath against the sin of his people that he lies facedown for forty days without food or water. Remember, this is not Moses' own sin that he is expressing humility and contrition for, but rather the sins of his people. When was the last time that any of us humbled ourselves before God by grieving over our own sin for even four minutes, let alone humbling ourselves over someone else's sin before God for forty days? We take sin lightly because we take God lightly. But Moses had a keen awareness of the weight of God's glory, and the heinousness of the people's idolatry floored him for forty days. God promises in 2 Chronicles 7:14 that "if my people who are called by my name humble themselves, and pray and seek my face and turn from their wicked ways, then I will hear from heaven and will forgive their sin and heal their land." God is seeking a people who will humble themselves and intercede for others.

Second, the intercessor seeks the Lord earnestly. Moses continues to recount his intercessory work in Deuteronomy 9:18–19: "I neither ate bread nor drank water, because of all the sin that you had committed, in doing what was evil in the sight of the Lord to provoke him to anger. For I was afraid of the anger and hot displeasure that the Lord bore against you, so that he was ready to destroy you." To seek the Lord earnestly is more a posture of the heart than anything else. But sometimes that invisible posture of humility and earnest seeking is expressed through visible practices, such as lying facedown and fasting. In this case, Moses' sincere brokenheartedness over his people's sin leads him to fast for forty days and nights. Of course, this is an exceptional and miraculous fast. We are not necessarily called or expected to fast forty days and nights from all food and water, as Moses did at least twice. But we do frequently see in Scripture multiday fasts—fasts that express both humility and an earnest seeking of the Lord. Fasting is frequently associated with the confession of sin, as with Moses in this passage. But fasting also accompanies earnest entreaties for God's protection, such as we read about in Ezra 8:21–23. Likewise, before Esther went before the king to entreat him to save her people, she asked all the Jews in Susa to fast on her behalf for three days (Esth. 4:16). Fasting is not a magic trick or a way of twisting God's arm, but God frequently chooses to honor such earnest seeking with answers.

Third, the intercessor pleads his case in prayer. We read in verse 26 of Deuteronomy 9, "And I prayed to the LORD, 'O Lord GOD, do not destroy your people.'" Moses does not argue that their sin does not deserve destruction, because it does deserve destruction. The wages of sin have always been death. But the basis of his request stands on three things that are very near to God's heart: his people, his promises, and his glory.

To begin with, Moses pleads God's ownership of his people in Deuteronomy 9:26: "do not destroy your people and your heritage, whom you have redeemed through your greatness, whom you have brought out of Egypt with a mighty hand." God had set his love on these people, not because they were worthy of it, but simply because he chose to love them. They were not worthy of that love at the beginning, and they are not worthy of it now. But Moses reminds God of how he has expressed that love in the past and of the price that he has already paid for that love.

Then Moses pleads God's promises, asking God, "Remember your servants, Abraham, Isaac, and Jacob" (Deut. 9:27). God had made promises to these patriarchs and sworn them by oath. God is faithful to his promises and cannot lie to his people. Moses is asking God to remember the patriarchs when he considers the judgment to deliver on Israel. He must remember that he promised to make this a great people and nation and to bring them into the land, which cannot very well be done if they are all dead.

Finally, Moses pleads with God to remember his own glory in Deuteronomy

9:28, "lest the land from which you brought us say, 'Because the Lord was not able to bring them into the land that he promised them, and because he hated them, he has brought them out to put them to death in the wilderness.'" The basic argument seems to be that if God destroys Israel, the nations (starting with Egypt) will mock God. God is righteously committed to his glory among all the nations on the earth. He proclaims in Psalm 46:10: "Be still, and know that I am God. I will be exalted among the nations, I will be exalted in the earth!" It is not simply a wish, but a statement of definite intent. Moses pleads with God that if he wipes out his people, it will ultimately work contrary to God's expressed purpose to be glorified among the nations. So Moses pleads for mercy based on the fact that they are God's people, to whom God has made promises, and by which God is to be glorified among the nations. Does God answer?

The resolution is only implied in Deuteronomy, but it is explicitly stated in the parallel passage of Exodus 32:14, "And the Lord relented from the disaster that he had spoken of bringing on his people." Moses' appeal regarding God's people, God's promises, and God's name reflects the priorities of God's own heart. When we see other prayers of intercession in the Bible, we see these same three priorities.[3] In our own prayers of intercession, we ought to follow these biblical examples, not only pleading our case in prayer aligning with God's own priorities, but also humbling ourselves and seeking the Lord earnestly. As we approach him, we should know that while his wrath is real, his disposition is to mercy. As Thomas Watson wrote: "The vial of wrath *drops*—but the fountain of mercy runs in *streams*. The sun is not so full of light—as God is of mercy."[4] God stands ready to pour out his abundant mercy, but he calls upon us to ask.

A theological issue raised by this passage needs to be addressed. Does the fact that God relents from bringing disaster on his people mean that our prayers can change God's mind? On the one hand, this is certainly how the text is presented to us, and we should not take lightly the fact that Moses' prayer appears to cause God to change his course. On the other hand, God is sovereignly executing his eternal decree, and nothing can change it. Christians tend to want to reduce this to an either/or proposition. Either

3. See, e.g., Neh. 9; Dan. 9:1–19; Joel 2:17. Christopher Wright, *Deuteronomy*, NIBC: Old Testament 4 (Hendrickson, 2007), 138.

4. Thomas Watson, *A Body of Divinity* (Banner of Truth, 1970), 96.

God's will is fixed and our prayers do not matter, or God's will is open and the future depends on us. But the biblical position is that while God's will is fixed, what we do matters. Even our prayers are part of God's appointed and preordained means of seeing his sovereign decree come to fruition. Christopher Wright helpfully brings these things together, explaining, "God not only allows human intercession, God *invites* it . . . and builds it into the decision-making processes of the heavenly council in ways we can never fathom."[5] We should pray earnestly and humbly without panic because God's sovereign will is going to be accomplished and he answers prayer. The people were saved because of Moses' intercession, but also Moses prayed because it was God's sovereign will to save his people.

Like Moses, we should intercede for God's people. We should humble ourselves and pray for repentance and revival. We should put together biblically informed cases for why we pray as we do for the lost, for the sick, for those who are under God's judgment. We should plead for the church by reminding God of his commitment to his people. We should pray for the advance of the gospel by reminding God of his commitment to be glorified among the nations. We should pray for our children by reminding God of his promises to us and to our children after us. For these things and many more, we ought to practice intercessory prayer. God's face toward his children is "yes."

The Future of Intercession

The next verses show us that God is going to continue his covenant with his people, despite their sin. Moses recounts in Deuteronomy 10:1–2: "At that time the Lord said to me, 'Cut for yourself two tablets of stone like the first, and come up to me on the mountain and make an ark of wood. And I will write on the tablets the words that were on the first tablets that you broke, and you shall put them in the ark.'" Moses does as God commands, and then he writes in verse 5: "Then I turned and came down from the mountain and put the tablets in the ark that I had made. And there they are, as the Lord commanded me." The fact that the covenant tablets are

5. Wright, *Deuteronomy*, 140.

still in the ark at the time that Moses is writing this nearly forty years later indicates that God continued to be Israel's God despite the people's many provocations of him in the wilderness years.

After this, we read that the journey continues, in Deuteronomy 10:6: "The people of Israel journeyed from Beeroth Bene-jaakan to Moserah. There Aaron died, and there he was buried. And his son Eleazar ministered as priest in his place." From the way that Moses communicates this, it sounds as though Aaron dies right away after the golden-calf incident. Aaron does eventually die, but he dies forty years later (Num. 33:37–39), indicating that Moses' intercession for him (Deut. 9:20) does prolong his life, although it does not ultimately allow Aaron into the promised land. Just as Moses will miss out on going in, so will Aaron. But while Aaron eventually dies, this is not the end of the priesthood. After his death, his son takes his place and there is a succession of priests within the tribe of Levi, which is set apart for a special work. Moses writes in Deuteronomy 10:8, "At that time the LORD set apart the tribe of Levi to carry the ark of the covenant of the LORD to stand before the LORD to minister to him and to bless in his name, to this day." "At that time" in verse 8 does not refer to when Aaron died, but rather refers to the golden-calf incident. That is when the Levites were set apart on account of their zeal for the Lord (Ex. 32:26–29). Only the descendants of Aaron could serve as priests, while the rest of the Levites functioned as subordinates to them, carrying out various tasks related to the tent of meeting and later the temple.

But as we look to the future of intercession, consider what Moses did while he was on the mountain this second time. All we read in Deuteronomy 10:10 is this: "I myself stayed on the mountain, as at the first time, forty days and forty nights, and the LORD listened to me that time also. The LORD was unwilling to destroy you." But what was Moses doing during his time on the mountain? We have a short summary of it in Exodus 32:30–32:

> The next day Moses said to the people, "You have sinned a great sin. And now I will go up to the LORD; perhaps I can make atonement for your sin." So Moses returned to the LORD and said, "Alas, this people has sinned a great sin. They have made for themselves gods of gold. But now, if you will forgive their sin—but if not, please blot me out of your book that you have written."

Moses' prayer to God is that he would forgive the people for their sin in response to Moses' request. Forgiveness does not mean that God simply forgets about sin or overlooks it. Forgiveness comes at a price, namely, that of blood. So Moses requests that if the sin cannot simply be forgiven, he would like to die in the place of his people. We may be tempted to think that this is a request to be eternally condemned, but our understanding of this is far more developed than Moses' would have been. Moses is asking to die, for as is seen in the judgment that the Levites inflicted, death is the penalty for this sin.[6] Moses is willing to shed his blood for the people.

God denies Moses' request, as is written in Exodus 32:33: "But the LORD said to Moses, 'Whoever has sinned against me, I will blot out of my book.'" God is not willing to accept Moses' offer to stand in the place of his people. We are not told why God does not accept it, but we know why from the rest of the Old Testament teaching about the sacrificial system. Moses is not suited to be the substitute for God's people. While Moses is not guilty of this sin of idolatry, he is by no means a pure and blameless sacrifice (Num. 20:12). The law makes it clear that sacrifices must be pure and blameless to bear the burden of another's guilt.[7] God's people needed another Intercessor, a better Mediator; God himself raises one up for his sinful and rebellious people.

Jesus is uniquely qualified to be our substitute because he alone has no sin. Moses was willing to die in the place of his people, but he was not able to do so because of his own sin. Jesus was both willing and able. As Paul explains it in 2 Corinthians 5:21, "For our sake he made him to be sin who knew no sin, so that in him we might become the righteousness of God." In a way that is beyond our ability to fully comprehend, Christ, who had no sin of his own, actually became sin through imputation. Our sins were placed on him as a spotless and pure sacrificial substitute, and he truly became guilty. Christ's death in our place is not a legal fiction. In a way that Moses could not, Christ became guilty of our sins and took our condemnation. The liability of our sins became his personal liability. This means that if Christ was guilty for us, then we are not guilty. If Christ was condemned for us, then we are not condemned. Christ was not only willing, but able to

6. Peter Enns, *Exodus*, NIVAC (Zondervan, 2000), 577.
7. Enns, 590.

shed his blood for his people, and he did. God accepted the sacrifice of the one for the many, and now it is finished!

Furthermore, in the exodus account, we see Moses intercede for the people on three different occasions. He is clearly committed to ensuring God's presence with them, even though they continually show their proclivity to sinning. As effective as Moses was at ensuring the continuing presence of God with his sinful people, he would eventually die. New priests would have to be continually raised up for God's people to ensure that they could continue in God's presence. Hebrews 7:23–25 explains how Jesus is greater:

> The former priests were many in number, because they were prevented by death from continuing in office, but he holds his priesthood permanently, because he continues forever. Consequently, he is able to save to the uttermost those who draw near to God through him, since he always lives to make intercession for them.

Jesus always lives to make intercession for his people, and he is able to save us to the uttermost. If Moses was partially effective at turning away God's wrath from his sinful people and ensuring that God's presence would continue with them into the promised land, how much more can we be confident of God's permanent presence with us on account of Christ's perfect intercession for us? For those who have trusted in Jesus the Intercessor, he will see to it that we make it to the promised land of the new heavens and earth.

If there had not been a mediator to stand in the gap between sinful Israel and its holy God, Israel would have never entered the promised land. Moses' work as the mediator between God and Israel anticipates the greater mediatorial work that Christ will perform in the new covenant. If Moses could effectively intercede on the Israelites' behalf so that they could receive what was promised despite Moses' own sin, how much more certain can we be that Christ's intercession will suffice to pardon all our sins and bring us into the promised land of God's forever kingdom (Heb. 9:15)?

In the Lord's Supper, Jesus said, "This is my blood of the covenant, which is poured out for many for the forgiveness of sins" (Matt. 26:28). Only by the shed blood of Jesus can our sins be forgiven. Because of what Christ has done for us, shedding his blood to seal the new covenant and bringing about the forgiveness of our sins, reconciling us to our Father, God always has a "yes" face toward us. We can come to him with all our needs, both for ourselves and also interceding for others, and know that his face toward us is "yes." The more we believe this, the more we will be able to come to him, even when we have sinned and fallen repeatedly. We come not because we are good, but because he is good.

So, brothers and sisters, because of who Jesus is and what he has done for us, as the writer of Hebrews urges, "Let us then with confidence draw near to the throne of grace, that we may receive mercy and find grace to help in time of need" (Heb. 4:16). May it not be said of us that we do not have because we do not ask. God's face is "yes" toward us. Will we come and ask him for what we need and also intercede on behalf of others?

19

What Does the Lord Require of You?

Deuteronomy 10:12—11:1

And now, Israel, what does the LORD your God require of you, but to fear the LORD your God, to walk in all his ways, to love him, to serve the LORD your God with all your heart and with all your soul, and to keep the commandments and statutes of the LORD, which I am commanding you today for your good? (Deut. 10:12)

Saving Private Ryan is the story of a mission that put many lives at risk to save one man. Private James Ryan is one of four brothers serving the U.S. Army during World War II. When three of the Ryan brothers are killed in action, General George C. Marshall is determined not to send their mother a fourth letter of condolence. So he orders a handpicked squad of Rangers to rescue Private James Ryan from behind enemy lines. They do indeed rescue him—at great cost. Near the close of the movie, Private Ryan is standing on a bridge surrounded by the bodies of those men who gave their lives to save him. Chief among them is Captain John Miller. With his dying breath, Captain Miller tells Private

Ryan what he requires in return for the gift that he has been given. He whispers: "Earn this. Earn it."

How can one man possibly earn what those men sacrificed to save him? How can a person ever repay such a debt? It is an incredible burden to live under, trying to make one's life justify that kind of extraordinary sacrifice. Some think of Christianity that way. They think that having received extraordinary grace freely, we must now live the rest of our lives trying to earn what we have been given. For those who have received God's grace, he does ask something of us, but it is not to try to earn the gift.

In Deuteronomy, Moses reminds the people of God that they have also received a gift. God rescued them from Egypt, and when they sinned and rebelled against him in the desert numerous times, he did not give them what they deserved. Rather, because of Moses' intercession for them and the promises made to Abraham, God recommitted to bring this sinful people into the promised land. It is a tremendous gift that they have been given. In response for the gift he has given, he does not ask them to earn it. He simply wants loyal love. In this chapter, we will consider how God has demonstrated his love to his people and how we are to reciprocate.

God Has Extended Persevering Grace and Asks for Loving Loyalty

Almost the entirety of Deuteronomy 9 and 10 has been a rehearsal of all the ways that Israel has not deserved its privileged position. But God has demonstrated his persevering grace toward his people and his willingness to renew the covenant that they broke on multiple occasions. It is in this context that we see the first instances of what God asks for or requires in response to his love. Moses writes in Deuteronomy 10:12–13, "And now, Israel, what does the Lord your God require of you, but to fear the Lord your God, to walk in all his ways, to love him, to serve the Lord your God with all your heart and with all your soul, and to keep the commandments and statutes of the Lord, which I am commanding you today for your good?" Each one of the five things described here is just a facet of the same precious jewel of loving loyalty to Yahweh. They all stand or fall together. One cannot love him and disregard his commandments. Likewise, to fear the Lord is to serve him wholeheartedly. As we consider these five facets of loving loyalty, we might distinguish between two postures of the heart and three active expressions of those postures.[1]

The postures are fear and love. Proper reverential fear of the Lord is not contrary to love, but a complement to it. God has sought to instill fear in his people, that we would keep his commandments. Love is not simply affection, as we tend to think of it, but covenant loyalty expressed in tangible actions of obedience. In the *Shema* of Deuteronomy 6:5, we saw that to love God with everything is the first and greatest commandment. It is an action to be obeyed more than a feeling to be felt. In the context of this holy fear and love of our God, we are to express those postures in the specific ways mentioned: walk in all his ways, serve him wholeheartedly, and keep his commandments. As J. A. Thompson writes, "Men in whom these attitudes are found will *walk* in God's ways, *serve* Him and *keep* His laws."[2]

To walk in the ways of our God is to imitate him.[3] A child who grows up walking in the ways of his or her father or mother approaches life in a similar way, perhaps with a similar vocation or set of values. To walk in God's ways is to follow in his footsteps, in much the same way that Jesus would later call his disciples to do. To serve the Lord wholeheartedly is the appropriate response to the covenant suzerain, and at the very least entails not serving other gods. To keep his commandments is precisely that: to pay careful attention to the stipulations of the covenant and do them. Obeying God's commands cannot be done apart from love and reverence. These qualities are foundational, and where they exist, the others will follow.

We should not overlook what Moses points out yet again regarding God's commandments: they are for the good of the people. God could ask or require of us any commandments he might wish, but he asks us to do only that which is for our good. God's law was a gift to God's people, not an arbitrary imposition of hoops for them to jump through. To disregard God's commands and to go our own way is to act not only against God, but against our own self-interest.

How has God persevered with you? How many times have we gone astray from him and yet he has remained loyal to us? In many ways, we represent

1. Daniel I. Block, *Deuteronomy*, NIVAC (Zondervan, 2012), 270.

2. J. A. Thompson, *Deuteronomy: An Introduction and Commentary*, TOTC (InterVarsity Press, 1974), 147.

3. This theme is repeated throughout Deuteronomy: 5:33; 11:22; 19:9; 26:17; 28:9; 30:16.

the prophet Hosea's wife, Gomer. Though she is married to Hosea, she continually goes back to other lovers, betraying her husband. He repeatedly takes her back. Eventually, her promiscuity gets her into such trouble that she becomes a cheap slave who needs to be redeemed. God tells Hosea, "Go again, love a woman who is loved by another man and is an adulteress, even as the LORD loves the children of Israel" (Hos. 3:1). So Hosea goes and pays to get his own unfaithful wife back. When he does, Hosea tells her: "You must dwell as mine for many days. You shall not play the whore, or belong to another man; so will I also be to you" (v. 3). To ask that his wife no longer act like a prostitute seems like a reasonable request, does it not? Hosea has persevered with her and asks for her loyalty and faithfulness in response to his grace. The lesson for Israel was that though the people were sinful, obstinate, and unfaithful at Horeb, Taberah, Massah, Kibroth-hattaavah, and Kadesh-barnea, their sin could not exhaust the store of God's grace and love for his people. The same is true for us: despite our unfaithfulness, God has remained faithful. Having redeemed us from our slavery to sin, he asks of us loving loyalty in response.

God Has Exercised Electing Love and Asks for Loving Responsiveness

Moses writes in Deuteronomy 10:14, "Behold, to the LORD your God belong heaven and the heaven of heavens, the earth with all that is in it." Here is a simple statement about God's ownership of everything. He owns all that is in the heavens, he owns all that is on the earth, and he owns even the earth itself. He could have set anything as his special treasure. He could have picked anyone to make the object of his affection. But he did not. We read with amazement verse 15: "Yet the LORD set his heart in love on your fathers and chose their offspring after them, you above all peoples, as you are this day." The word "yet" introduces the surprising truth that follows. Although God owns all and could have set his heart in love on anything and anyone that he made, he set his love on the patriarchs and their descendants. The knowledge of the greatness of God and his willingness to choose to love Israel should have astounded the people and humbled them, and it should do the same for us. We are not more astounded by God's love because we typically have too low a view of God and too high a view of ourselves. But if we estimated God properly as he is revealed in Scripture, and if we estimated ourselves properly as Scripture exposes us, we would be astounded that he chose to love us. It was as true then as it is today: we love God *because* he first loved us. Paul overflows with praise in Ephesians 1:3–6:

> Blessed be the God and Father of our Lord Jesus Christ, who has blessed us in Christ with every spiritual blessing in the heavenly places, even as he chose us in him before the foundation of the world, that we should be holy and blameless before him. In love he predestined us for adoption to himself as sons through Jesus Christ, according to the purpose of his will, to the praise of his glorious grace, with which he has blessed us in the Beloved.

God has chosen his beloved people before the foundation of the world so that we should be holy and blameless. He has predestined us for adoption as his sons. He has done this all to the praise of his glorious grace, which is given to us in Jesus. God's love of us is not to the praise of our goodness or anything in us, but rather to the praise of his glorious grace. The reason that God has chosen us is not found in us; it is found in him, and for that reason all praise goes to him for our salvation. The proper response to God's electing love is humility.

Charles Spurgeon writes: "Friends, if you want to be humbled, study election, for it will make you humble under the influence of God's Spirit. He who is proud of his election is not elect; and he who is humbled under a sense of it may believe that he is. He has every reason to believe that he is, for it is one of the most blessed effects of election that it helps us to humble ourselves before God."[4] But our response does not stop with humility. It must also lead to holiness from the heart. What follows then in Deuteronomy 10:16 is a call to that kind of response: "Circumcise therefore the foreskin of your heart, and be no longer stubborn." Within this verse we see that the effect of the circumcision of the heart is a responsiveness to God rather than stubborn resistance to him. The martyr Stephen calls for the same thing when he preaches to the Jewish people in the first century: "You stiff-necked people, uncircumcised in heart and ears, you always resist the Holy Spirit.

4. Charles H. Spurgeon, "Election," nos. 41–42 in *Sermons 1–53*, vol. 1 of *The New Park Street Pulpit*, Spurgeon Sermon Collection, Accordance electronic ed. (OakTree Software, 2004).

As your fathers did, so do you" (Acts 7:51). The uncircumcision of the heart and ears is indicated by a resistance to the Holy Spirit. There is a deadness to spiritual things in the heart that can be resolved only by a removal of the deadening veil on the heart and ears.

Some people characterize the faith of God's people in the Old Testament as being primarily external, whereas Christian faith is primarily internal. But that is a mischaracterization. Even in the Old Testament, the concern for God's people was not merely external but for the change of heart that the sign of circumcision was to represent. We read in Jeremiah 4:3–4: "For thus says the LORD to the men of Judah and Jerusalem: 'Break up your fallow ground, and sow not among thorns. Circumcise yourselves to the LORD; remove the foreskin of your hearts.'" The concern is for the heart. Likewise in Leviticus 26:41–42: "if then their uncircumcised heart is humbled and they make amends for their iniquity, then I will remember my covenant with Jacob, and I will remember my covenant with Isaac and my covenant with Abraham, and I will remember the land." The external sign under the old covenant is not the point, but the sign is to represent a heart-level transformation of responsiveness to God.

Circumcision was commanded under the covenant established with Abraham as an external marker of God's covenant relationship with his people. Every male child was to receive the sign of God's covenant in his flesh. But while the external sign was important, and to reject the sign was to reject the covenant, the external sign was not the point. Rather, the external sign of circumcision was to be a picture of an inner, invisible reality: a transformed heart. To have the external sign without the inner reality profited nothing.

As Paul writes in Romans 2:28–29: "For no one is a Jew who is merely one outwardly, nor is circumcision outward and physical. But a Jew is one inwardly, and circumcision is a matter of the heart, by the Spirit, not by the letter." Like baptism in the new covenant, circumcision represented the renewal of the heart by the work of the Holy Spirit. Some wonder why we Reformed believers baptize infants if baptism represents a change of heart that infants might not have experienced yet. They argue that having the external sign without the inner reality profits nothing, so we should wait until we see the inner reality before giving our children the sign of baptism.

We agree that merely having the external sign profits nothing. But that was also true in the Old Testament, and it did not prevent God from telling his people to put the sign of the covenant on their children. The people of God did not say, "What matters is the circumcision of the heart, so we are no longer going to put the sign of the covenant on children before they are transformed." No, in obedience to God's commands they put the sign of God's covenant promises on their children before they believed and raised them to know and respond to the sovereign, electing, persevering love of God. Today, we place the covenant sign on our children for the same reason that the people of God under the Mosaic covenant placed it on their children who had not yet experienced the change of heart that the Spirit must work in any person. It was and is a sign of what God promises to do for his people and what he has done through Christ's work on the cross (Col. 2:11–12).

But to be clear, the sign by itself, whether circumcision or baptism, counts for nothing. Paul writes in 1 Corinthians 7:19, "For neither circumcision counts for anything nor uncircumcision, but keeping the commandments of God." What matters primarily is not whether you have the outward circumcision, but that you have the invisible circumcision of the heart that reveals itself through responsive obedience to God's commandments. This flows from love and reverence. The visible sign of circumcision or baptism has value for those who experience the invisible and inward reality of what circumcision and baptism symbolize, but the symbols do not stand on their own and are not to be relied on as the basis of our standing with God.

Physical circumcision is straightforward enough, but how do we circumcise our hearts? This passage does not tell us, but we get a clue in Deuteronomy 30:6, 8: "And the LORD your God will circumcise your heart and the heart of your offspring, so that you will love the LORD your God with all your heart and with all your soul, that you may live. . . . And you shall again obey the voice of the LORD and keep all his commandments that I command you today." The circumcision of the heart in ourselves and our children is something that God himself will have to do for us. The chief command of God, to love him with everything, is a result of the circumcision of the heart that we cannot do for ourselves. We need a transformation that can come only from God himself. As Jesus will insist, "You must be born again" (John 3:7). We must experience the inner transformation of the heart that brings us from being God's sworn enemy to being a true lover of God. This is a work of his sovereign grace in the life of his chosen people. To be born again, to be circumcised of heart, is not the cause of God's election of sinners but the effect of his election of sinners. We must acknowledge our inability to love him as he deserves and ask him to do for us what we cannot do for ourselves.

God Has Distributed Tangible Mercy and Asks for Loving Imitation

We read in verses 17–18 of Deuteronomy 10: "For the Lord your God is God of gods and Lord of lords, the great, the mighty, and the awesome God, who is not partial and takes no bribe. He executes justice for the fatherless and the widow, and loves the sojourner, giving him food and clothing." The first verse emphasizes God's sovereignty over every other god and lord. He is supreme and sovereign to every superlative degree. Then verse 18 tells us the beneficiaries of God's supremacy: the fatherless, the widow, and the sojourner. God leverages his greatness, might, and awesomeness not primarily for the strong, but for the weak and vulnerable.[5] And what does he call us to do in response? He calls us to do likewise: "Love the sojourner, therefore, for you were sojourners in the land of Egypt" (Deut. 10:19). Our response to the greatness of God should be tangible demonstrations of love and mercy to the most vulnerable.

The "sojourner" (or "alien") refers to someone who has chosen to leave the security of his homeland and family to try to make a living in a foreign land.[6] Israelite law made special protections and provisions for vulnerable people among them, especially the widow, the orphan, and the foreigner residing among them. In this passage, it is the Lord himself who loves the sojourner and gives him food and clothing. Daniel Block writes, "Just as [God] is distinguished for his compassion to the widow, the fatherless, and the alien, so should his people be."[7] To love the foreigner among us is one of the ways that we are called to imitate God himself.[8] And in so doing, we will be recognizable as his people. How are we responding to the foreigners in our own midst? Does our love toward them reflect God's love? Christopher

5. Christopher Wright, *Deuteronomy*, NIBC: Old Testament 4 (Hendrickson, 2007), 149.

6. Block, *Deuteronomy*, 273.

7. Block, 277.

8. R. J. D. Knauth, "Alien, Foreign Resident," in *Dictionary of the Old Testament: Pentateuch*, ed. T. Desmond Alexander and David W. Baker (InterVarsity Press, 2003), 33.

Wright observes: "Love for aliens will always be the first feature of any society to evaporate in times of social pressure and conflict. . . . Xenophobia, exploitation, and precisely the kind of scapegoat politics that Israel suffered in Egypt are much more typical."[9] We have certainly seen this kind of treatment toward immigrants among us in the United States, but it is not to be so among the people of God. What about the other vulnerable populations among us? Are we imitating God's love toward widows by giving them a place in our lives, and toward orphans by seeing to it that they have families and loving care? God has used his power to extend his loving care toward us in our vulnerability, and he calls us to use what power and position we possess to extend the same to others.

God Has Done Mighty Works and Asks for Loving Obedience

We read of God's mighty acts in Deuteronomy 10:20–22: "You shall fear the Lord your God. You shall serve him and hold fast to him, and by his name you shall swear. He is your praise. He is your God, who has done for you these great and terrifying things that your eyes have seen. Your fathers went down to Egypt seventy persons, and now the Lord your God has made you as numerous as the stars of heaven." Moses references in these verses the loyalty that God's people are to show to him on account of the great things he did for them in rescuing them out of Egypt. But not only that, he reminds them of how God has multiplied the people of Israel greatly in fulfillment of his promises. What does God ask of his people in response? Moses tells us in 11:1, "You shall therefore love the Lord your God and keep his charge, his statutes, his rules, and his commandments always." What God asks from his people in response to his mighty works and his great love is our loving obedience. We have seen this theme repeatedly because it is so important.

As God's people, we are called to remember what he has done and the specific ways that he has shown grace, love, and mercy to us. Our response to that grace, love, and mercy is to trustingly walk in obedience to all that

9. Wright, *Deuteronomy*, 150.

he calls us to do. This obedience is not simply an outward conformity to a set of standards, but the fruit of a transformed heart. We live in obedience to God's commands not because of fear that God will cast us out, but because of love to him for what he has done. Charles Spurgeon writes:

> Christian men keep from sin because their nature abhors sin. Do not imagine we are kept back from sin because we are terrified with threats of damnation, we have no fear, except the fear of offending our loving Father. But we do not want to sin—our thirst is for holiness and not for vice. . . . You must have a religion that makes you hate the thing you once loved, and love that which you once hated—a religion that draws you out of your old life and puts you into a new life.[10]

That is precisely what we are offered in the gospel: a new life. Not one that we can earn or deserve, but one that is a sheer gift of grace to all who believe.

Saving Private Ryan ends with a powerful scene in which a now elderly Private Ryan is standing in the cemetery at Normandy. As he stands in front of Captain John Miller's grave, he tells him: "Every day I think of what you said to me that day on the bridge. I've tried to live my life the best I could. I hope that was enough. I hope that at least in your eyes, I've earned what all of you have done for me." His wife comes to his side by the grave, and he says to her: "Tell me I've lived a good life. Tell me I'm a good man." And his wife responds, "You are." But the viewer gets the feeling that Private Ryan is still not so sure that he has done enough to deserve their sacrifice.

One day, when we lay our heads down on our pillows for the last time, we may take the opportunity to look back on our lives and ask what we have done with what we have been given. In that moment, I pray, our thought will not be whether we have deserved the sacrifice that Jesus made for us. We could never live a life deserving of the sacrifice that Christ paid for us. Nor does he ask us to do so. His sacrifice was pure gift, sheer grace. We can thank God that Jesus' last words on the cross were not "Earn this," but rather "It is finished!" The debt is paid in full. What he asks of us is

10. Charles H. Spurgeon, "Election and Holiness," no. 303 in *Sermons 286–347*, vol. 6 of *The Metropolitan Tabernacle Pulpit*, Spurgeon Sermon Collection, Accordance electronic ed. (OakTree Software, 2012).

not that we try to earn what we have been freely given, but that we express the grateful and loving loyalty that such a sacrifice commands. If we have received his free gift, this is what he asks: that we love him, especially through obedience, and that we love others, especially the most vulnerable. These are not the conditions of the gift we have received, but the proper and grateful response to it.

20

Choices

Deuteronomy 11:2—32

See, I am setting before you today a blessing and a curse: the blessing, if you obey the commandments of the Lord your God, which I command you today, and the curse, if you do not obey the commandments of the Lord your God. (Deut. 11:26–28)

Americans are swamped by choices. I recall a time when my daughter and I went out for pizza, and I invited her to build whatever pizza she wanted. As we looked at the menu, making choices quickly became an overwhelming task. There were two options for crust, three options for size, four options for sauce, four options for cheese, seven options for meat, and sixteen options for vegetables. The number of choices was paralyzing. We settled on pepperoni and cheese.

Over the last several years, one of the fastest-growing grocery stores in the United States has been Aldi. That growth can be attributed to several things, but one of them is the simplicity of the shopping experience. Aldi strips down the grocery shopping experience to its bare minimum. Its stores are much smaller than others (roughly twelve thousand square feet compared to an average of forty thousand square feet for the typical grocery store), and consequently it offers far fewer choices than a more traditional grocery store today. The plethora of choices would seem to make people happier, but generally it has done the opposite. In every area of life, Americans have more choices available to us than ever before. We are faced with choices about where we are going to go to school, what we will study, whom we will marry, how we will spend our time, whom we will spend it with, and more. The sheer number of choices before us each day can be paralyzing. But what if we could reduce all those choices down to just one?

In Deuteronomy 11, Moses reduces the choices before Israel to one: obey God and choose the blessing or disobey God and choose the curse. It is that simple. The simplicity of this choice reflects the simplicity of the choice faced by Adam and Eve in the garden: obey and be blessed or disobey and be cursed. Here is the true fork in the road. Many of us worry too much over choices that do not really matter, and not enough about the choices that matter most. In the multitude of decisions that we are faced with every year, every week, every day, and even every hour, none is more important than this: will I choose the path of obedience and blessing, or disobedience and curse? The choice behind every other choice is whether it will be God's way or the wrong way, obedience or disobedience, blessing or curse. That choice is put before the people of Israel as they are about to enter the promised land, and it is set before each of us. Our choices matter, but none so much as the choice of obedience. As Moses sums up everything we have seen in the first ten chapters of Deuteronomy and prepares to lay out the particulars of God's commandments starting in chapter 12, he gives his readers two things to consider and one choice to make. When we are faced with a choice to obey or disobey, we need to consider two things.

Consider What God Does to Those Who Disobey His Word

The chapter begins with a call to love and obey God that sums up the message of Deuteronomy chapter 10 while also introducing chapter 11. Moses exhorts the people of Israel in 11:2, "And consider today (since I am not speaking to your children who have not known or seen it), consider the discipline of the Lord your God." Moses is directly challenging those of the present generation who have seen and heard of God's discipline. The word for "discipline" here includes the ideas both of punishment and of the lesson it teaches.[1] Their children might have some excuse for disregarding God's discipline, but not this present generation. The present generation of Israelites were children under twenty years old when their parents refused to go up from Kadesh-barnea and take the land, and some of them had not even been born yet. But they watched as every single one of the previous generation died in the wilderness according to God's promise. They saw what God does to those who disobey. They cannot claim ignorance about the outcome of disobedience.

Now Moses is going to give them a brief reminder of the same lesson through various illustrations. He continues in Deuteronomy 11:2–4:

> Consider the discipline of the Lord your God, his greatness, his mighty hand and his outstretched arm, his signs and his deeds that he did in Egypt to Pharaoh the king of Egypt and to all his land, and what he did to the army of Egypt, to their horses and to their chariots, how he made the water of the Red Sea flow over them as they pursued after you, and how the Lord has destroyed them to this day.

In the exodus event, God demonstrated his power against the Egyptians who refused to obey. Ten plagues were poured out on Egypt because Pharaoh refused to heed the voice of the Lord. When the people of Israel were delivered and Pharaoh decided to pursue them, God swept away the whole army. The implication of those last words, "to this day," is that the Egyptian army has still not recovered from the devastation that God brought upon them forty years earlier. Look at Egypt and consider what God does to those who disobey his Word.

But the people should not look at Egypt as though only pagans suffer for disobedience. God's people should also recall what God did to his own people who disobeyed his Word. Moses writes in Deuteronomy 11:5 that they should consider "what he did to you in the wilderness, until you came to this place." This is likely a reference to the discipline they experienced for not entering the promised land when first commanded to do so. It may also

1. Jeffrey H. Tigay, *Deuteronomy*, JPSTC (Jewish Publication Society, 1996), 110.

reference the various types of discipline they experienced at Horeb because of the golden calf, at Taberah for their grumbling, at Massah for their testing of the Lord, and at Kibroth-hattaavah for their sinful craving. Each place is to be a reminder to them of what God does to those who disobey his Word. The constant drumbeat is that disobedience brings death.

Next Moses points to one particularly terrifying story in Deuteronomy 11:6 as the people were to consider "what he did to Dathan and Abiram the sons of Eliab, son of Reuben, how the earth opened its mouth and swallowed them up, with their households, their tents, and every living thing that followed them, in the midst of all Israel." The story is told in Numbers 16. Dathan and Abiram, along with a man named Korah, organized a rebellion against Moses in the wilderness. In Numbers 16:3, we read: "They assembled themselves together against Moses and against Aaron and said to them, 'You have gone too far! For all in the congregation are holy, every one of them, and the Lord is among them. Why then do you exalt yourselves above the assembly of the Lord?'" These rebels wanted to be priests and felt that they were just as qualified to burn incense before the Lord as Moses and Aaron were. Moses immediately dropped to his face before the Lord. He told Korah, Dathan, and Abiram, as well as the 250 chiefs that they had riled up, to bring their censers and God would settle the matter. The next day, God opened up the earth, which swallowed these men and their families alive. Additionally, the 250 were consumed by supernatural fire from God. In one of the great marvels of human depravity, within twenty-four hours of this taking place, the congregation grumbled against Moses and Aaron again! God acted swiftly and killed 14,700 of them by a plague. What is the lesson? Disobedience leads to death.

Thus in Deuteronomy 11:7, Moses sums up the point in this first section: "For your eyes have seen all the great work of the Lord that he did." The people of God simply need to consider what God does to those who disobey him. They can look to Egypt, they can look to their own history, and what they will find in every place is that disobedience brings death. They have no reason to be ignorant. They have no reason to be confused. Consider what God does to those who disobey his Word.

We are to learn from these examples the same thing that Israel was to learn. The apostle Paul writes:

> Now these things took place as examples for us, that we might not desire evil as they did. Do not be idolaters as some of them were; as it is written, "The people sat down to eat and drink and rose up to play." We must not indulge in sexual immorality as some of them did, and twenty-three thousand fell in a single day. We must not put Christ to the test, as some of them did and were destroyed by serpents, nor grumble, as some of them did and were destroyed by the Destroyer. Now these things happened to them as an example, but they were written down for our instruction, on whom the end of the ages has come. (1 Cor. 10:6–11)

The lesson that we are to learn from Israel's disobedience is that we too will be tempted to disobey in terms of idolatry, sexual immorality, testing God, grumbling, and so on. But we must not disobey; it is the way of the curse. Has God not demonstrated plenty of good reasons for not disobeying? The outcome of disobedience is death. It is not safe to grumble. It is not safe to slander or gossip. It is not safe to sow discord in the church. It is not safe to dishonor our parents. Sometimes the consequences show up immediately, and sometimes the consequences are delayed. But we can be sure of this: God's Word repeatedly demonstrates that those who disobey his Word will suffer for it.

Consider What God Does for Those Who Obey His Word

Verse 8 of Deuteronomy 11 connects with what comes before it in verses 1–7. Because the people have seen what God does to those who disobey, Moses says in verses 8–9, "You shall therefore keep the whole commandment that I command you today, that you may be strong, and go in and take possession of the land that you are going over to possess, and that you may live long in the land that the Lord swore to your fathers to give to them and to their offspring, a land flowing with milk and honey." Two blessings attached to obedience in these two verses are going to be worked out through verse 25. The first blessing promised to the people for their obedience is that they will be strong and go in and possess the land. God has promised it to them, but they cannot expect to possess the promise while walking in disobedience to his commandments. This promise is further expanded on in verses 22–25:

> For if you will be careful to do all this commandment that I command you to do, loving the Lord your God, walking in all his ways, and holding fast to him, then the Lord will drive out all these nations before you, and you will dispossess nations greater and mightier than you. Every place on which the sole of your foot treads shall be yours. Your territory shall be from the wilderness to the Lebanon and from the River, the river Euphrates, to the western sea. No one shall be able to stand against you. The Lord your God will lay the fear of you and the dread of you on all the land that you shall tread, as he promised you.

These are extraordinary promises that God is holding out to his people, to drive out their enemies and give them a vast land to dwell in, but the blessing is connected with obedience.

The second blessing promised to the people for their obedience is to live long in the land. Moses goes on to describe how the land of Israel is going to be different from the land of Egypt. He explains in Deuteronomy 11:10, "For the land that you are entering to take possession of it is not like the land of Egypt, from which you have come, where you sowed your seed and irrigated it, like a garden of vegetables." Egypt produced crops primarily through vast systems of irrigation fed by the Nile River, and the people of Israel would have known this. These cleverly devised ways of watering the land were truly impressive features of human achievement. But the land that Israel is going to possess would not be sustained by great irrigation systems: "But the land that you are going over to possess is a land of hills and valleys, which drinks water by the rain from heaven, a land that the Lord your God cares for. The eyes of the Lord your God are always upon it, from the beginning of the year to the end of the year" (Deut. 11:11–12). God is personally watching over and caring for that land, and it gets its water from the rain he sends. But the blessing of the rain that leads to a fruitful and productive land is connected with the obedience of the people. Moses explains in verses 13–15:

> And if you will indeed obey my commandments that I command you today, to love the Lord your God, and to serve him with all your heart and with all your soul, he will give the rain for your land in its season, the early rain

> and the later rain, that you may gather in your grain and your wine and your oil. And he will give grass in your fields for your livestock, and you shall eat and be full.

The early rain came in October and November, enabling plowing after a dry summer, and the later rains came in March and April, making the land lush with green.[2] Both these rains were essential, and both came from God's hand. Now Moses tells the people that this blessing comes on an obedient people. If the people need rain to survive, and if God sends the rain, then it would be wise to be faithful to that God.[3] That is why in Deuteronomy 11:18–21 there is a repetition of the commands that we already saw in Deuteronomy 6. God's people need to be thoroughly grounded in God's Word, and they need to teach it to their children, that they all may walk in the way that God has promised to bless. To be clear: Israel is not earning this blessing. God gives the blessing as a gift. But it is a gift that will be enjoyed only by an obedient people.

Perhaps an illustration will help. One of our family's favorite customs on road trips is to stop at Dairy Queen. If we were to say to our children, "We love to give ice cream to obedient children," then when our kids got ice cream, they could not very well say that they earned it. We gave it to them because we love to give ice cream to obedient children. But they did meet the condition of enjoying the blessing of ice cream, which is obedience to their parents. What we are talking about here is the difference between *meritorious* conditions and *necessary* conditions. A meritorious condition earns a reward, while a necessary condition does not strictly earn anything. As one pastor puts it: "Meritorious conditions are about *doing*. Necessary conditions are about *describing* things that have to be there for the desired result to come about, but are there through no credit of our own."[4] Our children's obedient behavior did not merit ice cream, but it was the necessary condition that had to be met in order for them to enjoy it. Our obedience

2. J. A. Thompson, *Deuteronomy: An Introduction and Commentary*, TOTC (InterVarsity Press, 1974), 154.

3. Christopher Wright, *Deuteronomy*, NIBC: Old Testament 4 (Hendrickson, 2007), 154.

4. Jonty Rhodes, *Covenants Made Simple: Understanding God's Unfolding Promises to His People* (P&R Publishing, 2014), 61.

does not merit God's blessings, but obedience puts us in a position to enjoy the blessings that God loves to give freely to his children.

The next part of this illustration moves into the realm of the ridiculous—but stay with me. If our kids began to do a kind of pagan ice cream dance in the back seat, calling upon some god of their imagination to give them ice cream, we would most certainly not give them ice cream, lest they become confused. This is what God warns in Deuteronomy 11:16–17: "Take care lest your heart be deceived, and you turn aside and serve other gods and worship them; then the anger of the LORD will be kindled against you, and he will shut up the heavens, so that there will be no rain, and the land will yield no fruit, and you will perish quickly off the good land that the LORD is giving you." The people living in Canaan worshiped other gods. Baal was the Canaanite god that was said to be responsible for giving rain and fertility. Moses foresaw a time when the people of Israel were living in the land and their fearful hearts might be tempted to turn to other gods to look for rain. Yahweh makes it clear that this is not a good strategy and will yield exactly the opposite effect. Yet as we read the story of the Israelites through the rest of the Old Testament, we see them repeatedly worshiping Baal alongside Yahweh, clearly hoping to hedge their bets, but only bringing God's curse on themselves.

Idolatry never leads to God's blessing, and yet we too turn to the same idols again and again. The security that we are looking for from money can never deliver the ultimate blessing of security. The sense of significance that we are looking for from being a parent, from being successful in our work, or from achieving a goal can never be delivered by idols. Ultimate satisfaction cannot come apart from the Lord. Security, significance, peace, and purpose are all blessings that God gives freely to his children. We do not merit those blessings by our obedience; they are given freely to all who trust in Christ's meritorious work. But the necessary condition for enjoying those blessings is obedience. As Bryan Chapell writes, "God does not love us because we obey him, but we cannot know the blessings of his love without obedience."[5] Our obedience is not the basis of our salvation. But our enjoyment of our salvation is very much connected to our obedience. God's people then, and

5. Bryan Chapell, *Holiness by Grace: Delighting in the Joy That Is Our Strength* (Crossway, 2001), 12.

God's people today, should consider what God does to those who disobey him as well as consider what God does for those who obey him. Which brings us to the final choice.

Choose the Blessing of Obedience

Moses boils down the choice here in binary form in Deuteronomy 11:26–28: "See, I am setting before you today a blessing and a curse: the blessing, if you obey the commandments of the Lord your God, which I command you today, and the curse, if you do not obey the commandments of the Lord your God, but turn aside from the way that I am commanding you today, to go after other gods that you have not known." These are the only two options: blessing for obedience, curse for disobedience. To cement these two realities in the minds of his people, Moses instructs them in verses 29–30 to perform a ceremony on two mountains. We will look at this ceremony in detail when we get to Deuteronomy 27 in chapter 41. But for now, one mountain was to represent the blessing of obedience, while the other represented the curse of disobedience. There are only two options.

Again, we are brought back to the two trees in the garden of Eden (Gen. 2–3). The tree of life and the tree of the knowledge of good and evil represent the two choices that we all have: blessing versus curse. God's blessing brings life and well-being to a person. The curse of God is for a person to be left to corruption, death, judgment, and Satan.[6] While God's blessing entails abundance, community, and life, the curse brings scarcity, isolation, and death. Will we have God's blessing in God's way through obedience to his Word, or will we disobey God's Word and try to take God's blessing for ourselves according to our own way, as Adam and Eve did? There is no suspense.

Adam and Eve merited the curse of God, and so have we. God's curse meant that they were expelled from the garden, expelled from God's presence, and that they came under the condemnation of death. No longer would the land be fruitful and supply all their needs, but now there would be anxiety and scarcity surrounding their provisions. Later, Israel would make the same

6. Herman Bavinck, *Reformed Dogmatics*, ed. John Bolt, trans. John Vriend, vol. 3, *Sin and Salvation in Christ* (Baker Academic, 2008), 172.

choice, repeatedly disobeying God's commandments until the people had to be expelled from the land and suffer the consequences of their disobedience. Later still, we would all make the same choice. We know what it is like to live life under God's curse. If God's blessing depended on our earning it by perfectly keeping all his commandments, we could never experience it. This is why the good news of the gospel of God's grace in Jesus Christ is so good.

The gospel says that only one man ever earned God's blessings by perfect obedience to all his commandments. Through his earthly ministry, Jesus demonstrated that God's blessing was coming through him as he began to reverse the effects of the curse through healing the sick, feeding the hungry, enlightening the ignorant, setting captives free, and even raising the dead. That one man, Jesus Christ, who earned blessing, chose to be cursed in place of his cursed people. He died on the cross bearing the curse of sin, which is death and separation from God. This curse was symbolized through the crown of thorns he wore on his head (the thorns being a sign of the curse in Genesis 3:18). In bearing the curse, he removed the curse from us—the ones who properly deserved it. The apostle Paul writes, "Christ redeemed us from the curse of the law by becoming a curse for us—for it is written, 'Cursed is everyone who is hanged on a tree'—so that in Christ Jesus the blessing of Abraham might come to the Gentiles, so that we might receive the promised Spirit through faith" (Gal. 3:13–14). Christ bore the curse so that we might enjoy the blessing of God.

Not only that, but Jesus was raised from the dead and has entered the presence of God on our behalf, having merited for us all of God's richest blessings. We cannot earn these blessings; they are a gift of grace. But there is a necessary condition for experiencing them: faith. Paul writes: "For by grace you have been saved through faith. And this is not your own doing; it is the gift of God" (Eph. 2:8). The blessing of salvation is a gift freely given to all who believe, and even the believing is a gift. We must trust that Jesus died in our place for our sins, bearing our curse, and that he was raised again from the dead to reconcile us to God and grant us every spiritual blessing in the heavenly places (1:3). The blessings of the new covenant have already begun in that we are united to Christ and have received the indwelling presence of the Holy Spirit. Christ has opened up our full access to the throne of grace, and we are already seated with him in the heavenly places. But the fulfillment of the new covenant will not ultimately happen until death is finally defeated through our resurrection, the earth is renewed and cleansed of sin and its effects, and we see Jesus face to face. Because of what Jesus has done, those who trust in him will experience a new world where the curse of sin is no more. But we are not there yet.

Since we have received that gift of salvation, does the choice of obedience not matter anymore? It certainly does matter! Again, Chapell writes, "When God removes good works as a condition for his acceptance, he does not remove righteousness as a requirement for life."[7] God accepts us as his own on the basis of Christ's good work for us. That work is finished; we are God's forever! And having been set free by God from a cursed life of disobedience, we now desire to walk in the way of blessed obedience. Christ has satisfied the meritorious conditions for us to receive all of God's blessings by faith in him alone, but obedience remains the necessary condition for us to fully enjoy those blessings.

So let us consider the outcome of disobedience, let us consider the outcome of obedience, and let us choose the way of blessing through trusting in Jesus and obeying his commands.

7. Chapell, *Holiness by Grace*, 12.

21

Worship God Rightly

Deuteronomy 12:1–28

> *You shall surely destroy all the places where the nations whom you shall dispossess served their gods, on the high mountains and on the hills and under every green tree. . . . You shall not worship the* Lord *your God in that way.* (Deut. 12:2, 4)

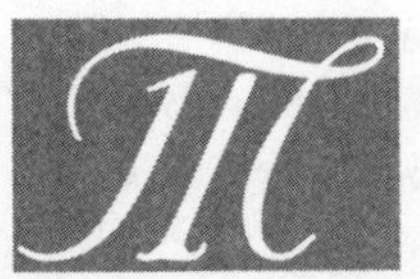

ost of the differences in religion are not important. What matters ultimately is that we all love one another." Have you ever heard a statement like that? We have all probably heard something like that because we live in a pluralistic age. Here is an example from Deepak Chopra, one of the bestselling authors of our day: "Christ-consciousness, God-consciousness, Buddha-consciousness—it's all the same thing."[1] To say that we live in a pluralistic age is to say that we live in a time when the dominant cultural narrative is that there are many equally true and valid ways to live in this world that will lead to ultimate wellness.

Kevin Vanhoozer is an American theologian who has been studying the effects of pluralism in our culture for some time. He identifies two

1. Quoted in Ajith Fernando, *Deuteronomy: Loving Obedience to a Loving God*, Preaching the Word (Crossway, 2012), 368.

pathologies that have developed from our pluralistic age.[2] The first is that it fosters a spirit of consumerism. Because there are so many different paths to the good life, we must choose among them. To do so, we take on a consumeristic posture to evaluate the many different brands of the same product: the Eternal One.[3] The second pathology that Vanhoozer observes in our pluralistic age is a spirit of cynicism. Pluralism functions like a centrifugal force that keeps people from settling on any one set of worldview convictions on which to base one's life. As a result, it is not surprising that Gen X, millennials, and Gen Z—the age group of younger adults today—make up the bulk of people in our population who do not claim any religious affiliation. How could any one religion or worldview know the answer to life's biggest questions about who we are and where we are going? In a pluralistic age, the only view that really encounters resistance is the one that claims to be exclusively true.

Vanhoozer sums up our cultural moment in this way:

> Our society does not appear to believe that there is any one way of being human that is superior to all others, nor that there are any universal human qualities that everyone should seek to cultivate. Human being has instead become an empty canvas, in which individuals are invited to create their own portraits: abstract art made flesh. Parents are even choosing names that could work for boys or girls, so that children can make their own choices about gender identity. The only thing our culture is sure it wants to preserve is freedom of choice. Yet, freedom without form is a vacuum, not a vocation.[4]

Indeed it is. Where does Christianity fit in a pluralistic age? Is God indifferent to whether people worship him directly if all religions ultimately lead to him anyway? Is there some worship that is acceptable to him and other worship that is not? As we head into the more detailed stipulations of God's covenant arrangement with his people that stretches from chapters 12 to 26 of Deuteronomy, the first chapters deal with the first commandments, which are matters of first importance, namely, the proper worship of God. Two things

2. The following observations are drawn from Kevin J. Vanhoozer, "Being Biblical in a Pluralistic Age," *Andrews University Seminary Studies* 57, no. 2 (2019): 305–26.

3. Vanhoozer, 314.

4. Vanhoozer, 315.

we should take away from this text that push back against the pluralism of our age are that whom we worship matters and that how we worship matters.

WHOM WE WORSHIP MATTERS

Chapter 12 of Deuteronomy marks the transition into the formal stipulations of the covenant. Verse 1 presents us with a summary of what chapters 12–26 are about: "These are the statutes and rules that you shall be careful to do in the land that the LORD, the God of your fathers, has given you to possess, all the days that you live on the earth." Chapters 5–11 gave us a broad overview, and chapters 12–26 will take us into the details. In chapters 12–26, we find many laws particular to Israel that overlap with the law code given in Exodus 20–23. Because of this, chapters 12–26 are sometimes referred to as the *Deuteronomic Code*. But this is not an additional law. Rather, this is "preached law" in the context of the renewal of the covenant as the people prepare to enter the land.[5] Everything that God calls his people to do in these chapters is a response to what he has done for them, as related in the earlier chapters. Thus far, we have seen the importance of keeping God's commandments, and that theme continues in earnest now.

The first command that Moses gives relates to the proper (and improper) worship of God. God alone is to be worshiped and not any idols in place of God or alongside God. Moses commands in Deuteronomy 12:2–4: "You shall surely destroy all the places where the nations whom you shall dispossess served their gods, on the high mountains and on the hills and under every green tree. You shall tear down their altars and dash in pieces their pillars and burn their Asherim with fire. You shall chop down the carved images of their gods and destroy their name out of that place. You shall not worship the LORD your God in that way."

One term that we see repeatedly in the Old Testament is "Asherim."[6] "Asherah" was the name of a Canaanite mother-goddess.[7] She was probably

5. Christopher Wright, *Deuteronomy*, NIBC: Old Testament 4 (Hendrickson, 2007), 158.

6. A survey of the passages referring to the Asherim gives us a clear sense of their idolatrous nature: Ex. 34:13; Deut. 7:5; 12:3; 1 Kings 14:15, 23; 2 Kings 17:10; 23:14; 2 Chron. 14:3; 17:6; 24:18; 31:1; 33:19; 34:3–4, 7; Isa. 17:8; 27:9; Jer. 17:2.

7. Along with the passages referring to the Asherim, we read of Asherah and the persistent influence of this deity in Israel in the following passages: Deut. 16:21; Judg. 6:25–26, 28, 30; 1 Kings 15:13; 16:33; 18:19; 2 Kings 13:6; 17:16; 18:4; 21:3, 7; 23:4, 6–7, 15; 2 Chron. 15:16; Mic. 5:14.

borrowed by the Canaanites from the Assyrians. Asherah came to be known in Canaanite religion as the goddess of fertility.[8] Those who served her would set up Asherim (or Asherah poles), which were symbols of the goddess, on the high places. The temptation for the people of God would have been to worship this goddess alongside Yahweh to try to secure her favor. But they were to have nothing to do with such idols. In fact, the Asherim were to be burned along with all the other trappings of idolatry. The Lord alone was to be worshiped, and all traces of rival gods were to be destroyed from the land.

When Moses says, "You shall not worship the LORD your God in that way" (Deut. 12:4), he is telling the people that there are proper ways of worshiping God and improper ways of worshiping God. Some worship pleases God, and some worship offends him. When God's people enter the land, they are not to mix their worship with the worship of the Canaanites whom they are driving out. Instead, they are to "destroy," "tear down," "dash in pieces," "burn," "chop down," and "destroy" all the remnants of their idolatrous worship (vv. 2–3). Clearly, God does not embrace the pluralistic spirit of the age.

This opposition to the Canaanite gods is further emphasized with the instruction in Deuteronomy 12:3 to "destroy their name out of that place." As Christopher Wright explains: "To remove the names of Canaan's gods was to remove *their* presence and *their* power, just as the putting of Yahweh's name in a place was to fill it with *his* availability and *his* nearness. But they could not coexist."[9] One name is to replace every other name. Such an idea would have been difficult for people to swallow then, and it seems even more difficult for people to accept now. The command to destroy the name of rival gods out of the land is in direct conflict with the pluralistic spirit of our age.

To be clear: political pluralism in a society that allows for religious freedom is a positive thing. We do not want to live in a culture in which people are not allowed to have their own religious convictions. Furthermore, we are not called to go about our community or the nations smashing idols and destroying other people's places of worship. Not even the Israelites were called to do that outside the land that God was giving them. But pluralism in the church and among the people of God is directly contrary to what the Bible

8. A. H. Sayce, *ISBE*, s.v. "Asherah," 1:318.

9. Wright, *Deuteronomy*, 159 (emphasis in original).

teaches. The pluralist insists that truth cannot be known absolutely and so all names and faces of the various deities of world religions can be equally valid and salvific.[10] But God's people know better and worship the Lord only.

In January 2021, an ordained minister, who also served as a U.S. representative, led the opening prayer to swear in the 117th Congress. He prayed as follows: "May the Lord lift up the light of his countenance upon us and give us peace . . . peace in our families, peace across this land, and dare I ask, O Lord, peace even in this chamber. . . . We ask it in the name of the monotheistic God, Brahma, and 'God' known by many names by many different faiths. Amen and awoman." People were most offended by his addition of "awoman" to "amen." But the deeper issue is what came before that. This pluralistic prayer is precisely the kind of thing that the text of Deuteronomy as well as the New Testament explicitly forbids as incompatible with the worship of the God of the Bible. In this view, the only name to be rejected is a name that refuses to accept its own relativity, which is, of course, exactly what our God refuses to do.

Christians must not acquiesce to the popular view that Jesus is just one god among many. Rather, we can trace the theme of this passage, in which one name will displace every other name, right through the Bible. We read in Isaiah 45:22–23: "Turn to me and be saved, all the ends of the earth! For I am God, and there is no other. By myself I have sworn; from my mouth has gone out in righteousness a word that shall not return: 'To me every knee shall bow, every tongue shall swear allegiance.'" There is no other God but God, and one day every knee and tongue will acknowledge it. The apostle Paul writes about Jesus in Philippians 2:9–11, "Therefore God has highly exalted him and bestowed on him the name that is above every name, so that at the name of Jesus every knee should bow, in heaven and on earth and under the earth, and every tongue confess that Jesus Christ is Lord, to the glory of God the Father." Jesus is the one before whom every knee will bow and every tongue will confess that he is Lord. His name will displace the name of every other so-called god. There is no salvation unless a person turns to this God in particular. He alone is the way, the truth, and the life.

We can see why Christianity is increasingly maligned when it refuses to accept that other ways to God, or the worship of various gods, are equally

10. Wright, 161.

valid. At the risk of rejection, we are called to be radically narrow in our devotion to God, while maintaining a tolerant posture of coexistence toward our unbelieving relatives, friends, and neighbors. We must be careful, in our insistence on Jesus' being the only way, not to malign or attack those with different convictions. We can be respectful of, peaceful toward, and tolerant of people with different religious convictions while still not accepting all views as equally valid. We will happily tolerate the existence of other religious convictions and treat those who hold those views with respect and dignity and love, but we will not participate in multifaith religious services where Jesus is named along with Allah or anything else. Such services are an insult to the faith of true believers in any of the major religions, each of which makes distinctive and mutually exclusive claims to truth.

We must also be on the lookout for more subtle ways that the pluralistic spirit of the age pollutes our own worship. One of the chief idols around the world today is Mammon. It is easy to slip into trusting in God *and* money. Western culture is also very much focused on the individual. We can easily begin to adapt an individualistic way of thinking into our Christianity that leads us to neglect the fellowship of God's people. Or we may breathe in the pluralistic air so deeply that we begin to believe that people without Christ are okay, quenching our evangelistic fervor. We are not to worship any gods alongside the one true God.

Did Israel obey the command to destroy the names of these gods from the land? The answer is emphatically no. If we were to read Deuteronomy alongside one of the books of the Deuteronomistic history, such as 2 Kings, we would quickly come to the conclusion that Israel's history is a recital of the people's consistent and flagrant disregard of God's covenant requirements.[11] Hundreds of years after Deuteronomy was written when Israel was overtaken by Assyria and carried into exile, this is the explanation given for why it happened:

> In the ninth year of Hoshea, the king of Assyria captured Samaria, and he carried the Israelites away to Assyria. . . .

11. Eugene Merrill writes, "Careful comparison between [Deuteronomy] and the Deuteronomistic history compels the reader to conclude that the history of Israel is the sorry recital of a systematic disregard of the covenant requirements so emphatically outlined by Moses." Eugene H. Merrill, "Old Testament History: A Theological Perspective," in *NIDOTTE*, 1:79.

> And this occurred because the people of Israel had sinned against the LORD their God, who had brought them up out of the land of Egypt from under the hand of Pharaoh king of Egypt, and had feared other gods and walked in the customs of the nations whom the LORD drove out before the people of Israel, and in the customs that the kings of Israel had practiced. And the people of Israel did secretly against the LORD their God things that were not right. They built for themselves high places in all their towns, from watchtower to fortified city. They set up for themselves pillars and Asherim on every high hill and under every green tree, and there they made offerings on all the high places, as the nations did whom the LORD carried away before them. And they did wicked things, provoking the LORD to anger, and they served idols, of which the LORD had said to them, "You shall not do this." (2 Kings 17:6–12)

Not only did Israel not destroy the idolatrous images of the nations, but the people set up their own. God warned them through many prophets to return to covenant fidelity, but they would not. Whom we worship matters, and Israel's history makes it clear that to worship other gods, either exclusively or alongside the one true God, leads only to destruction. We believe that one name is above every other name, and to him alone we give our allegiance and full devotion.

How We Worship Matters

The next two sections of the passage deal with two issues: Israel's worship at the place that God appoints (Deut. 12:5–7, 8–12) and the slaughter of animals for nonsacrificial purposes (vv. 13–19, 20–28). Deuteronomy 12:8 and 28 frame some specific commands about how God's people worship. Verse 8 describes "everyone doing whatever is right in his own eyes," while verse 28 describes "what is good and right in the sight of the LORD your God." Clearly, there is a way of worshiping that is right in God's sight and a way of worshiping that is right in man's sight—and they are not the same. The principle is that it is God, and not man, who determines the way that God is to be worshiped.

First, God tells the Israelites where they are to worship from this point forward in Deuteronomy 12:5–8:

> But you shall seek the place that the LORD your God will choose out of all your tribes to put his name and make his habitation there. There you shall go, and there you shall bring your burnt offerings and your sacrifices, your tithes and the contribution that you present, your vow offerings, your freewill offerings, and the firstborn of your herd and of your flock. And there you shall eat before the LORD your God, and you shall rejoice, you and your households, in all that you undertake, in which the LORD your God has blessed you.
>
> You shall not do according to all that we are doing here today, everyone doing whatever is right in his own eyes.

Worship in Israel took on a specific form and involved bringing various kinds of offerings and sacrifices listed in this passage and explained in far greater detail in Leviticus. Sacrifice was a fundamental component of worship, and it would have been costly for God's people. Once they moved into the land, those offerings and sacrifices were to be brought to one central worship location that God would show them. At first, that place was Shiloh (Josh. 18:1), then it was at Nob (1 Sam. 21), and then it was at Gibeon (1 Chron. 16:39). Eventually, that one central location was the temple in Jerusalem (1 Kings 8:4).[12] The primary unity of Israel's worship was based not on the fact that it was offered in one place, but on the fact that it was offered to only one God.[13] Confining worship to one place could help keep the focus of worship on the one true God and ensure that the priests could oversee proper worship. One of the persistent problems that the people of Israel would face was setting up worship in places besides the place that God had appointed for them (see, e.g., 1 Kings 12:26–14:20). The people of God were not to mix their worship with the worship of other gods in other places. Deuteronomy 12:13–14 warns explicitly against this: "Take care that you do not offer your burnt offerings at any place that you see, but at the place that the LORD will choose in one of your tribes, there you shall offer your burnt offerings, and there you shall do all that I am commanding you."

The second issue that this section deals with in Deuteronomy 12:15–27 is the regulations surrounding the eating of sacrificial food and nonsacrificial food. Moses clarifies in verses 15–19:

12. D. W. Gooding, *NBD*, s.v. "Tabernacle," 1145.
13. Wright, *Deuteronomy*, 162.

> However, you may slaughter and eat meat within any of your towns, as much as you desire, according to the blessing of the LORD your God that he has given you. The unclean and the clean may eat of it, as of the gazelle and as of the deer. Only you shall not eat the blood; you shall pour it out on the earth like water. You may not eat within your towns the tithe of your grain or of your wine or of your oil, or the firstborn of your herd or of your flock, or any of your vow offerings that you vow, or your freewill offerings or the contribution that you present, but you shall eat them before the LORD your God in the place that the LORD your God will choose, you and your son and your daughter, your male servant and your female servant, and the Levite who is within your towns. And you shall rejoice before the LORD your God in all that you undertake. Take care that you do not neglect the Levite as long as you live in your land.

Animals were allowed to be slaughtered for food anywhere within the land, and both the ceremonially clean and unclean could eat of that meat because it was not holy. They were explicitly forbidden from eating the blood, because the blood is the life, according to Deuteronomy 12:23.[14] Animals normally used in sacrificial worship could be eaten just like a deer or gazelle when those animals were slaughtered away from the place that God would choose; nothing was holy about them in themselves. But sacrificial food items were not to be eaten wherever people wanted. They were to be eaten at the place that God appointed and in the way that God appointed. When the people of God are enjoying all the benefits and fruitfulness of the land, they may be tempted to forget the Lord, as we saw in chapter 8. This chapter aims to help prevent that forgetfulness by encouraging them to specifically enjoy their eating and feasting in God's presence so as to remember where the blessings have come from. In a similar way, a discipline of regular prayer before or after meals helps us to remember where the blessings that we enjoy

14. Some people have suggested based on this verse (and Lev. 17:11) that because the "blood is the life," aborting a child before the blood is in the body means that a life is not taken. One problem with this view is that some creatures clearly have life that do not ever have blood at all, and a child is clearly alive in the womb, clearly a living organism, before there is blood. But there comes a point in the development of the child when life cannot be sustained without blood. At this point, blood and a beating heart become necessary for the sustaining of life. This seems to be the Bible's point about the life's being in the blood—not that there can be no life where there is no blood, but that blood ultimately sustains life that depends on it.

come from. We thank God for our work that enables us to make money, but our work is not the ultimate source of our blessings or our food. It is God who gives us the ability to earn wealth, and to him we give thanks. May our prayers before or after mealtimes serve to remind us of our true God and help us push back against the idols of our culture that tempt us.[15]

Note specifically the command in Deuteronomy 12:18, "And you shall rejoice before the Lord your God in all that you undertake." The worship of God and the living of life with and for him was not to be a drudgery but a joy. Of course, traveling to the appointed place of worship from various parts of Israel multiple times a year was no small undertaking, and it is easy to see how people could start to resent the inconvenience and expense of making the trip, leading their animals over a multiday journey, missing work, and so on. In the same way, to carve out time every week to gather with God's people for worship can seem like an inconvenient imposition. It might cost us time during which we could be working or playing. It involves bringing offerings that cost us financially as well as with our time and talent. It may feel that it is getting in the way of real life. But this is real life! And God calls his people to rejoice in their feasting together. They were not to feast like the people around them, for whom the feasting frequently entailed drunkenness and orgies. But this did not mean that they could not enjoy their meals with pure hearts and actions. We too should not feast like the world around us in drunkenness and carousing, but should instead feast with purity and joy.

Notice also in Deuteronomy 12:12 that the worship of God's people around these meals was to include males and females, sons and daughters, servants, and the Levites. They were not to leave any of God's people out of their worship. Everyone was to be included in the joyful worship and feasting of God's people, including those who could not contribute any of the meat or food for the sacrifices. In the New Testament, the Corinthian church was failing to include all the people in the celebration of the Lord's Supper, and Paul challenged them on it (1 Cor. 11:17–34). In the church in Acts 2:42–47, we see the ideal that God intended to characterize his people. They were to share all they had with one another in the context of a worshiping community.

15. Daniel I. Block, *Deuteronomy*, NIVAC (Zondervan, 2012), 321.

I experienced a reverse form of this principle while traveling alone in Jordan. It was during the time of Ramadan when Muslims fast during the day and feast after the sun goes down. I was on a long bus trip from the north end of the country to the south end at the Red Sea. At one point, the bus stopped at a little roadside store. Everybody on the bus got off and went inside, and I went along with them. They bought food and drinks, but after a brief survey of the place, I decided that I was not hungry. After we returned to the bus, the people all began eating and feasting together. I was perfectly content not to be eating anything, but when one of the men noticed that I was not eating, he gave me a sandwich and a Coke, intimating that he wanted me to share in the joy of the end of the fast. He knew that I was not a Muslim, and there was nothing sacred about that meal, but the invitation to share the joy was powerful. As Christians, we are not to share the sacred meal of the Lord's Supper with unbelievers. But we should be intentional and diligent to invite nonbelievers around our tables to share in the joy we have in Christ and in Christian fellowship. We should invite non-Christians to our Christmas and Easter parties to share in the joy of Christ's birth and resurrection; it may impact them more than we realize.

But what does all this have to do with us as Christians today? Namely this: God still cares about whom his people worship and how his people worship. We are not to worship other gods as does the culture around us, nor are we to worship God according to our own whims and preferences. Ligon Duncan identifies our challenges related to worship as evangelicals when he writes:

> Evangelicals do think that worship matters, but they also often view worship as a means to some other end than that of the glorification and enjoyment of God: some view worship as evangelism (thus misunderstanding its goal); some think that a person's heart, intentions, motives, and sincerity are the only things important in how we worship (thus downplaying the Bible's standards, principles, and rules for worship); and some view the emotional product of the worship experience as the prime factor in "good" worship (thus overstressing the subjective and often unwittingly imposing particular cultural opinions about emotional expression on all worshipers). Evangelicals believe these things about worship, but they do not think that there are

> many biblical principles about how to worship or what we are to do and not to do in worship.[16]

So is worship for the Christian simply whatever we want it to be? WCF 21.1 explains that "the acceptable way of worshipping the true God, is instituted by himself, and so limited by his own revealed will, that he may not be worshipped according to the imaginations and devices of men, or the suggestions of Satan, under any visible representation, or any other way not prescribed in the Holy Scripture." The regulative principle of worship is the idea that everything we do in worship is to be regulated by the Word of God.[17] God's Word itself supplies the content of Christian worship. Along with prayer, WCF 21.5 sets out the proper elements of biblical worship in the new covenant:

> The reading of the Scriptures with godly fear, the sound preaching and conscionable hearing of the Word, in obedience unto God, with understanding, faith, and reverence, singing of psalms with grace in the heart; as also, the due administration and worthy receiving of the sacraments instituted by Christ, are all parts of the ordinary religious worship of God: beside religious oaths, vows, solemn fastings, and thanksgivings upon special occasions, which are, in their several times and seasons, to be used in an holy and religious manner.

But we recognize that things have changed between the time of Deuteronomy and the present time, namely, that Christ has come and fulfilled all that the sacrificial rites of Old Testament worship entailed. Not only that, but the place of worship has also changed.

In John 4, Jesus, a Jew, was having a conversation with a Samaritan woman. Their forms of worship were different, but they were not equal. The Jews worshiped at Jerusalem, the place that God had appointed, while the Samaritans worshiped on Mount Gerizim. But even while the Jewish worship was correct at that point and the Samaritan worship was not, Jesus said, "The hour is coming when neither on this mountain nor in Jerusalem will you

16. J. Ligon Duncan III, "Does God Care How We Worship?," in *Give Praise to God: A Vision for Reforming Worship: Celebrating the Legacy of James Montgomery Boice*, ed. Philip Graham Ryken, Derek W. H. Thomas, and J. Ligon Duncan III (P&R Publishing, 2003), 25–26.

17. Duncan, 20.

worship the Father" (John 4:21). A change was occurring, and geographically central worship since the days of Deuteronomy was going to be replaced by something better. One theologian writes, "The temple worship of both rival sanctuaries is now being replaced by a spiritual form of worship that is not confined to one geographical location but, rather, is focused in the person of Jesus and in the community of his followers."[18] Through his death and resurrection, Jesus raised up a new temple, his body, and has become the proper focus of our worship (2:19–22). Jesus, not Jerusalem, is now the proper place where God is to be acknowledged and honored.[19] Jesus goes on to say that "the hour is coming, and is now here, when the true worshipers will worship the Father in spirit and truth, for the Father is seeking such people to worship him" (4:23).

This is what God is seeking from us: true worship. Worship that is not pluralistic, but exclusively focused on God himself as he is revealed as Father, Son, and Holy Spirit. Worship that is not according to our own designs or imaginations, but according to his Word. In our pluralistic age, let us recommit ourselves to worshiping God alone as he desires to be worshiped, through faith in Jesus Christ, his Son, and by the power of his Holy Spirit, according to what he has written in his Word.

18. Charles H. H. Scobie, *The Ways of Our God: An Approach to Biblical Theology* (Eerdmans, 2003), 593.

19. D. G. Peterson, *NDBT*, s.v. "Worship," 860.

22

Ruthlessly Resist Idolatry

Deuteronomy 12:29—13:18

For the Lord *your God is testing you, to know whether you love the* Lord *your God with all your heart and with all your soul.* (Deut. 13:3)

Google Maps is a great application. Except when it isn't. In 2019, a group of drivers in Colorado were all using Google Maps to get to Denver International Airport. A large crash in Aurora, Colorado, caused GPS (Global Positioning System) applications such as Google Maps to look for a quicker route to the airport. They found one, but it turned out to be a bigger problem than the traffic. One driver told reporters that she and about a hundred other drivers were led onto a dirt road. She thought to herself, "Well there are all these other cars in front of me so it must be OK." And she continued. What neither they nor Google Maps knew was that the road was impassable because of heavy rainfall. The first cars down the road ended up getting hung up in the mud, and then the cars behind them all got stuck as well. Thankfully, a few drivers with all-wheel-drive vehicles were able to get through and take some of the stranded travelers with them to the airport. But the Denver7 traffic anchor had these words of wisdom for people depending on GPS applications: "You are driving. Google Maps is not driving. . . . Google Maps is not perfect. You need to know where you are going and, if it does not look like that's where you should be going, turn around and try again."[1]

His words provide insightful counsel for God's people as well. We need to know where we are going, and if it looks like we are going the wrong way, we should turn around and try again. Much as Google Maps essentially enticed a whole cadre of drivers into an impassable road, there are many ways for God's people to be enticed into the mire of idolatry. Seeing lots of other people going one direction, a driver may rationalize that the road is safe. It is the same when people around us are engaged in idolatry; we may be more inclined to go along.

We are all susceptible to being ensnared by idolatry from the outside. This passage gives three explicit warnings about where those enticements to idolatry may come from. In addition to these external enticements, we cannot ignore the temptation from within. To paraphrase John Calvin: our own hearts are idol factories. We all have a sinful proclivity to turn good things into ultimate things and worship and serve the creature rather than the Creator. Between our own proclivity to idolatry and the enticements to idolatry around us, we must ruthlessly resist idolatry.

The word *ruthless* means "merciless," and it is the perfect word to describe our posture toward all enticements to idolatry. Moses warns all of God's people in Deuteronomy 12:29–30:

> When the LORD your God cuts off before you the nations whom you go in to dispossess, and you dispossess them and dwell in their land, take care that you be not ensnared to follow them, after they have been destroyed before you, and that you do not inquire about their gods, saying, "How did these nations serve their gods?—that I also may do the same."

He warns them before they go into the land that they need to watch out that they are not "ensnared" by idolatry. Idolatry is a trap. The people are not

1. Meghan Lopez, "From Detour to Disaster: Google Maps Got Dozens of Colorado Drivers in a Mud Mess on Sunday," Denver7.com, updated June 26, 2019, https://www.thedenverchannel.com/news/local-news/from-detour-to-disaster-google-maps-got-dozens-of-colorado-drivers-in-a-mud-mess-on-sunday, accessed March 17, 2022.

even to inquire about the gods of the Canaanites and how they worshiped because they would likely be inclined to do the same.

Moses goes on in Deuteronomy 12:31 to describe some of the horrors to which idolatry can lead: "You shall not worship the LORD your God in that way, for every abominable thing that the LORD hates they have done for their gods, for they even burn their sons and their daughters in the fire to their gods." Archaeological evidence shows that child sacrifice was indeed happening in Canaanite areas. Along with hundreds of urns containing the charred bones of children found in Phoenician colonies (such as Carthage), there are Egyptian reliefs depicting the practice in Canaan.[2] In these images, as the Egyptians are attacking Canaanite cities, the people of those cities are obviously involved in a religious ceremony. As they pray toward heaven, they are dropping the dead bodies of their sacrificed children over the wall in hopes of securing a victory.[3] Tragically, the practice of burning children as sacrificial offerings to idols was also done under the leadership of at least two of the kings of God's people (2 Kings 16:3; 17:17; 21:6). But who would sacrifice their own children? First, we must acknowledge that idolatry does not start with child sacrifice. It starts with the desire for something good, such as rain, or fertile soil or animals or people, or even protection from invaders. Eventually, things come to the point to which people's own desire for a good thing leads to a willingness to sacrifice their children for that good thing.

I imagine archaeologists and anthropologists' discovering the remains of tens of millions of unborn babies someday and wondering what kind of gods we must have served that required such vicious sacrifices. There are many reasons why people abort their children today. The most sympathetic of reasons is that a young woman has been abandoned by the father of the child and her own family. The mother feels that she has no choice; it will be her life or the baby's. It is not much different from the parents' throwing their children over the wall in hopes that by doing so their own lives will be saved. Less sympathetic reasons for abortion are given by Christian couples who sacrifice their children because they fear having to lower their standard

2. Jeffrey H. Tigay, *Deuteronomy*, JPSTC (Jewish Publication Society, 1996), 464.

3. In 2 Kings 3, when Israel attacks Moab, Mesha the king of Moab uses child sacrifice as a last resort when he sees that he cannot win the battle. Amazingly, it seems to work, and the Moabites repel Israel's attack.

of living if they were to add another child. Or by those parents who do not want to have to embrace the sacrifices that raising a child with disabilities would require.

Even for those of us who have not gone to the lengths of physically killing our children, some of us have sacrificed our children on the altar of our own success. Others are sacrificing our children on the altar of the idol of sports, academics, or cultural acceptability. Many are sacrificing our children's spiritual lives on the altar of our own comfort. Idolatry has been, and continues to be, one of the primary temptations of God's people. That is why Moses writes in Deuteronomy 12:32: "Everything that I command you, you shall be careful to do. You shall not add to it or take from it." We must ruthlessly resist idolatry, no matter which angle it may come from. This text highlights three sources of temptation to idolatry that must be resisted: spiritual deception, relational enticement, and cultural pressure.

Resist Spiritual Deception to Idolatry

The scenario is laid out for us in Deuteronomy 13:1–3: "If a prophet or a dreamer of dreams arises among you and gives you a sign or a wonder, and the sign or wonder that he tells you comes to pass, and if he says, 'Let us go after other gods,' which you have not known, 'and let us serve them,' you shall not listen to the words of that prophet or that dreamer of dreams." In both the Old Testament and the New Testament, God sometimes spoke to his people by way of prophecy or dreams. God spoke to Abraham in a dream; God spoke to Jesus' earthly father, Joseph, in a dream. These are legitimate ways in which revelation came to God's people. Additionally, God sometimes used signs and wonders to accompany or authenticate the message he gave through his prophets, such as when Elijah called down fire from heaven against the prophets of Baal. We will see later in Deuteronomy that one of the tests to determine whether a prophet is true or false is whether what he has prophesied comes to pass. But if that prophet goes on to say, "'Let us go after other gods,' which you have not known, 'and let us serve them,'" what should God's people do? Do not listen to that person, no matter how impressive his miracles are.

It is within the realm of possibility for a false prophet to arise and have dreams and visions and be able to authenticate his message with signs and wonders. In the book of Revelation, the second beast uses signs and wonders to get people to worship the first beast:

> It exercises all the authority of the first beast in its presence, and makes the earth and its inhabitants worship the first beast, whose mortal wound was healed. It performs great signs, even making fire come down from heaven to earth in front of people, and by the signs that it is allowed to work in the presence of the beast it deceives those who dwell on earth, telling them to make an image for the beast that was wounded by the sword and yet lived. (Rev. 13:12–14)

The second beast is a false prophet, using signs and wonders to lead people away from devotion to the true God. Jesus likewise warns us against being deceived: "For false christs and false prophets will arise and perform signs and wonders, to lead astray, if possible, the elect. But be on guard; I have told you all things beforehand" (Mark 13:22–23). Signs and wonders are not the ultimate indicators of truth; the Bible is. Perhaps the clearest point that the Bible makes is that we are to love the God of the Bible with all our heart, soul, and strength, which includes not having any other gods in our lives. If anyone rises up, performing miracles or wonders, and suggests that we are to pursue another god different from the one revealed in the Bible, we are not to listen, no matter who says it or what signs are performed.

Signs and wonders can be a tremendous gift to the church, but they can also be misleading. For this reason, Christians should not make signs and wonders or the pursuit of signs and wonders central to our faith, or we will be more easily led astray by them. Neither should we build our churches around signs and wonders, but we should rather build them around the Word of God. The plumb line of truth that teachers (or prophets) must align with is the gospel message about Christ's life, death, and resurrection. The apostle Paul affirms this in Galatians 1:6–8:

> I am astonished that you are so quickly deserting him who called you in the grace of Christ and are turning to a different gospel—not that there is another one, but there are some who trouble you and want to distort the gospel of Christ. But even if we or an angel from heaven should preach to you a gospel contrary to the one we preached to you, let him be accursed.

The issue here was teachers' coming to the church in Galatia and calling the people to follow a different god from the one revealed in the Bible through corrupting the gospel. Paul declares that if even he or an angel comes with a different message from the one contained in the Scripture, he is not to be listened to, but cursed. His point is that the apostolic gospel recorded in the New Testament is the only true foundation on which the church is to be built (Eph. 2:20).

When a false prophet arises among Israel, seeking to lead its people into idolatry, they are not to follow him. Instead, they are to recognize this as a test: "For the Lord your God is testing you, to know whether you love the Lord your God with all your heart and with all your soul" (Deut. 13:3). We have already seen in Deuteronomy that there is nothing that God does not know. But what the test of the false prophet reveals is the nature of our love and devotion to the one true God. The rise of a false prophet or false teaching provides occasion for the loyalty of God's people to be displayed. The evidence of our loyalty will be seen by the degree to which we do not go after other gods but live out the commands of Deuteronomy 13:4: "You shall walk after the Lord your God and fear him and keep his commandments and obey his voice, and you shall serve him and hold fast to him." The word order of each phrase here in the Hebrew emphasizes the people's devotion to Yahweh by putting his name first in each clause.[4] It sounds like this: "After the Lord your God you shall walk, him you shall fear, his commandments you shall keep, his voice you shall obey, him you shall serve, and to him you shall hold fast." These verbs are all familiar to us from other parts of Deuteronomy and reflect the wholehearted devotion that God requires of his vassal people. This is what covenant faithfulness looks like. But what about the false prophet?

He is to be dealt with severely. Moses directs in Deuteronomy 13:5:

> But that prophet or that dreamer of dreams shall be put to death, because he has taught rebellion against the Lord your God, who brought you out of the land of Egypt and redeemed you out of the house of slavery, to make you leave the way in which the Lord your God commanded you to walk. So you shall purge the evil from your midst.

4. J. G. McConville, *Deuteronomy*, ApOTC 5 (Inter-Varsity Press, 2002), 237.

To teach rebellion against Yahweh was a capital crime in Israel because to rebel against Yahweh was to rebel against Israel's suzerain. Moses reminds the people that it was God who delivered them from Egypt to be his special covenant people, and therefore anyone who would try to get them to rebel against God and go back into slavery to idols must be put to death. In so doing, they were "purging" or "burning" the evil from among them. False prophets were to be removed, not tolerated. If I were to get a cancer diagnosis and discover that there is a force within my body that is corrupting other parts of my body, I would be foolish to watch that happen without doing anything about it. Instead, I would immediately begin to rid my body of that dangerous disease. So also, false prophecy, false teaching, and any person who seeks to lead God's people away from faithfulness to him needs to be removed from the body.

Should false prophets therefore be put to death today? No. The execution of false prophets was limited to that time when God's people were a nation state and functioned as a theocracy. With the coming of Jesus and the global expansion of the gospel, the church is no longer to wield the sword and carry out executions on false prophets. The Presbyterian Church in America's *Book of Church Order* is correct when it states: "The power of the Church is exclusively spiritual; that of the State includes the exercise of force."[5] This is not to say that the church has always believed or practiced this precept. The history of the church is full of examples of false prophets and heretics (or suspected ones) being executed for trying to lead God's people astray. But to execute people like this is to fail to recognize the shift in the proper application of Deuteronomy under the new covenant. The appropriate response to false prophets at this point of redemptive history is not execution, but excommunication. Paul writes in 1 Corinthians 5:1–2: "It is actually reported that there is sexual immorality among you, and of a kind that is not tolerated even among pagans, for a man has his father's wife. And you are arrogant! Ought you not rather to mourn? Let him who has done this be removed from among you." After describing the process of excommunication of a man who would have been executed under the conditions of the Mosaic law, he then goes on to connect his teaching with Deuteronomy by quoting it:

5. *The Book of Church Order of the Presbyterian Church in America* (Office of the Stated Clerk of the General Assembly of the Presbyterian Church in America, 2021), 3–4.

"Purge the evil person from among you" (1 Cor. 5:13). If execution were still the appropriate response to false teachers and those who would lead others astray, we can be sure that Paul would have practiced execution. His zeal for God was unparalleled, and threat of punishment by the Romans would not have stopped him. But execution is not what he commands because it is no longer suitable in the gospel age. The ultimate judgment of church discipline is cutting a corrupting person out of Christian fellowship.

We may be tempted to look with disdain on the people of God in the Old Testament, or even our brothers and sisters in Christ through church history, who have used execution to deal with false prophets. We should not. The church was wrong to wield the sword, but we may be guilty of sinning in the opposite way. Christopher Wright observes:

> We respond to idolatrous, blasphemous evil not with a curse, but a shrug, and then have the gall to claim morally higher ground than ancient Israel. . . . If we can no longer identify with the scale of priorities and values that undergird Deuteronomy 13, it is manifestly not because we have acquired a greater appreciation of the value of human life, but because we have lost any sense of the awful majesty of God's reality.[6]

Our own tepid response to false teaching does not so much reveal our enlightened sensibility as much as it shows our comfort with idolatry.

Resist Relational Enticement to Idolatry

The second way in which God's people may be led astray into idolatry is through close family relationships. Moses warns against this in Deuteronomy 13:6–7:

> If your brother, the son of your mother, or your son or your daughter or the wife you embrace or your friend who is as your own soul entices you secretly, saying, "Let us go and serve other gods," which neither you nor your fathers have known, some of the gods of the peoples who are around you, whether near you or far off from you, from the one end of the earth to the other . . .

6. Christopher Wright, *Deuteronomy*, NIBC: Old Testament 4 (Hendrickson, 2007), 177–78.

Notice the close relational bonds mentioned. Who is closer than one's brother, child, spouse, or best bosom buddy? It is entirely possible that one of God's people may be tempted by his or her own spouse, child, or good friend. What are people to do when someone as close as this seeks to entice them to serve a god other than Yahweh? Moses goes on to say in Deuteronomy 13:8–10 that

> you shall not yield to him or listen to him, nor shall your eye pity him, nor shall you spare him, nor shall you conceal him. But you shall kill him. Your hand shall be first against him to put him to death, and afterward the hand of all the people. You shall stone him to death with stones, because he sought to draw you away from the LORD your God, who brought you out of the land of Egypt, out of the house of slavery.

The temptation will be to yield, or listen, or spare the person the consequences of his sin. But that is the wrong response. Instead, God's people are to be the ones who throw the first stones to put that person to death. Such a treatment of the one who would lead others into idolatry is supposed to be a deterrent against others' doing the same (Deut. 13:11).

We can all agree that this requirement is intense. It should be difficult for us to imagine doing this to our own brother, child, spouse, or best friend. We might even find ourselves saying, "I would never do that." Let me be clear: we are not called to do that. But this does not mean that God cares any less about our devotion to him. If we say to ourselves, "I would never do that even if I lived in ancient Israel," then what we are saying is that we have a loyalty deeper than our loyalty to God. In short, we have an idol. God cares about this underlying devotion as much in the New Testament as he does in the Old Testament. Listen to Jesus' words and notice the echo of Deuteronomy in Matthew 10:37: "Whoever loves father or mother more than me is not worthy of me, and whoever loves son or daughter more than me is not worthy of me." Or Luke 14:26: "If anyone comes to me and does not hate his own father and mother and wife and children and brothers and sisters, yes, and even his own life, he cannot be my disciple." God calls for such loyalty that everything else looks like hatred by comparison. Of course, Deuteronomy is not anti-family, and Jesus is not anti-family. But they were both passionately anti-idolatry, and the family may be the toughest and most subtle of enticements away from devotion to God.[7] If we have loyalty anywhere deeper than our loyalty to Jesus, then we have a functional god and savior in this world. That is what we are trusting to give our life purpose and meaning. This person or thing will lead us further away from our pure devotion to God. Resist.

Some of us may be the husband or wife or close friend who is leading one away from full devotion to Jesus. We must not do that. Let the warning about what is to be done to such a person show us the seriousness of our sin and lead us to repentance. If we are married to unbelievers and they consent to live with us, we are not to leave them (1 Cor. 7:12–13). Instead, we should pray for them and aim to win them through our conduct (1 Peter 3:1–2). But we are also not to let anyone or anything draw us away from our pure devotion to Jesus Christ. For those of us who are parents, we should beware that we may be enticing our children away from pure devotion to Jesus to pursue our idols.

RESIST CULTURAL PRESSURE TO IDOLATRY

The third scenario arises when a whole city has turned from the Lord. We read in Deuteronomy 13:12–15:

> If you hear in one of your cities, which the LORD your God is giving you to dwell there, that certain worthless fellows have gone out among you and have drawn away the inhabitants of their city, saying, "Let us go and serve other gods," which you have not known, then you shall inquire and make search and ask diligently. And behold, if it be true and certain that such an abomination has been done among you, you shall surely put the inhabitants of that city to the sword, devoting it to destruction, all who are in it and its cattle, with the edge of the sword.

The first thing that the Israelites are to do when they hear that a whole town has apostatized is to verify that it is true. (Joshua 22 is a description of just such an occurrence.) If it is true, the entire city is to be devoted to destruction,

7. Wright, 176.

meaning that every living thing in it is to be put to death and that Israel is to keep none of the spoil of the city. (The prohibition against keeping any of the spoil of the city would keep people from destroying a city under the pretense that it was apostate just to take the city's possessions.) The apostasy was treated like an infection, and the complete elimination of those who were carrying the infection served to protect the rest of God's people. In this case, the city itself has succumbed to the pressure to serve other gods, and the consequence is death. Ultimately, death and destruction come to the whole city because some family member or friend did not report the apostasy when it first developed. This person thought he was showing pity to his loved one but ended up bringing death to everyone.

A parallel concept in our own day is a church's allowing false teaching. The elders of the church, much like the elders of a city and the parents in a home, have a responsibility to see that no one in the fellowship is leading people astray. When the elders fail to do their job, all the people ultimately suffer through the spread of false teaching. We have said before that not all false teaching is equally dangerous. There are some matters in the Bible about which Christians can legitimately disagree and still share close fellowship with one another. But when central truths are distorted—particularly things about the person and work of Jesus—such corruptions are not to be tolerated. To allow heresy is to allow destruction to come upon a people. It is not loving to allow a false teacher or to allow a movement of false teaching to lead God's people astray.

There are numerous ways for God's people to be led astray into idolatry, as surely as those drivers were led astray by Google Maps into the mud. It can happen through spiritual deception, it can happen through the closest relationships we enjoy on earth, or it can happen through sharing in the general decline of an entire culture. But we must not be carried away into idolatry; we must ruthlessly resist it. The intensity with which this passage speaks of resisting idolatry is to be present in our own lives, even if we are not carrying out the death penalty on people who entice us. Instead, we are to put every trace of idolatry to death in our own lives when we see it rising up, because it will not be long before we see the kinds of sacrifices that our idols will demand.

When we go astray after any other god, that god will demand sacrifices and ultimately our lives. Every god out there requires sacrifices, but only one God became a sacrifice for us. This passage reminds us that we are all guilty of idolatry and deserve the death penalty. But the good news of the gospel is that the only one who did not falter in his devotion to God gave himself up as a sacrifice for us to pay the price of our idolatry. He took the judgment that our idolatry deserved so that we could experience the blessings of his obedience in our reconciled relationship with God. He gives this gift to all who receive it by faith alone. Having received this gift, we renounce our idols, and we freshly commit ourselves to resisting both internal and external enticements to worship them any longer. Every other god out there will ultimately demand our life, but the one true God who calls for our life first gave his life for us. Let us remember today what he has done for us, let us trust that his warnings against idolatry are good, and let us obey his command to have no other gods before him.

23

Be Distinctively Different

Deuteronomy 14:1–21

You shall not eat any abomination. (Deut. 14:3)

Those who enjoy eating Kellogg's Corn Flakes may be surprised to learn the origin of that classic breakfast cereal. John Harvey Kellogg and his brother Will were both steeped in the Adventist theological tradition in Battle Creek, Michigan. Ellen White was the self-proclaimed prophetess of Seventh-day Adventism, and during the 1860s, she claimed to have received revelations about diet and hygiene for her followers. Her directions for how to eat relied heavily on Genesis 1:29, and she advocated a strictly vegetarian diet. This diet, along with abstention from coffee, tea, alcohol, tobacco, and drugs, was intended to reduce people's inclinations to sexual sin.[1]

For those adopting this kind of diet in the nineteenth century, breakfast was an especially problematic meal. Breakfast typically consisted of potatoes, fried in the congealed fat from last night's dinner, or heavily cured and salted meats, such as bacon and ham. Others ate brown bread, milk toast, or graham

1. Paul addresses this kind of faulty thinking in Colossians 2:20–23.

crackers to start their day.[2] Having been discipled by Ellen White and her husband, and having completed medical school, Dr. Kellogg worked to come up with a grain-based, healthy breakfast that would be easy for mothers to prepare. In 1895, he came up with the answer: corn flakes. Today, many nutritionists and obesity experts would argue that the easy digestibility of processed cereals is not very healthy. Be that as it may, the Kellogg brothers revolutionized the American breakfast, propelled by the desire for a more biblical diet. Nor were the Kellogg brothers alone. In his book *Studies in Food and Faith*, James Jordan writes:

> Salvation through diet passed into the popular imagination through the writings of liberals like Horace Bushnell, sectarians like Kellogg and Charles Finney, and cultists like Mary Baker Eddy. As a result there is a pervasive orientation toward dietetic theology in American Christianity that colors our discussion of the Mosaic dietary laws.[3]

This passage in Deuteronomy 14, along with a very similar one in Leviticus 11, is sometimes used as the basis for these so-called biblical diets. Undoubtedly, Scripture contains principles of wisdom for how we should eat. But that is not what Deuteronomy 14 is about. Contrary to much popular belief, the food laws in this chapter are about not healthy eating, but holy living. The same is true for the somewhat mysterious commands that open and close this passage.

Three times in this passage, Israel's identity is firmly established. First, the Israelites are called "sons of the LORD your God" (Deut. 14:1). Then in Deuteronomy 14:2, Moses says, "You are a people holy to the LORD your God, and the LORD has chosen you to be a people for his treasured possession, out of all the peoples who are on the face of the earth." Then in verse 21, they are again described as holy to the Lord. The food laws in the chapter are not about the health of God's people, but are about the holiness of God's people! Everything in this passage confirms that God's people belong to him in a

2. Howard Markel, "The Secret Ingredient in Kellogg's Cornflakes Is Seventh-Day Adventism," *Smithsonian Magazine*, July 28, 2017, https://www.smithsonianmag.com/history/secret-ingredient-kelloggs-corn-flakes-seventh-day-adventism-180964247/, accessed March 25, 2022.

3. James B. Jordan, *Studies in Food and Faith* (Biblical Horizons, 1989), 8.

particular way, and this truth is to impact every single part of their lives, including how they mourn, how they eat, and how they worship. Even in the Old Testament, God does not say, "If you live this way, you will be holy." Instead, he says, "You are holy, and so therefore live this way." Holiness is not a position that we work ourselves up to every day, but a positional reality that we work out in everyday life. The indicatives of our identity precede the imperatives of our obedience. What we do should reflect who we are. To be holy means to be set apart for God. We are no longer our own and we no longer live for ourselves, and this holiness should be seen in every part of our lives.

Since the time of the New Testament, the food laws of Deuteronomy 14 are no longer in effect for God's people (Acts 10–11). But the principles that these laws were intended to teach are still integral. As God's covenant people, we are called to live *in* the world as distinctively different *from* the world. This passage lays out three categories in which our holiness should be seen.

We Should Be Distinctively Different in How We Mourn

The passage opens in Deuteronomy 14:1–2 with these words:"You are the sons of the Lord your God. You shall not cut yourselves or make any baldness on your foreheads for the dead. For you are a people holy to the Lord your God, and the Lord has chosen you to be a people for his treasured possession, out of all the peoples who are on the face of the earth." The Hebrew text emphasizes the identity of God's people: "sons you are . . . a holy people you are." Without these verses declaring who they are, the rest of the law in this passage would feel like something of an arbitrary imposition of a suzerain king on his vassal people. But these words change everything about how we read and interpret this passage.[4] What Moses says here to Israel is also true of Christians today. Paul writes in Romans 8:15–16: "For you did not receive the spirit of slavery to fall back into fear, but you have received the Spirit of adoption as sons, by whom we cry, 'Abba! Father!' The Spirit himself bears witness with our spirit that we are children of God." We are God's children not by birth, but by new birth and the gift of the Holy Spirit. We cannot take this privileged position for granted.

4. Daniel I. Block, *Deuteronomy*, NIVAC (Zondervan, 2012), 343.

The first implication of being a holy people is that "you shall not cut yourselves or make any baldness on your foreheads for the dead" (Deut. 14:1). This is a prohibition not against being bald, but against shaving part of one's hair as a religious ritual for the dead. Because the Israelites are holy, they must live as holy. Gashing and cutting the skin and shaving one's hair are mourning practices known throughout the world. They were also practiced in Israel and by Israel's neighbors.[5]

Cutting or gashing oneself as a ritual to deal with grief may seem like something from a distant time and place to many of us, but the fact is that self-harm and cutting are still practiced today by people we know and love. According to the National Health Service in the United Kingdom, grief is still one of the chief contributors to self-harm.[6] Recently, Australian tennis star Nick Kyrgios opened up on social media about cutting himself while experiencing depression. One study conducted across forty countries found that 17 percent of all people will self-harm at some point, and 45 percent of those will use cutting. According to emergency-room trends, there has been a 50 percent increase in self-harm among young females since 2009.[7] Of course, not all these people are necessarily mourning for the dead. They are mourning over who they think they should be, but are not. They are mourning over the mistakes they have made. They are mourning over the terrible things that have been done to them.

Though grief and mourning are as real for Christians as anyone else, as God's beloved children, we are not to express our grief in ways that are harmful. God has given us other resources to keep us from being swallowed up by our grief. Rather than wounding ourselves, we are to consider the wounds of Jesus. When we are aware of how we have fallen short, we remember that Jesus' blood has already been shed for our forgiveness. We must remember that the sins that others have committed against us do not reduce our value. We are tremendously valuable to God, as evidenced by the price he paid to make us his own. In the face of bereavement, Paul writes: "But we do not want you to be uninformed, brothers, about those who are

5. See, e.g., Isa. 15:2; 22:12; Jer. 16:6; 41:5; 47:5; 48:37; Ezek. 7:18; 27:31; Amos 8:10; Mic. 1:16.

6. National Health Service (UK), "Why People Self-Harm," https://www.nhs.uk/mental-health/feelings-symptoms-behaviours/behaviours/self-harm/why-people-self-harm/.

7. Recovery Village, "Self-Harm Statistics," updated August 30, 2024, https://www.therecoveryvillage.com/mental-health/self-harm/self-harm-statistics/.

asleep, that you may not grieve as others do who have no hope. For since we believe that Jesus died and rose again, even so, through Jesus, God will bring with him those who have fallen asleep" (1 Thess. 4:13–14). We grieve, yes, but not without hope. This is what is distinctively different about how we mourn as Christians.

We Should Be Distinctively Different in How We Eat

The bulk of the passage deals with eating. This segment begins with a general prohibition in Deuteronomy 14:3: "You shall not eat any abomination." "Abomination" is a strong word already used three times in Deuteronomy to refer to Canaanite idolatry (Deut. 7:25; 12:31; 13:14).[8] It reminds us that for Israel to eat any of what God had forbidden would be a form of covenant treachery.[9] Moses is going to address what may and may not be eaten in three categories: land creatures, sea creatures, and flying creatures. In 14:4–5, he tells the people which land animals may be eaten: "the ox, the sheep, the goat, the deer, the gazelle, the roebuck, the wild goat, the ibex, the antelope, and the mountain sheep." What do they have in common? Moses tells us in verse 6: "Every animal that parts the hoof and has the hoof cloven in two and chews the cud, among the animals, you may eat." Then in verses 7–8, we see that some animals part the hoof or chew the cud but do not do both. Any animal that does not part the hoof and chew the cud is "unclean" for God's covenant people. They are not to eat their meat, or even touch their carcasses.

Then we come to the distinction between various sea creatures; some are permissible and some are forbidden. The distinction is quite simple in Deuteronomy 14:9–10: "Of all that are in the waters you may eat these: whatever has fins and scales you may eat. And whatever does not have fins and scales you shall not eat; it is unclean for you." No specific examples are given here, nor are they given in Leviticus 11, where the laws regarding clean and unclean animals are laid out in detail. In short, bass would be okay, as would tilapia and mahi-mahi. But lobster, dolphin, and shrimp would be off-limits as "unclean" for God's people.

Then follows the third category of flying things that may and may not be

8. Christopher Wright, *Deuteronomy*, NIBC: Old Testament 4 (Hendrickson, 2007), 181.
9. Michael A. Grisanti, *NIDOTTE*, s.v. "תָּעַב," 4:316.

eaten. We read in Deuteronomy 14:11, "You may eat all clean birds." They are not listed for us here, but in the following verses Moses lists the ones that are unclean. In verses 19–20, he writes: "And all winged insects are unclean for you; they shall not be eaten. All clean winged things you may eat." Clearly, Moses is not aiming to recount the entire law in its specifics. He says, "All clean winged things you may eat," but he does not specify what those things are. One must refer to Leviticus 11. Among winged insects, the Israelites were not to eat any that walked on all six legs except those that have jointed legs to hop on the ground. So the grasshopper, the locust, and the cricket were okay. No particular birds are mentioned here or in Leviticus as being suitable to eat. Apart from the ones specifically named as unclean, all the rest could be eaten.

One final rule is given regarding what is not to be eaten, even if it is an otherwise clean animal or insect, in Deuteronomy 14:21: "You shall not eat anything that has died naturally. You may give it to the sojourner who is within your towns, that he may eat it, or you may sell it to a foreigner. For you are a people holy to the LORD your God." Anything that dies on its own is not to be eaten. The Israelites may give it to non-Jewish people and they may sell it, but they are not to eat it themselves. Why? Because they are holy. Now we can begin to see that the reasoning behind what is clean to eat and unclean is not primarily health-driven. If it were, it is unlikely that God would permit them to give it to the sojourner whom they are supposed to love. So why are some animals considered clean and others considered unclean?

Many people believe that clean animals are ones that are healthier for people. There are numerous problems with that view, one of which is why these laws would no longer be binding if they were established because they were good for our health. Others believe that these animals were used in Canaanite worship practices. Others think that unclean animals would simply have been repulsive to Israel, and still others think that unclean animals reflected some kind of divergence from the creational norm. The reality is, however, that we do not know why some are clean and some are unclean.

But we do know why Israel was to make a distinction between the clean and unclean. We are told explicitly in Leviticus 20:24–26:

> I am the LORD your God, who has separated you from the peoples. You shall therefore separate the clean beast from the unclean, and the unclean bird

> from the clean. You shall not make yourselves detestable by beast or by bird or by anything with which the ground crawls, which I have set apart for you to hold unclean. You shall be holy to me, for I the Lord am holy and have separated you from the peoples, that you should be mine.

The Israelites' food laws were symbolic of their distinctiveness as a people, while the distinction between clean and unclean animals corresponded symbolically to Israel and other nations. Christopher Wright observes:

> Just as from among all the nations of the earth God had chosen only Israel, so from among all the animals Israel must choose only those deemed clean for eating. The food laws were thus a daily reminder to Israel of their status and role in God's purpose and of the consequent call to holiness in other more morally significant areas of personal and social life.[10]

In the same way, we as God's people are called to live distinctively in every part of our lives. Consider one place where Peter connects these passages:

> But you are a chosen race, a royal priesthood, a holy nation, a people for his own possession, that you may proclaim the excellencies of him who called you out of darkness into his marvelous light. Once you were not a people, but now you are God's people; once you had not received mercy, but now you have received mercy.
>
> Beloved, I urge you as sojourners and exiles to abstain from the passions of the flesh, which wage war against your soul. Keep your conduct among the Gentiles honorable, so that when they speak against you as evildoers, they may see your good deeds and glorify God on the day of visitation. (1 Peter 2:9–12)

Because of who we are, every part of our lives should reflect the difference between us and "the Gentiles." Peter is writing to people who actually are Gentiles, but he counts these Gentiles as being part of the holy, covenant people of God. As a result, their conduct should reflect it, just as ours should.

Do we still need to keep these food laws? No. The passage we just read indicates why. The former distinctions between Jew and Gentile no longer

10. Wright, *Deuteronomy*, 82.

remain since Christ has come. Peter was the first to learn this through a vision he had in Acts 10. Peter had gone up to pray when

> he fell into a trance and saw the heavens opened and something like a great sheet descending, being let down by its four corners upon the earth. In it were all kinds of animals and reptiles and birds of the air. And there came a voice to him: "Rise, Peter; kill and eat." But Peter said, "By no means, Lord; for I have never eaten anything that is common or unclean." And the voice came to him again a second time, "What God has made clean, do not call common." This happened three times, and the thing was taken up at once to heaven. (Acts 10:10–16)

At that moment, some people came to take him to a Gentile's house to share the gospel. Peter continues, "And the Spirit told me to go with them, making no distinction" (Acts 11:12). Peter preached the gospel to the Gentiles, and the Spirit came upon them even as he did the Jews. There was no longer a distinction between Jews and Gentiles, and the food laws that indicated the distinction were no longer necessary. All such distinctions that would divide Christians from having fellowship with one another should also be broken down (Gal. 3:26–29). For this reason, at this point in redemptive history, any teacher requiring abstinence from particular foods should be understood as teaching something demonic (1 Tim. 4:1–5). Furthermore, Jesus declared that it is not what goes into our mouths that makes us unclean, but what comes out of our hearts (Mark 7:18–23). In saying this, he declared all foods clean. He also points us toward the moral heart of the law.

We should back up and consider what is meant by "clean" and "unclean."[11] For the Israelite, all of reality was divided into two categories: the holy and the common. If something or someone was not holy, it was considered common. For something or someone to be common is not necessarily to be sinful; it simply describes the ordinary ritual state of people and things.[12] The

11. Much of the following is dependent on the excellent work in Gordon J. Wenham, *The Book of Leviticus*, NICOT (Eerdmans, 1979), 19–29.

12. Though this is true, even in the Old Testament, the idea of purity/cleanness was being extended beyond ritual categories to the moral (Ps. 51:7, 10; Ezek. 36:33). It is also clear that the Old Testament emphasis on moral cleansing takes its vocabulary from ritual language. God teaches people to feel about sin as they are accustomed to feel about being in a state of uncleanness. See Christopher J. H. Wright, *Old Testament Ethics for the People of God* (InterVarsity Press, 2004).

category of common things and people can be further subdivided into the categories of clean and unclean things. Visually, we can illustrate it like this:

HOLY OR COMMON
(clean or unclean)

Most things are common, and the normal state of things is clean. But something that is clean can become unclean by being polluted through bodily processes, infirmities, or sin. Likewise, something that is holy can become common by being profaned. It looks like this:

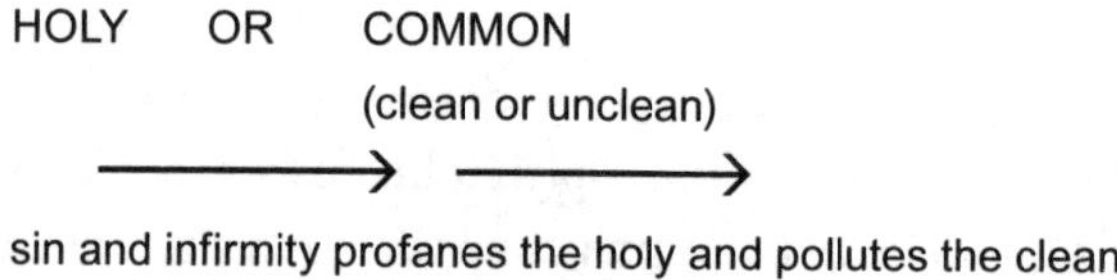

In a similar way, something unclean can become clean by means of cleansing or purifying through washings or sacrifices. Furthermore, that which is common and clean can be made holy through a process of sanctification, which usually includes the shedding of some kind of blood.

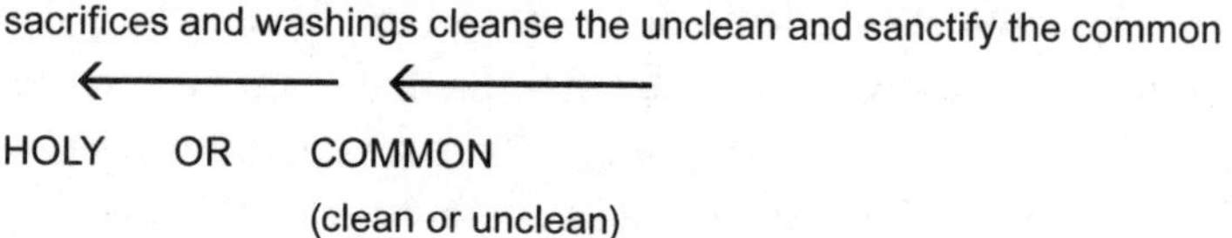

Putting it all together, it looks like this:

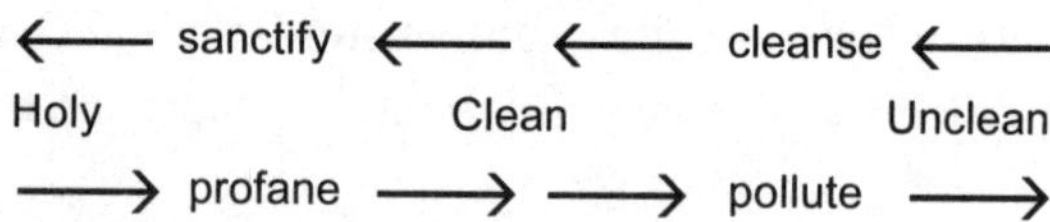

On two opposite ends of the spectrum are holiness and uncleanness. God is the ultimate holy reality, while on the ultimate end of the unclean reality is death. Apart from God and death, most things in between could fluctuate between being clean and unclean.[13] It is imperative that the holy never encounter the unclean. This is why Israel as God's holy people was to avoid contact with dead bodies and carcasses. It also helps us understand how radical a sacrifice it was for Holy Jesus to undergo death and burial, exposing himself to the ultimate uncleanness for us.

As we look closer, even among holy things and unclean things, there were various levels of gradation. For example, though all the people were holy, only the priests could come near to God's presence in the temple, and only the high priest could come into the Holy of Holies, and that only once a year after extensive rites of purification. The book of Leviticus was written to answer the question of how a people who are sinful and unclean could ever dwell in the presence of a holy God. The answer it gives is that only through sacrifices and the shedding of blood can the unclean become clean, and can the clean become holy and so dwell in God's presence.

And now we have new light from passages such as Hebrews 10:11–14:

> And every priest stands daily at his service, offering repeatedly the same sacrifices, which can never take away sins. But when Christ had offered for all time a single sacrifice for sins, he sat down at the right hand of God, waiting from that time until his enemies should be made a footstool for his feet. For by a single offering he has perfected for all time those who are being sanctified.

The sacrifice of Jesus has perfected his people for all time, making us forever fit to dwell in the presence of the Holy of Holies! As *unclean* sinners by birth and by choice, we are *dead* in our sins, but we can become a temple fit for God's own habitation through the cleansing, sanctifying blood of Jesus. When a person came into contact with someone or something unclean, the clean person became unclean. But when Jesus comes into contact with someone or something unclean, he makes the unclean clean. Jesus has sanctified even the grave for his people! We must all go to him and be made clean.

We are in a privileged position as God's children. We have been set apart from the world by him to live a distinctively different kind of life, and that privilege should affect every single part of our lives, including how we eat

13. Wright, *Old Testament Ethics for the People of God*, 297.

and with whom we eat. No longer should God's people be concerned about eating with sinners. Rather, these are precisely the kinds of people that Jesus ate with and that we should be eating with in light of the gospel.

We Should Be Distinctively Different in How We Worship

We close with one of the most enigmatic verses in all the Bible at the end of Deuteronomy 14:21: "You shall not boil a young goat in its mother's milk." This law stands out in the Torah because it is repeated three times (cf. Ex. 23:19; 34:26). Unfortunately, it is not clear in any case exactly why the law is there. Throughout much of the history of Judaism, this commandment has formed the basis for the prohibition of eating meat with dairy. This interpretation of the command likely developed sometime after the destruction of the temple in A.D. 70 and is almost certainly not what the commandment is about. In more recent times, a Ugaritic text was discovered that seemed to demonstrate definitively that boiling a kid goat in its mother's milk was a Canaanite practice. In that case, what was being forbidden here was worshiping like the Canaanites. It is possible that this is true, but it turns out that scholars were misreading the Ugaritic text, which did not actually refer to this practice.[14] Various other explanations have been given throughout history to explain this command, including the humanitarian explanation that it just seems cruel to do this.[15] While there is merit to some of these views, it is difficult to be certain about the purpose of this command. But when we consider the context that each mention of this law has in common, we start to get an idea of what it is about.

In both passages of Exodus where the command appears, it is in the context of bringing proper sacrifices and offerings to the Lord. Here in Deuteronomy, it is in the context of what the people may and may not eat. But immediately following these food laws are instructions about the bringing of offerings, connecting it with the two occurrences in Exodus. What is being

14. For an excellent academic treatment of the subject, see Tim Hegg, "You Shall Not Boil a Kid in Its Mother's Milk: The Interpretive History of a Curious Commandment," paper presented at the annual Evangelical Theological Society conference, Baltimore, MD, November 2013, 27, https://tr-pdf.s3-us-west-2.amazonaws.com/articles/you-shall-not-boil-a-kid-in-its-mothers-milk.pdf.

15. For this view, see Jeffrey H. Tigay, *Deuteronomy*, JPSTC (Jewish Publication Society, 1996), 140.

forbidden here is a particular way of preparing a sacrificial offering in the worship of the Lord. We are not told why it is forbidden. Perhaps because it was a Canaanite practice after all, but we do not know. What we do know is that God cares about how his people worship him, and this is one more way in which we are to be distinctively different in the world.

God used the Old Testament laws concerning holiness, cleanness, and uncleanness to teach his people the significance of their distinctiveness from the rest of the world, and the need for them to preserve holiness and cleanness in a world marked with ungodliness and moral filth.

It is through God's grace and Christ's work that we are cleansed and sanctified, and it is imperative that we be as diligent about our moral distinctiveness as Israel was its ritual cleanness. G. K. Chesterton was quoted as saying: "We do not want a church that will move with the world. We want a church that will move the world."[16] We wield this influence by being distinctively different from the world while still living in the world.

So having been cleansed and made holy by the blood of Christ, let us be distinctively different from the world in how we mourn, in how we eat, in how we worship—and in how we do everything—so that whether we eat or drink, we do all to the glory of God (1 Cor. 10:31).

16. J.John, "The Courage, Creativity and Charm of GK Chesterton," ChristianPost.com, November 4, 2021, https://www.christianpost.com/voices/the-courage-creativity-and-charm-of-gk-chesterton.html.

24

Growing Through Giving

Deuteronomy 14:22–29

You shall tithe all the yield of your seed that comes from the field year by year. (Deut. 14:22)

A man once came to Peter Marshall, the former chaplain of the United States Senate, with a concern about tithing. He said: "I have a problem. I have been tithing for some time. It wasn't too bad when I was making $20,000 a year. I could afford to give the $2,000. But you see, now I am making $500,000, and there is just no way I can afford to give away $50,000 a year." Dr. Marshall reflected on this wealthy man's dilemma, but he did not give any advice. He simply said: "Yes, sir. I see that you do have a problem. I think we ought to pray about it. Is that all right?" The man agreed, so Dr. Marshall bowed his head and prayed: "Dear Lord, this man has a problem, and I pray that you will help him. Lord, reduce his salary back to the place where he can afford to tithe."[1]

Some of us have experienced a similar problem: even as we have earned

1. Kevin G. Harney, *Seismic Shifts: The Little Changes That Make a Big Difference in Your Life* (Zondervan, 2005), 200.

more, we have given less. Perhaps at one point we were giving a tithe or more to our local church and kingdom work, but now it feels like too much. For the great majority of others, we have never given 3 percent of our income, let alone 10 percent. Tracing giving patterns in America, New Testament scholar Craig Blomberg reports that giving has mostly declined for the last century among American Christians.[2] The peak was in the 1920s, when Christian giving nearly topped 4 percent per person. Giving declined during the Great Depression and World War II and bottomed out in 1942 at around 1.5 percent. There was a slight increase in the 1950s and 1960s, followed generally by decreases, so that by 2009 giving was just over 2 percent.[3] The numbers continue to hover in the same vicinity.

In Deuteronomy 14:22–29, Moses gives God's people specific instructions about how much they are to be giving. Verse 22 directs, "You shall tithe." As a noun, the word "tithe" means "a tenth." If a person had ten pomegranates, he would give one as a tithe. The concept of the tithe first shows up in Genesis 14:20 in the story of Abram and Melchizedek. After winning a great military victory, Abram gives a tenth of his spoil to Melchizedek, the king of Salem. The tithe also appears in the story of Jacob in Genesis 28:22. These tithes were not commanded but appear to be expressions of gratitude in particular situations. The later Mosaic laws requiring tithing are given in Leviticus 27:30–33 and Numbers 18:21–32. While the particulars are difficult to nail down, we can say with certainty that God's people were called to give these tithes cheerfully. In addition to the compulsory tithes, other offerings were to be given both cheerfully and generously.

But cheerful and generous giving in the Old Testament was no easier than it is for people in the church today. Though God's expectations regarding giving are clear, so is our reluctance. The first reason for our reluctance is our fear that if we give, we will not have enough for ourselves. The people of Israel had better reasons to fear that lack than we do, but it remains a fear for many today. A second reason why people are reluctant to give is that they believe that those who need financial help are not deserving of it. A third reason that we are reluctant to give is that we simply do not want to.

2. Craig L. Blomberg, *Christians in an Age of Wealth: A Biblical Theology of Stewardship*, Biblical Theology for Life (Zondervan, 2013), 23.

3. Blomberg, 23–24.

But despite our fears and resistance, we should give generously, and three reasons are laid out in this passage.

We Should Give Generously so That We May Grow in Fear

The command to give the annual tithe is found in Deuteronomy 14:22: "You shall tithe all the yield of your seed that comes from the field year by year." From all their crops that they have grown, God's people are to take one out of ten for the Lord. Verse 23 tells us what they are to do with it: "And before the Lord your God, in the place that he will choose, to make his name dwell there, you shall eat the tithe of your grain, of your wine, and of your oil, and the firstborn of your herd and flock, that you may learn to fear the Lord your God always." The tithe from all their produce is to be eaten at the place that God chooses for the holy place, which will eventually be Jerusalem. It may surprise us that they will not be giving away the entirety of this tithe, but they are specifically commanded to eat it as part of their worship of God.

But this is where things start to get a little confusing. In Numbers 18:21–24, the tithe is presented as something that is to be given entirely to the Levites as compensation for the fact that they did not receive any land inheritance. The Levites were to be supported by the tithes and offerings of the people. The tithe eaten in Deuteronomy 14:23 is probably a reference to the same tithe shared with the Levites in Numbers 18:24, since it is unlikely that a family could eat the full tithe themselves in the time allotted.[4]

The Levites themselves are also commanded to give. According to Numbers 18:26, the Levites are to give "a tithe of the tithe" as their offering to the Lord, which would go to Aaron the high priest (Num. 18:28) and presumably the rest of the priests. Everybody gives. But the particulars of the tithe and how the various passages are harmonized are not laid out for us here. In Jewish tradition, the apparent discrepancies between the various texts regarding tithing are resolved by understanding three tithes. The first tithe went to the priests and Levites. The second tithe is the one that was to be consumed as a sacred meal in the place that God would choose. The third

4. Daniel I. Block, *Deuteronomy*, NIVAC (Zondervan, 2012), 358.

tithe is the "poor man's" tithe described later in Deuteronomy 14:28–29. It is likely that this third tithe was initially in place of the second tithe in the third and sixth years, but by the time of Josephus it was given in addition to the second tithe.[5]

But none of this is the focus of this passage. Instead, the people are instructed about the purpose of bringing this tithe to the place that God will choose and eating it there: "that you may learn to fear the LORD your God always" (Deut. 14:23). Part of the purpose of bringing the tithe was to instill in the people a proper sense of reverence for God.[6] To give him 10 percent is a reminder that he is their suzerain Lord who could rightfully demand all, but graciously allows his vassal people to keep 90 percent. The discipline of giving the tithe keeps them from forgetting where their ability to get wealth comes from (8:18). For people to give 10 percent of their produce to the Lord requires them to trust him that the remaining 90 percent is going to be sufficient to meet their needs through the year. As the people trust and God supplies, their fear of the Lord will grow. Those who have given sacrificially, not knowing where the money they needed would come from, know experientially how giving leads to growth in godly fear. When we give generously, we reverence God generously. When we do not give to the Lord, we do not grow in the fear of the Lord but our fear of him diminishes. When we do not give, we fail to recognize that he is the source of all that we possess. When we do not give, we miss the opportunity to see him provide more for us even as we are keeping less.

WE SHOULD GIVE GENEROUSLY SO THAT WE MAY GROW IN JOY

The next verses prescribe a remedy for what would have been a problem for many in Israel: hauling a large amount of produce a long distance. Moses explains in Deuteronomy 14:24–26:

> And if the way is too long for you, so that you are not able to carry the tithe, when the LORD your God blesses you, because the place is too far from you, which the LORD your God chooses, to set his name there, then you shall turn

5. For more, see David Henshke, *EDEJ*, s.v. "Tithing," 1310–11.
6. Eugene H. Merrill, *Deuteronomy*, NAC 4 (Broadman & Holman, 1994), 240.

> it into money and bind up the money in your hand and go to the place that the LORD your God chooses and spend the money for whatever you desire—oxen or sheep or wine or strong drink, whatever your appetite craves. And you shall eat there before the LORD your God and rejoice, you and your household.

Because hauling 10 percent of the produce may have been an enormous burden in the days before trucks and interstates, God made provision for the people. They could take their tithe of produce and convert it into silver, making it much easier to transport.[7] Once they arrived at the appointed place, they could then take the silver and spend it "for whatever you desire . . . , whatever your appetite craves" (Deut. 12:26). Here is a beautiful detail that is easy to overlook. While it was basically vegetable produce from the fields that they turned into silver to make the journey, they did not have to reconvert the silver back into vegetable produce. They could buy meat, wine, strong drink, and whatever else their appetite craved. In other words, God did not want this meal to be a boring and miserable one; he wanted it to be a party! He wanted their giving and their sharing of this meal together to increase the joy of everyone involved.[8]

Some of us have a commitment to being teetotalers from the consumption of all alcoholic beverages. I am one of those people. But for those of us committed to not consuming alcoholic drinks, whether in the form of wine, beer, or strong drink, we need to be clear that our conviction is a *personal* one, not a *biblical* one. The Bible does not prohibit God's people from consuming alcoholic beverages. It warns against the dangers of alcohol (Prov. 23:31; 31:4–5), and it most certainly condemns drunkenness as sin (Eph. 5:18), and there are times when drinking alcohol is not appropriate (Lev. 10:9; Rom. 14:15–21). But alcohol is one of God's good gifts when used appropriately (Ps. 104:14–15). Some of us have discovered that because even a

7. Actual money was not used in Israel until the fifth century B.C., so this would have been a conversion of the produce into various types of silver products.

8. The tithe is to be marked by joyful celebration in the worship of the one God. And the fact that all share in it symbolizes the oneness of the people of God. Gordon McConville, *Deuteronomy*, New Bible Commentary: 21st Century ed. (InterVarsity Press, 1994), 214. In a similar way, the Lord's Supper reminds us of the same reality of our unity in Christ. We eat of one bread and drink of one cup as a unified body. Additionally, we take the opportunity while remembering that unity to remember the parts of our body that are in need. If we are eating the Lord's Supper without remembering the needs of our body, we are not properly observing the Lord's Supper (cf. 1 Cor. 11:17–34).

little alcohol causes us to lose the ability to use it appropriately, it is better to avoid it altogether. But we should not expect others to embrace our personal conviction, nor should we be offended when others partake. It is perfectly biblical to do so, especially in the context of celebrating God's goodness.

When the wine ran out at the wedding that Jesus attended, he performed his first miracle to make sure that the party continued. God does not expect our reverence of him to be at the cost of joy! Nor should our joy come at the cost of reverence. But joy and reverence grow together in the heart of a true and generous worshiper of God. To bring the tithe and to mope around complaining about the cost is the opposite of God's desire for his people to rejoice in him and his provision. If we bring our offerings to God begrudgingly, we completely miss the point. Paul reminds us of that in 2 Corinthians 9:7: "Each one must give as he has decided in his heart, not reluctantly or under compulsion, for God loves a cheerful giver." If we are not cheerful as we give to the Lord and his work, we need to ask ourselves why.

Verse 27 of Deuteronomy 14 adds another reminder: "And you shall not neglect the Levite who is within your towns, for he has no portion or inheritance with you." Here we see instruction about not neglecting the Levite in the celebration of this meal because his sharing in it is dependent on the people sharing it with him and his family. The Levite was not going to be given any land in Israel because his job was to maintain the place of worship for God's people. Since that vocation did not generate income of its own as farming did, the people who were blessed by the temple ministry were called to give in support of the Levites. The apostle Paul uses this example as a basis for paying ministers of the Word in the New Testament: "Do you not know that those who are employed in the temple service get their food from the temple, and those who serve at the altar share in the sacrificial offerings? In the same way, the Lord commanded that those who proclaim the gospel should get their living by the gospel" (1 Cor. 9:13–14). Paul chose to forgo his right to be supported by the people and instead supported himself as a tentmaker. But he had a right, rooted in this Deuteronomic theology, to be supported in the ministry by the people to whom he ministered.

The same principle continues to this day, and it is one of the reasons why we should give to our local church. It is in our local church communities where we are ministered to through our various pastors and staff. Many others serve our churches purely as volunteers and devote themselves to this work, but some of us have been set apart by the church to give ourselves exclusively to church work. Since such work does not pay for itself, those who benefit from that ministry give to allow that ministry to continue and expand. If we are benefiting from the ministry of a local church, but we are not supporting the ministry of that church financially, we are not disregarding man, but God. We are missing out on the joy of obedience and the joy of giving. Not only that, but our lack of giving is limiting the church's ability to expand its ministry, which limits the spread of our joy in Christ. When we share what God has given to us with those who serve us, our own joy does not diminish, but increases.

We Should Give Generously so That We May Grow in Love

The next instruction regarding tithing in Deuteronomy 14:28–29 describes a tithe for the most vulnerable among the people:

> At the end of every three years you shall bring out all the tithe of your produce in the same year and lay it up within your towns. And the Levite, because he has no portion or inheritance with you, and the sojourner, the fatherless, and the widow, who are within your towns, shall come and eat and be filled, that the Lord your God may bless you in all the work of your hands that you do.

On a seven-year cycle, this special tithe was to be brought in the third and sixth years. As we saw earlier, it is difficult to say whether this tithe was in place of the normal annual tithe or in addition to it. From what we see in Deuteronomy, both here and in 26:12, it would seem that this tithe replaces the second tithe.[9] But by the time of Josephus, the Jews were practicing not only a tithe for the Levites and the second tithe to be eaten in the context of the festival, but this third tithe for the poor.[10] In either case, in the third and sixth years a tithe was kept right in the very towns in which the people lived. They were to "lay it up" to provide for the people in their community who did not possess land and therefore were most likely to be poor. The Levites would be responsible for seeing that these resources were appropriately

9. Henshke, "Tithing," 1311.

10. Timothy Keller, *Generous Justice: How God's Grace Makes Us Just* (Dutton, 2010), 197.

distributed to those who needed them; it was the job of the people to bring the resources. If all the people brought this tithe every three years, it would be enough that none of the people of God, or even the sojourners among them, would be destitute.

To give of what we have to our brothers and sisters in need, and even to others in our community, is not only an expression of love, but a way to grow in love. Not to give to those who are in need is to raise the question whether the love of God is in us at all. John writes: "By this we know love, that he laid down his life for us, and we ought to lay down our lives for the brothers. But if anyone has the world's goods and sees his brother in need, yet closes his heart against him, how does God's love abide in him? Little children, let us not love in word or talk but in deed and in truth" (1 John 3:16–18). To say that we love our fellow Christians without giving to them when they are in need is a failure of love. But when we see those needs and we lay down our lives in some small way for our brothers, we come to know love in a way that we cannot know otherwise. Love expresses itself in giving. We know from John 3:16, "For God so loved the world, that he gave . . ." Without giving, God's love for us would have availed nothing. But he gave his Son to become the sacrifice that paid the debt of our sins so that whoever believes in him would not perish, but have everlasting life. God's love did not diminish in the slightest when he gave us this most costly gift. In fact, if it were possible, the giving of this gift would have only deepened his love for us. When we grasp how dearly we have been loved by God and at what cost, we will find ourselves increasingly inclined to give in sacrificial ways to others.

It is difficult to determine precisely how the tithes worked. But the reason for the tithes is explicitly given to us. The first reason given was that the people would grow in the fear of the Lord. The second reason is given at the end of Deuteronomy 14:29, "that the LORD your God may bless you in all the work of your hands that you do." God's blessing on the community was connected to the willingness of those who had possessions to share with those who did not. When sharing happened, the whole community was blessed. God has numerous ways of taking care of his people. For some, he takes care of them by giving them the ability to create wealth. For others, he takes care of them by commanding those who have been blessed with the ability to create wealth to share it with those who have not. In this way,

God blesses all his people. Moreover, when his people give, all his people grow in fear, in joy, and in love.

The question that many people ask is whether Christians should still be tithing today. In the New Testament, Jesus chastises some of the Jews, who were diligently tithing of their various herbs but were neglecting justice and the love of God. He goes on to tell them that they should have been doing the latter, without neglecting the former (Matt. 23:23). In other words, giving the tithe was still a good idea, but it was to be part of a much bigger spirituality. Through the ministry of Jesus, the civil laws given to Israel concerning tithing were fulfilled and we are no longer under those laws, which is a good thing because it is difficult to sort out exactly what is required. But the general equity principles of these laws would suggest tithing as a *minimum* standard of Christian generosity and justice.[11] Randy Alcorn suggests thinking of tithing as the training wheels of giving.[12] For a child learning to ride a bicycle, riding with training wheels is not the ultimate goal. But the training wheels help the child learn to ride freely. So also tithing is not the ultimate goal, but it can be a helpful place to start learning how to give freely.

Parents should talk about giving with their children. We start children with training wheels on a bike not because we want them to stay on training wheels, but because we want them to learn to ride freely. In the same way, tithing can be a set of training wheels to help our children learn to give freely. We should teach our children early to think of everything they have as belonging to the Lord and to demonstrate that conviction by giving at least the first 10 percent. I am so thankful that my parents did that for me. It is difficult as an adult to go from giving nothing or 2 percent to giving 10 percent or more. So teach children early to give, and model it for them consistently.

Some think that to give a tithe or to use the tithe as the set of training wheels for giving is legalistic. Ultimately, it can be legalistic, as can reading our Bibles or attending worship services. But it does not have to be. And the reaction against tithing has not helped American Christians give more generously. It is quite possible that between the various tithes described in the Old Testament, the Israelites were giving something like 23 percent

11. Keller, 196.

12. Randy Alcorn, *Managing God's Money: A Biblical Guide* (Tyndale House, 2011), 121.

of their income. While the numbers on giving by Christians in churches varies from year to year, on average it is closer to 2.5 percent, which includes giving to the church, missions, and benevolence. Alcorn puts this data into perspective: "This statistic suggests that the Israelites were four times more responsive to the law of Moses than the average American Christian is to the grace of Christ!"[13] This should not be! By the way, if giving 10 percent feels legalistic, by all means, give 11 or 12 or 20 percent!

We need to consider our giving. We can examine our tax documents to realistically assess how much we are actually giving in a particular year. We should consider our income, and then consider our giving to the ministry of our local church. Are we giving at least 10 percent? If not, why are we giving less than the people of God under the old covenant, who did not have nearly the revelation of God's grace or promises that we have today? Do we fear that if we raised our giving to at least the level of God's people under the Mosaic covenant, God would not take care of our needs? Let us take a realistic assessment, and then let us step into cheerful and generous giving.

Malachi 3:10 is one place in Scripture where God's people are invited to put him to the test. The test is this: bring in the full tithe to the storehouse so that there would be food available for the Lord's purposes (namely, the support of the Levites and priests and care for the poor). If the people would do it, God promised to pour out such blessing (clearly financial in this case) on them as a nation that they would not be able to handle it. The link is made between Malachi 3:10–12 and what we see here in Deuteronomy 14:29. This promise was made to God's people under the Mosaic covenant, and God's people today should not necessarily expect a financial blessing in return for generosity. But will God be any less generous in providing for the needs of his people today under the more glorious terms of the new covenant? God is no man's debtor. He will never let us outgive him. But do not take my word for it. Test him.

Let me encourage all of us to first look up and then look within. Consider the Savior and the riches of his grace. When we were dead in sins, he made us alive with Christ and gave us a hope and a future. Consider how he brought us into his own family and surrounded us with love in the local church. Consider that it is he who gave us the ability to generate whatever

13. Alcorn, 119.

wealth we have, whether it is a lot or a little. Consider the promises he has given to us regarding his provision and his protection. Consider his great invitations, such as we find in Malachi, to test him in our giving and see that he pours out such blessing in our lives that we will not be able to hold it all. Consider the promised inheritance that awaits us in the new heavens and earth. Consider the promise extended to those who are diligent to store up treasures in heaven versus the futility of storing up treasures on earth.

Then look within. In light of all that God has given and promised, are we content with what we are giving? Does our giving reflect the true level of our own gratitude for what he has done? Does our giving reflect our trust in his promises of what he will do? Does our giving reflect a heart that is committed to storing up treasures in heaven rather than treasures on earth? Does our giving reflect a heart for justice and love for God's people? Consider how we will feel the moment we enter heaven and see what we spent on the things of this world, and what we invested in things that are eternal. At that point, it will be too late.

So let us remember God's faithfulness and his promises to provide. Let us trust him to do so. And let us give cheerfully and generously to him so that we may grow in fear, in joy, and in love.

25

Open Wide Your Hand

Deuteronomy 15:1–23

For there will never cease to be poor in the land. Therefore I command you, "You shall open wide your hand to your brother, to the needy and to the poor, in your land." (Deut. 15:11)

What causes poverty among a people? It depends, of course, on whom you ask.[1] If you were to ask people who dwell more on the left-wing side of the political spectrum, they would say that the causes of poverty are usually social forces beyond the ability of the poor to control: racial prejudice, economic deprivation, and other types of social injustice. Conversely, if you asked people who fall more on the right-wing side of the political spectrum, they would say that the causes of poverty are usually forces within the ability of the poor to control: the breakdown of the traditional family, the loss of important character traits such as hard work and discipline, and other bad habits or behavior. But what does the Bible say about the causes of poverty?

1. For the material in the next two paragraphs, I am indebted to Timothy Keller, *Generous Justice: How God's Grace Makes Us Just* (Dutton, 2010), 33–34.

When we come to the Bible, we find that the causes of poverty are far more balanced than either the political left or right would suggest. On the one hand, poverty is caused by oppression in the form of unfair judicial systems (Lev. 19:15), loans with exploitative interest rates (Ex. 22:25–27), and unjustly low wages (Jer. 22:13). Additionally, under the Mosaic law a great deal of instructions aimed to keep the disparities between the rich and poor from growing too large; when those disparities did grow, the responsibility fell on the wealthy and powerful (Prov. 13:23; Isa. 5:8–10; Amos 5:11–12; Mic. 2:1–2). Based on this survey, it sounds like the liberals are right. But the Bible says more. Sometimes natural disasters are the cause of poverty, whether it be famine, flood, fire, or even a disabling injury. To the credit of those on the right wing, the Bible would agree that sometimes laziness is a cause of poverty (Prov. 6:6–11), as well as a lack of discipline manifested in a variety of sinful ways (23:20–21). Poverty is not a simple problem. Solutions that suggest that the poor are not responsible for poverty or that society is not responsible for poverty both fall short of reality. We do not have space to consider everything the Bible says about this subject, but in this passage, we see a couple of ways in which God's people are to address the problem of poverty.

Two seemingly contradictory statements are juxtaposed in Deuteronomy 15. In verse 4, Moses states, "There will be no poor among you." Then in verse 11, he says, "For there will never cease to be poor in the land." Both are true. Verse 4 describes what should be the reality among God's people: there should be no poor among them, if they obeyed the commandments that God gave them in the law. But verse 11 takes into account the reality of the people of God. They are sinners, and they will fall short of what God requires. The result is that there will never be a shortage of the poor in the land. This perpetual reality of people in poverty should not make us cynical toward alleviating the suffering of the poor, but it should motivate us to openhanded giving. We should recognize the reality of verse 11, while being motivated by the vision of verse 4 to bring about the end of poverty.[2]

But there is a problem: us. From the days of Israel down to the present, rather than being openhanded, we are by nature tightfisted. We are afraid

2. Christopher Wright, *Deuteronomy*, NIBC: Old Testament 4 (Hendrickson, 2007), 196.

that if we forgive a debt, it will be more than we can afford. We are afraid that the person who appears to be in need is just taking advantage of us. We fear that if we open our hands, we will not have enough left for ourselves. These fears reflecting our scarcity mentality have been common to people ever since the fall in the garden of Eden. But in this passage, Moses is calling God's people to a radical kind of trust in God. He is calling them, and us, to faith. Because the Lord can be trusted, we can open our hands and give. Each one of the four segments of this passage has to do with trusting the Lord and opening our hands in some way.

We Can Trust God to Provide for Us When We Open Our Hands to Release a Debt

The first scenario in which God's people are to trust him has to do with debt forgiveness. We read in Deuteronomy 15:1–3: "At the end of every seven years you shall grant a release. And this is the manner of the release: every creditor shall release what he has lent to his neighbor. He shall not exact it of his neighbor, his brother, because the LORD's release has been proclaimed. Of a foreigner you may exact it, but whatever of yours is with your brother your hand shall release." This seventh year is called the sabbatical year. The same year is referred to in Exodus 23:10–11: "For six years you shall sow your land and gather in its yield, but the seventh year you shall let it rest and lie fallow, that the poor of your people may eat." The Hebrew phrase for "let it rest" is the same word translated in Deuteronomy 15:1 as "grant a release." In Exodus, the land is to be released in the seventh year from the burden of plowing, while in Deuteronomy the law is expanded to release human beings from the burden of debt.[3] In the seventh year when the land is to lie fallow and the people are not generating income, they could hardly make payments on their debts. So every sabbatical year, they do not have to.

The question is whether this release refers to the complete forgiveness of a debt, or simply to the release of the pledge of a debt.[4] It is difficult to

3. Wright, 188.

4. Robin Wakely, *NIDOTTE*, s.v. "שָׁמַט," 4:158.

determine from the Hebrew.[5] The ESV translation of Deuteronomy 15:3 suggests that it is the release of the entire remaining debt: "whatever of yours is with your brother your hand shall release." Whether temporary or permanent, the effect of the law was to give relief to the poor laboring under the crushing burden of debt. Debt was not to be an unending reality for God's people. The foreigner does not get the release. This is a benefit that is uniquely for the covenant people of God on the basis of the fact that they are brothers.

In Deuteronomy 15:4, God lays out the vision for his people when they obey: "But there will be no poor among you." Poverty is a reality, but it is not the vision that God desires for his people. One of the ways that the vision becomes a lived reality is through the forgiveness of debt. Imagine what it would be like if no one were carrying any unsecured debt. Families that can never catch up, let alone get ahead, would be free to begin saving. People who are constantly having to depend on the generosity of others to make minimum payments could have a fresh start. Debt is like a leech that just keeps sucking the lifeblood out of financial health. For this reason, God's people should avoid debt, especially unsecured debt, so that we can provide for our families and be free to give to others. A good rule to follow is that if we cannot afford to pay cash for something, then we cannot afford it at all. Exceptions can be made for the purchase of a reasonable home, which tends to appreciate in value, unlike most other major purchases. But Christians are called to be content with what we have and to resist the pull of materialism that leads to so much of contemporary indebtedness. When we have exceptional medical bills or long periods of unemployment and are tempted to take on credit-card debt, we should first go to our local church and see whether we can get help there.

But it is not primarily the forgiveness of debt that leads to the end of poverty among God's people; rather, it is the Lord's blessing that comes as they are openhanded toward one another:

5. It is also difficult, if not impossible, to determine what kind of loans this release covered. Since the release was specifically intended to relieve the poor, according to the Jewish *halakhah* the release did not include the forgiveness of unpaid wages, bills owed to shopkeepers for merchandise, and other types of secured loans. For more, see Jeffrey H. Tigay, *Deuteronomy*, JPSTC (Jewish Publication Society, 1996), 145.

> For the Lord will bless you in the land that the Lord your God is giving you for an inheritance to possess—if only you will strictly obey the voice of the Lord your God, being careful to do all this commandment that I command you today. For the Lord your God will bless you, as he promised you, and you shall lend to many nations, but you shall not borrow, and you shall rule over many nations, but they shall not rule over you. (Deut. 15:4–6)

The primary reason why there will be no poor among the people of God is that Yahweh is going to bless them in the land that he is giving to them. But in between the two promises of blessing is a key conditional statement: "if only you will strictly obey the voice of the Lord your God" (Deut. 15:5). If there are poor among them, it is because God's people are not obeying the voice of the Lord. For example, rather than forgiving the debts of their brothers, they continue to exact them. On the other hand, if they trust the Lord and obey his commands regarding debt and everything else, they will have an abundance. Not only that, but they will become a world bank with so much capacity that they can lend to many nations without having to borrow anything. As Proverbs 22:7 cautions, "the borrower is the slave of the lender." But if God's people will just obey his voice, none of them will be slaves of anyone. If they will each consider the interest of their brother and sister along with their own interest, then everyone will be better off. For the Israelites, to forgive a debt meant that they would not be repaid. It meant that they would have to look elsewhere for their provision, namely, to God. God promised to take care of them and bless them beyond measure, but would they trust him? And will we?

We are not under this law to forgive debts every seven years. But it does not mean that we cannot do so. God's promises to provide for us as Christians are no less certain than his promises to Israel. Perhaps someone owes us money. Maybe it is a little, or maybe it is substantial. We could consider releasing the person from that debt. If we decide to do so, we should tell the person why. We should explain that we were under a debt that we could not pay and that God forgave our debt. As a result, we are so thankful that we want to forgive that person's debt, and we are trusting God to provide what we need. Perhaps it is not a financial debt that someone owes us, but he has sinned against us. In this case, we have an explicit command to forgive the debt

(Matt. 6:12–15; 18:21–35; Col. 3:13). In the same way, this requires trusting in the Lord. To forgive a debt means that we are not making someone pay what he owes. Forgiveness (of a debt or of a sin) costs us. We feel that we are on the losing side—but that is where God invites us to trust him. We can trust God to provide for us when we open our hands to release a debt.

We Can Trust God to Provide for Us When We Open Our Hands to Give to the Needy

We read in Deuteronomy 15:7–8, "If among you, one of your brothers should become poor, in any of your towns within your land that the Lord your God is giving you, you shall not harden your heart or shut your hand against your poor brother, but you shall open your hand to him and lend him sufficient for his need, whatever it may be." The scenario is that someone from among God's people becomes poor. We are not told how the person became poor, but if he is one of God's people, he should not be allowed to remain in poverty. The American Puritan theologian Jonathan Edwards states it this way: "There ought to be none suffered to live in pinching want, among a visible people of God, who are able: unless in case of idleness, or prodigality, or some such case which the word of God excepts."[6] Those who will not work or those who insist on continually squandering what is given to them are choosing to remain in poverty, and the church is not responsible, though church discipline is likely in order. But toward the rest of the poor among God's people, they are commanded not to "harden your heart or shut your hand against your poor brother."

Neither heart nor hand is to be shut. The hard heart says, "You got yourself into this mess; you can get yourself out." The hard heart says, "Just get your act together." The hard heart says, "It is not my problem." The hard heart says, "There is so much need out there; if I help one, I will have to help all." We are called to be tenderhearted. But a tender heart by itself does not help the poor unless it is accompanied by an open hand. God's people should exhibit both the tender heart and the open hand. This is fitting for us as Christians who have received such kindness as we have from God! Again, Edwards writes:

6. Jonathan Edwards, *Works of Jonathan Edwards: Volume Two* (Banner of Truth, 1995), 163.

> How unsuitable is it for us, who live only by kindness, to be unkind! What would have become of us, if Christ had been so saving of his blood, and loth to bestow it, as many men are of their money or goods? or if he had been as ready to excuse himself from dying for us, as men commonly are to excuse themselves from charity to their neighbour? If Christ would have made objections of such things, as men commonly object to performing deeds of charity to their neighbour, he would have found enough of them.[7]

But right as we are about to open our hands and lend to those in need, a temptation will arise. We read in Deuteronomy 15:9, "Take care lest there be an unworthy thought in your heart and you say, 'The seventh year, the year of release is near,' and your eye look grudgingly on your poor brother, and you give him nothing, and he cry to the LORD against you, and you be guilty of sin." If we knew that next year was the year of release, we might be reluctant to lend to our brother in need because the debt would be forgiven soon. God warns, "Make sure that such a thought does not even enter your heart." That kind of calculation when giving to a fellow member of God's covenant people is unworthy of him and us. It is not simple stinginess, but sin. If we do not hear the cry of the poor among us, they will cry to the Lord, and we do not want to be in the position of answering to the Lord for ignoring their cries. Instead, we read in verses 10–11: "You shall give to him freely, and your heart shall not be grudging when you give to him, because for this the LORD your God will bless you in all your work and in all that you undertake. For there will never cease to be poor in the land. Therefore I command you, 'You shall open wide your hand to your brother, to the needy and to the poor, in your land.'" God will take care of us when we make it a point to take care of the poor. He will bless us in all that we undertake. Again, that might not be financial, but whatever form the blessing takes, we are better off with it than without it. God is no man's debtor. "Whoever is generous to the poor lends to the LORD, and he will repay him for his deed" (Prov. 19:17). When we are generous to those who are in need, we can be certain that God will honor it—if not in this life, in that which is to come. We can also add this one: "One gives freely, yet grows all the richer; another withholds what he should give, and only suffers want.

7. Edwards, 165.

Whoever brings blessing will be enriched, and one who waters will himself be watered" (11:24–25). Proverbs are not promises, but they are a description of wise behavior in light of how the world normally works. If we think we will be better off by withholding what we should give to the poor, we do not understand God's economy. In God's economy, the open hand will never be empty, while the tight fist will always lack. Edwards writes:

> To withhold more than is meet, tends as much to poverty, as scattering tends to increase. . . . Therefore, if you withhold more than is meet, you will cross your own disposition, and will frustrate your own end. What you seek by withholding from your neighbour, is your own temporal interest and outward estate; but if you believe the Scriptures to be the word of God, you must believe that you cannot take a more direct course to lose, to be crossed and cursed in your temporal interest, than this of withholding from your indigent neighbour.[8]

The question again is, will we trust God and open our hands to the poor?[9]

But then Deuteronomy 15:11 seemingly goes on to contradict verse 4 by saying, "For there will never cease to be poor in the land." Is this because the people will never actually care for the poor correctly? Or is it that there will just be a never-ending stream of people falling into poverty? It is hard to say. Edwards gives the following reason for this command:

> This is to cut off an excuse that uncharitable persons would be ready to make for not giving, that they could find nobody to give to, that they saw none who needed. God cuts off such an excuse, by telling us, that he would so order it in his providence, that his people every where, and in all ages, shall have occasion for the exercise of that virtue.[10]

Yet the fact that there will always be people in poverty is to lead not to a cynical posture toward the poor, but toward generous, openhanded giving:

8. Edwards, 168.

9. For more on this theme, readers should consult Jonathan Edwards's sermon "Christian Charity: Or, The Duty of Charity to the Poor, Explained and Enforced," in *Works of Jonathan Edwards: Volume Two*, 163–73.

10. Edwards, 163.

"Therefore I command you, 'You shall open wide your hand'" (Deut. 15:11). Jesus put it this way for his disciples: "Give to everyone who begs from you, and from one who takes away your goods do not demand them back. And as you wish that others would do to you, do so to them" (Luke 6:30–31). Jesus calls us to extend the Deuteronomic generosity even to our enemies, reflecting the mercy of our Father who is in heaven: "But love your enemies, and do good, and lend, expecting nothing in return, and your reward will be great, and you will be sons of the Most High, for he is kind to the ungrateful and the evil. Be merciful, even as your Father is merciful" (vv. 35–36). This does not forbid lending for business or charging reasonable interest in a person-to-person deal that benefits everyone, but the concern is particularly with the openhearted generosity that should be a defining mark of God's people.

In the early church, the vision of Deuteronomy became reality for a brief period. We read in Acts 4:32–35:

> Now the full number of those who believed were of one heart and soul, and no one said that any of the things that belonged to him was his own, but they had everything in common. And with great power the apostles were giving their testimony to the resurrection of the Lord Jesus, and great grace was upon them all. There was not a needy person among them, for as many as were owners of lands or houses sold them and brought the proceeds of what was sold and laid it at the apostles' feet, and it was distributed to each as any had need.

Why was there not a needy person among them? Not simply because people were giving 1 or 2 percent from their abundance, but because people were even selling assets to meet the immediate needs of their brothers and sisters. It was not the responsibility of the people to figure out where the money should go. They were simply to bring it to the church leaders, who would then distribute according to need.[11] In many North American churches, assets would not have to be sold to meet the needs of our brothers and sisters. But they could be. If we each simply walked in obedience to what we

11. For some givers today, relinquishing control of their giving to church leaders feels like bad stewardship. But if we cannot legitimately trust our church leaders with money, we need to join a church where we can.

learned in the previous chapter and committed ourselves to giving at least the 10 percent of our income required under the Mosaic law to our local churches, there would not be a needy person among us. We can trust God to provide for us when we open our hand to give to the needy.

We Can Trust God to Provide for Us When We Open Our Hands to Release Our Most Valuable Assets

The next scenario has to do with when a person is sold or sells himself or herself into indentured servanthood, usually to pay off a debt. In a quite literal way, the borrower becomes a slave of the lender. We read in Deuteronomy 15:12, "If your brother, a Hebrew man or a Hebrew woman, is sold to you, he shall serve you six years, and in the seventh year you shall let him go free from you." This is not the chattel slavery that was practiced in the United States and many other parts of the world. One key difference is that this is not a permanent position, but a temporary one as required by law. A provision is made in verses 16–17 for a person in this kind of servitude to stay in it for life, but it is a choice the servant makes because he or she wants to, not because he or she has to. But ordinarily, the servant is to be released. When released, the person is not to start out on his or her own at square one financially. Instead, we read in verses 13–15:

> And when you let him go free from you, you shall not let him go empty-handed. You shall furnish him liberally out of your flock, out of your threshing floor, and out of your winepress. As the Lord your God has blessed you, you shall give to him. You shall remember that you were a slave in the land of Egypt, and the Lord your God redeemed you; therefore I command you this today.

The Israelites' own experience of slavery is to give them compassion for those serving them. When they send a servant out, they are to "furnish him liberally." Even more specifically, they are to bless the servant as the Lord has blessed them. That is a liberal blessing! Without this financial blessing, the servant might very well end up selling himself into servitude again.

For an Israelite to let go of a faithful servant who has been working for him for up to six years may have felt like a tremendous sacrifice. That servant may have been his most valuable asset. Indeed, not only to let the servant go, but also to give him financial support on the way out the door might feel too costly. Moses addresses that issue before it arises in Deuteronomy 15:18: "It shall not seem hard to you when you let him go free from you, for at half the cost of a hired worker he has served you six years. So the LORD your God will bless you in all that you do." First of all, the master has received tremendous value from the person's service, so he is not to act as though this is an unbearable financial burden. Second, when the master releases this person with a generous sendoff, God will bless him in all that he does. Again, the question is: will God's people try to secure their own blessing by tightening their fists and being stingy, or will they open their hands to bless others, trusting that God will take care of blessing them?

It is hard to say what the modern equivalent of this situation might be. We might compare it to paying our employees generously rather than sparingly. To do so will certainly cut into the bottom line of the business, but it is hard to imagine a scenario in which doing so will not bring back a blessing upon the one who gives generously. Another possibility is how we react when some of our best people are leaving our company or organization to pursue other opportunities. Perhaps we feel that we are completely dependent on them and cannot afford to lose them. But then we must ask ourselves again where we believe our blessing comes from. Will we close our fists and seek to secure our blessing for ourselves, or will we trust the Lord and open our hand to others? Whatever the implications of this may be for Christians today, the passage says something plainly about God. He is not stingy and is eager to bless his people who demonstrate the same spirit of generosity.

We Can Trust God to Provide for Us When We Open Our Hands to Give Sacrificially to Him

The last section feels a bit out of place from the things that have gone before, but it is still addressing the same underlying question: will we trust the Lord and open our hands, or trust in ourselves and tighten our fists? Moses writes:

> All the firstborn males that are born of your herd and flock you shall dedicate to the LORD your God. You shall do no work with the firstborn of your herd,

> nor shear the firstborn of your flock. You shall eat it, you and your household, before the LORD your God year by year at the place that the LORD will choose. (Deut. 15:19–20)

The firstborn males belong to the Lord, and the people are prohibited from profiting from them through either their labor or their wool. Instead, they were to be sacrificed. If the firstborn had a blemish, it could not be used as a sacrifice, but it still could not be kept for the people's own profit. The difficulty in this is that the firstborn might be the *only* born. To give the firstborn to the Lord opened the people up to the risk of having nothing for themselves. The same is true with giving of the firstfruits of produce. But this is where God's people are called to trust.

The great challenge of this passage is the great challenge of giving for all of us: will we trust the Lord to provide for us? To help us with this, he has given us so many promises in his Word to strengthen our faith in his provision. Not only that, but he has given us a vision for a future where poverty is a thing of the past and where the burden of debt is no more. These commands, if they had been followed by God's people then, or if we faithfully apply their principles now, point us beyond the scarcity mentality of this world that makes us tightfisted. They bring us into the freedom that God intends for his children to enjoy that Jesus ultimately came to secure. One day, poverty will be no more. We should do what we can to make that future day today.

When Jesus began his ministry in Luke 4, he took one text as the paradigm for what he came to do. He quotes Isaiah 61 in Luke 4:18–21:

> "The Spirit of the Lord is upon me,
> because he has anointed me
> to proclaim good news to the poor.
> He has sent me to proclaim liberty to the captives
> and recovering of sight to the blind,
> to set at liberty those who are oppressed,
> to proclaim the year of the Lord's favor."
>
> And he rolled up the scroll and gave it back to the attendant and sat down. And the eyes of all in the synagogue were fixed on him. And he began to say to them, "Today this Scripture has been fulfilled in your hearing."

The aim of the Sabbath principle throughout the Old Testament is fulfilled in the ministry of Jesus. Through him, true freedom and rest will come. That includes freedom from debt, from oppression, from tightfistedness and all its effects. But it also includes freedom from the stinginess of our own hearts and the sin that so easily entangles. Even more, it includes freedom from the bondage of our debt to sin and the guilt we carry like chains. In Christ, we are truly free to love God with all our heart, soul, and strength, and we are free to love our neighbors as ourselves. In Christ, we know the love of God that expresses itself in such lavish generosity that we are brought into his family as children of the King, and so made confident to be generous to others.

Our Father is the King of the universe, and he has entrusted his people with certain resources. He implores us: "I want you to use these resources for my interests in my kingdom. Among the things I want you to do with them, I want you to be on the lookout for people in need, and I want you to give to them." Do we think that if we obey our Father's command, he is going to leave us in the lurch? Do we think we will ever lack for anything when we open our hands to him? Of course we will not. God has promised in his Word to provide for us and bless us, so let us trust and obey him by opening our hands to give.

26

Remember and Rejoice!

Deuteronomy 16:1–17

You shall remember that you were a slave in Egypt; and you shall be careful to observe these statutes. (Deut. 16:12)

One of the longest-running family reunions in West Virginia takes place annually on the Saturday before Memorial Day. My great-great-grandfather, Rev. C. J. Baker, instituted this reunion in 1918. Relatives gather at my grandmother's place, hitch up a hay wagon to a tractor, load it with food and people, and travel the three or so country miles to a hill, singing songs along the way. This hill that we call "Poplar" is in the middle of nowhere, West Virginia. To my knowledge, no one goes to this hill except for the one day a year that my family members gather on it because there is nothing there. Nothing, that is, except the bones and dust of our relatives, dating back to at least the early 1800s and probably longer. The most recent grave was dug in 1940. Not one of us who currently gather on the hill personally knew any of our relatives buried there. But while I was under my parents' roof, this was not a gathering to be missed for any reason. To this day, my dad has not missed one of these gatherings in his entire life, and the same is true for others. On that hill and among those graves we sing old hymns of the faith, someone from the family says a few words about why we gather, and we feast on some great down-home cooking. Then everybody goes home, some traveling twelve or more hours.

Why would anybody make it such a priority to go up to a place so hard to get to, gathering in a cemetery to remember people we did not even know and events we were not a part of? The reason is simple. There is something that we do not want to forget. Someone might object that we could meet anywhere, we could sing hymns any day, we could simply think about those people from home, and there is no need to go to all that trouble. Yet we know that there is something about the setting aside of time, the disruption of making a pilgrimage, and the ceasing from our ordinary routines that helps us to remember. This is true spiritually as much as in any other part of life.

We are prone to forget who God is and what he has done for us not just personally, but collectively. He is the source of *every* good thing we enjoy, and yet, amid the rush and busyness of life, we forget. When we forget, we become increasingly ungrateful, idolatrous, and rebellious. God in his wisdom has built reminders into the calendars of his people to help us remember and rejoice. One of these memorial days was called Passover, and in Exodus 12:14 God declared, "This day shall be for you a memorial day, and you shall keep it as a feast to the Lord; throughout your generations, as a statute forever, you shall keep it as a feast." Passover was just one of the three appointed times in the year when all the males were required to make a pilgrimage to a place that he would choose in order to remember important things about who God is and who they were. Deuteronomy 16:16 summarizes it this way: "Three times a year all your males shall appear before the Lord your God at the place that he will choose: at the Feast of Unleavened Bread, at the Feast of Weeks, and at the Feast of Booths."[1] These three feasts are the focus of this chapter. For each of them, we will consider the time, the place, the sacrifice, and the memory associated with the feast. As we will see, the feasts are no longer requirements for God's people, but to remember and rejoice in the Lord is no less important today than it was for the people of

1. More detailed information about these feasts can be found in Exodus 12, Leviticus 23, and Numbers 28–29.

Israel. As God's covenant people, we must remember God's rescue, God's generosity, and God's faithfulness, that we might rightly rejoice in him.

Remember God's Rescue

The first feast that we will consider has two constituent parts: the Passover and the Feast of Unleavened Bread.

The Time

The command regarding the Passover is given beginning in Deuteronomy 16:1: "Observe the month of Abib and keep the Passover to the Lord your God, for in the month of Abib the Lord your God brought you out of Egypt by night." The Passover was celebrated in the month of Abib (called Nisan after the exile) because this was the month in which the Passover took place. It started in the evening of the fourteenth day of the month (Ex. 12:18; Lev. 23:5). This typically fell in March or April of our calendar. The sacrifice was made in the evening at sunset (Deut. 16:6), just like the first Passover. The reenactment was a significant part of this memorial, as was the date. If the Israelites were busy on the fourteenth of Abib, they were not free to simply move the celebration to another day (though there is provision in Numbers 9 for what to do if they were unclean or on a journey that day). On the heels of the Passover came the seven days of the Feast of Unleavened Bread (Deut. 16:3). With each of these feasts, the people of God were to build their lives around these events rather than trying to cram the events into their busy schedules.

The Place

The Passover sacrifice was not to be made just anywhere, but in the place that the Lord chose (Deut. 16:2). In the original Passover, the sacrifice took place at each family's dwelling (Ex. 12:6). But not anymore. Moses emphasizes this in Deuteronomy 16:5–6: "You may not offer the Passover sacrifice within any of your towns that the Lord your God is giving you, but at the place that the Lord your God will choose, to make his name dwell in it." The sacrifice was to be taken up to the place of sacrifice, which would ultimately be the temple in Jerusalem. (The same is true with the other two festivals, so we need not mention the place again in those sections.)

The Sacrifice

The sacrifice was specified in Deuteronomy 16:2: "And you shall offer the Passover sacrifice to the LORD your God, from the flock or the herd, at the place that the LORD will choose, to make his name dwell there." The sacrifice could be from the flock *or* the herd. Originally, the sacrifice had to be from the flock, a year-old lamb (sheep or goat) without blemish (Ex. 12:3–6). Some think that because in Deuteronomy Israel was preparing to go and settle in the land, God allowed the required sacrifice to include cattle (i.e., "the herd").[2] More likely, Moses was talking about the other sacrifices that accompanied the Feast of Unleavened Bread in the week following the Passover sacrifice.[3] The point was that whether the sacrifice was from the flock (for Passover) or from the herd (for Unleavened Bread), the people were to sacrifice them not at home, but at the place that God would show them.

After the sacrifice of the Passover lamb on the fourteenth of Abib, the fifteenth through twenty-first would have been the Feast of Unleavened Bread (Ex. 12:14–20; Lev. 23:6). We read in Deuteronomy 16:4, "No leaven shall be seen with you in all your territory for seven days, nor shall any of the flesh that you sacrifice on the evening of the first day remain all night until morning." Then we read in verse 8: "For six days you shall eat unleavened bread, and on the seventh day there shall be a solemn assembly to the LORD your God. You shall do no work on it." During this whole festival, the people were not to eat leaven in their bread. On the seventh day, they had a solemn assembly. No one was to work on this day, but instead, they were to reflect on the significance of this festival. Some things are more important than working, such as remembering.

The Memory

The purpose of the annual Passover and Feast of Unleavened Bread was to help the people remember that they had been slaves in Egypt before God brought them out. We read in Deuteronomy 16:3: "You shall eat no leavened bread with it. Seven days you shall eat it with unleavened bread, the bread of affliction—for you came out of the land of Egypt in haste—that all the

2. Peter C. Craigie, *The Book of Deuteronomy*, NICOT (Eerdmans, 1976), 242.
3. Christopher Wright, *Deuteronomy*, NIBC: Old Testament 4 (Hendrickson, 2007), 202.

days of your life you may remember the day when you came out of the land of Egypt." As they ate the sacrifice of the Passover lamb and as they ate the unleavened bread, they were to remember the day that God had brought them out of Egypt.

Passover and Unleavened Bread were the central celebration of God's redemption of his people. Here the people of Israel would remember their life as slaves in Egypt under Pharaoh's oppression. It seems strange to us that they would eat "the bread of affliction." Who wants to remember their affliction while they are trying to rejoice? But God does not see remembering our affliction as antithetical to rejoicing. When the children asked the questions about why they ate the bitter herbs and the unleavened bread, the answer came in the story of God's deliverance of his people from their slavery and oppression.[4] Remembering what God has saved us from is central to the joy of our rescue. It is also worth noting that these people were all "remembering" something that they did not even experience firsthand. The generation that had experienced the exodus died in the wilderness. These people were now remembering the day of "their" departure from Egypt even though they had not even been there. But this event had shaped them as a people and they needed to remember, as surely as we need to remember.

It is good for us to remember what our life was like before we were rescued. Remember what it was like to be a slave to addiction. Remember the affliction of a guilty conscience. Remember the hopelessness, the misery of broken relationships, and the fear of death that once enslaved us. Remember the emptiness of living for money, the next high, the next party, or the next material possession. Remember the bread of affliction. Remember that day on which the Lord brought us out. Some of that freedom may have come to us years after we became Christians. Some of us may still be in strongholds from which we need to be rescued. Part of the value of eating the unleavened bread is that it reminded God's people of the misery of slavery, and remembering that should make them all the more diligent to avoid the idolatry that leads to slavery. One way for us to remember our affliction is to tell the story. When we tell the story of how Jesus saved us,

4. C. E. Armerding, "Festivals and Feasts," in *Dictionary of the Old Testament: Pentateuch*, ed. T. Desmond Alexander and David W. Baker (InterVarsity Press, 2003), 310.

and what Jesus saved us from, we get to relive and freshly rejoice in our salvation.

The freedom that the people of Israel experienced came through sacrifice, the sacrifice of the lamb without blemish, which became the primary Old Testament type by which to understand Christ's work of rescue. One theologian writes: "Like all the other sacrifices, it was expiatory. Animal life that was without blemish, so to speak not liable to death, was shed so that another life under judgment was spared. The beneficiaries were redeemed by blood not only from judgment but to be God's own possession."[5]

It was the Passover feast that Jesus chose to transform into a new institution that would commemorate his sacrificial death for his people. As surely as the blood of the Passover lamb over the doorposts of each home served to protect that home from judgment, so also the blood of Christ shields those covered by it from the wrath of God. At the Last Supper, the disciples were sitting around the table eating the Passover meal. We might have expected Jesus to pick up a piece of the mutton and hand it to his disciples, saying, "This is my body, which is given for you" (Luke 22:19). Instead, he picked up a piece of unleavened bread and identified it with his body. Why did he do this? Most likely, though identifying as the Lamb of God who takes away the sin of the world (John 1:29), he wanted to shift the focus in the future from the sacrifice to the need for ongoing spiritual nourishment.[6] Jesus was the Bread that came down from heaven that sustained the Israelites in the wilderness, and he is the Bread that continues to sustain his redeemed people today (6:32–41). We remember that in the Lord's Supper.

Sharing fellowship with Jesus carries with it the expectation that we will rid our lives of everything impure. Paul refers to the fulfillment of the Passover and the Feast of Unleavened Bread when he writes in 1 Corinthians 5:7–8: "For Christ, our Passover lamb, has been sacrificed. Let us therefore celebrate the festival, not with the old leaven, the leaven of malice and evil, but with the unleavened bread of sincerity and truth." We can remember every day, and especially at the Lord's Supper, that our Passover Lamb was slain and that we have been rescued from our slavery to sin, the fear of

5. Allan M. Harman, *NIDOTTE*, s.v. "Passover," 4:1045.
6. L. McFall, *NDBT*, s.v. "Sacred Meals," 751.

death, and the righteous wrath of God! As surely as the Israelites were to clean their homes of all leaven, so also we should cleanse our hearts of anything impure that is not consistent with his sacrifice. Let us remember God's rescue and rejoice!

Remember God's Generosity

The feast that God gave his people to help them remember his generosity is called the Feast of Weeks.

The Time

Moses instructs in Deuteronomy 16:9–10: "You shall count seven weeks. Begin to count the seven weeks from the time the sickle is first put to the standing grain. Then you shall keep the Feast of Weeks to the LORD your God with the tribute of a freewill offering from your hand, which you shall give as the LORD your God blesses you." After the first sickle is put to the grain, the Israelites were to count seven full weeks. At the end of those seven weeks, they celebrated the Feast of Weeks on the fiftieth day after Passover (Lev. 23:15–16). This would have taken place on the fourth day of Sivan (May-June), but we know it better as Pentecost. Like the other two festivals, it would take place at the place that God would choose (Deut. 16:11).

The Sacrifice

The people were to come to this festival "with the tribute of a freewill offering from your hand, which you shall give as the LORD your God blesses you" (Deut. 16:10). The sacrifice would have included bringing the firstfruits of their grain harvest and then, at the end of the seven weeks, an offering proportionate to how God had blessed them in the rest of the harvest.[7] If they had had a windfall year, they were to bring a windfall offering. The generosity of their giving was to reflect the generosity of God, which they were celebrating in this feast. It was to be a celebration that reflected God's generosity to all around, as we read in verse 11: "And you shall rejoice before the LORD your God, you and your son and your daughter, your male servant and your female servant, the Levite who is within your towns, the sojourner,

7. Jeffrey H. Tigay, *Deuteronomy*, JPSTC (Jewish Publication Society, 1996), 156.

the fatherless, and the widow who are among you, at the place that the Lord your God will choose, to make his name dwell there." They were commanded to rejoice before the Lord. Not only them, but also their children, their servants, Levites, sojourners, the fatherless, and widows. No category was to be left out of this feast regardless of ability to bring an offering.

Many of us think of holidays as "family-only" days. Perhaps sometimes they should be. But if our feasting never involves people who cannot afford to feast themselves, then our feasts can hardly be called Christian feasts. We should be intentional when we are celebrating God's generosity, such as at Thanksgiving, Christmas, and Easter, to think about including those who have no one to celebrate with, or who do not have the means to celebrate. Is this not what Jesus said in Luke 14? "When you give a dinner or a banquet, do not invite your friends or your brothers or your relatives or rich neighbors, lest they also invite you in return and you be repaid. But when you give a feast, invite the poor, the crippled, the lame, the blind, and you will be blessed, because they cannot repay you. For you will be repaid at the resurrection of the just" (Luke 14:12–14). Jesus is simply applying the teaching given to us in Deuteronomy regarding feasts to any expression of hospitality.

The Memory

Moses tells them in Deuteronomy 16:12 what to remember: "You shall remember that you were a slave in Egypt; and you shall be careful to observe these statutes." Perhaps while they were slaves, they could not eat the harvest that they had helped to produce. In any case, remembering that they had been slaves and now were not would naturally lead to rejoicing.

In the New Testament, it is not an accident that the Holy Spirit was poured out on the church on the day of Pentecost. We read in Acts 2:1, "When the day of Pentecost arrived, they were all together in one place." Into that place God's Spirit swept in, filling his people with his goodness. Christ's sacrifice, resurrection, and ascension led to the overflow of divine abundance in the outpouring of the Holy Spirit. On that day, Peter proclaimed the gospel, and three thousand souls were added to the family of God. It was the firstfruits of a global harvest that is still being reaped as God's people proclaim the gospel everywhere!

Indeed, the Holy Spirit himself is also spoken of as the firstfruits in Romans 8:22–23: "For we know that the whole creation has been groaning together in the pains of childbirth until now. And not only the creation, but we ourselves, who have the firstfruits of the Spirit, groan inwardly as we wait eagerly for adoption as sons, the redemption of our bodies." The Holy Spirit is our reminder that we have already received the firstfruits of new creation and our redemption, but we are still awaiting the fullness of God's new-creation work, especially the resurrection of our bodies. The presence of the Holy Spirit in us is evidence of the generosity of God that should be spilling out of our lives and into others through the kind of generous fellowship described in the book of Acts.

Remember God's Faithfulness

The people of God were reminded of God's faithfulness by keeping the Feast of Booths.

The Time

We read in Deuteronomy 16:13, "You shall keep the Feast of Booths seven days, when you have gathered in the produce from your threshing floor and your winepress." This festival would have taken place between the fifteenth and twenty-first of Ethanim/Tishri (September/October) (Lev. 23:34–40). It celebrated the ingathering of the summer fruits, such as grapes, figs, dates, and olives. The feast is also to involve all the people, whether they can contribute to it or not. Moses explains in Deuteronomy 16:14–15:

> You shall rejoice in your feast, you and your son and your daughter, your male servant and your female servant, the Levite, the sojourner, the fatherless, and the widow who are within your towns. For seven days you shall keep the feast to the Lord your God at the place that the Lord will choose, because the Lord your God will bless you in all your produce and in all the work of your hands, so that you will be altogether joyful.

God's blessing of them was so that the Israelites would be joyful. We ought to be joyful when we receive good gifts from God. We should not turn the gifts into gods, but there is nothing wrong with receiving a gift with thanksgiving. It is not uncommon for people to think that obeying God will make us less joyful. Consequently, we invent our own ways to try to be joyful in disobedience to God, not realizing that obedience is the only route to true joy. We must trust him in this.

The Sacrifice

It is not specified here what the people were to bring, but they were not to come with empty hands, as we read in Deuteronomy 16:16–17: "They shall not appear before the LORD empty-handed. Every man shall give as he is able, according to the blessing of the LORD your God that he has given you." To worship the Lord, remembering his faithfulness, without bringing a gift to share is unthinkable. Not only were the offerings that the worshipers would bring for each of these festivals to be enjoyed by the worshipers, but the vast majority would have gone to support the ongoing ministry of the priests and Levites who served the temple. Today, based on the same principle, we also are to bring to worship an offering proportional to how God has blessed us. Remembering God's faithfulness to us should lead us not only to rejoicing, but to a joyful kind of generosity.

The Memory

While the Feast of Booths was connected with the harvest of the summer fruits, it derives its name from what it was given to remember. Deuteronomy does not tell us what that is, but we read of it in Leviticus 23:42–43: "You shall dwell in booths for seven days. All native Israelites shall dwell in booths, that your generations may know that I made the people of Israel dwell in booths when I brought them out of the land of Egypt: I am the LORD your God." The people were to live in booths, or tents, to remind them of their wilderness wanderings and of God's faithful provision for them during that time. God had warned them earlier in Deuteronomy 6:10–12 that when they came into the land and enjoyed good things, they must be careful not to forget the Lord. Living in a tent for a week would have reminded them of their blessings, and also of God's faithfulness to provide for them during the forty years of their wanderings when they had no fields or vineyards or homes. This is one more reason why setting aside intentional times to remember and rejoice in the faithfulness of God is so important.

We know from later history that Israel did not keep these feasts well or often. In Nehemiah, we find a story recounted about the Feast of Booths. The people of God had been in exile on account of their many sins, and in Nehemiah a group of them had returned. Ezra the priest stood up and began to read the Book of the Law and explain what it meant. When the people heard it, they wept, for they realized how they had neglected God's commands (Neh. 8:9). The next day, the leaders, priests, and Levites came together with Ezra to study the law more intensively. They discovered this command to celebrate the Feast of Booths by living in booths (vv. 14–18). From the days of Joshua, they had not kept this feast. Joshua was the one who had led the people of Israel into the promised land after Moses died. This means that they kept God's law with regard to this command for basically one generation. But through the days of the Judges, of Samuel, of Saul, David, Solomon, and all the other kings, the days of Elijah and Elisha, the days of Isaiah and Jeremiah, the people of God did not obey this command. Is it any wonder that they failed to remember what God had done for them? Is it any wonder that they chased after other gods over and over and ultimately ended up in exile? The festivals were there to remind them of who God is, who rescued them from slavery, who provided for their daily bread, and who was going to bring the ultimate blessings that were still to come. By ignoring these intentional times of remembrance, they forgot.

So should we as Christians keep these feasts, or any feasts? The apostle Paul, writing to the Colossians, said: "Therefore let no one pass judgment on you in questions of food and drink, or with regard to a festival or a new moon or a Sabbath. These are a shadow of the things to come, but the substance belongs to Christ" (Col. 2:16–17). The issues of food and drink, festivals, new moon, and Sabbath were all pointing to realities fulfilled in Christ. Therefore, Christians are not to pass judgment on one another, nor to let others pass judgment on them, for either observing days, feasts, or festivals or not observing them. We do not have to celebrate the Feast of Weeks, the Feast of Booths, or the feast of Unleavened Bread. We also do not have to observe Christmas, Maundy Thursday, Good Friday, Easter, Ascension, or Pentecost. At some points in church history, Christians have not. On the other hand, we are free to observe such days if we recognize that they are just shadows that point us to the reality, which is found only in Christ. Given our proclivity to forget, it is probably wise for us to be intentional to remember.

Memorial days and feasts can help us to remember the most important things. It is why Americans pause on Memorial Day and remember the price of freedom paid by those who died for our liberty. It is why we recognize our wedding anniversaries. It is why Christians pause every Sunday to remember the rest that Christ has purchased for us and the freedom we have in him. It may not be a bad idea to create other intentional days to pause and reflect. For those of us who know the day we became a Christian or the day we were baptized, that would be a great day to set aside time to reflect on where we were and where God has brought us. All these are opportunities for us to push back against our proclivity to forget, and instead to remember and rejoice. A people always remembering and rejoicing in who God is and what he has done are far less likely to go after idols. The more we remember, the more we will rejoice.

So let us remember God's rescue, let us remember God's generosity, let us remember God's faithfulness, and let us rejoice!

27

Longing for Justice

Deuteronomy 16:18—17:13

Justice, and only justice, you shall follow, that you may live and inherit the land that the Lord your God is giving you. (Deut. 16:20)

Years ago, my wife and I lived in Dallas, Texas. Our apartment had a garage attached to it where I parked my bike. One day I came home from work and discovered the garage door pried open and my bike stolen. I promptly reported it to the police in hopes that they would go and search for the thief. When the officer arrived at the house, I told him what had happened, and he asked if I wanted to file a police report. I said: "Yes, of course. I want you to find my bike and the person who did this." He looked at me with a "bless your heart" kind of look and remarked: "Listen, you can fill out a report if you want to, but we are not going to get your bike back. And we are not going to look for this person. We have too many other issues to deal with." I was dumbfounded. I thought that this was what the police were supposed to do. I wanted justice, and the people entrusted with the task said that my issue was not important enough to merit their efforts. Fury and helplessness intermingled within me.

Have you ever been in that position, that someone wronged you and you had no recourse to make it right? Sometimes the system of justice that you are under works against you instead of for you. What if this were the case with every crime you experienced, not only petty theft, but grand theft, assault, homicide? Imagine a world in which there is no justice. Imagine having no recourse when robbed by a thief. Imagine being accused of a crime and being found guilty because the accuser bribed the judge. We take justice for granted, but we should not. Justice is not a given in society; it is a gift of God. Moreover, when justice is not practiced, evil flourishes. We need justice—both as a standard of right and wrong and as a system that enables the making of effective and binding judgments to set right the things that are wrong. This is largely what Deuteronomy 16:18–17:20 is all about in describing the work of judges and kings.

The work of judges and kings does not seem to logically follow the festivals in the passage before it. Grasping how this section of Deuteronomy is organized may help. One way of understanding how Deuteronomy 6–26 fits together is by seeing it as tracing the outline of the Ten Commandments.[1] For example, we have just passed through a section of the book on laws related to the sabbatical year and festivals that facilitate remembering who God is and what he has done. These commands are related to the fourth commandment. As we move into our current passage, they follow because they are related to the fifth commandment: "Honor your father and your mother" (Deut. 5:16). Nothing is said about fathers or mothers in this passage, but the fifth commandment is about honoring authority, and that is what this passage is defining.

In Deuteronomy 16:18, we meet the first of the four main types of authorities in Israel: judges, kings, priests, and prophets. At the risk of oversimplification, we could say, "Ideally, judges were meant to serve as the covenant's administrators, kings its guardians, priests its exemplars, and prophets its interpreters."[2] In Deuteronomy, authority is distributed among various leaders, which helps prevent the development of a concentration

1. For a brief overview of how this approach works, see John D. Currid, *Deuteronomy*, EPSC (EP Books, 2006), 17–21. While there does appear to be some correlation, there are exceptions.

2. Raymond Brown, *The Message of Deuteronomy: Not by Bread Alone*, The Bible Speaks Today (InterVarsity Press, 1993), 175.

of power. These checks and balances recognize the reality of sin and its effects when one person holds all the power. In this passage, the focus lies on the role of judges in maintaining a just society. The righteous practice of justice helps ensure that evil does not take root among God's people. When justice is not practiced, evil flourishes. In this passage, Moses lays out three threats to justice among the people of God that we must all be aware of and on guard against as the covenant people of God.

Corrupt Judges Are a Threat to Justice

In Deuteronomy 16:18–20, Moses gives the prescription for judges and warns of three ways in which they can be corrupted. The prescription is in verse 18: "You shall appoint judges and officers in all your towns that the Lord your God is giving you, according to your tribes, and they shall judge the people with righteous judgment." Judges are necessary because sin happens. Judges and officers were appointed in each city as a recourse for people to get resolution when wrongdoing had taken place. It is possible that these leading men among the elders were elected as judges, but it is hard to say with certainty.[3] Based on their function, they would have needed to be honorable and respectable people.[4]

The focus of this text is on their primary responsibility, which is to "judge the people with righteous judgment" (Deut. 16:18). Likewise, Deuteronomy 16:20 says that "justice, and only justice, you shall follow." The words translated "righteous" and "justice" are both the Hebrew word *ṣedeq*. In this context, the word indicates right behavior in relation to standards accepted in the community. It also entails the adjudication of such behavior, which is what the judges do according to the standard of God's law.[5] These judges are not to make judgments in any other way except in accordance with what is righteous as defined by God's Word. Biblical justice is built on a moral absolute—God's character—not on the shifting winds of cultural acceptability.[6]

3. Christopher Wright, *Deuteronomy*, NIBC: Old Testament 4 (Hendrickson, 2007), 204. In 2 Chronicles 19:11, the Levites served as officers.

4. In Job 29:7–25, Job gives us an illuminating picture of how he functioned as an elder-judge in Israel.

5. David J. Reimer, *NIDOTTE*, s.v. "צדק," 3:750.

6. Timothy Keller, "A Biblical Critique of Secular Justice and Critical Theory," Gospel in Life, https://quarterly.gospelinlife.com/a-biblical-critique-of-secular-justice-and-critical-theory/, accessed June 1, 2022.

One of the challenges in our modern context is that many people are calling for justice, but there is no agreed-upon standard by which to determine whether something is just or unjust. Philosopher Alasdair MacIntyre illuminates this challenge with an illustration. If a person unfamiliar with wristwatches is given a wristwatch and is asked whether it is a good or bad watch, the person cannot give an answer because he does not know what the wristwatch is *for*. Is it for hammering nails or for telling time? Only after the function is determined can a judgment be made. Likewise, unless we know what a human being is for, it is impossible to make any evaluation about what behavior is good or bad and therefore what justice is.[7] If the increasingly prevalent secular view is correct and humans are here by chance, then it will be impossible to agree on why we are here and thus what is just. But if there is a God who made us in his image, and he made us to glorify and enjoy him forever, then we can begin to identify what kind of behavior is just or unjust. Not only that, but we have a standard in God's law, and that standard is what these judges are to go by. But even if we have a perfect standard, if those entrusted with judging by that standard are corrupt, we will have injustice.

Three threats to just judges are highlighted in Deuteronomy 16:19: "You shall not pervert justice. You shall not show partiality, and you shall not accept a bribe, for a bribe blinds the eyes of the wise and subverts the cause of the righteous." The three commands given here are the three fundamental rules of judicial propriety found throughout the Bible.[8] It is forbidden to throw aside justice because of lesser concerns, such as taking care of a crony or lining one's pockets. Classes of people who have less social standing, such as the poor, sojourner, widow, and orphan, are the most likely to have their cases for justice perverted (Ex. 23:6; Deut. 24:17).[9] One of the most frequently condemned perversions of justice is bribery, which blinds the judge and prevents the righteous from getting justice.[10] God absolutely detests these corruptions of justice. Deuteronomy 10:17 reminds us why: "For the LORD your God is God of gods and Lord of lords, the great, the mighty, and the

7. Keller, "Biblical Critique of Secular Justice and Critical Theory."

8. Jeffrey H. Tigay, *Deuteronomy*, JPSTC (Jewish Publication Society, 1996), 160.

9. Most of us are on guard against being partial to the rich. But Leviticus 19:15 also warns us against being partial to the poor: "You shall do no injustice in court. You shall not be partial to the poor or defer to the great, but in righteousness shall you judge your neighbor." Partiality can go both ways.

10. This particular corruption is spoken against frequently: Ex. 23:8; Deut. 10:17; 27:25; 1 Sam. 8:3; 2 Chron. 19:7; Job 15:34; Pss. 15:5; 26:10; Prov. 6:35; 17:8, 23; Isa. 1:23; 5:23; 33:15; Ezek. 22:12; Mic. 3:11.

awesome God, who is not partial and takes no bribe." Those who execute justice must do so in a way that reflects the God of justice. Therefore, as Moses writes in Deuteronomy 16:20, "Justice, and only justice, you shall follow, that you may live and inherit the land that the LORD your God is giving you." Judges must rule in alignment with what God has set down in his Word. If they pervert justice—which they ultimately will—they will not be allowed to remain in the land. Not only that, but they will despair. As Christopher Wright observes, "Any society will have some levels of crime and some levels of injustice, but if the means of restitution and redress themselves become corrupt, then there is only despair."[11]

Behind the Beautiful Forevers[12] is a novel following the lives of a few families and individuals who are trying to survive. They scratch out their existence in a slum called Annawadi next to the Mumbai airport. To get a sense of the hopelessness of a world without justice, read this book. One young man named Abdul makes his living by rummaging through the dump in search of recyclables that he can sell to the recycling plant. He is falsely accused of a crime and is then extorted for a series of bribes from the police, the local slumlord, the hospital, and the special officer assigned to his case. The trial process is a farce, and though he is ultimately exonerated, there is no sense of justice. No one cares about what happened; people are concerned only with how they can profit from Abdul's misfortune. The young man laments the realization that though he wants to do right, the only way for him to survive is by becoming corrupt as well. The despair is tangible, and children in the community eat rat poison to escape it.

None of us live in a perfect justice system. But to the degree that we have any sense of justice in the places we live, we should give thanks to God. Those of us who live in the United States should not take for granted the degree to which our nation reflects these biblical convictions. We should pray for those who are entrusted with carrying out judgments in a society, for when they act as judges, they are carrying out a divine function in God's place. King Jehoshaphat's words to judges are still true today: "Consider what you do, for you judge not for man but for the LORD. He is with you in giving judgment. Now then, let the fear of the LORD be upon you. Be careful

11. Wright, *Deuteronomy*, 205.

12. Katherine Boo, *Behind the Beautiful Forevers: Life, Death, and Hope in a Mumbai Undercity* (Random House, 2012).

what you do, for there is no injustice with the LORD our God, or partiality or taking bribes" (2 Chron. 19:6–7). In any society, judges are carrying out a divinely ordained function. God is a God of justice, and any judge who makes judgments without respect to God and his righteousness will ultimately answer to the Judge of judges. This is true in the courts of law in our lands as well as the courts of our churches. Corrupt judges are a threat to justice.

IDOLATROUS WORSHIP IS A THREAT TO JUSTICE

Following on the heels of the instruction about judges comes these commands forbidding various forms of worship. At first the commands do not appear to follow until we understand that we cannot separate justice from right religion.[13] Remember, we cannot know what is right or wrong for humans unless we understand what humans are for. It is religion that gives the answer to that question. Idolatrous worship, including secularism, leads to wrong conclusions about what humanity is for, which eventually lead to injustice.

In Deuteronomy 16:21–22 and 17:1 are three specific prohibitions, followed in 17:2–7 with how to deal with them judicially. Here are the first two prohibitions: "You shall not plant any tree as an Asherah beside the altar of the LORD your God that you shall make. And you shall not set up a pillar, which the LORD your God hates" (Deut. 16:21–22). We dealt with Asherah poles in Deuteronomy 12:1–28 (chapter 21). By way of reminder, these were set up in honor of the Canaanite goddess of fertility. The Israelites' temptation was not to abandon Yahweh altogether as much as it was to hedge their bets by worshiping other gods alongside him. A desire to prevent syncretism is behind the prohibition on pillars' being set up. Despite the clear prohibitions, these were the sins that the prophets railed against as much as any other. Syncretistic worship was endemic among God's people,[14] and this idolatry led to injustice. An extreme example of this would be the practice of child sacrifice as the people of God worshiped the Ammonite god Molech (Lev. 20:1–5; Jer. 32:35). In our day, we do not worship Molech by name, but our idols demand sacrifices just the same, and they also lead us to injustice.

13. Gordon McConville, *Deuteronomy*, New Bible Commentary: 21st Century ed. (InterVarsity Press, 1994), 215.

14. Wright, *Deuteronomy*, 205.

Those who worship the idol of Mammon, for example, will likely withhold what they should give to others or perhaps use unjust means to acquire more wealth for themselves.

The third prohibition comes in Deuteronomy 17:1: "You shall not sacrifice to the LORD your God an ox or a sheep in which is a blemish, any defect whatever, for that is an abomination to the LORD your God." This is not so much an issue of idolatry as it is of dishonoring God (Mal. 1:6–8). Why would the people think that God would accept such an offering when their earthly rulers would not? It is possible that Canaanite religion did not prohibit offering defective animals and that the Israelites' doing so was a further reflection of their syncretistic worship.[15]

But the main focus of this section is on what to do when such idolatry is discovered:

> If there is found among you, within any of your towns that the LORD your God is giving you, a man or woman who does what is evil in the sight of the LORD your God, in transgressing his covenant, and has gone and served other gods and worshiped them, or the sun or the moon or any of the host of heaven, which I have forbidden, and it is told you and you hear of it, then you shall inquire diligently, and if it is true and certain that such an abomination has been done in Israel, then you shall bring out to your gates that man or woman who has done this evil thing, and you shall stone that man or woman to death with stones. (Deut. 17:2–5)

The particular crime described in Deuteronomy 17:2 is "transgressing his covenant" in the form of serving other gods. Remember, Yahweh is the Israelites' suzerain Lord, and as such he demands absolute loyalty for saving them, sustaining them, and protecting them. Worshiping other gods breaks that covenant and undermines their existence as a nation, since God will ultimately judge them and kick them out of his land if they are unfaithful. Therefore, if a person is guilty, then the community needs to join in condemning the sin and carrying out the execution.

But the stakes are high, since capital punishment is irreversible, so specific instructions are given about witnesses in Deuteronomy 17:6–7: "On the

15. Peter C. Craigie, *The Book of Deuteronomy*, NICOT (Eerdmans, 1976), 249.

evidence of two witnesses or of three witnesses the one who is to die shall be put to death; a person shall not be put to death on the evidence of one witness. The hand of the witnesses shall be first against him to put him to death, and afterward the hand of all the people. So you shall purge the evil from your midst." Two provisions are given to minimize the risk of injustice. First, no one can be executed on the testimony of one witness, which is just one person's word against another's. Second, when there is more than one witness, the witnesses have to cast the first stones. By having the witnesses cast the first stones, if they are lying, they are guilty of murdering an innocent person. Blood will be on their heads. But when they legitimately execute an idolater, they protect God's people from further contamination, and also from God's judgment on the community. This is why they must "purge the evil" from among them.

The people of God today are not to carry out civil judgments against idolaters. We most certainly are not to execute them. But when the apostle Paul applies this language of "purging the evil from among you" in 1 Corinthians 5, he is referring to the practice of church discipline. Those who persist in idolatrous sin of any nature in the church are to be removed from among the people of God. Allowing persons who call themselves Christians to continue in sin is to be complicit in the evil and to invite the judgment of God on the community. Therefore, elders have a particular responsibility to shepherd the flock and to pursue the purity of the church. But the rest of the church family has a responsibility to live by Matthew 18:15–17 as well. As is the case in Deuteronomy, Paul continues to affirm the necessity of at least two or three witnesses to make it more difficult for injustice to occur in the form of false accusations (2 Cor. 13:1; 1 Tim. 5:19).

Insolent People Are a Threat to Justice

Though some cases of justice are simple, many are not. God established through Moses a system of support for the more difficult cases. These judges, priests, and Levites were to be centrally located, eventually in Jerusalem. If a judge in a particular locale did not know how to handle a case, he could bring it to the central court (Deut. 17:8). Moses explains in Deuteronomy 17:9–10: "And you shall come to the Levitical priests and to the judge who is in office in those days, and you shall consult them, and they shall declare to you the decision. Then you shall do according to what they declare to you from that place that the Lord will choose. And you shall be careful to do according to all that they direct you." Once the case went to that next level, justice required that the lower levels enforce the judgment and that the people abide by it.[16] This is necessary for a stable system of law in any society. If higher-court judges hand down rulings that lower courts ignore, there will be no justice. Likewise, if courts hand down judgments that law enforcement ignores, there will be a corruption of justice.

Because of this, there is a firm warning against those insolent people tempted to disregard judgments in Deuteronomy 17:12–13: "The man who acts presumptuously by not obeying the priest who stands to minister there before the Lord your God, or the judge, that man shall die. So you shall purge the evil from Israel. And all the people shall hear and fear and not act presumptuously again." To disregard the court of referral was a serious crime threatening the social order. Even if the case in question had not been dealing with a capital offense, if the parties involved in the case disregarded the judgment, they were to receive capital punishment. The Israelites were to listen and follow the courts because ultimately it was God's will being delivered by the judges. To disregard these human judges was to disregard God.[17]

In the New Testament, we are likewise enjoined to show respect to authorities, including secular ones. Paul reflects the values of Deuteronomy when he writes in Romans 13:1–2: "Let every person be subject to the governing authorities. For there is no authority except from God, and those that exist have been instituted by God. Therefore whoever resists the authorities resists what God has appointed, and those who resist will incur judgment." We must not be so foolish as to think that disregarding human courts, judges, or officers somehow honors God. It is true that if authorities ask us to sin, we must not submit, but in matters of differing opinion, we are to be subject. Additionally, when we are on the receiving end of a judgment by either a civil court or a church court, we must receive that as though from

16. Second Chronicles 19:4–11 gives a picture of what all this looked like in practice among God's people under King Jehoshaphat's reforms.

17. Gary Smith writes, "To assume that these officials had no authority, that God had not spoken through them, and that the rights of each individual were not important to God would be an act of arrogant presumption." Gary V. Smith, *NIDOTTE*, s.v. "זִיד," 1:1069.

God himself. If there are avenues of appeal, then those may be utilized. But we are not free to disregard human courts or authorities. Practically speaking, if a civil court orders a person to pay a certain amount of child support, that person may appeal it, but may not simply disregard it. If a church court forbids someone to partake of the Lord's Supper on account of being in sin, to disregard that court is to disregard God. Those who disregard human courts fully deserve whatever judgment is to follow.

Is There Any Hope of Justice?

With these threats of corruption to those entrusted with justice, with the threats to the basis of justice, and with the threats to the enforcement of justice, do we have any hope for justice in this world? What about the fact that justice many times depends on people who are fickle? As Edward Dahlberg wrote, "Men are too unstable to be just; they are crabbed because they have not passed water at the usual time, or testy because they have not been stroked or praised."[18] It sounds cynical, but it is possible that a judge having a bad Tuesday may just decide to give everyone on the docket the maximum penalty. We live in a nation where justice is valued with many protections to help ensure that it happens, but even here, there is injustice.

If our hope of justice finally rests in this world, we will despair. In this world, there will be no perfect justice. We do not have the capacity to make things truly right even when the process of justice is functioning at its best. The adult daughter of a couple in our church was murdered in cold blood. One of the murderers was murdered himself sometime later. The other one was apprehended and sentenced to life in prison without the possibility of parole. The family was relieved to have the criminal process finished and they are thankful that the perpetrators have been judged, but in no way do they feel that things have been made right. No one can make them right. We must prize and work for justice, and we should be on guard against the ways in which it is corrupted in our courts and in our churches. What will carry us through, however, is not the hope of justice in the here and now, but the knowledge that one day there will be perfect justice. On the

18. Edward Dahlberg, *The Sorrows of Priapus*, in *Camp's Unfamiliar Quotations from 2000 B.C. to the Present*, by Wesley D. Camp (Prentice Hall, 1990), 164.

great day, the books will be opened and there will be a perfect judgment. Should we lose heart over continuing injustice in this world? Should we conclude like Abdul in Annawadi that the only way to live in this world is by becoming corrupt? What alternative do we have to despair or corruption? The alternative is prayer.

In Luke 18, Jesus told a parable so that his people would learn to pray for justice and not give up praying for it. A widow—someone with no standing in the community—was a victim of injustice. She came to a judge whom Jesus describes as having no respect for God or man. He was wicked and corrupt. He cared not about justice, but only about what he could get out of his position. The widow had nothing to offer him, so he had no interest in her case. But she kept coming to the judge and pleading, "Give me justice against my adversary" (Luke 18:3). But the judge refused. Eventually, she wore him down so much with her asking that even though he had no fear of God or respect for man, he gave her justice. Jesus' conclusion for his disciples is this: "And will not God give justice to his elect, who cry to him day and night? Will he delay long over them? I tell you, he will give justice to them speedily. Nevertheless, when the Son of Man comes, will he find faith on earth?" (vv. 7–8). If an unjust judge will give justice purely based on being worn down by petitions, how much more will the God of justice do it when his people call upon him? We have standing with God; we are his beloved children! He cares about justice more than we do. There will be justice. It may not be today, or tomorrow, or even in this life. But it will come. The question is, will we be faithfully working for it, praying for it, and waiting for it when he comes? How, then, should we live as we pray?

Jesus provides the model for us. Jesus was the most just person to have ever lived, and he suffered the greatest injustice ever perpetrated. How did Jesus handle injustice? Peter gives us a glimpse: "When he was reviled, he did not revile in return; when he suffered, he did not threaten, but continued entrusting himself to him who judges justly" (1 Peter 2:23). Jesus was able to endure the injustice of the present age by trusting that there will one day be perfect justice. He entrusted himself to God, the just Judge, knowing that perfect justice was coming, and so can we.

But God's perfect justice is also cause for alarm because when perfect justice comes, we will all be seen to be on the wrong side of it. Peter goes on to explain how God's perfect justice is good news for those who believe the gospel. He writes about Jesus, “He himself bore our sins in his body on the tree, that we might die to sin and live to righteousness” (1 Peter 2:24). God brought perfect justice against our sins that Jesus bore. Through the injustice that Jesus suffered at the hands of men, he paid the debt for our sins. Now perfect justice requires that God bring no condemnation on us because our sins have already been judged in Jesus. The one who has already borne our judgment is the one who is coming to judge the world!

Not only do we have nothing to fear of the judgment that is coming, but we have everything to look forward to. Every wrong will be made right, and perfectly so. As we wait, let us entrust our souls to our faithful Creator while doing good (1 Peter 4:19).

28

Godly Leadership

Deuteronomy 17:14–20

And when he sits on the throne of his kingdom, he shall write for himself in a book a copy of this law, approved by the Levitical priests. And it shall be with him, and he shall read in it all the days of his life. (Deut. 17:18–19)

Lyndon Johnson was the thirty-sixth president of the United States, and he loved to demonstrate his power over others. With a 6'3" tall and 210-pound frame, he was physically imposing. He used that frame to lean over those he was talking to—spitting, swearing, belching, or simply laughing in their faces. He once relieved himself on a Secret Service agent who was shielding Johnson from view. When the horrified agent realized what was happening, Johnson remarked: "That's all right, son. It's my prerogative."[1] But perhaps his favorite and most well-known power play was forcing subordinates to join him in the bathroom as he sat on the toilet. He would carry on his conversation as his underlings squirmed with discomfort.

1. Jenny Drapkin, "LBJ: The President Who Marked His Territory," Mental Floss, April 17, 2008, https://www.mentalfloss.com/article/18463/lbj-president-who-marked-his-territory, accessed June 7, 2022.

Moving through presidential history, we may recall the words of Richard Nixon. After authorizing illegal activities and resigning from office, he sought to explain his actions to interviewer David Frost by saying, "When the President does it, that means that it's not illegal."[2] Bill Clinton will always be remembered for how he abused his power in the Oval Office to take advantage of a young intern.

These are just three well-known examples from the realm of American presidents, but many more could be added from around the world, including business leaders, church leaders, and political leaders of every stripe. In many ways, the abuse of power feels more like the norm than the exception. Are these people corrupt when they step into power, or does power somehow corrupt them along the way? The answer is yes.

We have a phrase that is sometimes used to describe people in positions of power who are acting badly. We call them "drunk with power." Social science is finding that this phrase is very accurate. People drunk with power tend to be oblivious to what others think, more likely to pursue the satisfaction of their own appetites, and more likely to take risks. That sounds like a drunk person, because power lowers a person's inhibitions in a very similar way that alcohol does. Stanford Professor Deborah Gruenfeld, who focuses on the study of power, notes: "For most people, what we think of as 'power plays' aren't calculated and Machiavellian—they happen at the subconscious level. Many of those internal regulators that hold most of us back from bold or bad behavior diminish or disappear. When people feel powerful, they stop trying to 'control themselves.'"[3]

What we find in Deuteronomy, written more than three thousand years ago, is recognition that wielding power is dangerous for a sinful person. Therefore, when it comes to leadership in Israel, power needed to be distributed among a variety of people. The person who was most likely to hold the most power, the king, needed to have the firm checks and balances in place that this passage describes to protect him and everyone else. But though this passage focuses on Israel's kings, the principles here are true for any of us who

2. Richard M. Nixon, interview with David Frost, May 19, 1977, in *Camp's Unfamiliar Quotations from 2000 B.C. to the Present*, by Wesley D. Camp (Prentice Hall, 1990), 172.

3. Quoted in Vicki Haddock, "Power Is Not Only an Aphrodisiac, It Does Weird Things to Some of Us," SFGATE.com, November 19, 2006, https://www.sfgate.com/opinion/article/Power-is-not-only-an-aphrodisiac-it-does-weird-2546085.php, accessed June 8, 2022.

hold any position of power, including parents, teachers, administrators, law enforcement officers, public servants, coaches, and church or marketplace leaders. How can we wield power in such a way as to honor God and bless people? Or, to put it another way, what is required of godly leaders?

Godly Leaders Must Be Chosen

Moses begins by describing the scenario that will likely play out once the people settle in the land. He writes in Deuteronomy 17:14–15:

> When you come to the land that the Lord your God is giving you, and you possess it and dwell in it and then say, "I will set a king over me, like all the nations that are around me," you may indeed set a king over you whom the Lord your God will choose. One from among your brothers you shall set as king over you. You may not put a foreigner over you, who is not your brother.

God recognizes that his people will want to have a human king like the nations around them. Deuteronomy allows for a king but does not require one. This does not imply that the Israelites do not need leaders, only that they do not need a king. King is the only optional office; judge, priest, and prophet were all required. If they do have a king, Deuteronomy 17:14–20 provides the framework in which the king will be a blessing to the people as the embodiment of the law, rather than a curse as the embodiment of one drunk with power. Biblical history shows that Israel and Judah ended up with far more kings matching the description that 1 Samuel 8:10–18 warned against than the one prescribed by Moses.

Considering Deuteronomy 17:14–20 in light of the surrounding passages regarding judges, priests, and prophets, it is striking that kings get the least attention. The other three authorities are given specific instructions and duties, as well as explicit commands for the people to obey them. But when we come to the king, it says nothing whatsoever about his rights or authority or the need to obey him.[4] Multiple things that kings should not do are listed: amass wealth, armies, and harems—exactly the things that a king is most likely to do. But when it comes to positive commands about what

4. Jeffrey H. Tigay, *Deuteronomy*, JPSTC (Jewish Publication Society, 1996), 166.

he is supposed to do, only one responsibility is enumerated: he must copy, study, and obey God's instruction.[5] Jeffrey Tigay writes, "The aim of this law is to limit the king's power and to characterize him as essentially an optional figurehead who is as much subject to God's law as are the people as a whole."[6] In short, Queen Elizabeth II was a great picture of what an Israelite monarch was to be. Queen Elizabeth had little real power, but she was the embodiment of British ideals. So also, the king in Israel was to be a picture of what every Israelite should aspire to be, albeit with little governing power.

First, the selection of the king is to be a joint activity between God and his people. The people "set" the king over them (Deut. 17:14–15), but the one they set is the one "whom the LORD your God will choose" (v. 15). We see an example of this in 1 Samuel 16:1–13. The Lord sends the prophet Samuel to the house of Jesse in Bethlehem, "for I have provided for myself a king among his sons" (1 Sam. 16:1). Samuel goes there, and Jesse presents seven of his most likely sons to be king. But God instructs the prophet: "Do not look on his appearance or on the height of his stature, because I have rejected him. For the LORD sees not as man sees: man looks on the outward appearance, but the LORD looks on the heart" (v. 7). Then they bring in David from the field where he was keeping sheep, and the Lord tells Samuel that David is the one. The people and God both have a role to play in selecting the leader, but notice who does not have a role: the king himself. Israel's king is not to be one who dominates his way to power and imposes his rule. Rather, the people are to set him in place based on God's calling and choosing.

The second stipulation, which would seem to be addressed by the first, is that the king needs to be chosen "from among your brothers," meaning that a foreigner is not qualified. Probably the primary concern is to keep a foreigner from leading the people away from the true God to worship idols—as Herod did, for instance.

When we think about those whom we call to lead in our churches, we should seek to identify those whom God has chosen. In some churches and organizations, forceful personalities will push themselves to the front and into the lead. We should be careful not to assume that such people are called to lead in a church simply because they want to do so or have experience. We

5. Tigay, 166.
6. Tigay, 166.

must discern whom God is choosing. We do not have a prophet among us like Samuel to say simply, "This is the one." When we are in the process of calling pastors, or new elders or deacons, we do so with prayer, and ideally also with fasting.[7] We are seeking to discern who it is that God is choosing to lead us. *We* ultimately set the person in place, but we trust that we are setting in place the one whom *God* is choosing. When we find ourselves in a church or organization with an ungodly leader, it may be that we ignored obvious signs that this person is not chosen by God. But we also should not automatically assume that our process was flawed. Saul failed to be a godly leader, but that was on Saul, not on God or those who had put Saul into his position.

We should be prepared for God to choose people whom we would expect based on external qualifications (as he did Saul in 1 Samuel 9–10), but also be prepared for God to choose people we would not expect based on something in the heart (as he did David in 1 Samuel 16). Chief among the qualifications of any whom we put into leadership in the church or a Christian organization is that the person needs to be one of God's people. We cannot settle for good leadership when what we need is godly leadership. Numerous Christian organizations, schools, and even churches have been led astray by putting people into positions of leadership who are not followers of Jesus and have led the organization off course. In the same way, when a woman is choosing a husband, she is choosing the leader of her home. She must be certain that she does not choose someone who is not one of God's people who will lead her and her children astray. The world has many good leaders, but a godly leader must be one of God's people and chosen by him.

Godly Leaders Must Resist the Temptations of Leadership

As mentioned earlier, unlike the other offices in this section of Deuteronomy, no responsibilities are laid out. Instead, we see things that the king is absolutely not to pursue: money, sex, and power. Three thousand years later, these are *still* the primary temptations of leadership. We will consider them in more detail in the order described in Deuteronomy.

7. See the early church's example of prayer and fasting in choosing Saul and Barnabas for missionary efforts (Acts 13:1–2), as well as the choosing of elders for the church (14:23). In a similar way, when Jesus was choosing the disciples, he spent all night in prayer, fasting from sleep (Luke 6:12–13).

The Temptation of Power

The first temptation that the king and people must be on guard against is the temptation of power or the abuse of power. When people get power, one temptation is to try to get even more power. We read in Deuteronomy 17:16, "Only he must not acquire many horses for himself or cause the people to return to Egypt in order to acquire many horses, since the Lord has said to you, 'You shall never return that way again.'" This temptation to power is symbolized in the pursuit of horses and the development of a massive military. God does not forbid Israel from having a military, but he does not want the king to build an army so powerful that he would trust in it rather than in the Lord. Owning lots of horses—which were necessary for chariots and cavalry—would likely encourage the king to feel self-sufficient rather than being dependent on God.[8] The posture of the godly king is found in Psalm 20:7: "Some trust in chariots and some in horses, but we trust in the name of the Lord our God." Israel's trust is to be in the Lord for its defense, rather than in its military might.

Reflecting on Israel's history, when God's people lost a battle it was not because they lacked military strength. God demonstrated that he could give them victory with an army as small as three hundred men (Judg. 7:7). They could bring down a wall simply by marching around it with shouting and blasting trumpets (Josh. 6). God could even put enemies to flight without the army's doing anything (Isa. 37). The issue for their success was not building a massive military but trusting in the Lord. The clear implication of raising a mighty army was that Israel did not trust in the Lord.

Another temptation of power is to use that power as a basis for mistreating others in the service of oneself. That may be what is in view in the instruction that the king must not "cause the people to return to Egypt in order to acquire many horses" (Deut. 17:16). Some think that this is a reference to sending Israelites to become mercenaries in Egypt in exchange for more horses for the army.[9] Being in a leadership position and having power brings with it the temptation to use power to mistreat others to serve oneself.

While this problem can be frequently observed in the real world, it is also observable in the laboratory. Researchers once conducted something

8. Tigay, *Deuteronomy*, 167.

9. Raymond Brown, *The Message of Deuteronomy: Not by Bread Alone*, The Bible Speaks Today (InterVarsity Press, 1993), 179.

called the "cookie crumbles" experiment. They placed college students in groups of three and gave them an assignment to collaborate on a short policy paper about a social issue. In each group, one person was randomly assigned and empowered to evaluate the other two students and to give them points that would affect those students' ability to win a cash bonus at the end. Then the researchers casually brought out a plate containing five cookies to the three students. The students empowered with the ability to evaluate the other two not only ate more than their fair share of the cookies but were also more likely to chew with their mouths open and scatter crumbs across the table.[10] If just that much power can lead people to such disinhibited behavior, what might leading a Christian organization, a business, or a nation do to a person? Those of us who have any position of authority whatsoever must be on guard against our temptation to abuse that power or to trust in it.

The Temptation of Sex

We read in Deuteronomy 17:17, "And he shall not acquire many wives for himself, lest his heart turn away." Henry Kissinger described power as "the great aphrodisiac," noting how even unattractive men become desirable to women when they gain power. For this reason, when there is an unchecked increase of power, there is frequently an unchecked increase in sexual indiscretions. Such indiscretions certainly have the effect of turning one's heart away from the Lord. Examples are too plenteous to mention of men and women in positions of power using that power to abuse others or simply losing their inhibitions regarding sexual propriety.

While sexual sin is still a major temptation of those in leadership, in the ancient world, acquiring many wives was not primarily about sex. A large harem was a means of securing strategic alliances with other nations, and it was also a way of enhancing one's status in the eyes of others. Solomon and Ahab both secured many of these marriage alliances and tolerated or engaged in idolatry to do so. Very clearly, their hearts were led astray in the process. In some cultures, a harem or its functional equivalent is still a status symbol. In others, it is the accumulation of expensive items such as

10. I have not been able to locate this research, but am relying on the report of it in Haddock, "Power Is Not Only an Aphrodisiac, It Does Weird Things to Some of Us."

boats, cars, or homes. Increasingly today, investment in one's physical and mental health is becoming a symbol of status. Another status symbol may be the trips that we take or the people we are friends with on social media. Leadership carries with it a natural increase in status, but also the temptation to further enhance one's status, and however we do so, it has the potential to turn our hearts away from the Lord.

The Temptation of Excessive Wealth

The third warning is found in Deuteronomy 17:17: "nor shall he acquire for himself excessive silver and gold." Acquiring excessive wealth is a temptation of leadership and being in a position of power. Those with excessive wealth, like those with excessive armies, are likely to trust in it. When we trust in money to be our security, our comfort, and our chief problem solver, we will serve wealth rather than the Lord (Deut. 8:11–18). For political leaders, the accumulation of excessive wealth comes on the backs of unjust taxation or bribes. God wants to spare his people such abuse. Church leaders can also "tax" people in spiritually abusive ways by insisting on ever-increasing donations that primarily serve to advance the image of the leader, rather than the mission of the church. Business leaders face the temptation of acquiring a disproportionate amount of business profits at the expense of the people doing the work. No hard-and-fast rules are given here for numbers, simply the warning that if we are in a position of power, our temptation will be to exploit that position for our own financial gain. Deuteronomy does not tell us how much money is excessive. This calls for wisdom. What we should be aware of is that no one thinks he has excessive gold or silver. Some of us might think we are approaching the line, but none of us thinks that he is over the line into excess. This is why Jesus warns us to "watch out" for greed, because it is the kind of sin that we are unaware of when we are in it (Luke 12:15 NIV).

But who would want to do the hard work of being king or leader when he does not also get the trappings of power, wealth, and status? No one wants to do the hard work of ruling for nothing. No one, that is, except a shepherd with a heart for the sheep. These leaders see leadership not as a perk or a reward, but as a service to the people whom they are called to lead. George Washington is an example of one who resisted the temptations of leadership. After leading the United States to a very improbable victory in the Revolutionary War and serving as president, he could have become a sort of king. But rather than laying hold of his opportunity to enhance his own status and privilege by ruling America for the rest of his life, he voluntarily chose to set aside his power and retired to a private life. This humble setting aside of power is one of the reasons that Washington is so highly esteemed and considered one of the greatest men in history. He points us to an even greater leader, our Lord Jesus Christ. Jesus set aside even greater glory not only to become a private citizen, but to take on the form of a servant. He refused the opportunity to become king, and instead chose to bear the pain and humiliation of his people's sins. He ultimately gave his life so that his people could be free. He went to the grave and on the third day was raised again. Because of his humiliation, God has now highly exalted him to his own right hand. Jesus' greatness was seen in his humility, whereas many earthly leaders show their insignificance by attempting to prove their greatness.

Godly Leaders Must Be Subject to God's Word

The most extensive instruction given for a future king has to do with God's Word, where the keys to resisting the temptations of leadership are found. We read in Deuteronomy 17:18, "And when he sits on the throne of his kingdom, he shall write for himself in a book a copy of this law, approved by the Levitical priests." The king was to have his own copy of this Torah that he wrote with his own hand, approved by the Levitical priests to ensure its accuracy. What exactly "this law" refers to is not clear, but it may have been a section of Deuteronomy or possibly the whole book.[11] The effect of the teaching, though, is to establish the king not as the giver, but as the arch-reader of the law.[12]

If Israel is to have a king, this king will not *be* the law as the king was in Egypt. Furthermore, this king is not above the law, as in many examples throughout history. But this king must be subject to the law. Thus, he needs to write it with his own hand. Philo, a first-century B.C. Jewish philosopher, said that the king is to make his own copy because writing makes a more

11. Peter C. Craigie, *The Book of Deuteronomy*, NICOT (Eerdmans, 1976), 256.
12. J. G. McConville, *Deuteronomy*, ApOTC 5 (Inter-Varsity Press, 2002), 295.

lasting impression than does merely reading.[13] But writing it is not enough. Moses continues in Deuteronomy 17:19, "And it shall be with him, and he shall read in it all the days of his life, that he may learn to fear the LORD his God by keeping all the words of this law and these statutes, and doing them."[14] The king not only must write the law, but must read it. Moreover, he needs to learn to fear the Lord and to do what the law says.[15] To what end is he reading, learning, and doing the law? Verse 20 tells us: "that his heart may not be lifted up above his brothers, and that he may not turn aside from the commandment, either to the right hand or to the left, so that he may continue long in his kingdom, he and his children, in Israel." Persistent and attentive study of the Torah is to protect the king from both pride and disobedience, as well as the temptations of power. The law reminds him that he is not the ultimate king, but that he is subject to the ultimate King. He will answer to God for his rule as surely as the people will answer for their submission. If the king will faithfully submit himself to God and his law, he will enjoy a long reign in his kingdom, and his children too. Surely all of us who lead could benefit from the daily reminder that we are not higher than others, but subject to God and his Word like everyone else.

As Christopher Wright observes: "The law is to permeate the king's behavior in every sphere, whether political, administrative, judicial, or military. He should be a model of what was required of *every* Israelite."[16] In a similar way, when we come to the requirements for an elder or deacon in 1 Timothy 3, we see that the elder or deacon is to be a model of what every Christian should be. Specifically, he is to have only one wife, he is not to be a lover of money, and he is not to be violent or quarrelsome, but gentle.

13. Tigay, *Deuteronomy*, 168.

14. An interesting feature in the Hebrew text of Deuteronomy 17:19 is not visible in our English translations. In English it reads, "And it shall be with him, and he shall read in it all the days of his life." The first "it" in that sentence has a feminine referent, while the second "it" refers to a masculine object. In verse 18, "this law" (or Torah) is feminine in gender, while "book" is masculine. So verse 19 could be translated more specifically, "And this Torah shall be with him, and he shall read in the book all the days of his life." It seems to me that the point of the distinction is that he needs to carry the book, but that the Torah needs to be *with* him in a way that a physical book cannot be.

15. In Hebrew, "to learn" is a Qal imperfect verb, while "to fear," "to keep," and "to do" are all Qal infinitive constructs. Rather than translating the verse as the ESV does, it is preferable to translate this verse such that the king is to learn to fear, to keep, and to do: "to learn to fear the LORD his God, to keep all the words of this Torah, and to do these statutes" (cf. CSB translation).

16. Christopher Wright, *Deuteronomy*, NIBC: Old Testament 4 (Hendrickson, 2007), 209.

He is not to be one who is drunk with power, but rather sober-minded. He is warned against becoming puffed up with conceit and falling into condemnation (1 Tim. 3:6).

All of us who are called to leadership, especially in the home and in the church, must be continually subjecting ourselves to God's Word. We need to be reminded over and over that we are not above the people we lead and that we are not free to go our own way. Paul's words to Timothy are reminiscent of Deuteronomy's instruction to kings: "Devote yourself to the public reading of Scripture, to exhortation, to teaching. . . . Practice these things, immerse yourself in them, so that all may see your progress. Keep a close watch on yourself and on the teaching. Persist in this, for by so doing you will save both yourself and your hearers" (1 Tim. 4:13, 15–16). The chief concern of godly leaders is not leadership, but godliness. We can be godly without leading, but we must not lead without godliness. To paraphrase something I read once, our people need us as pastors to be humble more than they need us to be right. They need us to be men of prayer more than they need to hear us pray. They need us to be teachable even more than they need us to teach. They need us to be subject to the Word even more than they need us to make the Word our subject.[17]

One challenge we have in our churches and Christian ministries is that we sometimes sacrifice godliness on the altar of leadership ability. We have something we desire to get done and know that we need a strong leader to do it, so we look past the fact that the leader lacks godliness. Or in other cases, we have a leader who has a sin problem. Because we are afraid of the leadership implications if the sin were properly dealt with, we sweep the problem under the rug. This is an example of sacrificing godliness on the altar of leadership. Instead, we must pursue godliness first. Only in this way can those of us who are aiming to be godly leaders avoid the pitfalls of power.

We can sum up this viewpoint in the words of Robert Ingersoll, speaking of Abraham Lincoln: "Nothing discloses real character like the use of power. It is easy for the weak to be gentle. Most people can bear adversity. But if you wish to know what a man really is, give him power. This is the supreme test."[18] Even the best of leaders are susceptible to corruption, particularly

17. I am indebted to someone for these phrases, but I cannot remember whom.

18. Robert G. Ingersoll, *Abraham Lincoln: A Lecture* (C. P. Farrell, 1895), 52.

as they gain more power and influence. The more of it they have, the more that corruption will be revealed.

King Solomon provided a picture of what not to do. It is almost as though he read Deuteronomy 17 and decided to do just the opposite. He did not remember the law, and he did not do what it said. Solomon was renowned for accumulating enormous amounts of silver and gold. In fact, as we are told in 1 Kings 10:14, "Now the weight of gold that came to Solomon in one year was 666 talents of gold." That is approximately 49,950 pounds of gold in a year. Additionally, he took many wives. First Kings 11:3–4 relates: "He had 700 wives, who were princesses, and 300 concubines. And his wives turned away his heart." Just as God warned through Moses. Solomon also had a very large number of horses, and we are specifically told that he went to Egypt to get them (1 Kings 10:28). While the temple he built for the Lord was amazing, the palace he built for himself dwarfed it in size and took nearly twice as long to build (1 Kings 7). Not only that, but Solomon put people into slavery to accomplish it all (9:15–22). The world has seen many leaders of the King Solomon sort.

Now consider King Jesus, who was not lured by money and did not accumulate excessive silver and gold. In fact, he went through this world with a bare minimum of material possessions, not even having a place of his own in which to lay his head (Matt. 8:20). Jesus was not lured by sex or status symbols and did not collect a harem. Jesus did not take even one wife. He did not collect horses or raise up a great army, and he declined to defend himself. When he did ride, he rode humbly on a donkey. Zechariah 9:9 proclaims: "Rejoice greatly, O daughter of Zion! Shout aloud, O daughter of Jerusalem! Behold, your king is coming to you; righteous and having salvation is he, humble and mounted on a donkey." Who has ever heard of a humble king? This King does not build a temple, but he becomes the temple. Through his earthly life, death, and resurrection, he has commenced building a temple, not out of impressive stones, but with living stones (1 Peter 2:5).

He does not utilize slave labor to build his temple, but he builds his temple with former slaves whom he has set free. This King is not only devoted to God's Word; he is God's Word (John 1:1), and he is obedient to it even to the point of death on a cross (Phil. 2:8). He does not abuse his people to enrich himself, but he impoverished himself to make his people wealthy beyond measure (2 Cor. 8:9). Solomon lost almost the entire kingdom for his son

Rehoboam because he disregarded God's law (1 Kings 11:9–13), but Jesus' perfect obedience to God's law has secured his kingdom forever for all his people. Though he has every right to reign alone, he has made it so that we will reign *with* him forever (Rev. 22:5). The world has never seen a king like Jesus! Worship him! Serve him! Love him and devote yourself to him!

Here we have a true model of godly leadership that runs counter to so much political leadership, corporate leadership, and ecclesiastical leadership today. The temptations to power, prestige, and wealth are no less strong today than they were then. But Jesus shows us a better way, embodying in every way what the true godly leader should be. May those of us who are chosen to be leaders resist the temptations of power by subjecting ourselves to the Word and walking in the way of King Jesus.

29

Prophets, Priests, and Posers

Deuteronomy 18:1–22

I will raise up for them a prophet like you from among their brothers. And I will put my words in his mouth, and he shall speak to them all that I command him. (Deut. 18:18)

When Teddy Roosevelt was a boy, he was found repeatedly peeping through the open front door of the Madison Square Church. When the sexton invited him in to have a look around, little Roosevelt declined and ran away. This happened several times that morning. When Teddy got home, he told his mother about the invitations and his refusal to enter the church. She asked why he was afraid to go into the house of God and assured him that there was no danger in quietly looking around. Teddy confessed that he was afraid to go in because the zeal might jump out at him from under a pew or somewhere. "The zeal?" she asked. "What is the zeal?" Teddy didn't know, but thought that it was probably a large animal like an alligator or a dragon. His mother asked where he had learned about the zeal, and he told her that the minister had read about it from the Bible and that it frightened him. Using a concordance and looking up all the passages mentioning zeal, she found the one that terrified Teddy in the King James Version of Psalm 69:9, which reads, "For the zeal of thine house hath eaten me up."[1] Teddy was apparently afraid of being eaten up by the same "zeal" that ate Jesus (John 2:17). While he missed the meaning of the word "zeal," his instinct to fear the presence of the Lord was right. Our Lord is good, but he is not safe.

Ever since the first sin in the garden, humans attempting to enter God's presence risk being consumed by his holiness. The entire story of the Bible describes the lengths to which God went to enable sinful people to dwell in his holy presence and to hear his voice without being consumed. The existence of priests and prophets in Israel is a reminder of the distance that exists between God and humanity. The function of the prophets was to speak to the people on behalf of God because they were afraid that his voice would kill them (Deut. 5:24–28). He used Moses as a prophet to speak to them, and when the tent of meeting was established as God's dwelling place, the people could not come near because of God's holy presence. So God set apart the priests and the tribe of Levi to be representatives for the rest of the people in his presence. In this passage, God gives guidance regarding the roles of priests and prophets as they prepare to enter the land.

The formal offices of prophet, priest, and king in Israel have been fulfilled in the ministry of Jesus—the consummate Prophet, Priest, and King. But this text still provides some very practical instruction for us on the necessity of supporting God's servants, as well as appropriate and inappropriate ways to discern God's will in times of uncertainty.

We Should Support Those Who Serve God and His People

The tribe of Levi has been set apart for special service to God, as we read in Deuteronomy 18:1–2: "The Levitical priests, all the tribe of Levi, shall have no portion or inheritance with Israel. They shall eat the LORD's food offerings as their inheritance. They shall have no inheritance among their brothers; the LORD is their inheritance, as he promised them." Levitical

1. "Little Roosevelt and the Zeal" [1901?], newspaper article, Theodore Roosevelt Papers, Library of Congress Manuscript Division, Theodore Roosevelt Digital Library, Dickinson State University, https://www.theodorerooseveltcenter.org/Research/Digital-Library/Record?libID=o288665, accessed June 25, 2022.

priests are those Levites who are priests. (See diagram at the end of this chapter.) All priests are Levites, but not all Levites are priests.[2] The priests are a small subset of the Levites, specifically those who are descended from Moses' brother Aaron.[3] The priests had a special role in the service of the sanctuary, performing sacrifices and carrying the ark of the covenant when they were on the move. The other (nonpriestly) Levites served as keepers of the tabernacle in the early days and carried the furniture and structure of the tabernacle anytime they moved. After entering the land, many Levites were scattered through various towns, and they did not necessarily serve at the sanctuary, though they were free to do so (Deut. 18:6–8).[4]

Some of the responsibilities given to the priests and Levites wherever they were located were distinguishing between the holy and the profane and the clean and unclean, as well as teaching the people of God all the statutes that God had given them through Moses (Lev. 10:10–11).[5] The Levites also performed an important service for the rest of Israel by becoming the substitutes for each family's firstborn (Num. 3:40–51). As representatives of the people before God, they had no portion of the land assigned for their exclusive use. Instead, they were to live in select cities in each of the tribes where they could function as teachers, preachers, and moral examples before the rest of the people.

The Levites were supported by the tithes of the people (Num. 18:24), and the priests received portions of sacrificial offerings, the firstborn of the flock and herd, and a tithe of the tithe given to the Levites (Num. 18:25–28). We

2. The first words of Deuteronomy 18:1 introduce us to the Levite problem. The Hebrew literally says, "The priests, the Levites, and all the tribe of Levi." What is the relationship between priests and Levites? Jeffrey Tigay (among others) argues that Deuteronomy allows all Levites to become priests, not just the descendants of Aaron. This would seemingly contradict Numbers 3:1–10, where the priesthood is given to Aaron and his sons. A better reading of Deuteronomy 18:1 maintains the distinction between the priests and the Levites and sees verses 1–2 as applying to all Levites, verses 3–5 as referring to the Levitical priests, and verses 6–8 as referring to Levites who do not function as priests. For an excellent discussion of the issues, see D. A. Hubbard, "Priests and Levites," *NBD*, 956–62.

3. Gary Millar points out that the writer of Deuteronomy is obviously aware of divisions of function within the tribe of Levi as evidenced in Deuteronomy 10:8 and 31:25, but that those divisions are irrelevant to his message. What Moses is concerned about is Israel's treatment of the Levitical tribe as a reflection of the spiritual health of Israel. See J. Gary Millar, *Now Choose Life: Theology and Ethics in Deuteronomy*, NSBT 6 (Apollos, 1998), 128–29.

4. Christopher Wright, *Deuteronomy*, NIBC: Old Testament 4 (Hendrickson, 2007), 220.

5. Levites would perform their official duties from twenty-five years old to fifty, when they went into a sort of semiretirement with limited duties (Num. 8:24–26). See Hubbard, "Priests and Levites," 956.

read of the priests' provision in Deuteronomy 18:3–4: "And this shall be the priests' due from the people, from those offering a sacrifice, whether an ox or a sheep: they shall give to the priest the shoulder and the two cheeks and the stomach. The firstfruits of your grain, of your wine and of your oil, and the first fleece of your sheep, you shall give him." The priests' "due" is the Hebrew word *mšpṭ*. We typically translate this word as "justice" or "judgment," and in this context it refers to one's legal right.[6] This is what the priests deserve. The word *mšpṭ* does not denote charity; it indicates justice. This has implications for how we think about our giving to our local church. We may think of our giving to the ministry of our local church as "charity" that we donate when we feel like it. But Deuteronomy sees a failure to give to support these servants of God as a failure of justice. The prophet Malachi even describes it as stealing from God: "Will man rob God? Yet you are robbing me. But you say, 'How have we robbed you?' In your tithes and contributions" (Mal. 3:8).

The Levites have no land inheritance as a tribe. Levites do not have time to work the land because they are busy serving the Lord. Verse 5 of Deuteronomy 18 gives the reasoning as follows: "For the Lord your God has chosen him out of all your tribes to stand and minister in the name of the Lord, him and his sons for all time." Because God's people spiritually benefit from Levitical service, they are to share their material benefits with the Levites. This verse serves as the motivation to the people to treat the Levites with the appropriate generosity due to them. Just as Israel was chosen out of all the nations, Levi was chosen out of all the tribes. As all of Israel is called to depend on the Lord, the tribe of Levi is called to depend on Israel.[7]

The next verses deal with Levites who are not living at the central sanctuary. We read in Deuteronomy 18:6–8:

> And if a Levite comes from any of your towns out of all Israel, where he lives—and he may come when he desires—to the place that the Lord will choose, and ministers in the name of the Lord his God, like all his fellow Levites who stand to minister there before the Lord, then he may have equal portions to eat, besides what he receives from the sale of his patrimony.

6. BDB, s.v. "מִשְׁפָּט," 1049.
7. Wright, *Deuteronomy*, 214.

Just because he lives elsewhere does not mean that he is to be supported any less. No matter where he comes from to minister at the place that the Lord chooses, he is to receive the offerings just like the rest of the Levites. These portions are in addition to those that he gets from "the sale of his patrimony," the meaning of which is unclear in both English and Hebrew. It is possible that "the sale of his patrimony" refers to the sale of his own cattle, livestock, and beasts that he possesses (Num. 35:3). We cannot be sure. But what does this have to do with us today?

In the New Testament, those who serve in church leadership are never called priests. The word "priest" is applied only to Jesus (Heb. 7), or else (in plural) to the whole community of Christ-followers (1 Peter 2:9). In Christ, we are all priests and have immediate access to God. When Jesus was crucified, we are told, the veil in the temple separating sinful people from the Most Holy Place was torn in two. When Jesus died for our sins, what separated us from being in God's presence was removed. We can now approach the throne of grace with confidence—every single one of us—in a way that the people of Israel never could. The writer of Hebrews concludes, "Therefore, brothers, since we have confidence to enter the holy places by the blood of Jesus, by the new and living way that he opened for us through the curtain, that is, through his flesh, and since we have a great priest over the house of God, let us draw near with a true heart in full assurance of faith" (Heb. 10:19–22).

But though we all have this access, the New Testament still recognizes that there are people specially set apart for the work of priestly ministry who focus on teaching God's Word to God's people, as the Levites were to do. We want people like Ezra teaching in our churches: "For Ezra had set his heart to study the Law of the Lord, and to do it and to teach his statutes and rules in Israel" (Ezra 7:10). This was not Ezra's hobby or occasional pastime. His heart was set on *studying*, *doing*, and *teaching* God's Word. I believe that this specific order is intentional. It is not just studying and teaching, but *doing* that is to characterize those who minister to God's people. Likewise, Paul exhorted young Pastor Timothy: "Set the believers an example in speech, in conduct, in love, in faith, in purity. Until I come, devote yourself to the public reading of Scripture, to exhortation, to teaching. . . . Practice these things, immerse yourself in them, so that all may see your progress" (1 Tim. 4:12–13, 15). As ordained ministers devote their lives to this work, so also elders and lay leaders can do the same, though their time for doing so may be less because of the need to earn an income. It is tempting for us ministers to get caught up in things other than the ministry of God's Word. Some of us get caught up in the administrative leadership of the church. Others get caught up in counseling or putting out fires. Others get distracted by personal projects or interests. But the minister is set apart to *devote* himself to the ministry of the Word and prayer. We who are ministers, especially those of us focused on preaching and teaching, cannot allow ourselves to be sidetracked from our chief responsibility: to study, to do, and to teach God's Word to God's people.

Eugene Peterson captures the essence of a congregation's desire when they set apart a man for ordained ministry:

> Minister with word and sacrament to us in all the different parts and stages of our lives—in our work and play, with our children and our parents, at birth and death, in our celebrations and sorrows, on those days when morning breaks over us in a wash of sunshine, and those other days that are all drizzle. This isn't the only task in the life of faith, but it is your task. We will find someone else to do the other important and essential tasks. *This* is yours: word and sacrament.
>
> One more thing: we are going to ordain you to this ministry and we want your vow that you will stick to it. This is not a temporary job assignment but a way of life that we need lived out in our community. We know that you are launched on the same difficult belief venture in the same dangerous world as we are. We know that your emotions are as fickle as ours, and that your mind can play the same tricks on you as ours. That is why we are going to *ordain* you and why we are going to exact a *vow* from you. . . . There may be times when we come to you as a committee or delegation and demand that you tell us something else than what we are telling you now. Promise right now that you won't give in to what we demand of you. You are not the minister of our changing desires, or our time-conditioned understanding of our needs, or our secularized hopes for something better. With these vows of ordination we are lashing you fast to the mast of word and sacrament so that you will be unable to respond to the siren voices. There are a lot of other things to be done in this wrecked world and we are going to be doing at least some of them, but if we don't know the basic terms with which we are working, the

> foundational realities with which we are dealing—God, kingdom, gospel—we are going to end up living futile, fantasy lives. Your task is to keep telling the basic story, representing the presence of the Spirit, insisting on the priority of God, speaking the biblical words of command and promise and invitation.[8]

In return, churches are to support their ministers so that they can devote themselves to this work. Paul draws on the example set down here in Deuteronomy when he writes: "Do you not know that those who are employed in the temple service get their food from the temple, and those who serve at the altar share in the sacrificial offerings? In the same way, the Lord commanded that those who proclaim the gospel should get their living by the gospel" (1 Cor. 9:13–14). In Israel, the condition of the Levites would have reflected the spiritual health of Israel. If the Israelites were faithful to their own callings and responsibilities, the Levitical clan would have been adequately provided for.[9] The same is true in our churches and Christian organizations: if the church is functioning healthily, those who serve the church will be adequately provided for without needing to take on a "tentmaking" position.[10] We should support those who serve God and his people.

We Should Reject False Practices and False Prophets

When the people of Israel enter the land, Moses will no longer be with them. They might wonder how they will hear from God. Before he tells them, he makes it clear how they are *not* to hear from God. We are first going to consider false practices and then false prophets. We read of the false practices in Deuteronomy 18:9–12:

> When you come into the land that the LORD your God is giving you, you shall not learn to follow the abominable practices of those nations. There shall not be found among you anyone who burns his son or his daughter as

8. Eugene H. Peterson, *Working the Angles: The Shape of Pastoral Integrity* (Eerdmans, 1987), 24–25.

9. Wright, *Deuteronomy*, 215.

10. Of course, in some situations, such as when a church is being freshly planted or when the church is exceptionally impoverished, a minister might choose to be a tentmaker in the same way that the apostle Paul did. Such an approach is supported by the New Testament witness.

> an offering, anyone who practices divination or tells fortunes or interprets omens, or a sorcerer or a charmer or a medium or a necromancer or one who inquires of the dead, for whoever does these things is an abomination to the LORD. And because of these abominations the LORD your God is driving them out before you.

Deuteronomy 18:9–12 describes the kinds of practices that are not valid for God's people in terms of discerning the Lord's voice. The list is extensive in order to indicate that all the culturally approved ways of discerning the divine will are forbidden by God. First on the list is the forbidding of child sacrifice. God's people are to abhor the killing of children, both born and unborn.

Next, he lists a wide variety of practices that we will not detail here. "Anyone who practices divination or tells fortunes or interprets omens" (Deut. 18:10) is not to be found among God's people. These are all ways of attempting to know the future, such as the outcome of a battle or of an illness. There were many ways to do this in the ancient world. *Belomancy* attempted to interpret the way that arrows fall when they are shaken out of a quiver. *Hepatoscopy* was interpreting the configurations of the liver of a sacrificial animal. There was also a type of divination called *oleomancy* that sought to interpret the patterns formed when drops of oil are added to water. Some would attempt to discern divine messages by reading the flight patterns of birds or cloud formations.[11] But why try to make out secret messages when God speaks plainly in his Word?

Behind all these efforts at sorcery,[12] divination, and communicating with the dead is the desire to know, and thereby control, the future. Interestingly, these practices are not forbidden because they do not work. Rather, the Bible records cases in which the magicians of Egypt were able to duplicate some of the plagues and in which King Saul learned the outcome of a battle by consulting Samuel's ghost.[13] The issue is that the people are not looking to God for what they seek. God assigned prophets to communicate to his

11. Jeffrey H. Tigay, *Deuteronomy*, JPSTC (Jewish Publication Society, 1996), 173.

12. A sorcerer is a person who uses magic in some way. The Bible references several of these types, such as Simon the magician (Acts 8:9–24) and Bar-Jesus, who is also called Elymas the magician (13:6–12).

13. Tigay, *Deuteronomy*, 174.

people clearly and unambiguously, in ways that did not require strange and esoteric methods. Today we have his completed Word in the Bible. When the people of God go to these other methods, they are trying to circumvent God, and it is another form of unfaithfulness to him. The story of Saul's consulting the medium at En-dor is a good example of this.[14] When he sought information and God would not give it to him through the prophet on account of his disobedience, Saul went another route (1 Sam. 28:1–20).

People are practicing these things in my own community and nearly every other community in the United States. A quick Google search will reveal various kinds of palm readers, Tarot card readers, and even people who read coffee grounds. As I read reviews of these businesses in my own community, I understood better what people were seeking. Here is just one review that captures the essence of almost every review I read: "I will only go to M— going forward and highly recommend her to anyone who simply needs *guidance* and wants *answers* and a little *reassurance*!" (emphasis mine). Who does not want guidance, answers, and reassurance? We all seek these things as surely as the people in ancient Israel did. They are not bad desires. But how do we fulfill them? Not through the kinds of false practices described here. Nor through the consulting of horoscopes, astrological signs, Ouija boards, or anything else that is not seeking God himself. These false practices are to be rejected by God's people. He says in Deuteronomy 18:13–14: "You shall be blameless before the LORD your God, for these nations, which you are about to dispossess, listen to fortune-tellers and to diviners. But as for you, the LORD your God has not allowed you to do this."

What if we have been involved in these things? We should stop immediately. But we should also take heart that these sins are not unforgivable. Manasseh was one of the most wicked kings in all of Israel's history. It is almost as if Manasseh went right down the list of everything that Deuteronomy says not to do and did it. Among the long list of evil things he did, 2 Chronicles 33:6 records: "And he burned his sons as an offering in the Valley of the Son of Hinnom, and used fortune-telling and omens and sorcery, and dealt with mediums and with necromancers. He did much evil in the sight of the LORD, provoking him to anger." So God brought judgment on Manasseh for

14. Mediums are always mentioned alongside necromancers in the Bible (Lev. 19:31; 20:6, 27; Deut. 18:11; 1 Sam. 28:3, 9; 2 Kings 21:6; 23:24; 2 Chron. 33:6; Isa. 8:19; 19:3). It seems that there is significant overlap between them.

his wickedness, letting him fall into the hands of the Assyrians. Then we read: "And when he was in distress, he entreated the favor of the Lord his God and humbled himself greatly before the God of his fathers. He prayed to him, and God was moved by his entreaty and heard his plea and brought him again to Jerusalem into his kingdom. Then Manasseh knew that the Lord was God" (2 Chron. 33:12–13). Manasseh was involved in some of the worst kinds of sin imaginable. He burned his child alive to a false god. He was into witchcraft of every sort. Some readers may have been also. But hear this: God is willing to have mercy on mediums, necromancers, sorcerers, diviners, and everyone else. When Manasseh repented, God had mercy on him. Can we appreciate how eager God is to show mercy? Perhaps we have been involved in these sins and thought that there is no way that God could ever accept us. Rest assured, he will if we come to him with a humble heart, looking for mercy.[15]

In addition to rejecting false practices, we must reject false prophets. In Deuteronomy 18:20, Moses describes the kinds of prophets that we must reject: "But the prophet who presumes to speak a word in my name that I have not commanded him to speak, or who speaks in the name of other gods, that same prophet shall die." To say "thus says the Lord" when the Lord has not spoken thus is a sure ticket to death. God puts words into the prophet's mouth, but the prophet must not put words into God's mouth. Likewise, any prophet who speaks in the name of another god is to be put to death. The final two verses have to do with judging the authenticity of the prophet's message: "And if you say in your heart, 'How may we know the word that the Lord has not spoken?'—when a prophet speaks in the name of the Lord, if the word does not come to pass or come true, that is a word that the Lord has not spoken; the prophet has spoken it presumptuously. You need not be afraid of him" (Deut. 18:21–22). When a prophet speaks in the name of Yahweh, if the word does not come to pass, then God did not speak that word. The people of God need have no fear of a prophet whose words did not come to fruition. While prediction is an important means of establishing a prophet's credentials, it is not true that an accurate prediction necessarily indicates a true prophet. Deuteronomy 13:1–5 shows us that

15. For an interesting contemporary example of someone saved from such a life, see Doreen Virtue, "Please Don't Read My Books Anymore," *Christianity Today*, March 2022, 87–88.

false prophets can produce predictions, signs, and wonders that serve to lead people astray.

Today there are still false prophets operating in the context of the church who must be rejected. Those prophets who testify by saying "thus says the Lord" and their words do not come to pass should be rejected. First John 4:1 warns, "Beloved, do not believe every spirit, but test the spirits to see whether they are from God, for many false prophets have gone out into the world." Likewise, Paul warns against rejecting every kind of prophetic message when he writes, "Do not despise prophecies, but test everything; hold fast what is good" (1 Thess. 5:20–21). We test any contemporary words of prophecy against the words recorded for us in Scripture. We must reject false practices and false prophets.

WE SHOULD HEED THOSE WHO SPEAK FOR GOD

Rather than listening to these alternative sources for guidance and wisdom, the Lord will raise up a prophet like Moses from among the Israelites, as we read in Deuteronomy 18:15–18:

> The LORD your God will raise up for you a prophet like me from among you, from your brothers—it is to him you shall listen—just as you desired of the LORD your God at Horeb on the day of the assembly, when you said, "Let me not hear again the voice of the LORD my God or see this great fire any more, lest I die." And the LORD said to me, "They are right in what they have spoken. I will raise up for them a prophet like you from among their brothers. And I will put my words in his mouth, and he shall speak to them all that I command him."

God is going to raise up the prophet that they are to listen to. Notice the emphasis on the divine initiative here, as opposed to the way in which the nations went about trying to discern the divine will. *God* will raise up the prophet, and *God* will put *his* words in the prophet's mouth.[16] Moses functioned as the prophet mediating between God and his people during the wilderness years because they could not bear to hear God's voice. But

16. Patrick D. Miller, *Deuteronomy*, IC (John Knox Press, 1990), 151.

Moses is going to die before they go into the promised land. How will they know the voice of the Lord in the land? This is where the temptation to seek diviners, necromancers, sorcerers, and others will arise. But so will God's prophet arise. The mention of the singular prophet who will be raised up has caused some confusion. Some have sought to identify the prophet with a particular historical prophet such as Joshua or Jeremiah. Others see the role as a collective succession of prophets.[17] Better we should see a prophecy with two levels of fulfillment. On the one hand, this verse is clearly establishing the prophetic office in Israel that would continue through each generation. At the same time, it is ultimately pointing us forward to the Prophet of all prophets: the Messiah, Jesus.[18]

In Acts 3:22–26, Peter preached:

> Moses said, "The Lord God will raise up for you a prophet like me from your brothers. You shall listen to him in whatever he tells you. And it shall be that every soul who does not listen to that prophet shall be destroyed from the people." And all the prophets who have spoken, from Samuel and those who came after him, also proclaimed these days. You are the sons of the prophets and of the covenant that God made with your fathers, saying to Abraham, "And in your offspring shall all the families of the earth be blessed." God, having raised up his servant, sent him to you first, to bless you by turning every one of you from your wickedness.

Peter sees, and we should see, Jesus as the Prophet raised up like Moses who came first to the Jews to turn them from their wickedness. When his own people rejected him, he extended his ministry to Gentiles like us and continued that ministry through his apostles and the Scriptures that they wrote down.

Today, we must consider the prophetic invitation of Jesus to repent of our sins and to put our trust in him alone for our salvation. If we do, we will experience the blessing of eternal life here and now as well as participation in the new heavens and earth. If we do not, we will answer to God for our rejection of his Prophet, as described in Deuteronomy 18:19, "And whoever

17. Peter C. Craigie, *The Book of Deuteronomy*, NICOT (Eerdmans, 1976), 262.
18. John D. Currid, *Deuteronomy*, EPSC (EP Books, 2006), 289.

will not listen to my words that he shall speak in my name, I myself will require it of him." When a prophet that God appoints speaks in God's name, to disregard the prophet is to disregard God himself. God will come to the one disregarding his Word, and he will answer to God for disregarding it. The prophet of the Lord must be heard and heeded.

Jesus came bringing the Word, and he *is* the Word of God made flesh (John 1:1–14). While the people of God could not bear to hear God speak to them from Sinai, God took on flesh in the person of Jesus and came to dwell among us. To reject Jesus is to reject the Word of God. It remains popular today to think that there are many ways to know God, but Jesus said plainly: "I am the way, and the truth, and the life. No one comes to the Father except through me" (14:6). Yes, our sins have separated us from God since the days of the garden of Eden. We could not bear to be in God's presence or to hear his voice. But in his grace and mercy, through the work of Jesus Christ, our Great High Priest and Prophet, God has made a way for us to enjoy his presence and his voice once again.

Embrace Jesus as the Priest who has opened the way to God and as the Prophet who has brought us God's good news of our salvation. Then support those who remind you of these things, reject false ways of discerning God's will, and heed the message of those who bring you the true words of God.

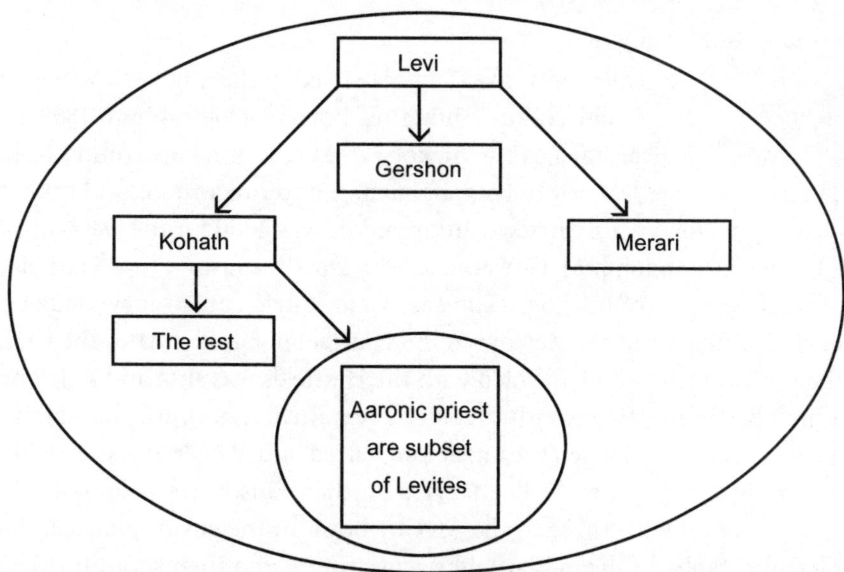

30

Protecting the Innocent and Purging the Guilty

Deuteronomy 19:1–21

Your eye shall not pity. It shall be life for life, eye for eye, tooth for tooth, hand for hand, foot for foot. (Deut. 19:21)

They called him the Devil. He lived in the Tug Fork Valley of the Appalachian Mountains. Born in a log cabin in 1839, he was as hard as the hickory trees that grew up around him. Though he never learned to read, he managed to run a successful timber business while raising thirteen children. Life was good for the Devil until 1878, when Randolph McCoy accused the Devil's cousin, Floyd Hatfield, of stealing some of his hogs. The case went to trial, and a jury made up of six Hatfields and six McCoys found Hatfield not guilty. After the trial, the McCoy juror who had sided with the Hatfields was shot and killed by a member of his own family. Tensions remained high until that fateful day in August 1882 when the anger and hatred boiled over. It was election day on Blackberry Creek. The Devil's brother, Ellison Hatfield, got into an altercation with three of the McCoy boys. In the ensuing melee, the McCoys stabbed Ellison Hatfield twenty times, and then shot him. The

Hatfields rescued their kin and brought Ellison back to their home. The Devil made a promise, "If Ellison dies, I'm going to kill the McCoy boys." Ellison did die, and the Devil captured the three McCoys, tied them to pawpaw bushes, and executed them in retaliation for his brother's death. The McCoys struck back. Over the next twenty-eight years, fifteen lives were lost in the back-and-forth retaliations between the Hatfields and the McCoys.

It may be the most famous family feud, but history is littered with stories of an injury, followed by a retaliation, followed by escalating violence and death. Such retaliatory feuds and vigilante justice destroy families, communities, and even nations. Where there are people, harm will be done, both accidental and intentional. We see it in the world around us every day. How can a society prevent these incidents from spiraling out of control? How should we as individuals respond to accidental or intentional offenses? We find instruction here.

Recall that this section of Deuteronomy is loosely following the order of the Ten Commandments. We have recently considered some of the implications of the fifth commandment by looking at the role of prophets, priests, judges, and kings among the people of God. With this passage, we come to the sixth commandment: "You shall not murder" (Deut. 5:17).[1] The major concern of this chapter is to give practical instruction on restraining evil and bloodshed in a community by protecting the innocent and purging the guilty, through the principle of just retribution described in Deuteronomy 19:21: "It shall be life for life, eye for eye, tooth for tooth, hand for hand, foot for foot."

The United States is not a theocracy in covenant with God. Rather, God's covenant is with his people in every nation. So all the particularities of the civil laws of Israel are not to be enforced in modern nations as the law of the land as though we were in the same position as Israel. But there is wisdom to be gained from considering how these things were applied among God's

1. The traditional translation, "Thou shall not kill," fails to capture the meaning of the Hebrew word *rāṣaḥ* because the law requires some killing. The term *rāṣaḥ* is not used to describe killing animals or killing in the context of war. "You shall not murder" is closer to the Hebrew, but still not quite right because the command forbids not only murder, but also what we might call manslaughter and negligent homicide. The best translation is probably something like "You shall not kill unlawfully," per J. Douma, *The Ten Commandments: Manual for the Christian Life*, trans. Nelson D. Kloosterman (P&R Publishing, 1996), 214–15.

people. We have a say in our own governance, and there are principles that can be applied in our homes and churches.

We Must Protect the Innocent

A government that does not protect the innocent is not worthy of the name. This is true for civil governments, as well as church governments and family structures. No government can perfectly protect the innocent, but when evil happens, the government is responsible to purge the guilty from its midst. But there is a tension. In a community where there is a concerted effort to purge the guilty, it is much more likely that the innocent will be unjustly punished. On the flip side, in a community where there is strong desire not to punish the innocent, it is far more likely that the guilty will not be purged. Neither alternative is acceptable. We serve a God who "will by no means clear the guilty" (Ex. 34:7; Num. 14:18). Yet at the same time, there are very strong protections here against accidentally prosecuting an innocent person. The innocent must not be punished and the guilty must be purged. That is what this section on the cities of refuge is all about.[2] Specifically, the government is to protect human life, protect private property, and protect the falsely accused.

Protect Human Life

In verses 1–3 of Deuteronomy 19, Moses commands the people to set apart three cities of refuge evenly dispersed throughout the land so that anyone who has accidentally killed someone can flee to one of them quickly. The purpose of these cities is described in verses 4–6:

> This is the provision for the manslayer, who by fleeing there may save his life. If anyone kills his neighbor unintentionally without having hated him in the past—as when someone goes into the forest with his neighbor to cut wood, and his hand swings the axe to cut down a tree, and the head slips from the handle and strikes his neighbor so that he dies—he may flee to one of these cities and live, lest the avenger of blood in hot anger pursue the manslayer

2. For more background information on cities of refuge, see Num. 35:9–34; Deut. 4:41–43; Josh. 20.

> and overtake him, because the way is long, and strike him fatally, though the man did not deserve to die, since he had not hated his neighbor in the past.

Here we have an example of when the city of refuge would be used. Such an unfortunate event could easily spark retaliation or escalating violence. A man is chopping down a tree and the axe head flies off and kills his neighbor. That man is guilty not of murder but of what we would call manslaughter. It was not an intentional killing; therefore, the man "did not deserve to die" (Deut. 19:6). The implication of that statement is that there *are* some people who do deserve to die, which we will consider in a moment. For now, the city of refuge is for someone who does not deserve to die to run to for refuge from the avenger of blood. The avenger of blood, literally "the redeemer of blood," is likely the next of kin who had an obligation to rectify losses to his relative when the relative could not do so. This would include redeeming him from slavery, redeeming his real estate, marrying his widow, and avenging his death.[3] The cities of refuge needed to be numerous and quickly accessible for someone fleeing the avenger of blood (vv. 8–9).[4]

Why is this so important? Deuteronomy 19:10 tells us: "lest innocent blood be shed in your land that the LORD your God is giving you for an inheritance, and so the guilt of bloodshed be upon you." God is trying to protect his people from the guilt of shedding innocent blood. If an avenger took the life of someone who was not guilty of murder, more innocent blood would be on the land. (We will consider the effects of innocent blood on the land when we cover Deuteronomy 21:1–9 in chapter 32.) If after investigation the elders determine that the death was in fact accidental, the manslayer must remain in the city of refuge until the death of the high priest (Num. 35:28). In some unexplained way, the high priest's death expiates the innocent

3. Jeffrey H. Tigay, *Deuteronomy*, JPSTC (Jewish Publication Society, 1996), 181.

4. It is difficult to say whether the total number of cities envisioned is six or nine. It may be that the original three are established in Deuteronomy 4:41–43 in the area east of the Jordan River. The reference to the enlarging of the territory in 19:8 would then refer to three additional cities that need to be set up when Israel enters the land west of the Jordan. Alternatively, the command to establish the three cities could refer to three on the west side of the Jordan in addition to the three already established on the eastern side of the Jordan, with an additional three after a further expansion of the land, which would bring the total to nine. If this is the proper interpretation, the Israelites' disobedience kept them from the envisioned expansion, and the total number of cities of refuge remained at six.

blood from the land. If the manslayer leaves before the high priest dies, then he is liable to be killed by the avenger. So even though it was an accidental killing, there is still a cost to the manslayer for the blood that was shed in the land. Without the protection of these cities of refuge, far more blood would have been shed.

When we think about the sixth commandment, we typically think only about what is forbidden, "You shall not murder." But as we study the Old and New Testaments, we see that the commandments not only forbid something, but command the opposite. The aim of the sixth commandment is not just that we would not murder, but that we would actively protect and preserve life. WLC 135 lays out in extensive detail what the sixth commandment requires of us:

> Q. What are the duties required in the sixth commandment?
>
> A. The duties required in the sixth commandment are, all careful studies, and lawful endeavors, to preserve the life of ourselves and others by resisting all thoughts and purposes, subduing all passions, and avoiding all occasions, temptations, and practices, which tend to the unjust taking away the life of any; by just defense thereof against violence, patient bearing of the hand of God, quietness of mind, cheerfulness of spirit; a sober use of meat, drink, physic [medicine], sleep, labor, and recreations; by charitable thoughts, love, compassion, meekness, gentleness, kindness; peaceable, mild and courteous speeches and behavior; forbearance, readiness to be reconciled, patient bearing and forgiving of injuries, and requiting good for evil; comforting and succoring the distressed, and protecting and defending the innocent.

This list is a better description of what it means to keep the sixth commandment. Cities of refuge provided the protection and defense of innocent life. The fight to end abortion is consistent with the sixth commandment, as is the fight to see innocent people on death row set free. Political and social efforts to reduce fatalities due to traffic problems, unhealthy work conditions, or violence in the streets are all in line with the sixth commandment. Policing strategies that lessen the likelihood of unnecessary lethal force are in keeping with the sixth commandment. Simply avoiding killing others unlawfully is important but not the full directive of the sixth commandment. In addition to not taking a life, we should actively protect and defend life.

Protect Private Property

We read in Deuteronomy 19:14, "You shall not move your neighbor's landmark, which the men of old have set, in the inheritance that you will hold in the land that the Lord your God is giving you to possess." What is being forbidden is taking the legal boundary marker and moving it over to increase one's own land at the expense of a neighbor. Admittedly, this verse feels a little out of place here and appears better suited to the commandment forbidding stealing. What does this have to do with cities of refuge, which come before it, or the witnesses, which come after it? It is difficult to say with certainty, but remember what we saw in WLC 135: "The duties required in the sixth commandment are, all careful studies, and lawful endeavors, to preserve the life of ourselves and others by resisting all thoughts and purposes, subduing all passions, and avoiding all occasions, temptations, and practices, which tend to the unjust taking away the life of any." Moving someone's property marker may end in mortal combat. Property disputes lead to feuds and killings all over the world on the personal level and the national level. In a just society, personal property needs to be protected by the force of law; otherwise, unjust violence is likely to follow.[5]

Protect the Falsely Accused

The third place where the innocent need to be protected is in the court of law: "A single witness shall not suffice against a person for any crime or for any wrong in connection with any offense that he has committed. Only on the evidence of two witnesses or of three witnesses shall a charge be established" (Deut. 19:15). We have considered the substance of this verse elsewhere, but in this context notice again how careful the biblical teaching is to avoid wrongly punishing an innocent person. A single witness is not enough. It would be too easy to punish the innocent. Those responsible for making judgments must err on the side of potentially letting the guilty go

5. The story of Ahab and Jezebel's utilizing false witnesses to murder the righteous Naboth and steal his vineyard is an illustration of this passage turned upside down for evil (1 Kings 21).

free rather than accidentally punishing the innocent. Perhaps the reason for this priority is that even though the guilty might temporarily escape judgment, perfect justice will come.

We continue to the situation of a false or malicious witness in Deuteronomy 19:16–20:

> If a malicious witness arises to accuse a person of wrongdoing, then both parties to the dispute shall appear before the LORD, before the priests and the judges who are in office in those days. The judges shall inquire diligently, and if the witness is a false witness and has accused his brother falsely, then you shall do to him as he had meant to do to his brother. So you shall purge the evil from your midst. And the rest shall hear and fear, and shall never again commit any such evil among you.

As we have seen earlier, there is a great danger in having only one witness as the basis for a guilty verdict, since there is a possibility that the witness is malicious. Therefore, two witnesses are the minimum requirement to establish guilt. This serves to protect the innocent.

In some cases, a witness may arise (Deut. 19:16), and someone may suspect that the witness is malicious. In that situation, both the accuser and the accused are carefully investigated by the priests and judges (probably local; otherwise, it would say "at the place that the LORD will choose"). If the accusation of false witness is proved, then whatever penalty was sought is to be handed down to the false witness himself. The motivation given, again, is to purge the evil from among Israel. But the deeper concern is to make sure that false witnesses do not put innocent victims at risk. Malicious witnesses threaten to bring bloodguilt on the whole community by leading the priests and judges to punish an innocent victim. Therefore, the punishment for those who endanger the whole community this way must be severe to serve as an example for all the people.

Deuteronomy 19:20 indicates that stiff penalties function as a deterrent to similar acts of wickedness: "And the rest shall hear and fear, and shall never again commit any such evil among you." When false witnesses or accusations are discovered, those cases need to be handled with the absolute strictest administration of justice and in the most public manner possible to deter others from doing something similar. This is especially important in our current system in which a false accusation can ruin someone long before the person ever gets the chance to set foot in a courtroom. We should also recognize that we can bear false witness through gossip and slander that can be just as damaging to a person as bearing false witness in a courtroom setting. The first segment is about protecting the innocent. In protecting the innocent, the priests and judges also protect themselves from bringing bloodguilt on the community. Deuteronomy is not soft on crime, and no just society should be.

We Must Purge the Guilty

We saw that a person who accidentally kills someone should be protected in the city of refuge. But for someone who intentionally takes a human life, Deuteronomy 19:11–12 is clear regarding how the murderer should be dealt with: "But if anyone hates his neighbor and lies in wait for him and attacks him and strikes him fatally so that he dies, and he flees into one of these cities, then the elders of his city shall send and take him from there, and hand him over to the avenger of blood, so that he may die." Notice the elements here of a person guilty of murder. There is a motive ("hates his neighbor"), premeditation ("lies in wait for him"), and follow-through ("attacks him and strikes him fatally so that he dies"). Murder generally starts with anger and hatred, which is why Jesus warns against it, and WLC 135 teaches that the sixth commandment requires "charitable thoughts, love, compassion, meekness, gentleness, kindness; peaceable, mild and courteous speeches and behavior; forbearance, readiness to be reconciled, patient bearing and forgiving of injuries." When we see anger and bitterness in our hearts, when we engage in aggressive behavior on the roads, we are moving toward murder. The city of refuge does not protect murderers. When a person in the city of refuge is investigated and it is determined that he intentionally killed someone, the elders are to have him brought back to his own city, and the family who was wronged will carry out the execution. This is not personal vengeance; this is community justice. He must be put to death, and not to do so is injustice. Verse 13 warns, "Your eye shall not pity him, but you shall purge the guilt of innocent blood from Israel, so that it may be well with you." The passage is telling us that when murder is committed, innocent blood stains the community. The only way to wash away that stain is for the blood of the murderer to be shed. Until then, the guilt of the crime remains on all the people.

Should nations today utilize the death penalty? Absolutely, if administered justly. In the case of the intentional taking of the life of another person, the one who took that life must die. Genesis 9:6 lays down the timeless principle that remains valid in any society: "Whoever sheds the blood of man, by man shall his blood be shed, for God made man in his own image." To destroy the image of God requires that the one who shed that blood be put to death. When we come to the New Testament, there is no repeal of this as an appropriate punishment for crime. Paul defends the right of civil authorities to implement capital punishment as one aspect of God's wrath, "for he is God's servant for your good. But if you do wrong, be afraid, for he does not bear the sword in vain. For he is the servant of God, an avenger who carries out God's wrath on the wrongdoer" (Rom. 13:4). Paul uses the word "avenger" to describe the role of the government in avenging innocent blood. A government that bears the sword in vain is failing the responsibility to practice justice, protect the innocent, and purge the guilty. It is certain that individuals are not to execute God's judgment. We are to forgive and love our enemies. It is the responsibility of civil authorities to uphold the sanctity of human life by executing murderers.

Many today both inside and outside the church reject capital punishment, including Pope Francis. He states that

> the death penalty is unacceptable, however grave the crime of the convicted person. It is an offence to the inviolability of life and to the dignity of the human person; it likewise contradicts God's plan for individuals and society, and his merciful justice. Nor is it consonant with any just purpose of punishment. It does not render justice to victims, but instead fosters vengeance. The commandment "Thou shalt not kill" has absolute value and applies both to the innocent and to the guilty. . . . It must not be forgotten that the inviolable and God-given right to life also belongs to the criminal.[6]

6. "Video Message of His Holiness Pope Francis to the 6th World Congress Against the Death Penalty," Oslo, June 21–23, 2016, https://www.vatican.va/content/francesco/en/messages/pont-messages/2016/documents/papa-francesco_20160621_videomessaggio-vi-congresso-contro-pena-di-morte.html, accessed July 1, 2022.

I submit the following in response to the pope's statement. First, capital punishment cannot contradict God's plan when God's plan explicitly prescribes it. Second, biblically speaking, retribution is the chief purpose of punishment, and the death penalty *is* consonant with it. Third, the death penalty may or may not foster vengeance in the hearts of victims, but that is beside the point. Christians are called to forgive our enemies, and we are not to take the lives of others for the sake of personal vengeance.The state, acting opposite of vengeance, has a responsibility to execute murderers in the enforcement of justice. Finally, his statement that "Thou shalt not kill" has absolute value and applies to the innocent and the guilty cannot be true and must be rejected. The very same books of Exodus and Deuteronomy that contain the sixth commandment also repeatedly call for the death of criminals, and so the commandment very clearly does *not* protect those guilty of capital crimes. We commend the Roman Catholic Church for its strong defense of life from conception until natural death, but this opposition to the death penalty is at odds with the Scriptures.[7] The guilty in a just society must be purged.

There is a threat, however, to bringing justice to the offender. The threat is pity. Verses 13 and 21 of Deuteronomy 19 both warn, "Your eye shall not pity." Those responsible for justice in a society may be tempted to shirk their responsibility because they pity the offender. While extenuating circumstances need to be considered when executing justice, such as the age or mental capacity of the offender, if the authorities responsible for carrying out justice neglect their duty, they will almost certainly bring more bloodguilt on the people. Everybody suffers when criminals have no fear of the governmental sword. Part of the function of government as it bears the sword serves as a restraint to sin in society. Singapore is well known for very severe penalties for crimes, including corporal punishment and capital punishment. Consequently, its citizens enjoy one of the lowest crime rates in the world. Contrast that with some of the "progressive" policing strategies being deployed in some American cities. When those breaking the law do not suffer, law-abiding citizens do suffer. Not only will evil flourish, but citizens will be left with few alternatives to taking the law into their own hands. This kind of vigilante justice rarely executes the aims of true justice

7. For more, see John M. Frame, *The Doctrine of the Christian Life*, Theology of Lordship (P&R Publishing, 2008), 704.

because it is frequently disproportionate. This is what verse 21 was written to protect against: "It shall be life for life, eye for eye, tooth for tooth, hand for hand, foot for foot."

This verse is referred to as the *lex talionis*, the law of retribution (the Latin *talionis* literally translates "retaliation," but "retribution" is a better word to describe the principle of Deuteronomy 19:21). Some think that this is a law of vengeance. It is not. The law of retribution was given to *limit* vengeance and disproportionate responses to evil actions. *Lex talionis* requires that the punishment fit the crime. The basic principle is that if one tooth is knocked out, it does not justify knocking out all of the offender's teeth. Furthermore, with the exception of life for life, the rest of the statement is probably not to be interpreted literally. The force of the phrases is to emphasize proportionate compensation for wrongs committed, which in many cases was monetary.[8]

In the United States justice system, our primary punishments are fines or incarceration. Interestingly, the Mosaic law does not prescribe incarceration for any crimes. Egypt, Assyria, Philistia, and Babylon all had prisons, but the law of Moses never specifies prison as a penalty for a crime. Instead, crimes punished by prison today were generally punished by beatings, restitution, or capital punishment. Our own society might benefit from the increased use of these other forms of punishment and less reliance on incarceration. Unfortunately, apart from the work of ministries such as Prison Fellowship, prisons as "correctional" facilities have been terrible failures. Generally speaking, people come out of prison worse than they went in, having been trained by more experienced criminals. Some offenses that we currently address with prison terms, such as theft, would be better addressed through corporal punishment and some form of work for repayment. Likewise, in terms of proportionate responses to crimes, capital punishment should be applied more frequently in cases involving the intentional taking of life.[9]

Does Jesus overturn *lex talionis* or do away with it? He says in the Sermon on the Mount: "You have heard that it was said, 'An eye for an eye and a tooth for a tooth.' But I say to you, Do not resist the one who is evil. But if anyone slaps you on the right cheek, turn to him the other also" (Matt. 5:38–39). One

8. Peter C. Craigie, *The Book of Deuteronomy*, NICOT (Eerdmans, 1976), 270. We can also compare this version of *lex talionis* with the slightly varying forms of it in Exodus 21:23–24 and Leviticus 24:17–21.

9. See Frame, *Doctrine of the Christian Life*, 699.

of my favorite authors (though not theologically reliable), Leo Tolstoy, held an extreme view. He believed that to have soldiers, police, or even magistrates was unchristian. He did not believe that we should resist evil in any way.[10] Others hold less extreme views but may think that Jesus forbids serving as soldiers or the practice of capital punishment. Is Jesus turning over the Mosaic law here? No, he is not. The teaching given in the Old Testament was a principle of justice not for individuals, but for the community as administered by judges who were responsible for law and order. Jesus, however, is specifically addressing Christian individuals. Individuals were utilizing *lex talionis* as justification for personal retaliation against others. Jesus is correcting this inappropriate use of the Mosaic teaching.

In our personal relationships, we are not to retaliate against those who sin against us, not even proportionately as the government is supposed to do. We forgive. Sometimes this means that we must allow ourselves to be defrauded by a fellow Christian without taking the person to a secular court (1 Cor. 6:1–8). This does not mean that we cannot prosecute crimes in court, but means that we leave justice to God and the courts rather than taking it into our own hands.

At the same time, when the state does not resist evil, it fails in the purpose for which it was given by God. The Bible strikes a most wise and careful balance. On the one hand, extreme diligence and care is needed to make sure that the innocent are not punished. On the other hand, when guilt is established, the Bible is not soft on crime. Lax prosecutors and overzealous prosecutors are both a threat to contemporary justice. When prosecutors are soft on crime, evil flourishes and the righteous suffer. At the same time, overzealous prosecutors who are eager to show that they are tough on crime expose themselves to all sorts of errors in trying to maximize the number of their convictions. Prosecutors should be concerned with seeing that the guilty are punished, but no less important is that the innocent are not punished. We should pray for those in our societies who are responsible for this aspect of justice because the effectiveness with which this responsibility is performed has a great deal to do with whether we can live peaceful and godly lives (1 Tim. 2:1–2).

10. His views are presented in a number of places, but a good summary can be found in chapter 1 of Leo Tolstoy, *The Kingdom of God Is Within You*, trans. Constance Garnett, vol. 1 (William Heinemann, 1894).

According to Deuteronomy, the primary purpose of punishing the guilty is retribution. The punishment is necessary not only to rectify the injustice done, but also to serve as an instructive deterrent to the rest of the community. There is a place in punishment for restitution, restraint, and even reformation of the offender. But I agree with theologian and ethicist John Frame, who argues that retribution is the key that holds the other motivations in their proper place. First, it aligns with the scriptural principle of *lex talionis*, an eye for an eye. People should receive the punishments they deserve, not more and not less. Second, the other motivations for punishment quickly become unjust if they are not based on someone's getting what he deserves for his crime. For example, if deterrence is our primary motivator, as it sometimes is in a community demanding "law and order," then some might justify punishing innocent people because it still adds deterrent value. If this is our motivation, then whether the person is guilty or not is not as important as the fact that the person appear guilty to the public.[11] When a government is functioning as it should in the world, in the church, and in the home, evil is restrained, bloodshed is minimized, and the righteous flourish.

Devil Anse Hatfield was as rough as they come. He wasn't nicknamed "Devil" by accident. But the Devil had a friend from his days in the Confederate army named Dyke Garrett. Garrett had earlier experienced a life-changing encounter with Jesus Christ. One day Dyke approached his friend and shared the gospel with him. He invited the Devil to go to a gospel meeting, and at the end of the meeting, at seventy-two years old, the Devil received Christ and repented of his sins. From there they went down to the waters of Island Creek, where Dyke baptized Devil Anse Hatfield for the remission of sins in the fall of 1911.[12] According to those who knew him, Devil Anse spent the rest of his days in peace, knowing that his many sins had been forgiven through the blood of the Lamb that was slain, washed away in the baptismal waters of a cold West Virginia creek. If the shed blood of the innocent Jesus can change a violent man such as Devil Anse into a man of peace, it can change you and me. One feud expert believes that the baptism not only ended the feud but impacted generations of Hatfields and others throughout the region. When Devil Anse died around ten years later,

11. I owe much of this discussion to Frame, *Doctrine of the Christian Life*, 695–98.

12. Robert Y. Spence, "Uncle Dyke Garrett," *e-WV: The West Virginia Encyclopedia*, rev. May 5, 2014, https://www.wvencyclopedia.org/entries/2023, accessed January 13, 2025.

it was the largest funeral ever held in Logan County, West Virginia. Some of the mourners are even said to have borne the name McCoy.[13]

The fact is that we too have a city of refuge, but it is a better refuge than the ones described in Deuteronomy. Our city of refuge is ready to receive both the innocent and the guilty alike. The Scripture testifies that we all have innocent blood on our hands. The Avenger of blood is hot on our trail, and we are all under a just sentence of death. But God provided a refuge in Jesus Christ. All who are guilty may flee to him and hide themselves in him for refuge. But Jesus is more than a city of refuge; he is also our High Priest. When he died, his death served to expiate the sins of all who have run to him for salvation. Through his death, God has judged our sins and given Christ what our sins deserved, in order that we might be recipients of his mercy. Because of the death of our High Priest, we need no longer fear the Avenger of blood.

Imagine how history would have been different had the Devil met Christ sooner. Imagine how our world would be different if more people knew him now. We cannot stop sin from happening. Violence, theft, and bearing false witness will be a part of our world until Jesus comes again. But as surely as we Christians must see to it that the innocent are protected and the guilty are punished, we must also share the good news of this gospel that is good news for the innocent and guilty alike: there is now no condemnation for those who are in Christ Jesus. The blood of the innocent was shed for the guilty once and for all. All who are covered in this blood, though our sins are like scarlet, will be washed white as snow.

13. Wendy Griffith, "Amazing End to the Hatfield-McCoy Feud," Daily Hatch, originally aired March 20, 2009, https://thedailyhatch.org/2012/06/01/great-great-granddaughter-of-devil-anse-hatfield-said-he-came-to-christ/, accessed July 1, 2022.

31

The Rules of War

Deuteronomy 20:1–20

Hear, O Israel, today you are drawing near for battle against your enemies: let not your heart faint. Do not fear or panic or be in dread of them, for the Lord your God is he who goes with you to fight for you against your enemies, to give you the victory. (Deut. 20:3–4)

When theologian R.C. Sproul was a boy, his father served overseas in the Army Air Corps. R.C. and his mother would listen to the newscasts daily at noon and six o'clock to hear updates on the latest casualties from the war. R.C. hated those times of day. The newscasts reminded him how vulnerable his father was and how quickly things could change for their family. Even though he was only a boy, he had some understanding that his father might not come back alive from the war.

Because of that fear, he hated the war, and he hated the concept of fighting altogether. He once went to his mother and told her that he wanted to write a letter to Adolf Hitler, Benito Mussolini, Joseph Stalin, Franklin Delano Roosevelt, and Winston Churchill, asking them to stop the war so that his daddy could come home. It was plain to him as a boy that what they were doing was wrong. His mother assured him that it was a good idea, but also that it would never work. He asked her: "But why do they need to hurt each other and kill each other? What good is there in that?"[1]

Countless others have asked the same question through the ages as wars have raged and devastated nations, communities, and families. In the 1970 antiwar song made famous by Edwin Starr, he sang memorably: "War . . . what is it good for? Absolutely nothing." He goes on to explain in the following verses that he despises war because it brings death to innocent people and tears to mothers' eyes.[2] It is easy to see how one could conclude that war is good for absolutely nothing.

War is a reality of our present existence in the world. It does indeed bring death and destruction to every sort of person and community. Between September 11, 2001, and the end of 2022, America spent $5.8 trillion waging war in Afghanistan, Iraq, Syria, and Pakistan. To appreciate how large that number is, imagine a stack of $1,000 bills. A million dollars would be a stack of $1,000 bills just over four inches high. A billion-dollar stack is about as tall as the Statue of Liberty. A trillion-dollar stack is 67 miles high.[3] So this is a stack of $1,000 bills nearly 402 miles high. Sadly, the financial toll is the least significant in terms of cost.

Since 1775, America has lost approximately 1.19 million active-service-member lives.[4] Perhaps the most heartbreaking statistic of them all is this one: since 2001, more than 130,000 veterans have taken their own lives.[5] As of this writing, that is more than sixteen suicides per day for the last twenty-two years. It is easy to see why many would conclude that war is good for nothing.

1. R.C. Sproul, *What Can I Do with My Guilt?*, Crucial Questions 9 (Reformation Trust, 2011), 27–28.

2. Barrett Strong and Norman Whitfield, "War," Sony/ATV Music Publishing LLC (1970).

3. Rachel Layne, "America's Price Tag for Two Decades of War: $5.8 Trillion," CBS News, updated September 1, 2021, https://www.cbsnews.com/news/afghanistan-cost-war-price-tag/, accessed July 6, 2022.

4. Department of Veterans Affairs, "America's Wars," https://www.va.gov/opa/publications/factsheets/fs_americas_wars.pdf, accessed July 6, 2022.

5. It was difficult to find a firm number on this. I took the average suicides per year between 2001 and 2019, then extrapolated that through the end of 2022, and then rounded down so as not to overstate the case. Data taken from Department of Veterans Affairs, "2021 National Veteran Suicide Prevention Annual Report," September 2021, https://www.mentalhealth.va.gov/docs/data-sheets/2021/2021-National-Veteran-Suicide-Prevention-Annual-Report-FINAL-9-8-21.pdf, accessed July 7, 2022.

Yet in Deuteronomy 20, we find specific instructions regarding war. In this section of Deuteronomy, Moses is working out the implications of the sixth commandment, which is best translated, "You shall not kill unlawfully." As we saw in the previous chapter, the sixth commandment does not prohibit the lawful use of capital punishment by the state. Here we will see that killing in the context of war is also not a transgression of the sixth commandment. At the same time, Deuteronomy does not allow a no-holds-barred approach to warfare. In fact, most of the laws here actually limit war by restricting the freedom of the military in terms of who may serve in battle and what can be done to conquered peoples and places. While some of what we will read seems harsh by modern standards, these laws actually limit the unrestrained destruction of life and property and are the oldest known rules of war.[6]

It should be noted again that neither America nor any other modern nation is a theocracy as Israel was under the terms of the old covenant. Likewise, modern Israel is not a theocracy in covenant with God as biblical Israel was. Therefore, no modern nations should be using this text as the basis for waging a holy war against any nations, peoples, or religious groups, and even biblical Israel did not do so beyond the conquest of Canaan. Moreover, the church has no warrant to wage military conflict. The apostle Paul reminds us that under the new covenant, "we do not wrestle against flesh and blood, but against the rulers, against the authorities, against the cosmic powers over this present darkness, against the spiritual forces of evil in the heavenly places" (Eph. 6:12). That is a significant development from the time that Deuteronomy 20 was written. The Israelites were engaged in spiritual warfare, but they were also engaged as God's people in physical warfare. Yet when Peter attempted to take up the sword to defend Jesus, Jesus rebuked him. The church is not to advance itself by the weapons of human warfare. Rather, the armor that we take up is righteousness, faith, salvation, truth, and the gospel of peace, and our weapon is the Word of God, all of which we may wield through prayer. Does this mean that there is no place for nations to wage war? No, it does not. One of the primary roles of the government, as we saw in the previous chapter, is to protect and defend its people. Jesus' teaching in the Sermon on the Mount regarding not resisting evil applies to private persons who have been personally offended, not to national governments.

6. Jeffrey H. Tigay, *Deuteronomy*, JPSTC (Jewish Publication Society, 1996), 185.

So why spend any time at all on this passage when we could simply go to Ephesians 6 to talk about spiritual warfare? Because this passage reveals to us something of God's heart for his covenant people and provides helpful instruction for us in engaging in our spiritual battles. The primary point that the people of God should take away from Deuteronomy 20 is that God fights for his people, so we should trust in his power, enjoy his gifts, and obey his commands.

God Fights for His People, so Trust in His Power

Deuteronomy 20:1 describes what will be a common scenario for God's people in warfare: "When you go out to war against your enemies, and see horses and chariots and an army larger than your own, you shall not be afraid of them, for the LORD your God is with you, who brought you up out of the land of Egypt." The expectation is that the people of Israel will go out to war. The question is not if, but when. When they do, they will see intimidating realities: horses, chariots, and superior numbers. All of these are the keys to victory in both ancient and modern warfare. Horses and chariots represent superior technology, and superior numbers mean strength. Yet God's people are not to be intimidated or afraid when they face this. Why not? "For the LORD your God is with you, who brought you up out of the land of Egypt" (Deut. 20:1). The same God who rescued them from superior numbers and technology when he rescued the Israelites from Egypt will be with them in the battles they will fight when they enter Canaan. We see this theme repeatedly in Deuteronomy.

Next, it is the priests' job to remind the people of these things so that they remember:

> And when you draw near to the battle, the priest shall come forward and speak to the people and shall say to them, "Hear, O Israel, today you are drawing near for battle against your enemies: let not your heart faint. Do not fear or panic or be in dread of them, for the LORD your God is he who goes with you to fight for you against your enemies, to give you the victory." (Deut. 20:2–4)

We can tell by the repetition of words forbidding fear that fear is going to be a serious temptation for God's people. Remember, Israel failed in its initial attempt to go into the land at Kadesh because of fear when seeing the size of the enemy and its fortified cities. So Moses tells the people in four different ways: "Let not your heart faint. Do not fear or panic or be in dread of them" (Deut. 20:3). The reason given, again, is that Yahweh is going with them to fight their enemies and give them victory. The spiritual leaders are there to remind them what is true. The people are called to remember, trust, and obey—specifically, to trust in God's power, as David taught the people to sing in Psalm 20:7: "Some trust in chariots and some in horses, but we trust in the name of the LORD our God." In the face of improbable odds, God is on our side.

Christians can take confidence that God is with them wherever they are: on the battlefield, in the classroom, in the workplace, or on the operating table. These truths regarding God's presence can still be clung to by soldiers in the face of actual battle today, and they have been clung to by Christians in battle through the ages. But while victory is assured for ancient Israel in these battles, this is not the case for Christians who are fighting in military combat today. Christian soldiers can be certain of God's comforting and sanctifying power through the presence of the Holy Spirit, but we have no promises of victory in modern military conflicts. In any given conflict between nations today, it is quite likely that there are Christians serving in the armies on both sides. Whose side is God on in such a conflict? We all have our opinions, but we do not *know*. This was not a problem in ancient Israel's battles because the people of God were all part of the one nation of Israel. The advance of Israel was the advance of God's mission in the world.

Today, God's mission is being advanced through his church, which is scattered among many nations. His purpose to rescue a people for himself from every tribe that will declare his excellencies amid this broken world is being accomplished through the triumph of the gospel over the unseen powers of darkness. These promises of victory from God are now best understood in the context of the spiritual battles we engage in, not the physical ones. As those who know that God is with us, as those who have seen his great power displayed through his works in Israel, through the triumph of the cross and resurrection of Jesus, we must have no fear of Satan, sin, death, and hell. We can take the gospel to hostile tribes and people without fear, knowing that victory belongs to the Lord. It does not mean that we will live, but it does mean that the gospel will prevail. Even if we die, we know that not even death can separate us from God's love. He will fight for us and ultimately raise us from the dead. Therefore, we must not fear, but trust his power.

GOD FIGHTS FOR HIS PEOPLE, SO ENJOY HIS GIFTS

The following verses are not what one would expect to find in a passage on waging war. We see here a list of exemptions from military service that reduce the already small army. Consider the first three exemptions in Deuteronomy 20:5–7:

> Then the officers shall speak to the people, saying, "Is there any man who has built a new house and has not dedicated it? Let him go back to his house, lest he die in the battle and another man dedicate it. And is there any man who has planted a vineyard and has not enjoyed its fruit? Let him go back to his house, lest he die in the battle and another man enjoy its fruit. And is there any man who has betrothed a wife and has not taken her? Let him go back to his house, lest he die in the battle and another man take her."

If a man has a new house, a new vineyard, or a new wife, he is exempt from military service. It would be a travesty for a man to have one of these good gifts of God and have his life cut off before he can enjoy it. Such a loss would suggest that a man was cursed. Later in Deuteronomy when Moses describes the curses that will fall to a people who are unfaithful to their suzerain King, he describes it this way: "You shall betroth a wife, but another man shall ravish her. You shall build a house, but you shall not dwell in it. You shall plant a vineyard, but you shall not enjoy its fruit" (Deut. 28:30).

Israel was not brought into the land simply to fight; the purpose of the fighting was to one day enjoy the gift of the land. God's intention for the Israelites was not that they would be in a constant state of fighting, but that through fighting they might enjoy rest from their enemies and the good gifts that God was giving. If enjoying homes, vineyards, and family life was lost, then the wars were pointless.[7] The people of Israel would fight, but they were not to see fighting as their norm; enjoying God's good gifts in the land was the norm, and fighting was the occasional requirement.

7. Peter C. Craigie, *The Book of Deuteronomy*, NICOT (Eerdmans, 1976), 274.

Many who are reading this commentary are goal-oriented people with an appreciation for success. But our measure of success and the goals we seek do not necessarily align with what God desires for us. Consider for a moment what God is doing in this passage. He is telling the army, right before they are going to go and fight to take a new piece of the land (or to defend a piece of the land), that if someone has not yet been able to enjoy the fruit of the fighting, he is to go home and enjoy it. The fighting is not the point; joy is the point. Fighting is how they get there.

What kind of God is this? One day in seven, he absolutely forbids his people to work. At multiple other points in the year, he commands them to stop working, and to intentionally feast together with all their household. He is not opposed to work, just as he is not opposed to war in some instances, but neither work nor war is the primary reason that we are here. Our chief end is to glorify God and to enjoy him forever. Sometimes we get overly caught up in working for God or even fighting for God so that we lose sight of our primary calling, which is to enjoy him and the good gifts he gives. Has God given us a home? It is okay for us to stay home sometimes and enjoy it. Has God given us a vineyard or a garden? These are wonderful gifts for us to enjoy. Have we left ourselves any time to enjoy them? Has God given us a husband or a wife? What a tremendous gift! Let us not be so busy pursuing things, battling, achieving, and accomplishing that we fail to enjoy the gifts.

Readers may be aware of the fable about the American businessman who went down to Brazil. There he met a simple fisherman who had a boat. Each day the fisherman would go out and catch enough fish to sell in the marketplace to feed his family. When he caught enough, he went home, enjoyed a siesta, played with his kids, and had dinner with his family. The next day, he got up and did it again. When the businessman saw this, he said to the fisherman: "You know, if you worked a little longer each day, you could catch more fish to sell in the market. With the extra money, you could also take out a loan and buy a second boat, hire another fisherman, and more than double the amount of profit you are bringing in at the market. With those increased profits, you could buy still more boats, hire more fishermen, and make even more money." The fisherman asked, "Why would I do that?" The businessman answered, "Then you could work less, come home in the evening, enjoy a siesta, play with your kids, and enjoy dinner with your family." The fisherman asked, "What do you think I'm doing now?"

We too can be so caught up in the "more" mentality that we fail to enjoy the gifts that we already have. This is not to say that work is bad, or that building a business is bad, or that we do not sometimes have to make sacrifices in the pursuit of our callings. Yet our norm should not be the struggle for more, but should be the enjoyment of the good gifts that God has given.

With that being said, under the terms of the new covenant, we have not been promised a land until Jesus returns and we inherit the earth. We have not been promised a spouse, a home, or a vineyard. In fact, some of those who faithfully follow Jesus in this world will explicitly lose these things. Is this also a travesty? No. Jesus asserts, "Truly, I say to you, there is no one who has left house or brothers or sisters or mother or father or children or lands, for my sake and for the gospel, who will not receive a hundredfold now in this time, houses and brothers and sisters and mothers and children and lands, with persecutions, and in the age to come eternal life" (Mark 10:29–30). We can enjoy God's good gifts even now, but when those gifts are forfeited for the sake of Christ and the advance of the gospel, we can be certain that it is not a travesty, but that he will more than repay whatever is lost.

The next exempt soldiers are the fearful:

> And the officers shall speak further to the people, and say, "Is there any man who is fearful and fainthearted? Let him go back to his house, lest he make the heart of his fellows melt like his own." And when the officers have finished speaking to the people, then commanders shall be appointed at the head of the people. (Deut. 20:8–9)

Despite the call not to be fearful, some will not trust and obey. They are not to be forced to go forward and fight, but instead are allowed to return home. Such people in the ranks would be like a wasting disease that spreads misery through the rest of the troops; better to not have them at all. Like the spies who brought back a bad report of the land of Canaan and caused the people to fear, faithless people can be contagious and convince others that their fears are rational. If they spread their faithlessness among God's soldiers, none of them will get to enjoy the good gifts that God is giving them. It is better that they go home. Underlying this ability to send all these exempt soldiers home is a confidence in God's power. The key to their victory will not be their numbers or even the strength of their army, but the fact that God fights for them. Therefore, they can trust him and enjoy his good gifts.

God Fights for His People, so Obey His Commands

In the remaining verses, Moses gives some specific commands for warfare that the people are to follow, since they know that God fights for them. There are two different sets of instructions for two different types of warfare.

Warfare with Cities Outside the Promised Land

At some point in the future, the expectation is that the Israelites will engage in war (for reasons not stated) with people in the area surrounding the promised land. In that case, the first thing they are to do is outlined in Deuteronomy 20:10–11: "When you draw near to a city to fight against it, offer terms of peace to it. And if it responds to you peaceably and it opens to you, then all the people who are found in it shall do forced labor for you and shall serve you." The people of God are to prefer peace and to avoid fighting if possible. If a city surrenders to them, they are allowed to make its inhabitants a vassal people and put the citizens to forced labor, but that is all. They are not to rape, pillage, terrorize, or engage in any of the other traditional activities involved with conquering. If the city rejects the terms, however, the instructions are given in verses 12–15:

> But if it makes no peace with you, but makes war against you, then you shall besiege it. And when the Lord your God gives it into your hand, you shall put all its males to the sword, but the women and the little ones, the livestock, and everything else in the city, all its spoil, you shall take as plunder for yourselves. And you shall enjoy the spoil of your enemies, which the Lord your God has given you. Thus you shall do to all the cities that are very far from you, which are not cities of the nations here.

Besieging the city is the next step, and because the Lord fights for the people of Israel, they will ultimately prevail. When they do, they are to kill all the men, presumably breaking the back of the enemy from resisting in the future.

But they are not to kill the women and children.[8] The plunder of the city is theirs to enjoy. They are to receive it also as God's gift to them.

But down in Deuteronomy 20:19–20 is one more command specific to warfare:

> When you besiege a city for a long time, making war against it in order to take it, you shall not destroy its trees by wielding an axe against them. You may eat from them, but you shall not cut them down. Are the trees in the field human, that they should be besieged by you? Only the trees that you know are not trees for food you may destroy and cut down, that you may build siegeworks against the city that makes war with you, until it falls.

When a siege was dragging on, sometimes an army would destroy all the surrounding fields and vegetation as a way of getting the inhabitants of the city to give up their resistance sooner. But God specifically prohibits this with a rhetorical question: "Are the trees in the field human, that they should be besieged by you?" (Deut. 20:19). The Hebrew of this question is difficult. But the translation here is likely, and the implication is that because the fruit trees are not enemy combatants, they should not be treated like enemies. If this interpretation is correct, while there is a utilitarian aspect to this in that the Israelites can enjoy the trees, the emphasis would seem to be more humanitarian in nature.[9] On the practical side, God means for them to have confidence that they will take the city, and it would be senseless for them to cut off their food supply once they have the victory. As we consider these instructions about warfare, we might not like it that Israel is going to attack cities and take captives, but the level of restraint stands out in the ancient world.

Warfare with Cities Inside the Promised Land

There is a different policy for dealing with the Canaanites. We already saw this when we considered Deuteronomy 7 in chapter 15, so the treatment here will be brief. With the Canaanites, Israel is not to offer peace. The people

8. Specific instructions are given in Deuteronomy 21:10–14 for how the women are to be treated.
9. Tigay, *Deuteronomy*, 190.

of God are to devote the Canaanites to complete destruction and leave no survivors because of their wickedness. God has put the people dwelling in the land of Canaan under the death penalty. Israel is not simply one army attacking a people; Israel is the sword in the hand of God executing his divine justice on the wicked. As it is appropriate for the state to wield the sword in carrying out justice against a murderer, so it is appropriate for ancient Israel to be the sword in God's hand carrying out justice on these child-sacrificing, necromancing, sexually immoral people. Israel has no right to refuse to deliver the justice that God is bringing to the Canaanites.

An additional reason for their complete destruction is given in Deuteronomy 20:18: "that they may not teach you to do according to all their abominable practices that they have done for their gods, and so you sin against the LORD your God." God wants to protect the lives of his own people. If Israel does not wipe out these Canaanites, then Israel is likely going to start doing the same things for which God is judging the Canaanites. Sadly, this is what happens, and God brings judgment on his own people. God would fight for his people, but they needed to trust and obey him. If they did not, they would find themselves in the same situation as the Canaanites.

Does this passage have anything to teach us about modern warfare? Perhaps.[10] Reflecting on Deuteronomy 20 should lead us to ask whether we can find avenues for compassion, human concern, and care for creation

10. Since Augustine in the fourth century, theologians and ethicists have tried to limit the resort to war and conduct in war once it has begun. This effort is known as *just-war theory*. The rules that govern going to war under this framework are as follows: (1) the only just cause is defense against violent aggression; (2) the only just intention is to restore a just peace to friend and foe alike; (3) the use of military force must be a last resort after negotiations and every other possibility; (4) the decision to wage war must be by the highest governmental authority. Once war has been entered into, the following should be considered: (5) a war must be for limited ends only, sufficient to repel aggression and redress injustice; (6) the means must be limited by proportionality to the offense; (7) noncombatants should be immune from intentional or direct attack; (8) combat should not be prolonged when there is no reasonable hope of success within these limits. See A. F. Holmes, "Just-War Theory," in *New Dictionary of Christian Ethics and Pastoral Theology*, ed. David J. Atkinson and David A. Field (InterVarsity Press, 1995), 521–22. John Frame demonstrates the challenges of attempting to utilize just-war theory in practice. He concludes: "Scripture does not try to micromanage humanitarianism in time of war. Rather, within some broad limits, it justifies doing whatever is needed to achieve a legitimate military objective. There are opportunities during war to minimize killing, and it is good to take advantage of them when we can. But the military objective comes first." John M. Frame, *The Doctrine of the Christian Life*, Theology of Lordship (P&R Publishing, 2008), 708–14. I am inclined to agree with Frame that while questions of just-war theory can be helpful checks on unnecessary devastation from war, they are only partly demonstrable from Scripture and are a guide rather than a rule.

in the midst of the death and destruction that characterize war.[11] Home and family, the enjoyment of life, and care for other persons are not to be completely set aside even amid the horrors of war.[12] Christopher Wright puts it helpfully:

> When we allow ourselves, then, to see past the slaughter of the Canaanites as a moral stumbling block to the other features of Deuteronomy's rules of war, we can hardly remain unimpressed. Without a Geneva Convention, Deuteronomy advocates humane exemptions from combat; requires prior negotiation; prefers nonviolence; limits the treatment of subject populations; allows for execution of male combatants only; demands humane and dignified treatment of female captives; and insists on ecological restraint. We may even, as in the case of slavery, detect something that seems to undermine war itself, even if only in whispers.[13]

Even with these mitigations, war remains hell.[14]

When we come to the New Testament, the idea of holy war as found in the Old Testament undergoes a transformation. In the New Testament, the battle is not an earthly one between God's people and the nations of the world, but rather a cosmic one between good and evil. God, the divine Warrior, takes on flesh in the person of Christ and dies on a cross for the sins of his people, bringing about an eventual end to the causes of suffering

11. Patrick D. Miller, *Deuteronomy*, IC (John Knox Press, 1990), 159.

12. Miller, 160.

13. Christopher Wright, *Deuteronomy*, NIBC: Old Testament 4 (Hendrickson, 2007), 230.

14. The three categories of views on war can be described as activism, pacifism, and selectivism. In their simplest definitions, the activist approach is that all wars are permissible and that the Christian is to be subject to the state regardless of the circumstances. The pacifist viewpoint is that all wars are wrong and that all Christian participation in war is likewise wrong. The selectivist approach would argue that there are some cases in which war is justified, as well as Christian participation in war. The activist approach fails to take into account the rest of the biblical ethic regarding our relationship to the state. The pacifist approach wrongly applies the teaching of Jesus meant for our personal responses to wrongdoing to the state, which has been charged with bearing the sword. The Bible does not prohibit Christian participation in warfare; therefore, when the state conscripts a Christian to be engaged in it, on what grounds may the Christian refuse? With regard to Christian pacifism, Helmut Thielicke describes it as a moral cop-out. He draws a parallel between a situation in which a Christian witnesses a murder and allows it to happen without trying to stop it. Thielicke makes the case that it is our responsibility not only to minister to the person who has been attacked by robbers (like the man on the Jericho road), but also to love our neighbor by preventing the crime. See R.C. Sproul, *How Should I Live in This World?*, Crucial Questions 5 (Reformation Trust, 2009), 66.

and death in the world. Christians are called to take up the fight, yet it is not a geopolitical conflict of armies that we are engaged in, but rather a spiritual battle against the rulers and powers behind this present darkness. Our armor is spiritual, and so are our weapons. Sadly, physical, geopolitical wars will continue to rage on earth until the end. But there will be an end.

At the end of history, all the cosmic powers of darkness along with the kings of the earth will make their final assault, not finally upon any one nation, but against the King of kings himself and his bride, the church. Revelation 20:7–10 describes the scene in apocalyptic language:

> And when the thousand years are ended, Satan will be released from his prison and will come out to deceive the nations that are at the four corners of the earth, Gog and Magog, to gather them for battle; their number is like the sand of the sea. And they marched up over the broad plain of the earth and surrounded the camp of the saints and the beloved city, but fire came down from heaven and consumed them, and the devil who had deceived them was thrown into the lake of fire and sulfur where the beast and the false prophet were, and they will be tormented day and night forever and ever.

Christians vary in their understanding of whether this is at the end of this present age or at the end of a future millennial age, but the point is that God will fight once again for his people and that his enemies will be cast into a lake of fire and eternal torment. In this way, through the destruction of Satan, death, and all those people aligned with his reign of death and destruction, God will bring peace to his people and peace on the earth.

And on that day, the promise of Micah 4:3–4 will be fulfilled:

> He shall judge between many peoples,
>   and shall decide disputes for strong nations far away;
> and they shall beat their swords into plowshares,
>   and their spears into pruning hooks;
> nation shall not lift up sword against nation,
>   neither shall they learn war anymore;
> but they shall sit every man under his vine and under his fig tree,
>   and no one shall make them afraid,
>   for the mouth of the Lord of hosts has spoken.

One day we will not need weapons, but employ only farm tools to work the good land that God is giving us in the new heavens and earth. We will all enjoy the good gifts that God intends to give us in the new creation. No one will have to tell us not to be afraid, because there will be nothing to fear. The one who will judge and bring that peace has already come the first time. Through his death on the cross, he has already disarmed his enemies (Col. 2:15). He has dealt the deathblow to death and extends the offer of peace to all his enemies. For those who accept his terms of peace, Jesus will put his yoke on us, a yoke that is easy and light (Matt. 11:30). But for those who refuse the offer of peace that Jesus is extending, the grace period will soon run out. There will be only destruction.

Do not miss the opportunity to share in the everlasting peace that the Prince of Peace offers. Whatever battles may be raging around us today, take heart: one day he will make all wars cease. Until then, we can be confident that God is fighting for us, so trust in his power, enjoy his gifts, and walk in obedience to his commands.

32

The Guilt of Innocent Blood

Deuteronomy 21:1–9

So you shall purge the guilt of innocent blood from your midst, when you do what is right in the sight of the Lord. (Deut. 21:9)

The woman and her husband had done a dastardly deed. They had killed a man in cold blood in their pursuit of prestige, position, and power. They got what they wanted. They had power to command armies and power to destroy their enemies, but they had no power to cleanse their consciences of the guilt of innocent blood. Upon returning from the murder, the husband looked at his bloody hands and asked, "Will all great Neptune's ocean wash this blood clean from my hand?" The answer, of course, was no. While the wife was more ruthless than her husband in the beginning, by the end, the blood on her hands had driven her mad. At one point, a physician came to observe the lady at night when she was sleepwalking. The lady rose from her bed, and though her eyes were open, she was not awake. She made her way to the basin and began to wash her hands, talking to herself along the way.

"Yet here's a spot. . . . Out, damned spot! out, I say! . . . What need we fear who knows it, when none can call our power to account?—Yet who would have thought the old man to have had so much blood in him. . . . Here's the smell of the blood still: all the perfumes of Arabia will not sweeten this little hand." After observing her condition, the doctor concluded: "Unnatural deeds do breed unnatural troubles: infected minds to their deaf pillows will discharge their secrets: More needs she the divine than the physician."[1] In his play *Macbeth*, William Shakespeare captures the reality of the guilt of innocent blood. What can wash away the stain that Lady Macbeth has on her hands? And what about the stain on the rest of the community? This conundrum is what Deuteronomy 21 was written to answer.

In this chapter, we continue to explore the implications of the sixth commandment: "You shall not kill unlawfully." We have seen the tremendous value that God places on human life in previous chapters. Human life is of such value that an unnatural death leaves a stain on the community that must be dealt with through another death. The shedding of innocent blood pollutes the community, and blood is on everyone's hands. If that is true, what does it mean for a nation that has shed the blood of more than 63 million innocent babies? What does it mean for a nation giving regular witness to mass shootings, gang violence, and one of the higher murder rates among developed nations? We can hold up our hands and say that we did not do it, but does that hold up in God's court? We may be rugged individualists who shun corporate responsibility, but what does our opinion matter to the Judge?

With an unusual passage such as the one before us, we need to be asking what God was teaching his covenant people through such a ritual. We know that the blood of animals can never erase bloodguilt. Nevertheless, this ritual was intended to teach something: life is of such value that it cannot be taken without cost. It further teaches us not simply that sin is personal and individual, but that it defiles communities and communities are responsible. Ultimately, it points us to the only final solution of bloodguilt on us all.

The Problem

We are introduced to the problem that this ritual will solve in verse 1 of Deuteronomy 21: "If in the land that the Lord your God is giving you to possess someone is found slain, lying in the open country, and it is not known who killed him . . ." A person is out traveling, or perhaps a farmer

1. William Shakespeare, *The Tragedy of Macbeth*, act 5, sc. 1.

is out working in the field, and discovers a dead body. The word used here for "slain" (*ḥālāl*) indicates that this is not a case in which someone was stung by bees, or had a heart attack, or otherwise collapsed on a journey. This person was obviously murdered. Deuteronomy 19:11–13 taught that if someone intentionally killed another person, the murderer must be put to death. Numbers 35:33–34 explains the absolute necessity of this:

> You shall not pollute the land in which you live, for blood pollutes the land, and no atonement can be made for the land for the blood that is shed in it, except by the blood of the one who shed it. You shall not defile the land in which you live, in the midst of which I dwell, for I the Lord dwell in the midst of the people of Israel.

Blood pollutes the land. Atonement needs to be made for the blood shed, but the only sufficient atonement is the blood of the one who shed it. In some ancient cultures, money could be paid in exchange for a life. But not in Israel. Those guilty of willful and intentional murder must be executed, not only because of the pollution of blood in the land, but because it is the price for snuffing the life from the image of God (Gen. 9:6).

While we are not under the same code of ritual purity as Israel was, we have some awareness of the way in which blood pollutes. Think, for example, of how we would feel if a real estate agent were showing us a home, saying, "By the way, you should know that someone was murdered here." It would have a different feel, would it not? So what were the people to do when the land was polluted with blood, but they had no culprit to execute for atonement?

The Solution

When the killer was unknown, the Israelites had a procedure. First, they needed to find the nearest city. We read in Deuteronomy 21:2 that "then your elders and your judges shall come out, and they shall measure the distance to the surrounding cities." The nearest city takes responsibility. We read in verse 3, "And the elders of the city that is nearest to the slain man shall take a heifer that has never been worked and that has not pulled in a yoke." A heifer is a young female cow that has not borne a calf. The Hebrew word *'eglah* might not directly translate to the English word *heifer*, and the CSB is right to translate it as "young cow." The most important point is that this cow also must never have pulled a yoke. While not stated, apparently putting a yoke on the animal contaminates it, and this ritual requires an unblemished specimen.[2] A female cow that has never been used for work was utilized for this ceremony to represent innocence and purity.

Next, instructions are given for what to do with this heifer in Deuteronomy 21:4: "And the elders of that city shall bring the heifer down to a valley with running water, which is neither plowed nor sown, and shall break the heifer's neck there in the valley." The "valley with running water" refers to a place that is not just seasonally running with water but has a perpetual source of water flowing through.[3] The land is not cultivated in any way. The reasons for this are not clear, though the unworked land may be parallel to the cow that has never been worked, but the remoteness of the location is important: far from human habitation, to avoid further pollution with blood. The continually flowing stream may indicate that if any blood was accidentally spilled in the performing of this ritual, it would be immediately washed away.[4]

At this remote location, the elders were to break the neck of the cow. There are five leading ideas about why this is to be done:

> It is either "a sacrifice, a symbolic or vicarious execution of the murderer, the representation of the penalty the elders will suffer if their confession of innocence is not true, the means of preventing the animal laden with guilt from returning to the community, or a reenactment of the murder which removes blood pollution from the inhabited to an uninhabited area."[5]

Given the context, we may be predisposed to see this as a sacrifice that atones for sin. Yet everything about the description of the killing suggests

2. Daniel I. Block, *Deuteronomy*, NIVAC (Zondervan, 2012), 489.

3. The only other use of this phrase *naḥal 'êtān* translated as "running water" in Deuteronomy 21:4 is translated as "ever-flowing stream" in Amos 5:24: "But let justice roll down like waters, and righteousness like an ever-flowing stream."

4. Yitzhaq Feder, "Breaking the Heifer's Neck: A Bloodless Ritual for an Unsolved Murder," TheTorah.com, 2018, https://thetorah.com/article/breaking-the-heifers-neck-a-bloodless-ritual-for-an-unsolved-murder.

5. Jeffrey H. Tigay, *Deuteronomy*, JPSTC (Jewish Publication Society, 1996), 473, quoting D. P. Wright, "Deuteronomy 21:1–9 as a Rite of Elimination," *CBQ* 49, no. 3 (July 1987): 388–89.

otherwise: the priests are not the ones killing the animal, they do not kill the animal at an altar, breaking the neck was not a sacrificial way to kill an animal,[6] no one sprinkles the blood, and the sacrifice is neither eaten nor burned. If this is a sacrifice, it runs counter to all the other ones. But if it is not a sacrifice, how can atonement be made? We will have to hold that question for the moment as we exercise care not to force the text into saying something that we think it should say, rather than what it actually says. Most likely, it is either a symbolic execution of the murderer or a reenactment of the murder itself.

One way of attempting to explain this ritual is by asking who or what the innocent and unblemished cow represents: does it represent the innocent victim, or does it represent the murderer? The innocence and purity of the cow is a strong clue, but first, another group is present at the killing of the cow and must be acknowledged. We read in Deuteronomy 21:5, "Then the priests, the sons of Levi, shall come forward, for the LORD your God has chosen them to minister to him and to bless in the name of the LORD, and by their word every dispute and every assault shall be settled." While the priests are present at the killing of the cow, they themselves do not kill the cow, which again confirms that this should not be seen as a sacrifice. Instead, they are there to function in their judicial capacity because "by their word every dispute and every assault shall be settled" (Deut. 21:5; cf. 17:8–12). The priests are there to hand down the decision regarding guilt or innocence and settle the matter. This gives a further clue to the meaning of the ritual. It makes more sense that they are introduced immediately after the killing of the cow because they are witnesses of the reenactment of the murder, after which they deliver their judgment, than that they appear right after the symbolic execution of the murderer to deliver their judgment of guilt or innocence. Therefore, we should see the killing of the cow as a symbolic reenactment of the murder, with the cow representing the innocent victim.

6. We cannot overestimate the significance of the method of putting the heifer to death. Why are the elders explicitly commanded to break its neck? The only other place where God's people are commanded to break the neck of an animal is Exodus 13:13: "Every firstborn of a donkey you shall redeem with a lamb, or if you will not redeem it you shall break its neck. Every firstborn of man among your sons you shall redeem." A donkey was inadmissible as an offering, and so this prescribed form of killing makes it very clear that the donkey is not a sacrifice. Nahum M. Sarna, *Exodus*, JPSTC (Jewish Publication Society, 1991), 67. The same would seem to be the case here in Deuteronomy 21.

Such an explanation makes the most sense of what the elders then say in Deuteronomy 21:6–7: "And all the elders of that city nearest to the slain man shall wash their hands over the heifer whose neck was broken in the valley, and they shall testify, 'Our hands did not shed this blood, nor did our eyes see it shed.'" When they say that their hands did not shed "this blood," whose blood does "this blood" refer to? They are referring to the heifer as a symbol of the innocent victim whose blood they did not shed, nor did their eyes see it shed. They wash their hands over the victim as a symbolic action that they did not do the evil deed of killing the innocent man. Meanwhile, what they say in verse 7 calls to mind the language of the courtroom:[7] "They shall testify, 'Our hands did not shed this blood, nor did our eyes see it shed.'" They did not kill the man, and they do not know who killed the man; therefore, they cannot make atonement for it. But this does not solve the problem of bloodguilt on the people. The heifer is not an atoning sacrifice (and this is key to understanding the passage).

After the killing of the heifer, the elders call out to God and say in Deuteronomy 21:8, "Accept atonement, O LORD, for your people Israel, whom you have redeemed, and do not set the guilt of innocent blood in the midst of your people Israel, so that their blood guilt be atoned for." The ESV's translators appear to have made the mistake of understanding the killing of the heifer to be an atoning sacrifice.[8] In Hebrew, the verb does not say, "Accept atonement, O LORD," but it is an imperative verb that simply means: "Atone, O LORD!"[9] (my translation). Whereas the priests are usually the ones who make atonement, in this case, God himself is the subject of the verb, called on to do what they cannot.[10] The next part of the prayer is that God would not set the guilt of innocent blood on the people. Since God is the one who sets the guilt among them, only God can remove it. What is more, the text assures us that he will in verse 9: "So you shall purge the guilt of innocent blood from your midst, when you do what is right in the sight of the LORD." This is the procedure by which the guilt of innocent blood will be purged from them.

7. The word is *'ānâ*. It does not always mean "to witness in a courtroom," but this makes the most sense in the context. See BDB, s.v. "עָנָה," 773.

8. They are not the only ones. The NIV uses the equally unhelpful "Accept this atonement." The CSB gets it right here: "LORD, wipe away the guilt of your people Israel whom you redeemed."

9. The verb *kpr* is piel imperative. "It is conceived that God in his sovereignty may himself provide an atonement or covering for men and their sins which could not be provided by men." BDB, s.v. "כפר," 497.

10. Block, *Deuteronomy*, 491.

God will not put the guilt of innocent blood in their midst, and their bloodguilt will be atoned for. But it leaves a question unanswered: where is God going to put the bloodguilt of this crime? Someone must pay. The answer to that question awaits the New Testament, though the Old Testament sacrificial system points forward to it. The ritual of the heifer provides a way for the people of God to purge the pollution of innocent blood from the community as they await the atonement for sin that only God can provide.

The Significance

What is the significance of this passage, and what is it here to teach us?

First, human life is inestimably precious, and we should treat it as such. Even though no one was present for the murder of this person, it does not mean that his death does not matter. While there are many strange aspects about this ritual, what should strike us is the expected response of an entire community through its civic, judicial, and religious leaders to just one single human death.[11] As our friends at the local pregnancy resource center remind us: "Every life matters." Additionally, this passage emphasizes just how wicked the crime of killing another human being is. As we have previously seen, this crime is so detestable that it requires the murderer to be put to death if found guilty. The value of life is upheld by taking the life of the one guilty of murder. No other punishment will suffice to cleanse the land of the bloodguilt on it. But even when the murderer was not found, a kind of solemn purging still needed to take place.

Though we live in a culture of death, we cannot be people who take human death lightly. Furthermore, the command to kill unlawfully does not forbid only the act itself, but all the steps that lead to that act, so that Jesus can say that even anger and insulting speech make us guilty of breaking the sixth commandment (Matt. 5:21–22). We must endeavor to keep not only our hands clean from unlawful killing, but our hearts as well. Are we harboring resentment? Do we have a temper that sometimes gets out of control? Are we promoting peace between our neighbors? Do we attempt to de-escalate the kind of rhetoric that is so prevalent around us that could easily turn to violence? It is the peacemakers who are blessed.

11. Christopher Wright, *Deuteronomy*, NIBC: Old Testament 4 (Hendrickson, 2007), 233.

Second, sin and guilt are not simply individual, but also have a communal aspect that should be dealt with communally. Raymond Brown writes:

> Criminals are accountable for their crimes but they are not *solely* responsible for them. The murderer grew up in a family and in a wider community which accepted some responsibility for his welfare and education. Was the life of his family happy and harmonious? Did his parents love him deeply? . . . Before he could read a word, the example of his parents was eloquent. Was he taught God's word: "You shall not murder", "Do not hate your brother", or "bear a grudge . . . but love your neighbour as yourself"?[12]

Some of us will recoil at the idea of any corporate responsibility for one person's crimes. But it is quite biblical. Our families and communities shape us, and each of us has a part in forming the identity of those communities.

Robert "Bobby" Crimo III was arrested for shooting up Fourth of July parade-goers in Highland Park, Illinois. As details began to emerge about the killer, the reports about his family upbringing were not pretty. When he was an infant, his mother pleaded guilty to leaving the two-year-old in a burning-hot car in a parking lot. Records show that police made visits to the house nearly twenty times from 2009 to 2014. Nine of those calls were for reports of domestic violence. At one point, authorities had labeled Bobby a "clear and present danger" for threatening to kill all his relatives. Within three months of that incident, his father sponsored Bobby's gun-license application so that he could purchase four guns, including the one used to murder seven people on July 4. When the press asked Bobby's dad about sharing any responsibility for this crime, his dad said: "They make me like I groomed him to do all this. . . . I've been here my whole life, and I'm gonna stay here, hold my head up high, because I didn't do anything wrong."[13] On one level, we can all agree that the elder Crimo did not pull any triggers. At the same time, we recognize that there is blood on his hands. But is he the only one who shares guilt?

12. Raymond Brown, *The Message of Deuteronomy: Not by Bread Alone*, The Bible Speaks Today (InterVarsity Press, 1993), 204–5.

13. Haley Brown and Gabrielle Fonrouge, "Crimo Dad Washes Hands of Guilt but Talked with Son About a Mass Shooting Night Before Highland Park Massacre," *New York Post*, July 6, 2022, https://nypost.com/2022/07/06/highland-park-shooter-robert-crimo-father-speaks-about-son/, accessed July 13, 2022.

Again, Brown points out what we are too quick to overlook when something like this happens:

> When things go wrong, people soon point the finger of bitter accusation. A public crime has been committed and such sins of commission must be punished. But what of those serious sins of omission which may have led up to the crime? Many things may not have been done for the offender, or they may have been poorly done. If he had been helped lovingly, that solitary man, hiding in the community, tormented by his guilt, might have been in peace.[14]

In other words, Bobby Crimo should be executed for shedding innocent blood. But the whole community, starting with his parents, should be asking questions about whether they were doing what they could to see to it that the Bobby Crimos of the world do not become mass shooters. Of course, asking these kinds of questions is painful because it seems that all it will do is to lead us to an overwhelming sense of guilt. It might. But perhaps this is exactly what we should feel so that we could come to a place of corporate repentance for creating a culture of death. Like it or not, we are a part of a culture that glorifies violence and devalues human life. We are reaping what we have sown.[15] Such knowledge would be too overwhelming for most of us to live with, except for the next thing we see.

Third, God has made provision for full atonement of our bloodguilt through the work of Christ. Some of us still do not feel that corporate guilt is a particularly pressing problem. But remember, we are part of a people who have murdered more than 63 million children since 1973 as of the time of this writing. Are our hands clean? We are a part of a people who took our country by violence and have committed a great deal of violence since then. Has *all* that bloodshed been justified, or might the guilt of innocent blood be on our hands? Or consider the ongoing violence in our country through the use of gun, knife, and fist—do we share any corporate responsibility for

14. Brown, *Message of Deuteronomy*, 205.

15. Interestingly, the nineteenth-century American abolitionist John Brown had a very strong sense of America's corporate guilt over slavery that motivated his efforts to free the slaves. He is best known for storming the armory at Harpers Ferry, West Virginia, in order to secure weapons to forcibly bring an end to American slavery. His last words before he was executed were written on a note and handed to a guard just before his death: "The sins of this land will not be purged away but with blood." The American Civil War seems to have been the fulfillment of Brown's pronouncement.

these evils in our land? Biblically speaking, we do. But even if we did not, we still carry the guilt of our own sins.

We carry the guilt of sexual sin. We carry the guilt of having known about evil deeds that were being done and not doing what we could to stop them. We carry the guilt of dishonesty and theft. We carry the guilt of the mistakes we made in raising our children and the way in which we see those mistakes expressing themselves in the lives of our adult children or grandchildren. What can we do with our guilt? How can we cleanse our hands of the blood?[16] We cannot. The prophet Jeremiah writes, "Though you wash yourself with lye and use much soap, the stain of your guilt is still before me, declares the Lord GOD" (Jer. 2:22). We cannot cleanse ourselves of our guilt. That "damned spot" will not be washed off our consciences, no matter how hard we scrub or how severely we beat ourselves up. Only through repentance and God's forgiveness can guilt be taken away. Even that forgiveness is based on a real atonement. Someone must pay for our sins. Any substitute must be innocent; otherwise, he has his own bloodguilt to die for.

The New Testament refers to the concept of innocent blood twice in the same chapter. In Matthew 27:4, Judas confesses to betraying "innocent blood" in reference to Jesus. Then, when Jesus was before Pilate and the people were clamoring for his crucifixion, we read: "So when Pilate saw that he was gaining nothing, but rather that a riot was beginning, he took water and washed his hands before the crowd, saying, 'I am innocent of this man's blood; see to it yourselves.' And all the people answered, 'His blood

16. In later Judaism, a number of practices and rites developed to deal with guilt, some of which may have arisen from this passage—specifically, something called the Ten Days of Penitence. According to Jewish scholar Jeffrey Tigay, the Ten Days of Penitence involved the following six elements: (1) Prayers for forgiveness and (2) confession of guilt from a month before Rosh Hashanah through Yom Kippur. (3) *Tashlikh*, which involved going to a body of water and reciting Micah 7:19, "You will cast all our sins into the depths of the sea," and other prayers while shaking out one's pockets. (4) *Kapparot*, which involved swinging a hen or rooster around over one's head for a day or two before Yom Kippur and reciting, "A life for a life . . . this is my substitute, this is my replacement, this is my atonement; this hen/rooster shall go to death but I shall go on to a long and pleasant life and peace," and then the animal is slaughtered, its intestines thrown to the birds, and the rest donated to the poor. (5) *Malkot*, which is ritual flagellation practiced by some Jews before Yom Kippur. (6) Fasting on Yom Kippur and at other times between Rosh Hashanah and Yom Kippur. Tigay concludes: "Like the ceremony of the broken-necked heifer, these prayers and ritual actions are complementary means of expiating guilt. In both cases, it is because expiation of guilt is so vital that numerous means were employed and redundance was not only disregarded but was considered a virtue." Tigay, *Deuteronomy*, 475–76. And yet the feelings of guilt still remain because there is only one way in which the stain of guilt can be removed: Jesus.

be on us and on our children!'" (vv. 24–25). Why did Pilate wash his hands? He did so because he knew that he was guilty, though he was claiming innocence. The people likewise accept responsibility for the bloodguilt of the crucifixion of Jesus. They are responsible for killing an innocent man (Luke 23:47). The innocent blood will cry out for vengeance; it requires death (Gen. 9:5). Except that this blood is different. In fact, this death of Jesus will provide the answer to the question of where the guilt of all the ages will ultimately be placed.

When Jesus' blood is shed, it cries out a different message from "vengeance!" Hebrews 12:24 says of Christians that "[you have come] to Jesus, the mediator of a new covenant, and to the sprinkled blood that speaks a better word than the blood of Abel." The blood of Christ speaks a better word than the blood of Abel, than the blood of our slain unborn children, than the blood of those wrongfully killed, than the blood of our nation's history of violence. All that blood cries for vengeance; it cries for the guilty to be put to death. But the blood of Christ cries out for mercy and forgiveness for his killers. In the ritual of the broken-necked heifer, the people of God acknowledge their helplessness to atone for sin, and so they cry out to God to atone for what they cannot. The blood of Christ is God's answer for the guilt on God's people. As the hymn writer William Cowper wrote, "There is a fountain filled with blood, drawn from Immanuel's veins; and sinners, plunged beneath that flood, lose all their guilty stains."[17] Like the perpetually flowing stream in which the elders symbolically wash away their guilt, Christ's blood perpetually washes away our guilt.

What can wash away our sin? Nothing but the blood of Jesus. The only agent strong enough to cleanse us from the guilt of innocent blood is the blood of Jesus. If we are aware of our guilty stains today, if we long to be clean, then we must plunge ourselves beneath the cleansing flow of Jesus' blood and let all our guilty stains be washed away once and for all. There is power in this blood! The stains that nothing else can cleanse, Jesus' blood can. The guilt of innocent blood is on us all. But hallelujah, the cleansing power of the blood of Jesus is greater still! What can wash away our sin? Nothing but the blood of Jesus.

17. William Cowper, "There Is a Fountain Filled with Blood" (1771).

33

Mitigating the Effects of Sin

Deuteronomy 21:10–23

But if you no longer delight in her, you shall let her go where she wants. But you shall not sell her for money, nor shall you treat her as a slave, since you have humiliated her. (Deut. 21:14)

Lee Ok-seon was simply running an errand for her parents when a group of uniformed men burst out of a car, attacked her, and dragged her into the vehicle. Little did Lee know as they drove away that she would never see her parents again. She was just fourteen years old.

That afternoon, a nightmare began for Lee that seemed like it would never end. She was taken to a so-called comfort station—a brothel that serviced Japanese soldiers—in Japanese-occupied China. There, this young girl became one of the tens of thousands of "comfort women" who were subjected to forced prostitution by the Japanese army between 1932 and 1945. How did this happen?

On December 13, 1937, Japanese troops began a six-week-long massacre that was later called the Rape of Nanking. In destroying that city, the soldiers are believed to have sexually assaulted from twenty thousand to eighty thousand Chinese women. The world was rightly horrified. The emperor, in an attempt to prevent such atrocities from happening again and further despoiling Japan's image, ordered the expansion of Japan's comfort stations. The idea was that these brothels of forced prostitution would satisfy the soldiers' sexual appetites with less outcry from the world.[1] It was a poor attempt to mitigate the effects of sin. It led to more kidnapping and sexual trafficking of women from all over southeast Asia, but mostly China and Korea.[2] It is estimated that 90 percent of these women were dead by the end of the war. It is an ugly, shameful, and wicked piece of world history.

Initially when we read this passage in Deuteronomy 21, we may be put off by aspects of it that seem horrifying. But then when we hear about what happened to women in China during World War II, we begin to see the wisdom and mercy of God in giving laws such as the ones we find here that serve to protect against the very wickedness witnessed in the twentieth century.

What we see in these four vignettes is the reality of life in a fallen world. Each one of these scenarios is unfortunate and sad. The fact that the laws in this passage must be given at all makes it clear that this is not the way life is supposed to be. God's intention was that his people would not be captives in war, that couples would not divorce, that his people would not have multiple wives, that children would be neither mistreated nor disobedient, and that no criminals would need to be executed. The world we live in is the world we deserve because of our rebellion, but it is not the way it is supposed to be. God, knowing the hardness of the human heart and the kinds of things that people would do, gave these laws to regulate and limit the negative effects of sin. These laws are not giving us a picture of the way that life is meant to be, but rather serve to illustrate God's mercy in limiting the negative impacts of the hardness of human hearts. These laws reflect the grace and mercy of God toward sinful humanity; they aim to minimize the misery of life under the curse of sin. Amid these depressing scenarios, we discover a ray of hope. One day the curse of sin will finally be removed and laws that mitigate the effects of sinful hearts will no longer be necessary.

1. Erin Blakemore, "The Brutal History of Japan's 'Comfort Women,'" History.com, updated July 21, 2019, https://www.history.com/news/comfort-women-japan-military-brothels-korea, accessed July 24, 2022.

2. Sadly, in 2007 it was revealed that the United States allowed those comfort stations to continue well past the war and that those stations ultimately served American soldiers as well. Not surprisingly, all nations involved would like to forget that this ever happened.

Before we consider the four scenarios, we should recognize the context of this passage once again. We have been considering the implications of the sixth commandment forbidding unlawful killing, and before that the fifth commandment regarding honoring parents. In this section, we see some of the weaknesses of reading Deuteronomy 12–26 as a straight exposition of the Ten Commandments.[3] Nevertheless, we can see how these passages relate to the Ten Commandments more broadly. Ultimately, these four sets of laws point us toward love of God and love of neighbor.

LAW MITIGATING THE EFFECT OF POWER IMBALANCE

Power imbalance is a reality of life in this fallen world. It is often used to exploit and harm others for one's own advantage. So long as sinful people are in the world, power will be abused, and people will suffer. Nowhere is this problem more evident than in a situation in which one army has conquered another. Historically, such situations have brought forth the worst in humanity, and frequently those who bear the brunt of the brutality are women and children. This law mitigates that reality in Israel. We read in Deuteronomy 21:10–14:

> When you go out to war against your enemies, and the LORD your God gives them into your hand and you take them captive, and you see among the captives a beautiful woman, and you desire to take her to be your wife, and you bring her home to your house, she shall shave her head and pare her nails. And she shall take off the clothes in which she was captured and shall remain in your house and lament her father and her mother a full month. After that you may go in to her and be her husband, and she shall be your wife. But if you no longer delight in her, you shall let her go where she wants. But you shall not sell her for money, nor shall you treat her as a slave, since you have humiliated her.

This statute does not sound good to twenty-first-century ears unless we compare it against the backdrop of the situation of the comfort women. It

3. For more on identifying the layout of Deuteronomy 12–26 with the Ten Commandments, see J. Gary Millar, *Now Choose Life: Theology and Ethics in Deuteronomy*, NSBT 6 (Apollos, 1998), 108.

is clearly written to protect a woman who would otherwise be defenseless and powerless. In the ancient Mediterranean world, a woman would have been completely subject to the sexual prerogatives of a conquering army. To this day, women in this situation are prone to the worst, most degrading forms of abuse.

But the law in Deuteronomy, while acknowledging that this will be one of the outcomes of war, refuses to allow for the shameful treatment of this non-Israelite image-bearer.[4] She is to be given a month to grieve her family (which was a standard length of time for mourning),[5] and she is not to be taken as a concubine or so-called comfort woman. The purpose of shaving her head and paring her nails is not entirely clear. Some of the early rabbis thought that these actions might make her unattractive to her captors so that they would think twice about marrying her. Others see these as rites of mourning for her old life. Some think they signify a change of her status by removing old clothing and the disposable parts of her body.[6] It is difficult for us to say with any certainty, but what is clear is that this whole section has to do with the care and well-being of the woman. If a man was going to engage in sexual relations with the captive, she must be taken as a wife. Such a thing was truly extraordinary in the ancient world. She is not a plaything; she is a person. If a man establishes a sexual relationship with this woman, he brings himself under all the obligations of a husband to a wife.[7]

Sadly, because of the hardness of human hearts, sometimes marriages end in divorce. If the man decided that he did not want to be married to the woman anymore, he had to let her go free. She could not become his slave or anyone else's, "since you have humiliated her" (Deut. 10:14). This word is hard to define precisely, but it is sometimes used in the Old Testament as a description of violation, humiliation, or sexual assault.[8] It is deeply shameful for a man to take one of these women, humiliate her, and then decide not to fulfill the commitments of marriage to her. Such a provision

4. These are not Canaanite women, because those were to be devoted to destruction. These are the enemies who are far away and living outside the land that God was giving his people (Deut. 20:10–15).

5. There is no mention of this woman's having been married before or mention of her mourning her husband; therefore, it seems likely that only unmarried women are in view.

6. Jeffrey H. Tigay, *Deuteronomy*, JPSTC (Jewish Publication Society, 1996), 194.

7. Tigay, 194.

8. Such as Gen. 34:2; Judg. 19:24; 20:5; 2 Sam. 13:12, 14, 22, 32.

would have caused a man to think carefully about whether he truly wanted to be married, and the thirty-day waiting period would have helped minimize the impulsiveness of such a situation.

Again, we may read this passage and feel ethically superior to the Old Testament and think that women are in a much better position today. In some ways they are. But one way in which women today are not better off is illustrated by men's respect for their sexuality. Biblically speaking, for a man to have sex with a woman is to engage himself to provide for her all the rights of a wife. This is why the biblical order is always to make the commitment, to establish the covenant, and then to consummate the marriage with sex. The commitment and covenant must come first. No man or woman should engage in sex with anyone who has not made a covenant commitment of marriage. Otherwise, that man or woman is basically consenting to be used as a concubine. But even concubines had some rights and protections, which is far more than most men and women can count on when they give themselves away sexually today.

People are giving themselves away sexually for nothing, and many are moving in together with no commitments made. Some are living sexually with someone to whom they are not married, and others are thinking about it and do not understand why they should not. For one person to ask another person to move in with him or her, to live in a sexual relationship as though they were married, without giving the lifelong commitment of love and provision of marriage, should be the consummate insult. That person is saying: "I want to have sex with you and enjoy you and enjoy all the benefits of marriage, but I am not ready to commit the rest of my life to you. After all, I may discover things about you that I don't like, and I would like to reserve the right to trade you in if someone better happens to come along. Don't get me wrong—I think you're great. But if there's somebody better than you who is willing to take me, I would like to keep that option open. Meanwhile, continue to give me the most intimate parts of yourself to enjoy, and I promise not to hurt you until doing so suits my interests."[9] Even if we do not respect God, we should at least respect ourselves enough not to fall for that.

9. The immensely popular secular psychologist Jordan B. Peterson makes this case very well in numerous books and lectures. Not only is sex outside marriage sinful biblically, but from a purely secular point of view, Peterson would say that it is just plain foolish.

Some people say that marriage is "just a piece of paper," but this statement cannot be taken seriously. If a person truly believed that marriage was "just a piece of paper," then it would be no big deal to sign the piece of paper and commit to the relationship, "till death do us part." Others decide to live together as a way to save money on rent. But one's dignity and honor before God is worth so much more than rent. Even the captive foreign woman was to be respected enough to be taken as a wife and not simply as a live-in girlfriend. How much more so should we respect the children of God!

With the law detailing how the captive woman is to be treated, we see that God's heart here is for the powerless who are susceptible to abuse. This is still the reality of power dynamics in many relationships today. As God's covenant people, we should be intentional to ensure that we are not abusing power, and that we are doing what we can to help protect those who are susceptible to abuse.

Law Mitigating the Effect of Partiality in the Home

The next law has to do with another situation very strange to our twenty-first-century ears. It is a case of a polygamous marriage in which the husband is playing favorites. Moses explains in Deuteronomy 21:15–17:

> If a man has two wives, the one loved and the other unloved, and both the loved and the unloved have borne him children, and if the firstborn son belongs to the unloved, then on the day when he assigns his possessions as an inheritance to his sons, he may not treat the son of the loved as the firstborn in preference to the son of the unloved, who is the firstborn, but he shall acknowledge the firstborn, the son of the unloved, by giving him a double portion of all that he has, for he is the firstfruits of his strength. The right of the firstborn is his.

Let us first consider polygamy, and then focus on the law itself. We may be tempted to scoff at polygamy and to think of ourselves as being far above such silliness and far more morally advanced. But it is a bit more complicated than that. While polygamy was clearly present among God's people in the

Old Testament, it was not as extensive as is sometimes supposed. It was largely limited to kings and others in high positions.[10] While it is never commanded in the Bible, it is tolerated in the Old Testament. But what Jesus said about divorce in Matthew 19:8 could also be applied to polygamy: "from the beginning it was not so." God's creational intention for marriage was a man and a woman in a lifelong, one-flesh union. Given that marriage was used as a metaphor for the exclusive relationship between God and his people, God clearly intended the marriage relationship to be exclusive.[11] Furthermore, the stories relating polygamous practice generally carry their own warning of the pitfalls of such a scenario (see, e.g., the stories of Abraham and Jacob).

Nevertheless, as a concession God allowed polygamy as a social practice and gave laws intended to minimize its negative effect, such as the one we are reading here. We do not practice polygamy in our culture, but we do practice divorce extensively. If we were to ask a random sampling of Americans which is worse, nearly all would say polygamy. But ethically, divorce appears to fall even shorter of the creational ideal than polygamy. Christopher Wright argues: "Whereas polygamy is a kind of 'expansion' of marriage beyond the monogamous limit intended by God, divorce is a severing destruction of marriage. . . . Polygamy multiplies relationships where God intended a single relationship; but divorce destroys that relationship altogether."[12] I am not advocating that polygamy is biblical, but only that the ubiquity of divorce in our culture has caused us to take marriage far more lightly than the Bible does.

In the hypothetical household that Moses describes, as in any polygamous household, the husband has a favorite wife. The other wife is said to be "unloved," though literally in the Hebrew the word is "hated." His love for the one is evidently greater than his love for the other. As a result of this, he may be tempted to give the right of the firstborn to the son of his favored

10. In this particular context about war, some think that polygamy may have been a way of dealing with a shortage of men who had died in battle. See Peter C. Craigie, *The Book of Deuteronomy*, NICOT (Eerdmans, 1976), 282.

11. Christopher J. H. Wright, *Old Testament Ethics for the People of God* (InterVarsity Press, 2004), 330.

12. Wright, 332.

wife, rather than to the son who is the legitimate firstborn. Why is this a big deal? Because the firstborn typically received double the inheritance of the other sons. The reason is that the firstborn was primarily responsible for the aging parents and for the rest of the family after the patriarch had died. To give the right of the firstborn to another son was to dishonor and shame the firstborn.

The concept of the right of the firstborn was a cultural concept in Israel and not one that continues among God's people, unless it does so culturally. But the negative effects of partiality are still very much a reality, and this passage warns us against shamefully mistreating any of the children in our homes, whether they are ours by birth, adoption, or a blended-family relationship. No parent wants to admit that he or she has favorites or is partial. But even if we are partial, we should endeavor to treat all the children under our care with dignity, respect, and love, as our Father in heaven treats us.

Law Mitigating the Effect of Rebellious Children

Having just considered the responsibility of parents to their children, we now consider the responsibility of children to their parents. We read the scenario in Deuteronomy 21:18–20:

> If a man has a stubborn and rebellious son who will not obey the voice of his father or the voice of his mother, and, though they discipline him, will not listen to them, then his father and his mother shall take hold of him and bring him out to the elders of his city at the gate of the place where he lives, and they shall say to the elders of his city, "This our son is stubborn and rebellious; he will not obey our voice; he is a glutton and a drunkard."

What is being described here is not a naughty toddler who keeps digging in the trash can, or even a teenager who experiments with alcohol. This is a son characterized by gluttony and drunkenness, who stubbornly refuses to obey his parents. The parents have done their part to exercise biblical discipline, and yet still the son refuses to heed their instruction. The parents are at their wits' end. Frankly, they are concerned about the well-being of the rest of their family and potentially the community if this young man goes on living as he is. This law gives them recourse to protect themselves and their community from such a rebel. While the crime was initially against the parents, they are not the ones to carry out the execution. The execution is carried out by the elders because the son's sins do not affect simply the family, but the community itself.[13] Therefore, he needed to be punished by representatives of the community to purge the evil from their midst and to inspire others to resist their rebellious inclinations. Both mother and father are required to bring the rebellious son. This is further protection for children from being victims of either a father or a mother who is disinclined toward a particular offspring. If the elders concur with the parents' judgment, as we read in Deuteronomy 21:21: "Then all the men of the city shall stone him to death with stones. So you shall purge the evil from your midst, and all Israel shall hear, and fear."

We have no record of this punishment's being handed down in Israel, but this does not mean that it did not happen. We may think that we have come a long way since parents were allowed to hand over rebellious children to the authorities to receive a death sentence. But have we really? The stability of the family is the foundation of a strong community. When families are broken down or devalued, both the church and the culture will see the effects. Proverbs 19:18 states, "Discipline your son, for there is hope; do not set your heart on putting him to death." To fail to discipline one's child in the Old Testament context was to raise a rebel and set him up for execution. Even in a situation like this one in which discipline was exercised, children sometimes go astray. As parents today, we have no less responsibility to discipline and train our children. While rebellious children will not be put to death by stoning, if we do not teach them to honor appropriate authorities (which starts with honoring their parents), we may well be setting them up for a premature death.

Patrick Miller writes, "The parents are the first rank of persons whose authority must be acknowledged in order for human community to work in behalf of goodness and peace."[14] If respect of authority is not learned in

13. Craigie, *Deuteronomy*, 284–85.
14. Patrick D. Miller, *Deuteronomy*, IC (John Knox Press, 1990), 167.

the home, it is not likely to be learned anywhere. Who is responsible for teaching children to honor their father and mother and so to honor all legitimate authorities in their lives and in so doing to honor God himself? It is not the children's job to teach this to themselves. It is the role of parents. But that requires parents to own the authority that God has given and to use it to serve their children.

We have multiple challenges in this regard, but here are two. First, in the modern West, there has been a temptation for parents to function as their child's friend more than their authority. The result is that parents are unable to say no to the things that a parent should say no to for the protection of their child. A corollary to this problem is that many parents are carrying a great deal of guilt because they are not involved in their child's life to the degree that they want to be. It may be because a divorce has resulted in limited custody, or it may be that work or other interests prevent time together. The effect is that with limited time with their child, no parents want to spend it feeling that they are making their child hate them. Whatever the cause, children are robbed of the training and instruction they are to receive in their formative years regarding the biblical imperative to honor parents and every other authority appointed by God.

The second problem is a cultural idea suggesting that discipline promotes violence. There are types of so-called discipline that are abusive, but controlled corporal punishment without anger, exercised in the context of a loving family, is a tool for teaching children that disregarding authority carries painful consequences.[15] And those consequences do not get less painful as they get older.

Our children are likely to encounter the authority of law enforcement after parents, teachers, and coaches. According to numerous studies, how our youth experience police officers is very much connected to how our youth engage with them. When it comes to being arrested, for example, here is what numerous studies have found:

15. From my brief survey of the psychological studies regarding corporal punishment, they generally refer to spanking or hitting in anger. I certainly agree that this kind of discipline may ultimately lead to short- or long-term psychological issues. Biblical corporal punishment should never seem like an angry or out-of-control violent reaction to misbehavior, but instead, a careful and calculated delivery of appropriate consequences for wrongdoing.

> Other than having a prior record, a youth's demeanor or "contriteness" was the most crucial factor in police decisions to arrest. A youth who is respectful is more likely to receive a warning, whereas a youth with a negative attitude or who disrespects police officers is four times more likely to be taken into custody or arrested.[16]

It is the parents' job to teach children that exhibiting a negative attitude or disrespect toward authority is likely to lead to bad outcomes. It is not the job of the police, the coach, or the teacher. Increasingly, our culture undermines the trust of legitimate authorities, and this leads to more frequent negative outcomes. Parents can undermine legitimate authorities not only with our words, but also by our actions. In our increasingly polarized culture, it is not uncommon for people to speak of political authorities or church authorities with a complete lack of respect. Our children pick up on this, and it shapes their view of authority and what it means to honor that authority.

This case from Deuteronomy shows us that even in a loving family with diligent parents, some children will grow up rebellious and bring a curse on their own heads. But if we neglect to discipline them, we will almost certainly raise children who will become a scourge on both our families and the community.[17] If it becomes apparent that such a child is going to become a danger to society, then it is the responsibility of the parents to look after the interests of not only their family, but also the community. At the present time in the United States, a long line of young men in their late teens and early twenties have become mass shooters. In some cases, the parents are aware that something is wrong with their sons, but they do not know what to do about it. The general equity discernible from the laws in Deuteronomy 21 shows us that when a child becomes a threat to the greater community, the parents have a responsibility to hand that child over to the civil authorities and to allow those authorities to do their work of protecting the community.

16. Development Services Group, Inc., "Interactions Between Youth and Law Enforcement," Literature Review, Office of Juvenile Justice and Delinquency Prevention, updated January 2018, https://www.ojjdp.gov/mpg/litreviews/Interactions-Youth-Law-Enforcement.pdf, accessed July 24, 2022.

17. I do not mean to imply that corporal discipline is the only kind of discipline that is biblical or helpful. Parents can take numerous approaches to discipline that evolve as their children grow and that take into account the unique personality of each child. Some forms of discipline are more effective for some children than others.

LAW MITIGATING THE EFFECT OF CAPITAL CRIMES

The final law has to do with the execution of a criminal, and specifically what is done with his body after the fact: "And if a man has committed a crime punishable by death and he is put to death, and you hang him on a tree, his body shall not remain all night on the tree, but you shall bury him the same day, for a hanged man is cursed by God. You shall not defile your land that the LORD your God is giving you for an inheritance" (Deut. 21:22–23). The man was not executed by hanging; he was likely stoned. After the execution, they hung his body up on a tree as a warning and example to others. The law did not command that step, but it recognized that this was a common practice.[18] The law prevented the ongoing humiliation of that man and his family, as well as the defiling effect of a hung-up corpse on the land. Without getting overly graphic, if a body were left hanging, it would not be long before animals and birds would come and scatter parts of it and further spread the impurity.[19] Instead of leaving him up, he must be taken down and buried that day.[20]

There is some question about the phrase "for a hanged man is cursed by God." What is meant by this? A man is not cursed by God because he is hung on a tree, but he is hung on a tree because he is cursed by God. To break the law of God and thereby to incur the death penalty and be hung up was the ultimate symbol of receiving God's curse. It was a formal and final separation from the community of God's people.[21] This is what makes Paul's use of this language in Galatians so stunning. The apostle writes in Galatians 3:10–14:

> For all who rely on works of the law are under a curse; for it is written, "Cursed be everyone who does not abide by all things written in the Book of the Law, and do them." Now it is evident that no one is justified before God by the law, for "The righteous shall live by faith." But the law is not of faith, rather "The one who does them shall live by them." Christ redeemed

18. Craigie, *Deuteronomy*, 285.

19. Tigay, *Deuteronomy*, 198. We can see the concept illustrated in the buying of the scattered corpses of Gog's army in Ezekiel 39:11–16.

20. Joshua reflects obedience to this law when various Canaanite kings were killed, hung up, and then removed by evening in Joshua 8:29; 10:26–27.

21. Craigie, *Deuteronomy*, 286.

> us from the curse of the law by becoming a curse for us—for it is written, "Cursed is everyone who is hanged on a tree"—so that in Christ Jesus the blessing of Abraham might come to the Gentiles, so that we might receive the promised Spirit through faith.

The fact that these laws exist in Deuteronomy reminds us that we live in a world under the curse. What is more, the Bible tells us repeatedly that because of our sin, we all deserve to live and to die under the curse.

But in love, God set about a plan to rescue us sinful and cursed people from the fate we deserved. Christ redeemed us from the curse of the law by becoming a curse for us. What is more, the manner of his death and crucifixion dramatically portrayed the meaning of his death. He was hung on a tree, cursed of God, not for his own sins but for the sins of all who believe. He was painfully separated from God, and from the family of God, to grant us admission into the family of God. The law had been broken by every one of us. We were under its curse. But thanks be to God—Christ was cursed so that we might be blessed through faith in him alone! For all who trust in Christ, we have the assurance that the blessings of God will flow as far as the curse is found, and laws mitigating sin will be needed no more.

34

Rules for Everyday Life

Deuteronomy 22:1–12

You shall not see your brother's ox or his sheep going astray and ignore them. You shall take them back to your brother. (Deut. 22:1)

María Gabriela de Faría is a popular actress who was spotlighted for her support of animal rights. In an interview with *Global Heroes*, she was asked this question: "What is one good choice that everyone can make to improve the world around them?" She answered: "Question everything. And then question some more. Look for your own truth, LIVE your own truth, instead of repeating anybody else's." Such an approach is one that we have all become familiar with and may even embody. De Faría encourages her audience to make a daily practice of asking, in the context of meditation, "What do I need today?" because "the only person that will know what works for you is you."[1] Such a question is not particularly problematic in and of itself; the problem is that it is often asked *by* itself. Being cognizant of our own needs

1. Osvoldo Ponton, "María Gabriela de Faría on Growth, Empowerment, and Inspiring Positive Change," Global Heroes, https://www.globalheroes.com/maria-gabriela-de-faria-empowerment/, accessed August 15, 2022.

is not wrong, but living our lives as though the fulfillment of our needs were the meaning of life is contrary to biblical wisdom. We are largely a people, both inside and outside the church, turned inward on ourselves and inclined to live without respect to God or others. Though it is generally accepted wisdom today that we should pursue our own fulfillment, if everyone did this it would be horrific. Imagine living in a world where our orienting question was "What do I need today?" We would not be free, as some imagine, but we would be slaves to the tyranny of self.

The people of Israel had been slaves in Egypt for more than four hundred years before God graciously rescued them and set them free. When he set them free, he did not command them to go into the promised land and "LIVE their own truth." He revealed the truth to them and called them to live in obedience to it. It was not freedom from obligations or cultural norms that would make them happy, but obedience to God's good commands in response to his saving love. For Christians, we too have been set free from the slavery of our sinfulness and selfishness by the blood of Jesus. The apostle Paul writes in Galatians 5:13–14: "For you were called to freedom, brothers. Only do not use your freedom as an opportunity for the flesh, but through love serve one another. For the whole law is fulfilled in one word: 'You shall love your neighbor as yourself.'" True freedom is expressed through living a life of love for God and others, which is the fulfillment of God's law.

In Deuteronomy 22, God gives his people some instructions about how to live a life of love as free people. The verses in this section feel like a hodgepodge of commandments and do not initially strike us as relevant, since they are part of the civil law that expired with the nation of ancient Israel. But a deeper look reveals that they do have some connectivity with one another, and the principles of general equity underlying these commands are strikingly contemporary and relevant. We will break these verses down into six positive statements that strike back against our selfish orientation and move us toward the freedom of loving God and neighbor.

Look Out for Your Neighbor's Best Interests

This principle is laid out in the first four verses of Deuteronomy 22 in the context of an agricultural community. We read in verse 1: "You shall not see your brother's ox or his sheep going astray and ignore them. You shall take them back to your brother." Seeing someone's ox or sheep going astray is unlikely for many of us today. But livestock still get loose in many parts of the world and through much of human history. When we notice our brother's animal wandering away from his farm or property, we might be tempted to ignore it. The Hebrew literally says here and in verse 4, "[Do not] hide yourself from them." Our natural reaction is not to get involved. After all, it will likely be time-consuming to corral the stray animal and return it to our brother. It will be much easier to say, "Not my animal, not my problem." But such a statement runs counter to both the law of God and the heart of God. While the problem of our brother's fugitive animal is not our fault, in love we make it our responsibility. To care for other people means to care for what they own and to give practical help to them when they need it.[2]

A very practical application of this is still common in agricultural communities. On several occasions while staying with my grandparents in a farming community, I recall riding in their car and seeing that one of the neighbor's cows was loose. They stopped the car, we got out, and we tried to corral the animal back into the fenced area. Occasionally it was easy, and sometimes it was a major hassle. But they were following the principles of love in a very practical way.

Like the lawyer in Luke 10:29, we may be inclined to ask Jesus, "Who is my neighbor?" Moses continues in Deuteronomy 22:2: "And if he does not live near you and you do not know who he is, you shall bring it home to your house, and it shall stay with you until your brother seeks it. Then you shall restore it to him." The person whom we are to love enough to inconvenience ourselves for may not live near us, and we may not even know the animal's owner. No matter. We must bring the animal to our own house until the owner comes looking for it. When he does, we give the animal back to him. This verse teaches us that we are to do such a service not only for our family members or people we know, but for anyone. Just because we do not personally know someone does not mean that we do not owe that person brotherly love. A parallel passage in Exodus goes even further and teaches us that just because we do not like a person (or the person does not like us) does not excuse us from the requirements of brotherly love: "If you meet your enemy's ox or his donkey going astray, you shall bring it back to him. If you

2. Christopher Wright, *Deuteronomy*, NIBC: Old Testament 4 (Hendrickson, 2007), 240.

see the donkey of one who hates you lying down under its burden, you shall refrain from leaving him with it; you shall rescue it with him" (Ex. 23:4–5).

This responsibility to look out for our neighbor's or enemy's animals extends beyond animals, as Deuteronomy 22:3–4 goes on to explain: "And you shall do the same with his donkey or with his garment, or with any lost thing of your brother's, which he loses and you find; you may not ignore it. You shall not see your brother's donkey or his ox fallen down by the way and ignore them. You shall help him to lift them up again." Whether it is a donkey, a coat, a blanket, a wallet, or anything else that belongs to him, we must not ignore it. Instead, we should do what we can to help minimize his loss. Likewise, verse 4 tells us that when we see our brother in need of help, such as rescuing his donkey or ox from a ditch, we should not pass on by as though it were not our problem. If our brother needs help, we can assume that God has put us there to help him. Our brother's problem may not be our fault, but in love we make his problem our responsibility as we have ability to help.

When we recognize that Jesus and the apostle Paul were thoroughly grounded in the theology of Deuteronomy, we can better understand some of the things they taught. For example, when Jesus told the story of the good Samaritan, he was not advocating a new level of care for one's neighbor, but was simply bringing to light what had already been written in the law, particularly about love for our enemies. Likewise, when the apostle Paul called on the members of the church to bear one another's burdens, this was not a new teaching but comes straight out of the Old Testament.

If we see someone whose car is broken down along the road, we might be tempted to hide our eyes. Instead, we should offer to help. When we see that our neighbors are out of town and smoke appears to be rising from the roof, we should call someone to come and help. Shortly before Hurricane Irma hit our community in 2017, a man and his son came over and spent hours helping me board up the windows of our house. Thankfully, they had not awakened that morning asking, "What do I need today?" After the hurricane, many from our church went around helping one another and strangers remove trees, recover property, and restore assets. Such helping is directly in line with the teaching of this text.

The book of Deuteronomy does not envision a community where everyone asks, "What do I need today?" but envisions one where the covenant people of God love in practical ways, looking out for the best interests of others. We do not take advantage of our neighbors' misfortune; rather, we try to alleviate the suffering of their misfortune at our own expense. As we see in both the Old and New Testaments, this commitment includes doing such things not only for our brothers and sisters in Christ, but also for our enemies.

Embrace the Distinction Between Male and Female

Without warning, Moses abruptly changes topic in Deuteronomy 22:5: "A woman shall not wear a man's garment, nor shall a man put on a woman's cloak, for whoever does these things is an abomination to the Lord your God." The connection of this verse with the one before it is not clear, nor is it clear what prompted the giving of this law. Why would a woman wear a man's garment, or a man put on a woman's cloak, and why is it forbidden? Our text does not explain.

Some think that dressing as the opposite sex would allow for intermingling with that sex and thus facilitate sexual sin. Others hold that transvestism is abominable because it was a perverse means of sexual stimulation or because it may have been used in certain pagan magical rites.[3] Adding to the complexity of the question is that the words used for what the man or woman is wearing are not synonymous. The word used for a man's garment (*kheli*) is quite broad, covering the ideas of a vessel, utensil, weapon, armor, or jewelry.[4] The word used for a woman's cloak (*simlath*) is more specific to a mantle or outer garment. Most likely, the activity described here is forbidden because it blurs the sexual differences that God created in Genesis 1:27. This is how traditional Jewish *halakhah* understands it, as summed up by Jeffrey Tigay: "Women may not wear armor or clothing, hairdos, or other adornments that are characteristic of men, nor may men wear what is characteristic of women (what is characteristic of each sex is defined by local practice)."[5] But what is the big deal?

The problem with wearing clothes of the opposite sex was that it confused what is proper for one sex with what is proper for the other. We should still account for different cultural expressions. For example, kilts in Scotland

3. Jeffrey H. Tigay, *Deuteronomy*, JPSTC (Jewish Publication Society, 1996), 200.
4. BDB, s.v. "כָּלָה," 479.
5. Tigay, *Deuteronomy*, 200.

and long male skirts in Myanmar are not considered feminine, while a man wearing a dress in North American culture is aiming to blur lines. In December 2020, musician Harry Styles became the first man on the cover of Vogue magazine. He was featured wearing a dress. In the accompanying interview, he said:

> Clothes are there to have fun with and experiment with and play with. What's really exciting is that all of these lines are just kind of crumbling away. When you take away "There's clothes for men and there's clothes for women," once you remove any barriers, obviously you open up the arena in which you can play. . . . It's like anything—anytime you're putting barriers up in your own life, you're just limiting yourself. . . . I've never really thought too much about what it means—it just becomes this extended part of creating something.[6]

At the time of writing, Harry Styles is recognized as a generational voice—and this is what the voice is saying. He admits that he has not really thought about it, but still declares that dressing is no more than a creative act and that one should be free to do whatever he wants. The actress and director Olivia Wilde is quoted in the same magazine with her interpretation of what Styles is doing:

> To me, he's very modern . . . and I hope that this brand of confidence as a male that Harry has—truly devoid of any traces of toxic masculinity—is indicative of his generation and therefore the future of the world. I think he is in many ways championing that, spearheading that. It's pretty powerful and kind of extraordinary to see someone in his position redefining what it can mean to be a man with confidence.[7]

This message is the current cultural narrative. Essentially, many of our problems could be solved if men just put on dresses and acted more like women. But what does the biblical text say? Male and female are not interchangeable. A distinction is made in the creation accounts between male and female in terms of role and the physical anatomy appropriate for each.

6. Hamish Bowles, "Playtime with Harry Styles," *Vogue*, November 13, 2020, https://www.vogue.com/article/harry-styles-cover-december-2020, accessed August 12, 2022.

7. Bowles, "Playtime with Harry Styles."

Additionally, a sex-specific distinction is made in Genesis 3 when the curse is handed down, reflecting our differences as male and female. In the Old and New Testaments, we see some commands directed specifically to males or females. In a scholarly article on this verse, Dr. Hilary Lipka concludes:

> It is evident from both the gender roles prescribed in the legal collections and the depictions of gendered behavior in other parts of the Bible, that upholding a binary gender system was of significant importance to biblical authors, who clearly delineated gender specific roles, spaces, behaviors, attire, tasks, and tools. . . . Men should look and act like men and women should look and act like women. One's public presentation of his or her gender should be clear, not subject to confusion.[8]

In our current cultural context, debates about masculinity and femininity have helpfully highlighted that there is not just one way to be male or one way to be female. Not all men enjoy hot rods, hunting, and sports. Not all women enjoy cooking, crafts, and makeup. When we have these narrow categories for what it means to be male or female, people who are outside those categories get confused about who they are. Our culture adds to this confusion by telling a man who enjoys musicals that he must be gay because men do not like those things. Or a woman who enjoys physical sports must be gay because that is not what women enjoy.

At the same time, we must resist the incessant attempts to remove the distinctions between male and female today. Men are not women, women are not men, and there are demonstrable physiological and psychological differences between us that should be embraced, not denied. Men should not be "dressing up" as women to compete in women's sports. Women should not be "dressing up" as men to enter military combat.[9] Husbands should not

8. Hilary Lipka, "The Prohibition of Cross-Dressing," TheTorah.com, 2018, https://thetorah.com/article/the-prohibition-of-cross-dressing, accessed August 14, 2022.

9. Such a statement will likely offend many in our cultural moment, and it is an inference from the text rather than a direct scriptural command. I am not saying that women should not be allowed to serve in our nation's military as they have done sacrificially for a very long time. But putting them on the ground in combat is contrary to almost the entirety of human history. There have been exceptions, but generally speaking, combat has been something that men have sought to protect women from. Our cultural obsession with destroying lines between male and female now has us celebrating putting women in harm's way when most of human history would have seen this as deeply shameful.

pretend to be helpers in the home when they are called to be heads of their households, and wives should not pretend to be heads of their households when they are called to be helpers.

Our young men need to hear that God made them men. The church must affirm this louder than the culture is denying it. Being masculine is not a problem, and godly men do not need to put on dresses to prove that they have no traces of toxic masculinity. To be aggressive, assertive, and decisive is not toxic, though everything needs to be made obedient to Christ. The apostle Paul urges men in 1 Corinthians 16:13 to "act like men, be strong." It is good for men to act like men and for women to act like women, when we are pursuing Christlikeness and cultivating the fruit of the Spirit.

Men's dressing in drag is contrary to the spirit of this text. While we have the right to oppose such behavior in the public square in the spirit of a sane and moral society, we must be careful not to communicate to people who experience this confusion that they are not welcome in the church. Sin distorts and separates and creates confusion. What transvestites need is not our condemnation and judgment, but our invitation into a relationship with Jesus, where we are all discovering a better way to be human than cultural pressures are suggesting.

Steward God's Resources Wisely

We read in Deuteronomy 22:6–7: "If you come across a bird's nest in any tree or on the ground, with young ones or eggs and the mother sitting on the young or on the eggs, you shall not take the mother with the young. You shall let the mother go, but the young you may take for yourself, that it may go well with you, and that you may live long." Like other verses in Deuteronomy, this one surprises us. The people of God are forbidden from taking both the young birds or eggs and the mother bird. The basic logic would be that if one takes only the mother, both the mother and the young birds or eggs will die because the young depend on the mother. Take the young, and the mother can go on and reproduce again. This reasoning is common sense in terms of protecting our food sources but hardly seems worthy of the promise attached to it: "that it may go well with you, and that you may live long." This is the same promise attached to the fifth commandment, which is about honoring our father and mother (Deut.

5:16; Eph. 6:3). How are these two commands within the same ballpark of importance such that this great promise would accompany both?

The Jewish rabbis explicitly referred to this law as "the least of the commandments."[10] And from it they deduced the importance of the whole law, since the same theological justification is used for the commandment in Deuteronomy 22:6–7 as for keeping the fifth commandment. Jesus states in Matthew 5:19, "Therefore whoever relaxes one of the least of these commandments and teaches others to do the same will be called least in the kingdom of heaven, but whoever does them and teaches them will be called great in the kingdom of heaven." These verses teach us the continuing relevance of even the least of God's law for God's covenant people. But that is not the only reason why it is here.

As God's people, we are not to be ignorant of our impact on the resources that God has given for us to steward and enjoy. Extremist views on one side might advocate the elimination of humanity so that creation may thrive. Extremists on the other side might advocate the reckless use of everything we can without regard to the consequences on the environment, the poor, or future generations. God has given us real responsibility for the stewardship of the earth as his viceregents. Instead of either of these approaches, we should allow long-term wisdom to set limits to short-term greed.[11] We are pushing back against the "what do I need today?" mentality and the greed that would harm our future selves and future generations. It is biblical to use the earth's resources to supply human needs. It is also biblical to consciously limit our consumption of resources as an act of loving concern for our neighbors and future generations. Why can we not hold these two truths together?

Minimize the Risk of Harm to Your Neighbor

We read in Deuteronomy 22:8, "When you build a new house, you shall make a parapet for your roof, that you may not bring the guilt of blood upon your house, if anyone should fall from it." People used to spend significant time on their roofs, and without a parapet or railing, it was quite possible that

10. Wright, *Deuteronomy*, 242.
11. Wright, 241.

someone could fall to his or her death. God's people cannot be indifferent to this possibility. Our neighbor's safety is our concern. The same biblical concern today requires us to have fences around our swimming pools to protect children from accidentally wandering into them. The law of the parapet means that we should keep our guns locked in safes so that people do not accidentally harm themselves or others. While building codes are a hassle, such codes aim to protect life, and we can thus embrace them as reflections of godly concerns in a community. Until we reflect deeply on laws such as this one, I do not think that we fully appreciate just how pro-life God is.

How should this passage inform how we think about gun control in America? People on both sides of this issue are frequently driven by political talking points rather than biblical convictions. The biblical conviction that we must have is that all life is sacred, and as God's people we should be at the forefront of helping to preserve life. Some Christians believe that the best way to do so is by putting more restrictions on gun ownership and reducing the number and types of weapons available. Other Christians believe that the best way to preserve life is not by restricting gun ownership but by getting guns into the hands of more people who can stop bad guys. Christians can disagree on the right approach to the issue. Yet we must agree on the sanctity of human life, and the driving force of our view should not be the Constitution or political talking points but the Word of God. When our aim is minimizing the risk of harm to our neighbor rather than defending our entrenched political views or long-held personal convictions, we are free to change our minds on an issue as more information comes to light.

Or what about universal healthcare? Christians can have differing views on this complicated issue, but those views should not be rooted in our personal best interests, nor in what our political party's viewpoint is, nor in what is most advantageous for us financially, but rather in which approach best protects the lives of our neighbors (which includes our own families). Some may conclude that privatized medicine is the best course and others that socialized medicine is the best course, but as Christians, we must ensure that our viewpoint has as its driving motivator the desire to preserve life because that is God's heart. This passage teaches us that our neighbor's safety is worth our inconvenience. What is in the best interests of my neighbor?

While this is the guiding principle, we must admit that there are limits. For example, knowing that driving a car could threaten my neighbor's life might lead us to the conclusion that we should never drive a car. This would be an undue burden going beyond what the general equity of the law requires. Back to the text, if we truly wanted to minimize the risk of harm to ourselves or our neighbor, we might forbid access to the roof of the house altogether. But this too would seem to be an undue burden. The law of the parapet was a reasonable provision in ancient Israel for the safety of a family and its neighbors. Christians today should also consider how to minimize the risk of harm to our neighbors, guided by both wisdom and a genuine desire to protect life.

Maintain Spiritual Integrity

The next section refers to mixing things. Moses writes in Deuteronomy 22:9–11: "You shall not sow your vineyard with two kinds of seed, lest the whole yield be forfeited, the crop that you have sown and the yield of the vineyard. You shall not plow with an ox and a donkey together. You shall not wear cloth of wool and linen mixed together." This is one of the laws that people like to point to today when they say: "Oh, you say that the Bible prohibits homosexuality? Well, it also prohibits wearing two types of cloth. Since you do that, why shouldn't others practice homosexuality?" We can point such people to the helpful distinctions between the moral law, which endures forever, and those ceremonial and civil aspects of the law, which ended with biblical Israel. But as to this specific set of laws about mixing, we really do not know what these laws are about. They do not appear to fit into that category of moral law that continues to apply directly to all people everywhere. Instead, I believe these laws prescribed practices for ancient Israel that were intended to point beyond themselves to spiritual realities. For one thing, Paul writes in 2 Corinthians 6:14, "Do not be unequally yoked with unbelievers." He is making a spiritual application of Deuteronomy 22:10. One reason suggested as to why the ox and donkey are not to plow together is that the ox was clean and the donkey was unclean (Lev. 11:1–8). In this case, the prohibition would be a reminder to God's people that the clean and unclean were not to be linked together, meaning especially intermingling God's people with pagans.

While these commands refer to specific things that the people of God were not to do in the context of the Mosaic covenant, they are a symbol of a continuing spiritual reality and the importance of avoiding syncretism and maintaining our spiritual integrity.

Remember God's Commandments

The last law in this section concerns tassels on garments. Moses commands in Deuteronomy 22:12, "You shall make yourself tassels on the four corners of the garment with which you cover yourself." What is the purpose of these tassels on the four corners of the garment? Moses does not explain, but takes for granted what is written in Numbers 15:38–39, which provides more background to this commandment. There the Lord says:

> Speak to the people of Israel, and tell them to make tassels on the corners of their garments throughout their generations, and to put a cord of blue on the tassel of each corner. And it shall be a tassel for you to look at and remember all the commandments of the Lord, to do them, not to follow after your own heart and your own eyes, which you are inclined to whore after.

This command was given to help God's people remember all the commandments of God and to remind them not to follow their own hearts or eyes. Here is a good reminder for all of us: Do not follow your heart; follow God's commandments.

Jesus rebuked the scribes and Pharisees in his day for making their tassels extra-long as a self-righteous demonstration of their piety: "They do all their deeds to be seen by others. For they make their phylacteries broad and their fringes long" (Matt. 23:5). But Jesus was not opposed to the practice. In fact, he wore his garment with tassels on the four corners. We know this because of a couple of stories recounted in the Gospels. In one of them, a woman who had suffered from a discharge of blood for twelve years, keeping her in a perpetual state of ritual uncleanness, came up to Jesus and touched one of these tassels, receiving a healing (9:20–22).[12]

12. Others did the same thing. Mark 6:56 relates: "And wherever he came, in villages, cities, or countryside, they laid the sick in the marketplaces and implored him that they might touch even the fringe of his garment. And as many as touched it were made well."

Making tassels to wear on our garments is no longer a necessary practice, but being intentional to remember God's commandments certainly is. We are called to live distinctively as God's covenant people in this world. To do that, we must not be conformed to the thinking and practices of our culture, such as the idea that fulfillment can be found if we all just live for ourselves. Instead, this passage reminds us repeatedly that obedience to God's commands in response to God's grace is the path to fulfillment. Jesus models this kind of self-giving love. Jesus was perfectly fulfilled in heaven from eternity past. Moreover, when humanity fell into sin and under God's righteous condemnation, it was not Jesus' fault. Out of love for us, though we were his enemies, Jesus made our fallen condition his own responsibility. He gave himself up to live the life we should have lived and die the death we should have died so that we could be saved from the misery of living for ourselves. He set us free from a life turned inward so that we might experience the joy of living for God and being a blessing to others.

Jesus offers this gift of freedom to all who will receive it by faith alone. If we have received it, then let us demonstrate it by living out these very practical rules for everyday life for God's glory, the good of our neighbor, and our everlasting joy.

35

Sex Is a Community Affair

Deuteronomy 22:13–30

If a man is found lying with the wife of another man, both of them shall die, the man who lay with the woman, and the woman. So you shall purge the evil from Israel. (Deut. 22:22)

Kevin felt like someone had died. His wife had asked him for a divorce because she said that he was working too much. While that may have been true, it turns out that she was also having an affair with a man they both knew. This case took place in North Carolina, which is one of seven states that (as of 2024) still has the "alienation of affection" law. Kevin sued the man he held responsible for breaking up his marriage and alienating his wife from him. The court agreed and awarded a judgment of $750,000 in Kevin's favor.

While such laws and judgments are rare today, they do reflect a scriptural principle: sex is a community matter. The relationship between Kevin's wife and her lover was not victimless. The breakup of that marriage impacted not only Kevin, but their families and their friends. The court's decision to punish the adulterer reflects the fact that society has an interest in the preservation of marriages and some measure of sexual integrity. Not everyone agrees, however.

Supreme Court Justice John Harry Blackmun wrote in a dissenting opinion from the 1986 *Bowers v. Hardwick* decision that "how a person engages in sex should be irrelevant as a matter of state law. . . . In a diverse nation such as ours, we must preserve the individual freedom to choose, and not to imply that there are any 'right' ways of conducting relationships."[1] The idea that there are no right ways to conduct relationships flies in the face not only of the Bible, but of nearly all of human history. Along with establishing norms of language and commerce that enable communication and business, cultures also establish norms of marriage, family, and sex.

We all have an interest in the sexual integrity of our neighbors. Imagine that you and your spouse are friends with another couple. One member of that couple engages in an affair. Consequently, the marriage becomes contentious and ends in divorce. Do the actions of those two consenting adults in the bedroom not have an impact on your life? Suppose that someone's private pornography addiction continues to lead to diminished intimacy with his spouse that leads to a coldness in the relationship and a functional (if not actual) breakdown in the marriage. Will their children not be affected by their private and personal sexual decisions? When sexual sin leads to 40 percent of children in the United States being born into families without a married mother and father, and consequently those children grow up with a challenged childhood that leads to a greater proclivity toward all sorts of social ills, does our society not bear the weight of those personal and private decisions?[2] The novelist Wendell Berry puts it succinctly: "Sex, like any other necessary, precious, and volatile power that is commonly held, is everybody's business."[3]

Deuteronomy reflects that reality. The laws in this section appear to be an exposition of the seventh commandment, "You shall not commit adultery" (Deut. 5:18). As we have seen with other commandments, the fullness of the seventh commandment is not exhausted by simply not having sex outside of one's marriage. It is far more extensive and is a matter of the heart, as

1. Quoted in Lauren F. Winner, *Real Sex: The Naked Truth About Chastity* (Brazos Press, 2005), 47.

2. Elizabeth Wildsmith, Jennifer Manlove, and Elizabeth Cook, "Dramatic Increase in the Proportion of Births Outside of Marriage in the United States from 1990 to 2016," Child Trends, August 8, 2018, https://www.childtrends.org/publications/dramatic-increase-in-percentage-of-births-outside-marriage-among-whites-hispanics-and-women-with-higher-education-levels, accessed August 25, 2022.

3. Quoted in Winner, *Real Sex*, 49.

Jesus highlights in Matthew 5:27–28: "You have heard that it was said, 'You shall not commit adultery.' But I say to you that everyone who looks at a woman with lustful intent has already committed adultery with her in his heart." But the law must deal with practical matters surrounding the stuff of everyday life in the land, a significant part of which has to do with marriage and sexuality. This passage teaches us that matters of sex are not isolated from the rest of life, and that God's covenant people are called to live with sexual integrity of heart and body.

Sexual Integrity Is a Community Affair

We first encounter a law that aims to protect sexual integrity before marriage and inside marriage. The situation is described in Deuteronomy 22:13–14: "If any man takes a wife and goes in to her and then hates her and accuses her of misconduct and brings a bad name upon her, saying, 'I took this woman, and when I came near her, I did not find in her evidence of virginity' . . ." The new husband is accusing his wife of not being a virgin when he married her. The motive in this case is that he does not like her and wants to be rid of her. So he accuses her of having been unfaithful before their marriage. If this happens, then we read what must happen next in verses 15–17:

> then the father of the young woman and her mother shall take and bring out the evidence of her virginity to the elders of the city in the gate. And the father of the young woman shall say to the elders, "I gave my daughter to this man to marry, and he hates her; and behold, he has accused her of misconduct, saying, 'I did not find in your daughter evidence of virginity.' And yet this is the evidence of my daughter's virginity." And they shall spread the cloak before the elders of the city.

The parents of the girl are now involved because they received the bride price for the girl. The man has accused them of giving him something less than he paid for in the bride price. They must also defend family honor. So the parents bring the evidence of her virginity to the elders in the city gate. The required involvement of the elders means that this is not a private family matter, but a community matter. The parents spread out the cloak that somehow proves her virginity. How it did so is not clear. It was common in the ancient Near East for a garment to be kept, demonstrating with bloodstains that the hymen had been ruptured when the marriage was consummated. We know that this is not very good proof of virginity today, but at the time it was a common test. Another possibility is that this is a reference to menstrual cloths that prove that the woman was not pregnant when she was given to the man.[4] We simply do not know. The point is that the parents are able to demonstrate that their daughter had lived with sexual integrity within their home and that this was a false charge.

In that case, Moses continues in Deuteronomy 22:18–19, "then the elders of that city shall take the man and whip him, and they shall fine him a hundred shekels of silver and give them to the father of the young woman, because he has brought a bad name upon a virgin of Israel. And she shall be his wife. He may not divorce her all his days." Accusing his wife of sexual sin was a serious matter, bringing shame on the young woman and, by extension, her family. Therefore, the man is to be publicly whipped for his sin, and he must pay a very significant sum of money for the damage he has done to the woman and her family. The fine is to be paid to the father because if it were paid to the bride, the husband would end up retaining it himself.[5] In addition to the fine, the man who wanted to divorce his wife could never divorce her. While that does not sound like a particularly pleasant prospect for the wife, there were very few options for a single woman at that time. Remaining married to this kind of man at least ensured that she would be provided for and have the opportunity to raise children, which was central to the life of a woman in Israel.

But what if the parents cannot prove that their daughter has lived with sexual integrity? We read in Deuteronomy 22:20–21: "But if the thing is true, that evidence of virginity was not found in the young woman, then they shall bring out the young woman to the door of her father's house, and the men of her city shall stone her to death with stones, because she has done an outrageous thing in Israel by whoring in her father's house. So you shall purge the evil from your midst." Moses refers to sex before marriage as "whoring in her father's house." Sex outside the context of marriage, for

4. For an extensive scholarly treatment of these issues, see Gordon J. Wenham, "*Bĕtûlāh*, a Girl of Marriageable Age," *Vetus Testamentum* 22, no. 3 (July 1972): 326–48.

5. Eugene H. Merrill, *Deuteronomy*, NAC 4 (Broadman & Holman, 1994), 303.

a man or a woman, is tantamount to prostituting oneself, except that there is no payment. Under the terms of the Mosaic covenant, the penalty for engaging in sex this way was death. Execution was to happen outside the young woman's father's door because only her public death at the hands of the community could remove the disgrace from her family and community.

It is hard for us to fathom that a person would be executed for having sex outside marriage. To be clear, under the new covenant, sexual sin does not and should not carry the death penalty. These laws were part of the civil law that expired with ancient Israel. But rather than looking back and dismissing these as primitive people who should lighten up about sex, perhaps we should look at our own nonchalant attitudes and ask whether we are taking sex too lightly. This law reminds us that as parents, we bear some responsibility for our children's living with sexual integrity while in our homes. We not only should be modeling sexual integrity, but should be teaching it to those living under our roof. This includes establishing good boundaries to limit the opportunities for sexual sin, and also maintaining a relationship in which these things can be honestly discussed with our children as they mature. Sexual integrity is a community affair.

SEXUAL SIN IS A COMMUNITY AFFAIR

We now come to a series of sexual sins and how they are to be handled when they occur.

A Case of Adultery

We read in Deuteronomy 22:22: "If a man is found lying with the wife of another man, both of them shall die, the man who lay with the woman, and the woman. So you shall purge the evil from Israel." This is classic adultery, when one or both parties in the sexual relationship are married to someone else. More than any other illicit sexual behavior, adultery is unfaithfulness in the context of a covenant commitment. The marriage covenant commitment reflects God's covenant commitment to his people. Unfaithfulness to that marriage commitment was the social equivalent to cheating on God.[6] It is a form of treason that strikes at the heart of the household and its stability.

6. Peter C. Craigie, *The Book of Deuteronomy*, NICOT (Eerdmans, 1976), 160.

Consequently, the appropriate penalty under the law was death for both the guilty man and woman. There is no sexual double standard here.

While our civil laws no longer call for death in the case of adultery, the sin is no less serious today than it was then. It still strikes at the heart of the stability of the household and greatly increases the likelihood of children and others' suffering and drifting from faithfulness to God. The community suffers from adultery together and must address it together.

A Case of Implied Consent

The next two laws provide guidelines for determining when a woman is innocent or guilty in a sexual encounter. We read in Deuteronomy 22:23–24:

> If there is a betrothed virgin, and a man meets her in the city and lies with her, then you shall bring them both out to the gate of that city, and you shall stone them to death with stones, the young woman because she did not cry for help though she was in the city, and the man because he violated his neighbor's wife. So you shall purge the evil from your midst.

Here we have a very difficult text in which Moses is trying to determine whether this sinful sexual act was carried out forcibly or consensually.[7] In both the ancient world and today's world, it can be difficult to determine whether a sexual act was consensual. The implication of these verses is that if a man and woman have sex within city limits, this was a consensual act "because she did not cry for help." The assumption is that everyone was living in close enough quarters that a cry would be heard and someone would stop the attack. Early Jewish interpreters say that this guideline was not absolute, as commentator Jeffrey Tigay writes: "Philo, Josephus, and halakhic sources hold that this guideline is not absolute: whether in town or in the country, evidence that there was no one who could have saved her, that she resisted, or that her life was threatened if she resisted, would establish innocence; evidence to the contrary would establish guilt."[8]

7. Nations are still trying to create better laws to prevent sexual assault, determine consent, and ensure that the guilty do not go unpunished. For an example of one such law recently enacted in Spain, see https://www.dailymail.co.uk/news/article-11148663/Spain-brings-yes-means-yes-rape-laws-following-notorious-gang-sex-attack.html.

8. Jeffrey H. Tigay, *Deuteronomy*, JPSTC (Jewish Publication Society, 1996), 207.

Unfortunately, some have used this text to tell sexual assault survivors today that if they did not call out or fight during the attack, then it must have been consensual. Obviously, this is hurtful to those who have suffered such attacks and may already feel guilt and shame because they feel as though they could have done more to prevent the attack. We must be very careful in how we handle this text, knowing that this is a circumstance that many women and men have experienced.

We know that sometimes victims have cried out and no one has come to their aid. This does not make them guilty, nor does it make the assault consensual. We also know that in some cases, especially when the attacker is known, people have a freeze response. The person being attacked does not consent to the violence, and yet cannot move or speak. In the horrifying event of anyone's being attacked in this way, the biblical text would encourage the person to cry out and resist if he or she is able, and perhaps the attacker will flee or help will come. But if victims are unable, they can still cry for help after the attack by going to a parent, a pastor or counselor, or a trusted friend. Assault victims are not guilty of anything; they are not responsible for what happened to them, and they are not in trouble. Our homes and our churches need to be safe places for people to cry out after the fact.

In this particular case, the Hebrew text makes it clear that the woman was not violated but consented to the sinful act. Consequently, she shares in the penalty of the crime against her future husband, her father, and her community. That is not the case with the next situation.

A Case of Sexual Assault

Before we say any more about sexual assault, we recognize that some will think that we should not go down this dark path. Others will think that this is better left to the counselor's office. But if the statistics on sexual assault are accurate, then this subject impacts a very large number of people in our churches. Those people need to hear about it honestly and compassionately from the pulpit. Moses writes in Deuteronomy 22:25–27:

> But if in the open country a man meets a young woman who is betrothed, and the man seizes her and lies with her, then only the man who lay with her shall die. But you shall do nothing to the young woman; she has committed no offense punishable by death. For this case is like that of a man attacking and

> murdering his neighbor, because he met her in the open country, and though the betrothed young woman cried for help there was no one to rescue her.

In this scenario, a man "seizes" (*khzq*) a betrothed young woman and lies with her. This word makes it clear that consent is not involved. Rather than considering her guilty until proven innocent, she is declared innocent unless proven guilty.[9] Not only does the text make it clear that she does not deserve to die (unlike in some shame-and-honor cultures to this day), she is identified as the victim of a violent crime, like murder. Connecting sexual assault with murder rightly recognizes that those who suffer sexual assault do experience a type of death. The expectation is that the survivor will report this attack in order that the rapist gets the penalty suitable to the crime of sexually assaulting a betrothed woman, which is death.

Second Samuel 13 tells the tragic story of Tamar, King David's daughter. The king's son Amnon could not lawfully have his half-sister. So with the help of a despicable friend, he schemed to get her alone, and then he "seized" (*khzq*, my translation) her. She resisted him, she pleaded with him, but he would not listen to her voice, and he raped her. Then he hated her and sent her away. She pleaded with him not to send her out, but again, he would not listen to her voice. Devastated, she left his presence and encountered her brother Absalom. She somehow made known what had happened to her, but he also did not listen to her voice. Surely trying to say the right thing, he said a terribly wrong thing: "Now hold your peace, my sister . . . ; do not take this to heart" (2 Sam. 13:20).

"Hold your peace"? "Do not take this to heart"? Tamar had had a hope, she had had a future; she was a princess with dreams of being a wife and mother. In that culture, those dreams had been torn from her hands in one selfish moment by a man who used her and then threw her out. She would now live her life as a desolate woman (2 Sam. 13:20). When she had cried out, the people around her responsible for giving her justice told her to be quiet and not to take it personally. That was wrong. To the Tamars (female and male) who have suffered and been sinned against in this way, do not hold your peace. Cry out. Tell someone, and keep telling until someone really

9. Sandra L. Richter, "Rape in Israel's World . . . and Ours: A Study of Deuteronomy 22:23–29," *JETS* 64, no. 1 (2021): 66.

listens. Grieve and lament what has been lost and what has been stolen. I believe Tamar's desolation related to her being alone, suffering in silence, forbidden from giving voice to the shattering pain she had suffered. In our churches, we cannot allow survivors of sexual assault to suffer alone. We must listen to their voices.

A Case of Seduction

Some have also seen the following case as sexual assault, but a careful look at the text reveals otherwise. Moses continues in Deuteronomy 22:28–29: "If a man meets a virgin who is not betrothed, and seizes her and lies with her, and they are found, then the man who lay with her shall give to the father of the young woman fifty shekels of silver, and she shall be his wife, because he has violated her. He may not divorce her all his days." Many read this and are appalled that the woman is forced to marry the man who assaulted her. But the word "seize" (*thfsh*) here is a different word from the one used in the context of the sexual assault in verse 25 and in the story of Tamar. This word (*thfsh*) does not imply that force was used, nor does the word translated "violated." The word "violated" (*innah*) in this context refers to lowering the woman's social status.[10] That this is a case of seduction is confirmed by a parallel passage in Exodus 22:16–17: "If a man seduces a virgin who is not betrothed and lies with her, he shall give the bride-price for her and make her his wife. If her father utterly refuses to give her to him, he shall pay money equal to the bride-price for virgins." If a man seduces and has sex with an unmarried woman, he does not simply move on. He must pay the bride price and make her his wife, unless the father refuses. Otherwise, because of the way that the seducer has lowered her social status, the woman was not likely to find a husband in that culture and would be in a desperate situation. This law was meant to protect women and to discourage casual flings.

Virginity is not so highly valued in Western culture today, and having a sexual relationship is probably not going to keep a woman or man from getting a spouse. But when 40 percent of children in the United States are being born out of wedlock, leaving mothers to fend for themselves, we can hardly say that our society's approach to casual sex is in the best interests of women.

10. Richter, 67.

This law also teaches us that to engage in sex with another person is never a casual affair. Sex is a covenant-forming and covenant-renewing act that carries with it lifelong obligations of a one-flesh relationship. This law does not establish that reality but reflects that reality. The apostle Paul confirms this principle in 1 Corinthians 6:16: "Or do you not know that he who is joined to a prostitute becomes one body with her? For, as it is written, 'The two will become one flesh.'" Casual sex and hookups with a prostitute or another consenting adult fail to appreciate that sex bonds us to another person, whether we want it to or not.

In the movie *Vanilla Sky*, Tom Cruise plays a man-about-town who has a fling with a blonde whom he was never serious about. But she was serious, and she begins stalking Cruise. When she eventually corners him, she speaks real wisdom about sex that sounds like the Bible in contemporary language: "Don't you know that when you sleep with someone, your body makes a promise whether you do or not."[11] God created sex to unite two people, and just because we think it is no big deal does not mean that sex does not accomplish the bonding that God created it to do. The biblical command is not to engage in sex until marriage, and not to engage in sex outside marriage.

As we have read through these laws, we have seen that sexual integrity and sexual sin are both handled with deathly seriousness. Both in the wider culture and inside the church, we take matters of sexuality much less seriously. But the emotional and spiritual impact of our collective sexual sin has taken a tremendous toll on the church and our society. So what should we do?

We should practice sexual integrity, which means avoiding all sexual relationships except with one's own husband or wife. Again, the apostle Paul writes, "For this is the will of God, your sanctification: that you abstain from sexual immorality; that each one of you know how to control his own body in holiness and honor, not in the passion of lust like the Gentiles who do not know God" (1 Thess. 4:3–5). Those of us who know God should demonstrate a different sexual ethic from the culture around us. In part, this means recognizing that our culture is wrong in its emphasis on sex as being private. If a member of the church is unmarried and engaging in sex, or a fellow believer is being unfaithful to his or her spouse, that is the business of the person's brothers and sisters in Christ. As Christians, we need

11. Quoted in Winner, *Real Sex*, 88.

to encourage and challenge each other to walk with sexual integrity, which includes forsaking pornography as well as sexual sins directly involving other people. But what happens when we fall? How do we respond to a brother or sister in Christ who has sinned sexually?

Redemption After Sexual Sin Is a Community Affair

If our brothers and sisters in Christ are not aware of their sin, or they are not repenting of their sin, we have a responsibility to show it to them and follow the principles of Matthew 18. Unrepentant sexual sinners under the new covenant are not executed, but if they remain unrepentant, they are ultimately excommunicated. We see an example of this in 1 Corinthians 5:1–2, where a man continued to have his father's wife. That man was breaking the law described in Deuteronomy 22:30, which carried the death penalty under the Mosaic covenant. Nearly all agree that the prohibition here has in view a sexual relationship with one's stepmother, which would have been far more common than a sexual relationship with one's own mother (which is also prohibited). Most of the biblical material about incest relates to this stepmother relationship. Part of the temptation in a household would have been that the son and the father's new wife would likely have been much closer in age. In the biblical narratives, we can see that Reuben is guilty of this sin (Gen. 35:22), as is Absalom in a different sort of way (2 Sam. 16:21–22). As the apostle Paul condemns this kind of relationship and requires the removal of the persistent sexual sinner from Christian fellowship, so we must do with those who refuse to repent of sin.

How should we respond to brothers and sisters who know that they have sinned and are repenting of their sin? We should respond as Jesus did toward repentant sexual sinners. In Luke 7:36–50, a woman, who was also a prostitute, came to Jesus and fell at his feet, washing them with her tears, hair, and kisses. One of the Pharisees who saw it was dismayed that Jesus would let this sinner touch him. So Jesus told him a short story to this effect: "A moneylender had two debtors. One owed him five hundred denarii; the other owed him fifty. Neither of them could pay, so he canceled the debt of both. Which would love him more?" They answered that the one with the bigger debt forgiven would love more. Jesus turned and looked at the sexual sinner weeping at his feet and said to the Pharisee: "'Therefore I tell you, her sins, which are many, are forgiven—for she loved much. But he who is forgiven little, loves little.' And he said to her, 'Your sins are forgiven. . . . Your faith has saved you; go in peace'" (Luke 7:47–50). She was forgiven right then and there, no waiting period required.

For those who are broken under the guilt and shame of sexual sin today, come to Jesus. Fall at his feet and love him. How? By recognizing that he came to die for our sexual sin. He bore the guilt, he bore the shame, he bore the judgment of all our sexual sins, even our worst ones. If we reject his death for us, we are still in the guilt and shame and under the judgment for our sins. But if we accept it, if we say, "I am a sinner, and his death was for my sins," then our sins were taken away with the shedding of his blood and buried with him in the tomb. As surely as Jesus came forth to new life out of that tomb, we have also been brought from death to new life in him. We have a new start. Consequences from our former life of sin will not disappear. We will need to take responsibility for the consequences of those sexual sins and the people we have hurt. But we can now face those consequences, confident and at peace, for Jesus is with us, God is for us, and the Holy Spirit is inside us.

What should our posture be, as a body and as individuals, toward sexual sinners? We must condemn the sin, but welcome, forgive, and receive the repentant sinner. How many times? Even seven times? Jesus says "seventy-seven times" (Matt. 18:22). Some might think that urging those who have been sexually sinned against through sexual assault, abuse, or adultery to forgive their abusers is too much to ask. This is certainly understandable. It is not fair that they have to live with this, that they have to go through this, and that they have to suffer this way. It is not right. But it is reality, and if anyone knows the difficulty of this, Jesus does. He suffered and forgave the worst of sins. Because he loves us, he also calls us to forgive those who have sinned against us, because he knows that holding onto unforgiveness will destroy us. He does not tell us to forgive to make us miserable; he tells us to forgive that we may be free.

To be clear, forgiving someone does not mean that what happened was okay or that there will not be consequences. Forgiveness does not mean the restoration of trust. Forgiveness does not mean that a marriage will survive broken vows. Forgiveness does not mean that a sexual abuser will not spend time in jail. Forgiveness means that the one sinned against does not have to remain in the prison of anger, hatred, and bitterness or shame. Through our relationship with Christ and the forgiveness that we ourselves have received, we can learn to forgive those who have sinned against us—even in the worst possible ways.

For those who are understandably having difficulty forgiving someone who sinned against them in seemingly unforgivable ways, there is biblical counseling. In a gentle and patient way and with biblical resources, a counselor can help someone come to a place of forgiveness so that the person may experience the freedom that can come only through the gospel. The way of healing in Jesus can be just as much a reality as the hurt we feel today.

Sex is a community affair. Therefore, by the power of the Holy Spirit, let us walk with sexual integrity of heart and body, let us condemn sexual sin, and let us look to Jesus not only for forgiveness of our sexual sins, but also for the grace to forgive those who have sinned against us.

36

Holiness Among God's People

Deuteronomy 23:1–14

Because the Lord your God walks in the midst of your camp, to deliver you and to give up your enemies before you, therefore your camp must be holy, so that he may not see anything indecent among you and turn away from you. (Deut. 23:14)

After the passing of Queen Elizabeth II, many people shared stories of her life and their encounters with her. One such story is told by Vaughan Roberts. Back in 1966, England's soccer team won the World Cup. The captain of the team, Bobby Moore, had the privilege of leading his team up to the royal box to receive the trophy from the hands of Queen Elizabeth herself. An interviewer later asked him how he felt going up to get the trophy from the queen. Moore described how mortified he was as he approached the queen because he saw that she was wearing pristine white gloves and his own hands were completely covered with mud from the soccer field. So as he walked up the thirty-nine steps to the royal box, he kept wiping his hands on his shorts, and then wiped them on the velvet cloth in front of the royal box in a desperate attempt to get them clean before he touched her. Roberts makes the connection for us:

> If Bobby Moore was worried about approaching the Queen with his muddy hands, how much more horrified should we be at the prospect of approaching God? Because of our sin, we are not just dirty on the outside; our hearts are unclean. And God doesn't just wear white gloves; he is absolutely pure, through and through.[1]

In Deuteronomy 23, God's covenant people are given some specific instructions about who can and who cannot enter the assembly of the Lord to worship him. Other instructions are given concerning what the people must do to keep the camp clean because the holy God dwells in their midst. The laws in Deuteronomy 23:1–14 may sound quite strange to us, and indeed they are strange. But God gave them to his people through Moses so that his sinful and unclean people could enjoy the benefit of fellowship with him even though he is "holy, holy, holy" (Isa. 6:3). The ceremonial rules regarding ritual purity in Israel have come to an end through the ministry of Jesus, whose blood alone can take away the defilement of our sin. The rules about who can be in the assembly of the Lord and how God's people should live knowing that God is present in our midst are no less instructive for us than for them. Because God is holy and dwells among his covenant people, we must be holy as he is holy.

Because God Is Holy, We Must Keep the Assembly Holy

In Deuteronomy 23:1–8, directions are given about who may enter the assembly of the Lord. The assembly of the Lord is the covenant people of God gathered in his presence.[2] They might gather to discuss war, deal with legal cases, establish a king, or worship.[3] The Greek translation of this verse uses the word *ekklēsia*, which in the New Testament is usually translated as "church." The church is the holy assembly of God's people gathered, especially for the purpose of worship. A person may have been an Israelite and a member of the covenant community by birth, but that did

1. Vaughan Roberts, *The Porn Problem* (Good Book Company, 2018), 51.
2. Peter C. Craigie, *The Book of Deuteronomy*, NICOT (Eerdmans, 1976), 296.
3. Jeffrey H. Tigay, *Deuteronomy*, JPSTC (Jewish Publication Society, 1996), 210.

not necessarily qualify the individual for full participation in community worship.[4] In this passage, we see three groups of people excluded to protect the sanctity of the holy assembly.

The Sexually Broken Man Is Excluded from the Holy Assembly

We read in Deuteronomy 23:1, "No one whose testicles are crushed or whose male organ is cut off shall enter the assembly of the Lord." This is one of those verses that have somehow never made it onto a bumper sticker or refrigerator magnet. In any case, the verse prohibits an emasculated male from entering the assembly of the Lord. A man's testicles may have been accidentally crushed, though more likely what is being described here is something done intentionally to make him a eunuch. Typically, just before puberty a boy destined to be a eunuch would have his testicles crushed.[5] Similarly, one's male organ may have been accidentally cut off, but more likely this describes an intentional situation of surgical removal with the aim of changing one's gender.[6] It turns out that harmful genital mutilation has been around for a long time.

Under the law, a man in this situation would not have been allowed into the holy assembly. In our day, some men are still voluntarily having their male organs removed in the process of transitioning from male to female. Of course, one cannot become a female simply by cutting off one's male organ. To be either male or female is not an assignment that a physician makes when a person is born, but a determination that God makes before the foundation of the world. In a very few situations, a person does not fit squarely into the traditional category of male or female, but even in these rare instances, in most cases it is simple for a physician to determine whether the person is male or female.

Despite this fact and contrary to the Hippocratic oath that many physicians pledge to uphold, some will surgically remove a physically healthy male's organ to try to solve a complex mental and emotional disorder. No Christian physician should participate in such genital mutilation, and no scientifically advanced nation should allow such procedures to be performed on its citizens, and certainly not on its children. As Christians, we should extend love and

4. Eugene H. Merrill, *Deuteronomy*, NAC 4 (Broadman & Holman, 1994), 309.
5. Daniel I. Block, *Deuteronomy*, NIVAC (Zondervan, 2012), 534n2.
6. Block, 534n2.

compassion to those struggling with the incredibly disorienting idea that they have been born in the wrong body and not mock such people's pain. At the same time, in love we must extend the hope of the gospel and encourage those we know and love to seek treatment from Christian counselors who can help them work through to a place of healing.

Under the law here, a man who has gone through such a surgery would have been forever banned from assembling with the people of God. Does this mean that those whose sexual organs have been messed up intentionally or accidentally are forbidden from worshiping in our churches? Before we answer, we will consider the second group excluded.

The Person of Illegitimate Birth Is Excluded from the Holy Assembly

Moses writes in Deuteronomy 23:2: "No one born of a forbidden union may enter the assembly of the Lord. Even to the tenth generation, none of his descendants may enter the assembly of the Lord." What is described here is traditionally known as a bastard in older versions of the Bible, but also includes those born as a result of incest or prohibited degrees of relationship.[7] Even though the child born of such a forbidden union is innocent of the circumstances of his or her birth, the defect prohibits the child from entering the assembly of the Lord. The same is true for the person's descendants even to the tenth generation, which is another way of saying "forever" (Deut. 23:3).[8] The sanctity of the holy assembly must be protected. Does this mean that a person born of such a union is not welcome to worship God with us today? Before we answer, let us go on and consider the third group excluded.

Those from Nations That Opposed God's People Are Excluded from the Holy Assembly, Either Permanently or Temporarily

Moses writes in Deuteronomy 23:3–4:

> No Ammonite or Moabite may enter the assembly of the Lord. Even to the tenth generation, none of them may enter the assembly of the Lord forever, because they did not meet you with bread and with water on the way, when

7. BDB, s.v. "מזר," 561.
8. Tigay, *Deuteronomy*, 211.

> you came out of Egypt, and because they hired against you Balaam the son of Beor from Pethor of Mesopotamia, to curse you.

Ammonites and Moabites are forbidden from ever being a part of the holy assembly because they did not support—and even resisted—God's purposes for his holy people.[9] Specifically, Moab is called out for hiring Balaam to curse the people of God (Num. 22:1–6). When the king of Moab hired Balaam, the king said: "Come now, curse this people for me, since they are too mighty for me. Perhaps I shall be able to defeat them and drive them from the land, for I know that he whom you bless is blessed, and he whom you curse is cursed" (v. 6). Those words should sound familiar because they are almost exactly what God had promised to Abraham many years before: "I will bless those who bless you, and him who dishonors you I will curse" (Gen. 12:3). The question is, who has the power to bless and curse? Balaam did attempt to curse God's people, but he could not do so. Deuteronomy 23:5 explains, "But the LORD your God would not listen to Balaam; instead the LORD your God turned the curse into a blessing for you, because the LORD your God loved you." God's love for his people not only prevented Balaam from cursing them, but actually caused Balaam to pronounce blessings over them. What a wonderful reminder that the worst that our enemies try to do to us must ultimately be turned in the hand of our God for our good and blessing!

Though Balaam could not curse the people of God, God still brings the Moabites under a curse for the attempt and forbids them from ever being part of his holy assembly. He also forbids the people of God from pursuing Moab's and Ammon's good (Deut. 23:6). These nations have opposed God's purposes for his people; therefore, they can never fully be part of his people.[10]

Alongside the Ammonites and Moabites, two other nations are mentioned in a significantly different light. Moses writes in Deuteronomy 23:7–8: "You

9. One difficulty that has been almost entirely ignored by evangelical commentators is the fact that Deuteronomy 2:29 describes the Moabites as having supplied Israel with food and water. McConville suggests that the implication that Moab actually helped Israel may just be the rhetoric of war. J. G. McConville, *Deuteronomy*, ApOTC 5 (Inter-Varsity Press, 2002), 349. Additionally, Moab and Ammon were nations produced from an incestuous union described in Genesis 19:30–38, which may be the connection with Deuteronomy 23:2. Yet the explicit reason given for their exclusion is not their incestuous heritage but their opposition to God's purposes for his people.

10. We know that this law was later applied in the days of Nehemiah (Neh. 13:1–3).

shall not abhor an Edomite, for he is your brother. You shall not abhor an Egyptian, because you were a sojourner in his land. Children born to them in the third generation may enter the assembly of the LORD." A couple of things are surprising about these two verses. First, the fact that Edom (Esau) is Israel's (Jacob's) brother is sufficient reason for Israel not to abhor the Edomites, even though the Edomites did not let the Israelites pass through their land when they were coming out of Egypt (Num. 20:14–21). Second, the Israelites are not to abhor the Egyptians because they sojourned in Egypt. It is interesting that Moses refers to their more than four hundred years in Egypt as "sojourning." Perhaps this is because the slavery portion was only the latter part of those many years. Regardless, Edomites and Egyptians will eventually be allowed into the assembly of the Lord in the third generation—but of course, only if they abandon their gods to serve the one true God alone.

These verses teach us that God has the right to accept or deny admission into his holy assembly. It is not the people of God who get to decide who may be a part of his assembly; it is God himself. The keeping out of these various people seems harsh to us, but only because we have such a low view of God's holiness and sovereignty. Few things offend us more than the idea that God chooses who may worship him or come into his presence. Yet even within the Old Testament, we see God's making a way for those excluded from his assembly to ultimately be included in his assembly if they forsake their false gods and put their trust in him alone. The book of Ruth is the story of a Moabite woman's being included in Israel as part of the people of God. Not only was she included, but her great-grandson (David) became the greatest king in Israel's history (Ruth 4:17), and her many times great-grandson (Jesus) became the greatest King in all history (Matt. 1:5–6, 16)!

In addition to the story of Ruth, we read another word of hope for those excluded from full membership in the holy assembly offered through the prophet Isaiah:

> Let not the foreigner who has joined himself to the LORD say,
> "The LORD will surely separate me from his people";
> and let not the eunuch say,
> "Behold, I am a dry tree."
> For thus says the LORD:

"To the eunuchs who keep my Sabbaths,
who choose the things that please me
and hold fast my covenant,
I will give in my house and within my walls
a monument and a name
better than sons and daughters;
I will give them an everlasting name
that shall not be cut off.

"And the foreigners who join themselves to the LORD,
to minister to him, to love the name of the LORD,
and to be his servants,
everyone who keeps the Sabbath and does not profane it,
and holds fast my covenant—
these I will bring to my holy mountain,
and make them joyful in my house of prayer;
their burnt offerings and their sacrifices
will be accepted on my altar;
for my house shall be called a house of prayer
for all peoples."
The Lord GOD,
who gathers the outcasts of Israel, declares,
"I will gather yet others to him
besides those already gathered." (Isa. 56:3–8)

What a tremendous set of promises God extends to the foreigner, to the sexually broken, and to all the outcasts in Israel! Isaiah declares a day when the true people of God will include all those who hold fast to God's covenant, regardless of their nationality, physical defects, or illegitimate births. While we get glimpses of it in the Old Testament, this radical inclusion comes to its fullest expression through the proclamation of the gospel. It is remarkable when we read the story of the Ethiopian eunuch in Acts 8 and discover that one of the earliest singled-out converts to Christianity was both a eunuch and a foreigner, and he was reading the book of Isaiah![11] The Spirit explicitly

11. Christopher Wright, *Deuteronomy*, NIBC: Old Testament 4 (Hendrickson, 2007), 248.

led Philip to go to this man and tell him the good news about Jesus. As soon as the man believed, God provided water for him to be baptized with and thus be fully identified with the holy assembly of God's people!

Under the old covenant, no eunuch could have fully been a part of the holy assembly of God's people. Likewise, no man who attempted to transition to a female could have enjoyed fellowship in the presence of God. But under the new covenant, even someone who has undergone a sex-change operation can have access into the presence of God—not on the basis of the person's own holiness or wholeness, but on the basis of the holiness of Jesus Christ imputed to all who repent and believe the gospel. The same goes for people from every nation, tribe, and tongue, even those who explicitly opposed God's work as the apostle Paul did (1 Cor. 15:9). No one is left out, no one is excluded, and all can be a part of the holy assembly by keeping God's covenant through faith.

What does this mean for us? It means embracing Jesus Christ as our Lord and Savior. It means trusting that his death on the cross paid the debt for our sins, our brokenness, and all our imperfections. It was his death that fulfilled the law of God, opening the way for all of God's chosen people to come in (Eph. 2:11–22). Jesus opens the way for full participation in the worshiping community of God's people, not just for Israelites, but even for Moabites. Not just for the ritually clean, but for the ritually unclean. Not just for the moral, but for the immoral. Faith in Jesus alone is what is required for someone to be a full participant in God's holy assembly.

Because God Is Holy, We Must Keep Ourselves from Every Evil Thing

We read in Deuteronomy 23:9, "When you are encamped against your enemies, then you shall keep yourself from every evil thing." Keeping oneself from every evil thing would seem to be a good thing to do all the time, not simply when encamped against one's enemies. The word "evil" (*ra'*) here may mean "unclean," though there is a better word for that (*tame'*) if this is the point. For a member of God's holy people, keeping oneself from evil and uncleanness was important all the time, but it was especially important during holy war. We should also remember that the various rules in Israel that related to purity and cleanness were for the people's own protection.

God is holy, and he calls his people to be holy. When the holy encounters someone or something unclean, it is like putting a butter knife into an electrical outlet. God's people must not be so careless.

Verses 10–14 of Deuteronomy 23 appear to give two specific examples of the kinds of "evil" things from which the people of God need to keep themselves. Moses writes in verses 10–11: "If any man among you becomes unclean because of a nocturnal emission, then he shall go outside the camp. He shall not come inside the camp, but when evening comes, he shall bathe himself in water, and as the sun sets, he may come inside the camp." A "nocturnal emission" is literally a "chance or accident of the night."[12] In today's parlance, it is typically referred to as a "wet dream." The Bible is less squeamish on these topics than most of us are, though Deuteronomy is helping us to overcome our squeamishness. The fact is that the Bible deals with the real stuff of life and equips us with how to think about real-life issues such as nocturnal emissions.

Is a nocturnal emission sinful? The Hebrew words themselves give us a clue by calling it a "chance or accident of the night." Those who have experienced a nocturnal emission (and those who study such things) know that it is an involuntary occurrence usually connected with a sexual dream. Some people have a measure of control over their dreams, but most people do not. Generally, nocturnal emissions do occur more frequently when a person has been dwelling on sexual thoughts or even intentionally exposing himself to sexually stimulating material, so sin may be involved. But that is not always the case. Particularly for teenagers and young men who are practicing self-control and not engaging in sexual sin (such as masturbation or any kind of sexual intercourse outside marriage), there is an increased likelihood of a nocturnal emission. Such would have been the case with these young men in the army, who were not engaging in sexual intercourse with their wives (or anyone else). In the army camp of Israel, the fact that the man who had a nocturnal emission had to go outside the camp as unclean does not necessarily mean that his nocturnal emission was sinful, but rather that it was contrary to God's designs for seminal emission and incompatible with the holiness of the camp. But no punishment was to be handed down for this, unlike in the case of adultery and other sexual sins. We should not

12. BDB, s.v. "קָרֶה," 899.

expose ourselves to sexually stimulating material, whether pornography in its more graphic forms or softer forms such as most music videos and much of what is on social media. Aiming to guard our hearts, particularly by guarding what our eyes see, is a key step (especially for men) in minimizing sexual stimulation. Richard Baxter directs, "Suffer not your thoughts, or tongue, or actions to run sinfully upon that in the day, which you would not dream sinfully of in the night."[13] Stoking our lust by intentionally exposing ourselves to stimulating material is sin.

At the same time, especially during our teen years and beyond, sexual desire is very strong, and hormones are normally changing. To experience sexual desire for a person of the opposite sex is a God-given desire, though it must be brought into submission to Jesus, and we should not dwell on such thoughts. Nevertheless, it is very common for teens, especially males, to experience a nocturnal emission. What should we do if it happens? If we have been dwelling on sexually stimulating thoughts, then we ought to confess that to God and possibly to a friend, and ask God's forgiveness. But in any case, we ought not to dwell on this or beat ourselves up for it. We should immediately give it to Jesus, whose blood cleanses us from every sin and uncleanness, and resolve to keep our hearts and minds holy by directing them to that which is honorable, lovely, and pure (Phil. 4:8).

The second "evil" situation is found in Deuteronomy 23:12–13: "You shall have a place outside the camp, and you shall go out to it. And you shall have a trowel with your tools, and when you sit down outside, you shall dig a hole with it and turn back and cover up your excrement." The basics of this situation are that the army camp needs to have a latrine area separate from the living quarters of the soldiers. A hole is to be dug, and then later covered over once a person has made the "deposit." The health of many people around the world could be dramatically improved just by practicing this one simple, sanitary procedure. But the primary point is not about hygiene. It is about holiness—namely, God's holiness. The reason why they must bury their excrement outside the camp is given in verse 14: "Because the LORD your God walks in the midst of your camp, to deliver you and to give up your enemies before you, therefore your camp must be

13. Richard Baxter, *A Christian Directory*, in *The Practical Works of Richard Baxter*, 4 vols. (Soli Deo Gloria, 2008), 1:341.

holy, so that he may not see anything indecent among you and turn away from you."

Deuteronomy 23:14 is the key to this whole section.[14] It is God's presence among his people that calls for holiness among them, including what they are to do when they are unclean and how to keep that which is unclean away from God's presence. The evil thing from which they are to be diligent to keep themselves is not the emission of semen or defecation, both of which are part of God's design for us. What was evil was being unclean in the presence of the holy God and not being cognizant of God's presence in their midst.

When we think about our sins, what bothers us most about them? That we feel defeated by them? That they make us miserable? While those things are true, they reflect a self-centered view of sin. We mostly think of sin in terms of how it affects us. But we need to increasingly see sin as an offense against a holy God. First and foremost, our sins should grieve us because they grieve the heart of our God. We can become comfortable and familiar with our sins, but God never does. He hates them, and we should hate them for his sake.

Practically speaking, this means that we, like Israel, out of reverence for God, need to "keep [ourselves] from every evil thing." What does that mean? When we come to the New Testament and the ministry of Jesus, we discover that God's primary concern is not with matters of ritual purity or impurity, but with ethics, morality, justice, and matters of the heart. The Pharisees in Jesus' day were caught up in ritual purity, and Jesus redirects their thinking: "Do you not see that whatever goes into the mouth passes into the stomach and is expelled? But what comes out of the mouth proceeds from the heart, and this defiles a person. For out of the heart come evil thoughts, murder, adultery, sexual immorality, theft, false witness, slander. These are what defile a person. But to eat with unwashed hands does not defile anyone" (Matt. 15:17–20). Jesus presses beyond ritual purity to the holiness of heart that the law was aiming at. The things that pass into our mouths will pass out the other end and can be dealt with by burial. But the matters of the heart that Jesus addresses can be buried only at the foot of the cross. What

14. J. Gary Millar, *Now Choose Life: Theology and Ethics in Deuteronomy*, NSBT 6 (Apollos, 1998), 138.

the Pharisees, and all of us, must keep from are the kinds of sins that arise from our own hearts. How can we do this practically?

First, we must acknowledge that it is God himself who cleanses our hearts by faith (Acts 15:9) and makes us holy by the blood of Jesus (1 John 1:7). If we have not trusted in Christ, we are not holy, and we cannot be clean, no matter how good our lives look on the outside. But no matter how messy our lives are on the outside, if we have put our trust in Jesus, we are clean. On that basis, we are accepted by God into his holy family, the church. Then, as part of his holy people and recognizing that he dwells not only in our midst, but in our hearts, we must be diligent to put away all sin. Paul writes, "Since we have these promises, beloved, let us cleanse ourselves from every defilement of body and spirit, bringing holiness to completion in the fear of God" (2 Cor. 7:1). We could go right down the list of all the things Jesus mentioned that defile us. By the power of the Spirit dwelling in us, we must put away those things as contrary to the heart of God. In their place, we are now to bring forth the fruit of the Spirit (Gal. 5:22–24). God dwells within us. Because that is true, we need to remove from our life all that is contrary to his holiness.

Bobby Moore was conscious of his dirty hands as he went up to Queen Elizabeth to receive that World Cup trophy, and he sought to cleanse them before he got there. We may be conscious of our own dirty hands today too. We cannot cleanse our hands before we come to our holy God, but he invites us to come to him as we are, dirty as we may be, and he will cleanse us of every stain (1 John 1:9). So let us go to him. As his covenant people made clean, let us be diligent to keep ourselves from every evil thing that would offend his holiness and prevent our happiness.

37

Do Not Take Advantage

Deuteronomy 23:15—24:4

You may charge a foreigner interest, but you may not charge your brother interest, that the Lord your God may bless you in all that you undertake in the land that you are entering to take possession of it. (Deut. 23:20)

It has been said, "The difference between Western culture and other cultures is that in the West human beings exploit other human beings, whereas elsewhere in the world, it is the other way around."[1] To take advantage of other human beings, or to exploit them, seems as natural to us as breathing. Hardly a day goes by that I do not receive a phone call, email, or text message from some unscrupulous person trying to take advantage of me by way of a scam. Odds are that the same is true for you. In 2020, nearly half of all U.S. citizens became victims of some form of identity theft. In 2021, Americans reported losing more than $5.8 billion to fraud, an increase of $2.4 billion from 2020.[2]

1. "Reflections," *Christianity Today*, May 22, 2000, 84.

2. Federal Trade Commission, *Consumer Sentinel Network Data Book 2021*, February 2022, https://www.ftc.gov/system/files/ftc_gov/pdf/CSN%20Annual%20Data%20Book%202021%20Final%20PDF.pdf.

But taking advantage of others comes in many forms besides scams and fraud. Just across our southern border, human smugglers known as "coyotes" charge anywhere from $7,000 to $15,000 to bring migrants across the border from South and Central America. Throngs of people trying to escape the poverty of failed states have no better hope than to put their lives and savings into the hands of these cartels, which might enslave, assault, or even kill them along the way. Likewise, criminals in eastern Europe and other parts of the world promise young ladies jobs and modeling careers, only to steal their passports and trap them in the living hell of sexual trafficking.

Closer to home, a nationwide study of state lotteries by the Howard Center for Investigative Journalism at the University of Maryland found that lottery retailers are disproportionately clustered in lower-income communities in every state. Why is that? Because those with less money to spend are the most likely to spend it on lottery tickets. The study also revealed the practice of establishing check-cashing businesses in poor neighborhoods that charge exorbitant fees for instant cash and that then sell those same people lottery tickets. While most of my fellow Floridians who support the lottery do so because of the money it puts into the education system, the fact is that state lotteries transfer money from the lowest 10 percent of Americans to the rest of us who benefit from the education. Our lotteries are disproportionately milking the poor and minorities to pay for education. This is not acceptable, and it is not how God intended humans to live. While we cannot control the behaviors of the world at large, as God's covenant people we are called to show the world a different way to be human.

As we have seen at numerous points along the way, much of Deuteronomy 12–26 is tracing the outline of the Ten Commandments. In this passage, several of the laws appear to relate to the eighth commandment, "You shall not steal" (Deut. 5:19). The correlation of each command to the eighth commandment is not perfect, but we can see a pattern. Each of these loosely connected laws is calling God's people to live differently from the world around them. Specifically, we can say that as God's covenant people, we must not take advantage of our neighbors, but instead we should seek their best interests. In other words, we should love them. Discussing how to do so will take up the rest of this chapter.

Do Not Take Advantage of the Refugee Slave

Moses writes in Deuteronomy 23:15–16: "You shall not give up to his master a slave who has escaped from his master to you. He shall dwell with you, in your midst, in the place that he shall choose within one of your towns, wherever it suits him. You shall not wrong him." Here we have one of the most stunning laws in all the Old Testament, especially when compared to the rest of the ancient world. In the ancient Near East, there were not only laws forbidding running away, but also international treaties requiring allied states to extradite runaway slaves.[3] But Israel was to be a sanctuary nation. When a slave escaped from his master and came to the people of God, they were not to give him up to his master. If a slave was merely a piece of property, then it would not be right *not* to return the slave. We have already seen in Deuteronomy that if a man's animal breaks loose, his neighbor has a responsibility to return it to him, or at least take care of it for him until the owner comes seeking it. But clearly, a slave is not a piece of property. If the slave gets free, he is to remain free. He is not to be taken advantage of but treated well. The refugee was free to live within one of the Israelite towns wherever he pleased. For one of God's people to return the slave would be to "wrong him." Of course, there are other ways to wrong people who have fled their homes and are living with only the clothes on their back. But God's people are not to wrong them.

These verses became one of the rallying points for American abolitionists in the 1800s after the passage of the Fugitive Slave Act in 1850.[4] The act required Americans to return slaves to their masters, even across state lines.[5] It also forbade hiding or helping runaway slaves. It is hard to imagine a law more contrary to the one we find in Deuteronomy. So how did Christians in the nineteenth-century American South read these verses in Deuteronomy so as to justify returning slaves to their masters? One argument was that because their slave-owning brothers in the South were not pagans, to return

3. Jeffrey H. Tigay, *Deuteronomy*, JPSTC (Jewish Publication Society, 1996), 215.

4. The full text of the act can be read here: https://www.battlefields.org/learn/primary-sources/fugitive-slave-act.

5. One antislavery hymn from that era went like this: "Where human law o'errules divine, Beneath the sheriff's hammer fell My wife and babes—I call them mine,—And where they suffer, who can tell? The hounds are baying on my track, O Christian! will you send me back?" "The Fugitive Slave to the Christian" (1844).

a slave to his master was not like returning a slave from Israel to a heathen land.[6] Additionally, the more sophisticated defenders of the institution of slavery did not claim to actually own the person of the slave, but simply claimed the right to the slave's labor.[7]

Nevertheless, a minister by the name of William Thayer printed a sermon demonstrating that the Fugitive Slave Act was unbiblical.[8] From these verses in Deuteronomy, Thayer deduced three truths: (1) The existence of this law in Deuteronomy implied a wrong in slavery itself. Even if the law protected only people fleeing to Israel from other nations, it still implied that those slaves were escaping a wrong. (2) This law implied that a slave had a right to his freedom, and Moses' words would have induced a slave to attempt to get freedom. If freedom were not right, Moses would have been inducing people to sin. (3) It implied that the master had no right to withhold freedom from his slave, and so to hold him in slavery was to do injustice to the slave. Ultimately, Americans came to the same conclusion, but not without a fight.

We do not have legalized slavery in the West today. But we do have many people fleeing to Western nations as refugees from oppressive conditions that may be very similar to that of slavery. I do not believe that this text gives instructions for how any nation needs to act with regard to immigrants and refugees. No modern nation is God's covenant people. But I do believe that the general equity of these biblical laws tells us, as the church, what our posture should be toward those fleeing to us for refuge: a posture of welcome, support, and safety. If the churches in our local communities

6. Moses Stuart, *Conscience and the Constitution* (Crocker & Brewster, 1850), 30–32.

7. "The true definition of the term, as applicable to the domestic institution in the Southern States, is as follows: Slavery is the duty and obligation of the slave to labor for the mutual benefit of both master and slave, under a warrant to the slave of protection, and a comfortable subsistence, under all circumstances. The person of the slave is not property, no matter what the fictions of the law may say; but the right to his labor is property, and may be transferred like any other property, or as the right to the services of a minor or an apprentice may be transferred. Nor is the labor of the slave solely for the benefit of the master, but for the benefit of all concerned; for himself, to repay the advances made for his support in childhood, for present subsistence, and for guardianship and protection, and to accumulate a fund for sickness, disability, and old age. The master, as the head of the system, has a right to the obedience and labor of the slave, but the slave has also his mutual rights in the master; the right of protection, the right of counsel and guidance, the right of subsistence, the right of care and attention in sickness and old age. He has also a right in his master as the sole arbiter in all his wrongs and difficulties, and as a merciful judge and dispenser of law to award the penalty of his misdeeds." E. N. Elliott, *Cotton Is King, and Pro-Slavery Arguments* (Pritchard, Abbott & Loomis, 1860), vii.

8. William M. Thayer, "A Sermon on Moses' Fugitive Slave Bill," preached at Ashland, MA, November 3, 1850 (Charles C. P. Moody, 1850), 6.

across this country (and others) reached out to those coming to us to help them find a place to live, learn our language, navigate a very lengthy and expensive immigration process, and, most importantly, know and follow Jesus, the current immigration problem could become an immigration blessing. Every nation has a right to determine who may cross its borders and under what conditions for the good of its citizens. Christians may have differing ideas about what those policies should be. But as private citizens, Christians should have no confusion over how to treat the person made in God's image standing before us.

Do Not Take Advantage of the Sinful Vices of Others

Moses continues expounding on what love looks like when he writes:

> None of the daughters of Israel shall be a cult prostitute, and none of the sons of Israel shall be a cult prostitute. You shall not bring the fee of a prostitute or the wages of a dog into the house of the Lord your God in payment for any vow, for both of these are an abomination to the Lord your God. (Deut. 23:17–18)

Two things are forbidden: being a cult prostitute and using the proceeds from prostitution as payment for a vow. A cult prostitute (*kadesh*) is literally a "holy person," not in the sense of morally pure, but "set apart." The more common word for "prostitute" is *zonah*. Scholars debate whether cult prostitutes were ever present in ancient Israel, or anywhere else in the ancient Near East during the biblical period.[9] If there were in fact men and women performing sexual services in the worship of foreign gods, it was likely a reflection of the common belief that the processes of nature were controlled by the relationships between various gods and goddesses. The worshipers believed that by engaging in sexual intercourse with devotees of the shrine, this would encourage gods and goddesses to do the same, which would lead to fertility for their own herds and fields.[10] But whether these are cult prostitutes or prostitutes of the more traditional variety, it is safe to say that none of God's covenant people should be prostitutes of any sort. In our technological age,

9. For the case that they likely did not exist, see Jeffrey H. Tigay, "Excursus 22: The Alleged Practice of Cultic Prostitution in the Ancient Near East," in *Deuteronomy*, 480–81.

10. Jackie A. Naudé, *NIDOTTE*, s.v. "קָדֵשׁ," 3:883.

people can now earn money by prostituting themselves online through images and video. This would also be precluded by God's commands.

The text goes beyond forbidding prostitution among God's people and adds that the fee of a prostitute and the wages of a dog (probably a reference to the male prostitute) are not to be given in payment of any vow. Money earned through sexual sin or sexual exploitation is not fit for fulfilling a vow to a holy God. We could even say more broadly that money gained from any objectionable sources is not fit for a gift to the Lord. If money earned is not fit for being given to our God, then we should conclude that it is not fit for us to earn it at all.

Are there other sources of income that are not fit for giving to the Lord's work? We might add that money gained through extortion, through immoral business dealings, through theft, or through taking advantage of the poor is all considered dirty money. Rather than trying to list every possible source of dubious income, we should reflect on the sources of our income, including the companies that we are invested in. Are we making money from exploited persons? Are we profiting from people's addictions?

When I was still a college student and just getting into investing, one of the first stocks I bought was Philip Morris, the old tobacco company. But as I grew in my walk with Christ, I was convicted that I should not be a partial owner (albeit a very small one) in a company that makes its money by getting people hooked on nicotine while giving them cancer. It was a personal decision, but we each must apply what we understand of the Scripture to our particular situations. In our current economy, it is difficult to be involved at all without being somehow connected with unrighteous wealth. One alternative is to withdraw from the marketplace completely, but that would run counter to our role as salt and light. Instead, we should evaluate the sources of our income and determine whether we can offer that money to our holy God without shame.

I am reminded of two stories of the redemption of people who gained money in sinful ways. The first is Zacchaeus, who exploited people as a tax collector (Luke 19:1–10). After he met Jesus, he more than repaid to people what he had stolen. The second is the story of the woman in Luke 7:36–50 who is described as a sinner, a polite way of saying that she was a prostitute. When she met Jesus, she took an alabaster jar filled with precious perfume. It is hard to imagine that she got this alabaster jar from any source other than her work as a prostitute. When she met Jesus, she fell at his feet and broke the jar to anoint him. The others present recoiled at her gift, but Jesus saw it as a beautiful thing. He received the offering of the prostitute. To be clear, this was not the payment of a vow. Nor is it an endorsement of making money as a prostitute. But it is a visible sign that for those who have made money in ways they regret and seek to be reconciled to God through Jesus, they can be, and they may even give of what they have gained in wrong ways as a sign of the sincerity of their repentance.

Do Not Take Advantage of the Poor

The next law promotes love of neighbors by forbidding us from taking financial advantage of them. Moses continues in Deuteronomy 23:19–20:

> You shall not charge interest on loans to your brother, interest on money, interest on food, interest on anything that is lent for interest. You may charge a foreigner interest, but you may not charge your brother interest, that the Lord your God may bless you in all that you undertake in the land that you are entering to take possession of it.[11]

The people of God were not to charge interest to others in the family of God. When we think of interest, we think of our modern banking system and loans taken for the purchase of a home or to expand a business. But in ancient Israel, the kind of loan being referred to here was taken out because a man did not have money to keep a roof over his head or food on the table. He was in a desperate situation and came to his brother for help in a time of need. To charge interest to one's brother or sister in the faith at a time like this was to profit from that person's destitution.[12] Instead of asking how he could profit from his neighbor's desperate condition, the brother should have been seeking to get his neighbor out of that condition as quickly as possible.

11. This is very similar to that which is laid down in Leviticus 25:35–37: "If your brother becomes poor and cannot maintain himself with you, you shall support him as though he were a stranger and a sojourner, and he shall live with you. Take no interest from him or profit, but fear your God, that your brother may live beside you. You shall not lend him your money at interest, nor give him your food for profit."

12. Deuteronomy 24:12 indicates that some borrowers among the people of God might not be poor. Even in such a case, the prohibition against charging interest would apply.

The prohibition against charging interest did not mean that it was wrong to make money from lending altogether or that it is wrong today. Secured bank loans take into account that there are risks in lending money as well as opportunity costs. Such loans can mutually benefit the borrower and the lender. In Israel's marketplace, finances and goods could be exchanged for interest, so long as the exchange was with a foreigner and not one of the people of God. (For clarity, we need to make a distinction between the foreigner and the sojourner. The foreigner was someone like a merchant who was in Israel to buy and sell goods and do business, while the sojourner had become part of the community.)[13] The reason annexed to this command against charging interest was that "the LORD your God may bless you in all that you undertake in the land" (Deut. 23:20). Moses indicates that someone who charged interest to his brother or sister was exchanging the blessing of God for a small bit of interest. It took only a moment of reflection to realize that the little bit of money that might be earned from interest was a poor substitute for God's blessing. Rather than trying to profit from his brother's destitution at the expense of God's blessing, he would be wise to remember the words of Proverbs 19:17, "Whoever is generous to the poor lends to the LORD, and he will repay him for his deed."

The principle deduced from this Deuteronomic law is that we should not take advantage of another person's destitution or seek to profit from it. This extends beyond our friends and family as well. Jesus said: "And if you lend to those from whom you expect to receive, what credit is that to you? Even sinners lend to sinners, to get back the same amount. But love your enemies, and do good, and lend, expecting nothing in return, and your reward will be great, and you will be sons of the Most High, for he is kind to the ungrateful and the evil" (Luke 6:34–35). As private individuals, we should give freely, even to our enemies.

We also find implications for our churches, where we may encounter brothers or sisters in need. Biblically speaking, there are practical benefits to being a part of the family of God. In our local church and many others, we encourage our members in financial need to turn to their church family for help, rather than turning to a credit card. We will help them. Part of that help may be determining whether they really need whatever it is they are

13. Daniel I. Block, *Deuteronomy*, NIVAC (Zondervan, 2012), 548.

thinking of financing with a credit card. Part of that help might be retooling their budget with them so that they are not under such financial pressure in the future. But part of that help might be either lending or giving them money they need at no interest so that they do not create a pile of debt that they cannot escape. There are benefits of being in a family, including a church family, and this is one of them. We cannot promise that if someone is not a member of our church, we will help, but if the person is a member, we will help somehow, because we are one body, and others' problems are our problems.[14]

Do Not Take Advantage of the Lord

After forbidding taking advantage of one another financially, the law now forbids taking advantage of the Lord. Moses continues in Deuteronomy 23:21–23:

> If you make a vow to the Lord your God, you shall not delay fulfilling it, for the Lord your God will surely require it of you, and you will be guilty of sin. But if you refrain from vowing, you will not be guilty of sin. You shall be careful to do what has passed your lips, for you have voluntarily vowed to the Lord your God what you have promised with your mouth.

This law is about making formal commitments to God in the form of vows.[15] On the one hand, these verses do not require anyone to make vows. Vows are voluntary commitments. If we do make a vow, however, it becomes binding, and if we break it, we are guilty of sin. For example, one common and informal vow made among those in school sounds like this: "Lord, I am not ready for this test today. But if you will get me through this, I promise that I will start reading my Bible and will not be so unprepared for another test again!" Breaking a vow is a form of stealing because what has been vowed belongs to another person—in this case, God.[16] Therefore, we should be

14. In Galatians 6:10, Paul continues to uphold the differing levels of priority in our care toward those inside and outside the church: "So then, as we have opportunity, let us do good to everyone, and especially to those who are of the household of faith." We seek to do what we can for all, but we make our brothers and sisters in Christ a priority.

15. Ecclesiastes 5:4–7 includes very similar instruction.

16. Block, *Deuteronomy*, 548–49.

very careful in making vows, and once we have made them, we should be very careful to fulfill them.

We do not frequently make vows to the Lord under the new covenant except in a few instances. One of those instances is when a man takes his ordination vows as an elder or deacon.

Another occasion is when a person is baptized or makes membership vows to a local church. We strongly encourage church membership, but taking membership vows should not be done lightly. One of those vows in many churches is a commitment to "support the church in its worship and work to the best of your ability." This is not a vow that anyone should make lightly. Disregarding these vows or breaking them is not simply breaking them with the church, but breaking them with the Lord of the church. When we vow to give something, we must give it, and to not give it is to steal back what we have promised.

A third common occasion of vows is that of wedding vows. These vows are made to a new husband or wife, but they are also made in the presence of God. He is a witness to the commitment we are making, and when we break that commitment, he is likewise a witness of it. Such vows are not to be entered into lightly, nor are they to be broken once made. To keep one's vows is a mark of righteousness. The psalmist asks in Psalm 15:1, "Who shall dwell on your holy hill?" A number of characteristics are described, but two of them are laid out for us in this passage: "He . . . who swears to his own hurt and does not change; who does not put out his money at interest" (Ps. 15:2–5). Sometimes keeping our vows is painful, but that is what we do because that is who we are. The reason why we make vows to begin with is that we realize that what we are vowing is a good thing to do, but also that a time might come when we do not want to do it. In such times, our vow serves as a means of holding us fast to what we declared was important in a clearer moment. Our identity as God's people must work its way out in very practical ways, such as keeping our word and sharing our resources.

Do Not Take Advantage of Your Neighbor's Generosity

Not taking advantage of the Lord leads into a law forbidding taking advantage of a neighbor's generosity. Moses writes: "If you go into your neighbor's vineyard, you may eat your fill of grapes, as many as you wish, but you shall not put any in your bag. If you go into your neighbor's standing grain, you may pluck the ears with your hand, but you shall not put a sickle to your neighbor's standing grain" (Deut. 23:24–25). Here is a similar principle to the one regarding interest. Neighbors have a responsibility to take care of one another's needs. But this is not to be taken advantage of by scurrilous people who go and raid their neighbor's vineyard or field. The intention is that none of God's people should starve while there is food available, and at the same time no one should make their living from a generous neighbor's back. This social safety net in ancient Israel allowed the hungry to pluck grain and eat grapes from anyone's field or vineyard. In the New Testament, Jesus' disciples made use of this principle when they passed through a field, plucking ears of grain with their hands (Luke 6:1). The land was the Lord's, after all, and all its produce came from him. So no one was to take advantage of the social safety net by going beyond gleaning to essentially reaping a neighbor's crops.

One thing that this passage shows us is that among the people of God, a hungry brother's need for food supersedes a crop-holding brother's rights to his entire harvest. In other words, the man with the farm has a *right* to all the produce from his land. But if his brother has a *need* for sustenance, his need supersedes the farmer's right to harvest all his own produce.[17]

What if we in the church started thinking this way about our possessions and even our work? On the one hand, those of us who are working have a right to the entirety of what we earn. But what if a brother or sister is in need of food or shelter? That person's need supersedes our rights. To value our things above people runs counter to the command to love our neighbor as ourselves. There is no requirement to give per se, but to refuse to do so runs counter to love of neighbor,[18] and those who are beneficiaries of generosity must not take advantage. If we have a need, this passage tells us, we are right to go to the family of God to seek help without shame. It also

17. Christopher J. H. Wright, *Old Testament Ethics for the People of God* (InterVarsity Press, 2004), 312–14.

18. Or consider this example that we also find in the New Testament. We have a right to eat or drink whatever we want. But our brother stumbles when we drink wine. Which is the higher priority: our rights or our brother's weakness? The answer Paul gives in line with Deuteronomy is that our brother's weakness takes priority over our rights (Rom. 14:20–21; 1 Cor. 8:11–13).

warns that we do not have a right to make our living from the generosity of God's people.

Do Not Take Advantage of a Divorce

We now come to the only law in the Old Testament regarding divorce. Indeed, the law itself is not even regulating divorce, but considers a specific case in which remarriage is not allowed after divorce. Without regurgitating the entirety of Deuteronomy 24:1–4, we can paraphrase it this way: Bill divorces Sally because of some "indecency" in her, and she goes off and marries Mike. If Mike dies or divorces Sally, Bill is not allowed to remarry Sally "after she has been defiled, for that is an abomination before the LORD" (Deut. 24:4).

Why was it considered defiling for Bill to remarry Sally after she has been married to Mike? No one knows for certain. There are as many interpretations of these verses as there are commentators. This passage was even a subject of debate in Jesus' day between two major rabbinical schools. But in keeping with the character of Deuteronomy, it is likely that part of the purpose of this law was to protect the weaker person from being taken advantage of. It may have been aimed at keeping the man from casually divorcing his wife, since he knew that he could not remarry her if she remarried. It may have been aimed at keeping the first husband from potentially profiting from the wealth of her second marriage by taking her back again after it ended. But ultimately, the aim is protection.

Jesus makes it clear that divorce is not God's design for marriage (Matt. 19:1–12). His intention is that a marriage would last a lifetime, but because of the hardness of human hearts, allowances are made for divorce. As we have seen in previous chapters, part of the design of the law is to try to mitigate the negative effects of sin. In this instance, the wife is protected from the capricious designs of her husband. There was a major power imbalance in ancient Israel between the husband and wife. This law would have helped level the playing field to some degree. Divorce laws should do precisely that: help minimize the negative effects of the divorce to all parties involved.

Currently in the United States, there is more parity between men and women than there was in Israel. In some cases, a man may still have the upper hand in a divorce and take advantage of the situation. But it is also quite possible for the woman to take advantage of the situation. Among God's people, even in an unfortunate situation such as divorce, neither party should aim to take advantage.

What we have seen in each of these laws is that God's intention for his people is that we would live differently from the world around us. It might be a dog-eat-dog world out there, but it is not to be so among the people called by his name. When we are tempted to take advantage of another, we remember Jesus. Jesus had all the power. He could have rightfully taken advantage of his position over us. But instead of taking advantage, he laid down his position and took our place. He came to bear the judgment that our taking advantage of each other deserved. He paid the debt that we all owed. Now all of us who trust in him are free. We owe nothing anymore, which means that we do not need to take from one another. The only thing we owe, as God's people, is the debt of love. The apostle Paul sums it up beautifully:

> Owe no one anything, except to love each other, for the one who loves another has fulfilled the law. For the commandments, "You shall not commit adultery, You shall not murder, You shall not steal, You shall not covet," and any other commandment, are summed up in this word: "You shall love your neighbor as yourself." Love does no wrong to a neighbor; therefore love is the fulfilling of the law. (Rom. 13:8–10)

Love does no wrong to a neighbor. Love does not take advantage of a neighbor's difficult situation. Love does not exploit a neighbor's weakness. Rather, love seeks the good of others. Exploiting others may seem like second nature, and it is. But our first nature is made after the image of God, and through faith in Christ we are being remade in that image. We are no longer a people who take advantage of others, but having been loved by God, we now love one another. Instead of taking advantage of one another, let us love our neighbor as we love ourselves.

38

A Compassionate People

Deuteronomy 24:5–25:4

You shall not pervert the justice due to the sojourner or to the fatherless, or take a widow's garment in pledge, but you shall remember that you were a slave in Egypt and the Lord your God redeemed you from there; therefore I command you to do this. (Deut. 24:17–18)

In 2022, Hurricane Ian wreaked massive destruction on many in our church in Naples, Florida. In the aftermath of the hurricane, I witnessed something beautiful. I saw people set aside their work and go into people's flooded homes to haul out all their ruined possessions. I saw people put their own interests aside to take up sledgehammers and crowbars to tear out moldy drywall and flooring for their neighbors. I saw people open their homes to make room for displaced people. I saw people open their checkbooks to help meet the needs of people whom they would never meet. I saw people open their veins to give their blood to others who needed it even more than they did. I saw young and old alike serving together, making meals, scrubbing floors, and giving their own beds away to help people in their time of need. I saw a compassionate people in action. Or to put it another way, I saw the God of compassion made manifest through the people called by his name.

Our English word *compassion* comes from a Latin word meaning "suffer with." To show compassion is to enter the suffering of another in an effort to minimize or reduce it. Witnessing this kind of compassion left a tremendous impression on me, because while compassion is a biblical response to human suffering, ever since the fall, it is no longer the natural response. In an acute situation such as a natural disaster, both Christians and non-Christians alike will respond with compassion because we are all made in the image of the compassionate God. But in the day-to-day suffering of life, our proclivity is to forget that we were objects of God's compassion. Because we are born rebels against God, our natural response to human need is to think only of ourselves, and the result is that we frequently fail to show compassion. Rather than helping the poor, we are inclined to despise them for not working harder or smarter. Rather than sharing with struggling immigrants in our midst, we remind them that they did not have to come here. Rather than loving the addicted, we judge them for their weakness. Rather than having compassion on those enslaved to debt, we remind them that it serves them right.

But these verses in Deuteronomy call forth a different response from God's covenant people. Moses reminds the people of God that they were once enslaved, without hope, and unable to help themselves. Yet God stepped into their misery, demonstrated compassion, and rescued them from their affliction. Now in this series of loosely connected laws, he calls forth the same kind of compassion to be demonstrated by his covenant people.[1] As Christians, we are no longer under the law, but we are very much bound by the law of love, which finds expression through the laws in this passage. We will meditate on these laws in seven specific situations, so that we might be fashioned into a compassionate people who respond to the hurts of the world around us with the compassion that we ourselves have received.

1. There are four aspects to compassion: (1) Cognitive: recognizing that there is suffering. (2) Affective: feeling emotionally moved by that suffering. (3) Intentional: wishing there to be relief from that suffering. (4) Motivational: a readiness to take action to relieve that suffering. See Hooria Jazaieri, "Six Habits of Highly Compassionate People," *Greater Good Magazine*, April 24, 2018, https://greatergood.berkeley.edu/article/item/six_habits_of_highly_compassionate_people, accessed October 6, 2022.

HAVE COMPASSION ON THE NEWLY MARRIED

The first law in this section shows God's concern for newlyweds. Moses writes in Deuteronomy 24:5: "When a man is newly married, he shall not go out with the army or be liable for any other public duty. He shall be free at home one year to be happy with his wife whom he has taken." The Hebrew text is clearer than our English translation. It literally says that the newly married man is free for one year and that "he shall make happy his wife." God's law recognizes that the establishment of a household takes time and effort. Good marriages do not happen by accident. The phrase about "making his wife happy" probably has in view the conception of a child. Bearing children is a biblical value, and accomplishing it in a healthy marriage requires time and intimacy.

Unfortunately, we do not have the same protections for those who serve in our military as ancient Israel did. Extended deployments have been a reality for many newlyweds, and they take a definite toll on marital satisfaction and longevity. Newly married couples should make a concerted effort, in the first year particularly, to develop their relationship and enjoy the blessings of being married. They should avoid jobs requiring extensive travel shortly after getting married. They should reduce extracurricular activities and instead focus on spending time together and creating deep relational bonds. The seeds that a couple sows in those early years are not enough to make a marriage last a lifetime, but they are an invaluable start and strong foundation on which to keep building.

This law is primarily directed to the community surrounding the newly married couple. We should do our part not to impose burdens on a newly married couple that would keep them separated for extended periods. One of the early blessings in my own marriage was that my wife and I did not have to spend a night apart for nearly four years after getting married. That is by no means required by this law, but many new marriages could reap the benefits of such a commitment. Families of newly married couples should do what they can to avoid contributing to a newlywed couple's spending time apart. Churches can be supportive by asking newlyweds to take a temporary break from their areas of service or responsibility as they invest in this most precious of human relationships. Christian employers should be cognizant of the need for their newly married employees to establish a foundation with their new spouses. As people who treasure marriage as one of God's gifts, how can we as a covenant community have compassion on the newly married and bless them?

Have Compassion on Those in Debt

Three sections in this passage have to do with how the creditor is to relate to the debtor with compassion. The first way is by protecting the debtor's life. Moses writes, "No one shall take a mill or an upper millstone in pledge, for that would be taking a life in pledge" (Deut. 24:6). Without a little cultural context, this verse does not make sense. When a person took on a debt, the lender would have a lien on the debtor's property. If the debtor did not pay, the creditor would seize what had been agreed on in advance, or whatever he wanted.[2] This law forbids the mill or upper millstone from being taken by the lender, since these objects were essential to survival.[3] Without a mill or upper millstone, a person or family could not prepare food to eat. While the lender had a right to get some collateral or pledge of repayment, it must be within reason and must not threaten the life of the borrower. The life of a person is more important than the debt owed! Historically, the mill or upper millstone was probably of little value to the lender. The purpose in seizing those items would not have been to satisfy the debt but to pressure the debtor to repay by depriving him of something essential for survival.[4] God's people are not to use such tactics that do not reflect the compassion that we have received from him.

The second way in which the creditor is to show compassion is by preserving the debtor's dignity. Instead of going into the house to get the pledge, the lender is to wait outside while the borrower brings it out. We read in Deuteronomy 24:10–11: "When you make your neighbor a loan of any sort, you shall not go into his house to collect his pledge. You shall stand outside,

2. The Hebrew word translated as "pledge" may refer to the concept of collateral for a loan, or it may refer to the confiscating of property as distraint for unpaid debts. In either case, the primary emphasis of the law remains clear. See Robin Wakely, *NIDOTTE*, s.v. "חָבַל," 2:6–8.

3. Likewise in Job 24:3, the wicked are condemned for taking the ox of a widow. So the principle of Deuteronomy 24:6 is extended to other items essential to a debtor for survival.

4. Jeffrey H. Tigay, *Deuteronomy*, JPSTC (Jewish Publication Society, 1996), 223.

and the man to whom you make the loan shall bring the pledge out to you." This restriction serves to protect the dignity of the borrower in the sight of his family and community. Just because a person borrows from a lender does not mean that he loses his right to privacy or dignity. The character Marius in Victor Hugo's classic novel *Les Misérables* resisted going into debt at great personal cost, suffering every kind of privation to avoid doing so. To him, debt was the beginning of slavery. As Hugo writes, "a creditor is worse than a master, for the master is master only of your person whereas a creditor is master of your dignity and can give it a beating."[5] He is correct, and this is precisely what creditors among the people of God are *not* to do.

The third way that a creditor is to show compassion is by honoring the humanity of the borrower. One of the primary pledges that would be given is a cloak, probably because this is one of the only pieces of personal property that a debtor might own. If that is the case, then God's people must be compassionate and return the cloak to the man to sleep in so that he does not freeze. We read in Deuteronomy 24:12–13: "And if he is a poor man, you shall not sleep in his pledge. You shall restore to him the pledge as the sun sets, that he may sleep in his cloak and bless you. And it shall be righteousness for you before the LORD your God." It is not likely that one night without his cloak would lead a man to die of exposure, but he was sure to be miserable. God's compassionate people are not to put the poor through that kind of misery. At this point, the less compassionate part of ourselves might say, "If the man gets his cloak back every night before bed, then he will never feel the pressure to pay back the loan." Be that as it may, God's covenant people are to be a compassionate people and honor the humanity of our debtors.

Lenders are to act on their faith in the Lord, honoring his Word. While it is true that a lender may never get repaid, his godliness will benefit him in important ways. First, the poor man will bless the lender (Deut. 24:13). To be blessed by the poor is a blessing that goes straight to God's heart. Second, the demonstration of such compassion will be righteousness before the Lord (v. 13). He is not describing forensic righteousness, which is the basis of our justification, but rather the very practical expression of deeds that are pleasing to God.

5. Victor Hugo, *Les Misérables*, trans. Christine Donougher, Penguin Classics Deluxe ed. (Penguin Books, 2015), 616.

Job provides us with a picture of the practical righteousness that God desires from his covenant people:

> I delivered the poor who cried for help,
> and the fatherless who had none to help him.
> The blessing of him who was about to perish came upon me,
> and I caused the widow's heart to sing for joy.
> I put on righteousness, and it clothed me;
> my justice was like a robe and a turban.
> I was eyes to the blind
> and feet to the lame.
> I was a father to the needy,
> and I searched out the cause of him whom I did not know.
> I broke the fangs of the unrighteous
> and made him drop his prey from his teeth. (Job 29:12–17)

A lender who is willing to accept the blessing of the poor and the satisfaction of having done something pleasing to God in place of a loan repayment is a lender who has been transformed by God's grace and compassion.

In Deuteronomy 24:17–18, we see similar laws prescribed, along with a command to remember how God dealt with his people: "You shall not pervert the justice due to the sojourner or to the fatherless, or take a widow's garment in pledge, but you shall remember that you were a slave in Egypt and the Lord your God redeemed you from there; therefore I command you to do this."

The antidote to perverting justice, risking a widow's well-being, and all the other abuses of debtors is for the Israelites to remember their own slavery in Egypt and how God rescued them. They know what it is to be helpless and poor. They are not to become oppressors.[6] God not only created his people, but redeemed his people, and he has a right to command his people how to treat others justly and with compassion.

We have repeatedly seen throughout Deuteronomy that the practical righteousness that God calls forth from his people begins with remembering

6. In most revolutions throughout history, when the oppressed take power, they become oppressors themselves. It is not to be the case among God's covenant people.

what God has done for us and then acting accordingly. We may have fellow Christians in our debt. Debtors should pay back their debts, especially if they are Christians. But the emphasis in this passage is on the lender. While we may ask for debts to be repaid by our brothers and sisters, we must do so in a way that protects their lives and livelihood, preserves their dignity, and honors their humanity. Such is God's heart toward us, and remembering this should move us to the same kind of compassion, not only in money matters, but in all matters.

Have Compassion on Victims of Trafficking

Kidnapping and any other form of human trafficking are condemned by the law in Deuteronomy. Moses writes: "If a man is found stealing one of his brothers of the people of Israel, and if he treats him as a slave or sells him, then that thief shall die. So you shall purge the evil from your midst" (Deut. 24:7). Notice that the penalty for trafficking a human is death because trafficking is a kind of "social murder."[7] The death penalty was not applied for stealing things; but if someone stole a person, that was worthy of death. As Myrto Theocharous concludes in her excellent essay on the subject, "The physical, psychological, and social effects human trafficking has on the victims do constitute a type of 'death' that demands to be confronted with an analogous severity in the way we perceive it, and its graveness needs to be reflected in the Church's approach to this crime."[8]

The primary way in which we can have compassion on victims of trafficking is by seeking justice on their behalf. As citizens, we can support our judicial system. As the people of God, we are to purge the evil from our midst. We should not tolerate in our churches any who participate in any part of human trafficking. If a person views pornography, that person is a participant. The viewer may not be the one enticing women (or kidnapping them), but the viewer is creating the demand that is driving an increasing supply of trafficked women and children. There are many reasons why God's people must have nothing to do with pornography, but one of them is that

7. Peter C. Craigie, *The Book of Deuteronomy*, NICOT (Eerdmans, 1976), 307.

8. Myrto Theocharous, "Stealing Souls: Human Trafficking and Deuteronomy 24:7," in *For Our Good Always: Studies on the Message and Influence of Deuteronomy in Honor of Daniel I. Block*, ed. Jason S. DeRouchie, Jason Gile, and Kenneth J. Turner (Eisenbrauns, 2013), 508.

we are to have compassion on trafficked persons, rather than sharing in their abuse and exploitation.

Have Compassion for Your Neighbor's Health

This next law seems to come out of nowhere. Moses writes in Deuteronomy 24:8: "Take care, in a case of leprous disease, to be very careful to do according to all that the Levitical priests shall direct you. As I commanded them, so you shall be careful to do." Leprous disease was likely not what we know as Hansen's disease today, but rather was any kind of infectious skin problem. Leviticus 13–14 gives extensive instruction about these skin issues as well as the process for being counted clean. The priests were responsible for diagnosing and dealing with such outbreaks, much as public health officials would do today.[9] Moses emphasizes that the priests are to be obeyed first because they have a responsibility to preserve the purity of God's people, and secondarily to help stop the spread of infection.

Then Moses writes a warning in Deuteronomy 24:9: "Remember what the Lord your God did to Miriam on the way as you came out of Egypt." In Numbers 12, God gave Miriam leprosy[10] because she spoke against God's servant Moses (Num. 12:8). Moses seems to be using her example to warn the people; disregarding the priests' instructions will have consequences. The moral purity and the physical health of God's people are not to be neglected because an infected person is inconvenienced by the law.

While this passage is difficult, like the others it is compassionate. To disregard the instructions of the priests' authority, as Miriam did, was to disregard the health of one's neighbor. Such an action runs counter to the law of love. We should be conscious of how our actions impact our neighbor's health. If we know that our child is sick, we are likely not loving our neighbor well when we send our child to school. During the days of COVID-19, many refused to observe any of the public health measures as infringements on personal freedom. The law of love would instead ask how to minimize the

9. Christopher Wright, *Deuteronomy*, NIBC: Old Testament 4 (Hendrickson, 2007), 257.

10. Most commentators fail to ask why God uses Miriam's situation as an example. She had leprosy, yes, but her sin was speaking against Moses and leprosy was the consequence. It seems to be a warning that if the Israelites neglect to heed the priests' directives regarding leprosy, they can likewise expect negative consequences for endangering their neighbors' health.

risk of harm to our neighbor's health. We can debate where the limits are to looking out for our neighbor's health, but our basic posture should be one of compassion for our neighbor's health and well-being, not rigorous insistence on our rights.

HAVE COMPASSION ON THOSE WHO WORK FOR YOU

The people in any society most likely to suffer oppression are those without the adequate ability to defend their rights, such as the poor, the widow, the orphan, and the sojourner. God's people must not oppress them. Moses writes in Deuteronomy 24:14–15: "You shall not oppress a hired worker who is poor and needy, whether he is one of your brothers or one of the sojourners who are in your land within your towns. You shall give him his wages on the same day, before the sun sets (for he is poor and counts on it), lest he cry against you to the LORD, and you be guilty of sin." A variety of ways of oppressing such people are listed in the Bible, such as using false scales (Hos. 12:7), delaying or withholding payment to a laborer (Jer. 22:13), and bribery, usury, and profit at the expense of the poor or the sojourner (Ezek. 22:12, 29). The purpose of the oppression is generally the accumulation or preservation of wealth at the expense of one's neighbor.[11] In this case, the hired worker, poor and needy, is being oppressed; his wages are being withheld. The worker described here is living hand to mouth. He has no savings. The day's wages were for the day's needs. If such a man cries out to the Lord, the one withholding his wages will be held accountable (e.g., James 5:4).

This law calls employers to think about the impact of their payment practices on their employees. Many of us work in jobs for which our pay is sufficient that we can receive it once or twice a month without feeling financial pressure. Others can live on weekly paychecks. But there are people who need to be paid immediately because that payment is the source of their next meal. Employers must demonstrate a compassionate heart and be sensitive. It is expressly forbidden to take advantage of someone's work and withhold payment just because it suits the employer.

Along these same lines, Moses writes in Deuteronomy 25:4, "You shall not muzzle an ox when it is treading out the grain." This verse is familiar

11. I. Swart, *NIDOTTE*, s.v. "עָשַׁק" 3:554.

to us because of how the apostle Paul applies it in the New Testament. In its original context, it meant that the people of God needed to show compassion to the animals that worked for them. While an ox was treading out the grain, he had a right to enjoy some of it, and to prevent him from doing so was cruel.

But the law is not exhausted by this application. Already in the New Testament, the apostle Paul draws out the principle underlying this law and uses it as the basis for arguing that those who preach the gospel should make their living from the gospel (1 Cor. 9:9; 1 Tim. 5:18). Consider how Paul applies this passage in 1 Corinthians 9:9–10: "Is it for oxen that God is concerned? Does he not certainly speak for our sake? It was written for our sake, because the plowman should plow in hope and the thresher thresh in hope of sharing in the crop." Paul is giving us a clue here about how to apply Old Testament law in the New Testament context. He says that this law was written for us, for followers of Jesus. He shows us how to apply a culturally specific Old Testament law under the terms of the new covenant.[12] It calls us to ask the question whether there are people working for us who do not get to share in the fruits of their labor. For those who hold private companies, are the people who are doing much of the work getting an appropriate share of the profits? To withhold pay that should be given is a form of stealing and breaking the eighth commandment. We are called to have a heart of compassion toward those who work for us, whether in our businesses, in our yards, or anywhere else.

Have Compassion on the Poor

The next group of laws about being compassionate toward the poor has the same motivation as the previous laws. We read in Deuteronomy 24:19: "When you reap your harvest in your field and forget a sheaf in the field, you shall not go back to get it. It shall be for the sojourner, the fatherless, and the widow, that the Lord your God may bless you in all the work of your

12. Christopher Wright writes, "Paul's hermeneutical assumption is that we can recognize the moral will of the same God behind the specific, culture-related Israelite injunction and the principle that he applies to practical rights and responsibilities within the Christian Church." Christopher J. H. Wright, *Old Testament Ethics for the People of God* (InterVarsity Press, 2004), 316. While this law itself expired with biblical Israel, Paul demonstrates what the "general equity thereof may require." See WCF 19.4.

hands." Moses then goes on in verses 20 and 21 to say the same thing about olive trees and grapes. The farmer has a right to the entirety of the harvest in the field, grove, or vineyard, except for the very last part. He is to leave some of the harvest intentionally for the most vulnerable in the population to collect for themselves. If he leaves some of the fruit on the vine and produce in the field, he will receive the blessing of the Lord on all his work. It is a question of trust: will he trust in his harvest for his provision, or will he trust in the Lord of the harvest? The Bible is not opposed to harvesting a profit, but compassion toward the poor and vulnerable is more important than the bottom line.

This method of providing for the poor and vulnerable in Israel still allowed the poor to do something for their provision. No one brought the olives, grapes, or sheaves and dropped them at the feet of the poor. The poor had to go into the field and collect the sheaves; they had to climb the trees and get the remaining olives; they had to work the vineyard and find the remaining grapes. There was effort involved. When caring for the poor, we should look for ways to enable them to provide for themselves, and ways that *encourage* industriousness rather than *penalize* it.

What are some practical ways that we can have compassion on the most vulnerable among us today that allows them to earn provisions? The government attempts to do this through policy, but it is far more effective when it is done privately and through individuals. One of the best ways to help the working poor is to pay them well for a job well done. Likewise, those who lead companies or serve on boards might ask this question: what would it look like to leave some olives on the tree as additional provision for those in our company who have less? In other words, rather than maximizing profit by paying employees the minimum necessary, what would it look like to leave more gleanings for the working poor in our business or organization? At the same time, we should recognize that some of the poor genuinely cannot do for themselves and need a handout. The wisdom of God's Word allows God's people to be discriminating about the shape that compassion should take rather than applying a one-size-fits-all solution.

The motivation is given again in Deuteronomy 24:22: "You shall remember that you were a slave in the land of Egypt; therefore I command you to do this." This is the third time in this passage that the people are commanded to remember. Remembering has been a consistent theme all the way through

Deuteronomy. In this case, their memory that they were slaves in the land of Egypt is to motivate the compassion necessary to leave behind some of their crop so that the working poor would be provided for. We should not miss the theological underpinning of these very specific ethical commands. As God's covenant people, we are to reflect God's character, which has been revealed in his actions toward us and on our behalf. Christopher Wright observes, "The primary, compelling and repeated reason why, if you had been an Israelite, you were supposed to observe this compassionate law towards the weak, the enslaved or the impoverished was that this is the way God had actually behaved towards you, when you were in similar conditions."[13] And it is true for us as Christians as well. When we were dead in sin, he made us alive. When we were weak, he rescued us. When we were lost in sin, he came and found us. When we were poor, he became poor to make us rich. These images are given to us over and over, and we are not to forget. Instead, we are to embody these gospel realities in our practical deeds toward others. It is not simply because such actions provide opportunities for evangelism, though they do. But we are to be this kind of people because it is right and righteous in God's sight.

Have Compassion on the Innocent and the Guilty

The final section here is about justice. We read in Deuteronomy 24:16: "Fathers shall not be put to death because of their children, nor shall children be put to death because of their fathers. Each one shall be put to death for his own sin." Only the one guilty of a crime should pay for the crime. We see some exceptions to this in the Old Testament in extraordinary cases,[14] but this is the principle. It does not mean that children will not be affected by the sins of their fathers (Deut. 5:9), but means that the individual responsible for the crime must accept the legal punishment of the law. We must have compassion on the innocent and not punish them for crimes that they did not commit, and must also be sure to punish those who are guilty.

13. Wright, *Old Testament Ethics for the People of God*, 300.

14. For example, the case of Achan in Joshua 7.

But even while bringing justice, we are not to forget compassion for the criminal:

> If there is a dispute between men and they come into court and the judges decide between them, acquitting the innocent and condemning the guilty, then if the guilty man deserves to be beaten, the judge shall cause him to lie down and be beaten in his presence with a number of stripes in proportion to his offense. Forty stripes may be given him, but not more, lest, if one should go on to beat him with more stripes than these, your brother be degraded in your sight. (Deut. 25:1–3)

We observe several things here, some of which we have already seen in Deuteronomy. First, justice means that the innocent are acquitted and the guilty are condemned. Second, the guilty are to be punished in proportion to their offense. Unfortunately, the chief aim of our criminal justice system today appears to be the rehabilitation of the offender. Consequently, the focus is on helping offenders be restored to society as soon as possible. This should not be the focus of criminal justice. The justice system is to acquit the innocent and punish the guilty. It is the role of the church to see offenders redeemed through the proclamation of the gospel. While the state can have a secondary purpose of helping to rehabilitate offenders through getting them sober, educating them, and teaching them employable skills, it must not lose sight of its first responsibility. When the state steps out of its proper sphere of bringing justice to criminals for the sake of rehabilitation, more people suffer.[15] This does not mean that rehabilitation should not be an aim of the justice system, but it should be secondary to the aim of justice.

Third, punishment should be limited by the humanity of the guilty person. We are talking in this specific case about a dispute, not about a murder or some other capital crime. In this case, a proper punishment would be corporal punishment. The guilty person is to be punished in

15. Consider the examples in Memphis, Tennessee, where two criminals were released early for different reasons and went on to take innocent lives when they should have been in prison. If the state had kept its focus on punishing the guilty where it belonged, the innocent in these cases would not have suffered. "In Memphis, Renewed Attention on Violence After Shooting Rampage," *New York Times*, September 8, 2022, https://www.nytimes.com/2022/09/08/us/memphis-shooting-gun-violence.html.

the presence of the judge so that the sentence is properly executed. The maximum penalty for an offense of this sort was forty lashes. Later the Jews capped the punishment at thirty-nine. In case the one delivering the punishment miscounted, they did not want to go over forty. The reason why going over forty was problematic was that "your brother [would] be degraded in your sight."

What is it about forty-one lashes that is degrading, while forty lashes is appropriate? We are not told. But the aim of the punishment was to see to it that the punishment fit the crime without being a gross maltreatment of a brother. Among the people of God under the new covenant, we do not exercise any kind of discipline except that which is spiritual. The state is responsible for wielding the sword to administer justice. Notice that showing compassion to the guilty does not mean reducing his sentence or forgoing his punishment, but it means respecting his humanity while delivering the punishment that his crime deserves.

Though corporal punishment is forbidden in most nations today for humanitarian reasons, I believe it would be more humane than prison in many instances. Prisoners are frequently assaulted while incarcerated, and many others suffer horrendous sexual assault, both of which fates are far less humane than state-supervised, measured corporal punishment. Additionally, incarcerating people means that they are removed from their families, leaving children to grow up without a father (or in some cases mother) in the home and no one to provide. As for whether corporal punishment is inhumane, I prefer to side with the Bible than modern conceptions of what is humane. God made man in his image, and God prescribed corporal punishment for particular crimes in the Bible. We should not think we are more humane than God himself by rejecting corporal punishment and simultaneously embracing a prison system that is far more degrading.

In seven different areas, we have seen God hold forth a vision of a compassionate people. These laws do not exhaust the limits of our compassion but point us toward other applications that reflect the same compassionate heart. Ideally, we can begin to see that simply trying to keep all these laws will not effectively make us compassionate. What we need is a new heart, a new disposition that reflects the grace and mercy that we ourselves have received. When we apprehend God's compassion toward us in coming to rescue us from our dreadful condition, we ourselves will begin to reflect that compassion in the ways described in this text and more.

May we be intentional to meditate on God's compassionate acts toward us, especially in the gospel. And may we in turn express that same compassionate heart toward others.

39

Love Protects in a Selfish World

Deuteronomy 25:5–19

And if the man does not wish to take his brother's wife, then his brother's wife shall go up to the gate to the elders and say, "My husband's brother refuses to perpetuate his brother's name in Israel; he will not perform the duty of a husband's brother to me." (Deut. 25:7)

The Hunger Games[1] tells the story of a poor girl named Katniss growing up in a dystopian world where the political class has lost complete touch with human compassion. Every year, two young representatives are chosen from each of the twelve districts to compete in the Hunger Games. These "tributes" fight to the death in a gladiator-type arena until only one remains, all for the entertainment of the Capitol.

This is the unquestioned reality every year until Katniss comes along and breaks the Games. First, when her younger sister is chosen as tribute,

1. Suzanne Collins, *The Hunger Games* (Scholastic Press, 2008).

Katniss steps in and takes her place as a substitute. Such a self-sacrificial act catches the attention of the Capitol because people do not do that for one another. In the arena, alliances are formed among the strong to kill the weak first, but there Katniss develops a friendship with Rue, the smallest tribute in the Games. Katniss fights to keep Rue alive, despite the rules and incentives to kill her. This loving loyalty prompts another competitor from Rue's district named Thresh to show mercy to Katniss when he could have killed her. Her actions are turning the Games upside down and changing how others play.

As the Games develop, it becomes clear that Katniss is competing not against the other tributes, but against the system, against the Gamemakers behind the scenes. In the end, only two tributes remain: Katniss and her compatriot from District 12 named Peeta. Rather than claim the glory and honor due to the victor, Katniss and Peeta plan to eat poison berries to kill themselves rather than each other. At the last moment, the Gamemakers intervene and change the rules, knowing that they have been beaten. In a system in which those in power gain their strength by dividing up the population and turning them against one another, Katniss's acts of love and compassion for others break the system by bringing people together. The powers of the Capitol understand this and try to take her out.

Katniss is a picture of what the people of God are to be in this world, living according to the values of the true King and short-circuiting the powers behind this present darkness. Throughout Deuteronomy, God calls his people to this kind of radical living. In a world that puts self first, God's people put the interests of others ahead of their own. In a world where many seek to take advantage through dishonesty, God's people are honest even when it hurts. In a world that seeks to divide, God's people are breaking down boundaries with love. When we live this way, we push back against the spiritual forces of evil in the heavenly places and on the earth and can even change how other people play the game.

As the people of God prepare to go into the land, they will face multiple threats that could prevent them from flourishing and becoming a light to the nations. In this passage, three of these threats are addressed with some protective measures to safeguard the family, the economy, and the covenant community.

Love Protects the Family

The first set of commands aim to protect individual family lines from extinction:

> If brothers dwell together, and one of them dies and has no son, the wife of the dead man shall not be married outside the family to a stranger. Her husband's brother shall go in to her and take her as his wife and perform the duty of a husband's brother to her. And the first son whom she bears shall succeed to the name of his dead brother, that his name may not be blotted out of Israel. (Deut. 25:5–6)

This command notes a tragic situation. Two brothers dwell together along with two wives. One of the brothers dies, without a son to carry on the family name or to receive the family inheritance. To prolong his name and protect the family inheritance, the widow is not to marry outside the family, but instead the surviving brother is to take his dead brother's widow for his own wife.[2] The first son she gives birth to will be considered the son of her first husband. That son will receive his dead "father's" share of the family possessions and carry on the name of that "father," even though his birth father is still alive. This concept, referred to as levirate marriage (from Latin *levir*, "husband's brother"), was widely practiced

2. Some might object to this and point to Leviticus 20:21: "If a man takes his brother's wife, it is impurity. He has uncovered his brother's nakedness; they shall be childless." These two laws seem to be contradictory, and if the couple is going to be childless, wouldn't that defeat the purpose of levirate marriage? This does appear to be a difficulty. In fact, the Jewish Talmud has a lengthy and very detailed tractate (Tractate Yevamot) devoted to this whole concept. According to some critical scholars, these chapters of Leviticus were written much later and by a different author (referred to as H) than other parts of the law, including Deuteronomy 25. At this point in Israel's history (they argue), levirate marriage was no longer accepted and expressly forbidden. The promise that "they shall be childless" is understood as an explicit undermining of the practice of levirate marriage. See, e.g., E. L. Feinstein, "Sexual Prohibitions in the Bible and the ANE: A Comparison," TheTorah.com, 2018, https://www.thetorah.com/article/sexual-prohibitions-in-the-bible-and-the-ane-a-comparison. But there is a reasonable resolution to the tension between these two laws in the Talmudic tradition. The Talmudic resolution is that the two prohibitions in Leviticus (Lev. 18:16; 20:21) are a generality, and that the law here in Deuteronomy is the exception. So generally, a man must not marry his brother's wife. But if his brother had no children and died, in that case, he must. Jeffrey H. Tigay, *Deuteronomy*, JPSTC (Jewish Publication Society, 1996), 232.

in the ancient Near East and is still practiced in some parts of the world today.[3]

The reason is given in Deuteronomy 25:6: "that his name may not be blotted out of Israel." Having a name in Israel was important, and the continuation of that name was equally important. The child would be called "___, son of ___." Even if a man died before inheriting the fullness of God's promises to Abraham, through his descendants he might be understood to be enjoying the fulfillment of those promises. We may think this approach strange, but we have our own ways of doing much the same today. Many of us are named for someone else in our family or we have named one of our children after a deceased relative. It is a way to see the memory of a loved one continue into the next generation.

But levirate marriage did not always work as prescribed. A man could refuse for any number of reasons: he might not like his brother's widow; he might believe that with his brother dead and heirless, he could get a larger share of their father's estate; he might not want to create a rival for his wife if he is already married; or he might decide that it is too costly to care for another wife and child who are not his own or that it would diminish the estate he planned to leave to his own children.[4] Whatever the selfish reason, if a man did not want to marry his brother's widow, there was a process described in Deuteronomy 25:7: "And if the man does not wish to take his brother's wife, then his brother's wife shall go up to the gate to the elders and say, 'My husband's brother refuses to perpetuate his brother's name in Israel; he will not perform the duty of a husband's brother to me.'" Clearly, in this context, for a man to refuse to perpetuate his brother's name through levirate marriage was to fail to love his deceased brother and his widow. The elders were then to give it their best effort to convince the selfish man. If after they implored him he continued to refuse to do what was right, a particular ceremony was prescribed in verses 8–10. The woman was to remove his sandal, spit in his face, and declare that this is what such a man deserves who would not love his brother enough to build up his brother's

3. For an interesting example of how this issue is being addressed by Christians in a contemporary context, see M. E. Baloyi, "The Christian View of Levirate Marriage in a Changing South Africa," *Journal of Sociology and Social Anthropology* 6, no. 4 (2015): 483–91.

4. Tigay, *Deuteronomy*, 232–33.

house.[5] Since he refused to build up his brother's house, his own house would carry a bad name.[6]

The de-sandaling and face-spitting ceremony was not the way it was supposed to be, but was another concession to the hardness of man's selfish heart. The brother of the dead man had a choice: he could do what was honorable in God's sight by continuing his brother's line, giving his heir a share of the inheritance, and providing for his brother's widow. Or he could act shamefully: seeking the wealth of his dead brother's estate to maintain and increase his own children's estate.[7] We still face similar choices every day. Will we put our own desires and interests above our responsibilities to our family and community?[8]

This is a strange custom for us as people who are living under the new covenant. Clearly, aspects of this law are rooted in Israel's cultural history and its relationship to the land. We do not see any confirmation of this practice in the New Testament.[9] Rather, levirate marriage was inseparably connected with the possession of the land of Israel, part of the civil law that expired with that nation. The inheritance of the land takes on greater significance under the new covenant as we prepare to inherit the new heavens and earth, something that death will not keep any of us from enjoying.

The apostle Paul might have levirate marriage in mind when he writes in 1 Timothy 5:8, "But if anyone does not provide for his relatives, and especially for members of his household, he has denied the faith and is worse than an unbeliever." He then goes on to talk about appropriate care for widows. Under the law, families and widows were taken care of through levirate marriage. Paul does not prescribe that practice when he addresses

5. The historical particulars of what the sandal-removal ceremony symbolized are difficult to say with certainty, but the intent of the ceremony is clearly to shame the man and free the widow to go forward and remarry outside the family. A version of this sandal ceremony, today called *halizah*, is found in Ruth 4:7–12. For an example in modern Judaism of how this ceremony functions today, see Jeremy Sharon, "Jerusalem Rabbinical Court Refuses to Let Widow of 13 Years Remarry," *Jerusalem Post*, September 4, 2014, https://www.jpost.com/israel-news/jerusalem-rabbinical-court-refuses-to-let-widow-of-13-years-remarry-374371.

6. Tigay, *Deuteronomy*, 234.

7. Michael D. Matlock, "Obeying the First Part of the Tenth Commandment: Applications from the Levirate Marriage Law," *JSOT* 31, no. 3 (March 2007): 310.

8. J. Gary Millar, *Now Choose Life: Theology and Ethics in Deuteronomy*, NSBT 6 (Apollos, 1998), 142.

9. It is, however, in the background of the Sadducees' question to Jesus about the resurrection in Matthew 22:23–33.

how to take care of them, but we can see that the general equity of that law remains relevant. Still today, it is important that we not put our own selfish interests ahead of caring for our family members. Selfishness was and is a threat to the family.

A second threat to the family is found in the strange law of Deuteronomy 25:11–12: "When men fight with one another and the wife of the one draws near to rescue her husband from the hand of him who is beating him and puts out her hand and seizes him by the private parts, then you shall cut off her hand. Your eye shall have no pity." On the one hand, the scenario is clear: two men are fighting when one man's wife steps in and rescues her husband by seizing his assailant's private parts. Such an action strikes us as noble and even heroic. But Moses says that this woman's hand must be cut off and that though people might be tempted to show her pity, they must not do so. Why would people be tempted to have pity? Because her motive was good; she was trying to save her husband!

What is wrong with the woman's action? Jewish and Christian scholars have wrestled with this question for a long time, but the most likely reason why her action is punished so severely is that it threatens the man's reproductive ability.[10] Her action has the potential to harm the man to such a degree that he is unable to father children. Although injury is not specifically mentioned in this passage, a parallel Middle Assyrian law does mention injury similar to this.[11] Also, Deuteronomy 25:5–10 just reaffirmed the importance of carrying on the family name. Damaging a man's genitals not only would threaten his reproductive ability, but might also keep the man from being a part of the assembly of the Lord (Deut. 23:1).[12] Cutting off the hand appears to be a proper punishment for someone who cut off another's family line.

One threat to the continuance of the family is the early departure of a man without producing any offspring. A second threat is a selfish brother-in-law

10. Other reasons for why the punishment is so severe are summarized well in Marc Cortez, "The Law on Violent Intervention: Deuteronomy 25.11–12 Revisited," *JSOT* 30, no. 4 (June 2006): 431–47.

11. Jeffrey H. Tigay, "Excursus 24: Improper Intervention in a Fight," in *Deuteronomy*, 485.

12. What do we make of this with regard to modern self-defense? Women are frequently taught that this part of the anatomy is where they should kick or hit a man. Is this unbiblical? I do not believe so. If a man is attacking a woman, then he is bringing upon himself the immediate consequences of his actions. As Tigay observes, the Bible seems to penalize women for using this tactic only when they are intervening in a fight between others, not when they are being attacked themselves. See Tigay, "Excursus 24," 486.

who refuses his familial obligations. A third threat to the continuance of the family is damage to a male that would prevent him from being able to father offspring. These laws together serve to communicate just how important being fruitful and multiplying is to God. The seriousness with which this passage protects a person's ability to reproduce should be a corrective for us. Our own modern reluctance to have children, reflected in a declining birth rate, should also be questioned in light of the tremendous value placed on raising godly offspring (Mal. 2:15). Frequently, the reluctance to have children or adopt children is rooted in the same selfish desires and pursuits that this passage (and others in the Bible) condemns, such as having less time and money for me. At the same time, Christ himself did not have children, nor did the apostle Paul. The priorities of the kingdom are even greater than those of family. For those called to be practical eunuchs for the sake of the kingdom, reproduction can still occur through the proclamation of the gospel and the raising of spiritual children, something that all of us are called to do. Selfishness is also a threat to that kind of reproduction, and we must resist it.

Love Protects the Economic Interests of Others

Thankfully, the next verses are much more straightforward! Moses describes laws that prohibit dishonesty in the workplace:

> You shall not have in your bag two kinds of weights, a large and a small. You shall not have in your house two kinds of measures, a large and a small. A full and fair weight you shall have, a full and fair measure you shall have, that your days may be long in the land that the Lord your God is giving you. For all who do such things, all who act dishonestly, are an abomination to the Lord your God. (Deut. 25:13–16)

When buying, one would want to use heavy weights to get the most product for a price. Likewise, when selling, one would want to use light weights to give the least product for a price. The same went with measures. Without standardized forms of measurement, it was much easier to cheat on such things. But such cheating is stealing from others what properly belongs to them. These practices would erode the trust necessary for an economy and a society to properly function, resulting in more poverty and suffering. God refers to people who are dishonest in their business dealings as "an abomination." That is strong language, and certainly language that we do not want to describe us.

Dishonesty is condemned throughout the Bible. We should ask ourselves where we are tempted to be dishonest in our business practices. My family started a little hobby business a few years ago, stringing tennis rackets. We have learned that there are numerous ways to cheat people in that business. For example, if we are stringing several rackets in a row, we may forget to change one of the settings between rackets. Rather than starting over, which would cost time and money, we might be tempted to give the incorrectly strung racket to the customer and hope that he or she does not notice. We have also seen people charge customers for one type of string, but secretly substitute a cheaper string in its place, knowing that the customers would not notice. Those in the restaurant business may be tempted to add charges to a bill to increase their tips. Others might be tempted to be dishonest to avoid taxes. Those who sell real estate or vehicles might be tempted to withhold information to ensure that a sale goes through. Others might be tempted to bill for hours they have not actually worked for a client. There are a million ways to be dishonest. The people of God are not to practice any of them. If deceptive practices are common in an industry, then breaking out and acting counterculturally will be a difficult but worthy task.

In addition to more traditional forms of dishonesty, today there is a phenomenon known as *quiet quitting*. Quiet quitters are those who are not psychologically engaged in their work and are doing the bare minimum to get by.[13] In many jobs, it is easy to be lazy and get away with it. Management shortcomings are helping to create this kind of bare minimalism, but as God's people, we must recognize that not doing what we are being paid for is a form of dishonesty. We are not called to be workaholics, but we are called to work honestly and give our best to those who have hired our skills and labor. Even if we are not being closely supervised, we know that God is watching, and it is God whom we always aim to please. The apostle Paul speaks directly to this in Colossians 3:22–24: "Bondservants, obey in

13. Jim Harter, "Is Quiet Quitting Real?," Gallup Workplace, September 6, 2022, https://www.gallup.com/workplace/398306/quiet-quitting-real.aspx, accessed October 12, 2022.

everything those who are your earthly masters, not by way of eye-service, as people-pleasers, but with sincerity of heart, fearing the Lord. Whatever you do, work heartily, as for the Lord and not for men, knowing that from the Lord you will receive the inheritance as your reward. You are serving the Lord Christ." Neither quiet quitting nor dishonesty of any other sort has a place in the life of a Christian. If we need to change jobs, then so be it. Wherever we find ourselves, we must work heartily as for the Lord.

When I preached on this concept to my congregation, one of our high schoolers took it to heart. She went into her part-time job that week with the enthusiasm of one working for Jesus. Immediately her supervisor commented that she had never seen anyone else do such good work, and our high schooler gave witness to Jesus. In a world where people are tempted to be dishonest to their own advantage and so threaten the economic well-being of all, the people of God are called to be honest, even when it threatens our own economic well-being.

Love Protects the Covenant Community

The final piece of this section directs the covenant community what to do to the Amalekites once they are settled in the land. Moses writes in Deuteronomy 25:17–19:

> Remember what Amalek did to you on the way as you came out of Egypt, how he attacked you on the way when you were faint and weary, and cut off your tail, those who were lagging behind you, and he did not fear God. Therefore when the Lord your God has given you rest from all your enemies around you, in the land that the Lord your God is giving you for an inheritance to possess, you shall blot out the memory of Amalek from under heaven; you shall not forget.

Amalek failed to show pity to the people of Israel. Even though the Amalekites were not God's covenant people, they would be judged as a nation for their merciless treatment of Israel in its helpless condition, as well as for their attacking the weakest among the people of God who were lagging behind.[14]

14. We see a similar pronouncement of judgment on "secular" nations in Amos 1–2.

It is a serious warning to all modern nations that even though we are not in covenant with God as Israel was, there will be judgment for nations of the earth that refuse to show pity to the weakest and most vulnerable, even in war.

The bigger issue with the Amalekites was the fact that they had sought to interfere with the plan of God for his newly redeemed people. God had just rescued his people and was bringing them to Sinai, where he would confirm them as his covenant people and give them his law. Right there, the Amalekites sought to destroy God's people and disrupt his plan of redemption and blessing for all the nations through Israel.[15] Such hubris would have devastating consequences for Amalek.

The instructions here are not a guide for how nations today should deal with their enemies, nor are they a justification for modern genocide. Rather, the Amalekites represent all the forces of evil that resist the kingdom of light and salvation. As surely as the Amalekites were doomed, so also are all those forces that oppose the work of God in the world today. As Christians, we remember that our battle is not with flesh and blood. Paul reminds us in Ephesians 6:12, "For we do not wrestle against flesh and blood, but against the rulers, against the authorities, against the cosmic powers over this present darkness, against the spiritual forces of evil in the heavenly places." We fight these battles not with swords or guns but by taking up the armor of God and with prayer. In this way, we tread down our foes while rescuing those who have been taken captive by the enemy to do his will. Our enemy surely is ruthless, as ruthless as Amalek was toward the weak and vulnerable in Israel. We can expect that as Amalek pursued the young, the wounded, and the isolated, so our enemy seeks to do the same. But we must not back down. We must not be ignorant of the battle. We must take up the fight and stand firm in the faith while standing together.

ALL THINGS NEW

In *The Hunger Games*, Katniss is a picture of what the people of God are to be in this world, practicing selflessness and love and undermining the powers behind this present darkness. She points beyond herself to the one

15. Daniel I. Block, *Deuteronomy*, NIVAC (Zondervan, 2012), 595.

who, like her, had every right to stay out of the fray, but willingly stepped into the mess for our sake. Our Hero refused to play by the rules of the kingdom of darkness and intentionally chose the weak and made them his own. Our Hero refused to enrich himself at the expense of others and instead impoverished himself to make others rich. Rather than using his power to destroy his enemies, he chose to die in our place to make us his own. Because of his selfless acts, Jesus broke the world system and disarmed the powers of darkness. Death could not hold him, and he rose on the third day and is now making all things new. Those of us who trust in him join in the resistance to this present darkness that he is bringing down.

In a world that either devalues children altogether or worships them, we cherish them and disciple them and seek to spiritually reproduce in them as well. In a world that threatens the economic well-being of all for selfish gain, we put the interests of others ahead of ourselves. In a world that seeks to demonize every opponent, we do good to our fleshly enemies, recognizing that our true opponents are really demons. When we live this way, we push back against the spiritual forces of evil in the heavenly places and on the earth. Love protects the family by looking out for one another's interests, love protects the economy by practicing honesty before the Lord, and love protects the covenant community by focusing our efforts on fighting the right enemy. As we carry out the actions of love, we will resist and ultimately undermine the works of a selfish world until Christ returns to consummate his kingdom of love once and for all.

40

Grateful People Are Obedient People

Deuteronomy 26:1–19

You have declared today that the Lord *is your God, and that you will walk in his ways, and keep his statutes and his commandments and his rules, and will obey his voice. And the* Lord *has declared today that you are a people for his treasured possession, as he has promised you, and that you are to keep all his commandments.* (Deut. 26:17–18)

Four college wrestlers were looking for antlers in the Shoshone National Forest in Wyoming. About the time Brady Lowry noticed evidence all around him that a bear was nearby, a grizzly came charging through the bushes and tackled him. When Lowry put up his arm to protect his face, the bear gnashed down on the arm and broke it. Lowry's wrestling buddy, Kendell Cummings, saw the bear mauling his friend. He knew in that moment that he could turn and run or that he could try to save his friend. He decided to save his friend. When yelling and throwing things at the bear did not work, Cummings began to hit the bear and pull its hair. Eventually, he yanked hard on the bear's ear, causing the bear to turn on him. The bear knocked Cummings down and began to maul him while Lowry got away. After a time, the bear relented in its attack. When Cummings got up to yell for his friend, the bear came back and attacked him a second time, doing serious damage to Cummings's head and face. Eventually, the bear left him for dead, and the four men were able to reconnect and make it back to safety.

What do you suppose the young man Brady said after his friend Kendell rescued him? This is what he said: "I can't even express how grateful I am for him [Kendell]. . . . I don't know what I'm going to pay him back, I don't. I owe him everything."[1] Gratitude is the natural response to rescue. We do not have to tell anyone to thank the person who saved his life. If he understands at all how much danger he was in, he will give thanks from the heart—so long as he remembers.

In Deuteronomy 26, we are coming to the end of a major section (Deut. 12–26) where the detailed stipulations of the covenant are spelled out between the suzerain Lord and his vassal people. In this section, Moses prescribes rituals and recitations to remind the people of what God has done for them. Their grateful response to God's grace should find expression in obedience to his commands. While we have repeatedly seen that theme in Deuteronomy, it is fitting that at the conclusion of the giving of these laws, gratitude expressed through obedience is given an exclamation point. It serves as a transition to the blessings and curses of the covenant soon to come. For us as the people of God living under the terms of the new covenant, the laws in this passage have found their fulfillment in the ministry of Jesus Christ. Nevertheless, we will see that even under the new covenant, gratitude for God's grace expresses itself in obedient worship, obedient giving, and obedient living.

Give Thanks for God's Grace Through Obedient Worship

Recall that at this point the people of God are in the plains of Moab and have not crossed into the promised land. But they are on the verge of doing so. God is preparing them for how to respond when they do.

1. Leo Wolfson, "Wyoming Hero: College Wrestler Jumps on Grizzly to Save Friend," *Cowboy State Daily*, October 17, 2022, https://cowboystatedaily.com/2022/10/17/wyoming-hero-college-wrestler-jumps-on-grizzly-to-save-friend/, accessed October 21, 2022.

First, Moses reminds them that obedient worship acknowledges God's provision:

> When you come into the land that the LORD your God is giving you for an inheritance and have taken possession of it and live in it, you shall take some of the first of all the fruit of the ground, which you harvest from your land that the LORD your God is giving you, and you shall put it in a basket, and you shall go to the place that the LORD your God will choose, to make his name to dwell there. (Deut. 26:1–2)

God has promised his people that they will enjoy harvests that they did not plant (Deut. 6:10–12) and that in future years, when they do plant, it will still be God who is making the land fruitful to provide for their needs (11:13–17). They are to respond by bringing the firstfruits to God as an offering and acknowledgment that he is the source of the blessings they enjoy.

Second, Moses teaches them that obedient worship acknowledges God's faithfulness. Moses continues in Deuteronomy 26:3–4: "And you shall go to the priest who is in office at that time and say to him, 'I declare today to the LORD your God that I have come into the land that the LORD swore to our fathers to give us.' Then the priest shall take the basket from your hand and set it down before the altar of the LORD your God." When the people come in and bring the firstfruits, they are to make this declaration that they have come into the land. God was faithful to fulfill his promise. It is likely that while this action was to be performed the first time Israel experienced a harvest in the land, it was not to be the last time. The mention in verse 3 of "the priest who is in office at that time" suggests that this ceremony would be performed throughout the generations.[2] Because forgetting was one of Israel's chief dangers (Deut. 8:11–20), it is likely that God intended this to be done every year as a reminder of God's faithfulness. The firstfruits of the land are a visual reminder of the fact that God has been faithful to fulfill his promises and bring his people into the land. But God's faithfulness extends beyond the fruitfulness of the land. It includes everything he did to bring them there.

Third, obedient worship acknowledges God's rescue. After laying down the firstfruits, the worshiper was to acknowledge God's salvation of him

2. Jeffrey H. Tigay, *Deuteronomy*, JPSTC (Jewish Publication Society, 1996), 238.

personally. He was to do so by retelling the story of what God had done for his people. This was the story of rescue and grace that God wanted his people to recount so that they did not forget his redeeming blessing. Moses writes in Deuteronomy 26:5: "And you shall make response before the LORD your God, 'A wandering Aramean was my father. And he went down into Egypt and sojourned there, few in number, and there he became a nation, great, mighty, and populous.'" This quotation is probably a reference to Jacob, who not only went down to Egypt with his sons, but married Leah and Rachel, who were both Aramean women.[3] The word translated "wandering" usually means either "perishing" or "straying." In either case, the aim of the recitation is to contrast the wandering and homeless existence of Israel's fathers with the people's present possession of this amazingly fertile land and stable existence.[4] While Jacob and his immediate descendants were just sojourners there, the people bringing the offering were at home in their own land.

Then the worshiper is to recall what happened to his ancestors in Egypt: "And the Egyptians treated us harshly and humiliated us and laid on us hard labor. Then we cried to the LORD, the God of our fathers, and the LORD heard our voice and saw our affliction, our toil, and our oppression. And the LORD brought us out of Egypt with a mighty hand and an outstretched arm, with great deeds of terror, with signs and wonders" (Deut. 26:6–8). Here is the centerpiece of Israel's gospel. In Egypt the people were harshly treated, oppressed, and enslaved. But they cried out to God, and he came and rescued them through the hand of Moses. He brought them out when they had no way out. He brought them through the sea when there was no way across. It was a mighty salvation! But God did more than bring this nation out of Egypt. The worshiper is to continue recalling the story in Deuteronomy 26:9–11:

> "And he brought us into this place and gave us this land, a land flowing with milk and honey. And behold, now I bring the first of the fruit of the ground, which you, O LORD, have given me." And you shall set it down before the LORD your God and worship before the LORD your God. And you shall rejoice

3. Peter C. Craigie, *The Book of Deuteronomy*, NICOT (Eerdmans, 1976), 321.
4. Tigay, *Deuteronomy*, 240.

> in all the good that the Lord your God has given to you and to your house, you, and the Levite, and the sojourner who is among you.

God brought them into this good land and blessed them in every way. He was the source of the blessings they enjoyed, so when they come to worship, they should acknowledge his rescue. The joy of this celebration not only was for individuals, but was to be shared by all in the household, as well as by the Levites and sojourners, who had no land of their own. The blessings of God's salvation overflowed from the lives of his people into all those around them.

The explicit giving of thanks to God when bringing the firstfruits in worship would have continually reminded the people that what they enjoyed was a result of God's grace. It was not the gods of Canaan that gave them a fruitful harvest, but the God who rescued them out of Egypt. Like Israel, we face a continual temptation to ascribe our blessings to our commitment to success, our hard work, or our capitalist system. These things are not unimportant, but they are secondary causes. God is the First Cause of each of those things, and it is appropriate when we give back to him to remember that he is the Giver of every good gift.

Additionally, our worship of God should reflect the same joy in our rescue that Israel experienced. While the Israelites could recount the specific instance of their slavery and oppression in Egypt followed by God's miraculous rescue of them through the exodus, we have an even greater story of rescue. Here is how Paul describes it in Ephesians 2:1–6:

> And you were dead in the trespasses and sins in which you once walked, following the course of this world, following the prince of the power of the air, the spirit that is now at work in the sons of disobedience—among whom we all once lived in the passions of our flesh, carrying out the desires of the body and the mind, and were by nature children of wrath, like the rest of mankind. But God, being rich in mercy, because of the great love with which he loved us, even when we were dead in our trespasses, made us alive together with Christ—by grace you have been saved—and raised us up with him and seated us with him in the heavenly places in Christ Jesus.

These realities should fuel our worship each Sunday and every other day of the week. We look to our past and see our sins forgiven, and we look to the present with gratitude for resurrection life. If we have in fact been saved, then we should give thanks for the gift of salvation by worshiping God only.

Give Thanks for God's Grace Through Obedient Giving

The gift of God's grace and salvation impacts not only the worshiper himself, but his household and others around him. One way by which worshipers of God are to express gratitude is through obedient giving. We read in Deuteronomy 26:12, "When you have finished paying all the tithe of your produce in the third year, which is the year of tithing, giving it to the Levite, the sojourner, the fatherless, and the widow, so that they may eat within your towns and be filled . . ." The expectation here is that every third year, God's people were going to give a tithe to the most vulnerable people among them (cf. Deut. 14:28–29). This practice is what we refer to as mercy ministry, or benevolence. One-tenth of all their produce every third year was to be given to meet the needs of people who did not have land or were not able to produce for themselves.

The emphasis in this passage, however, is not primarily on the giving, but on what the worshiper is to say when he gives:

> Then you shall say before the Lord your God, "I have removed the sacred portion out of my house, and moreover, I have given it to the Levite, the sojourner, the fatherless, and the widow, according to all your commandment that you have commanded me. I have not transgressed any of your commandments, nor have I forgotten them. I have not eaten of the tithe while I was mourning, or removed any of it while I was unclean, or offered any of it to the dead. I have obeyed the voice of the Lord my God. I have done according to all that you have commanded me." (Deut. 26:13–14)

There are numerous ways by which we can say "I love you" to God. But none is better than to declare, "I have obeyed the voice of the Lord my God." In this instance, obedience takes the form of giving to those who are in need, and obeying all the particular aspects of how that giving was to be done in ancient Israel. When we obey God in gratitude for what he has done for us, we are saying "I love you" in a way that pleases him above all else. He delights in our obedience, in both the big and small things. We demonstrate love for God not primarily by what we say or what we sing, but by how we walk in obedience to all his commands. Giving is one of those areas. Those who recognize that they have been given much are to demonstrate that reality by giving liberally to others.

But this is not the end of the worshiper's statement to God. God commands the worshiper to pray for his continued blessing on his people in Deuteronomy 26:15: "Look down from your holy habitation, from heaven, and bless your people Israel and the ground that you have given us, as you swore to our fathers, a land flowing with milk and honey." God wants his people to ask for his blessing on his people, and here that blessing is in a very material form. It is not wrong to ask God for material blessings for ourselves and the rest of God's people, so long as we never confuse the blessings with the God who blesses.

We should also recognize that the prayer for continued blessing is conditioned on continued obedience. This does not mean that obedience merits God's blessing, or that blessing is deserved because of obedience. God's blessing for his people is already written into his promises and what he has done for his people. The prayer is not saying, "We have obeyed; therefore, you must bless us," but rather: "You have blessed us and we have responded with obedience. So now please continue to bless us and we will continue to obey."[5]

For those of us living under the new covenant, the precise law of the tithe as it was expressed in ancient Israel is no longer binding on us as Christians. But the underlying principle of giving to the Lord as a response to his grace and giving to others as the overflow of our joy remains in effect. God's eagerness to bless those who give generously also remains in effect. When we think about how much to give as Christians, we can think of the tithe as a starting point. This is what God required of his people that he rescued out of Egypt and brought into the land of Canaan. We are participants in that story of rescue through our ingrafting into the people of God through faith in Jesus Christ (Rom. 11:17–24; Gal. 3:29; Eph. 2:11–13). But not only have we seen God rescue us from slavery in Egypt, we have also seen him rescue us through the death and resurrection of his only Son! Not only are

5. The concept here is expressed in Christopher Wright, *Deuteronomy*, NIBC: Old Testament 4 (Hendrickson, 2007), 272.

we being brought into a small Middle Eastern plot of land like Israel, but our promised land is the entire new heavens and new earth! How much grace has God bestowed on us! Is returning to God 10 percent an adequate expression of our gratitude for what he has done for us?

We should not forget that as surely as God promised to bless his people's obedience in matters of giving, the New Testament confirms and strengthens them for those who give cheerfully! The apostle Paul writes in 2 Corinthians 9:10–13:

> He who supplies seed to the sower and bread for food will supply and multiply your seed for sowing and increase the harvest of your righteousness. You will be enriched in every way to be generous in every way, which through us will produce thanksgiving to God. For the ministry of this service is not only supplying the needs of the saints but is also overflowing in many thanksgivings to God. By their approval of this service, they will glorify God because of your submission that comes from your confession of the gospel of Christ, and the generosity of your contribution for them and for all others.

As the people of God give generously, God will enrich his people to give even more generously, just as he promised Israel. Their submission to the command to give will flow from their "confession of the gospel of Christ." Cheerful and obedient giving is a response to our reception of God's grace in Christ.

Practically, this means that if we are recipients of God's grace in Christ, we should be aiming to give at least 10 percent of our income to the ministry of our local church as God's storehouse (Mal. 3:10). While the law of the tithe expired with the civil laws of Israel, the principle remains an instructive starting point for grace giving. In addition to giving to support the ministries of our local church, it is appropriate to give benevolence offerings that are used to meet the needs of people in our church and community. In the church I pastor, we do that through a mercy ministry fund collected after communion on the first Sunday of each month. As we give cheerfully and obediently, we may also ask God to continue to pour out his blessing on us, that we may be able to increase and give even more generously going forward.

GIVE THANKS FOR GOD'S GRACE THROUGH OBEDIENT LIVING

With the stipulations of the law having been laid down in detail through chapters 12–26, these final verses of Deuteronomy 26 serve as a summary of God's call to his vassal people. God's people must obey. Moses writes in verse 16: "This day the LORD your God commands you to do these statutes and rules. You shall therefore be careful to do them with all your heart and with all your soul." We have considered in detail what God requires of his people. In short, he requires obedience. We must remember what he has done, we must trust in his character, and we must obey his commands. Without rehashing those details again, we can sum up all his commands under two headings: love God and love your neighbor. The details of that principle have been spelled out in the Ten Commandments and elsewhere, but it is as simple as love. If we want to demonstrate that we are grateful for what God has done for us in Christ, there is no better way than obedience. Jesus said, "If you love me, you will keep my commandments" (John 14:15). We are not to substitute religious rituals for our obedience; God detests that. Nor are we to give money as a substitute for obedience. Such activities are to be an expression of our loving obedience, not a replacement for it.

Two more reasons are given in this passage that sum up why we must obey. First, God's people must obey because of who we are. Moses writes in Deuteronomy 26:17, "You have declared today that the LORD is your God, and that you will walk in his ways, and keep his statutes and his commandments and his rules, and will obey his voice." The people of Israel declared that they were the people of Yahweh and that they would walk in his ways and obey him. When we profess our faith in Christ, we profess that we will walk in his ways and obey his commandments. We profess that he is our Lord. If you have not made a public profession like that at the front of some church, find out what the process is in your church and begin to take those steps. It is important to make a public profession and identify ourselves as Christians if we are. If we are, then we must obey his voice.

But it is not just we who have made a public proclamation of who we are. The Lord has also made a declaration: "And the LORD has declared today that you are a people for his treasured possession, as he has promised you, and that you are to keep all his commandments" (Deut. 26:18). God claims the people of Israel as his own. He gives his people his law because we are his treasured possession.[6] Just as we give rules to our children because they are our treasured possessions, God gives his law to his beloved people. Why did he choose Israel? Why did he choose us? No reason is given in the Bible except that he loved us. He has demonstrated that love in ways that we have seen again and again, especially through the work of Christ. If we wonder whether we are God's treasured possession, we just need to look at the cross to see the price he paid for us. It was through the shedding of the blood of his only Son that our sins were atoned for and that we have peace with God. If you have not trusted in Christ's shed blood to take away your sins, you have no peace with God. But today, if you call on the name of the Lord, you will be saved through faith in Jesus. You can know that you are his treasured possession and, as such, begin to walk in loving obedience to his commands. God's people must obey because of who we are.

Second, God's people must obey because of what God will do. As we faithfully walk in obedience to his commands, he promises in Deuteronomy 26:19 that "he will set you in praise and in fame and in honor high above all nations that he has made, and that you shall be a people holy to the LORD your God, as he promised." As the people of God obey his commands, God is going to raise them up so that through the demonstration of wisdom they embody, they will be a light to the nations. Through Israel's obedience, the rest of the nations will desire to come to the one true God.

Sadly, we know the rest of the Old Testament story. The people of Israel did not keep God's covenant. Not only did they not become a light to the nations, but they were kicked out of the land! Yet God's intention to bless the people of every nation (including us) did not come to an end. Through Israel came the one true Israelite: Jesus Christ was the perfectly obedient man of Israel. Only Jesus could say without reservation or hesitation: "I have obeyed the voice of the LORD my God. I have done according to all that you have commanded me" (Deut. 26:14). He never disobeyed, he was never selfish, and he always perfectly loved God and loved his neighbor. Out of love for God and love for neighbor, he was obedient in everything, even to the point of dying on the cross (Phil. 2:8). Because of his obedience, he was

6. Romans 11:11–24, Ephesians 2:11–22, and 1 Peter 2:9–10 confirm that believing Gentiles are heirs with believing Jews of God's covenant promises.

lifted up and exalted in praise, fame, and honor above all (v. 9). He is the Light that is drawing all nations to God the Father (John 8:12; 12:32). When we come to him in faith, we too are lifted up along with him and exalted. As we read in Ephesians 2:5–7:

> Even when we were dead in our trespasses, [God] made us alive together with Christ—by grace you have been saved—and raised us up with him and seated us with him in the heavenly places in Christ Jesus, so that in the coming ages he might show the immeasurable riches of his grace in kindness toward us in Christ Jesus.

Even now in and through the church, God is showing his great grace in kindness. Since we are recipients of that grace, it is only fitting that we express our loving gratitude through obedient worship, obedient giving, and obedient living.

41

Cursed

Deuteronomy 27:1–26

"Cursed be anyone who does not confirm the words of this law by doing them." And all the people shall say, "Amen." (Deut. 27:26)

Do you believe in curses? Hollywood certainly does, and for good reason. One suspected curse is attached to the screenplay of a 1963 novel called *The Incomparable Atuk*. The actual content of the story is not of interest. But in 1979, writer Tod Carroll adapted the novel for film. He landed his good friend John Belushi to play the lead role. Sadly, Belushi was found dead of a drug overdose in his hotel room before the film could be made.

After Belushi, the comedian and actor Sam Kinison was recruited for the lead role. Kinison accepted, and production began in 1988. Unfortunately, Kinison's behavior coupled with his alcoholism led to the production's being halted for a time. Shortly after they began again, Kinison was killed by a drunk driver. After Kinison, the screenplay made its way to another actor named John Candy. Candy agreed to play the lead role in 1993. But shortly after finishing production for what would be his last film, Candy was found dead in his hotel room, probably of a heart attack, which may have been a consequence of his lifelong smoking habit, obesity, and occasional dabbling with cocaine.

In 1996, actor Chris Farley was approached to play the lead role. Along with him, another comedian by the name of Phil Hartman was considering taking a role alongside Farley. Tragically, neither would make it. Farley was soon found dead of a drug overdose at thirty-three years old, the same age as his idol, John Belushi. The next year, Hartman was killed by his wife, who was found to have alcohol, cocaine, and Zoloft in her system at the time of the crime. After all this, film executives finally seized the script, and the film remains unmade.[1]

So is there a curse of *Atuk*, or is it all just coincidence? It does seem that there is a curse, though not in any mysterious, shamanistic sense. The curse is addiction to alcohol and drugs, accompanied by a series of life decisions by extraordinarily talented people that led them to early graves. In other words, the curse is not a magical mystery, but rather the working out of the consequences of poor choices, either by the actors themselves or by those around them.

God's curse is similar in that the actions described in this passage will bring about negative consequences, but God is also supernaturally involved in bringing the curse as surely as he is involved in bringing the blessing. Over the next four chapters of Deuteronomy, the people of God are going to be presented with a choice: blessing or curse. The meanings of those two words will be filled out in exquisite—and sometimes disturbing—detail. But amid the details, we must not lose sight of the big picture and the basic choice: life and good or death and evil. It is a choice we all face every single day, a choice that goes all the way back to the garden of Eden with its two trees: the tree of life, which is blessing, and the tree of the knowledge of good and evil, which would lead to the curse. The decision seems easy enough to make at a distance, but we fail to appreciate the power of the serpent, who seeks to undermine our trust in God so that we too will choose the way of curse and death. If we are going to avoid the curse, we need to be clear on what the law requires, clear on who we are, clear on the consequences of disobedience, and clear on the remedy for disobedience.

1. Much of the material for this introduction comes from Chad Glapion, "The Curse of Atuk," *Inside the Simulation*, May 18, 2021, https://medium.com/inside-the-simulation/the-curse-of-atuk-28896a18e29f, accessed October 27, 2022.

To Avoid the Curse, We Need to Be Clear on What the Law Requires

After coming to the end of the covenant stipulations section from Deuteronomy chapters 12–26, a transition is introduced in verse 1 of chapter 27: "Now Moses and the elders of Israel commanded the people, saying, 'Keep the whole commandment that I command you today.'" Moses is described in the third person here. It is a reminder to us that while Moses is the primary author and source of the content of Deuteronomy, others were involved in bringing it to its final form.[2] Moses' message in verse 1 is a reaffirmation of what he has been saying throughout Deuteronomy: God's people must keep God's law. The whole commandment refers to everything he has commanded in Deuteronomy.[3]

Stone monuments are introduced that will help the people of God remain clear on what he requires. The basic principle is that the faintest ink is better than the strongest memory. We read in Deuteronomy 27:2–3: "And on the day you cross over the Jordan to the land that the Lord your God is giving you, you shall set up large stones and plaster them with plaster. And you shall write on them all the words of this law, when you cross over to enter the land that the Lord your God is giving you." Plastering or whitewashing these stones made it possible for them to be written on.[4] The actual content written on the stones likely includes all the laws from chapters 12–26 at least, if not more of Deuteronomy. Verse 4 commands that these stones be set up on Mount Ebal, which will become the mountain associated with God's curse for breaking the law that is written. Then Moses reemphasizes in verse 8, "And you shall write on the stones all the words of this law very plainly." The idea behind the clear communication of the Word is that no one can be confused about what God requires.

From this instruction, we can draw the following principles about God's law. First, it is imperishable and unchanging, and we are reminded of this by the fact that it is written in stone. We do not write in stone things that we intend to change. The law of God reflects the heart of God, and therefore

2. Peter C. Craigie, *The Book of Deuteronomy*, NICOT (Eerdmans, 1976), 28–29.

3. Jeffrey H. Tigay, *Deuteronomy*, JPSTC (Jewish Publication Society, 1996), 247.

4. It is not clear if the text was engraved through the plaster into the stone, or if the plaster served as a clean surface for writing in ink or paint. See Tigay, 248.

it cannot change unless God changes. As Jesus declared, "For truly, I say to you, until heaven and earth pass away, not an iota, not a dot, will pass from the Law until all is accomplished" (Matt. 5:18). People would not hate God's law if it just moved enough to allow pet sins. But God's law stands like a stone, unmoved and unmovable in the face of our sinful ways and attitudes. As Robert Murray M'Cheyne preached: "It is an unchangeable law, for He is an unchangeable God. Therefore, ungodly men have an unchangeable hatred to that holy law."[5]

Second, God's law is intelligible. While aspects of it are more complicated for us reading it thousands of years later, the law's basic principles are simple enough for a child to understand. Therefore, it should be made plain to the people of God. It is summarized in the Ten Commandments and even more so in the two Great Commandments to love God and love neighbor. But the law also contains some particular instructions, as well as promises and threats—none plainer than Deuteronomy 27:26, "Cursed be anyone who does not confirm the words of this law by doing them."

That verse reminds us, third, that the law is not optional: it is obligatory. We cannot simply decide that we are going to live in a world without God's law. It is as much a law of the universe as the law of gravity. We can no more live contrary to God's law without being hurt than we can live contrary to the law of gravity. If we ignore it, it will break us. The teaching that we have already seen and will see in Deuteronomy makes it plain that the law is not just for writing or for hearing, but for doing.[6] And it is for these three reasons and more that the unbeliever hates God's law, because what the law requires, the unbeliever cannot and does not want to give: wholehearted obedience.

Even as we consider what the law requires, we should not lose sight of the fact that this monumental expression of God's law comes to the people after their experience of his grace in bringing them out of Egypt and into the land he promised. These stones will be a reminder of God's covenant law, and the land they stand on will be a reminder of God's covenant faithfulness. As Christopher Wright puts it, "Even in physical symbolism, the law is

5. Quoted in Andrew A. Bonar, ed., *Memoir and Remains of Robert Murray M'Cheyne* (1844; repr., Banner of Truth, 2019), 429.

6. Raymond Brown, *The Message of Deuteronomy: Not by Bread Alone*, The Bible Speaks Today (InterVarsity Press, 1993), 263–64.

grounded in grace."[7] So to be clear, what does the law require? The law requires wholehearted obedience. That is no less true for us under the new covenant than it was for Israel.

To Avoid the Curse, We Need to Be Clear on Who We Are

After telling the Israelites what to do with these stone monuments upon entering the land, Moses and the Levitical priests remind them of who they are in Deuteronomy 27:9–10: "Then Moses and the Levitical priests said to all Israel, 'Keep silence and hear, O Israel: this day you have become the people of the Lord your God. You shall therefore obey the voice of the Lord your God, keeping his commandments and his statutes, which I command you today.'" These verses underline something that we have repeatedly seen regarding the relationship between God's covenant and the obedience of his people. Look at the relationship between verses 9 and 10. Verse 9 says that "you have become the people of the Lord your God." This is who you are, and it is purely by God's grace and not because of anything that you have done. They already were the people of God, but this ceremony was a renewal of that reality. Then look at the implications of this new identity in verse 10: "You shall therefore obey the voice of the Lord your God, keeping his commandments and his statutes." The connection between God's covenant and the obedience of his people could not be any clearer: We are not his people because of our obedience. We are his people, and therefore we must obey. God's covenant relationship with us is a gift that he has sovereignly bestowed. He has chosen us by grace to be his treasured possession; we could not earn it or deserve it. Our obedience is a grateful expression of God's acceptance.

If we do not understand this fundamental concept, our Christian life will be like running on a treadmill. We will always be wondering whether we have done enough good for God to accept us as his people: have we gone to church enough, read our Bibles enough, prayed enough, shared the gospel enough, avoided sin enough, or done good enough to be accepted by God? We will always feel as though we are running toward God but never getting any closer because that is how a treadmill works. Instead, these verses confirm

7. Christopher Wright, *Deuteronomy*, NIBC: Old Testament 4 (Hendrickson, 2007), 276.

what the rest of the Bible teaches us: we are chosen, loved, and accepted not because of anything we have done, but in spite of what we have done! When the reality of this message touches our hearts, we will want to walk in God's ways because we will love him as he ought to be loved!

So to be clear, who are we? We are the covenant people of God, called to walk in his ways as a response to his gracious salvation.

To Avoid the Curse, We Need to Be Clear on the Consequence of Disobedience

After reminding them of who they are, Moses charges the people in Deuteronomy 27:12–13: "When you have crossed over the Jordan, these shall stand on Mount Gerizim to bless the people: Simeon, Levi, Judah, Issachar, Joseph, and Benjamin. And these shall stand on Mount Ebal for the curse: Reuben, Gad, Asher, Zebulun, Dan, and Naphtali." Half the tribes will stand on Mount Ebal and half on Mount Gerizim. It is not clear why the tribes are divided as they are between the mountains. The best explanation is probably their maternal relationship to Jacob. Those tribes that descended from Jacob's legitimate wives (Leah and Rachel) are on the mountain of blessing. Those that descended from their servants (Zilpah and Bilhah), along with Reuben and Zebulun, are on Mount Gerizim, representing the curse.[8] Because these mountains were a significant journey into the land that God had promised, the people would not be able to fulfill this ritual on the actual day that they crossed into the land (Deut. 27:2), but the spirit of the command is to do it as a matter of first importance.

The location that God chooses for this ceremony is not random. All the way back in Genesis 12, we read: "When they came to the land of Canaan, Abram passed through the land to the place at Shechem, to the oak of Moreh. At that time the Canaanites were in the land. Then the LORD appeared to Abram and said, 'To your offspring I will give this land.' So he built there an altar to the LORD, who had appeared to him" (Gen. 12:5–7). God made the promise of this land to Abram at Shechem. Now the people of God are going to be in the land that God promised Abram, and God wants them to observe this ceremony of shouting from one mountain to another with a

8. Craigie, *Deuteronomy*, 330.

valley in between them. The city that lies in the valley between Mount Ebal and Mount Gerizim is none other than Shechem. Continued possession of the land that was promised at Shechem will depend on whether the people remain faithful to God's covenant and receive the blessings of Mount Gerizim, or whether they are unfaithful and bring on themselves the curses of Mount Ebal. The promise seems to hang in the balance between these two mountains, in much the same way that God's promise in the garden of Eden hung in the balance between the two trees. Now in the new Eden of the promised land, God's people will be visually reminded by these two mountains of the choice that is always before them: obedience and blessing in the land that God gave them versus disobedience and curse with exile from the land.

In Deuteronomy 27:14–26, twelve curses are laid down for infractions of the covenant that God is entering into with his vassal people. The Levites were to declare the curses for disobedience, and the people were to agree that these actions deserved God's curse by affirming each statement with the word "Amen." The list here is not exhaustive of the things that bring God's curse, nor is it a summary. It is rather a representative list. We will not revisit all these cursed activities because we have seen them elsewhere in Deuteronomy. But if we step back and look at them together, we see that one thing that these infractions of the covenant have in common is that they would have been difficult for humans to prosecute.[9] For example, the man committing idolatry would be easy enough to convict, but not if he worships his idol in secret (Deut. 27:15). Dishonoring father or mother can be explicit and vocal, but it can also be done secretly in the heart (v. 16). Moving a neighbor's landmark would be easily deniable (v. 17). Misleading a blind man, refusing justice to a vulnerable person, having sex with a close relative or animal, murdering someone in secret, and taking a bribe are all difficult sins to prosecute. But these curses remind us that even if man does not see, God sees. One example is in verse 24: "'Cursed be anyone who strikes down his neighbor in secret.' And all the people shall say, 'Amen.'" This verse does not mean that the person who murders his neighbor in broad daylight is not condemned. It is a warning; the curse comes even if no one knows what we have done.

The most common form of striking down a neighbor in secret today is

9. Tigay, *Deuteronomy*, 247.

abortion. A person or couple seeking an abortion used to go to a clinic to terminate the life of the child in the womb. The uncomfortable and visible nature of that process likely kept some people from aborting their children. Now, however, the abortion pill is mailed to those seeking an abortion; children can be killed without anyone's knowing. As of 2020, 54 percent of children killed in the womb are killed with the "morning-after pill."[10] Even if no one sees us go into Planned Parenthood to get an abortion, we have not avoided God's eye.[11] Those who do these things might escape the justice of man, but they will not escape the justice of the God who sees. That is not only true of abortion; it is also true about our sexual sin. It is true about our withholding from the vulnerable the justice due to them. It is true of the secret idolatries in our hearts. None of these sins escape God's eye. To keep God's law rightly is not a matter of mere external conformity and avoiding being caught, but it is a matter of being changed from the inside out so that we *want* to walk in God's ways.

In addition to being primarily secret in nature, these sins are also relational. The curses here are aimed at those who break their relationships with God and others through sin, whether it is idolatry, dishonoring parents, stealing land, harming the vulnerable, sexually perverted behavior, or murder. Actions or intentions that harm relationships are incompatible with God's blessing and attract his curse instead.[12] We cannot claim to be loving God while mistreating our neighbor in any way. All who do such things, whether it is murder or a hateful word, are under a curse. Deuteronomy 27:26 sums it all up in this way: "'Cursed be anyone who does not confirm the words of this law by doing them.' And all the people shall say, 'Amen.'"

10. Rachel K. Jones, Elizabeth Nash, Lauren Cross, Jesse Philbin, and Marielle Kirstein, "Medication Abortion Now Accounts for More than Half of All US Abortions," Guttmacher Institute, February 2022, https://www.guttmacher.org/article/2022/02/medication-abortion-now-accounts-more-half-all-us-abortions, accessed October 17, 2022.

11. This view of abortion is not a result of current political debates. Christians have always understood the taking of a baby's life in the womb to be murder. An early-second-century Christian document called the *Didache* says, "Thou shalt do no murder, thou shalt not commit adultery, thou shalt not corrupt boys, thou shalt not commit fornication, thou shalt not steal, thou shalt not deal in magic, thou shalt do no sorcery, thou shalt not murder a child by abortion nor kill them when born" (Did. 2:2). The consistent Christian ethic through the ages has recognized the killing of a child in the womb to be sin, while recognizing that in some cases it may be necessary to save the life of the mother.

12. J. McKeown, "Blessings and Curses," in *Dictionary of the Old Testament: Pentateuch*, ed. T. Desmond Alexander and David W. Baker (InterVarsity Press, 2003), 85.

The consequence of disobedience to God's law is to be under the curse of the law. If we have broken any part of God's law, at any point, in any way, we are under the curse of the law. This passage does not set out all that the curse entails; we will see that when we come to Deuteronomy chapter 28. For now, it is enough to know that we all are cursed: "for all have sinned and fall short of the glory of God" (Rom. 3:23). But even within this passage handing down the curse, there is hope.

To Avoid the Curse, We Need to Be Clear on the Remedy for Disobedience

Earlier in the chapter, we passed over the instructions regarding the altar to be built on Mount Ebal. Moses instructs in Deuteronomy 27:5–7: "And there you shall build an altar to the Lord your God, an altar of stones. You shall wield no iron tool on them; you shall build an altar to the Lord your God of uncut stones. And you shall offer burnt offerings on it to the Lord your God, and you shall sacrifice peace offerings and shall eat there, and you shall rejoice before the Lord your God." After building this altar of uncut stones, the Israelites were to make sacrificial offerings and rejoice on this mountain representing the curse. If we were to go on reading, we would see that in Joshua 8:30–35, the people of God under Joshua's direction followed the instructions of this passage and did what Moses commanded.

In the early 1980s, archaeologists excavated a stone ruin on a ridge beneath the summit of Mount Ebal. While it is impossible to be sure, it appears to be a stone altar made with uncut stones with a ramp leading up to it (Ex. 20:26). Some archaeologists believe that it could be the ruins of the altar commanded in this passage. The site dates broadly between 1220 and 1150 b.c., which would be the approximate time when Joshua would have fulfilled the commands of this passage if the late date for the exodus is correct.[13] Later, in 2019, a group of archaeologists were sifting the dirt from that earlier excavation and came across an iron amulet that was folded in half. When they were finally able to read and interpret it, they announced what it said in March 2022: "Cursed, cursed, cursed—cursed by the God *Yhw.*

13. K. A. Kitchen, *On the Reliability of the Old Testament* (Eerdmans, 2003), 232–34. I am not making a case for a late date for the exodus, only stating the relative time period.

You will die cursed. Cursed you will surely die. Cursed by *Yhw*—cursed, cursed, cursed."[14] This is not the kind of positive message that we tend to see printed on bookmarks at the local Christian bookstore. Why would anyone possess this amulet with such a negative message?

Dr. Scott Stripling, the archaeologist who led the research on this amulet, explains:

> This is a self-imprecatory curse, with the author saying that they are binding themselves, saying that these curses will happen to them if they violate God's covenant. More importantly, the amulet was found in the altar context. This was to say that if they broke the covenant, they would come to the altar as taking responsibility for their actions.[15]

The worshiper who carried this amulet had a stern reminder of the curse for covenant disobedience. He went to the altar on the mount of cursing, and at that place sacrifices were made that could enable him to rejoice in spite of the curse.

This is a picture of the hope that was coming later on a mount of cursing called Calvary. On that mountain, the only person to have lived faithfully to God's covenant bore the curses of the covenant on himself so that the blessings of the covenant could come to us. Like the Israelites rejoicing on the mount of cursing, we too can rejoice in the shadow of the cross, knowing that the curse of God has been absorbed by our substitute when he turned that cross into an altar where he paid the debt for our sins! We rejoice not because there is no curse in the New Testament, but because the curse was absorbed by another in our place.

While there was to be a blessing from Mount Gerizim, not one word of blessing was actually announced. All the Israelites heard was the curse. The apostle Paul gives us a commentary on this in Galatians 3:10: "For all

14. The primary value of this amulet from an archaeological perspective is that it would be the earliest form of Hebrew writing ever discovered, which would further support the historical reliability of the Old Testament. Nathan Steinmeyer, "An Early Israelite Curse Inscription from Mt. Ebal?," Biblical Archaeology Society, April 25, 2022, https://www.biblicalarchaeology.org/daily/biblical-artifacts/inscriptions/mt_ebal_inscription/, accessed October 16, 2022.

15. Quoted in Adam Eliyahu Berkowitz, "Does 'Curse Amulet' Prove the Discovery of Joshua's Altar on Mount Ebal?," *Jerusalem Post*, April 3, 2022, https://www.jpost.com/christianworld/article-703046, accessed October 24, 2022.

who rely on works of the law are under a curse; for it is written, 'Cursed be everyone who does not abide by all things written in the Book of the Law, and do them.'" If we rely on works of the law, we are under a curse. The curse comes on everyone who does not do all that is written in the law, and none of us do. God provided a remedy for all of us who are under a curse. Paul continues in verses 13–14, "Christ redeemed us from the curse of the law by becoming a curse for us—for it is written, 'Cursed is everyone who is hanged on a tree'—so that in Christ Jesus the blessing of Abraham might come to the Gentiles, so that we might receive the promised Spirit through faith."

Christ died in such a way as to redeem us from the curse by becoming a curse for us. We who should have been cursed can now go free and receive the blessing of Abraham. Christ's death was substitutionary; he was our substitute. His death was penal; he bore the penalty due to us for our sins. The effect of Christ's work on the cross is that the curse laid down in the law now has nothing more to do with us.[16] In the language of Deuteronomy 27: Christ went up Mount Ebal to bear the curse for our breaking of the law, so that we might go up Mount Gerizim to enjoy the blessings of his obedience to the law. Note also that God did not call his people to worship him on Mount Gerizim, in the context of their self-righteous works. Instead, he called for worship on Mount Ebal, in the context of their sin and failure—but also the place where the atoning sacrifice was made.[17]

If we are aware that we are under God's curse for breaking his law, then there is an answer. If we are terrified of the curse of God coming upon us, then we must flee to Jesus Christ to find our rest and refuge. Christ has fully answered the law's demands. Christ has fully absorbed the curse that the law proclaims for sinners. He has redeemed us from the curse of the law by becoming a curse for us. Now we do not need to fear the law, but we are freed to love the law! M'Cheyne writes:

> You have no more to fear from the law than you will have after the judgment-day. Imagine a saved soul after the judgment-day. When that awful scene is past; when the dead, small and great, have stood before that great white throne; when the sentence of eternal woe has fallen upon all the unconverted,

16. Leon Morris, *The Apostolic Preaching of the Cross* (Eerdmans, 1965), 55.
17. My thanks to Richard D. Phillips for this insight.

> and they have sunk into the lake whose fires can never be quenched; would not that redeemed soul say, I have nothing to fear from that holy law; I have seen its vials poured out, but not a drop has fallen on me? So may you say now, O believer in Jesus! When you look up on the soul of Christ, scarred with God's thunderbolts; when you look upon His body, pierced for sin, you can say, He was made a curse for me; why should I fear that holy law?[18]

While the curse of the law is real, so is the fact that Christ became a curse for us to redeem us from what we rightly deserved. Does this mean that we now ignore God's law and sin however we want, since there is no more curse for us? No! Thomas Watson writes: "Mercy is not for them that sin and fear not, but for them that fear and sin not. God's mercy is a holy mercy; where it pardons it heals."[19] If we have received his mercy, it is a healing mercy that changes our hearts toward God's law and leads us to walk in obedience to it from a posture of holy fear and love.

To be clear, the remedy for disobedience is for a substitute to bear the curse of the law in our place. That remedy is Jesus Christ. You who are under the curse of the law, run to Christ today. For those who are in Christ, let us remember who we are, rejoice in what he has done, and gratefully walk in obedience to all his holy commands.

18. Quoted in Bonar, *Memoir and Remains of Robert Murray M'Cheyne*, 429–30.
19. Thomas Watson, *A Body of Divinity* (Banner of Truth, 1970), 97.

42

The Blessings of Obedience and the Curses of Disobedience

Deuteronomy 28:1—29:1

But if you will not obey the voice of the Lord your God or be careful to do all his commandments and his statutes that I command you today, then all these curses shall come upon you and overtake you. (Deut. 28:15)

He was just a ten-year-old kid when he got into his first fight. A bully took one of his pet pigeons. When he ran after the bully, the bully ripped the bird's head off and threw it at him. The kid started throwing punches, and the bully went down. The kid's name was Mike Tyson. After taking the bully out, Tyson said: "I just wanted more and more and more. I wanted to crush the world to my feet."[1] In some

1. Quoted in Scoop Malinowski, "Biofile Mike Tyson Interview," Mr Biofile, October 12, 2022, https://mrbiofile.com/2022/10/12/biofile-mike-tyson-interview/, accessed November 4, 2022.

ways, he did. Coming from an incredibly broken home and having suffered much growing up, Mike Tyson became the youngest boxer ever to win a heavyweight title, at age twenty. He was the first heavyweight boxer to hold the WBA, WBC, and IBF titles simultaneously and is widely considered one of the greatest fighters of all time. But he also spent time behind bars for sexual assault, he has had various alcohol- and drug-related issues, and though he earned more than $400 million from boxing, he went bankrupt in 2003.

Yet through the ups and downs, one thing has remained constant in Tyson's life: pigeons. He still cares for more than a thousand of them today. When asked why, Tyson responds: "What I love about birds is what we can't get from human beings which is loyalty. . . . As long as he's alive and his heart is pumping, he'll come back."[2] The unstated implication is that humans do not. It is a sad thing when a man must look to a bird to find loyalty because he cannot find it among his own kind.

What Tyson found in his pigeons, God is looking for from his people: loyalty. He desires a people who will not leave him or forsake him, who will not worship other gods besides him, who will obey his commands, honor him as Lord, and keep coming back to him as long as their hearts are pumping. While this kind of loyalty will yield blessings beyond imagination, disloyalty is threatened with curses unspeakable. But such loyalty is hard to find. As Proverbs 20:6 reminds us, "Many a man proclaims his own steadfast love, but a faithful man who can find?"

Our trouble is that we want God on our terms. We want a god who will punish evildoers, but who will also make an exception for us. We want a god who will be satisfied with our occasional participation in the life of the church, our token efforts at doing good, our uncostly living, and our unsacrificial service.[3] We want a god who does not mind if we have a couple of other gods on the side. But these verses leave no room for such an approach to life with God. There are no exceptions. Obedience leads to blessings untold, while disobedience leads to curses unspeakable.

2. Quoted in Malinowski, "Tyson Interview."

3. Raymond Brown, *The Message of Deuteronomy: Not by Bread Alone*, The Bible Speaks Today (InterVarsity Press, 1993), 269.

Obedience Leads to Blessings Untold

Because we are covering a very large section of text, we will just dip in here and there to get a flavor of the blessings. We can break this down into three sections: the condition, the blessings, and the cause.

The Condition

Moses goes out of his way to spell out the condition of blessing as clearly as possible. He writes in Deuteronomy 28:1–2: "And if you faithfully obey the voice of the Lord your God, being careful to do all his commandments that I command you today, the Lord your God will set you high above all the nations of the earth. And all these blessings shall come upon you and overtake you, if you obey the voice of the Lord your God." What God is calling for from his people is faithful obedience to his voice and carefulness to do all his commandments. This is not the first time that we have seen this condition in Deuteronomy, but here the command has added emphasis.

The blessings that God will lay out for the Israelites are going to "come upon you and overtake you." The word "overtake" is a hunting term connected with the idea of pursuing something successfully.[4] In this case, God's blessings will go after his obedient people and find them. In case it needs to be said a little louder for the people in the back, we read in Deuteronomy 28:13–14, "And the Lord will make you the head and not the tail, and you shall only go up and not down, if you obey the commandments of the Lord your God, which I command you today, being careful to do them, and if you do not turn aside from any of the words that I command you today, to the right hand or to the left, to go after other gods to serve them." We get the feeling that Moses does not want to leave any room for them to say, "How were we supposed to know that you wanted us to obey and not worship other gods?" So, reemphasizing the same points, he calls them to obey, not to turn aside, and not to go after other gods.

The Hebrew word translated as "obey" is related to the word *hear*. To hear God's voice, in Hebrew thought, is not simply to hear, but to do what he says: to heed. Obedience is not only an Old Testament concern. The apostle James makes this same connection when he writes, "But be doers of the

4. Robin Wakely, *NIDOTTE*, s.v. "נָשַׂג," 3:164.

word, and not hearers only, deceiving yourselves" (James 1:22). Those of us who are parents know what obedience is. When we command our children at bedtime, "Go brush your teeth," what happens next? Obedience involves stopping whatever else they are doing, making their way to the bathroom, putting toothpaste on a toothbrush (preferably their own), and brushing their teeth. But experience tells us that there are all sorts of ways for this to go wrong. Our children might just ignore us—intentionally because they do not want to do it, or unintentionally because they are absorbed in something. They might talk back and complain. They might give excuses about why they cannot do it. They might hit the floor and start crawling like an inchworm. They might start a fight with a sibling, or put soap on someone else's toothbrush, or ask for food because they just realized that they are hungry, or decide that they are too tired to do it, or just stand there holding the toothbrush. None of these is obedience. Some of these responses are close to our own response when God commands us not to lie or spread disinformation. How do we respond when God commands us to forgive those who have sinned against us or when he tells us to rest and give him one day out of seven? It matters. The condition of blessing is obedience.

The Blessings

Verses 1–13 of Deuteronomy 28 all contain specific blessings promised to the people of Israel that are inseparably connected with obedience to God's covenant stipulations. There is some repetition in these, so we are going to group them into four categories to handle them collectively.

Exaltation

Deuteronomy 28:1 says that "the Lord your God will set you high above all the nations of the earth." He is going to make Israel great above the rest of the nations. His aim in doing so is that the nations would be blessed by desiring what the people of Israel have through their relationship with Yahweh.

Fruitfulness

We read in Deuteronomy 28:3–4: "Blessed shall you be in the city, and blessed shall you be in the field. Blessed shall be the fruit of your womb and the fruit of your ground and the fruit of your cattle, the increase of your herds and the young of your flock." The city is the place of trade, and the field is the place of agriculture, and in both places the Israelites will prosper as a people. God will also bless them with fertility for themselves and their animals, and their land will be fertile as well. Children are a blessing, as are growing flocks and productive fields. These are all blessings that require our work, but can happen only by God's creative will.

Abundance

"Blessed shall be your basket and your kneading bowl" (Deut. 28:5). The basket was the instrument used for gathering produce and the kneading bowl for making bread.[5] This means that the harvest is going to be plentiful, resulting in lots of food to enjoy and share. It is hard for us to appreciate this promise of plenty in our culture of abundance, but for people in a subsistence culture, the blessing of not worrying about where the next meal is coming from is unfathomable.

Victory

We read in Deuteronomy 28:6–7: "Blessed shall you be when you come in, and blessed shall you be when you go out. The LORD will cause your enemies who rise against you to be defeated before you. They shall come out against you one way and flee before you seven ways." Whatever the people of Israel are doing, they will experience success. They are not a large nation, they do not have a great military, and yet God says that he will see to it that they are victorious in conflict.

The Cause

Deuteronomy 28:7–13 expands further on these themes, but we get the idea. The important contribution we see in these verses is that the blessings that are going to come on God's people are not just the natural benefits of good living. Rather, the blessings will come because God is going to bring them. In verses 7–13, we see seven occurrences of "The LORD will" or "he will," referring to the Lord. God is going to shower them with blessings, taking care of all their needs, exalting them as a model nation, and filling

5. Jeffrey H. Tigay, *Deuteronomy*, JPSTC (Jewish Publication Society, 1996), 258.

their land with children and livestock, with plenty of food and victory over all their enemies, so that they can be secure and at peace. That is a good life! It is a life inseparably connected with obedience.

DISOBEDIENCE LEADS TO CURSES UNSPEAKABLE

As we did with the blessings, we will step into the curses just enough to get a sense of them, and to guide us we will consider them under the same three headings of the condition, the curses, and the cause.

The Condition

The "if . . . then" condition leading to these horrific curses is laid out first in Deuteronomy 28:15: "But if you will not obey the voice of the LORD your God or be careful to do all his commandments and his statutes that I command you today, then all these curses shall come upon you and overtake you." Such a thought was a tremendous encouragement when thinking of blessings, but to know that we will not be able to escape the curses should put the fear of God in us. That is precisely the purpose of these curses.

The Curses

The first thing to notice about the curses is that this section is about four times as long as the blessing section, stretching from verses 15 through 68 of Deuteronomy 28. Why are so many more curses than blessings listed? There are several possibilities. In other ancient treaties that follow the same pattern as Deuteronomy, the curse section was typically longer than the blessing section. In some of those ancient treaties, no blessings were even mentioned, just threats for disobedience. Another possible reason for the longer curse section is that sometimes people are more motivated to avoid consequences than to gain rewards. My inclination is toward a third view, which holds that Moses had a pretty good idea that the curse section of this passage was going to be a lot more relevant for the covenant people of God than the blessing section. In fact, the curses in this section so accurately reflect the curses that Israel later suffered that some critical scholars think this passage had to be written after the events occurred. For those who believe in a sovereign God who directs the course of history and who inspires his prophets to write things before they occur, we have no such issue with the accuracy of the descriptions in this section. What are the curses to follow if the people persist in disobedience to God?

Humiliation

Rather than Israel's being exalted above the nations, we read in Deuteronomy 28:43–44: "The sojourner who is among you shall rise higher and higher above you, and you shall come down lower and lower. He shall lend to you, and you shall not lend to him. He shall be the head, and you shall be the tail." The people of God will sink even lower than the underprivileged sojourner dwelling among them.[6] Rather than having abundance to share, they will have to borrow. This will not be the extent of their humiliation, but will comprise just one small piece of it.

Barrenness

Rather than Israel's being fruitful, we see the flip side of those promised blessings from Deuteronomy 28:3–6 in verses 16 and 18: "Cursed shall you be in the city, and cursed shall you be in the field. . . . Cursed shall be the fruit of your womb and the fruit of your ground, the increase of your herds and the young of your flock." In both trade and agriculture, the people will lack. Wombs will be barren for both people and livestock, and the land will not produce.

Futility

In Deuteronomy 28:31–34, Moses captures the sense of the futility of life under the curse:

> Your ox shall be slaughtered before your eyes, but you shall not eat any of it. Your donkey shall be seized before your face, but shall not be restored to you. Your sheep shall be given to your enemies, but there shall be no one to help you. Your sons and your daughters shall be given to another people, while your eyes look on and fail with longing for them all day long, but you shall be helpless. A nation that you have not known shall eat up the fruit of your

6. Peter C. Craigie, *The Book of Deuteronomy*, NICOT (Eerdmans, 1976), 347.

> ground and of all your labors, and you shall be only oppressed and crushed continually, so that you are driven mad by the sights that your eyes see.

Imagine that. Everything we work for constantly being taken from us before we have the chance to enjoy it. Raising children, only to have them taken from us and being helpless to save them. This kind of futility and injustice would drive anyone mad, and the curse of futility is expanded even further in Deuteronomy 28:38–42.

Lack

Moses writes in Deuteronomy 28:17, "Cursed shall be your basket and your kneading bowl." Again, this is the reverse of the blessing from verse 5. But it is not just that the Israelites will go without a meal every now and then. He is warning of famine of the worst kinds. Verses 54–57 speak of the most refined men and women among them as being so hungry that they will eat their children and their afterbirth, and they will refuse to share with their remaining living relatives. The horror of that kind of lack is unfathomable. Moses continues in verses 47–48:

> Because you did not serve the Lord your God with joyfulness and gladness of heart, because of the abundance of all things, therefore you shall serve your enemies whom the Lord will send against you, in hunger and thirst, in nakedness, and lacking everything. And he will put a yoke of iron on your neck until he has destroyed you.

When God made his people abound, they did not serve him as he deserved. Now God is going to allow them to serve their enemies in total lack.

Exile

Finally, the Israelites will suffer defeat at the hands of their enemies and God will put them out of the land:

> And the Lord will scatter you among all peoples, from one end of the earth to the other, and there you shall serve other gods of wood and stone, which neither you nor your fathers have known. And among these nations you shall find no respite, and there shall be no resting place for the sole of your

> foot, but the LORD will give you there a trembling heart and failing eyes and a languishing soul. Your life shall hang in doubt before you. Night and day you shall be in dread and have no assurance of your life. In the morning you shall say, "If only it were evening!" and at evening you shall say, "If only it were morning!" because of the dread that your heart shall feel, and the sights that your eyes shall see. And the LORD will bring you back in ships to Egypt, a journey that I promised that you should never make again; and there you shall offer yourselves for sale to your enemies as male and female slaves, but there will be no buyer. (Deut. 28:64–68)

The picture is one not only of being exiled from the land but of returning to the slavery of Egypt. It is a reverse exodus. But the situation will be so dire that when the Israelites want to become slaves of their enemies, there will not be a buyer for them.

The Cause

The Lord will bring these things on the people. His judgment will stalk the offender until it overtakes him (Deut. 28:15) as surely as his blessings will follow the obedient (v. 2). The curses culminate in Deuteronomy 28:63: "And as the LORD took delight in doing you good and multiplying you, so the LORD will take delight in bringing ruin upon you and destroying you." Is this the awful God of the Old Testament that people warned us about? Peter Craigie writes, "The potential actions of God described in [these verses] are not the mindless or capricious acts of an unknown and malevolent deity; they are the just acts of a righteous God whose covenant love would have been spurned by his own people."[7] Our God is absolutely committed to covenant loyalty to his people, and he calls for loyalty in return.

The cumulative effect of this whole section is to leave us with the impression that disloyalty to God is horrific if God will do these things to deter his people from going astray, or to bring them back once they have gone astray. Later in Israel's history, the people would experience these curses of disobedience. God used the exile to sanctify the Israelites and then restore them to the land under the leadership of Ezra and Nehemiah. By means of these curses, God brought his people back to himself. Clearly, in these

7. Craigie, 351.

curses God is not forsaking his people, but his gifts to them are different. Instead of giving them rain, he is now going to give them drought and famine (Deut. 28:24) as a way of turning them back from disaster.[8] As terrible as these curses are, they are not as bad as the ultimate end of disobedience. Through these terrible things, God seeks to rescue his people from a worse fate that awaits them if they persist in disobedience and sin.

Any one of these situations would be absolutely devastating, yet here is what we should consider: hell is worse than all of this. As bad as it would feel to be in such destitution that we would eat our children and not share with other family members, hell is worse. As horrific as it would be to have loved ones assaulted before our eyes, hell is worse. The terrors of this passage cannot begin to sound the depths of the despair, the hopelessness, the pain, the anger, the regret, the selfishness, and the misery of hell. What Deuteronomy 28:15–68 describes is life without God's presence in blessing and with his presence only in the form of judgment. Yet even so, God's blessing is present in some way because there is opportunity to repent, there is opportunity for a change of direction, there are still the gifts of sunshine, love, and family, and not everything is as bad as it could be. But in hell, the last remaining vestiges of God's blessing will be completely removed. There will be no more opportunity to repent, no more ability to have a different future, no more enjoyment of any of God's blessings.

Here is the very real picture that the Bible gives us of life apart from God and separation from him eternally. It is not a scare tactic, but a realistic warning. Currently, you may be living your life in rebellion against God and saying, "This is not so bad." But it is "not so bad" only because of God's mercy. When God withdraws his mercy, it will be worse than you could ever fathom.

FINAL CONSIDERATIONS

As we conclude this chapter, there are three things to consider. First, God has made provision for the forgiveness of the disobedient. None of these curses are inevitable. God does not bring them on the people for slipping up here and there, even if they repent. His patience stretches on and on, but

8. Gordon J. Wenham, *The Book of Leviticus*, NICOT (Eerdmans, 1979), 331.

there comes a point when the rebelliousness of the people requires more severe forms of discipline to save them from themselves. Judgment is not ultimately God's last word to his people, nor does it prove that he has rejected his people. Forgiveness was present under the law, for these believers were under the same covenant of grace as we are. The difference is that they did not know that the sacrifices of atonement they were making were pointing forward to the infinitely precious blood of Jesus that takes away the sins of all of God's people. One blessing under the gospel is to know that Christ has fulfilled the law's demands for obedience on behalf of his people. Paul writes in Philippians 3:8–9:

> Indeed, I count everything as loss because of the surpassing worth of knowing Christ Jesus my Lord. For his sake I have suffered the loss of all things and count them as rubbish, in order that I may gain Christ and be found in him, not having a righteousness of my own that comes from the law, but that which comes through faith in Christ, the righteousness from God that depends on faith.

We are declared righteous in the sight of God and heirs of every blessing on account of Christ's righteousness imputed to us by faith alone. We may be disobedient, but we do not have to face the curse. If we have been walking in disobedience to God's commands, we should not just keep on going. Rather, we must repent and go to Jesus for the forgiveness of our sins and commit ourselves to walking in obedience.

Second, the New Testament is as serious about obedience as the Old Testament is. Some are under the impression that obedience is an optional extra in the life of a Christian. After all, if Christ has fulfilled the law for us, what have we to do? Obedience is not optional. It is the only proper response to God's saving grace, just as it was for Israel. The late Westminster theologian John Murray wrote:

> It is one of the most perilous distortions of the doctrine of grace, and one that has carried with it the saddest records of moral and spiritual disaster, to assume that past privileges . . . guarantee the security of men irrespective of perseverance in faith and holiness. Believers under the gospel continue in the covenant and in the enjoyment of its privileges because they continue

> in the fulfillment of the conditions; they continue in faith, love, hope, and obedience. True believers are kept unto the end, unto the eschatological salvation; but they are kept by the power of God *through faith*. . . . It is not reached irrespective of perseverance, but through perseverance. And this means nothing if it does not mean concentrated obedience to the will of Christ as expressed in his commandments.[9]

If we have made peace with any sin in our lives, it is time to wage war once again. Hebrews 3:12–14 warns: "Take care, brothers, lest there be in any of you an evil, unbelieving heart, leading you to fall away from the living God. But exhort one another every day, as long as it is called 'today,' that none of you may be hardened by the deceitfulness of sin. For we have come to share in Christ, if indeed we hold our original confidence firm to the end." Only those who persevere in faith and obedience share in Christ.

Third, the blessings of obedience and the curses of disobedience remain in effect. The New Testament does not speak of Christians' being under God's curse (for Christ took the curse for us [Gal. 3:13–14]), but it does speak of our experiencing the discipline of God (1 Cor. 11:27–30; Heb. 12:5–11). In his book *Holiness by Grace*, Bryan Chapell describes what can and cannot change in our relationship with God. What can change is our fellowship with God, our experience of his blessing, our assurance of his love, and his discipline. What cannot change is our sonship, his desire for our welfare, and our security in his love and affection for us.[10]

The shape of discipline for the people of Israel was very much physical and national, whereas in the new covenant, discipline is not so limited and may come in many forms. God brings hardship on his people, whether described as curses, discipline, or judgments, not only because we deserve

9. John Murray, *Principles of Conduct: Aspects of Biblical Ethics* (Eerdmans, 1984), 199–200.

10. Chapell's complete lists are as follows:

WHAT CAN CHANGE	WHAT CANNOT CHANGE
Our fellowship	*Our sonship*
Our experience of his blessing	*His desire for our welfare*
Our assurance of his love	*His actual affection for us*
His delight in our actions	*His love for us*
His discipline	*Our destiny*
Our sense of guilt	*Our security*

Bryan Chapell, *Holiness by Grace: Delighting in the Joy That Is Our Strength* (Crossway, 2001), 196.

it, but because he loves us and wants to correct our foolish ways (Deut. 8:5; Pss. 38:2; 94:12; Jer. 30:11; 31:18; Heb. 12:5–11).[11] Amos 4:6–12 laments the fact that despite God's judgments, his people still did not return to him. When we encounter hard things, we should use it as an opportunity for self-reflection on whether it might be related to any disobedience or sin in our life. At the same time, in both the Old and New Testaments, we are warned against assuming that hardship in anyone's life, including our own, is a direct result of covenant disobedience (Job 1–2; Ps. 73; John 9; 2 Cor. 11:16–30). We do know that for those who are in Christ, even those things that seem like curses in this life will become blessings to us. For those who are not in Christ, even those things that look like blessings will become curses. Alexander Maclaren puts it succinctly:

> Though the connection between well-doing and material gain is not so clear now, it is by no means abrogated, either for nations or for individuals. Moral and religious law has social and economic consequences, and though the perplexed distribution of earthly good and ill often bewilders faith and emboldens scepticism there still is visible in human affairs a drift towards recompensing in the world the righteous and the wicked.[12]

For the covenant people of God under the terms of the new covenant, obedience to God's commandments is no less important than it was to the covenant people of God under the Mosaic covenant. The enjoyment of God's blessings in the new covenant is no less connected to our obedience than it was for the people under the Mosaic covenant.[13] Those blessings cannot be

11. Wenham, *Book of Leviticus*, 330–31.

12. Alexander Maclaren, *Deuteronomy, Joshua, Judges, Ruth, and First Book of Samuel, Second Samuel, First Kings, and Second Kings, Chapters I to VII*, vol. 2 of *Expositions of Holy Scripture* (Eerdmans, 1944), 27.

13. Evangelicals frequently mistake God's relationship to the people of Israel as one based on a covenant of works, while those of us under the new covenant relate to God as under a covenant of grace. That is incorrect. The proper understanding is that those under the Mosaic covenant and those under the new covenant are under different administrations of the one covenant of grace (see chapter 7 of the WCF for more). Faith working itself out in loving obedience is what God required of the people of Israel, and it is what he requires of us. Neither the obedience of the people of Israel nor that of Christians today in any way earns acceptance with God. We receive that acceptance by faith in Christ alone. And that faith then obeys God's commands in loving gratitude, which is simply walking on the path of blessings that Christ has purchased for us. Christ has earned the blessings for us, but we cannot enjoy them apart from the path of obedience to God's commands. Murray writes:

earned; they are given freely in Christ. Yet we cannot enjoy those free blessings apart from obedience.[14] The hardships connected to disobedience are no less real for the people of God under the new covenant than they were for the people of God under the Mosaic covenant. The disciplinary function of the curses for the covenant people of God under the Mosaic covenant is no less loving than the disciplinary function of hardship for the covenant people of God under the new covenant. Finally, the threats of eternal separation for perpetual disloyalty are no less real for the people of God under the new covenant than for the people of God under the Mosaic covenant.

While our English Bibles end the chapter after verse 68, the Hebrew and Greek Old Testament conclude the passage at Deuteronomy 29:1: "These are the words of the covenant that the LORD commanded Moses to make with the people of Israel in the land of Moab, besides the covenant that he had made with them at Horeb." It is most likely that "these are the words of the covenant" refers to everything that has come before, rather than what comes after. Moses is not referring to a separate covenant from the one made at Horeb, but is writing of a renewal of that covenant by reestablishing and expanding on the covenant stipulations laid down there and concluding with this reminder of the curses that will follow upon disobedience.

May we all heed the promise and the warning of this text. Does God's wrath seem overly severe? It is only a reflection of his perfect moral character and hatred of all sin, which must be judged. But if his wrath is severe, how much more severe is his love—a love that would send his one and only Son to bear the wrath of our covenant-breaking in our place and secure our perseverance to the end by the merit of his faithfulness, not ours. The blessings and curses are before us. If we will embrace the God who loved us and gave himself up for us to forgive our sins and to reconcile us to himself,

---

> We may therefore sum up the matter by saying that the holiness of God demanded conformity to his holiness, that holiness was of the essence of the covenant privilege, that holiness was the condition of continuance in the enjoyment of the covenant blessings and the medium through which the covenant privilege realized its fruition. Holiness is exemplified in obedience to the commandments of God. Obedience is therefore entirely congruous with, and disobedience entirely contradictory of, the nature of God's covenant with Israel as one of union and communion with God.
>
> In all of this the demand of obedience in the Mosaic covenant is principally identical with the same demand in the new covenant of the gospel economy.

Murray, *Principles of Conduct*, 198–99.

14. See O. Palmer Robertson, *The Christ of the Covenants* (Baker, 1981), 184–85.

if we will walk in his ways and keep going back to him as long as our hearts beat in our chests, he will bless us now and in eternity with blessings beyond telling. But if we will not be faithful to him, if we insist on going our own way and living apart from him, if we will not show him the same loyalty that even a pigeon will show to its master, he will ultimately give us what we seek: an eternity bereft of all his goodness. Choose wisely.

43

The Things That Are Revealed

Deuteronomy 29:2–29

The secret things belong to the Lord *our God, but the things that are revealed belong to us and to our children forever, that we may do all the words of this law.* (Deut. 29:29)

It was a cold Christmas night in 1776 when General George Washington led the battered remnants of his army across the Delaware River. The army was in terrible shape because of previous battles and a lack of food, but Washington was committed to making a surprise attack on the Hessian soldiers in Trenton, New Jersey. The Hessian commander, Colonel Johann Rall, was at a Christmas party that night. As an experienced commander, he could not fathom that the colonials would mount an attack. Around midnight, a local farmer came to the door of the party, bringing Colonel Rall a message. A servant took the note and gave it to Rall. Unfortunately for Rall, he was in the middle of a holiday card game and stuffed the note into his pocket without reading it. At daybreak, Washington and his troops attacked amid a freezing sleet. The bleary Hessians, surprised by the attack, were soon overwhelmed. Nine hundred of the Hessian soldiers were taken captive, and Colonel Rall was mortally wounded.

When a physician cut away Rall's clothing to treat his wounds, a note fell from his pocket. That note was a warning from the farmer that Washington was going to attack. If Rall had heeded the message, he might have lived to see the American troops defeated and Washington taken captive. Instead, from his deathbed the colonel lamented before he died: "If I had read this, I would not be here."[1] Everything he needed to know had been revealed, but he had failed to profit from it because he did not read it and did not heed its warning.

Moses does not want the people of Israel to make the same mistake. God revealed to his people everything they needed to know for life in the land through this book of Deuteronomy. But since the revelation itself is not enough, in Deuteronomy 29 Moses begins his third speech and brings together all the main threads in order to show the importance of heeding the message.

Remember God's Grace in Establishing His Covenant

In the opening verses, Moses points the Israelites back to their history with the Lord. In doing so, he makes two things plain.

First, God's saving acts must be spiritually discerned. We read in Deuteronomy 29:2–4:

> And Moses summoned all Israel and said to them: "You have seen all that the LORD did before your eyes in the land of Egypt, to Pharaoh and to all his servants and to all his land, the great trials that your eyes saw, the signs, and those great wonders. But to this day the LORD has not given you a heart to understand or eyes to see or ears to hear."

Much of the present generation about to cross into the land had not directly witnessed God's mighty acts of salvation in Egypt. The people had heard of

1. Quoted in Rick Beyer, *The Greatest Stories Never Told: 230 Tales from History to Astonish, Bewilder, and Stupefy*, Reader's Digest special ed. (Reader's Digest Association, 2008), 260–61.

them and were beneficiaries of them, and they had also seen God do other mighty works on the way to the plains of Moab where they now stand, but at this point in the text, they have not yet understood.

Moses goes on to remind the people of what God has done for them in Deuteronomy 29:5–6: "I have led you forty years in the wilderness. Your clothes have not worn out on you, and your sandals have not worn off your feet. You have not eaten bread, and you have not drunk wine or strong drink, that you may know that I am the LORD your God." God has supernaturally sustained his people for those forty years. They have not been living on bread or drinking wine or strong drink, which would have been the ordinary sources of provision. Instead, God has provided miraculous manna from heaven and water from rocks to sustain them. His purpose is explicit: "that you may know that I am the LORD your God" (Deut. 29:6). What an incredibly gracious God!

Then he reminds the Israelites of the victories he has given them over the tribes on the east side of the Jordan in Deuteronomy 29:7–8: "And when you came to this place, Sihon the king of Heshbon and Og the king of Bashan came out against us to battle, but we defeated them. We took their land and gave it for an inheritance to the Reubenites, the Gadites, and the half-tribe of the Manassites." When we add all of this up, Moses is reminding them of the miraculous deliverance, provision, and victory that God has given. He wants them to see it so that their hearts will be bound in covenant loyalty to this gracious God. Thus far, they have not understood it, though.

To understand why the people have not discerned what these miracles were intended to reveal to them, we need to go back to Deuteronomy 29:4: "But to this day the LORD has not given you a heart to understand or eyes to see or ears to hear." There is a type of seeing, hearing, and understanding that transcends our physical capacities. This verse makes it clear that such spiritual discernment is a gift of God. John Calvin writes that "a clear and powerful understanding is a special gift of the Spirit, since men are ever blind even in the brightest light, until they have been enlightened by God."[2] It is entirely possible to physically see what God has done, and yet not truly

2. John Calvin, *Commentaries on the Four Last Books of Moses, Arranged in the Form of a Harmony*, trans. Charles William Bingham, Calvin's Commentaries (Baker, 2005), 1:389.

see.[3] The people of Israel need God to do for their hearts what they cannot do for themselves (Deut. 30:6). As Paul will later write in Ephesians, they need the eyes of their hearts enlightened (Eph. 1:16–18).

But this raises a challenging theological question: if people do not understand, see, or hear spiritually because God has not enabled them, then isn't God to blame for our spiritual obtuseness? No. Our spiritual blindness is a result of our own sin and rebellion against God, and it is a testimony to the hardness of our hearts apart from his enlightening grace. As sinful people, in the arrogance of our hearts, we would blame God for our blindness, rather than humbly crying out to him to give us the sight and understanding that we do not deserve. God's saving acts must be spiritually discerned, and this spiritual discernment is a gift of his grace.

The second truth that Moses makes plain is that God's saving acts call for an obedient response. Because of God's rescue, God's provision, and the victory that God accomplished for the Israelites over Sihon and Og, Moses draws the following conclusion in verse 9 of Deuteronomy 29: "Therefore keep the words of this covenant and do them, that you may prosper in all that you do." Our obedience is not the way by which we become God's people, but the evidence that we are God's people. Those who have not seen, heard, or understood what God has done for them are not capable of walking in obedience to God's covenant commands. They must first be set free.

The great hymn writer Charles Wesley captured this twofold reality of God's enlightening grace and his call for obedience. He wrote in his classic hymn, "Long my imprisoned spirit lay fast bound in sin and nature's night."[4] By "nature's night" he is referring to the darkness of understanding that we are in on account of our sin. But into that darkness, God brings his light: "Thine eye diffused a quick'ning ray; I woke, the dungeon flamed with light; my chains fell off, my heart was free; I rose, went forth, and followed thee." God brought light into that spiritual darkness and set the prisoner free. In response to that freedom, Wesley walked out of that dark dungeon and began to follow Jesus. This is what an enlightened and freed heart does: it freely follows God's commandments.

3. Likewise, Jesus frequently appends the phrase "he who has ears to hear, let him hear" (e.g., Matt. 11:15; Mark 4:9; Luke 8:8), indicating the reality that many who listen to him will not really hear him because of this spiritual darkness.

4. Charles Wesley, "And Can It Be That I Should Gain" (1738).

When I was in college, I desperately desired to grasp salvation, to know that I was forgiven. I spent weeks reading the Scriptures, but I could not make it happen; I could not see. One evening as I was listening to my roommate's worship music, I was singing along with "Open the Eyes of My Heart," and as I sang that song, God did open the eyes of my heart! I saw that what Christ had done was enough for me. I could not open my eyes for myself. I was hungry enough to search for it, and even this hungering and seeking were the product of God's grace in my life. He had to open my eyes, though. If you are blind to what God has done, and if you hear the words of the gospel but you have not really heard the gospel, then ask him to open the eyes of your heart. You will know that he has done so when your heart is set free and you actually desire to follow him—not for what he will do, but because of what you understand that he has already done.

Embrace Your Place in God's Covenant

If we are going to benefit from what God has done, then we must embrace our place in God's gracious covenant.

First, every individual is called to respond. This invitation is for every individual who hears the invitation now, and for those who follow. Moses writes in Deuteronomy 29:10–12:

> You are standing today, all of you, before the LORD your God: the heads of your tribes, your elders, and your officers, all the men of Israel, your little ones, your wives, and the sojourner who is in your camp, from the one who chops your wood to the one who draws your water, so that you may enter into the sworn covenant of the LORD your God, which the LORD your God is making with you today.

The importance of embracing this covenant by every member of the people of God is made clear in this passage. It is not enough that the elders of the people enter the covenant on behalf of the rest, or that the heads of the families do so. Each man, woman, and child, the sojourner among them, the one who chops wood and carries water—every single one must personally embrace this covenant from the heart. Peter Craigie writes, "The health and vitality of the whole community depended on the health and vitality of the religious commitment of each individual within it."[5] Every single one must enter it in the same way. There is no special path for the upper class or the working class, the young or the old.

We embrace the covenant according to Deuteronomy 29:13, "that he may establish you today as his people, and that he may be your God, as he promised you, and as he swore to your fathers, to Abraham, to Isaac, and to Jacob." This is the central covenant promise down through the ages, starting with Abraham: that he will be our God and we will be his people.[6]

Second, future generations are called to respond. These covenant promises are available not simply to the generation of people standing there, but also to their children who will come after them. Moses continues in Deuteronomy 29:14–15, "It is not with you alone that I am making this sworn covenant, but with whoever is standing here with us today before the Lord our God, and with whoever is not here with us today." Each successive generation was to embrace personally God's covenant and his promises from the heart.

Under the new covenant in Christ, these covenant promises radically expanded to all the Gentiles, as Peter said in Acts 2:38–39: "And Peter said to them, 'Repent and be baptized every one of you in the name of Jesus Christ for the forgiveness of your sins, and you will receive the gift of the Holy Spirit. For the promise is for you and for your children and for all who are far off, everyone whom the Lord our God calls to himself.'" The expansion of the promises to the Gentiles does not lessen the importance of God's covenant promises for our own children, but further confirms it. He still promises to be a God to us and to our children after us.

Presbyterian and Reformed Christians believe in the continuity of God's covenant promises from one generation to another. We believe that the children of God's covenant people are included in God's covenant promises until those children explicitly reject their portion, as Esau did. For this reason, we give the children of believers the sign of the covenant, which is baptism, even before they can embrace the covenant themselves. Because they are children of believers, they get to enjoy the outward benefits of being a part of God's covenant people that the children of unbelievers do

5. Peter C. Craigie, *The Book of Deuteronomy*, NICOT (Eerdmans, 1976), 359.
6. E.g., Gen. 17:7; Ex. 6:7; Lev. 26:12; Jer. 7:23; 11:4; 30:22; Ezek. 36:28.

not get to enjoy. When the children of believers are of sufficient age to understand the terms of the new covenant, and that they must embrace God's covenant promises themselves and put their trust in Jesus Christ alone for salvation, to understand that they too are called to walk in obedience to his commandments, then they must embrace the covenant promises personally. The doctrine of the inclusion of believers in the covenant of grace in no way detracts from the need for regeneration, repentance, and faith. Everyone who is a part of God's covenant people embraces the covenant promises in the same way. We must stop trusting in ourselves and our good works. We must stop thinking that we are okay on our own, and instead fling ourselves on God's mercy, trusting that he will not cast us out. Every individual is called to embrace his or her place among God's covenant people by trusting in Jesus Christ. Each generation of believers is responsible to impress these covenant promises on their children, that they too will respond to God's gracious offer of salvation.

BEWARE BETRAYING THE GOD OF THE COVENANT

God is faithful to do all that he has promised, but in addition to the blessings that he promises to deliver, he also promises curses for those who betray him. We have seen in Deuteronomy chapters 12–26 many ways that we can go astray from God's commands, but in this passage two specifically heinous forms of betrayal are named.

First, there is idolatry. Repeatedly through Deuteronomy and the rest of the Old and New Testaments, the worshiping of idols is strictly warned against and forbidden. Moses writes in Deuteronomy 29:16–18: "You know how we lived in the land of Egypt, and how we came through the midst of the nations through which you passed. And you have seen their detestable things, their idols of wood and stone, of silver and gold, which were among them. Beware lest there be among you a man or woman or clan or tribe whose heart is turning away today from the LORD our God to go and serve the gods of those nations." Idolatry includes worshiping rival gods, but it also includes fearing, trusting, or loving anything else with the fear, trust, or love that only the true God deserves. The people are called to beware of their hearts' turning from God. It could be a man or woman, it could be a clan, or it could even be a whole tribe turning away. Likewise, not only individuals, but families and churches can turn away from God to serve the gods of our culture.

What idols are we most prone to go after as Americans? Money remains one of our biggest temptations. Political and sexual identities are increasingly the things that people are looking to for meaning and hope in this world, rather than God. Sports have become a tremendous idol in our culture. To see how important this is to us, look at how much money is spent on youth sports all the way through the professional leagues. Whatever we are regularly willing to put before worship on Sundays probably has idol status in our lives. We must beware of things that turn our affections from God.

Second, there is willful disobedience. Moses continues with this second habit to beware of in Deuteronomy 29:18–19: "Beware lest there be among you a root bearing poisonous and bitter fruit, one who, when he hears the words of this sworn covenant, blesses himself in his heart, saying, 'I shall be safe, though I walk in the stubbornness of my heart.' This will lead to the sweeping away of moist and dry alike." Here is the person who knows what God requires and determines in his heart that he will be safe even though he rejects God's way and goes his own way. The person who follows his wayward heart is described as "a root bearing poisonous and bitter fruit." The writer of Hebrews also warns us against such people: "See to it that no one fails to obtain the grace of God; that no 'root of bitterness' springs up and causes trouble, and by it many become defiled" (Heb. 12:15).

Everyone who has God's Word has two options in any situation: follow God's Word, or follow the stubbornness of one's own heart. This word for "stubbornness" shows up several times in the Old Testament, and each time it is in a context of the people's rejecting God's Word and stubbornly following their own hearts.[7] It always leads to disaster, not only for themselves, but for the other people they have defiled. Raymond Brown writes:

> That is one of the most frightening things about human sin—it dulls our perception and warps our judgment. It corrupts our thinking and distorts our values. Sin parades itself in a subtly attractive guise; we do not see it for the horror it truly is. It liberalizes our outlook, professing to release us from

7. A survey of the following passages reveals how common a problem this was for God's people: Deut. 29:19; Ps. 81:12; Jer. 3:17; 7:24; 9:14; 11:8; 13:10; 16:12; 18:12; 23:17.

> outdated traditions and mere social conventions. Instead of listening to what God says to us in his word, we listen to the changing, vacillating dictates of our own minds and the equally corrupt judgments of others.[8]

We are tempted to "follow our heart" in many situations, but the most destructive areas tend to be in relationships. For instance, God's Word warns against marrying those who do not follow Christ (1 Cor. 7:39; 2 Cor. 6:14). Yet people decide to follow their hearts rather than the Word of God. Or a Christian husband or wife starts to feel that the marriage is not everything that he or she hoped it would be. Another woman or man begins to give the unhappy spouse the attention that he or she deserves. Sparks fly. The married man or woman decides that he or she must follow his or her heart, without regard to the spouse and children, let alone the God who detests adultery and the breakup of families. Why would we trust our hearts rather than God's Word? Did we create the world or design the human eyeball? Do we create hurricanes and hold the earth in orbit? Do we suppose that God revealed his Word for other people who are not as smart as we are? We are free to follow our hearts, but if we do, we should beware of the consequences.

Third, the consequences of betrayal will testify to God's faithfulness. Here is a stiff warning for those who know what God's Word says, and then decide that they are going to do what they want because they suppose that God will forgive them afterward. We read in Deuteronomy 29:20, "The LORD will not be willing to forgive him, but rather the anger of the LORD and his jealousy will smoke against that man, and the curses written in this book will settle upon him, and the LORD will blot out his name from under heaven." Those who willfully go on sinning against God, assuming that they can repent whenever they wish, fail to appreciate that repentance from sin is a gift of God's grace. A man cannot simply decide that he is going to repent of sin. Left to his own devices, he will only go deeper into sin, confusion, and disaster. God has every right to allow us to go on hardening our hearts. That is probably what is being described here. God's refusal to forgive indicates the idolater's refusal to repent.[9] Because of that refusal to repent, great wrath is going to come upon this sinner, as described in detail

8. Raymond Brown, *The Message of Deuteronomy: Not by Bread Alone*, The Bible Speaks Today (InterVarsity Press, 1993), 276.

9. Christopher Wright, *Deuteronomy*, NIBC: Old Testament 4 (Hendrickson, 2007), 288.

in verses 21–23. The whole nation of Israel would ultimately experience the consequences of the people's stubborn hearts. Rather than God's standing by to allow Israel to prosper in sin, God will show his faithfulness by bringing the curses on them that he promised. When people see the ruin of such lives, as we read in verses 24–28,

> all the nations will say, "Why has the LORD done thus to this land? What caused the heat of this great anger?" Then people will say, "It is because they abandoned the covenant of the LORD, the God of their fathers, which he made with them when he brought them out of the land of Egypt, and went and served other gods and worshiped them, gods whom they had not known and whom he had not allotted to them. Therefore the anger of the LORD was kindled against this land, bringing upon it all the curses written in this book, and the LORD uprooted them from their land in anger and fury and great wrath, and cast them into another land, as they are this day."

The destruction of sinners will be a warning to others that though people may be unfaithful to God's covenant, he will be faithful to deliver the promised curses on all who reject him.

Because of God's faithful judgment, we must beware falling into idolatry or following our own hearts rather than God's Word. One mark of growing Christian maturity is an increasing distrust of one's own desires while simultaneously depending more on God's Word. Do not betray him. Do not tempt him. Do not test him. Do not grieve his Holy Spirit. Instead, having remembered his grace toward us, having embraced our place in his covenant promises, let us live not by what is in our hearts, but by what he has revealed.

Live by What Is Revealed

Moses concludes this section with an important statement in Deuteronomy 29:29: "The secret things belong to the LORD our God, but the things that are revealed belong to us and to our children forever, that we may do all the words of this law." What does this verse mean? Several options have been presented. Targum Jonathan suggests that the meaning is that secret sins are known to God and he will punish them, but that the sins that are not secret are the responsibility of the people to punish. After having heard that the sins of one bitter root can bring destruction on the whole people, the people would be encouraged by this verse that such destruction will not come if they deal with sin properly.[10]

A more likely possibility is that "secret things" refers to the secrets that God has reserved for himself and hidden from humanity. We are not called to live our lives by those things, nor are we held responsible for them. But the things that God has revealed in his Word—those things belong to us as his people, and we are responsible to obey what he has revealed, "that we may do all the words of this law."[11] We must treasure the things that God has revealed in his Word that are able to make us wise for salvation through faith in Christ!

What was only partially revealed in the Old Testament through sacrifices, signs, and symbols has been more clearly revealed in the New Testament. The first responsibility of everyone who hears the Word of God is to obey the gospel. Acknowledge and confess that you are a sinner who has betrayed God. Believe that Jesus Christ came to do for you what you could not do for yourself, by living his life in obedience to all of God's commands, but dying on the cross as a betrayer of the covenant. He died in our place. Because he had no sin of his own, he did not remain dead but was raised on the third day and ascended into heaven, from which he gives the gift of salvation and the promise of the Holy Spirit to all who believe. By the power of the Spirit at work in us, we can now walk in obedience to God's commands. We not only can, but want to.

These revealed truths belong not only to us, but also to our children. By virtue of being born into our households, our children have a right to be taught the things of God. If we are not teaching biblical truth to our children in the home, and we are not bringing them to Sunday school and worship, where are they going to learn these things? The things that have been revealed are not simply things to know, but truths to be obeyed by all of God's people.

10. Jeffrey H. Tigay, *Deuteronomy*, JPSTC (Jewish Publication Society, 1996), 283.
11. J. G. McConville, *Deuteronomy*, ApOTC 5 (Inter-Varsity Press, 2002), 419.

Let us look back and remember what God has done for us at the cross, and if we do not grasp it, let us ask him to open the eyes of our hearts. May we embrace our place in God's covenant through faith in Jesus, every one of us. Let us beware of idols and following our hearts, which will surely lead us astray, and instead live by the truths revealed in God's Word for us and our children. If we will diligently practice these things, we can be sure that the grace we have received was not received in vain.

44

Choose Life

Deuteronomy 30:1–20

I call heaven and earth to witness against you today, that I have set before you life and death, blessing and curse. Therefore choose life, that you and your offspring may live. (Deut. 30:19)

The young man was full of promise. But he was also full of himself. Not content to live under his father's roof, he demanded his inheritance before his father even died so that he could strike out on his own. The father gave it to him, and the son went off to live far from his father's house. In that far country, he quickly squandered all that he had been given in reckless living. At the same time, a famine struck the land, and he was in a very bad way. He hired himself out to a farmer to take care of pigs, but no one took care of him. He was so hungry, he envied the pigs' food. He had reached the low point of his life. In that low place in the far country, as we read, "when he came to himself, he said, 'How many of my father's hired servants have more than enough bread, but I perish here with hunger! I will arise and go to my father, and I will say to him, "Father, I have sinned against heaven and before you. I am no longer worthy to be called your son. Treat me as one of your hired servants"'" (Luke 15:17–19).

Jesus told that parable in Luke 15. The story is simple, yet it resonates throughout the world and across generations. Many people have had a similar experience. Having been brought up in a good home and knowing the truth, they rebel against it and run wild into a far country. They might get entangled in a string of bad relationships. Or they might find themselves addicted to drugs, alcohol, or sex. They might wind up behind bars or deep in debt or on the run. But eventually, the fortunate ones come to a place where they realize what they have lost.

Some of us may be in the far country today. We are present in our churches, but our hearts are far from our Father's house. Perhaps we have hit rock bottom. Figuratively speaking, we are so personally impoverished that we envy what the pigs have; we have gone far from home, lost in the wilderness of life.

Moses anticipates that Israel is going to be in this situation. The Lord is clear throughout Deuteronomy: those who flagrantly break his covenant and disobey his commandments will be cast out of the land. We know from Israel's history that after a long and repeated rejection of God's offer of life, he eventually gave the people what they deserved and exiled them to Babylon. But judgment is not God's final word to his people. This passage reminds us that no matter how far we have drifted or run from God's good plan, the option to choose life is still before us. Moses writes these verses to a people who will one day find themselves in the far country. He pleads with them, and with us, to choose life.

The Condition of Life

God gives life freely, even to rebels, but this does not mean that life has no conditions. Moses knows that the people of God are going to go astray, be cursed, and live in exile outside the land that God promised. He also knows that judgment is not the final word. He writes in Deuteronomy 30:1–3:

> And when all these things come upon you, the blessing and the curse, which I have set before you, and you call them to mind among all the nations where the Lord your God has driven you, and return to the Lord your God, you and your children, and obey his voice in all that I command you today, with all your heart and with all your soul, then the Lord your God will restore

> your fortunes and have mercy on you, and he will gather you again from all the peoples where the LORD your God has scattered you.

Three verbs represent the constituent parts of one movement: *remember*, *return*, and *obey*.

First, *remember*. When Israel is in the far country and all these things come upon the people, as Moses continues, "you call them to mind among all the nations where the LORD your God has driven you" (Deut. 30:1). A point will come as they experience the consequences of their disobedience that they will remember what God said about the blessing and the curse, and they will realize that they are experiencing the curse. But that is not enough to enjoy the blessing.

After remembering, second, they must *return*. The Israelites cannot stay in the far country but must return from there to the Lord whom they have left. Deuteronomy 30:2 urges them to "return to the LORD your God, you and your children." A return requires some measure of trust. A person in the far country will not likely return home unless he trusts that home is better than where he is. Prodigals must have some hope that if they return, they will not be cast out.

While remembering and returning are essential, there is one final verb: *obey*. Obedience is essential. Moses continues in Deuteronomy 30:2, "Obey his voice in all that I command you today, with all your heart and with all your soul." Disobedience to God's voice had led the Israelites to the far country. Obedience allows them to enjoy the blessings of home.

The three parts of this movement are a description of repentance. WSC 87 describes repentance in this way: "Repentance unto life is a saving grace, whereby a sinner, out of a true sense of his sin, and apprehension of the mercy of God in Christ, doth, with grief and hatred of his sin, turn from it unto God, with full purpose of, and endeavour after, new obedience." Notice the elements of calling to mind the reality of sin and separation from God, trusting that the mercy of God is available in Christ, which leads to turning from sin to God with the intention of new obedience. This is precisely what we are to do when we find ourselves in the far country. The catechism adds that this is "a saving grace," which means that it is a gift that God gives.

If we are far from God, we must call these things to mind. We must remember what God has done for us and what he promises to do. We cannot run from his goodness in disobedience any longer, but we must return to the Lord. Where we are explicitly ignoring his commands, we must turn around and renew our commitment to obedience. He will not cast us out if we come to him in humble repentance. There is no life with God apart from repentance. We cannot go on loving our sin and loving God. We must leave behind one or the other.

Legend has it that one way to catch a monkey is by placing an attractive temptation, such as a piece of fruit, inside a jar. The opening of the jar must be large enough that the monkey can put his hand in, but small enough that the monkey cannot pull his hand out when it is balled up into a fist, grasping the object. When the monkey sees the treat in the jar, he reaches in without a problem and takes hold of the treat, but now he cannot get his hand back out. The monkey must either hang on to the treat and be caught or let go of the treat and be free. It is the same with our sin. If we continue to love it and cling to it, we will remain forever trapped. We must let go of it to fully take hold of the true God. As an encouragement to returning to the Lord, the promise of life is held out.

The Promise of Life

God promises renewed life for his covenant-keeping people. These are people who had been disobedient. They did not have a perfect record. The expectation is that this is a people who were carried off into exile as a result of their unfaithfulness to the covenant. But if they will remember, return, and obey, look what God promises to do for them:

First, God will restore and gather. Moses writes in Deuteronomy 30:3–4 that "then the Lord your God will restore your fortunes and have mercy on you, and he will gather you again from all the peoples where the Lord your God has scattered you. If your outcasts are in the uttermost parts of heaven, from there the Lord your God will gather you, and from there he will take you." What the people had lost on account of sin and disobedience, God will restore in the context of mercy. This includes bringing them back into the land from which they had been exiled on account of their sin. The books of Ezra and Nehemiah recount God's faithfully delivering on this promise many years later when he brought the Israelites back into the land from their Babylonian captivity.

Second, God will prosper. We read in Deuteronomy 30:5: "And the Lord your God will bring you into the land that your fathers possessed, that you may possess it. And he will make you more prosperous and numerous than your fathers." Similarly in verse 9: "The Lord your God will make you abundantly prosperous in all the work of your hand, in the fruit of your womb and in the fruit of your cattle and in the fruit of your ground. For the Lord will again take delight in prospering you, as he took delight in your fathers." The fruitfulness and prosperity that they will lose through covenant-breaking, God will delight in restoring to them. When Israel later returned to the land under the leadership of Ezra and Nehemiah, God prospered the nation. The temple that had been destroyed in the Babylonian invasion was rebuilt.

Third, God will transform. He will not leave the Israelites as they are but will actively be at work in them, as we read in Deuteronomy 30:6: "And the Lord your God will circumcise your heart and the heart of your offspring, so that you will love the Lord your God with all your heart and with all your soul, that you may live." After being circumcised in heart, the people and their offspring will love God rightly. That love will express itself in obedience, as described in verse 8: "And you shall again obey the voice of the Lord and keep all his commandments that I command you today."

Outward circumcision was never an end in itself, but it was to be an external sign of an internal reality. The apostle Paul writes: "For no one is a Jew who is merely one outwardly, nor is circumcision outward and physical. But a Jew is one inwardly, and circumcision is a matter of the heart, by the Spirit, not by the letter. His praise is not from man but from God" (Rom. 2:28–29). The change of heart required to love God and walk in his commandments is a transformation that God works in the heart of his people. The point is not that obedience saves us or makes us God's covenant people. Rather, obedience is evidence of the fact that a person has experienced the circumcision of the heart; this makes someone a true part of the people of God. As Jonty Rhodes puts it, "God's law lays out the path which the Spirit empowers us to walk."[1]

There is no sense in which any of these blessings are merited or deserved. These are gifts that God gives, and the condition for the reception of these

1. Jonty Rhodes, *Covenants Made Simple: Understanding God's Unfolding Promises to His People* (P&R Publishing, 2014), 168.

gifts is believing repentance, which is also God's gift. The condition is emphasized again in Deuteronomy 30:10: "when you obey the voice of the LORD your God, to keep his commandments and his statutes that are written in this Book of the Law, when you turn to the LORD your God with all your heart and with all your soul." God is not reluctant to bless his people! All over Deuteronomy, he is pleading with them to walk in his ways, that he might shower his blessings on them. Hear God's heart expressed by the psalmist: "Hear, O my people, while I admonish you! O Israel, if you would but listen to me! There shall be no strange god among you; you shall not bow down to a foreign god. I am the LORD your God, who brought you up out of the land of Egypt. Open your mouth wide, and I will fill it" (Ps. 81:8–10). The Lord is no reluctant blesser! God is eager to fulfill his promises, but he will not bless disobedience. Therefore, when we are far from God, we must recall this, repent by turning away from our sin to the one who promises not to cast us out, and commit ourselves to new obedience. While the promises of this passage were specific to Israel in terms of their content, we can be sure that under the new covenant God's promises are not any less.

The Objections to Life

In the next verses, Moses anticipates what the objections to obeying the voice of the Lord may be from a reluctant people. We read the objections in Deuteronomy 30:11–13: "For this commandment that I command you today is not too hard for you, neither is it far off. It is not in heaven, that you should say, 'Who will ascend to heaven for us and bring it to us, that we may hear it and do it?' Neither is it beyond the sea, that you should say, 'Who will go over the sea for us and bring it to us, that we may hear it and do it?'" Moses attempts to help his people understand that God's commandments are not too difficult. God has not hidden what he requires from his people, nor has he dangled his requirements so far out of reach that only a few can grasp them. This emphasis distinguishes biblical revelation from other ideas such as Scientology and Freemasonry. In those religions, you must pay money and be granted access to higher levels of revelation, and not everyone can know the deepest secrets. But biblical revelation is available to all who will hear it and receive it. Not everything is easy to understand, but everything is available.

Despite this availability, some people think: "Well, God's requirements are just way too much. Since I cannot keep his commandments perfectly, I won't even try." Such an attitude betrays a misunderstanding of the law. The law is not described in the Old Testament as being impracticable or impossibly idealistic. Christopher Wright observes:

> The idea that God deliberately made the law so exacting that nobody would ever be able to live by it belongs to a distorted theology that tries unnecessarily to gild the gospel by denigrating the law. The frequent claims by various psalmists to have lived according to God's law are neither exaggerated nor exceptional. They arise from the natural assumption that ordinary people can indeed live in a way that is broadly pleasing to God and faithful to God's law, and that they can do so as a matter of joy and delight. This is neither self-righteousness nor a claim to sinless perfection, for the same psalmists are equally quick to confess their sin and failings, fully realizing that only the grace that could forgive and cleanse them would likewise enable them to live again in covenant obedience.[2]

We see numerous examples of this kind of delight in walking in God's law. It does not refer to sinless perfection but reflects a heart aligned with God's law and a desire to obey because of his transforming work.

Those who see the law as burdensome and ungracious fail to appreciate the law for what it is. Alexander Maclaren writes:

> The possession of the law is a blessing because its authoritative voice ends the weary quest after some reliable guide to conduct, and we need neither try to climb to heaven, nor to traverse the wide world and cross the ocean, to find certitude and enlightenment enough for our need. They err who think of God's commandments as grievous burdens; they are merciful guide-posts. They do not so much lay weights on our backs as give light to our eyes.[3]

The quest of trying to figure out right and wrong on our own leads to cultural anxiety and political striving. We are not left to figure out what is

2. Christopher Wright, *Deuteronomy*, NIBC: Old Testament 4 (Hendrickson, 2007), 290.

3. Alexander Maclaren, *Deuteronomy, Joshua, Judges, Ruth, and First Book of Samuel, Second Samuel, First Kings, and Second Kings, Chapters I to VII*, vol. 2 of *Expositions of Holy Scripture* (Eerdmans, 1944), 26.

pleasing to God and beneficial for man, but rather, the Lord lays it out for us in exquisite detail. This is a gift!

Moses emphasizes this point about the Word's not being too distant or difficult in Deuteronomy 30:14: "But the word is very near you. It is in your mouth and in your heart, so that you can do it." For the people of Israel, the law was not merely an external code disconnected from the heart. It certainly could be, but that was not the aim. Rather, it was to be in their mouths and hearts. The apostle Paul speaks to these verses in his letter to the Romans. He contrasts two types of righteousness: the righteousness that the Jews of his day believed they possessed because of lawkeeping, and the righteousness that comes by faith in Christ. He writes:

> For Moses writes about the righteousness that is based on the law, that the person who does the commandments shall live by them. But the righteousness based on faith says, "Do not say in your heart, 'Who will ascend into heaven?'" (that is, to bring Christ down) "or 'Who will descend into the abyss?'" (that is, to bring Christ up from the dead). But what does it say? "The word is near you, in your mouth and in your heart" (that is, the word of faith that we proclaim); because, if you confess with your mouth that Jesus is Lord and believe in your heart that God raised him from the dead, you will be saved. (Rom. 10:5–9)

The righteousness that comes by faith does not attempt to go up to heaven and bring Christ down, nor does it attempt to go and raise Christ from the dead. Rather, the righteousness that comes by faith recognizes that Christ has already done both. He has already come to the earth to fulfill all righteousness. He has already risen from the dead for our justification. In order to be saved, we need only "confess with [our] mouth that Jesus is Lord and believe in [our] heart that God raised him from the dead." Wherever we may be today, he is only a whisper away. That brings us to the choice of life.

The Choice of Life

Moses reduces all Deuteronomy down to a simple binary choice: life or death. The path of life involves obedience to God's commands and walking in his ways. Moses writes in Deuteronomy 30:15–16:

> See, I have set before you today life and good, death and evil. If you obey the commandments of the LORD your God that I command you today, by loving the LORD your God, by walking in his ways, and by keeping his commandments and his statutes and his rules, then you shall live and multiply, and the LORD your God will bless you in the land that you are entering to take possession of it.

If the Israelites will obey, they are promised life, multiplication, and blessings beyond measure in the land that God is giving them.

The alternative to life, however, is death. Moses says in Deuteronomy 30:17–18: "But if your heart turns away, and you will not hear, but are drawn away to worship other gods and serve them, I declare to you today, that you shall surely perish. You shall not live long in the land that you are going over the Jordan to enter and possess." This statement takes us all the way back to Genesis 3 and the garden of Eden. The choice was life or death. The serpent came to the woman and assured her that she could choose the option of death and she would "not surely die" (Gen. 3:4). She believed the serpent rather than God. The people of Israel also have a choice: to choose life, or to choose death by turning away from God, ignoring his voice, and serving idols. It is a spiritual death that will culminate in physical death under the curse.

Given these options, choose life! Moses, speaking as God's representative, is not ambivalent to the choice that the people make. He is not like the salesman who gets a commission whether the customer makes a purchase or not. He is rather like a father pleading with a son whose life hangs in the balance. With heaven and earth called as witnesses to this covenant, Moses implores the Israelites to choose life:

> I call heaven and earth to witness against you today, that I have set before you life and death, blessing and curse. Therefore choose life, that you and your offspring may live, loving the LORD your God, obeying his voice and holding fast to him, for he is your life and length of days, that you may dwell in the land that the LORD swore to your fathers, to Abraham, to Isaac, and to Jacob, to give them. (Deut. 30:19–20)

Life in God's land enjoying God's blessing is what Moses wants for the people, and it is what God desires to give. The choice is theirs.

We do not have to read far beyond Deuteronomy to see that Israel chose death. God was tremendously patient with his people's waywardness and their idolatry, but ultimately they brought the covenant curses on themselves and were sent into the far country. Yet God did not leave his people there to languish in the misery of their sin. Instead, God sent a second Adam to make a better choice. The Word of God himself took on flesh and dwelt among us. He himself kept the requirements of the covenant, perfectly loving God and his neighbor, obeying the voice of God even to the point of death on a cross. In his death, he was cursed, taking our place as covenant-breakers. Then he rose from the dead, breaking the power of the curse and securing the blessing for all who will trust in him. By this saving work, Jesus delivered us from the curse of the law to life in his gospel. It is by faith in Jesus Christ that we are saved, not by our keeping of God's law. He is our life, Moses declares, to those who under the law could have only death.

That God is our life means even more for those of us who know Jesus than it did for the people of Israel. Likewise, to be promised long life in the land means even more for us than it did for them. To love God, to be loved by God, and to be in union with him are what give us the true life. The one who is joined to Jesus by the Holy Spirit truly lives, and the one who is not joined to Jesus is dead, even while he lives.[4] Life for the believer means not just a hundred years in the land of Israel, but eternity in the new heavens and the new earth. Meanwhile, death means far more than a mere passing into oblivion; rather, it means passing into eternal, conscious torment away from the goodness of God. The choice is before us all.

When Jesus told the parable of the prodigal son who was in the far country, he did not leave us hanging as to how the father would receive the son who returned home from the pigsty. He says of the prodigal in Luke 15:20–24:

> And he arose and came to his father. But while he was still a long way off, his father saw him and felt compassion, and ran and embraced him and kissed him. And the son said to him, "Father, I have sinned against heaven and before you. I am no longer worthy to be called your son." But the father said to his servants, "Bring quickly the best robe, and put it on him, and put a ring on his hand, and shoes on his feet. And bring the fattened calf and kill

4. Maclaren, 28.

> it, and let us eat and celebrate. For this my son was dead, and is alive again; he was lost, and is found." And they began to celebrate.

God offers salvation life to all those who are in the far country and desire to come home. He will meet us on the way, shower us with love, and restore and prosper us beyond our wildest dreams, so that we will live as his children. Why stay away from a love like this? Why go on trying to make our own way and figuring it out on our own, only to serve up more heartbreak for ourselves and others? But we must choose. To have an intellectual knowledge of the gospel is not enough. To delay the choice is to choose death. Remember the goodness of our God, trust his loving heart to receive and welcome sinners, return to him in faithful obedience, and abide in his love. Choose life.

45

Strong Foundations in Seasons of Uncertainty

Deuteronomy 31:1–29

Be strong and courageous. Do not fear or be in dread of them, for it is the Lord your God who goes with you. He will not leave you or forsake you. (Deut. 31:6)

In late autumn, half of all American college football fans are calling for the head of their favorite team's coach. At dining-room tables and around televisions, we hear familiar phrases such as "He's a bum," "This team will never get any better as long as that guy is at the helm," and "Since when did we decide to settle for mediocrity?" My own alma mater is a mess. We could not afford the obscene amount of money that it would cost to fire our coach, so we fired the athletic director instead; he is the one who had gotten us into such a bad contract. This is the nature of college football today. People have confidence that with the right leadership, any program can be successful.

Sometimes changing the head coach makes a significant difference. Other times, it sets the team back another four years while the next guy comes in, fails, and gets sent packing like his predecessor. A change in leadership does not always bring about a change in outcome; it does always bring a season of uncertainty.

In Deuteronomy 31, the people of Israel are facing the uncertainty of a leadership transition. Moses announces that he is about to die; he is, after all, 120 years old. Their leader is departing just as the Israelites are about to face their greatest challenge. Moses has brought them out of Egypt and led them for forty years, and he is the only leader they have known. Who and what will they be able to depend on when they cross the Jordan and face the enemies that caused their parents' faith to shrivel up and die?

We too go through seasons of uncertainty. It may be a leadership transition in our church or workplace or nation. It may be the concern surrounding a delicate health situation. It may be the uneasiness of a tenuous marriage or the continued life of someone we depend on. We may be passing from one season of our life across a Jordan River moment into an unknown land without knowing what to expect. When we enter seasons of uncertainty, Deuteronomy 31 teaches us that we can discern four strong foundations on which our faith can rest.

Foundation 1: God's Presence Is the Foundation of Our Strength and Courage at All Times

In Deuteronomy 31:1–8, Moses is speaking to all Israel gathered. He announces his impending departure in verse 2: "I am 120 years old today. I am no longer able to go out and come in. The LORD has said to me, 'You shall not go over this Jordan.'" Moses explains that he is old and no longer able to lead the people as he used to do.[1] Additionally, God has told him that he will not cross the Jordan on account of his own sin and failure to believe (Num. 20:12). But the people need not be fearful, for God himself will go over before them. Moses continues in Deuteronomy 31:3–5:

> The LORD your God himself will go over before you. He will destroy these nations before you, so that you shall dispossess them, and Joshua will go over at your head, as the LORD has spoken. And the LORD will do to them as he

1. At the same time, this must be balanced with the statement in Deuteronomy 34:7 that "his eye was undimmed, and his vigor unabated." The fact that Moses was 120 recalls what he wrote that the Lord said in Genesis 6:3: "Then the LORD said, 'My Spirit shall not abide in man forever, for he is flesh: his days shall be 120 years.'"

> did to Sihon and Og, the kings of the Amorites, and to their land, when he destroyed them. And the LORD will give them over to you, and you shall do to them according to the whole commandment that I have commanded you.

Joshua 3 records that God did indeed go over before the Israelites, as represented by the ark of the covenant. The Lord would give them victory over the nations in Canaan, just as he did over Sihon and Og on the east side of the Jordan, and Joshua would be their leader. Then in Deuteronomy 31:6, Moses gives them a little extra encouragement that they are going to need: "Be strong and courageous. Do not fear or be in dread of them."

Anytime people are commanded to be strong and courageous, it is because they are going to encounter something that will provoke a response of weakness and fear. To feel weak or afraid is not sinful in itself; it may become sinful, however, if it keeps us from doing what God is calling us to do. God does not just command his people not to be afraid, but gives us solid reasons for why we need not be afraid: "for it is the LORD your God who goes with you. He will not leave you or forsake you" (Deut. 31:6). The same God who gave victory over the Egyptians and over Sihon and Og is the God who is going to fight for his people in Canaan. He will not leave or forsake them. What that means is that fear-based disobedience is irrational.

Imagine a child, accompanying his father into a dark room. The father knows exactly what is in the room and promises the child that no matter what they encounter, the child need not be afraid or run away. For that child to go running out of the dark room and away from the father would be senseless and even more dangerous than to be in the dark with the father. Likewise, our Father promises not to leave or forsake us. Why, then, would we leave and forsake him through disobedience or running away from where he is calling us to go?

In times of uncertainty, those of us who believe that God is with us should be strong and courageous. That is a firm foundation for living at any time, especially an uncertain time.

Foundation 2: God's Appointed Leaders Are the Ordinary Means by Which God Brings Us into What He Has Promised

As we move into Deuteronomy 31:7–8, Moses now addresses Joshua directly and gives him the same command that he gave to all the people:

> Then Moses summoned Joshua and said to him in the sight of all Israel, "Be strong and courageous, for you shall go with this people into the land that the Lord has sworn to their fathers to give them, and you shall put them in possession of it. It is the Lord who goes before you. He will be with you; he will not leave you or forsake you. Do not fear or be dismayed."

Joshua is personally encouraged by a very similar message from Moses that Moses gave to the whole congregation. The Lord promises not to leave or forsake Joshua, and Moses again exhorts him not to fear or be dismayed as God uses him to lead the people into possession of the promise.

Leadership of any sort is a frightening prospect. To lead people is to take them to a place where they may not want to go. Leadership involves uncertainty. It also involves taking shots, either from the enemy or from the people themselves. Unsurprisingly, many people do not want to lead. Yet someone must lead, and God continues to call leaders in the home, church, and community. The same promise of God's presence can be expected for leaders who do his will. Of course, the people of God are led not by any man exclusively, but always by God himself. Yet God uses called men to exercise his leadership among the people of God. In the context of the church, we believe that God does not use just one man, but uses a plurality of men to lead his people.

As a leader, Joshua needed a special charge, which we read of in Deuteronomy 31:14–15:

> And the Lord said to Moses, "Behold, the days approach when you must die. Call Joshua and present yourselves in the tent of meeting, that I may commission him." And Moses and Joshua went and presented themselves in the tent of meeting. And the Lord appeared in the tent in a pillar of cloud. And the pillar of cloud stood over the entrance of the tent.

The Lord wanted Moses and Joshua to get into the tent of meeting because God was going to commission Joshua to lead after Moses' death. The Lord appeared in a pillar of cloud, the same phrase used to describe the glory cloud that had led them in the desert (Ex. 13:21), probably to prevent Moses and Joshua from seeing him, which would not have been safe for them. From the pillar, the Lord spoke to Moses first (Deut. 31:16–22), and then in Deuteronomy 31:23, the Lord solemnized Joshua's selection: "And the LORD commissioned Joshua the son of Nun and said, 'Be strong and courageous, for you shall bring the people of Israel into the land that I swore to give them. I will be with you.'" Although the word "LORD" does not appear in the Hebrew, the third-person masculine singular "he commissioned" most likely refers to the Lord, considering what he had said in verse 14. The Lord appoints Joshua with the same direct charge to have strength and courage. He tells Joshua what he is going to do: bring the people into the land that God had promised. He also gives Joshua that most assuring of promises that we all need in the face of impossible tasks: "I will be with you."

None of us have been called to lead the people of Israel into the promised land, but we have been called to lead our families to know and serve the Lord. We have been called to be faithful witnesses to Jesus in our places of work, study, and play. We have been called to face difficult circumstances with faith and trust, not to be afraid, to love our enemies, to forgive those who have hurt us deeply, and to give thanks in all circumstances. Some of these callings may be overwhelming, but we are to be strong and courageous. The same God will be with us. He will not be in a pillar of cloud or attending the ark of the covenant, but he has taken up residence within the hearts of all who call on his name by his Holy Spirit. When Jesus came to earth and was born of the virgin Mary, his name was called Immanuel, which means "God with us." The Advent and Christmas season is our reminder that God is forever with us, and that we can face with strength and courage whatever is before us, no matter what may be happening to us as leaders or what may be happening in the absence of leadership.

Foundation 3: God's Word Gives Us Needed Direction About How to Be, What to Do, and How to Return

After Moses reminds the people of God's presence in this time of uncertainty, and after he reminds Joshua of the same thing, we read in Deuteronomy 31:9, "Then Moses wrote this law and gave it to the priests, the sons of Levi, who carried the ark of the covenant of the LORD, and to all the elders of Israel." Moses wrote down Deuteronomy and gave it to the priests and elders. If any wonder why we believe that Moses is the primary author of Deuteronomy, this is the reason.[2] The text says so!

Then we read in Deuteronomy 31:10–11, "And Moses commanded them, 'At the end of every seven years, at the set time in the year of release, at the Feast of Booths, when all Israel comes to appear before the LORD your God at the place that he will choose, you shall read this law before all Israel in their hearing.'" After Moses wrote it down, the priests were responsible to ensure that at the end of every seven years during the Feast of Booths, Deuteronomy should be read. Recall that Deuteronomy follows the format of secular suzerain-vassal treaties. It was standard practice for the suzerain to give a copy of the treaty to the vassal people to keep in the sanctuary of their god under the care of their priests so that it could be read from time to time.[3] When the leader of the vassal people died, his successor would need to be approved by the suzerain and agree to the conditions of the covenant. That is what is being described here. While there is a change in leadership of the vassal people from Moses to Joshua, the terms of the covenant remain the same.

We should also appreciate the context in which the law was to be publicly read. The "year of release" was the year of canceling debts and releasing slaves, a reminder of God's own deliverance of his people and the gift of his law in the context of grace. Likewise, the Feast of Booths was a time of remembering the goodness of the Lord in giving them a harvest to enjoy. So the reading of the law would have come in the context of remembering God's gracious salvation of his people and his ongoing provision.[4]

The commands continue in Deuteronomy 31:12–13:

> Assemble the people, men, women, and little ones, and the sojourner within your towns, that they may hear and learn to fear the LORD your God, and be careful to do all the words of this law, and that their children, who have not known it, may hear and learn to fear the LORD your God, as long as you live in the land that you are going over the Jordan to possess.

2. John D. Currid, *Deuteronomy*, EPSC (EP Books, 2006), 439.

3. J. A. Thompson, *Deuteronomy: An Introduction and Commentary*, TOTC (InterVarsity Press, 1974), 290–91.

4. Christopher Wright, *Deuteronomy*, NIBC: Old Testament 4 (Hendrickson, 2007), 295–96.

The law is to be read to everyone: men, women, children, and sojourners. The wisdom of God's Word is for all his people to enjoy, not just men and not just adults. The aim is that "they may hear and learn to fear the LORD your God, and be careful to do all the words of this law," and that their children would too. The Word of God reveals to us how we should be, what we are to be doing, and how to return home when we go astray. The principles in God's Word stand forever, and they are true in times of certainty as well as uncertainty. Even when we do not know what else to do, we know that we can obey God's Word.

Sometimes we underestimate what children can absorb from sitting in a worship service and listening to the preaching of God's Word. The teaching in the sermon on Sunday mornings is not enough for a child to grow to maturity in the faith. Instruction needs to be supplemented with Sunday school and teaching at home, as described in Deuteronomy 6. But being present in the worship service, being attentive to the message, actively taking notes or doodling to stay focused, and not frequently getting up to go to the bathroom are all great strategies for children to gain from hearing the Word each week. It can be difficult for parents, but there is great biblical and historical precedent for the practice. It probably was not easy to keep the little children of Israel focused for the extended time it would have taken to read through Deuteronomy, but it was important, so they did it.

The written Word was to do something else for God's people: it was to call them back when they went astray. We read in Deuteronomy 31:24–26, "When Moses had finished writing the words of this law in a book to the very end, Moses commanded the Levites who carried the ark of the covenant of the LORD, 'Take this Book of the Law and put it by the side of the ark of the covenant of the LORD your God, that it may be there for a witness against you.'" The ark of the covenant was a box that contained several important items. It included the Ten Commandments, a jar of the manna that God had used to sustain his people in the wilderness, and Aaron's staff that miraculously budded. Alongside the ark was to be the book of Deuteronomy, or at least a significant portion of the book. The purpose of the book was the same as the purpose of the song that we will explore in the next chapter: to be a witness against them. In other words, when they break the covenant and experience consequences, they will not be able to say, "How could we know that this was going to happen?" Instead, they will know that these things are happening because they have broken the covenant.

Then Moses goes on to point out why this witness is going to be necessary:

> For I know how rebellious and stubborn you are. Behold, even today while I am yet alive with you, you have been rebellious against the LORD. How much more after my death! Assemble to me all the elders of your tribes and your officers, that I may speak these words in their ears and call heaven and earth to witness against them. For I know that after my death you will surely act corruptly and turn aside from the way that I have commanded you. And in the days to come evil will befall you, because you will do what is evil in the sight of the LORD, provoking him to anger through the work of your hands. (Deut. 31:27–29)

When Israel is told to do one thing, the people's inclination is to do something different. They refuse to change their mind, even when it is hurting them. Moses has been with them forty years, so he knows who he is dealing with. Since they have been this way while he has been with them, he is certain that they are going to get worse when he is gone. When they do the evil that they are sure to do, they are going to suffer. Moses is telling them this because he wants them to act contrary to their basest instincts. If they will continually expose themselves to this Word, then when they go astray, God will use it to show them the way back home.

Nehemiah 8–9 provides us with a historical example of this. After Nehemiah led some of the exiles back to the promised land, they finally did what they had long neglected: they read from the book. We read in Nehemiah 8:8, "They read from the book, from the Law of God, clearly, and they gave the sense, so that the people understood the reading." The priests were going line by line, with the Levites reading God's Word and explaining to the people what it meant. They were preaching. The people responded with confession, repentance, and obedience to the Word. One of the things we learn in Nehemiah is that though God had commanded this reading to be done every seven years at the Feast of Booths, the people stopped obeying the command to dwell in booths during the feast after the days of Joshua and did not resume obeying it again until the days of Nehemiah. The Feast of Booths described in Nehemiah 8 was celebrated in 445 B.C. Joshua would have likely died sometime in the 1300s.[5] So for more than nine hundred years, the people of God ignored this command.

Surely they suffered from failing to take in God's Word. In many churches and homes today, we are likewise starving God's people of God's Word. Sometimes people suggest that pastors could shorten the service by removing the Scripture reading before the sermon, or by just reading a few select verses. This is a common practice in the evangelical church today. But the people of God should hear from God, and we can be certain that they will hear from him through the reading of the Word. Pastors should also try to supplement that reading by giving the people the sense of the text through expository preaching, just as was done in the days of Nehemiah. To neglect the Word is to neglect the firm foundation that God has given us for all times, and especially for uncertain times.

Foundation 4: God's Unchanging Character Gives Us Confidence That We Can Always Depend on Him to Do What He Has Promised

Though everything else may change in the world around us, God never does. When his people go astray from him and start to pursue idols, he will respond as he promised. We read the bad news about the future for God's people in verses 16–18 of Deuteronomy 31:

> And the Lord said to Moses, "Behold, you are about to lie down with your fathers. Then this people will rise and whore after the foreign gods among them in the land that they are entering, and they will forsake me and break my covenant that I have made with them. Then my anger will be kindled against them in that day, and I will forsake them and hide my face from them, and they will be devoured. And many evils and troubles will come upon them, so that they will say in that day, 'Have not these evils come upon us because our God is not among us?' And I will surely hide my face in that day because of all the evil that they have done, because they have turned to other gods."

5. This estimate is based on the "early" date of the exodus in 1446 B.C. Even with the late date of the exodus, we are still talking about more than seven hundred years of ignoring this command.

There are four parts to what is going to happen. First, Moses is going to die. Second, the people will be spiritually unfaithful and chase after the idols of Canaan. Third, God will be angry, forsake them, and allow them to be devoured by their enemies. Fourth, amid their misery the people will ask, "Have not these evils come upon us because our God is not among us?" Since God's unstated desire at that point is that the people will repent, he instructs Moses to write down a song and teach it to the people, as is explained in Deuteronomy 31:19–22:

> "Now therefore write this song and teach it to the people of Israel. Put it in their mouths, that this song may be a witness for me against the people of Israel. For when I have brought them into the land flowing with milk and honey, which I swore to give to their fathers, and they have eaten and are full and grown fat, they will turn to other gods and serve them, and despise me and break my covenant. And when many evils and troubles have come upon them, this song shall confront them as a witness (for it will live unforgotten in the mouths of their offspring). For I know what they are inclined to do even today, before I have brought them into the land that I swore to give." So Moses wrote this song the same day and taught it to the people of Israel.

The purpose of the song (which we will consider in the next chapter) is to be a witness against them. They will sing it and their kids will sing it, and when all the terrible things come upon them for their rebellion, the song will remind them that God has told them so. The song will serve to "confront" them.

It seems that the Lord takes a pretty dim view regarding his people, saying, "I know what they are inclined to do even today, before I have brought them into the land that I swore to give" (Deut. 31:21). He knows that they have a proclivity for sinning and idolatry. While some might see this as pessimism, it is a realistic view of human nature after the fall.

It is not just the people of ancient Israel who, when "they have eaten and are full and grown fat, . . . will turn to other gods and serve them" (Deut. 31:20). Many years ago, in the late 1600s and early 1700s, the Puritan minister Cotton Mather noted the decline in godliness in America: "Religion brought forth Prosperity, and the daughter destroyed the mother."[6] Have we not seen this pattern repeat itself? Our inclination to forget the Lord when life is easy is a partial explanation for the widespread neglect of the Christian faith today. We have had many years of relative ease, having our needs provided for, not having to fight, struggle, and depend on the Lord or on each other. Nobody wants to live a hand-to-mouth existence, but we do tend to flourish spiritually when we struggle physically. So in his mercy, when prosperity leads us astray from the true God, sometimes God will remove our prosperity so that we will seek him once again. Though we are faithless, he remains faithful. Though we abandon him, he will not forsake us.

When we think on the biblical story, Israel's unfaithfulness did lead to God's temporary removal of his presence from among them, but he did not permanently forsake his people. John explains that at the first advent, "the Word became flesh and dwelt among us, and we have seen his glory, glory as of the only Son from the Father, full of grace and truth" (John 1:14). Not only that, but Jesus the Son, the Word made flesh, suffered the curse that our sins deserved. That is why Jesus cried out on the cross, "My God, my God, why have you forsaken me?" (Matt. 27:46). He was forsaken on the cross, not for his own sins, but for ours. Now that our sins have been removed, we need never fear being abandoned by our God. In fact, after Jesus was raised from the dead, he commissioned his disciples to go and make disciples, our own version of possessing the land that God has promised. In the face of that fearsome task, Jesus promises, "I am with you always, to the end of the age" (28:20). What greater confidence do we need in times of uncertainty?

Whatever we may be facing today, we must rest our faith on these four foundations. God is with us, and therefore we can be strong and courageous to face what is coming. Human leaders will come and go, but God is the leader who will always ensure the fulfillment of his promises to his people. God's Word is a firm foundation that teaches us how to be, what to do, and how to return if we go astray. Finally, though we may falter, God never fails, and he never changes. We can trust him to do what he has promised. These strong foundations are a solid resting place for our faith through seasons of uncertainty.

6. Cotton Mather, *Magnalia Christi Americana: Or, The Ecclesiastical History of New-England; from Its First Planting, in the Year 1620, unto the Year of Our Lord 1698*, Seven Books 1 (Silas Andrus and Son, 1855), 63.

46

When You're on the Rocks, Look to the Rock

Deuteronomy 31:30—32:47

The Rock, his work is perfect, for all his ways are justice. A God of faithfulness and without iniquity, just and upright is he. (Deut. 32:4)

Music has an incredible ability to bore a hole into our brains and bury content so deep, it seems that we could never get it out, even if we wanted to. It creates associations that even dementia cannot break. If I hear the words "West" and "Philadelphia" in the same sentence, there is a 100 percent chance that I will start rapping the lyrics to *The Fresh Prince of Bel-Air.* If I hear the phrase "at the end of the day," anyone around can prepare themselves to hear me sing in my best *Les Misérables* singing voice, "At the end of the day you're another day older, and that's all you can say for the life of the poor." My kids give me a hard time because this happens so frequently. Someone will utter a word or phrase, and I break into song. My parents did the same thing. I realize now that they could not help it.

This phenomenon is one of the reasons why music is such a powerful aid to memory. According to an article in the *New York Times*, "Though scientists used to believe that short- and long-term memories were stored in different parts of the brain, they have discovered that what really distinguishes the lasting from the transient is how strongly the memory is engraved in the brain."[1] Music is one of those things that help engrave things into our brains. Dr. Michael Thaut, professor of music and neuroscience, observed, "It would be a virtually impossible task for young children to memorize a sequence of 26 separate letters if you just gave it to them as a string of information."[2] But if you teach it to them with a song, even preschoolers can learn the alphabet with ease.

We do not know what the tune of this song in Deuteronomy 32 would have been, but though the message is largely depressing, we can imagine that the music would have been somewhat catchy. It seems likely to me that when certain phrases of the song would be spoken in conversation, such as a teenager's asking his father, "Dad, could you help me move this rock?," his father may have burst out singing:[3] "The Rock, his work is perfect, for all his ways are justice. A God of faithfulness and without iniquity, just and upright is he" (Deut. 32:4)—inevitably causing his children to sigh and roll their eyes. But this was the point of teaching the people the song. When Israel settled in the land and began to drift away from faithfulness to God, this firmly implanted song would remind the people of the judgment that unfaithfulness would bring about, and the Lord's prevailing commitment to keep them as his people.

In fact, the song takes on the form of a lawsuit brought by a suzerain Lord against an unfaithful vassal, explaining how the vassal broke the terms and is going to receive the judgment due to him. But unlike most lawsuits, this one is in the form of a song. Also unlike other lawsuits, this one adds a note of hope for redemption that is missing from any other covenant lawsuit in

1. Natalie Angier, "In One Ear and Out the Other," *New York Times*, March 16, 2009, https://www.nytimes.com/2009/03/17/science/17angi.html, accessed December 8, 2022.

2. Angier, "In One Ear and Out the Other."

3. When I preached this sermon, I wrote a catchy little tune for Deuteronomy 32:4 that I sang multiple times during the message. The idea was to demonstrate in real time the power of song to help us remember. The experience was memorable for preacher and congregation alike, though I am not sure that the song stuck.

the ancient world.[4] If I were to title Moses' song today, I would call it "When You're on the Rocks, Look to the Rock." It is a reminder to us, when we find ourselves on the rocks of life, that there is one Rock whose work is perfect and whose ways are just. God has not changed since this song was written, and neither have the fundamental issues that people face. Memorizing and singing this song would have encouraged the people of God to look to the Rock in five ways that are still appropriate for his people today.

ASCRIBE PERFECTION TO YAHWEH

The song begins with a call to the heavens and earth to be witness to the song and the greatness of the God described in Deuteronomy 32:1–2: "Give ear, O heavens, and I will speak, and let the earth hear the words of my mouth. May my teaching drop as the rain, my speech distill as the dew, like gentle rain upon the tender grass, and like showers upon the herb." Remember that Moses' aim with this song, and God's aim, was to teach and instruct. Even though the content is difficult, his prayer is that the content would drop like gentle rain, dew, and showers, and that the people would receive it with the same eagerness as grass and herb receive moisture. Moses desires this teaching to be received by the people because of the central focus of its content as described in verse 3: "For I will proclaim the name of the LORD; ascribe greatness to our God!" In this song, Moses aims to proclaim Israel's covenant-keeping God, Yahweh, and to lead the people to ascribe greatness to him. Those who sing this song should have a bigger view of God after they sing it. Our aim in worship and with the songs we sing together is the same as this one: that the things we sing would cause us to ascribe greatness to God.

In Deuteronomy 32:4, aspects of God's greatness and perfection are summed up in two very poignant sentences: "The Rock, his work is perfect, for all his ways are justice. A God of faithfulness and without iniquity, just and upright is he." This line sets the scene for everything that follows. If we could remember these truths about God when our lives are on the rocks, we

4. J. A. Thompson, *Deuteronomy: An Introduction and Commentary*, TOTC (InterVarsity Press, 1974), 297.

would be tremendously comforted. That God is described as the Rock speaks to his unchanging character: his strength, stability, and permanence.[5] The contrast with his people is palpable. His work is "perfect," and all his ways are "justice," which means that he never makes a mistake and never does what is wrong. He is a God of faithfulness and without iniquity who is just and upright in all his ways.

Part of what makes life so hard when we find ourselves on the rocks is that we are tempted to believe that God either has messed up or is treating us unfairly. It is an honest struggle, and we should comfort ourselves with the description of God in Deuteronomy 32:4. As we give praise to the Rock for his character, justice, and unfailing faithfulness, we will find our hearts strengthened, even while we are struggling with our faith.

I have walked with faithful Christians through many difficult times and trials over the years. One of the marks of those who come through those trials more beautiful than they went in is their resolute commitment to ascribe greatness and perfection to Yahweh. Their faith grew stronger as they looked to the unchanging God and focused on praising him. As we do so, we also become more conscious of our own imperfections.

Acknowledge the Imperfections of Yahweh's People

We often discover as we give praise to God for who he is that we see ourselves more clearly. In Israel's case, the people's imperfections are painfully spelled out in the song. We might sum up their imperfections under three headings:

First, *they are a crooked and twisted people.* In contrast to God's faithfulness, God's people have dealt corruptly with him. We read in Deuteronomy 32:5, "They have dealt corruptly with him; they are no longer his children because they are blemished; they are a crooked and twisted generation." They are described literally as his "non-children" because they are "blemished," a word usually used to describe animals not fit for sacrifice. They have dealt corruptly because they are crooked and twisted. Jesus uses a similar description for God's people in his own day (Matt. 17:17). The apostle Paul alludes to this passage when he writes that true believers will stand out in

5. Daniel I. Block, *Deuteronomy*, NIVAC (Zondervan, 2012), 750.

a crooked and twisted generation: "Do all things without grumbling or disputing, that you may be blameless and innocent, children of God without blemish in the midst of a crooked and twisted generation, among whom you shine as lights in the world" (Phil. 2:14–15). Too frequently, like Israel, we look more like our crooked and twisted generation than lights in the world.

Second, *they are a people who trample grace.* What is particularly heinous about God's people's actions toward him is how gracious he has been. We read in Deuteronomy 32:6: "Do you thus repay the LORD, you foolish and senseless people? Is not he your father, who created you, who made you and established you?" God has been so generous, and this is how they repay him. He brought them into existence, gave them a land, and made them his possession among all the nations, as we read in verses 7–9: "Remember the days of old; consider the years of many generations; ask your father, and he will show you, your elders, and they will tell you. When the Most High gave to the nations their inheritance, when he divided mankind, he fixed the borders of the peoples according to the number of the sons of God. But the LORD's portion is his people, Jacob his allotted heritage."

As the Most High, God is sovereign over all nations. But he took special interest in the Israelites, and they trampled on his grace. The passage goes on to describe God's tender care for his people in Deuteronomy 32:10: "He found him in a desert land, and in the howling waste of the wilderness; he encircled him, he cared for him, he kept him as the apple of his eye." He rescued them from barrenness and treasured them for his own. Moses continues in verses 11–12, "Like an eagle that stirs up its nest, that flutters over its young, spreading out its wings, catching them, bearing them on its pinions, the LORD alone guided him, no foreign god was with him." God is compared to an eagle, catching his people when they are falling and carrying them on his wings, guiding them into a good future. Moses writes in verses 13–14:

> He made him ride on the high places of the land,
>   and he ate the produce of the field,
> and he suckled him with honey out of the rock,
>   and oil out of the flinty rock.
> Curds from the herd, and milk from the flock,
>   with fat of lambs,

rams of Bashan and goats,
with the very finest of the wheat—
and you drank foaming wine made from the blood of the grape.

God provided for his people's needs. The implication is that they were helpless and unable to feed themselves, but he provided for them in impossible scenarios. How, though, did God's people respond to the tremendous blessings he showered on them? "But Jeshurun grew fat, and kicked; you grew fat, stout, and sleek; then he forsook God who made him and scoffed at the Rock of his salvation" (Deut. 32:15). The word "Jeshurun" is related to the Hebrew word meaning "upright." God's so-called upright people grew fat on his provisions and then scoffed at the God who had given them.

We should be indignant that anyone would treat God this way, yet we also trample on his grace. We call out to him when we are on the rocks, only to forget him when we have been delivered. As we sit down to eat the food that he has provided, we forget to acknowledge him with thanks because we are consumed with our devices. As he fills our bank accounts, we are reluctant to give him back a portion of what he has blessed us with. Not to mention that he has blessed us with the gift of salvation and the promise of eternal provision!

Third, *they are a people unmindful of God*. The third way in which our imperfections are evident is in how quickly we forget God. We read in Deuteronomy 32:16–18:

They stirred him to jealousy with strange gods;
with abominations they provoked him to anger.
They sacrificed to demons that were no gods,
to gods they had never known,
to new gods that had come recently,
whom your fathers had never dreaded.
You were unmindful of the Rock that bore you,
and you forgot the God who gave you birth.

Consider how personally God takes our idolatry. He is not indifferent, but takes it personally when we are not mindful of him and put our hope and trust in idols. How might he feel when we treasure something or someone more than we treasure him? What does it do to his heart when our hope is set on a political candidate rather than on him? We are like the cheating wife who assures her husband that it is nothing personal, but other men just give her something that her husband does not. Meanwhile, the faithful husband is gut-wrenched and angry.

We must begin to take our sin seriously in light of the perfection of our God and Father. No more can we live like the crooked and twisted generation around us, but through faithful obedience to our God we must shine like lights in the world. We must not trample his gracious care and provision but rather, with grateful hearts, respond to him with loving obedience. We cannot tolerate any rival gods beside him. As we look to the Rock, we should see how we are not like him, and then confess and repent of these things.

Recognize the Justice of Yahweh

In Deuteronomy 32:19–35, after having leveled the case against his unfaithful people, God promises justice toward his people and vengeance toward his adversaries.

In response to their rejection of him, the Lord is going to hide his face from his people and watch what happens. He says in Deuteronomy 32:19–21:

> The LORD saw it and spurned them,
> because of the provocation of his sons and his daughters.
> And he said, "I will hide my face from them;
> I will see what their end will be,
> for they are a perverse generation,
> children in whom is no faithfulness.
> They have made me jealous with what is no god;
> they have provoked me to anger with their idols.
> So I will make them jealous with those who are no people;
> I will provoke them to anger with a foolish nation."

Just as they made him jealous with "no god," he will make them jealous with "no people." He is going to use foreign peoples to bring judgment on them.

This statement of judgment on Israel later kindles a flame of hope in the apostle Paul for the "no people" nations![6] Paul quotes Deuteronomy 32:21 in Romans 10:19. Then in Romans 11:11, he goes on to explain the implications: "So I ask, did they [Jews] stumble in order that they might fall? By no means! Rather, through their trespass salvation has come to the Gentiles, so as to make Israel jealous." In other words, Israel's unfaithfulness in seeking "no-gods" leads God to respond by seeking "no-people," meaning Gentiles like us. His extension of the covenant promises of salvation to Gentiles is intended to make the physical children of Abraham jealous, that they might stop rebelling against God and receive the free gift of salvation through faith in Jesus, even as the Gentiles have. God's mercy is evident even in his judgment! This redemptive motive is important to remember as we read Deuteronomy 32:22–25, describing the judgments for their unfaithfulness, including disasters, hunger, plague, wild beasts, and the sword.

Then God says in Deuteronomy 32:26–27 that he would have destroyed the Israelites completely, "had I not feared provocation by the enemy, lest their adversaries should misunderstand, lest they should say, 'Our hand is triumphant, it was not the LORD who did all this.'" The Lord determines not to wipe them out completely to spare his reputation. Furthermore, he will bring judgment on those very nations that he had sent as agents of judgment on his people.

In addition to judgment on his people, the Lord also promises vengeance toward his adversaries. Verses 28–35 of Deuteronomy 32 are a bit difficult to follow, but it helps to know that the song is now talking about God's enemy, the foreign nation that God will use to judge his people. The song continues in verses 28–31:

> For they are a nation void of counsel,
>   and there is no understanding in them.
> If they were wise, they would understand this;
>   they would discern their latter end!
> How could one have chased a thousand,
>   and two have put ten thousand to flight,
> unless their Rock had sold them,

6. Christopher Wright, *Deuteronomy*, NIBC: Old Testament 4 (Hendrickson, 2007), 301.

> and the LORD had given them up?
> For their rock is not as our Rock;
> our enemies are by themselves.

The nations are ignorant. They do not see how God gave his own people into their hand. The enemies think it is their gods who gave them victory, but it was God, the true Rock. God will demonstrate that power to them in time, as he says in Deuteronomy 32:34–35: "Is not this laid up in store with me, sealed up in my treasuries? Vengeance is mine, and recompense, for the time when their foot shall slip; for the day of their calamity is at hand, and their doom comes swiftly." God promises that those enemies that attack God's people will ultimately be the objects of God's vengeance.

Later, the apostle Paul quotes this verse to encourage Christians in his day not to seek revenge on those who harm them because God is still the one who will bring vengeance (Rom. 12:19). The writer of Hebrews uses this verse to warn those who should know better not to trample on the grace of God because the Lord will repay (Heb. 10:30). As we consider the justice of the Lord, we should be encouraged by both those applications. On the one hand, we ought not to avenge ourselves, for God is our Avenger. At the same time, we should not trample on his grace because the Lord will bring judgment on all his enemies.

TREASURE THE COMPASSION OF YAHWEH

God will not allow the enemies of his people to trample on them forever. Deuteronomy 32:36–38 begins with a treasure of grace in the midst of judgment:

> For the LORD will vindicate his people
> and have compassion on his servants,
> when he sees that their power is gone
> and there is none remaining, bond or free.
> Then he will say, "Where are their gods,
> the rock in which they took refuge,
> who ate the fat of their sacrifices
> and drank the wine of their drink offering?

Let them rise up and help you;
  let them be your protection!"[7]

God will have compassion on his people and step in to vindicate them when "their power is gone." It was their strength and self-assurance that led them to spurn the Lord and align with other gods. That strength must be demolished for them to realize their need for God's strength.[8] The taunt about the other gods could be directed to either the nations or the people of Israel—really, anyone who trusts in a rock other than the Rock. When life is on the rocks, both God's people and his enemies will see that every other rock will fail. Often, we must hit rock bottom and see the futility of idolatry before we turn from lifeless rocks to the living Rock.[9]

If our life is currently on the rocks, this exhortation may be hard to hear. It is difficult to wrap our minds around God's allowing tremendously difficult things into our lives to expose our self-dependence or our trust in idols, but this is his compassion. Far worse than a life on the rocks, or even at rock bottom, is a life cut off from the living Rock. When the devil begins to taunt that God does not care or that he has abandoned us, our Rock will have compassion to vindicate our trust in him. First we must come to the end of ourselves, our self-reliance, and our trust in idols.

In the end, God will demonstrate his superiority over the foolishness of trusting in anyone but him. The song continues in Deuteronomy 32:39–41:

See now that I, even I, am he,
  and there is no god beside me;
I kill and I make alive;
  I wound and I heal;
  and there is none that can deliver out of my hand.
For I lift up my hand to heaven
  and swear, As I live forever,

7. The Hebrew word translated "vindicate" in Deuteronomy 32:36 could also be translated "judge." The word "vindicate" is more likely in this context, given the parallelism with the second phrase, "and have compassion on his servants." Psalm 135:13–14 appears to echo this sentiment: "Your name, O Lord, endures forever, your renown, O Lord, throughout all ages. For the Lord will vindicate his people and have compassion on his servants."

8. Peter C. Craigie, *The Book of Deuteronomy*, NICOT (Eerdmans, 1976), 387.

9. Craigie, 387.

if I sharpen my flashing sword
  and my hand takes hold on judgment,
I will take vengeance on my adversaries
  and will repay those who hate me.

When God is ready to vindicate and rescue his people by carrying out judgment on his enemies, there is none who will be able to stop him. This should be a frightening prospect for unbelievers, but a tremendously comforting truth for all who are looking to the Rock. His compassion for his people will lead to the destruction of our enemies. But who are our enemies? Not flesh and blood, though we may suffer at the hands of people. Our enemies are the world system that stands opposed to righteousness, justice, love, and God. Our enemies are our own flesh that resists God and his good purposes. Our enemies are the devil and the demonic forces that seek to steal, kill, and destroy. Our last enemy to be defeated is death (1 Cor. 15:26).

Our enemies continue to persist in this world and make life difficult for Christians. But our enemies are already defeated. When Christ died on the cross, he disarmed our enemies by taking away the list of accusations that stood against us (Col. 2:15). We all had a debt that we owed and could not pay, and with his death he paid those debts. Now the accusations against us have no foundation. There is nothing to keep us from reconciliation with our God. We who were not his people now are his people, and nothing can separate us from his love (Rom. 8:38–39). Because Christ rose from the dead, defeating death, all who trust in him will share in that triumph. God's compassion for his people is seen most clearly in the cross. It is a compassion that we ought to treasure continually.

Rejoice in and Respond to the Deliverance of Yahweh

While this song has covered some difficult ground, it closes with a call to give praise to God.[10] We read in Deuteronomy 32:43: "Rejoice with him, O heavens; bow down to him, all gods, for he avenges the blood of his children and takes vengeance on his adversaries. He repays those who hate him and

10. Deuteronomy 32:43 is fraught with textual difficulties, as indicated by the extensive footnotes in our English Bibles.

cleanses his people's land." We see two reasons to rejoice in deliverance and one way to respond to deliverance in this verse.

First, Israel is to rejoice in the restored relationship. The text refers to God's people once again as "his children." While their idolatry caused God to withdraw, he has drawn near once again in compassion. Not only that, but it says that he "cleanses his people's land." The Hebrew word here for "cleanses" is often translated "atone." He will somehow atone for the sins that defile his people and their land without destroying the people themselves.

Second, they are to rejoice in the judgment of their enemies. God will deliver his people Israel, and ultimately the church, through bringing judgment on our enemies. We are not told how God will be able to save his people while bringing judgment on their sin, but the New Testament resolves the question for us. God took on flesh and the sins of his people. He judged our sin in Christ so that it might be properly addressed without destroying us. This victory has already been won at the cross, and we can rejoice in the judgment of our sin in Christ. We can continue to rejoice even today as we await the final victory at Christ's return, when evil will be eradicated from the earth.[11]

Third, the Israelites are to respond with loving obedience to the law. Moses clearly warns those of us who have experienced God's gracious salvation how to respond in Deuteronomy 32:45–47 after he concludes the song:

> And when Moses had finished speaking all these words to all Israel, he said to them, "Take to heart all the words by which I am warning you today, that you may command them to your children, that they may be careful to do all the words of this law. For it is no empty word for you, but your very life, and by this word you shall live long in the land that you are going over the Jordan to possess."

The proper response to God's salvation is to rejoice and to walk in obedience to his law. Rejecting it and going our own way will land us on the rocks, but as we walk in obedience, trusting in the Rock, we may enjoy a long life, and eternity beyond it.

11. The "song of Moses" and "the song of the Lamb" in Revelation 15:2–4 are pictures of our ultimate rejoicing in God's deliverance through final judgment on our enemies.

47

Last Words

Deuteronomy 32:48—33:29

This is the blessing with which Moses the man of God blessed the people of Israel before his death. (Deut. 33:1)

"I only regret that I have but one life to lose for my country." Those are the famous last words of the twenty-one-year-old American patriot Nathan Hale before he was hanged as a spy by the British in 1776. Except for the power of his last words, we might have never heard of Nathan Hale. Instead, his last words have become the interpretive lens through which we look at his short life.

My father-in-law, Dr. Robert Johnstone, is an anesthesiologist, and he occasionally hears people's last words. In an article he wrote for the *Journal of the American Medical Association*, he observed, "While last words are forever, the opportunities to speak them or hear them are fleeting, and usually unrecognized."[1] He goes on to recount how, as a young physician, he first heard the last words of a patient. The man died unexpectedly in the recovery room after surgery. His last conversation had been in the operating room related

1. Robert E. Johnstone, "A Piece of My Mind: Last Words," *Journal of the American Medical Association* 295, no. 14 (April 12, 2006): 1624.

only to his positioning on the table and his breathing from the face mask. After the man died, Dr. Johnstone reflected on the man's insignificant last words. He writes: "I wished he'd said something profound, warm, or loving to pass along, but he hadn't. If either of us had known the future, we'd have spoken differently."[2] We would also speak differently if we knew that we were saying our last words. Moses had that privilege—and that responsibility.

The last words of Moses are found in Deuteronomy 33. Unlike those who die unexpectedly, Moses is speaking very intentionally, knowing that his death is near. He knows it because of God's directions to him in Deuteronomy 32:49–50: "Go up this mountain of the Abarim, Mount Nebo, which is in the land of Moab, opposite Jericho, and view the land of Canaan, which I am giving to the people of Israel for a possession. And die on the mountain which you go up, and be gathered to your people." Deuteronomy reminds us why Moses will speak his last words on the east side of the Jordan in verses 51–52: "because you broke faith with me in the midst of the people of Israel at the waters of Meribah-kadesh, in the wilderness of Zin, and because you did not treat me as holy in the midst of the people of Israel. For you shall see the land before you, but you shall not go there." We will consider the meaning of these verses more fully in the next chapter, but for now, they set the scene for Moses' last words.

Moses will not be going any farther with the people, and so he must tell them now what they must remember later. With his final words, he pronounces blessings on each of the tribes, just as Jacob did at the end of his life. What Moses tells the people of God as they head into the dangers, trials, and fearsome obstacles that they are about to encounter is simple, yet profound. The same truths that would carry them through the challenges before them will also carry us. Moses' final message is that God loves you, God is for you, and God is with you.

God Loves You

The passage is introduced in Deuteronomy 33:1: "This is the blessing with which Moses the man of God blessed the people of Israel before

2. Johnstone, 1624.

his death." The phrase "man of God" appears many times in the Old Testament and usually refers to a prophet, or a person through whom God speaks.[3] Even as Moses speaks, we are reminded that he speaks for God. With his introductory words, he reminds us that God loves his people. We read in verse 2, "The LORD came from Sinai and dawned from Seir upon us; he shone forth from Mount Paran; he came from the ten thousands of holy ones, with flaming fire at his right hand." Despite textual and interpretive difficulties, the overall intention is clear. Moses is referring to the momentous event when God gave his people the law. The "holy ones" references angels. When the New Testament speaks of the law of Moses as having been mediated by angels (see Acts 7:53; Gal. 3:19; Heb. 2:2), it is probably because of these verses. God's appearance to his people at Sinai, terrifying as it was, demonstrated his love for them. Moses emphasizes it in Deuteronomy 33:3–4: "Yes, he loved his people, all his holy ones were in his hand; so they followed in your steps, receiving direction from you, when Moses commanded us a law, as a possession for the assembly of Jacob." The point is that the law was a gift to a people he loved so that he might rule over them. Moses writes in verse 5, "Thus the LORD became king in Jeshurun, when the heads of the people were gathered, all the tribes of Israel together." With God's deliverance of his people and the gift of his law, God becomes King in Jeshurun (another name for "Israel," meaning "upright"). Even though Moses is going to be passing on, God is their King, and he will be with them in the next phase of their journey.

Evidence of God's love is also found in how he came to us, not at Sinai, but at Bethlehem. At Sinai he came with lightning and thunder, and none could approach even the mountain, but at Bethlehem he came to us as a baby. He was still a King, but approachable by all. Through Jesus at Bethlehem, God calls us to follow him, because he loves us. That is why he came, and that is why he will come again.

3. Besides Deuteronomy 33:1, consider also: Josh. 14:6; Judg. 13:6, 8; 1 Sam. 2:27; 9:6–8, 10; 1 Kings 12:22; 13:1, 4–8, 11–12, 14, 21, 26, 29, 31; 17:18, 24; 20:28; 2 Kings 1:9–13; 4:7, 9, 16, 21–22, 25, 27, 40, 42; 5:8, 14–15, 20; 6:6, 9–10, 15; 7:2, 17–19; 8:2, 4, 7–8, 11; 13:19; 23:16–17; 1 Chron. 23:14; 2 Chron. 8:14; 11:2; 25:7, 9; 30:16; Ezra 3:2; Neh. 12:24, 36; Ps. 90 (heading); Jer. 35:4. Additionally, the apostle Paul uses the phrase in 1 Timothy 6:11 and 2 Timothy 3:17.

God Is for You

Moses pronounces formal blessings on the people in Deuteronomy 33:6–25. Many of these blessings are difficult for us to appreciate, but the point is to assure the people that God is for them.[4] The first blessing is for the firstborn of Jacob in verse 6, "Let Reuben live, and not die, but let his men be few." The tribe of Reuben is granted life, but that life is limited because of the sin of their namesake. Reuben slept with his father's concubine (Gen. 35:22). The tribe will continue because God is for them, but it will not be great.[5] The second blessing is for Judah in Deuteronomy 33:7: "Hear, O Lord, the voice of Judah, and bring him in to his people. With your hands contend for him, and be a help against his adversaries." Judah's blessing is that God will hear his voice and that God will fight for him against his foes.

The third blessing is for the tribe of Levi beginning in Deuteronomy 33:8–9:

> Give to Levi your Thummim,
> and your Urim to your godly one,
> whom you tested at Massah,
> with whom you quarreled at the waters of Meribah;
> who said of his father and mother,
> "I regard them not";
> he disowned his brothers

4. Simeon is not mentioned anywhere in the blessings. Some think that perhaps it is because of Simeon's involvement in the violence at Shechem and Jacob's allusion to it in his blessing of Simeon and Levi (Gen. 49:5–7). But if this were the case, it does not explain why Levi receives such a tremendous blessing in Deuteronomy 33 and Simeon is not mentioned. It has also been suggested that because Simeon's allotment was within the territory of Judah, he is not mentioned specifically. An alternative suggestion was given to me in private correspondence with Dr. Iain Duguid of Westminster Theological Seminary regarding Simeon and Levi. In his view, both Simeon and Levi are cursed with scattering in Genesis 49 because of the Shechem event, but that curse works its way out differently. Simeon is dispersed within Judah and largely disappears, while Levi is faithful at the golden-calf incident and so sees its curse reversed into a blessing—it is still scattered as a tribe, but now scattered in order to serve all twelve tribes. Both messages are important: parents' sins have consequences for their children, but the Lord can reverse the curse through his grace.

5. Both ancient versions and modern translations differ over whether the second line of Reuben's blessing is a wish for great numbers (NASB) or for few (ESV). The Hebrew is literally "may his men be a number," which echoes the expression "men of number" and refers to men of small number (e.g., Gen. 34:30). See J. G. McConville, *Deuteronomy*, ApOTC 5 (Inter-Varsity Press, 2002), 466.

and ignored his children.
For they observed your word
and kept your covenant.

Moses is referring to the way in which the Levites were willing to take up their sword against their own family members who were engaged in worshiping the golden calf (Ex. 32:25–29). As a result of their loyalty to the Lord, Deuteronomy 33:10–11 reports that they have received the priesthood. The priests then were responsible for giving guidance by the Urim and Thummim (Deut. 33:8), teaching the law (v. 10), and leading in worship (v. 10).

The next blessing is for Benjamin in Deuteronomy 33:12: "Of Benjamin he said, 'The beloved of the LORD dwells in safety. The High God surrounds him all day long, and dwells between his shoulders.'" Benjamin is beloved and therefore safe in God's care. The next and longest blessing (in English word count) is for Joseph and the two tribes that come from him, Ephraim and Manasseh in verses 13–17. The emphasis of the blessing is on material provision (Deut. 33:13–16) and military might (v. 17).

After Joseph is the blessing for Zebulun, which also includes Issachar, in Deuteronomy 33:18–19: "And of Zebulun he said, 'Rejoice, Zebulun, in your going out, and Issachar, in your tents. They shall call peoples to their mountain; there they offer right sacrifices; for they draw from the abundance of the seas and the hidden treasures of the sand.'" These tribes are invited to rejoice because their material provision from the sea and the seashore will be so great, they will hold sacrificial festivals of thanksgiving.[6] It is not clear why these landlocked tribes will enjoy such provision from the seas, but it is clear that God is for them.

The next blessings are for Gad, Dan, and Naphtali, which include prominence in military victory (Deut. 33:20–21) and an abundance of favor (v. 23). The last blessing is reserved for Asher in Deuteronomy 33:24–25: "And of Asher he said, 'Most blessed of sons be Asher; let him be the favorite of his brothers, and let him dip his foot in oil. Your bars shall be iron and bronze, and as your days, so shall your strength be.'" Asher's name means "happy," and so this tribe will be. It is not clear what dipping his foot in oil signifies, but it is apparently a good and joyful symbol. The bars of iron and

6. Peter C. Craigie, *The Book of Deuteronomy*, NICOT (Eerdmans, 1976), 399.

bronze are a description of the tribe's security and safety, that they may live out their happy days protected. Their strength will last as long as their lives.

What do these blessings have to do with readers today? One answer is that the blessings that God gave to his people through Moses were a tremendous indication that God was for them. He was for them not only en masse, but with particular blessings for the tribes, reflecting their unique situations. As great as these blessings were that were given through Moses, we who are in Christ have been blessed even more so! Ephesians 1:3 exults, "Blessed be the God and Father of our Lord Jesus Christ, who has blessed us in Christ with every spiritual blessing in the heavenly places." Those blessings include our election, our predestination, our adoption, our redemption, our forgiveness, our inheritance, and the gift of the Holy Spirit! We have been given every spiritual blessing in the heavenly places in Christ Jesus. What more could God do to show that he is for us than to give us Jesus Christ, and in Jesus Christ to give us all these blessings? In addition to the blessings that we all share in Christ, our Father knows our individual needs as well and provides for us accordingly. After reflecting on the blessings that we have been given in Romans 8, the apostle Paul declares: "What then shall we say to these things? If God is for us, who can be against us? He who did not spare his own Son but gave him up for us all, how will he not also with him graciously give us all things?" (Rom. 8:31–32). God is for you. He gave you Jesus. As greatly as the people of Israel were blessed, we can be confident that no blessing will be withheld from those who trust in Jesus.

God Is with You

In the final verses, Moses proclaims the uniqueness of our God and his special relationship to his people. What better legacy could we leave with those we love than a reminder of God? Consider these seven truths:

First, God is with you as your unique rescuer. Moses proclaims in Deuteronomy 33:26, "There is none like God, O Jeshurun, who rides through the heavens to your help, through the skies in his majesty." God is unique in all the universe for many reasons. He alone is infinite, eternal, and unchangeable. He alone rides through the heavens to rescue his people. The word "Jeshurun" is used again as another name for his people. In 32:15 it was used ironically, but here it is meant sincerely.

Recently in a neighborhood near our church, some walkers noticed the sound of a kitten crying out from a storm drain. After trying unsuccessfully to locate the kitten, they called others to help. These good neighbors actually went down into a manhole in search of this kitten crying out for rescue. After four days, the county got involved. Groups of county employees were using the best electronic and technical equipment to try to locate this kitten. Cameras mounted on robots were dispatched into the drains without success. Eventually, county workers cut up the asphalt road to find the helpless kitten, and after many days and many dollars, this stray kitten without a name or an owner was rescued. In a happy ending, the kitten was adopted into a loving family and, because of the proximity of the rescue to Christmas, was given the name Mistletoe. As dramatic and as costly as that rescue was, it pales in comparison to the rescue of the God who rides through the heavens to the help of his people. Our God went all the way from heaven to earth, and then to the cross, to rescue his people. Though we were not a people, he gave us a name and adopted us into his own family at the infinite cost of the blood of his only Son. This God who went to such lengths to rescue you is with you.

Second, God is with you as your eternal dwelling place. Moses writes in Deuteronomy 33:27, "The eternal God is your dwelling place." God is eternal, and he is the place where his people find rest forever. If God is our dwelling place, then we are always home, no matter where we are, because he is always with us. If our home is destroyed through flood or fire, if we move from place to place, our dwelling place in which we find rest and security has not changed. The language of "dwelling place" was also frequently used to describe God's abode in heaven (e.g., 1 Kings 8:30; 2 Chron. 6:30) and God's abode on earth in the temple (e.g., 2 Chron. 6:39; Ps. 74:7). But in Ephesians 2:22, the apostle Paul tells us that in Christ something incredible has happened: "In him [Christ] you also are being built together into a dwelling place for God by the Spirit." Not only is God our eternal dwelling place, but in Christ, we are the dwelling place of the eternal God! This truth was pictured in the incarnation of Jesus when he took up residence in the womb of the virgin Mary, and it is continually fulfilled through the indwelling of the Holy Spirit in every believer. God is with us as surely as he was with Mary in the womb.

Third, God is with you as your unfailing support. We read in Deuteronomy 33:27 that "underneath are the everlasting arms." When you cannot stand on your own, underneath you are God's everlasting arms, forever holding you up. Years ago, I ran the St. Louis Marathon. The conditions were not particularly favorable that day, so I ended up more dehydrated than usual. When I crossed the finish line and was walking down the finishing chute, my calf muscles in both legs locked up completely. It was so sudden and painful that I shouted out loud. As I was about to hit the ground and cause a pileup in the finishing chute, some unknown stranger put his arms under me and held me up until I could get out of the path of traffic for more help. I did not know he was there until I started to go down. Often it is not until we are falling that we recognize the everlasting arms underneath us.

Back in the late 1800s, a successful author, businessman, and devout Presbyterian layman named Anthony Showalter received some sad letters from two different friends about losses they had experienced. Anthony wrote back letters of encouragement that included Deuteronomy 33:27 about the everlasting arms. As he concluded the letters, the thought occurred to him that this theme would make a great hymn.[7] So he jotted down the chorus and music, which, with the help of his friend Elisha Hoffman, would become a beloved hymn in 1887: "What a fellowship, what a joy divine, leaning on the everlasting arms; what a blessedness, what a peace is mine, leaning on the everlasting arms."[8] Our fellowship with the Lord is marked by his holding us up with his everlasting arms. My favorite verse in the hymn is the last one: "What have I to dread, what have I to fear, leaning on the everlasting arms? I have blessed peace with my Lord so near, leaning on the everlasting arms." If he is with us and holding us up, we have nothing to fear.

Fourth, God is with you as your unbreachable security. We read in Deuteronomy 33:27–28: "And he thrust out the enemy before you and said, 'Destroy.' So Israel lived in safety, Jacob lived alone, in a land of grain and wine, whose heavens drop down dew." It is worded as a statement of something that is finished, but at the time of writing, it had not yet taken place. The enemy had not been thrust out, and Israel was not yet living in safety. But Moses is declaring it as the future that will be because of the God who is with the people. He will be their unbreachable security and

7. Kenneth W. Osbeck, *Amazing Grace: 366 Inspiring Hymn Stories for Daily Devotions* (Kregel, 1990), 87.

8. Elisha A. Hoffman and Anthony J. Showalter, "Leaning on the Everlasting Arms" (1887).

will remove their enemies before them. These verses remind the Israelites that the path ahead of them is not going to be one of peaceful existence and quiet solitude, but will be one of fearsome battles and opposition. Yet in the midst of it, God will be with them because this is the path on which he is calling them to walk.[9] So he will also be with us.

Fifth, God is with you as your unexpected happiness. Moses writes in Deuteronomy 33:29: "Happy are you, O Israel! Who is like you, a people saved by the LORD." The people of God are happy because they are unique on the earth. The Israelites are a people who have been saved, unexpectedly and undeservedly, and so are we! The people of Israel have been saved through the plagues in Egypt, the parting of the Red Sea, the miraculous provision of manna and water in the wilderness, and their military victories over Sihon and Og. They have been saved dramatically!

Our salvation is so much more dramatic. Consider our hopeless condition: dead in sin, lost in the darkness—blind, deaf, and unable to help ourselves. "But God, being rich in mercy, because of the great love with which he loved us, even when we were dead in our trespasses, made us alive together with Christ—by grace you have been saved—and raised us up with him and seated us with him in the heavenly places in Christ Jesus" (Eph. 2:4–6). Nothing about our salvation can be expected, nothing taken for granted. Happy are we, a people saved against all odds! God defeated our enemies, pulled us out of the miry bog, set our feet on the Rock, and gave us a new name, a new life, and a new future.

Sixth, God is with you as your shield of help. A shield is used for defense and protection against the enemy's arrows and sword strikes. In Deuteronomy 33:29, Moses describes God as "the shield of your help." God is with you as your shield of defense, and he does not fail. Even when we are struck, wounded, and suffering, God is our shield. This truth is best summarized in a line from the first answer of the Heidelberg Catechism, "He also preserves me in such a way that without the will of my heavenly Father not a hair can fall from my head; indeed, all things must work together for my salvation." God is with us as our shield, and without the will of our Father, not an arrow can come near, nor can a hair fall from our heads. He does allow some difficult things into our lives, including some painful things. Yet whatever

9. Craigie, *Deuteronomy*, 403.

he allows to come to us must work for our salvation. Nothing gets past our shield of defense except what works for our salvation.

Seventh, God is with you as your sword of triumph. God is not only our defense, but our offense. The final description of God with us is in Deuteronomy 33:29: "and the sword of your triumph! Your enemies shall come fawning to you, and you shall tread upon their backs." The people of Israel will have victory over their enemies as they go into the land. But victory over enemies is not just for them, and it is not just victory over human enemies. Christians, God is our sword of triumph! Yes, that besetting sin that will not seem to die—one day we will tread on its back. Yes, the grave that holds our loved ones today and one day our bodies as well—we will tread on its back. Yes, we will even tread on the devil himself! As Paul encourages us in Romans 16:20, "The God of peace will soon crush Satan under your feet." God will crush him . . . under our feet!

The Greatest Blessing

What does Moses want the people of God to know with his last words? God loves you, God is for you, and God is with you. He wants them to know this so that they will remember, trust, and obey. Before Jesus ascended to heaven, his own last words strike the same chord: "And behold, I am with you always, to the end of the age" (Matt. 28:20). As he sends his people out, not to take the land of Canaan, but to take the nations by making disciples, we too must remember, trust, and obey the God who loves us, is for us, and is with us.

Just before he died, the poet Samuel Taylor Coleridge wrote some of his last meaningful words to his godchild: "On the eve of my departure, I declare to you, that health is a great blessing; competence, obtained by honourable industry, a great blessing; and a great blessing it is to have kind, faithful, and loving friends and relatives; but that the greatest blessing, as it is the most ennobling of all privileges, is to be, indeed, a Christian."[10]

And so it is. For to be a Christian is to know beyond a shadow of a doubt that God loves you, God is for you, and God is with you. Do you know this? Then remember, trust, and obey.

10. Quoted in John D. Currid, *Deuteronomy*, EPSC (EP Books, 2006), 492–93.

48

Unfulfilled Longings

Deuteronomy 34:1–12

Moses was 120 years old when he died. His eye was undimmed, and his vigor unabated. And the people of Israel wept for Moses in the plains of Moab thirty days. Then the days of weeping and mourning for Moses were ended. (Deut. 34:7–8)

At the Hudson Theatre in New York in December 2022, an apparently inebriated heckler interrupted a production of Arthur Miller's classic play *Death of a Salesman*. The lead actor, Wendell Pierce, eventually broke character and tried to plead with the woman to leave, even offering to give her a refund himself. At one point, Pierce can be heard in a video recording saying in frustration, "I've waited too long for this!"[1] Too long for what? In the seventy-year history of the play on Broadway, Pierce is just the sixth man to play the lead role and the first black man to do so. He has described this role as being the pinnacle of his nearly forty-year acting career. Yet this drunken patron threatened to leave him with his career-defining longing unfulfilled.

1. Margaret Hall, "Wendell Pierce Talks Down Unruly Audience Member at *Death of a Salesman*," *Playbill*, December 28, 2022, https://playbill.com/article/wendell-pierce-talks-down-unruly-audience-member-at-death-of-a-salesman, accessed December 28, 2022.

Coincidentally, *Death of a Salesman* is largely about the theme of unfulfilled longings. The play tells the story of Willy Loman, a middle-aged salesman who is struggling to come to terms with his own failures and unfulfilled longings in pursuit of the American Dream. Willy is a complex and flawed character, filled with regrets and a deep sense of disillusionment. He is constantly trying to live up to his own expectations and the expectations of others, but he is unable to succeed, largely because of himself. Earlier in his life, Willy made a mistake, a very costly one, that would haunt him for the rest of his days. When all his attempts to eradicate his mistake fail, he takes his own life as a final desperate attempt to make it right. *Death of a Salesman* continues to resonate with audiences because it forces us to hold a mirror up to ourselves. Willy's feelings of failure and regret are emotions that we can all relate to because we have all experienced them at some point.

Like Willy Loman, Moses was also flawed. Though he was a gifted leader, he was unable to experience the fulfillment of the greatest object of his life. Like Willy, Moses was haunted by the mistakes of his past, one in particular. Because of that failure, despite his best efforts, Moses was unable to fulfill his longing to lead the Israelites into the promised land; he died before he was able to see the culmination of his life's work. Moses' unfulfilled longings are a reminder of the consequences of sin and the sobering limitations of every human life.

The fact is, unless Jesus returns first, we will all die with unfulfilled longings. We will have goals that we did not accomplish, things that we did not say, books that we did not write, places that we did not visit, changes that we did not make, and growth that did not happen. Death is the jagged rock on which our unfulfilled longings will be dashed. Facing this reality is the greater part of wisdom. As we conclude our series on Deuteronomy, we can draw at least four lessons from Moses' death.

Death Comes to the Best of Us and to the Rest of Us

We have been prepared for the death of Moses through multiple references in Deuteronomy (Deut. 1:37; 3:23–29; 31:2, 14, 16, 27–29; 32:48–52).[2] The Lord was explicit in Deuteronomy 32:49–51:

2. Christopher Wright, *Deuteronomy*, NIBC: Old Testament 4 (Hendrickson, 2007), 312.

> Go up this mountain of the Abarim, Mount Nebo, which is in the land of Moab, opposite Jericho, and view the land of Canaan, which I am giving to the people of Israel for a possession. And die on the mountain which you go up, and be gathered to your people, as Aaron your brother died in Mount Hor and was gathered to his people, because you broke faith with me in the midst of the people of Israel at the waters of Meribah-kadesh, in the wilderness of Zin, and because you did not treat me as holy in the midst of the people of Israel.

Between that passage and this one, Moses blessed the people with his last words. Then Moses did as he was told. We read in Deuteronomy 34:1, "Then Moses went up from the plains of Moab to Mount Nebo, to the top of Pisgah, which is opposite Jericho." It is possible that "Pisgah" is an alternative name for Mount Nebo, but the word in Hebrew means "ridge," and the verse could be rendered "to Mount Nebo, the summit of the ridge."[3] From there, God shows Moses all the promised land and declares in verses 4–6:

> "This is the land of which I swore to Abraham, to Isaac, and to Jacob, 'I will give it to your offspring.' I have let you see it with your eyes, but you shall not go over there." So Moses the servant of the Lord died there in the land of Moab, according to the word of the Lord, and he buried him in the valley in the land of Moab opposite Beth-peor; but no one knows the place of his burial to this day.

Moses died on the mountain before crossing into the promised land. The text adds further detail in Deuteronomy 34:7: "Moses was 120 years old when he died. His eye was undimmed, and his vigor unabated." Though Moses was 120 years old, he did not die from old age. Moses died on account of his sin at the waters of Meribah-kadesh when he struck the rock and broke faith with the Lord. He did not treat the Lord as holy (Deut. 32:51). We may think it unfair that Moses should die because of this one sin, but the very law that Moses delivered to the people puts that protest to rest. As he wrote, "Each one shall be put to death for his own sin" (24:16). The apostle Paul would later explain, "For the wages of sin is death" (Rom. 6:23). That was true for Moses, and he was the best of us. How much more is it true for the rest of us!

3. Peter C. Craigie, *The Book of Deuteronomy*, NICOT (Eerdmans, 1976), 404.

We may say that Moses' sin was just one dark mark amid 120 years of faithfulness, but such a statement reveals our ignorance about the nature of sin. Moses' one sin at that rock tells us everything we need to know about Moses' condition. As Alexander Maclaren puts it, "One little mark under the armpit of a plague-sufferer tells the physician that the fatal disease is there."[4] Moses too was afflicted by that dreadful condition far worse than any plague that the world has ever known. Moses was born a sinner. So he sinned. Thus, he died. Not even the greatest will escape the horrible consequences of the least sin. Neither will we. In the death of Moses, we are reminded that the curse of sin remains; even the greatest are not free of the grip of death.

But in Deuteronomy 34:5, Moses is called "the servant of the LORD." Earlier, in 33:1, Moses was identified as "the man of God." Striking about both statements is that they come right on the heels of verses explaining that he will not be entering the land because of his sin. It is difficult for many of us to hold these two realities together: that a man can be a true man of God, and yet also have failures. But the Old and New Testaments demonstrate repeatedly that being a "man of God" does not mean that we never fail. It means that the overarching character of our lives is one of love and trust in the Lord and obedience to his commandments. David sinned tremendously and was still known as a "man of God" (2 Chron. 8:14) and a "man after [God's] own heart" (1 Sam. 13:14). Likewise, Peter failed tremendously, and yet Jesus restored him (John 21:15–19), and he became a significant pillar in the early church and down to this day. We could add many more examples. The point is that it is God who defines us and not our failures. There is only one man who never failed, and we look to Jesus for the righteousness that we do not possess.

Business Will Remain Unfinished and Longings Will Remain Unfulfilled

Moses was able to see the land, but he was not able to enter it. We read in Deuteronomy 34:1–3, "And the LORD showed him all the land, Gilead as

4. Alexander Maclaren, *Deuteronomy, Joshua, Judges, Ruth, and First Book of Samuel, Second Samuel, First Kings, and Second Kings, Chapters I to VII*, vol. 2 of *Expositions of Holy Scripture* (Eerdmans, 1944), 79.

far as Dan, all Naphtali, the land of Ephraim and Manasseh, all the land of Judah as far as the western sea, the Negeb, and the Plain, that is, the Valley of Jericho the city of palm trees, as far as Zoar." I have been on Mount Nebo several times, but I have yet to see all that the Lord showed Moses because of dust, dirt, and clouds. This does not mean that the Bible is being untruthful. It is quite likely that Moses saw with prophetic vision as the Lord showed him what the natural eye could not see. He saw the entirety of the promised land. If we imagine Moses as standing on a clock at 3 o'clock, the tour worked its way around the promised land counterclockwise. After the Lord showed it to him, as we read in verse 4: "And the LORD said to him, 'This is the land of which I swore to Abraham, to Isaac, and to Jacob, "I will give it to your offspring." I have let you see it with your eyes, but you shall not go over there.'" Moses will see the land, but he will not enter it. That longing will remain unfulfilled. Here the Pentateuch comes full circle. In Genesis, God promised Abraham that he was going to give him this land. Now at the end of the Pentateuch, Moses stands poised, but he will not receive what was promised. Death will stop him short of fulfilling the longing that sustained him. Many others continue to follow suit.

Arthur Stanley, a former dean of Westminster Abbey, observed in the nineteenth century:

> To labor and not to see the end of our labor; to sow and not to reap; to be removed from this earthly scene before our work has been appreciated and when it will be carried on not by ourselves but by others—is a law so common in the highest characters of history, that none can be said to be altogether exempt from its operation.[5]

When we look to the world of the arts, we remember Emily Dickinson, who is now widely considered one of the greatest poets of all time, but her work was not appreciated until after she was gone. In the realm of politics, we remember Abraham Lincoln, who is now considered by many to be one of the greatest American presidents, but he was killed before he got to see the fruits of his labor.

5. Arthur Penrhyn Stanley, *Lectures in the History of the Jewish Church* (J. Murray, 1883), n.p., quoted in Dennis Prager, *The Rational Bible: Deuteronomy: God, Blessings, and Curses*, ed. Joseph Telushkin, Alperson ed. (Regnery Faith, 2022), 504.

There is one example that is even more striking: Martin Luther King Jr. In "I've Been to the Mountaintop," a message he gave the night before he was assassinated, he alluded to Moses' death before entering the promised land:

> Well, I don't know what will happen now. We've got some difficult days ahead. But it doesn't matter with me now. Because I've been to the mountaintop. And I don't mind. Like anybody, I would like to live a long life. Longevity has its place. But I'm not concerned about that now. I just want to do God's will. And He's allowed me to go up to the mountain. And I've looked over. And I've seen the Promised Land. I may not get there with you. But I want you to know tonight, that we, as a people, will get to the Promised Land.[6]

He too died with an unfulfilled longing, and the same will be true for us.

Dr. King spent his life laboring for something that was meaningful in the scope of eternity. Abraham Lincoln spent his life laboring for something that made a difference in the lives of many. Moses also died in the pursuit of a worthy goal. But what about us? It is far better to die with a worthy longing unfulfilled than to die having fulfilled an unworthy longing. Maclaren writes: "It is easy for a man to secure immediate consequences of an earthly kind; easy enough for him to make certain that he shall have the fruit of his toil. But quick returns mean small profits; and an unfinished life that succeeds in nothing may be far better than a completed one, that has realized all its shabby purposes and accomplished all its petty desires."[7] Death will come to us all unless the Lord returns, and we will all die with unfinished business. The question that we should be asking ourselves is whether the chief business of our lives is even worth the pursuit. May we say like William Carey, who spent his life seeking to reach the lost in India: "I'm not afraid of failure. I'm afraid of succeeding at things that don't matter."[8] Moses died short of the goal, but it was a goal worthy of the pursuit. Is yours?

6. Quoted in Prager, 504.

7. Maclaren, *Deuteronomy*, 82.

8. Quoted in Tim Challies, "How to Avoid the Worst Form of Failure," Challies.com, June 13, 2016, https://www.challies.com/articles/how-to-avoid-the-worst-form-of-failure/.

No One Is Indispensable, and the World Will Move On

After Moses dies, we read in Deuteronomy 34:8–9: "And the people of Israel wept for Moses in the plains of Moab thirty days. Then the days of weeping and mourning for Moses were ended. And Joshua the son of Nun was full of the spirit of wisdom, for Moses had laid his hands on him. So the people of Israel obeyed him and did as the Lord had commanded Moses." It is hard for us to imagine such a thirty-day period of mourning, as Israel did for Moses. By comparison, when Queen Elizabeth II died, the United Kingdom began only a ten-day period of mourning her death, even though she was perhaps the best-loved monarch in the nation's storied history. Moses was worthy of such a prolonged period of mourning.[9] Verses 10–12 remind us of his uniqueness:

> And there has not arisen a prophet since in Israel like Moses, whom the Lord knew face to face, none like him for all the signs and the wonders that the Lord sent him to do in the land of Egypt, to Pharaoh and to all his servants and to all his land, and for all the mighty power and all the great deeds of terror that Moses did in the sight of all Israel.

No one shared intimate fellowship with God as Moses did. No one did signs as Moses did. No one delivered God's people as Moses did. Remember his extraordinary life!

Moses was born into seemingly impossible circumstances, since the pharaoh of Egypt had ordered the killing of all male Hebrew children to quell the growing population of Hebrews in the country. But Moses' mother managed to save him by placing him in a basket and setting him adrift on the Nile. He was discovered and raised by Pharaoh's daughter, who hired Moses' own mother to nurse him. As a young man, Moses received a privileged education in the ways of the Egyptian elite, but he never forgot his Hebrew heritage. After killing an Egyptian who was mistreating a Hebrew slave, Moses spent the next forty years in obscurity as a shepherd in Midian, being prepared for the great calling of his life, to be the shepherd of Israel. When

9. His brother Aaron was also mourned for thirty days (Num. 20:29).

he was eighty (Ex. 7:7), God called him to confront Pharaoh and lead the people out of slavery in Egypt and into the promised land. After a series of miraculous plagues, Pharaoh relented, and Moses led the Israelites on a perilous journey through the wilderness. Despite countless challenges and obstacles, Moses remained a steadfast and compassionate leader, providing guidance and inspiration to an enormous horde of unruly people on the way to the promised land.

The New Testament writer of Hebrews also held Moses up as an example worthy of imitation:

> By faith Moses, when he was born, was hidden for three months by his parents, because they saw that the child was beautiful, and they were not afraid of the king's edict. By faith Moses, when he was grown up, refused to be called the son of Pharaoh's daughter, choosing rather to be mistreated with the people of God than to enjoy the fleeting pleasures of sin. He considered the reproach of Christ greater wealth than the treasures of Egypt, for he was looking to the reward. By faith he left Egypt, not being afraid of the anger of the king, for he endured as seeing him who is invisible. By faith he kept the Passover and sprinkled the blood, so that the Destroyer of the firstborn might not touch them. (Heb. 11:23–28)

Moses was hardcore: he loved God and he loved the people of God. He was a shepherd, a leader, a prophet, and a preacher. He suffered so much for God's people and from God's people. We should honor this man and strive to be like him, a man worthy of imitation. What a life he lived! But then he died, and after thirty days of mourning, Joshua took over.

No one is indispensable. The world moved on after Moses. Similarly, the world will move on after us. Such realizations are not pleasant, especially when some of us have been significant people in the world: founders, leaders, and change-makers in every area of life. But none of us compares to the influence that Moses had on the world—perhaps second in history only to Jesus. The people mourned for him thirty days and then moved on. It will not take that long for the world to move on from us.

Such knowledge gives valuable perspective. Many of us are trying desperately to please people who will simply move on once we are gone.

Some are throwing away meaningful relationships in pursuit of the approval of people who will not think twice about us after we have expired. Still others doggedly pursue success under the illusion that we will attain some sort of immortality. Others are literally working ourselves to death, thinking that without us, everything will fall apart. The truth is that none of us is indispensable and that the world will move on when we are gone.

"All of this has been a downer," you might say. If this world were all there was, we would have good reason to be depressed because most assuredly we are all going to die, we will leave unfinished business, and people will forget about us sooner than we care to admit. But there is one other thing that we should take away from this last message in Deuteronomy.

One Day, Death Will Be Swallowed Up in Victory and Every Longing Will Be Fulfilled

After Moses, and after Deuteronomy, comes Joshua. He will be the one to lead the people of God into the fulfillment of the land of promise. Even he was not able to lead the people into the rest that they longed for. Those who died in the land also died with a sense of longing. Hebrews 4:8–10 speaks of a greater rest: "For if Joshua had given them rest, God would not have spoken of another day later on. So then, there remains a Sabbath rest for the people of God, for whoever has entered God's rest has also rested from his works as God did from his." There is a greater rest that awaits God's people than they enjoyed in the promised land. The promised land was only a pointer to the ultimate rest, security, and satisfaction of every longing that nothing in this world could satisfy. It would take a Prophet greater than Moses, a Mediator of a better covenant than the one made at Sinai, and a better Warrior than Joshua to satisfy these longings. That greater Prophet came. The greater Joshua rose up. A better covenant was ratified. While Moses was a servant in the household of God, Jesus Christ is the only begotten Son of the Father (Heb. 3:1–6).[10] While Moses was used to accomplish the exodus from Egypt, Jesus would bring about a new exodus from the grip of sin, death, and hell, and by it he would deliver all his people, including

10. Craigie, *Deuteronomy*, 407.

Moses and Joshua. While Moses died with unfinished business, Jesus said with his last breath, "It is finished" (John 19:30). While Moses spoke with God face to face, in the face of Jesus we see God.

While Moses was not able to enter the land in his lifetime, he did ultimately enter the land. Nearly fifteen hundred years later, Moses appeared on one of those mountains that he must have seen off in the distance from Mount Nebo. He was there with the great prophet Elijah and the one greater than all, Jesus Christ. We read in Luke 9:30–31, "And behold, two men were talking with [Jesus], Moses and Elijah, who appeared in glory and spoke of his departure, which he was about to accomplish at Jerusalem." Moses and Elijah were chosen to come and minister to Jesus and prepare him for his departure, an amazing privilege given to the man who would die before entering the land. But the Greek text adds even more interest to this encounter. While our English text says that they "spoke of his departure," the Greek text says that they "spoke of his exodus, which he was about to accomplish at Jerusalem."[11] Jesus' death on the cross would be not simply a departure, but the initiation of a new exodus—not to lead the people of Israel out of slavery to Pharaoh in Egypt, but to lead people from every nation out of slavery to sin, death, and hell. By Jesus Christ's bearing the judgment of death and hell that our sins deserved, the very law delivered by Moses could no longer condemn any who put their faith in Christ, including Moses. The law's requirements were satisfied. Through the resurrection of Jesus Christ, finally everything old would be made new, everything wrong would be made right, and everything sad would come untrue.

A reader might say: "No amount of good in the future can make up for what I have suffered or lost in this world. No amount of ultimate fulfillment can compensate me for the unfulfilled longings I have today." This is an understandable objection. But consider what C. S. Lewis writes in *The Great Divorce*: "That is what mortals misunderstand. They say of some temporal suffering, 'No future bliss can make up for it' not knowing that Heaven, once attained, will work backwards and turn even that agony into a glory."[12] Our current unfulfilled longings will one day be a glorious thing to behold

11. Douglas F. Kelly, *Deuteronomy: A Mentor Expository Commentary* (Mentor, 2022), 469.
12. C. S. Lewis, *The Great Divorce* (Macmillan, 1946), 67.

when every longing is more than met in the infinite abundance of Jesus. There is no longing so great that the God who put it in us cannot fulfill it.

Those who have longed for love in this world will be satisfied. Those who have been empty will be filled. Those who have desired glory will be glorified beyond their wildest dreams. Those who have longed to give creative expression to intense feelings will have full capacity. Those who have longed for security and stability will never feel it more than when all things are made new. When we know that this world is not the only world and this life is not the only life that we are ever going to have, we can face the realities of death and unfulfilled longings with cheerful courage. Timothy Keller writes: "The resurrection means we can look forward with hope to the day our suffering will be gone. But it even means that we can look forward with hope to the day our suffering will be glorious."[13]

As we close this book, let us remember from the life of Moses that death will come to us all; there are no exceptions. Likewise, we will all die with unfinished business, and the question is whether that business is worth pursuing. Once we are gone, we will be replaced, and the world will move on. What distinguishes the one who trusts in the greater Moses, the greater Joshua, the Lord Jesus Christ himself, is that death will not be the end, but only the beginning of a greater story, in which no longing is so great that it will not be more than satisfied when we see him face to face.

We have this hope. Let us live faithfully as God's covenant people. Let us remember who he is and what he has done for us. Let us trust him to be true to all that he has promised, and let us obey him with a heart full of love and gratitude. Amen.

13. Timothy Keller, *King's Cross: The Story of the World in the Life of Jesus* (Dutton, 2011), 224.

Afterword

Arthur Miller wrote:

> There is a certain immortality involved in theatre, created not by monuments or books but through the knowledge an actor carries with him to his dying day that, in an empty and dusty theatre, on a certain afternoon, he cast a shadow of a being that was not himself but a distillation of everything he had ever thought or felt. All the unsingable heartsong that the ordinary man may feel but never utter he gave voice to and, by that, he somehow joins the ages.[1]

But I do pray that these pages cast a shadow of a Being worthy of our endless praise and far greater than anything we have ever thought or felt.

1. Quoted in Edward Goodman, *Make Believe: The Art of Acting* (Charles Scribner's Sons, 1956), 121.

Bibliography

Alcorn, Randy. *Managing God's Money: A Biblical Guide*. Tyndale House, 2011.

Alexander, T. Desmond, Brian S. Rosner, D. A. Carson, and Graeme Goldsworthy, eds. *New Dictionary of Biblical Theology*. InterVarsity Press, 2000.

Allen, Charles L. *God's Psychiatry*. Revell, 1988.

American Psychological Association. *Stress in America 2019*. November 2019. https://www.apa.org/news/press/releases/stress/2019/stress-america-2019.pdf. Accessed July 15, 2023.

Angier, Natalie. "In One Ear and Out the Other." *New York Times*, March 16, 2009. https://www.nytimes.com/2009/03/17/science/17angi.html. Accessed December 8, 2022.

Armerding, C. E. "Festivals and Feasts." In *Dictionary of the Old Testament: Pentateuch*, edited by T. Desmond Alexander and David W. Baker. InterVarsity Press, 2003.

Atchley, Paul. "You Can't Multitask, So Stop Trying." *Harvard Business Review*, December 21, 2010. https://hbr.org/2010/12/you-cant-multi-task-so-stop-tr. Accessed January 6, 2022.

Baloyi, M. E. "The Christian View of Levirate Marriage in a Changing South Africa." *Journal of Sociology and Social Anthropology* 6, no. 4 (2015): 483–91.

Bavinck, Herman. *Our Reasonable Faith*. Translated by Henry Zylstra. Eerdmans, 1956.

———. *Reformed Dogmatics*. Edited by John Bolt. Translated by John Vriend. Vol. 3, *Sin and Salvation in Christ*. Baker Academic, 2008.

Baxter, Richard. *A Christian Directory*. In *The Practical Works of Richard Baxter*. 4 vols. Soli Deo Gloria, 2008.

Bennet, Arthur. *The Valley of Vision: A Collection of Puritan Prayers and Devotions*. Banner of Truth, 2002.

Berkhof, Louis. *Systematic Theology*. Banner of Truth, 1958.

Berkowitz, Adam Eliyahu. "Does 'Curse Amulet' Prove the Discovery of Joshua's Altar on Mount Ebal?" *Jerusalem Post*, April 3, 2022. https://www.jpost.com/christianworld/article-703046. Accessed October 24, 2022.

Beyer, Rick. *The Greatest Stories Never Told: 230 Tales from History to Astonish, Bewilder, and Stupefy*. Reader's Digest special ed. Reader's Digest Association, 2008.

Blakemore, Erin. "The Brutal History of Japan's 'Comfort Women.'" History.com. Updated July 21, 2019. https://www.history.com/news/comfort-women-japan-military-brothels-korea. Accessed July 24, 2022.

Block, Daniel I. *Deuteronomy*. NIVAC. Zondervan, 2012.

Blomberg, Craig L. *Christians in an Age of Wealth: A Biblical Theology of Stewardship*. Biblical Theology for Life. Zondervan, 2013.

Bonar, Andrew A., ed. *Memoir and Remains of Robert Murray M'Cheyne*. 1844. Reprint, Banner of Truth, 2019.

Boo, Katherine. *Behind the Beautiful Forevers: Life, Death, and Hope in a Mumbai Undercity*. Random House, 2012.

The Book of Church Order of the Presbyterian Church in America. Office of the Stated Clerk of the General Assembly of the Presbyterian Church in America, 2021.

Bowles, Hamish. "Playtime with Harry Styles." *Vogue*, November 13, 2020. https://www.vogue.com/article/harry-styles-cover-december-2020. Accessed August 12, 2022.

Brattson, David W. T. "Abortion and the Early Church." Christians for Social Action. January 10, 2017. https://christiansforsocialaction.org/resource/abortion-and-the-early-church/. Accessed November 10, 2021.

Bridges, Jerry. *The Discipline of Grace: God's Role and Our Role in the Pursuit of Holiness*. NavPress, 1994.

Bromiley, Geoffrey W., ed. *International Standard Bible Encyclopedia*. 4 vols. Zondervan, 1979–88.

Brown, Francis, S. R. Driver, and Charles A. Briggs. *The New Brown-Driver-Briggs Hebrew and English Lexicon*. Hendrickson, 2005.

Brown, Haley, and Gabrielle Fonrouge. "Crimo Dad Washes Hands of Guilt but Talked with Son About a Mass Shooting Night Before Highland Park Massacre." *New York Post*, July 6, 2022. https://nypost.com/2022/07/06/highland-park-shooter-robert-crimo-father-speaks-about-son/. Accessed July 13, 2022.

Brown, Raymond. *The Message of Deuteronomy: Not by Bread Alone*. The Bible Speaks Today. InterVarsity Press, 1993.

Calvin, John. *Commentaries on the Four Last Books of Moses, Arranged in the Form of a Harmony*. Translated by Charles William Bingham. 4 vols. Calvin's Commentaries. Baker, 2005.

———. *Institutes of the Christian Religion*. Edited by John T. McNeill. Translated by Ford Lewis Battles. Library of Christian Classics 20. Westminster John Knox Press, 1960.

———. "The Sixth Sermon upon the First Chapter on Saturday the 15th of April 1555." In *Sermons on Deuteronomy*. https://www.monergism.com/sermons-deuteronomy-ebook.

———. "The Twelfth Sermon Which Is the Second upon the Second Chapter on Friday the 25th of April 1555." In *Sermons on Deuteronomy*. https://www.monergism.com/sermons-deuteronomy-ebook.

Case, Thomas. "A Treatise of Afflictions." In *Select Works*. Soli Deo Gloria, 1993.

Challies, Tim. "How to Avoid the Worst Form of Failure." Challies.com. June 13, 2016. https://www.challies.com/articles/how-to-avoid-the-worst-form-of-failure/.

Chapell, Bryan. *Holiness by Grace: Delighting in the Joy That Is Our Strength*. Crossway, 2001.

Chapman, Gary. *The Five Love Languages: How to Express Heartfelt Commitment to Your Mate*. Northfield, 1992.

Clark, Mark. *The Problem of God: Answering a Skeptic's Challenges to Christianity*. Zondervan, 2017.

Collins, John J., and Daniel C. Harlow, eds. *Eerdmans Dictionary of Early Judaism*. Eerdmans, 2010.

Collins, Suzanne. *The Hunger Games*. Scholastic Press, 2008.

Cortez, Marc. "The Law on Violent Intervention: Deuteronomy 25.11–12 Revisited." *JSOT* 30, no. 4 (June 2006): 431–47.

Craigie, Peter C. *The Book of Deuteronomy*. NICOT. Eerdmans, 1976.

Currid, John D. *Deuteronomy*. EPSC. EP Books, 2006.

Dahlberg, Edward. *The Sorrows of Priapus*. In *Camp's Unfamiliar Quotations from 2000 B.C. to the Present*, by Wesley D. Camp. Prentice Hall, 1990.

Department of Veterans Affairs. "America's Wars." https://www.va.gov/opa/publications/factsheets/fs_americas_wars.pdf. Accessed July 6, 2022.

———. "2021 National Veteran Suicide Prevention Annual Report." September 2021. https://www.mentalhealth.va.gov/docs/data-sheets/2021/2021-National-Veteran-Suicide-Prevention-Annual-Report-FINAL-9-8-21.pdf. Accessed July 7, 2022.

Development Services Group, Inc. "Interactions Between Youth and Law Enforcement." Literature Review. Office of Juvenile Justice and Delinquency Prevention. Updated January 2018. https://www.ojjdp.gov/mpg/litreviews/Interactions-Youth-Law-Enforcement.pdf. Accessed July 24, 2022.

DeYoung, Kevin. "Do the Ten Commandments Have Authority over New Testament Christians?" The Gospel Coalition. October 23, 2018. https://www.thegospelcoalition.org/blogs/kevin-deyoung/ten-commandments-authority-new-testament-christians/. Accessed November 4, 2021.

———. *The 10 Commandments: What They Mean, Why They Matter, and Why We Should Obey Them*. Crossway, 2018.

Douma, J. *The Ten Commandments: Manual for the Christian Life*. Translated by Nelson D. Kloosterman. P&R Publishing, 1996.

Downs, Tim. *Head Game*. Thomas Nelson, 2007.

Drapkin, Jenny. "LBJ: The President Who Marked His Territory." Mental Floss. April 17, 2008. https://www.mentalfloss.com/article/18463/lbj-president-who-marked-his-territory. Accessed June 7, 2022.

Duncan, J. Ligon, III. "Does God Care How We Worship?" In *Give Praise to God: A Vision for Reforming Worship: Celebrating the Legacy of James Montgomery Boice*, edited by Philip Graham Ryken, Derek W. H. Thomas, and J. Ligon Duncan III. P&R Publishing, 2003.

Earls, Aaron. "Most Teenagers Drop Out of Church When They Become Young Adults." Lifeway Research. January 15, 2019. https://lifewayresearch.com/2019/01/15/most-teenagers-drop-out-of-church-as-young-adults/. Accessed January 6, 2022.

Edwards, Jonathan. *The Blank Bible*. Vol. 24 of *The Works of Jonathan Edwards*, edited by Stephen J. Stein. Yale University Press, 2006.

———. *The "Miscellanies": Entry Nos. a–500*. Vol. 13 of *The Works of Jonathan Edwards*, edited by Thomas A. Schafer. Yale University Press, 1994.

———. *Works of Jonathan Edwards: Volume Two*. Banner of Truth, 1995.

Elliott, E. N. *Cotton Is King, and Pro-Slavery Arguments*. Pritchard, Abbott & Loomis, 1860.

Enns, Peter. *Exodus*. NIVAC. Zondervan, 2000.

Estes, Daniel J. *Hear, My Son: Teaching and Learning in Proverbs*. NSBT 4. Apollos, 1997.

Feder, Yitzhaq. "Breaking the Heifer's Neck: A Bloodless Ritual for an Unsolved Murder." TheTorah.com. 2018. https://thetorah.com/article/breaking-the-heifers-neck-a-bloodless-ritual-for-an-unsolved-murder.

Federal Trade Commission. *Consumer Sentinel Network Data Book 2021*. February 2022. https://www.ftc.gov/system/files/ftc_gov/pdf/CSN%20Annual%20Data%20Book%202021%20Final%20PDF.pdf.

Feinstein, E. L. "Sexual Prohibitions in the Bible and the ANE: A Comparison." TheTorah.com. 2018. https://www.thetorah.com/article/sexual-prohibitions-in-the-bible-and-the-ane-a-comparison.

Fernando, Ajith. *Deuteronomy: Loving Obedience to a Loving God*. Preaching the Word. Crossway, 2012.

Foster, Richard J., and James Bryan Smith, eds. *Devotional Classics: Selected Readings for Individuals and Groups*. Rev. ed. Zondervan, 2005.

Frame, John M. *The Doctrine of the Christian Life*. Theology of Lordship. P&R Publishing, 2008.

France, R. T. *The Gospel of Matthew*. New International Commentary on the New Testament. Eerdmans, 2007.

Glapion, Chad. "The Curse of Atuk." Inside the Simulation. May 18, 2021. https://medium.com/inside-the-simulation/the-curse-of-atuk-28896a18e29f. Accessed October 27, 2022.

Goodman, Edward. *Make Believe: The Art of Acting*. Charles Scribner's Sons, 1956.

Goodwin, Thomas. *The Works of Thomas Goodwin*. Vol. 2. Tanski, 1996.

Gouin, Joseph O. "God Always Has a 'Yes' Face." *Iron Mountain Daily News*, October 22, 2018. https://www.ironmountaindailynews.com/lifestyles/life/2018/10/god-always-has-a-yes-face/. Accessed February 10, 2022.

Griffith, Wendy. "Amazing End to the Hatfield-McCoy Feud." Daily Hatch. Originally aired March 20, 2009. https://thedailyhatch.org/2012/06/01/great-great-granddaughter-of-devil-anse-hatfield-said-he-came-to-christ/. Accessed July 1, 2022.

Groves, Sara. "Painting Pictures of Egypt." SaraGroves.com. https://www.saragroves.com/song-lyrics/painting-pictures-of-egypt. Accessed February 4, 2022.

Haddock, Vicki. "Power Is Not Only an Aphrodisiac, It Does Weird Things to Some of Us." SFGATE.com. November 19, 2006. https://www.sfgate.com/opinion/article/Power-is-not-only-an-aphrodisiac-it-does-weird-2546085.php. Accessed June 8, 2022.

Hall, Margaret. "Wendell Pierce Talks Down Unruly Audience Member at *Death of a Salesman*." *Playbill*, December 28, 2022. https://playbill.com/article/wendell-pierce-talks-down-unruly-audience-member-at-death-of-a-salesman. Accessed December 28, 2022.

Harney, Kevin G. *Seismic Shifts: The Little Changes That Make a Big Difference in Your Life*. Zondervan, 2005.

Harris, Joshua. *Dug Down Deep: Unearthing What I Believe and Why It Matters*. Multnomah, 2010.

Harter, Jim. "Is Quiet Quitting Real?" Gallup Workplace. September 6, 2022. https://www.gallup.com/workplace/398306/quiet-quitting-real.aspx. Accessed October 12, 2022.

Hegg, Tim. "You Shall Not Boil a Kid in Its Mother's Milk: The Interpretive History of a Curious Commandment." Paper presented at the annual Evangelical Theological Society conference, Baltimore, MD, November 2013. https://tr-pdf.s3-us-west-2.amazonaws.com/articles/you-shall-not-boil-a-kid-in-its-mothers-milk.pdf.

Heid, Markham. "You Asked: Is Social Media Making Me Miserable?" *TIME*, August 2, 2017. https://time.com/4882372/social-media-facebook-instagram-unhappy/. Accessed November 9, 2021.

Henry, Matthew. "Complete Commentary on Deuteronomy 1." In *Henry's Complete Commentary on the Bible*. https://www.studylight.org/commentaries/eng/mhm/deuteronomy-1.html.

Heschel, Abraham Joshua. *God in Search of Man: A Philosophy of Judaism*. Jewish Publication Society, 1959.

Holmes, A. F. "Just-War Theory." In *New Dictionary of Christian Ethics and Pastoral Theology*, edited by David J. Atkinson and David A. Field. InterVarsity Press, 1995.

"How Sports Fans Choose Their Teams: Readers Share Their Stories." *New York Times Magazine*, July 5, 2017. https://www.nytimes.com/2017/07/05/magazine/how-sports-fans-choose-their-teams-readers-share-their-stories.html. Accessed January 6, 2022.

Hugo, Victor. *Les Misérables*. Translated by Christine Donougher. Penguin Classics Deluxe ed. Penguin Books, 2015.

"Impossible to Serve God and Mammon." Bible Hub. https://biblehub.com/sermons/pub/impossible_to_serve_god_and_mammon.htm. Accessed January 13, 2025.

Ingersoll, Robert G. *Abraham Lincoln: A Lecture*. C. P. Farrell, 1895.

"In Memphis, Renewed Attention on Violence After Shooting Rampage." *New York Times*, September 8, 2022. https://www.nytimes.com/2022/09/08/us/memphis-shooting-gun-violence.html.

Irwin, Tim. *Impact: Great Leadership Changes Everything*. BenBella Books, 2014.

Jackson, Liane. "Balance of Power: Money and Inequity in the Judicial System." *ABA Journal*, September 1, 2019. https://www.abajournal.com/magazine/article/balance-of-power. Accessed September 2, 2021.

Jazaieri, Hooria. "Six Habits of Highly Compassionate People." *Greater Good Magazine*, April 24, 2018. https://greatergood.berkeley.edu/article/item/six_habits_of_highly_compassionate_people. Accessed October 6, 2022.

J.John. "The Courage, Creativity and Charm of GK Chesterton." ChristianPost.com. November 4, 2021. https://www.christianpost.com/voices/the-courage-creativity-and-charm-of-gk-chesterton.html.

Johnstone, Robert E. "A Piece of My Mind: Last Words." *Journal of the American Medical Association* 295, no. 14 (April 12, 2006): 1624.

Jones, Rachel K., Elizabeth Nash, Lauren Cross, Jesse Philbin, and Marielle Kirstein. "Medication Abortion Now Accounts for More than Half of All US Abortions." Guttmacher Institute. February 2022. https://www.guttmacher.org/article/2022/02/medication-abortion-now-accounts-more-half-all-us-abortions. Accessed October 17, 2022.

Jordan, James B. *Studies in Food and Faith*. Biblical Horizons, 1989.

Keller, Timothy. "A Biblical Critique of Secular Justice and Critical Theory." Gospel in Life. https://quarterly.gospelinlife.com/a-biblical-critique-of-secular-justice-and-critical-theory/. Accessed June 1, 2022.

———. *Counterfeit Gods: The Empty Promises of Money, Sex, and Power, and the Only Hope That Matters*. Dutton, 2009.

———. *Generous Justice: How God's Grace Makes Us Just*. Dutton, 2010.

———. *King's Cross: The Story of the World in the Life of Jesus*. Dutton, 2011.

Kelly, Douglas F. *Deuteronomy: A Mentor Expository Commentary*. Mentor, 2022.

Kitchen, K. A. *On the Reliability of the Old Testament*. Eerdmans, 2003.

Knauth, R. J. D. "Alien, Foreign Resident." In *Dictionary of the Old Testament: Pentateuch*, edited by T. Desmond Alexander and David W. Baker. InterVarsity Press, 2003.

Larson, Craig Brian. *750 Engaging Illustrations for Preachers, Teachers, and Writers*. Baker, 2007.

Larson, Craig Brian, and Phyllis Ten Elshof, eds. *1001 Illustrations That Connect: Compelling Stories, Stats, and News Items for Preaching, Teaching, and Writing*. Christianity Today International, 2008.

Layne, Rachel. "America's Price Tag for Two Decades of War: $5.8 Trillion." CBS News. Updated September 1, 2021. https://www.cbsnews.com/news/afghanistan-cost-war-price-tag/. Accessed July 6, 2022.

Lewis, C. S. *The Great Divorce*. Macmillan, 1946.

Lipka, Hilary. "The Prohibition of Cross-Dressing." TheTorah.com. 2018. https://thetorah.com/article/the-prohibition-of-cross-dressing. Accessed August 14, 2022.

"Little Roosevelt and the Zeal." [1901?] Newspaper article. Theodore Roosevelt Papers. Library of Congress Manuscript Division. Theodore Roosevelt Digital Library. Dickinson State University. https://www.theodorerooseveltcenter.org/Research/Digital-Library/Record?libID=o288665. Accessed June 25, 2022.

Lopez, Meghan. "From Detour to Disaster: Google Maps Got Dozens of Colorado Drivers in a Mud Mess on Sunday." Denver7.com. Updated June 26, 2019. https://www.thedenverchannel.com/news/local-news/from-detour-to-disaster-google-maps-got-dozens-of-colorado-drivers-in-a-mud-mess-on-sunday. Accessed March 17, 2022.

Luther, Martin. *Table Talk of Martin Luther.* Translated by William Hazlitt. Lutheran Publication Society, n.d.

Maclaren, Alexander. *Deuteronomy, Joshua, Judges, Ruth, and First Book of Samuel, Second Samuel, First Kings, and Second Kings, Chapters I to VII.* Vol. 2 of *Expositions of Holy Scripture.* Eerdmans, 1944.

Malinowski, Scoop. "Biofile Mike Tyson Interview." Mr Biofile. October 12, 2022. https://mrbiofile.com/2022/10/12/biofile-mike-tyson-interview/. Accessed November 4, 2022.

Manetsch, Scott M. *Calvin's Company of Pastors: Pastoral Care and the Emerging Reformed Church, 1536–1609.* Oxford Studies in Historical Theology. Oxford University Press, 2013.

Markel, Howard. "The Secret Ingredient in Kellogg's Cornflakes Is Seventh-Day Adventism." *Smithsonian Magazine,* July 28, 2017. https://www smithsonianmag.com/history/secret-ingredient-kelloggs-corn-flakes-seventh-day-adventism-180964247/. Accessed March 25, 2022.

Marshall, I. Howard, A. R. Millard, J. I. Packer, and Donald J. Wiseman, eds. *New Bible Dictionary.* InterVarsity Press, 1996.

Mather, Cotton. *Magnalia Christi Americana: Or, The Ecclesiastical History of New-England; from Its First Planting, in the Year 1620, unto the Year of Our Lord 1698.* Seven Books 1. Silas Andrus and Son, 1855.

Matlock, Michael D. "Obeying the First Part of the Tenth Commandment: Applications from the Levirate Marriage Law." *JSOT* 31, no. 3 (March 2007): 295–310.

McConville, Gordon. *Deuteronomy.* ApOTC 5. Inter-Varsity Press, 2002.

———. *Deuteronomy.* New Bible Commentary: 21st Century ed. InterVarsity Press, 1994.

McKeown, J. "Blessings and Curses." In *Dictionary of the Old Testament: Pentateuch,* edited by T. Desmond Alexander and David W. Baker. InterVarsity Press, 2003.

McRobbie, Linda Rodriguez. "Total Recall: The People Who Never Forget." *Guardian,* February 8, 2017. https://www.theguardian.com/science/2017/feb/08/total-recall-the-people-who-never-forget. Accessed February 4, 2022.

Merrill, Eugene H. *Deuteronomy.* NAC 4. Broadman & Holman, 1994.

Millar, J. Gary. *Now Choose Life: Theology and Ethics in Deuteronomy.* NSBT 6. Apollos, 1998.

Miller, C. John. *Saving Grace: Daily Devotions from Jack Miller.* New Growth Press, 2014.

Miller, Patrick D. *Deuteronomy.* IC. John Knox Press, 1990.

Morris, Leon. *The Apostolic Preaching of the Cross.* Eerdmans, 1965.

Motyer, Alec. *Roots: Let the Old Testament Speak.* Edited by John Stott. Christian Focus, 2009.

Murray, John. *Principles of Conduct: Aspects of Biblical Ethics.* Eerdmans, 1984.

National Health Service (UK). "Why People Self-Harm." https://www.nhs.uk/mental-health/feelings-symptoms-behaviours/behaviours/self-harm/why-people-self-harm/.

Nixon, Richard M. Interview with David Frost. May 19, 1977. In *Camp's Unfamiliar Quotations from 2000 B.C. to the Present*, by Wesley D. Camp. Prentice Hall, 1990.

Ortlund, Dane. *Gentle and Lowly: The Heart of Christ for Sinners and Sufferers.* Crossway, 2020.

Osbeck, Kenneth W. *Amazing Grace: 366 Inspiring Hymn Stories for Daily Devotions.* Kregel, 1990.

Owen, John. *The Mortification of Sin in Believers.* Religious Tract Society, 1799.

Packer, J. I. *Knowing God.* InterVarsity Press, 1973.

Peterson, Eugene H. *Working the Angles: The Shape of Pastoral Integrity.* Eerdmans, 1987.

Ponton, Osvoldo. "María Gabriela de Faría on Growth, Empowerment, and Inspiring Positive Change." Global Heroes. https://www.globalheroes.com/maria-gabriela-de-faria-empowerment/. Accessed August 15, 2022.

Prager, Dennis. *The Rational Bible: Deuteronomy: God, Blessings, and Curses.* Edited by Joseph Telushkin. Alperson ed. Regnery Faith, 2022.

Recovery Village. "Self-Harm Statistics." Updated August 30, 2024. https://www.therecoveryvillage.com/mental-health/self-harm/self-harm-statistics/.

"Reflections." *Christianity Today*, May 22, 2000, 84.

Rhodes, Jonty. *Covenants Made Simple: Understanding God's Unfolding Promises to His People.* P&R Publishing, 2014.

Richter, Sandra L. *The Epic of Eden: A Christian Entry into the Old Testament.* IVP Academic, 2008.

———. "Rape in Israel's World . . . and Ours: A Study of Deuteronomy 22:23–29." *JETS* 64, no. 1 (2021): 59–76.

Roberts, Vaughan. *The Porn Problem*. Good Book Company, 2018.

Robertson, O. Palmer. *The Christ of the Covenants*. Baker, 1981.

Rushing, Richard, ed. *Voices from the Past: Puritan Devotional Readings*. Banner of Truth, 2009.

Sarna, Nahum M. *Exodus*. JPSTC. Jewish Publication Society, 1991.

Scobie, Charles H. H. *The Ways of Our God: An Approach to Biblical Theology*. Eerdmans, 2003.

Shakespeare, William. *The Tragedy of Macbeth*.

Sharon, Jeremy. "Jerusalem Rabbinical Court Refuses to Let Widow of 13 Years Remarry." *Jerusalem Post*, September 4, 2014. https://www.jpost.com/israel-news/jerusalem-rabbinical-court-refuses-to-let-widow-of-13-years-remarry-374371.

Spence, Robert Y. "Uncle Dyke Garrett." *e-WV: The West Virginia Encyclopedia*. Rev. May 5, 2014. https://www.wvencyclopedia.org/entries/2023. Accessed January 13, 2025.

Sproul, R.C. *How Should I Live in This World?* Crucial Questions 5. Reformation Trust, 2009.

———. *What Can I Do with My Guilt?* Crucial Questions 9. Reformation Trust, 2011.

Spurgeon, Charles H. "Caleb—The Man for the Times." No. 538, preached November 1, 1863. Spurgeon Sermon Collection. Accordance electronic ed. OakTree Software, 2012.

———. "Election." Nos. 41–42 in *Sermons 1–53*. Vol. 1 of *The New Park Street Pulpit*. Spurgeon Sermon Collection. Accordance electronic ed. OakTree Software, 2004.

———. "Election and Holiness." No. 303 in *Sermons 286–347*. Vol. 6 of *The Metropolitan Tabernacle Pulpit*. Spurgeon Sermon Collection. Accordance electronic ed. OakTree Software, 2012.

Stanley, Arthur Penrhyn. *Lectures in the History of the Jewish Church*. J. Murray, 1883.

Steele, Richard. "Sermon XIV: What Are the Hinderances and Helps to a Good Memory in Spiritual Things?" In *Puritan Sermons 1659–1689 in Six Volumes*. Vol. 3. Richard Owen Roberts, 1981.

Steinmeyer, Nathan. "An Early Israelite Curse Inscription from Mt. Ebal?" Biblical Archaeology Society. April 25, 2022. https://www.biblicalarchaeology.org/daily/biblical-artifacts/inscriptions/mt_ebal_inscription/. Accessed October 16, 2022.

Stuart, Moses. *Conscience and the Constitution*. Crocker & Brewster, 1850.

Swoboda, A. J. *Subversive Sabbath*. Brazos Press, 2018.

Tan, Kim Huat. "The Shema and Early Christianity." *Tyndale Bulletin* 59, no. 2 (2008): 181–206.

Thayer, William M. "A Sermon on Moses' Fugitive Slave Bill." Preached at Ashland, MA, November 3, 1850. Charles C. P. Moody, 1850.

Theocharous, Myrto. "Stealing Souls: Human Trafficking and Deuteronomy 24:7." In *For Our Good Always: Studies on the Message and Influence of Deuteronomy in Honor of Daniel I. Block*, edited by Jason S. DeRouchie, Jason Gile, and Kenneth J. Turner. Eisenbrauns, 2013.

Thomas, I. D. E., comp. *The Golden Treasury of Puritan Quotations*. Banner of Truth, 1989.

Thompson, J. A. *Deuteronomy: An Introduction and Commentary*. TOTC. InterVarsity Press, 1974.

Tigay, Jeffrey H. *Deuteronomy*. JPSTC. Jewish Publication Society, 1996.

Tolstoy, Leo. *The Kingdom of God Is Within You*. Translated by Constance Garnett. Vol. 1. William Heinemann, 1894.

Tozer, A. W. *The Knowledge of the Holy*. Harper & Row, 1961.

VanGemeren, Willem A., ed. *New International Dictionary of Old Testament Theology and Exegesis*. 5 vols. Zondervan, 1997.

Vanhoozer, Kevin J. "Being Biblical in a Pluralistic Age." *Andrews University Seminary Studies* 57, no. 2 (2019): 305–26.

"Video Message of His Holiness Pope Francis to the 6th World Congress Against the Death Penalty." Oslo, June 21–23, 2016. https://www.vatican.va/content/francesco/en/messages/pont-messages/2016/documents/papa-francesco_20160621_videomessaggio-vi-congresso-contro-pena-di-morte.html. Accessed July 1, 2022.

Virtue, Doreen. "Please Don't Read My Books Anymore." *Christianity Today*, March 2022, 87–88.

Watson, Thomas. *A Body of Divinity*. Banner of Truth, 1970.

Wenham, Gordon J. "*Bětûlāh*, a Girl of Marriageable Age." *Vetus Testamentum* 22, no. 3 (July 1972): 326–48.

———. *The Book of Leviticus*. NICOT. Eerdmans, 1979.

———. "The Gap Between Law and Ethics in the Bible." *Journal of Jewish Studies* 48, no. 1 (Spring 1997): 17–29.

Wildsmith, Elizabeth, Jennifer Manlove, and Elizabeth Cook. "Dramatic Increase in the Proportion of Births Outside of Marriage in the United States from 1990 to 2016." Child Trends. August 8, 2018. https://www.childtrends.org/publications/dramatic-increase-in-percentage-of-births-outside-marriage-among-whites-hispanics-and-women-with-higher-education-levels. Accessed August 25, 2022.

Wilkin, Jen. *Ten Words to Live By: Delighting in and Doing What God Commands*. Crossway, 2021.

Willard, Dallas. "Live Life to the Full." *Christian Herald* (UK), April 14, 2001. https://dwillard.org/articles/live-life-to-the-full. Accessed September 2, 2021.

Winner, Lauren F. *Real Sex: The Naked Truth About Chastity*. Brazos Press, 2005.

Wolfson, Leo. "Wyoming Hero: College Wrestler Jumps on Grizzly to Save Friend." *Cowboy State Daily*, October 17, 2022. https://cowboystatedaily.com/2022/10/17/wyoming-hero-college-wrestler-jumps-on-grizzly-to-save-friend/. Accessed October 21, 2022.

Wood, David J. "The Best Life: Eugene Peterson on Pastoral Ministry." *Christian Century*, March 13, 2002. https://www.christiancentury.org/article/2002-03/best-life. Accessed September 2, 2021.

Wright, Christopher J. H. *Deuteronomy*. NIBC: Old Testament 4. Hendrickson, 2007.

———. *Old Testament Ethics for the People of God*. InterVarsity Press, 2004.

Wright, D. P. "Deuteronomy 21:1–9 as a Rite of Elimination." *CBQ* 49, no. 3 (July 1987): 387–403.

Index of Scripture

Index of Subejcts and Names

Available in the Reformed Expository Commentary Series

Old Testament

Genesis, by Richard D. Phillips
1 Samuel, by Richard D. Phillips
2 Samuel, by Richard D. Phillips
1 Kings, by Philip Graham Ryken
2 Kings, by Philip Graham Ryken
Ezra & Nehemiah, by Derek W. H. Thomas
Esther & Ruth, by Iain M. Duguid
Job, by Douglas Sean O'Donnell
Psalms 42–72, by Richard D. Phillips
Psalms 73–106, by Richard D. Phillips
Ecclesiastes, by Douglas Sean O'Donnell
Song of Songs, by Iain M. Duguid
Daniel, by Iain M. Duguid
Hosea, by Richard D. Phillips
Jonah & Micah, by Richard D. Phillips
Zephaniah, Haggai, Malachi, by Iain M. Duguid
and Matthew P. Harmon
Zechariah, by Richard D. Phillips

Available in the Reformed Expository Commentary Series

New Testament

The Incarnation in the Gospels, by Daniel M. Doriani, Philip Graham Ryken, and Richard D. Phillips
Matthew, by Daniel M. Doriani
Luke, by Philip Graham Ryken
John, by Richard D. Phillips
Romans, by Daniel M. Doriani
2 Corinthians, by Trent Casto
Galatians, by Philip Graham Ryken
Ephesians, by Bryan Chapell
Philippians, by Dennis E. Johnson
Colossians & Philemon, by Richard D. Phillips
1 & 2 Thessalonians, by Richard D. Phillips
1 Timothy, by Philip Graham Ryken
2 Timothy & Titus, by Daniel M. Doriani and Richard D. Phillips
Hebrews, by Richard D. Phillips
James, by Daniel M. Doriani
1 Peter, by Daniel M. Doriani
1–3 John, by Douglas Sean O'Donnell
Revelation, by Richard D. Phillips